DAVID BUSCH'S

Sony α a7CR/a7C II

GUIDE TO
DIGITAL PHOTOGRAPHY

DAVID D. BUSCH

David Busch's Sony® α a7CR/a7C II
Guide to Digital Photography
David D. Busch

Project Manager: Jenny Davidson
Technical Editor: Darrell Young
Layout: Bill Hartman
Cover Design: Mike Tanamachi
Indexer: Valerie Haynes Perry
Proofreader: Mike Beady

ISBN: 979-8-88814-196-0
1st Edition (1st printing, September 2024)

© 2024 David D. Busch

All images © David D. Busch unless otherwise noted

Rocky Nook, Inc.
1010 B Street, Suite 350
San Rafael, CA 94901
USA
www.rockynook.com

Distributed in the UK and Europe by Publishers Group UK
Distributed in the U.S. and all other territories by Publishers Group West

Library of Congress Control Number: 2024937111

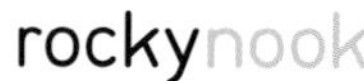

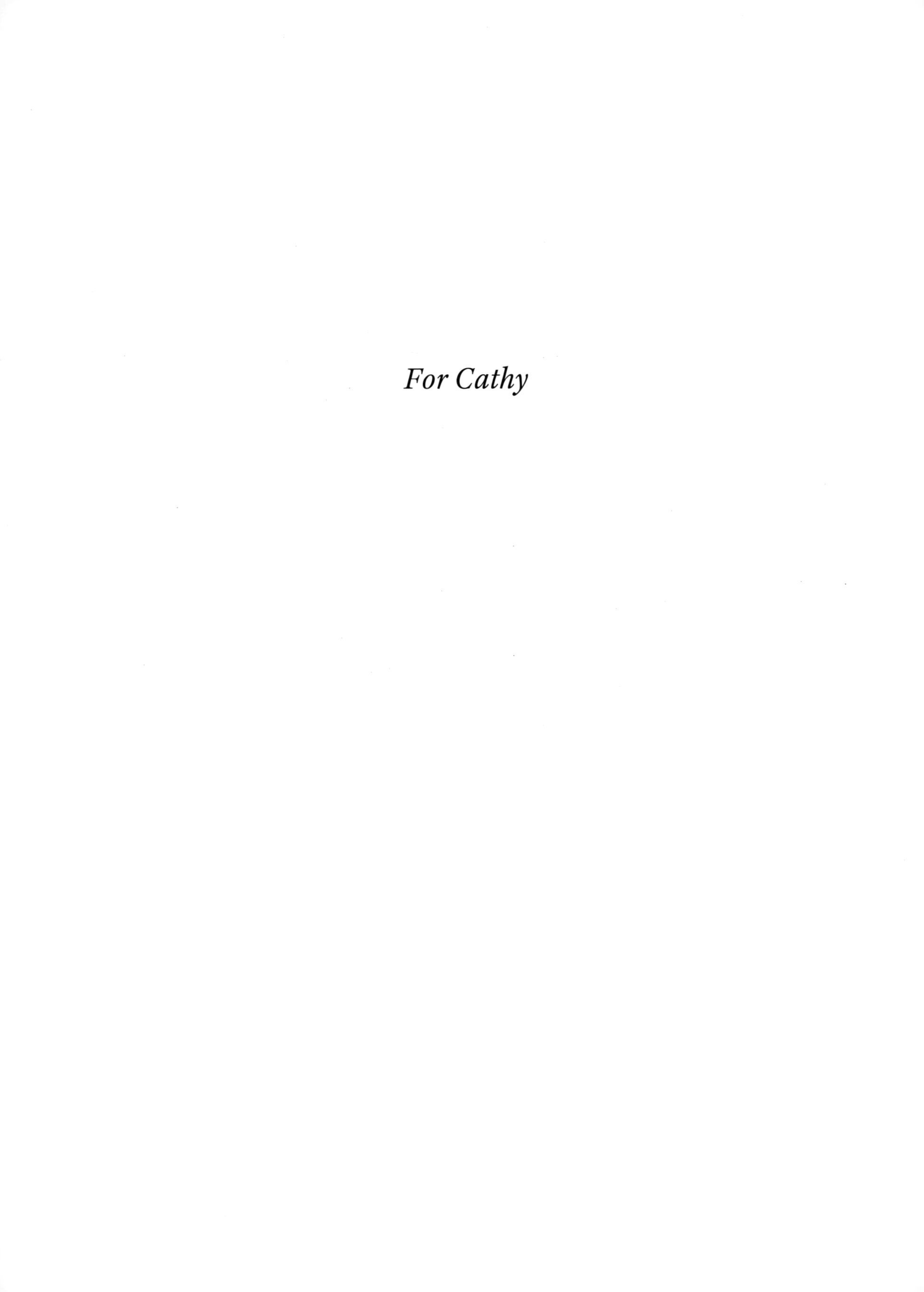

For Cathy

Acknowledgments

Thanks to everyone at Rocky Nook, including Scott Cowlin, managing director and publisher, for the freedom to let me explore the amazing capabilities of the Sony a7CR/a7C II in depth. I couldn't do it without my veteran production team, including project manager, Jenny Davidson. Also, thanks to Darrell Young, technical editor; Bill Hartman, layout; Valerie Hayes Perry, indexing; Mike Beady, proofreading; Mike Tanamachi, cover design; and my agent, Carole Jelen, who has the amazing ability to keep both publishers and authors happy.

About the Author

With more than 3 million books in print, **David D. Busch** is the world's #1 bestselling camera guide author, and the originator of popular series like *David Busch's Pro Secrets, David Busch's Compact Field Guides,* and *David Busch's Quick Snap Guides.* He has written dozens of hugely successful guidebooks for Sony and other digital SLR models, including the all-time #1 bestsellers for several different cameras, as well as many popular books devoted to photography, including *Mastering Mirrorless Photography.* As a roving photojournalist for more than 20 years, he illustrated his books, magazine articles, and newspaper reports with award-winning images. He's operated his own commercial studio, suffocated in formal dress while shooting weddings, and shot sports for a daily newspaper and an upstate New York college. His photos and articles have appeared in *Popular Photography, Rangefinder, Professional Photographer,* and hundreds of other publications. He's also reviewed dozens of digital cameras for CNet and other CBS publications.

When About.com named its top five books on Beginning Digital Photography, debuting at the #1 and #2 slots were Busch's *Digital Photography All-In-One Desk Reference for Dummies* and *Mastering Digital Photography.* Busch has had as many as 18 books listed in the Top 100 of Amazon.com's Digital Photography Bestseller list—simultaneously! Busch's 300-plus other published books include bestsellers like *Digital SLR Cameras and Photography for Dummies.*

Busch is a member of the Cleveland Photographic Society (www.clevelandphoto.org), which has operated continuously since 1887. Visit his website at http://www.sonyguides.com.

Contents

Exposure/Color Menu   215

Focus and Playback Menus   239

CHAPTER 9

Network and Setup Menus 277

CHAPTER 10

Movie-Making Basics   335

Preface

The Sony a7C II and a7CR, in addition to being great all-around cameras in their own right, leverage one of the key reasons why mirrorless cameras became so popular initially: their remarkably compact size and light weight. Either of these full-frame cameras give you all the most-desired features of other mirrorless models, squeezed into a form factor roughly the same size as Sony's a6700 APS-C offering.

Do you need a camera with resolution to spare? The a7C II includes a 33-megapixel sensor that captures enough detail to satisfy the most discerning landscape, commercial, or portrait photographer's needs. The a7CR sets the bar even higher with a 60 megapixel sensor and a Pixel Shift feature that lets you combine up to 16 separate images to create astonishing images with an effective 240 megapixels of resolution. With advanced autofocus, five-axis anti-shake image stabilization built into the camera body, and 4K video capabilities, the a7C II and a7CR come close to being "do-everything" models.

Indeed, in less than a decade and a half, Sony has become the acknowledged innovator in mirrorless technology with a lineup of cameras that are smaller, lighter, faster to focus, and loaded with cutting-edge features. So, it's no wonder you're excited about your new Sony a7C II/a7CR. With all these features at your disposal, you don't expect to take good pictures with such a camera—you demand and anticipate *outstanding* photos.

Unfortunately, your gateway to pixel proficiency is dragged down by the limited instructions provided by Sony. Over the years, Sony has reduced its printed guidebooks to mere pamphlets and relegated essential detailed instructions to online HTML-based guides and PDF versions that are difficult to navigate. And, sad to say, not everything you need to know is included.

What you really need is a guide that explains the purpose and function of the basic controls, how you should use them, and *why*. That's what I am giving you in this book. If you want a quick introduction to focus controls, flash synchronization options, how to choose lenses, or which exposure modes are best, this book is for you. If you can't decide on which basic settings to use with your camera because you can't figure out how changing ISO or white balance or focus defaults will affect your pictures, you need this guide.

Introduction

With Sony's latest dynamic duo, the a7CR and a7C II, Sony has packaged up an impressive roster of advanced capabilities and stuffed them into a pair of compact, fully featured bodies. A new, more logically arranged menu layout gives you easy access to extensive customization features, including a powerful autofocus system that allows you to track humans, animals, birds, insects, cars, trains, and planes with remarkable precision. Many of the a7C II and a7CR's other features are significant upgrades from previous models.

Of course, once you've confirmed that you made a wise purchase, the question comes up, *how do I use this thing?* The skimpy pamphlet included with the camera is no help at all. All the cool features of the a7C II/a7CR can be mind-numbing to learn, if all you have as a guide is the mediocre online manual offered for the camera. Basic functions and options are explained, but there's really very little about *why* you should use particular settings or features, and the organization may make it difficult to find what you need. Multiple cross-references may send you flipping back and forth between two or three sections of the book to find what you want to know. The basic manual is also hobbled by black-and-white line drawings and tiny pictures that aren't very good examples of what you can do.

I sincerely believe that this book is your best bet for learning how to use your new camera, and for learning how to use it well. The roadmap sections use large, color pictures to show you where all the buttons and dials are, and the explanations of what they do are longer and more detailed. I've tried to avoid overly general advice, including the checklists and recipes you'll find in other manuals on how to take a "sports picture" or a "portrait picture" or a "travel picture." If you want to know where you should stand to take a picture of a quarterback dropping back to unleash a pass, there are plenty of books that will tell you that. This one concentrates on teaching you how to select the best autofocus mode, shutter speed, f/stop, or flash capability to take, say, a great sports picture under any conditions.

This book is aimed at Sony veterans as well as newcomers to digital photography. Both groups can be overwhelmed by the options the a7C II and a7CR offer, while underwhelmed by the explanations they receive in their Help Guide, which some suspect was written by a Sony employee who last threw together instructions on how to operate a camcorder or PlayStation game console.

Although this book's main focus is *still* photography, I *will* devote a lot of space to helping you get up to speed on using the a7C II and a7CR's video capabilities. After all, these cameras are capable of capturing awesome, professional-level movies and a variety of Picture Profiles you can use to squeeze the last bit of dynamic range from your video.

Who Am I?

After spending many years as the world's most successful unknown author, I've become slightly less obscure in the past few years, thanks to a horde of camera guidebooks and other photographically oriented tomes. You may have seen my photography articles in the late, lamented *Popular Photography, Rangefinder, Professional Photographer,* and dozens of other photographic publications. But, first, and foremost, I'm a photojournalist and made my living in the field until I began devoting most of my time to writing books. Although I love writing, I'm happiest when I'm out taking pictures, which is why I spend many winters ensconced in the Florida Keys, dividing my time between writing books and taking photographs. You'll find images of many of these visual treats within the pages of this guide.

Like all my digital photography books, this one was written by someone with an incurable photography bug. I've worked as a sports photographer for an Ohio newspaper and for an upstate New York college. I've operated my own commercial studio and photo lab, cranking out product shots on demand and then printing a few hundred glossy 8 × 10s on a tight deadline for a press kit. I've served as a photo-posing instructor for a modeling agency. People have actually paid me to shoot their weddings and immortalize them with portraits. I even prepared press kits and articles on photography as a PR consultant for a formerly dominant (and now vestigial) Rochester, NY company. My trials and travails with imaging and computer technology have made their way into print in book form an alarming number of times, including hundreds of volumes on photographic topics.

Like you, I love photography for its own merits, and I view technology as just another tool to help me get the images I see in my mind's eye. But, also like you, I had to master this technology before I could apply it to my work. This book is the result of what I've learned, and I hope it will help you master your Sony a7C II/a7CR.

I'd like to ask a special favor: let me know what you think of this book. If you have any recommendations about how I can make it better, visit my website at www.sonyguides.com, click on the E-Mail Me tab, and send your comments, suggestions on topics that should be explained in more detail, or, especially, any typos. (The latter will be compiled on the Errata page you'll also find on my website.) I really value your ideas and appreciate it when you take the time to tell me what you think! Some of the content of the book you hold in your hands came from suggestions I received from readers like yourself. If you found this book especially useful, tell others about it. Visit http://www.amazon.com/dp/B0CHDR83N2 and leave a positive review. Your feedback is what spurs me to make each one of these books better than the last, and if enough of you like what I've done, Rocky Nook may be moved to ask me to follow up with a new book the next time Sony introduces one of its photographic innovations. Thanks!

Meet Your Sony Alpha a7C II/a7CR

The Sony a7C II and a7CR *can* be incredibly easy to use, right out of the box, especially if you already have some experience with digital photography. As ridiculous as it may seem, these advanced cameras can be used in point-and-shoot mode simply by rotating the large mode dial on the top-right panel to select the Program (P) label or green Intelligent Auto icon. (See Figure 1.1.) If you've charged the battery, mounted a lens, and inserted a formatted memory card into the camera, flip the power switch to On. (It's concentric with the shutter-release button on top of the camera.) I'll provide tips on performing these tasks later in this chapter if you need help. Otherwise, you're ready to start taking your first pictures.

As you peer through the viewfinder or examine the monitor (the rear LCD screen), the scene your camera will capture is shown, with the current shooting mode displayed in the upper-left corner of the frame. Compose your image, and press the shutter-release button when you're ready to take your first shot. That's all there is to it. The a7C II and a7CR are smart enough to produce a pretty good shot without much input from you. In this book, I'm going to help you go beyond *pretty good* to consistently great.

Although you can begin shooting as soon as you unbox your new camera, it's not a bad idea, once you've taken a few orientation pictures, to go back and review the basic operations of the a7C II or a7CR from the beginning—if only to see if you've missed something. The two cameras operate quite

similarly—the most important difference between the two is that the a7C II has a 33-megapixel sensor, while the a7CR sports Sony's ultra-high-resolution 60-megapixel imager.

This chapter is my opportunity to introduce new owners to their cameras and review the setup procedures for those among you who are already veteran users. I aim to help ease the more timid (even those few who have never before worked with an interchangeable-lens camera) into the basic pre-flight checklist that needs to be completed before you really spread your wings and take off. For the uninitiated, as easy as it is to use initially, your camera *does* have some dials, buttons, and menu items that might not make sense at first but will surely become second nature after you've had a chance to review the instructions in this book.

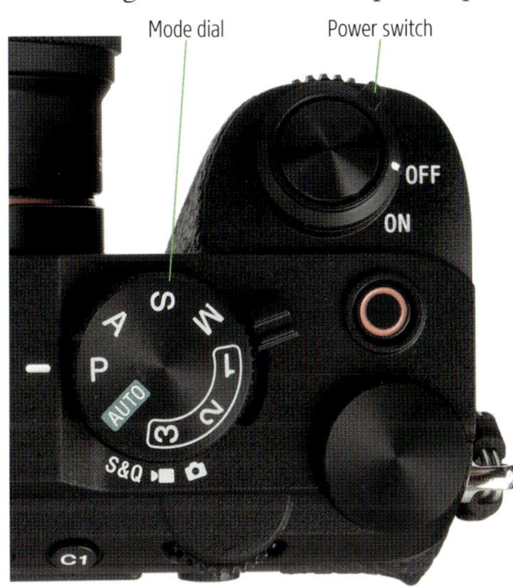

Figure 1.1 Select Program or Auto and take a picture.

But don't fret about wading through a manual to find out what you must know to take those first few tentative snaps. I'm going to help you hit the ground running with this chapter (or keep on running if you've already jumped right in). If you *haven't* had the opportunity to use your camera yet, I'll help you set it up and begin shooting in minutes. You won't find a lot of operational detail in this chapter. Indeed, I'm going to tell you just what you absolutely *must* understand, accompanied by some interesting tidbits that will help you become acclimated. I'll go into more depth and even repeat some of what I explain here in later chapters, so you don't have to memorize everything you see. Just relax, follow a few easy steps, and then go out and begin taking your best shots—ever.

DIFFERENT STROKES…

One of the challenges of writing a guidebook like this is satisfying the needs of both veteran E-mount users as well as newcomers to Sony cameras (which now includes the hordes who jumped to the Sony mirrorless world from other camera platforms). Believe it or not, while the a7C II and a7CR attract both photo enthusiasts and professional photographers, a surprising number of less experienced shooters have found these cameras appealing, too.

So, whether you're an advanced shooter looking to improve your comfort level with the features of these well-designed (yet complex) cameras or you are looking forward to starting from a more modest level of photographic expertise, I hope you'll find the advice I'm about to offer in this chapter—or beyond—useful. If you like, you can zip right through the basics, and then dive into learning a few things you probably didn't know about your a7C II or a7CR. Sony veterans might want to skim through the material in this chapter and move on. I promise I didn't charge you extra for it; even in the days of digital publishing it's not possible to provide *only* the material a particular reader needs, and nothing else.

Your Out-of-Box Experience

Your Sony a7C II/a7CR comes in an attractive box that's sparsely populated when compared to previous a7-series cameras—Sony no longer supplies a battery charger, cables, or even a printed user guide. You'll need to obtain your own, as well as a memory card, as one is not included. If you don't purchase the camera as a kit with a lens, the contents consist of the camera itself (with eyepiece, body, and hot shoe caps attached), a battery, neckstrap, and some starter leaflets that include instructions for accessing Help Guides online.

The first thing to do is to carefully unpack the camera and double-check the contents with the checklist on one side of the box. While this level of setup detail may seem as superfluous as the instructions on a bottle of shampoo, checking the contents *first* is always a good idea. It's better to know *now* that something is missing so you can seek redress immediately.

LENS NOMENCLATURE

In the discussion of lenses that follows, you're going to find me describing certain E-mount lenses using their full, formal product names, which can be rather unwieldy. For example, if you check Sony's website, you'll see that the basic kit lens is officially known as the Sony FE 28-60mm f/4-5.6 Full-frame Standard Zoom Lens. However, for the most part in this book, I'll use shorter, more compact nomenclature—usually just the focal length and aperture—when there is little chance of confusion.

So, check the box at your earliest convenience, and make sure you have (at least) the following:

- **Sony a7C II or a7CR body.** These are hard to miss. The camera is the main reason you laid out the big bucks, and yours is tucked away inside a nifty protective envelope you should save for re-use in case the camera needs to be sent in for repair. It almost goes without saying that you should check out the camera immediately, making sure the color LCD on the back isn't scratched or cracked, the battery/memory card door and connection port doors open properly, and, when a charged battery is inserted and lens mounted, the camera powers up and reports for duty. Out-of-the-box defects in these areas are rare, but they can happen. It's probably more common that your dealer played with the camera or, perhaps, it was a customer return. That's why it's best to buy your camera from a retailer you trust to supply a factory-fresh camera.

- **Lens.** Depending on where you live, the Sony a7C II or a7CR may be available in several different configurations—often the body alone, or packaged in several different kits that include a lens. The options may include the new compact Sony FE 24-50mm f/2.8G lens (which cost about $1,100 when introduced), or the less expensive Sony FE 28-60mm f/4-5.6 kit lens referenced earlier. It is frequently bundled with the a7C II, and available separately for about $500.

  Other options include the FE 28-70mm f/3.5-5.6 OSS optic (a budget lens), the Sony Zeiss Vario-Tessar T* FE 24-70mm f/4 ZA OSS lens, or even the premium Sony FE 24-70mm f/2.8 GM II (G Master) lens. The latter replaced an earlier Mark I 24-70mm f/2.8 G Master that was excellent, so you know the latest iteration is superb.

  My recommendation: I already owned the Zeiss Vario-Tessar 24-70mm f/4, so the next time I purchased a full-frame Sony camera, I went with the FE 24-105mm f/4 zoom. *You probably do not need both lenses* because the 24-105mm lens completely overlaps the range of the 24/28-70mm optics. You might make an exception for the 24-70mm f/2.8 G-Master II if you do *a lot* of shooting in the shorter focal length neighborhood and want a super-sharp lens with a fast f/2.8 maximum aperture. If you want a slightly wider lens, the Sony 20-70mm f/4G is also excellent.

  As the owner of a camera with either 33 or 60 megapixels, you probably won't be satisfied with the low-cost 28-70mm f/3.5-5.6 OSS lens, as it's not the sharpest lens in the drawer. The Zeiss 24-70mm version is a bit better, and its constant maximum aperture gives you f/4 (rather than f/5.6) at the 70mm setting. The f/2.8 G-Master II is the best of all, and my guess is that, despite its greater bulk, it will be the preferred lens among those investing in either of these cameras.

  Owning *any* lens in this particular zoom range is a matter of personal style and preference. Many shooters tend to "see" images as "wide-angle/perspective distortion/maximum depth-of-field" shots or, conversely, as "longer lens/selective focus" photos. If you are in either camp, eschewing all these lenses and putting the money toward a different lens is a good option. I use my Sony Vario-Tessar T* FE 16-35mm f/4 ZA OSS lens quite often and have been relying on the 24-105mm zoom more frequently as a "walk-around" lens.

- **Info-Lithium NP-FZ100 battery.** This is the power source for your Sony camera. Charge yours as soon as possible.

  My recommendation: Although this 2280 mAh battery is more than twice as powerful as the NP-FW50 furnished with some of Sony's earliest full-frame mirrorless cameras, it's smart, nay, *essential* to have more than one battery pack. Although relatively small in size, these cameras gulp power, and, even with the generous standards Sony cites in its literature, each is likely to last for no more than 560 (a7C II) or 530 (a7CR) still shots or roughly 165/155 minutes of non-stop video capture. (The figures given vary depending on whether you are using the electronic viewfinder or LCD monitor screen to frame your image, plus other factors.) Buy *more*, and stick to Sony-brand products. Off-brand packs have been known to fail quickly, sometimes in potentially destructive ways.

- **GP-X2 Grip extension.** This aluminum grip extender fits both cameras, but is furnished only with the a7CR. (See Figure 1.2.) Owners of the a7C II can purchase one as an add-on for about $160.

Many, especially those coming from the dSLR world of larger cameras, find the extra size and road-hugging weight better from an ergonomic standpoint.

My recommendation: Any a7C II owner who feels they require one of those should try one out to confirm their need. You might be able to acquire this grip at a good price from a7CR user who decides this add-on isn't their cup of tea. An even less-expensive option is the SmallRig Bottom Mount plate (about $30), which provides similar functionality and adds an Arca-Swiss-compatible plate.

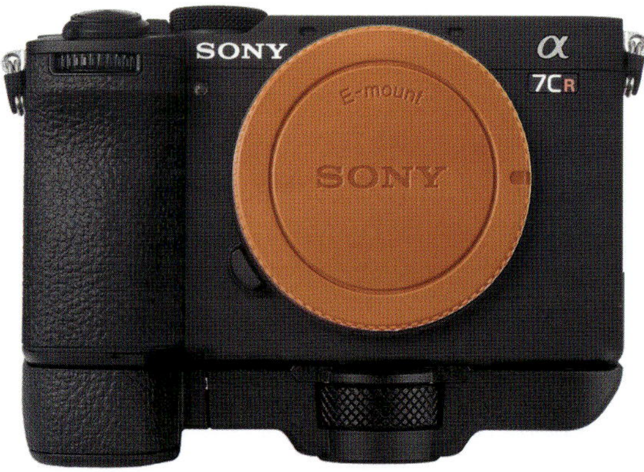

Figure 1.2 Many find the GP-X2 Grip extension provides a more comfortable grip.

- **Body cap.** This accessory will already be attached to the camera body if you purchase your a7C II/a7CR without a lens.

My recommendation: Purchase an extra body cap. With mirrorless cameras like the a7C II/a7CR series, it is especially important not to leave the sensor unprotected. If you lose your body cap, mount a lens as a "body cap" until you purchase spares. A body cap is essential when packing your camera for compact travel. Owners in the USA will find cheap body and rear lens caps at www.laserfairepress.com, too. You'll find both available in official Sony orange (see Figure 1.2), which I think are easier to find within the dark confines of most camera bags.

- **Shoulder strap.** Sony provides a suitable neck or shoulder strap, with the Sony logo subtly worked into the design.

My recommendation: While I am justifiably proud of owning a fine Sony camera, I never attach the factory "Steal Me" strap to my camera. It's not very adjustable, and, while useful for showing off to your friends exactly which nifty new camera you bought, the Sony strap also can serve to alert observant unsavory types that you're sporting a model that's worthy of their attention.

Using a traditional strap that attaches to the neckstrap loops, a hand strap, or some other way to hold your camera is a personal preference. I usually opt for a more serviceable traditional strap with quick-release clips. I strongly prefer this type over holsters, slings, chest straps, or any support that dangles my camera upside down from the tripod socket and allows it to swing around too freely when I'm on the run. Give me a strap I can hang over either shoulder, or sling around my neck, and I am happy.

- **Multi-interface shoe cap.** This plastic piece slides into the camera's multi-interface shoe on top of the camera (what we used to call a "hot shoe") and protects the contacts from dirt, moisture, and damage when you don't have an electronic flash, microphone, or other accessory attached.

  My recommendation: If you are *very* careful about how you insert an external flash or microphone into the multi-interface shoe, and avoid drenching moisture, you can remove this piece and leave it off for the rest of your life. I *have* lost shots while fumbling with protective covers and manage to lose the shoe cap with alarming frequency. If you misplace yours, USA shooters can get a replacement from www.laserfairepress.com for a few bucks. (Nobody gets rich selling these items for a few dollars, but these are provided as a service because a key previous source for them has gone out of business.)

- **Eyepiece cup.** This rubber accessory is already installed on the electronic viewfinder eyepiece when you receive the camera; if you want to remove it, slide it up.

- **Application software (not included).** Sony stopped providing a software CD in the package ages ago, even before CD/DVD drives ceased being standard equipment with new computers. The first time you power up the camera, it will display the current URL for your country where you can download imaging software for the a7C II/a7CR. Be sure to get the latest free Imaging Edge software. It's a great RAW processor and editor and has a remote application for tethered shooting (with your a7C II/a7CR connected to a laptop or other computer).

- **Printed instruction manual (not included).** The camera comes with a Startup Guide pamphlet and Reference Guide leaflet with some basic start-up instructions. A 573/574-page Help Guide to the camera's operation can be accessed online in HTML format or downloaded as a more useful PDF file from Sony's esupport.sony.com website. The box will also contain warranty and registration information and assorted pamphlets listing available accessories.

Initial Setup

The initial setup of your Sony a7C II/a7CR is fast and easy. You just need to charge the battery, attach a lens (if that hasn't already been done), and insert a memory card. I'll address each of these steps separately, but if you already feel you can manage these setup tasks without further instructions, feel free to skip this section entirely. You should probably at least skim its contents, however, because I'm going to list a few options that you might not be aware of.

Battery Included

Your Sony a7C II/a7CR is a sophisticated hunk of machinery and electronics, but it needs a charged battery to function, so rejuvenating the NP-FZ100 lithium-ion battery pack should be your first step. Sony says that a fully charged power source should theoretically be good for as many as 530 to 490 shots when using the power-hungry viewfinder or up to 560 shots when working with the more juice-frugal LCD monitor screen. Expect around 100 minutes (or more) of typical video capture, which includes standby time, zooming, and turning the camera on or off from time to time. When shooting continuously, you may be able to stretch a single battery for as much as 160 minutes of continual video capture. Theoretically. I frequently (always) deplete my batteries more quickly than that. Sony's estimates are based on standard tests defined by the Camera & Imaging Products

Association (CIPA). If you often use the camera's Wi-Fi feature (discussed later), you can expect to take even fewer shots before it's time for a recharge. This is an InfoLithium battery, so the camera can display the approximate power remaining with a graphic indicator.

Remember that all rechargeable batteries undergo some degree of self-discharge just sitting idle in the camera or in the original packaging. Lithium-ion power packs of this type typically lose a small amount of their charge every day, even when the camera isn't turned on. Li-ion cells lose their power through a chemical reaction that continues when the camera is switched off. So, it's very likely that the battery purchased with your camera, even if charged at the factory, has begun to poop out after the long sea voyage on a banana boat (or, more likely, a trip by jet plane followed by a sojourn in a warehouse), so you'll want to revive it before going out for some serious shooting.

I own eight NP-FZ100 batteries (so far). You won't need that many, but in addition to my a7C II and a7CR, I also own other cameras that use the same battery, including the a1 and a9 III. I keep a fresh battery in the camera at all times. Nevertheless, I always check battery status before I go out to shoot, as some juice may have been siphoned off while the camera sat idle. I go to the Network > Network Option tab and turn Airplane Mode on (as described in Chapter 9) when I don't need Wi-Fi features.

THIRD-PARTY BATTERIES

I don't recommend using third-party batteries, even though they may cost one-third the price of Sony's own batteries. It makes little sense to risk damaging an expensive camera body just to save a few dollars on such a crucial component. Your camera may display a compatibility warning message when many of these batteries are inserted. While the latest-generation knock-offs seem to work better, many have reduced capacity, and there's no guarantee that the third parties selling them will be able to issue timely recalls if needed. While some owners have had no problems, and swear by their Wasabi, Watson, Neewer, or DTSE batteries, I don't think it's worth the risk.

Charging the Battery

As I noted earlier, Sony no longer includes a charger with their cameras, which is probably for the best. Generic 5V 2A (10W) power adapters for electronic devices have proliferated to the point that it's common to own a dozen of them, and most manufacturers have stopped supplying them. More to the point, most of us have begun using the later-generation beefed-up units compatible with the Power Delivery (PD) specification. Their Gallium Nitride (GaN) technology makes such chargers smaller and safer with built-in protection from short circuits, over-voltage, over-current, over-charging, over-heating, and short circuits. Rated for up to 100W (so they can be used with power-hungry laptops), commercially available AC adapters have multiple ports, including those for your camera's USB Type-C connector.

If you really go through a lot of batteries (or own multiple Sony cameras that use the NP-FZ100 pack), you might consider the NPA-MQZ1K Multi-Battery Adapter Kit. At $400, it sounds pricey (it is!). However, it comes with two NP-FZ100 batteries (normally about $80 each), which means that, effectively, you're paying "only" $240 for the charger itself. The charger is extremely versatile: it can charge up to four NP-FZ100 batteries simultaneously but can be converted to a compact two-battery charger for use while traveling. (See Figure 1.3.) Even better, the charger can serve as a power pack

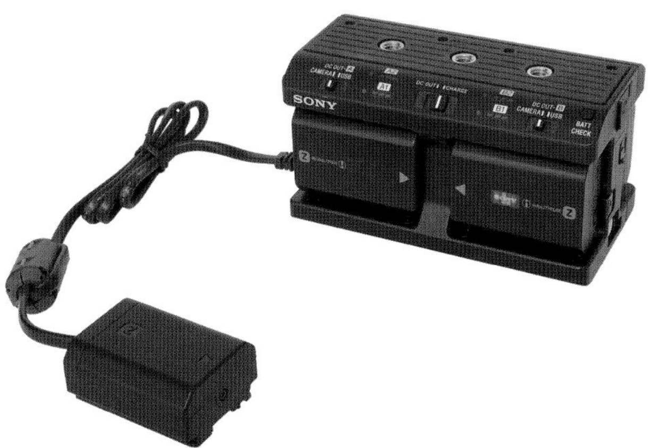

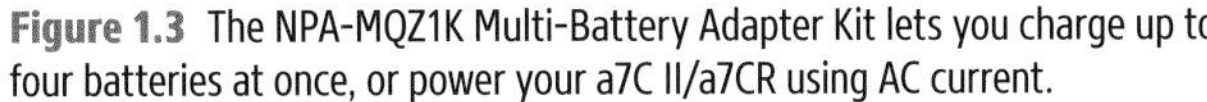

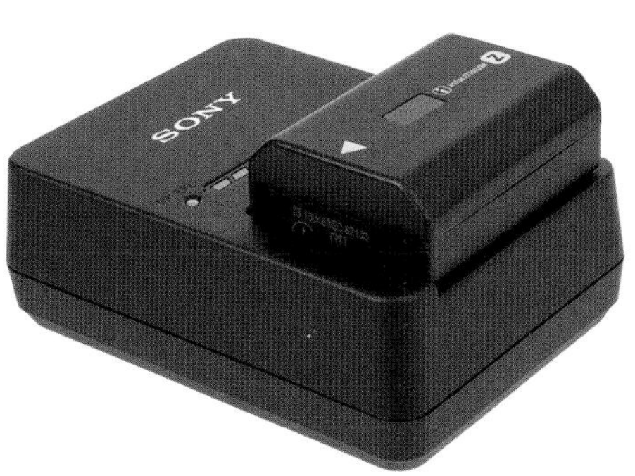

Figure 1.3 The NPA-MQZ1K Multi-Battery Adapter Kit lets you charge up to four batteries at once, or power your a7C II/a7CR using AC current.

Figure 1.4 The Sony BC-QZ1 charger allows rejuvenating your battery outside the camera, so you can keep shooting with a spare battery.

when outfitted with fully charged batteries. A dummy battery plugs into the battery compartment of the a7C II/a7CR (or, with a supplied adapter, into any E-mount camera that uses the puny NP-FW50 batteries). Two USB ports allow rejuvenating other devices that use USB cable charging (including your smartphone!). It has six standard 1/4"-20 mounting sockets so it can be mounted to support systems (like the cages videographers use to attach external viewfinders and other accessories).

I also use the Sony BC-QZ1 charger that Sony formerly packaged with their cameras, as I have several of these dedicated chargers left over from earlier camera purchases. (See Figure 1.4.) Priced at around $100, they've largely been supplanted by the less expensive (and more versatile) Power Delivery chargers, but if you own one, they will work perfectly well with your a7C II/a7CR's batteries. Charging the battery with the BC-QZ1 external charger is easy; just slide the battery in, connect to AC power, and the charger's yellow status light will begin to glow, accompanied by three green LEDs that illuminate progressively as charging proceeds, to let you know when the battery is fully charged. The yellow LED will extinguish when the cycle is over.

When hiking I rely on a 44,000 mAh lithium-ion power "brick," which also can recharge my phone, my tablet, and, in a pinch jump start a car. The brick comes with its own 12V DC charger, so I can keep it topped up using my vehicle's accessory outlet (what we used to call a "cigarette lighter" socket). I also have a more compact 22,000 mAh pack that I keep in my camera bag.

You can charge your battery when it's still in the camera, if you like. When you're ready to charge the battery internally, turn the camera Off. Then, connect one end of the optional USB Type-C cable into your power source, and the other into the camera's USB terminal on the left end of the body. (See Figure 1.5.)

Whether you charge from a computer's USB port or household power, a Charge light next to the camera's USB/charging port glows yellow, without flashing. It continues to glow until the battery completes the charge and the lamp turns off. Note that charging takes place *only* when the camera is powered off. If you turn the camera on, the Charge light will turn off, and a "plug" icon appears to the right of the battery symbol on the display, indicating the camera is being powered externally.

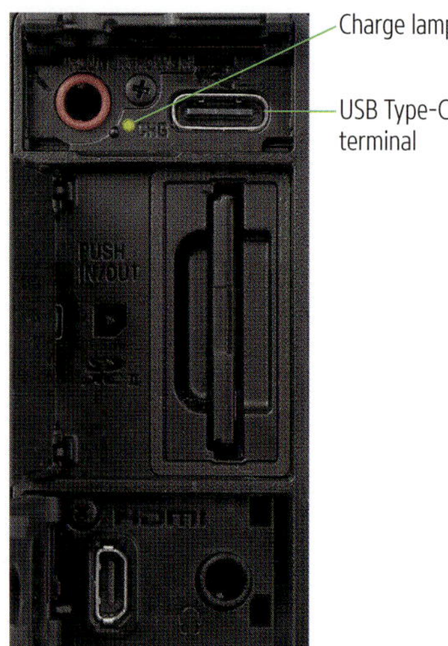

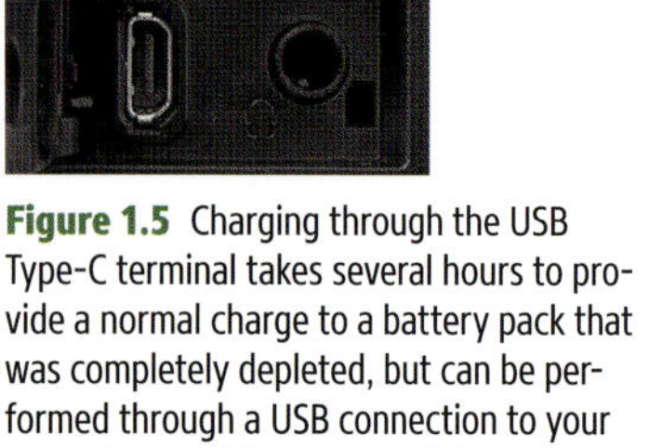

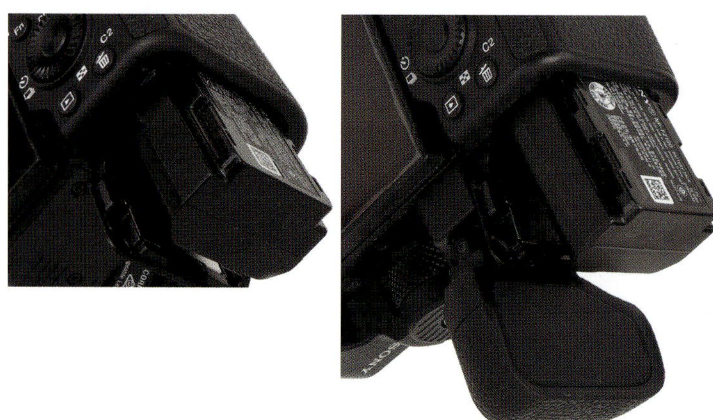

Figure 1.5 Charging through the USB Type-C terminal takes several hours to provide a normal charge to a battery pack that was completely depleted, but can be performed through a USB connection to your computer, or with an appropriate power brick or AC adapter.

Figure 1.6 Install the battery in the camera; it only fits one way (left). The Grip Extension GP-X2 allows access to the battery compartment (right).

In practice, the full charge may be complete as long as about one hour *after* the charging lamp turns off, so if your battery was really dead, don't stop charging until the additional time has elapsed. Be sure to plan for charging time before your shooting sessions, because it takes several hours in a warm environment to fully restore a completely depleted battery.

If the charging lamp flashes after you insert an externally charged battery into the camera, that indicates an error condition. Remove it and re-insert it. To insert/remove it, slide the latch on the bottom of the camera, open the battery door, and press a blue lever in the battery compartment that prevents the pack from slipping out when the door is opened; then, ease the battery out. To insert it, do so with the contact openings facing into the compartment (see Figure 1.6, left). If you have the Grip Extension GP-X2 installed, the section covering the battery door pivots to allow access (see Figure 1.6, right). Fast flashing that can't be stopped by re-inserting the battery indicates a problem with the battery. Slow flashing (about 1.5 seconds between flashes) means the ambient temperature is too high or low for charging to take place.

Mounting a Lens

My recommended lens-mounting procedure emphasizes protecting your equipment from accidental damage, and minimizing the intrusion of dust. If your camera has no lens attached, select the lens you want to use and loosen (but do not remove) the rear lens cap. I generally place the lens I am planning to mount vertically in a slot in my camera bag, where it's protected from mishaps but ready to pick up quickly. By loosening the rear lens cap, you'll be able to lift it off the back of the lens at the last instant, so the rear element of the lens is covered until then.

After that, remove the body cap that protects the camera's exposed sensor by rotating the cap toward the shutter-release button. You should always mount the body cap when there is no lens on the camera, because it helps keep dust out of the interior of the camera, where it potentially can find its way onto the sensor. This is a particular issue with mirrorless cameras like the a7C II and a7CR. Although you can tell the camera to close the shutter when power is off, the shutter itself needs protection from accidental damage.

If you've mislaid your body cap, you should try to locate one through Sony or another vendor if you possibly can; a camera body should never be left with its sensor or shutter completely exposed.

Once the body cap has been removed, remove the rear lens cap from the lens, set the cap aside, and then mount the lens on the camera by matching the raised white alignment indicator on the lens barrel with the white dot on the camera's lens mount (see Figure 1.7). Rotate the lens away from the shutter release side of the camera until it seats securely and clicks into place. (Don't press the lens-release button during mounting.) Some lenses ship with a hood. If that accessory is included, and if it's bayoneted on the lens in the reversed position (which makes the lens/hood combination more compact for transport), twist it off and remount with the rim facing outward. A lens hood protects the front of the lens from accidental bumps, and reduces flare caused by extraneous light arriving at the front element of the lens from outside the picture area.

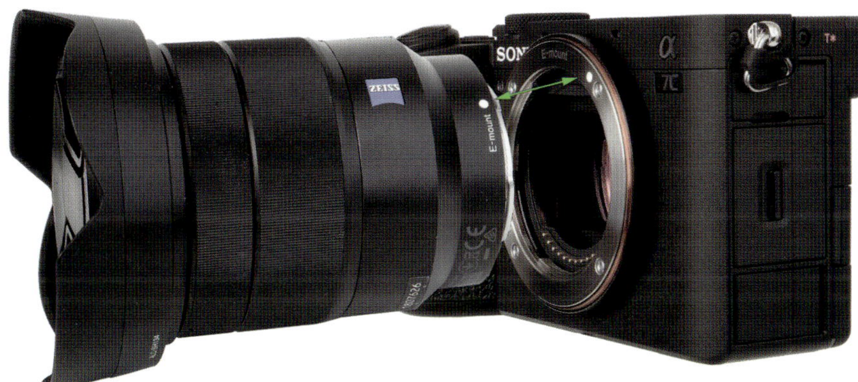

Figure 1.7 Match the raised white dot on the lens with the white dot on the camera mount to properly align the lens with the bayonet mount.

Turn on the Power

Locate the On/Off switch that is wrapped around the shutter-release button and rotate it to the On position. The LCD display will be illuminated. If you bring the viewfinder up to your eye, a sensor will detect that action and switch the display to the built-in electronic viewfinder instead. You can disable this automatic switching using the Select Finder/Monitor entry in the Finder/Monitor group of the Setup menu tab. I'll show you how to navigate the new Sony menu system to find this setting in the section that follows this one. After one minute of idling (the default), the a7C II and a7CR go into standby mode to save battery power. Just tap the shutter-release button to bring the camera back to life. (You can select a specific time using the Power Setting Option > Power Save Start Time option in the Setup menu, as I discuss in Chapter 9.)

When the camera first powers up, you may be asked to set the date and time. The procedure is self-explanatory (although I'll explain it in more detail in Chapter 9). You can use the left/right directional buttons to navigate among the date, year, time, date format, and daylight saving time indicator, and use the up/down buttons to enter the correct settings.

Once the Sony a7C II and a7CR are satisfied that they know what time it is, you will be viewing a live view of the scene in front of the lens—on the LCD screen or in the viewfinder when held up to your eye—whenever you turn the camera on. The view is superimposed with many items of data over the display; these provide a quick method for checking many current camera settings, including current shutter speed and aperture (f/stop), shooting mode, ISO sensitivity, and other parameters.

Adjusting the Diopter Setting

The a7C II and a7CR are equipped with a built-in electronic viewfinder or EVF, a small high-resolution (2,359,296 pixels) OLED (organic light-emitting diode) screen that can be used instead of the LCD monitor screen for framing your photos or movies. A sensor detects your eye at the viewfinder and shuts off power to the LCD when you are using the EVF. Usually, when you're learning to use the camera's many features, you'll rely on the LCD screen's display, but when you're actually taking photos, you'll sometimes want to use the EVF instead. You can also use it to review your photos or video clips and navigate menu selections.

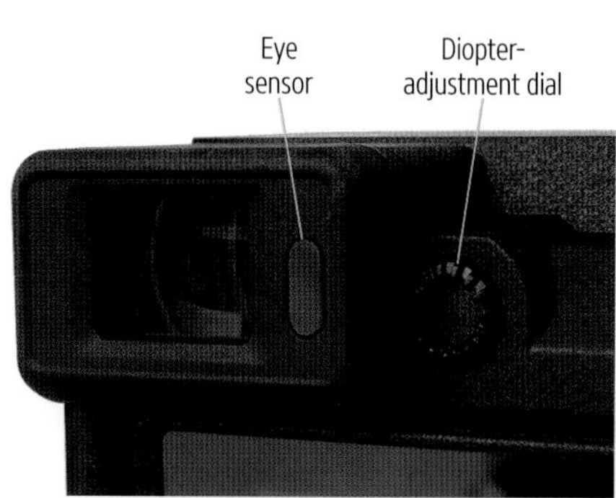

Figure 1.8 Diopter-adjustment dial and eye sensor.

If you wear glasses and want to use the EVF without them, or if you find the viewfinder needs a bit of correction, rotate the diopter-adjustment dial located to the right of the viewfinder window (and shown in Figure 1.8). Adjust the dial while looking through the viewfinder until the image appears sharpest.

Inserting a Memory Card

You can't take actual photos without a memory card inserted in your camera, although if you have the Release without Card entry in the Shooting > Shutter/Silent menu page set to Enable, you can pretend to shoot. In that case, if you don't have a card installed, the camera will sound as if it's taking a photo (when using the mechanical shutter, of course), and it will display that "photo." However, the image is only in temporary memory and not actually stored; you'll get a reminder about that with a flashing orange NO CARD warning at the upper left of the LCD. If you go back later and try to view that image, it will not be there. So, be sure you have inserted a compatible card with adequate capacity before you start shooting stills or videos.

The memory card slot is located beneath the middle door on the left side of the camera. Open the door and insert the card end with the contacts first, with the label facing the back of the camera (see Figure 1.9). You should remove the memory card only when the camera is switched off. The metal contacts go into the slot first; the card simply will not fit into the slot if it is incorrectly oriented.

Close the door, and your pre-flight checklist is done! (I'm going to assume you'll remember to remove the lens cap when you're ready to take a picture!) When you want to remove the memory card later, just press down on the card edge that protrudes from the slot, and the card will pop right out.

My recommendation: Given the fast continuous shooting speeds available with the a7C II/a7CR, you'll want to consider a speedy memory card of the UHS-II (Ultra High Speed II) type, with a V90 rating. Such a card will have a *minimum* sequential write speed (that is, storing your image or video on the card) of 90MB/second, which is fast enough for either camera's fastest continuous still shooting rate and 4K video capture capabilities. The actual *maximum* sequential write speed of the card is likely to be some-what higher. SD cards also have a maximum *read* speed, too, which is useful when it comes time to transfer your

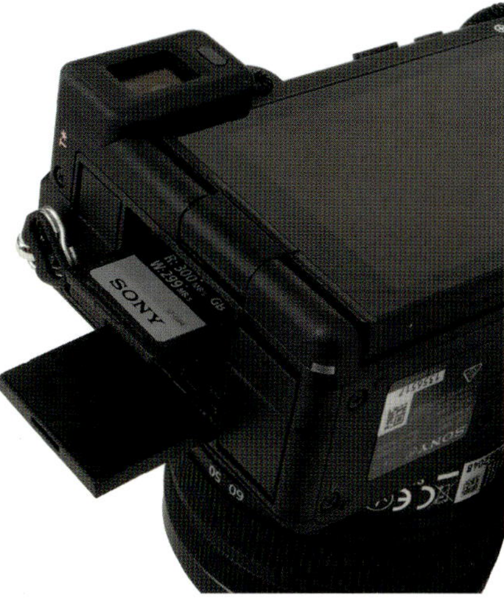

Figure 1.9 Insert a memory card in the slot on the underside of the camera.

images from the memory card to your computer. Vendors typically tout their cards' read speed and downplay the write speed, which can be half as fast. SanDisk, for example, doesn't supply the write speed at all in its specification.

In addition, capacity matters when you're using a camera with a 33 or 60 megapixel sensor. If you're buying new, rather than re-using old cards, if your budget is limited, purchase at least two fast 64GB cards (so you'll always have a backup). If your pockets are a little deeper, 128GB and 256GB memory cards can be more attractive, especially when you're on vacation and shooting a lot each day.

HOW MANY SHOTS?

The Sony a7C II and a7CR provide a fairly accurate estimate of the number of shots that your memory card will hold. This number is visible near the top-left corner of the display (next to the memory card icon) in standard live view. It is only an estimate, because the actual number will vary, depending on the capacity of your memory card, the content of the image itself, and the aspect ratio (proportions) of the image. (The a7C II/a7CR can use traditional 3:2 proportions, 4:3, 1:1 [square format], and 16:9 [HDTV] aspect ratios.) Some photos may contain large areas that can be more efficiently squeezed down to a smaller size. If you change the file format (from JPEG to RAW or from a large JPEG to a small JPEG, for example), the number will change. The Shooting > Media > Display Media Info setting will show you how many images you can capture at your current settings, and how much movie-shooting time you can squeeze out of your memory card.

Table 1.1 shows the number of shots you can expect using typical memory cards. Although the a7C II/a7CR can shoot more than 10,000 images with a high-capacity card, the maximum number of recordable images displayed on the LCD or viewfinder will never exceed 9,999.

TABLE 1.1 Typical Number of Shots with 64GB/128GB Memory Cards

	SONY A7C II		SONY A7CR	
	64GB	**128GB**	**64GB**	**128GB**
JPEG Light	9,000	19,000	4,900	9,000
JPEG Standard	6,800	13,000	3,300	6,700
JPEG Fine	4,800	9,600	2,300	4,700
JPEG Extra Fine	2,300	4,700	1,200	2,500
HEIF Light	14,000	28,000	6,500	13,000
HEIF Standard	10,000	21,000	4,800	9,000
HEIF Fine	7,700	15,000	3,600	7,200
HEIF Extra Fine	5,400	10,000	2,500	5,000
RAW & JPEG (Compressed RAW)	1,000	2,100	590	1,100
RAW & HEIF (Compressed RAW)	1,100	2,400	640	1,300
RAW (Compressed RAW)	1,400	2,800	780	1,500
RAW & JPEG (Lossless Compressed RAW: L)	1,000	2,000	530	1,000
RAW & HEIF (Lossless Compressed RAW: L)	1,100	2,200	570	1,100
RAW (Lossless Compressed RAW: L)	1,200	2,600	680	1,300
RAW & JPEG (Uncompressed RAW)	660	1,300	360	720
RAW & HEIF (Uncompressed RAW)	690	1,300	380	770
RAW (Uncompressed RAW)	770	1,500	420	860

Menu Navigation Quick Start

You may need to format your memory card before shooting, and to do that, you'll need to start learning how to use your camera's menu navigation system. Recent Sony cameras, including the a7C II and a7CR, have converted to an entirely new menu system that's more logically arranged by function, and easier to navigate once you get used to it. Owners of previous Sony full-frame cameras may be lost at first, so I'm including this menu navigation quick start. I'm going to provide just the basics: keep in mind that Sony gives you multiple controls for navigation, including the touch screen and directional buttons, but I'll keep things simple for now. Figure 1.10 shows the basic components of a typical menu screen. They are as follows:

- **Menu tabs.** The column at far left displays the top-level menu *tabs*, which each contain *groups* with associated entries. There are seven individual tabs, which are, starting at the top:
  - **My Menu (Gray).** You can set up your own customized menus to reside here, installing the entries from any of the other tabs for quick access. The tab has just one group: My Menu Setting, with options that allow you to add/delete, sort, and arrange pages of favorite entries. I'll explain every entry for this tab in Chapter 6.
  - **Main Menu (Black/White).** This is a graphic menu with 18 of the most frequently accessed adjustments arrayed for quick access. (See Figure 1.11.)

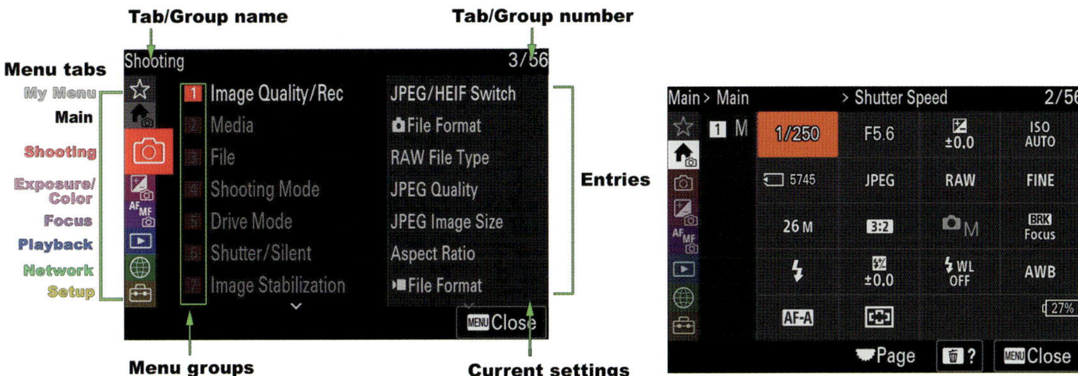

Figure 1.10 Menu layout.   **Figure 1.11** Main menu.

- **Shooting (Red/Orange).** This tab includes commands for handling image quality, recording media and files, shooting modes, USB streaming, drive modes, shutter option, image stabilization, optical/digital zoom, and shooting display. This tab is also covered in Chapter 6.

- **Exposure/Color (Magenta).** This tab includes groups with options for exposure, metering, flash, white balance, color rendition, and overexposure warnings. You'll learn about exposure and color control in Chapters 3 and 7.

- **AF/MF (Violet).** Here you'll find groups with all the controls you need to set focus parameters, and the aids built-into the camera to make focusing more accurate and convenient. Chapters 4 and 8 explain all the focus options you'll need to operate your a7C II or a7CR.

- **Playback (Blue).** This tab has entries that will enable you to review, manage, edit, and delete the photos you've taken. These are all explained in Chapter 8.

- **Network (Green).** The a7C II/a7CR include a broad range of Wi-Fi, Bluetooth, and wired LAN options, all controlled through this tab.

- **Setup (Yellow).** This tab has a host of options you may not use on an everyday basis—such as Area/Date settings, custom control definitions for various dials and buttons, USB connectivity, and output to external monitors and recorders.

- **Tab/group name / Tab/group number.** The top line of the screen displays the name of the current tab and group, such as Shooting, shown at top left in Figure 1.10. You start with 56 groups in all, and the "page" of the current group is shown at top, in this case, 3/56.

- **Menu groups.** After you've highlighted a top-level menu tab, you can use the directional controls (explained next) to gain access to all the menu groups available for that tab. Each group will have its own number, which will appear as you scroll among the groups. In Figure 1.10, the first group, Image Quality/Recording, is shown highlighted and the numeral 1 in the second column from the left is highlighted in the red/orange used for the Shooting tab. But see the following sidebar "Paths."

- **Group entries.** The remainder of the screen shows the available entries for the currently highlighted group, with their current settings.

> **PATHS**
>
> Throughout this book, I will use the ***Tab > Group > Entry > Option Name*** hierarchy to point you to a specific entry, for example:
>
> **Shooting > Shutter/Silent > Shutter Type > Mechanical Shutter.**
>
> I am going to *omit* the number that precedes the group, because Sony, unfortunately, *changes* the group number depending on your shooting mode. For example, with the S&Q/Movie/Still dial set to Still photos, the Shutter/Silent group is shown as **6 Shutter/Silent.** The same group is available in Movie and S&Q modes, but it's renumbered as **5 Shutter/Silent.** Only the group number changes, not the *actual path*, so to avoid confusion, I will not use the group number.

- **General controls.** Near the bottom of the screen shown earlier in Figure 1.10 you'll find a downward-pointing triangle indicating that this particular group has additional entries beyond those shown, accessed by scrolling down. The Trash icon can be pressed to retrieve some Help for the highlighted entry. Press the MENU button to back out of the menu system.

As mentioned earlier, you can use a variety of controls to navigate the camera's options, whether you're wending your way through the menu system or specifying a particular AF point or zone within a frame. I'll give you a complete guide to using the controls in Chapter 2. For this quick start, all you'll need is the MENU button, located on the top panel to the right of the viewfinder window and the directional buttons located on the control wheel in the lower right of the back of the camera, as seen in Figure 1.12. The figure shows a "flow chart" of the menu system at far right, accompanied by images of the control wheel up/down "buttons" (the top and bottom edges of the wheel, marked with green triangles), and the right directional "button" (the right edge of the wheel, marked with a yellow triangle).

Starting at the top of the figure, here's your roadmap:

- **Top row.** Use the up/down buttons to scroll within the eight Menu tabs. The Shooting tab is highlighted. You can press the right directional button to move from the Menu tab list into the list of groups available within the highlighted tab group.

- **Second row.** Use the up/down buttons to highlight the group you want to work with. The Image Quality/Rec group is highlighted. The available groups are shown, each assigned a number. You may have to scroll down to see all of them available in the Shooting and Setup groups. Press the right directional button to access one of the numbered groups.

- **Third row.** The up/down buttons can be used to scroll among the entries found within the group you've selected. In this case, the JPEG/HEIF Switch entry is highlighted. Press the right button to see the options available with the highlighted entry.

- **Bottom row.** Several choices are shown, such as the highlighted JPEG option. For some entries, the options may include additional screens of sub-options within that setting. Use the up/down button to highlight the radio button for the option you want to activate, or, if sub-options are offered, use the right button to navigate to the additional choices. When the setting you want is highlighted, press the control wheel's center button to confirm.

- **Exiting.** For each of these levels, pressing the MENU button will Close/Exit the screen.

Navigating the Sony Menu System

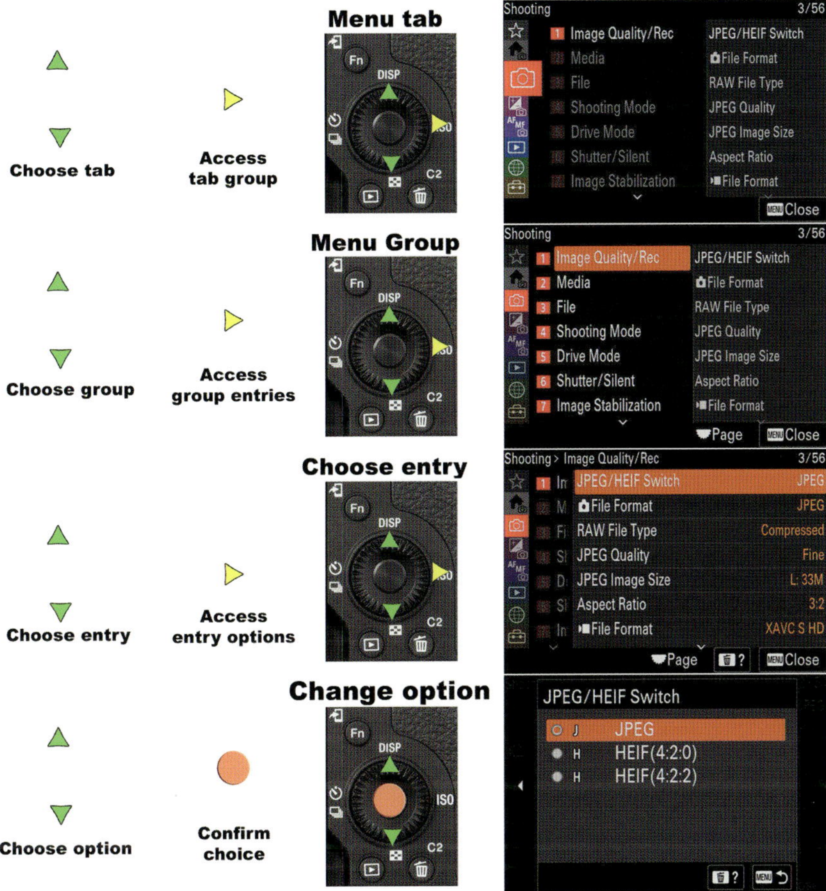

Figure 1.12 Navigating the menus.

Formatting a Memory Card

There are three ways to create a blank memory card and two of them are at least partially wrong. Here are your options, both correct and incorrect:

- **Transfer (move) files to your computer.** You'll sometimes decide to transfer (rather than copy) all the image files to your computer from the memory card (either using a direct USB cable transfer or with a card reader and appropriate software, as described later in this chapter). When you do so, the image files on the card can be erased leaving the card blank. Theoretically. This method does *not* remove files that you've labeled as Protected (by choosing Protect from the Playback > Selection/Memo > Protect menu during review), nor does it identify and lock out parts of your card that have become corrupted or unusable since the last time you formatted the card. Therefore, I recommend always formatting the card after transferring the image files, rather than simply moving the image files. The only exception is when you *want* to leave the protected/unerased images on the card for a while longer, say, to share with friends, family, and colleagues.

- **(Don't) Format in your computer.** With the memory card inserted in a card reader or card slot in your computer, you can use Windows or Mac OS to reformat the memory card. Don't even think of doing this! The operating system won't necessarily arrange the structure of the card the way the camera likes to see it (in computer terms, an incorrect *file system* may be installed). In particular, cards larger than 32GB must be initialized using the exFAT format, and while your computer may offer exFAT as an option, it may default to a different scheme. The only way to ensure that the card has been properly formatted for your camera is to perform the format *in the camera itself*. The only exception to this rule is when you have a seriously corrupted memory card that your camera refuses to format. Sometimes it is possible to revive such a corrupted card by allowing the operating system to reformat it first, then trying again in the camera to restore the proper exFAT system.

- **Shooting menu format.** Use the recommended method to format a memory card in the camera, with the Shooting > Media > Format entry, as described next.

To format a memory card, just follow these steps, using the menu system I just described above:

1. **Press MENU.** When you press the MENU button, the menu screens shown earlier will appear on the LCD monitor or electronic viewfinder. If you've previously selected a menu entry, the camera will remember that and return to *that menu screen* with the most recently used item highlighted with an orange bar.

2. **Navigate to Shooting > Media > Format.** The screen that appears is shown at top in Figure 1.13. It has three options: Format, Recover Image DB (to restore the card's picture database), and Display Media Information (to view the number and type of still photo and video files on the memory card).

3. **Select Format.** If Format is highlighted, you can simply press the control wheel center button to proceed, or, highlight the Format entry and press the right directional button. When the screen shown at the bottom of the figure appears, you have three choices:

   - **Enter (default).** Press the control wheel center button to proceed with a Quick Format, which will zero out the memory card's pointers to any files stored on the memory card. The data itself is not erased; only the "table of contents" is removed. Note that after a Quick Format, the process can sometimes be reversed using special recovery software (available online via Google) if you have not written any additional information to the card.

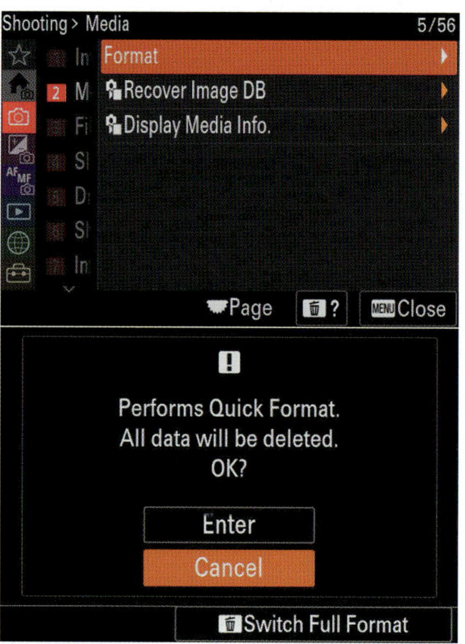

Figure 1.13 Formatting a memory card.

- **Cancel.** If you change your mind, highlight Cancel and press the center button.
- **Switch to Full Format.** Press the Trash button to perform a Full Format instead of the Quick Format. This process takes a bit longer and cannot be undone, but it can make the memory card work faster and more efficiently by eliminating the odd gaps (fragmentation) in the file structure that builds up when multiple Quick Formats allow the camera's operating system to write new photos into the gaps rather than in contiguous sectors of the media. A Full Format can lock out defective sectors, as well.

4. **Format.** After the formatting process is completed, you can press MENU to exit the menu system.

Selecting a Shooting Mode

When it comes time to select the shooting mode and other settings on the a7C II/a7CR, you may start to fully experience the "feel" of the user interface. The mode dial, shown in Figure 1.14, is the control you'll use to select one of the camera's shooting modes. Just below it is the Still/Movie/S&Q dial, which allows you to switch among shooting still photos, capturing movies, or shifting into Slow and Quick (S&Q) video mode.

The S&Q modes let you capture time-lapse/slow-motion and quick-motion video clips when you press the red Movie button. Quick-motion rates of up to 120X normal speed can also be selected. I'll show you how to use these in Chapter 6. For now, make sure the Still/Movie/S&Q dial is in the Still position, and rotate the mode dial above it to select a shooting mode, such as Auto/Scene Selection mode, discussed next.

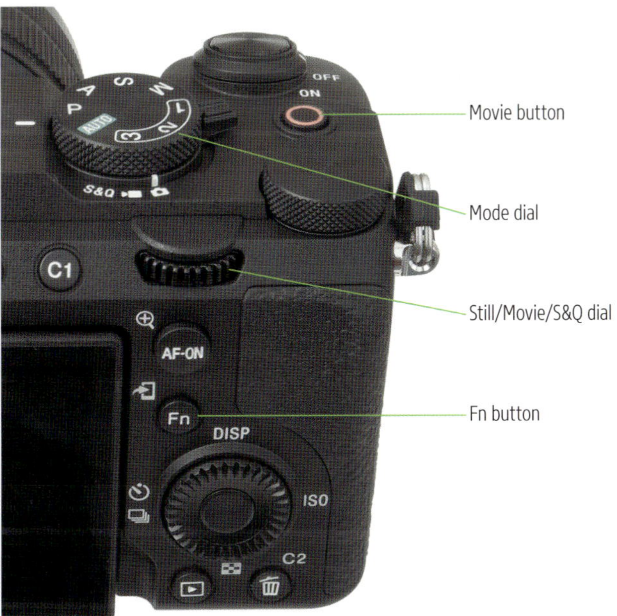

Figure 1.14 Mode dial and Still/Movie/S&Q dial.

Intelligent Auto/Scenes Selection

Sony has combined the traditional separate Scene (SCN) position on the mode dial with its Intelligent Auto function. In either mode, the camera makes most of the decisions for you (except when to press the shutter). When you rotate the mode dial to the green AUTO position, you can use the up/down buttons to select either Intelligent Auto (see Figure 1.15, left) or Scene Selection (see Figure 1.15, right).

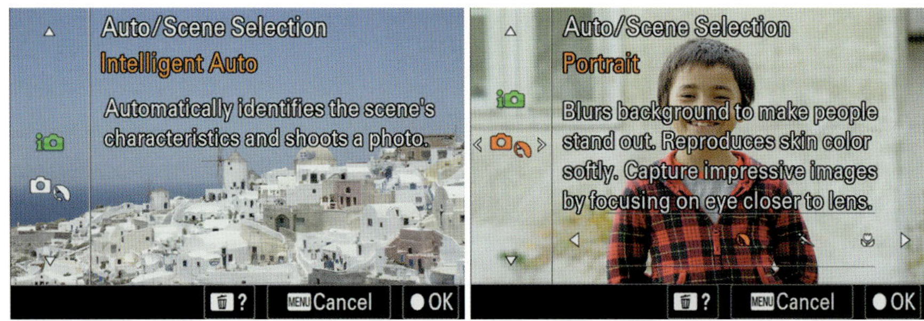

Figure 1.15 Choose Scene Intelligent Auto (left) or Scene Selection mode (right).

When Intelligent Auto is active, the camera will evaluate your scene and switch to one of the 12 Scene modes listed below. An icon representing the active scene mode will appear in the upper-left corner of the camera display. (Figure 1.16 shows each of the icons that may appear.) Note that even if you've disabled Subject Recognition, as described in Chapter 3, the camera will use it anyway in Intelligent Auto mode, as it is required for Portrait, Infant, Night Portrait, and Backlight Portrait scene modes. Scene detection may be incorrect if you're using the digital zoom feature, discussed in Chapter 4.

Even though the camera is choosing a Scene mode automatically, you can still adjust the brightness and color tone of the image and the amount of background focus. The available scene modes the camera may choose on your behalf are as follows:

- **Portrait.** With the Portrait setting, the camera uses settings to blur the background and sharpen the view of the subject, while using soft skin tones. External flash will fire in low light if you have attached it and powered it up.

- **Infant.** Optimizes settings for photographing small children, using bright, vivid colors.

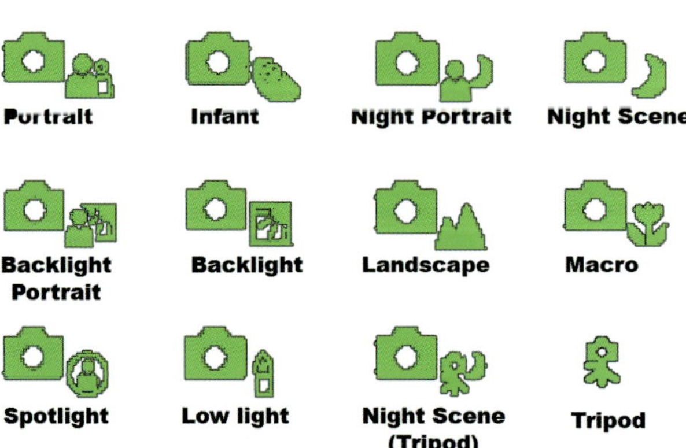

Figure 1.16 Scene icons appear in the upper-left corner of the display.

- **Night Portrait.** Choose this mode when you want to illuminate a subject in the foreground with flash, but still allow the background to be exposed properly by the available light. Be prepared to use a tripod or to rely on the SteadyShot image stabilization feature to reduce the effects of camera shake. If there is no foreground subject that needs to be illuminated by the flash, you may do better by using the Night Scene mode, discussed next. Remember that you must attach and power up the external flash before taking a shot if you want the flash to fire.

- **Night Scene.** This mode uses slower shutter speeds to provide a useful exposure, but without using flash. You should use a tripod to avoid the effects of camera shake that can be problematic with a slow shutter speed.

- **Backlight Portrait.** This is like the Portrait setting but compensates exposure for lighting coming from the rear.

- **Backlight.** Provides exposure compensation for backlight for subjects that are not portraits.

- **Landscape.** Select this scene mode when you want a maximum range of sharpness (instead of a blurred background) as well as vivid colors of distant scenes. External flash will never fire in this mode.

- **Macro.** This mode is helpful when you are shooting close-up pictures of a subject such as a flower, insect, or other small object. External flash will fire in low light, but the flash may be too bright for a subject that's very close to the camera.

- **Spotlight.** This setting compensates for subjects that are illuminated by a small, direct light source, as in stage performances and concerts.

- **Low Light.** This special mode is designed for use in low light. The camera will set a high ISO (sensitivity) level to enable it to use a fast shutter speed to minimize the risk of blurring caused by camera shake.

- **Night Scene (Tripod).** This mode also uses slower shutter speeds, including those long enough to make use of a tripod mandatory.

- **Tripod.** Deploys *really* low shutter speeds, making a tripod almost mandatory. Image stabilization is not going to help you much.

If you choose Scene Selection instead, the seven available Scene modes are slightly different from the Intelligent Auto selections. Their parameters can also be modified using the camera's My Image Style feature described in Chapter 7. Your choices include:

- **Portrait.** With the Portrait setting, the camera uses settings to blur the background and sharpen the view of the subject, while using soft skin tones. External flash will fire in low light if you have attached it and powered it up.

- **Sports Action.** The a7C II/a7CR shoots images continuously while the shutter release is pressed down all the way, capturing a sequence of images. The camera selects faster shutter speeds to freeze the action.

- **Macro.** This mode is helpful when you are shooting close-up photos. An attached external flash will fire under low-light conditions if powered up.

- **Landscape.** Select this scene mode when you want a maximum range of sharpness (instead of a blurred background) as well as vivid colors of distant scenes. External flash will never fire in this mode.

- **Sunset.** Settings are optimized for the warm tones of sunset and sunrise images.
- **Night Scene.** This mode uses slower shutter speeds to provide a useful exposure, but without using flash. A tripod is recommended.
- **Night Portrait.** This mode allows you to use an optional flash to illuminate your main foreground subject, while using a shutter speed slow enough to capture the background much of the time.

Other Modes

The mode dial also includes three semi-automatic modes (Program, Aperture Priority, and Shutter Priority), which allow you to provide more input over the exposure and settings the camera uses, and a fully Manual mode. (These modes are referred to as PASM, for short.) I'll provide additional tips on how and when to use these in Chapter 3. The other positions represent three Memory Recall settings, which are "slots" to register frequently used settings. I'll explain how to use the memory settings in Chapter 6. The mode dial options include:

- **P (Program auto).** This mode allows the a7C II/a7CR to make the basic exposure settings, but you can still override the camera's settings to fine-tune your image.
- **A (Aperture Priority).** Choose this mode when you want to use a particular lens opening (called an aperture or f/stop), especially to control how much of your image is in focus. The camera will set the appropriate shutter speed after you have set your desired aperture using either the front or left rear dial.
- **S (Shutter Priority).** This mode is useful when you want to use a particular shutter speed to stop action or produce creative blur effects. You dial in your chosen shutter speed with the front dial or the left rear dial, and the camera will set the appropriate aperture (f/stop) for you.
- **M (Manual).** Select this mode when you want full control over the shutter speed and the aperture (lens opening), either for creative effects or because you are using a studio flash or another flash unit not compatible with the camera's automatic flash metering. You also need to use this mode if you want to use the Bulb setting for a long exposure, as explained in Chapter 3. You select both the aperture (with the front dial) and the shutter speed aperture (with the rear dial on the camera back). There's more about this mode, and the others, in Chapter 3.
- **1/2/3 (Memory Recall).** These three positions on the mode dial, simply marked 1, 2, or 3, aren't actually exposure modes. Instead, they correspond to one of three different groups of settings that you've previously stored in an internal memory storage "slot" (register) numbered 1, 2, and 3. You can use the memory registers to set up the a7C II/a7CR for specific types of shooting scenes, and then retrieve those settings from the mode dial.

Choosing a Metering Mode

You might want to select a particular exposure metering mode for your first shots, although the default high-tech Multi (short for multi-zone or multi-segment) metering is probably the best choice while getting to know your camera. If you want to select a different metering pattern, you must not be using Intelligent Auto; in that mode, the camera uses Multi metering and that cannot be changed.

To change the metering mode, press the Fn button, located to the upper left of the control wheel, as seen at left in Figure 1.17. The Function menu screen, shown at upper right in the figure, appears. Use the up/down (green triangles at left in the figure) and left/right (yellow triangles) controls to highlight the Metering Mode icon in the Function menu. Then, press the center button to produce the screen shown at lower right in the figure. Use the up/down buttons to reach Multi, Center (for center weighted), Spot, Entire Screen Averaging, and Highlight metering selections. Press the center button to confirm your choice and return the camera to shooting mode.

The metering options are as follows:

- **Multi metering.** In this standard metering mode, the camera attempts to intelligently classify your image and choose the best exposure based on readings from 1,200 different zones or segments of the scene. You can read about this so-called "evaluative" or "Multi-pattern" metering concept, as well as the other four options, in Chapter 3.

- **Center metering.** The camera meters the entire scene but gives the most emphasis (or weighting) to the central area of the frame.

- **Spot metering.** The camera considers only the brightness in a very small central spot, so the exposure is calculated only based on that area. You can set the size of the metering circle to Standard or Large (press the left/right buttons to switch when Spot is highlighted), and either link the spot to a focusing point or fix it to the center position, as I'll explain in Chapter 3.

- **Entire Screen Averaging.** This mode sets exposure based on the mean value (in the arithmetic, rather than vengeful sense) of all the tones in the frame, which means the exposure will remain constant even if your subject moves around within the frame.

- **Highlight metering.** Emphasizes preserving tones in the highlights of an image to avoid overexposure, possibly at the expense of shadow detail. I'll show you how to balance exposures for lighter and darker images in Chapter 3.

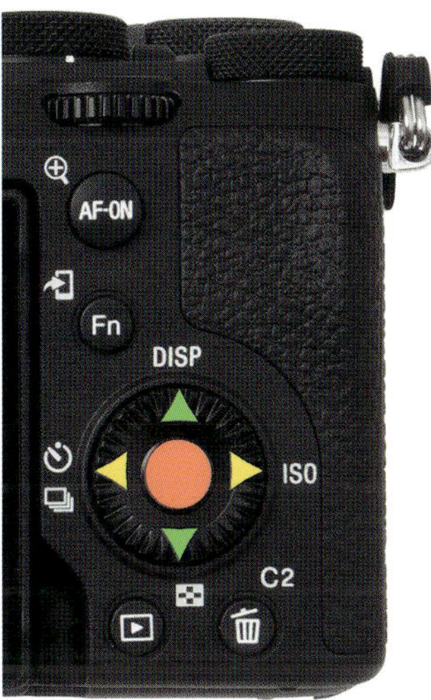

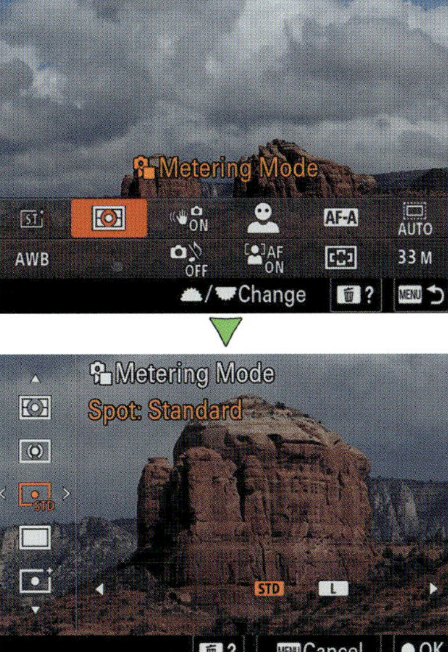

Figure 1.17 Setting the metering mode.

Choosing a Focus Mode

The focus mode can be selected using the same Function menu you used to specify the metering mode. It's located fifth from the left in the top row of the Function menu. Press the center button, and a screen similar to Figure 1.18 pops up. Focus mode determines *when* focus is established. The choices that are available when using P, A, S, or M mode are as follows:

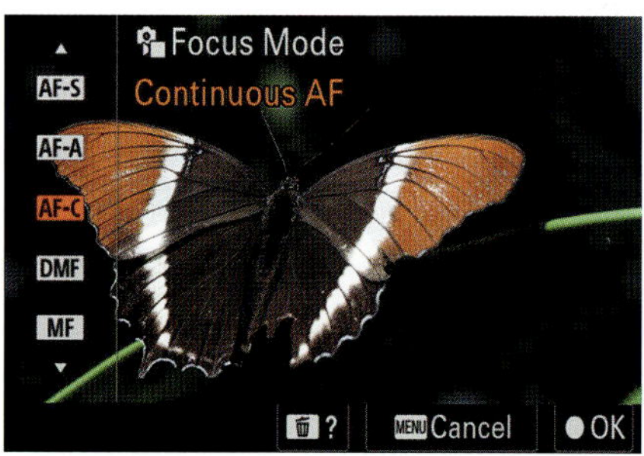

Figure 1.18 Choosing a focus mode.

- **Single-shot AF (AF-S).** This mode, sometimes called *single autofocus*, sets focus after you touch the shutter-release button and the camera beeps to confirm focus (unless you've turned the beeps off). The active focus point(s) is shown in green on the screen and a green dot appears in the bottom-left corner of the display. The focus will remain locked as long as you maintain contact with the shutter-release button, or until you take the picture. If the auto-focus system is unable to achieve sharp focus (because the subject is too close to the camera, for example), the green focus confirmation dot in the lower-left corner will blink. This mode is best when your subject is relatively motionless as when you're taking a portrait or landscape photo.

- **Continuous AF (AF-C).** This mode, sometimes called continuous servo or continuous tracking focus by photographers, sets focus when you partially depress the shutter button, but continues to monitor the frame and refocuses if the distance between the camera and the subject changes. (This allows it to continuously focus on a person walking toward you, for example.) No beep sound is provided. A green dot surrounded by two brackets (curved lines) appears to indicate that the camera is not having a problem achieving and maintaining focus. If the camera should fail to acquire focus, the green dot disappears, and the brackets remain. Continuous AF is a useful mode for photographing moving subjects.

- **Automatic AF (AF-A).** When using AF-A the a7C II/a7CR will switch between AF-S and AF-C to account for a subject that is moving intermittently. When shooting continuously, even if AF-A is set the camera will automatically shift into AF-C mode *after* the first exposure in the series.

- **DMF (Direct Manual Focus).** This setting allows you to manually adjust focus after autofocus has been confirmed, using the focus ring on the lens.

- **Manual Focus.** This mode allows you to focus by rotating the focus ring on the lens. You can use the available magnification and Focus Peaking as aids to manual focus. I'll describe their use in Chapter 4.

Selecting a Focus Area

The Sony a7C II and a7CR are equipped with an advanced hybrid autofocus system using both phase detection and contrast detection. I'll explain what those are and how they work in detail in Chapter 4. In Intelligent Auto and Scene modes, the focus area that will set focus is selected automatically by the camera; in other words, the AF system decides which part of the scene will be in sharpest focus. In the semi-automatic P, A, and S mode, and in the manual M exposure modes, you can allow the camera to select the focus point automatically, or you can specify which focus point should be used with the Focus Area feature.

You can set the camera to one of the focus area modes using the Function menu, as described earlier, or by pressing the C2 button located on the bottom-right rear panel of the camera. The Focus Area icon is fifth from the left in the bottom row. When you press the center button, the screen shown in Figure 1.19 appears. By default, Focus Area will be set to Wide (multi-point autofocus). Scroll up/down until you reach the option you want to use and press the center button to confirm your selection. (The button is located in the middle of the control wheel that resides to the immediate right of the LCD screen.) There are six autofocus area options, described in detail in Chapter 4. Here's a brief overview of the options:

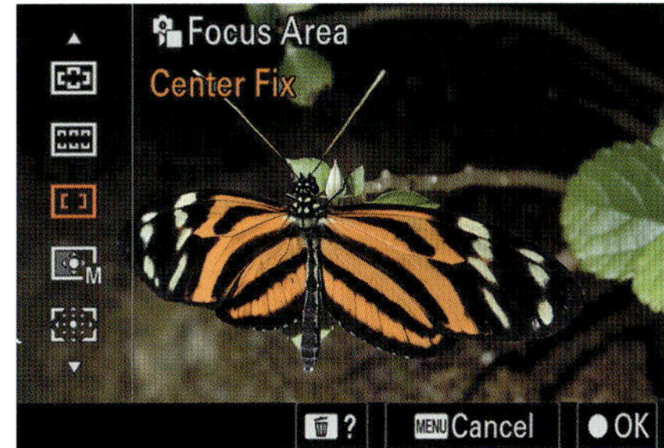

Figure 1.19 Choose Focus Area from this scrolling list.

> ### MOVING THE FOCUS AREA
>
> In shooting mode, the control wheel's center button by default toggles the behavior of the left/right/down buttons between two modes. Press it to switch between:
>
> - **Focus area movement.** If you select Zone, Spot, or Expand Spot focus areas (only), the up/down/left/right directional buttons can be used to move the focus area around the screen.
> - **Button functions.** When focus area movement is not enabled, the left directional button produces the Drive Mode/Self-timer screen; the right button produces the ISO setting screen; and the down button serves as a zoom out/image index button.

- **Wide.** The a7C II/a7CR automatically chooses the appropriate focus area or areas; often, several subjects will be the same distance from the camera as the primary subject. The active AF area or areas are then displayed in green on the LCD monitor or in the viewfinder, depending on which display you're using.
- **Zone.** In this mode, a frame that encompasses nine focus areas appears on the LCD while you're shooting. You can move this grid around the frame with the left/right/up/down directional buttons, and the camera will select which of the focus areas to use to focus within the zone you specify.
- **Center Fix.** The camera *always* uses the focus area in the center of the frame, so it will focus on the subject that's closest to the center in your composition. If you have owned a previous Sony model, this mode was called simply Center.

- **Spot.** After you select this option from Focus Area, you can use the left/right directional buttons to specify Small, Medium, or Large focus areas. Then, while viewing your subject, you can move the focus frame (rectangle) around the screen to your desired location, using the directional buttons. This was called Flexible Spot in previous Sony cameras. Adjust the focus frame so it covers the most important subject in the scene; I'll discuss this topic in more detail in Chapter 4, where I'll cover many aspects of autofocus (as well as manual focus), including some not covered in this Quick Start chapter.

- **Expand Spot.** Like standard Spot, in this mode, if the camera is unable to lock in focus using the selected focus point, it will also use the eight adjacent points to try to achieve focus. Sony previously labeled this mode as Expand Flexible Spot. You can move the focus area using the directional buttons.

- **Tracking.** In this mode, the camera locks focus onto the subject area that is under the selected focus spot when the shutter button is depressed halfway. Then, if the subject moves (or you change the framing in the camera), the camera will continue to refocus *on that subject*. You can select this mode *only* when the focus mode is set to Continuous AF (AF-C). You can activate it for any of the five focus area options described above. That is, once you've highlighted Tracking on the selection screen, you can then press the left/right directional buttons and choose Wide, Zone, Center, Flexible Spot, or Expand Spot.

SWITCHING AF AREAS/POINTS

You can set separate AF points and AF areas for horizontal and two different vertical orientations (horizontal upside-down is not supported) using the Focus > Focus Area > Switch Vertical/Horizontal AF Area entry, described in Chapter 4.

Other Settings

There are a few other settings you can make if you're feeling ambitious, but don't feel bad if you postpone using these features until you've racked up a little more experience with your Sony a7C II/ a7CR. By default, these camera features will be at Auto, so the camera will make a suitable setting.

Adjusting White Balance and ISO

If you like, you can custom-tailor your white balance (overall color balance) and the ISO level (sensitivity) as long as you're not using Intelligent Auto. To start out, it's best to leave the white balance (WB) at Auto, and to set the ISO to ISO 200 for daylight photos or to ISO 400 for pictures on a dark, overcast day or indoors when you'll be shooting with an external flash. You can adjust white balance with the White Balance entry in the Function menu (it's at the far left in the bottom row) or by pressing the C1 button (located to the right of the MENU button and shown earlier in Figure 1.14). ISO can be set using the ISO button (the right directional button on the control wheel), or by pressing MENU and navigating to Exposure/Color > Exposure > ISO. **Note:** If the directional buttons have been toggled to select focus point, press the center button to switch back to button functions.

Using the Self-Timer

If you want to have time to get into the photo before the tripod-mounted camera takes the actual shot, the self-timer is what you need. You can select the self-timer using the Drive Mode button (the left directional button on the control wheel in Figure 1.17). Hold the Drive Mode button and rotate the control wheel to highlight either Self-Timer choice (described next). The dial also includes Single Shooting; High+, High-, Medium-, and Low-speed continuous; and various Bracketing options.

When the Drive Mode screen is visible, scroll up/down through the various options until you reach either the Self-timer (Single) or Self-timer (continuous) options. When the former is highlighted, press the directional buttons to choose 2-, 5-, or 10-second durations. With the Self-timer continuous choice, you can also specify either 3 or 5 images to be taken after the timer elapses. Press the center button to confirm your choice and a self-timer icon will appear on the LCD monitor. Press the shutter release to lock focus and exposure and to start the timer. The self-timer lamp will blink, and the beeper will sound (unless you've silenced it in the menu) until the final two seconds when the lamp remains lit.

The multiple image option is handy if you are taking family group pictures with a few known inveterate blinkers to be pictured. Note that the self-timer setting is "sticky" and will still be in effect for multiple shots, even if you turn the camera off and power up again. When you're done using the self-timer, reset the camera to one of the other Drive Mode options.

Quick Start to Movie Making

I'm going to talk in more detail about your movie-making options in Chapters 10 and 11. For now, though, I'll give you enough information to get started, in case a cinematic subject wanders into your field of view before you get to that chapter. The overrides you have set for certain aspects while shooting still photos will apply to the video clip that you'll record; these include exposure compensation, White Balance, any Creative Look, Metering Mode, Subject Recognition, D-Range Optimizer, and Lens Compensation. You'll even retain your aperture setting if the camera is in A mode or the shutter speed if it's in S mode. You also get access to the settings for the movie file formats (XAVC S HD and XAVC S 4K modes we'll explore later in this book) and the resolution in the Record Setting item of the Camera Settings II section of the menu.

After you start recording, you can change the aperture or the shutter speed; either step will make your movie brighter or darker as you'll notice while viewing on the EVF or LCD while making the adjustments. However, you can also set plus or minus exposure compensation for that purpose while filming. The a7C II and a7CR provide an effective Continuous Autofocus in Movie mode and sound is recorded in stereo with the built-in mics located on the front panel of the cameras.

Let's save the discussion of those aspects for Chapters 10 and 11. For the moment, let's just make a basic movie. With the camera turned on, aim at your subject, and locate the red Movie record button located on the top panel to the right and behind the shutter button. You don't have to switch to Movie mode using the Still/Movie/S&Q dial; the Movie mode position simply gives you access to more movie-shooting controls, including the ability to adjust shutter speed and aperture.

Compose as you wish and press that button once to start the recording, and again to stop it; don't hold the button down. The camera will adjust the focus and exposure automatically, and you can zoom while recording, if you have a zoom lens attached to the camera.

After you finish recording a video clip, you can view it by pressing the Playback button at the lower right of the LCD screen, then pressing the center button to start the movie displayed. While a movie is being played back, press the down button to access an operation panel with playback controls. (See Figure 1.20.) Highlight the control you want to use with the directional buttons. I'll explain the use of these buttons in more detail in Chapter 10. From left to right at the bottom of the figure, they are: Previous Movie File, Fast-Rewind, Pause/Resume, Fast-Forward, Next Movie File, Photo Capture, Sound Volume Adjustment, and Close Operation Panel.

Figure 1.20 Movie playback options.

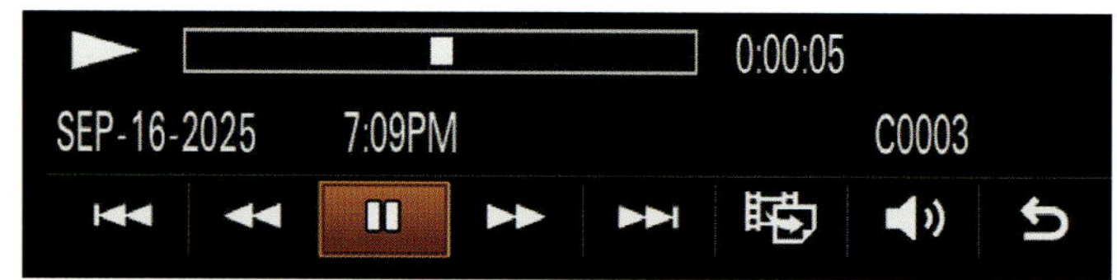

Reviewing the Images You've Taken

The Sony a7C II and a7CR have a broad range of playback and image review options. I'll cover them in more detail in Chapter 2. Initially, you'll want to learn just the basics for viewing still photos, so I'll assume you have taken only such images. Note that, as always, you have several options—the left/right edges of the control wheel or either rear dial can all be used to view the previous or next image. For now, I'll stick to just one image review method in the list that follows. (**Note:** These cameras have *two* rear dials, plus the dial-like control wheel. Sony dubs the dials Rear Dial L [left] and Rear Dial R [right]. They may share a function or each have individual functions, as I will point out.) After shooting some video or JPEG and/or RAW photos, here's how to view them:

- **Playback (Display the most recently taken image).** Press the Playback button. (It's the small button with a > symbol located to the lower right of the LCD monitor screen.) If you have shot both still photos as well as movie clips, the a7C II/a7CR will show both in playback mode. Just press the control wheel's center button to play the movie. Images shot using continuous shooting or interval shooting will be stacked together. To view individual images in the group, press the center button.

- **View a previous image.** Press the left directional button or rotate either rear dial clockwise.

- **View the next image.** Press the right directional button or rotate either rear dial counterclockwise.

- **Change information displayed.** While viewing a photo, press the DISP button (top directional button) repeatedly to cycle among the available displays: views that have no recording data, full recording data (f/stop, shutter speed, image quality/size, etc.), and a thumbnail image with histogram display. (I'll explain all these in Chapter 2.)

- **Delete current image.** Press the lower-right button, marked with a C2 (Custom 2) label and trash can icon, to delete the currently displayed image.

- **Rotate image.** While the image is displayed, press the MENU button and choose Playback > Edit > Rotate. Select Rotate, followed by pressing the center button, to rotate the image on the screen 90 degrees. Successive presses of the center button rotate the image 90 degrees each time. (You won't likely need this feature unless you have disabled automatic rotation, which causes the camera to display your vertically oriented pictures already rotated. I'll explain how to activate/deactivate automatic rotation in Chapter 8.)

- **Zoom.** Press the AF-ON/Zoom In (Enlarge) button located to the right of the viewfinder window to zoom into the image. Rotating the control wheel on the back of the camera also allows you to zoom in and out. You can also scroll around inside the image using the directional buttons. To exit this screen and return to normal view, press the MENU button.

- **Access thumbnail/calendar view.** While in Playback mode, press the down button to display an index screen showing either 9 or 30 thumbnail images (select the number using the Image Index option in the Playback > Playback Option > Image Index entry). Keep scrolling downward to view the thumbnails of the next images (assuming you have shot lots of photos). Scroll to the thumbnail of the photo you want to view and press the center button; the photo will then fill the screen. In default Date View mode, the a7C II/a7CR arranges index images by date shot, and includes a calendar view you can use to look for pictures taken on a specific date. (See Figure 1.21.) (When the left bar of the playback screen is highlighted, press the center button to toggle between Calendar and Date View modes.) You can also choose to play back images using Folder View, or display only specific video file formats. I'll explain those options in more detail in Chapter 8.

VIEWING BURSTS

Capturing bursts of shots in continuous shooting modes produces a lot of separate images—up to 8–10 frames per second. Sony lets you speed up picture review by optionally "nesting" each burst sequence into a single "stack," which is represented by a single image overlaid on a "pile" icon. If you decide you do want to look at each image in the burst, press the center button to drill down into the stack, then press the left/right controls to view the images. Press center again to return to normal view. Enable Playback > Playback Option > Display as Group entry to activate the stacking feature.

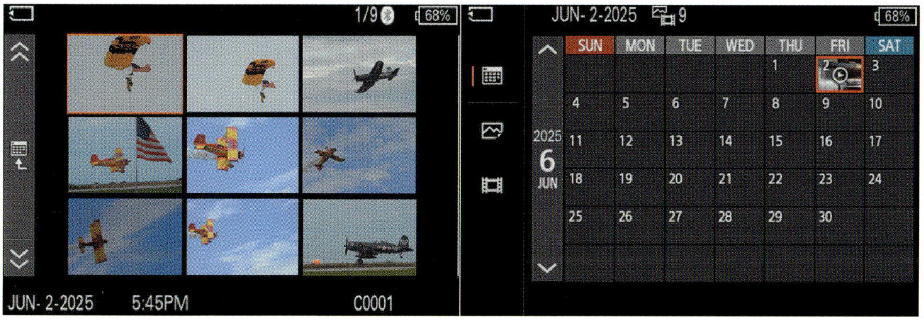

Figure 1.21 Viewing thumbnails (left) and calendar view (right).

Transferring Files to Your Computer

The final step in your picture-taking session will be to transfer the photos and/or movies you've taken to your computer for printing, further review, or editing. (You can also take your memory card to a retailer for printing if you don't want to go the do-it-yourself route.) Your a7C II/a7CR allows you to print directly to PictBridge-compatible printers, without downloading the photos to a computer, and to create print orders right in the camera. It also offers an option for selecting which images to transfer to your computer.

For now, you'll probably want to transfer your images by either using the USB cable from the camera to the computer or by removing the memory card and transferring the images with a card reader. The latter option is ordinarily the best because it's usually much faster and doesn't deplete the camera's battery. However, you might need to use a cable transfer when you have the cable and a computer but no card reader. (You might be using the computer at a friend's home, for example.)

Here's how to transfer images from a memory card to the computer using a card reader:

1. Turn off the camera.
2. Slide open the memory card compartment door and press on the card, which causes it to pop up, so it can be removed from the slot.
3. Insert the memory card into a memory card reader accessory that is plugged into your computer. Your installed software detects the files on the card and offers to transfer them. The card can also appear as a mass storage device on your desktop; in that case, you can open that and then drag and drop the files to your computer.

To transfer images from the camera to a Mac or PC computer using the USB cable:

1. Turn off the camera.
2. Open the port door on the left side of the camera (the upper door, marked with the candelabra-like USB symbol) and plug an optional USB Type-C cable into the USB port inside that door.
3. Connect the other end of the USB cable to a USB port on your computer.
4. Turn on the camera. From this point on, the method is the same as in entry 3 in the card reader list above.

Wireless File Transfer

Your a7C II and a7CR are also equipped with built-in Bluetooth/Wi-Fi which provide many options, including a method for wireless transfer of image files to a Mac or Windows computer when connected to a wireless network. This is a multi-faceted topic, so I won't begin to discuss it here; instead, you'll find full coverage in Chapter 9.

Your Camera Roadmap   2

The official manuals for the a7C II and a7CR are available only as online HTML "Web Manuals," which you can also download as PDF files. Sony calls these documents "Help Guides," which many take to mean that the average user needs a lot of help to use them. They're 500-plus pages long and include page upon page of tiny black-and-white drawings impaled with dozens of callouts. No less than *nine* pages are devoted just to *labeling* the 250-plus individual icons that can appear in the viewfinder and LCD monitor screen. Seeking information about a specific feature is a lot like being presented with a world globe when what you really want is to locate the capital of Brazil.

I'll take a somewhat different approach in this book, particularly in this "roadmap" chapter. Rather than provide you with a satellite view, I'll give you a street-level map that includes close-up, full-color photos of the camera from several angles, with a smaller number of labels clearly pointing to each individual feature. And, I don't force you to flip back and forth among dozens of pages to find out what a component does. Each photo is accompanied by a brief description that summarizes the control's functions, so you can begin using it right away. *Only when a feature deserves a lengthy explanation do I direct you to a more detailed write-up later in the book.*

Using Cross-References

"I wish I could learn everything I need to know about a feature in one place!"

Some readers find cross-references inconvenient. They'd like to open the book to one page and read *everything* there is to know about using, for example, the bracketing feature. Unfortunately, it's not possible to explain everything there is to know about every button and control (or indeed, any feature of either camera) with anything less than a mammoth 100-page chapter.

But it is possible to tell you what you absolutely *must* know to get started. So, if you're wondering what the right directional button on the control wheel does (it summons the ISO adjustment screen), I'll tell you up front, rather than have you flip to several pages. This book is not a scavenger hunt. But *after* I explain how to select continuous shooting, I *will* provide a cross-reference to a longer explanation later in the book that clarifies the use of the various drive modes, the self-timer, and exposure bracketing. Unfortunately, it's impossible to understand some features without having a background in what related features do. Explanations of how to bracket exposures aren't useful for those who need to first understand all the available exposure options.

So, my strategy is to provide you with introductions in the earlier chapters, covering simple features completely, and relegating some of the in-depth explanations to later chapters. For veteran enthusiasts, the introductions may be all they need; less-experienced photographers will be glad I didn't make unwarranted assumptions about what they already know. Feedback from readers has told me that this kind of organization works best for the broadest possible audience working with cameras as sophisticated as the Sony a7C II and a7CR. (Remember, you were a beginner once, too, and can always skip any sections if you feel you won't benefit from a refresher.)

In all cases, however, by the time you finish this chapter, you'll have a good understanding of every control and of the various roles each can take on. I'll provide a lot more information about items in the menus and submenus in Chapters 6, 7, 8, and 9, but the following descriptions should certainly satisfy the button pusher and dial twirler in you.

Front View

When thinking about any given camera, we always imagine the front view. That's the view that your subjects see as you snap away, and the aspect that's shown in product publicity and on the box. The frontal angle is, essentially, the "face" of a camera like the Sony a7C II or a7CR. But, not surprisingly, most of the "business" of operating the camera happens *behind* it, where the photographer resides. The front of the camera has very few controls and features to worry about. These few controls are most obvious in Figure 2.1:

- **Self-timer lamp/AF illuminator.** This bright LED flashes while your camera counts down the 2-, 5-, or 10-second self-timer. In 5- and 10-second modes, the lamp blinks at a measured pace off and on at first, then switches to a constant glow in the final moments of the countdown. When the self-timer is set to 2 seconds, the lamp stays lit throughout the countdown. Stop the self-timer, once initiated, by pressing the shutter release a second time. This lamp also serves as the AF (autofocus) Illuminator, emitting its orange-red glow in dark conditions to help the camera's autofocus system achieve sharp focus. You can enable/disable the AF illuminator in the Focus > AF/MF > AF Illuminator menu entry.

- **Front dial.** Adjusts various settings. It's often used in conjunction with the rear dials to control pairs of adjustments, such as shutter speed and aperture.

Figure 2.1

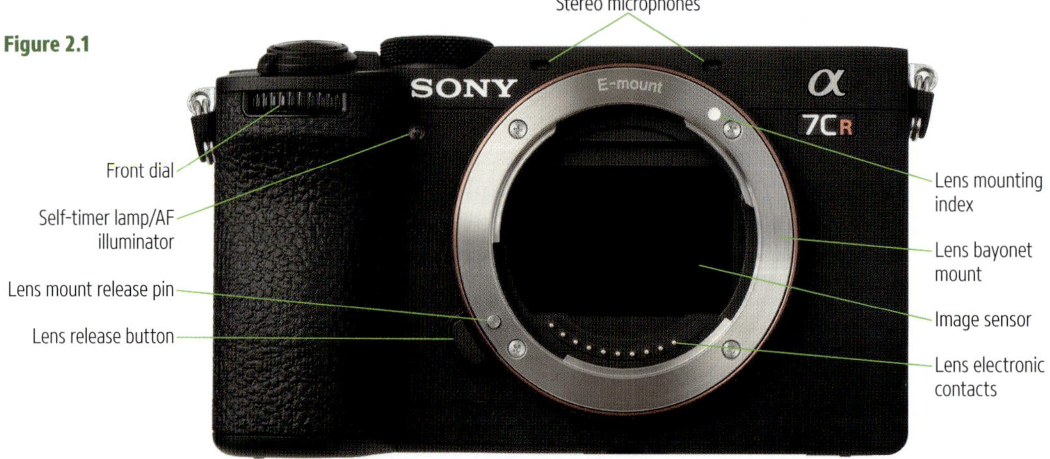

- **Stereo microphones.** A pair of microphones on the front of the camera can capture stereophonic audio while making movies.
- **Lens release button.** Press and hold this button to unlock the lens so you can rotate it to remove the lens from the camera.
- **Lens mount release pin.** Retracts when the release button is pressed, to allow removing the lens.
- **Lens mounting index.** Match this recessed, white index button with a similar white indicator on the camera lens's mount to line the two up for attaching the lens to the a7C II/a7CR.
- **Lens bayonet mount.** Grips the matching mount on the rear of the lens to secure the lens to the camera body. While both cameras have a sturdy mount fully capable of supporting many longer lenses, it's always a good idea to hold one hand under a very long lens and, if using a tripod or monopod, attach the support to the tripod socket of the lens (if available), rather than the one on the bottom of the body.
- **Lens electrical contacts.** These metal contact points match up with a similar set of points on the lens, allowing for communication with the camera about matters such as focus and aperture.
- **Image sensor.** This fairly ordinary-looking little rectangle is the heart and soul of your digital camera. On these cameras, their EXMOR R sensors are CMOS (complementary metal-oxide semiconductor) devices, approximately 35.7 × 23.8 mm in size, with 60 megapixels (a7CR) or 33 megapixels (a7C II) of resolution.

In Figure 2.2, you can see the terminals/ports hidden under the port covers that provide a modicum of protection from dust and moisture for the internal connectors:

- **Microphone jack.** Allows connecting an external stereo microphone to provide better audio recording than the built-in mics.

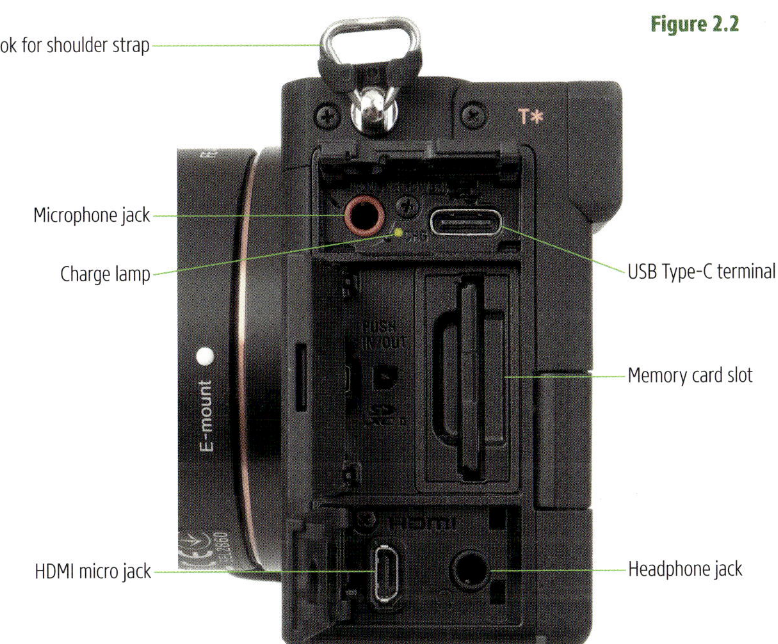

Figure 2.2

- **Headphone jack.** You can monitor audio as you shoot video and listen to your movies during playback by plugging an external headphone into this jack.

- **HDMI micro jack (Type D).** If you'd like to see the images from your camera on a television screen/monitor or direct output to a video recorder, you'll need to buy an HDMI cable (not included with the camera) to connect this port to an HDTV set or monitor. You can also link to an external video recorder and output video to both the memory card and recorder. Be sure to get an HDMI Type-A-to-HDMI-Type-D cable; it has a full-size, standard male HDMI connector on one end and a micro HDMI connector on the other.

- **USB Type-C terminal.** You can use this USB Type-C port to connect your camera to your computer. This connection can be used to upload images to the computer. You can also use this port to charge the battery while it's in the camera, and to upgrade the firmware to the latest version available for your respective camera, using a file downloaded from the Sony support website. The same port serves as a charging port when the USB cable is connected to a powered USB port on your computer or an AC charging adaptor or power pack. You can also operate the camera using the free Imaging Edge Desktop software linked to your computer with a USB-C cable.

- **Charge lamp.** This yellow LED glows steadily while battery charging is underway, and the camera is powered by an external source.

- **Hook for shoulder strap.** Attach your strap to this loop.

- **Memory card slot.** Your SD card goes in here, contacts end first, with the label facing the back of the camera.

The Sony a7C II/a7CR's Business End

The back panel of the a7C II/a7CR is where many of the camera's physical controls reside. As I noted earlier, some can perform several functions, depending on the context. Most of the controls on the back panel are clustered on the right side of the body, labeled in Figure 2.3:

- **MENU button.** Press to enter the multi-tabbed menu system described in Chapter 1. This button also serves to exit many functions, including menu settings and playback zoom. A Menu/Exit label will appear in the viewfinder or LCD monitor in that case.

- **Viewfinder.** Look into this window to activate the eye-level electronic viewfinder (EVF), an internal OLED (organic LED) display with 2,359,296 dots of resolution, utilizing a Zeiss T* Coating to reduce reflections. On top of this, a customizable frame rate is available for this EVF, with options of either 60 fps or 120 fps.

  The viewfinder shows 100 percent of the frame at .70X magnification with a 50mm lens focused to infinity, making it equal to the optical viewfinders found in traditional digital SLR cameras. I actually like it much better in many circumstances, such as when shooting in dim light, when the view is quite bright. You can frame your composition and see the information on the electronic viewfinder's display.

  While some shooters will use the rear-panel LCD monitor for framing their photos instead of the electronic viewfinder, the latter offers some benefits. On sunny days, when the LCD display is often obliterated by glare, the EVF is preferable. You might also want to use it for reviewing

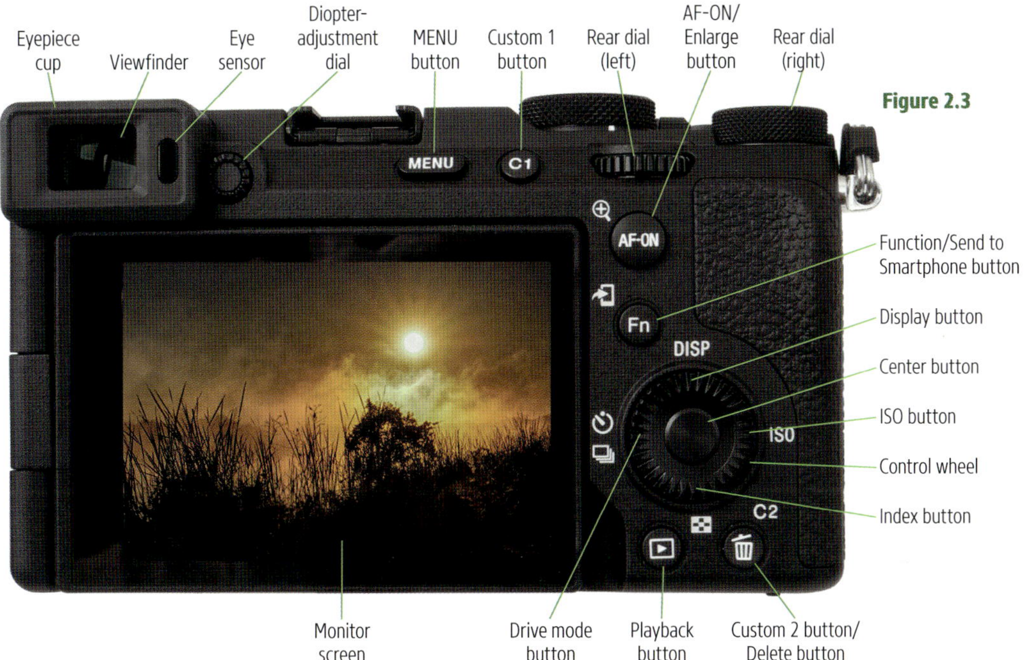

your images and video clips in Playback mode. Holding the camera pressed up against your face helps provide extra steadiness to reduce camera shake (and image blurring) at very slow shutter speeds. (Even the in-body 5-axis SteadyShot stabilization, or the optical SteadyShot included in some lenses, is not a panacea and is more effective when the camera is at least somewhat stable.) Both EVF and LCD monitors can be used with the camera's focus peaking and focus magnification features, which makes it easier to achieve sharp focus manually.

- **Eye sensor.** This solid-state device senses when you (or anything else, unfortunately) approach the viewfinder; the camera then triggers a switch that turns off the back-panel LCD, activates the viewfinder screen, and starts the autofocus system. You can enable or disable either of these features, as I'll explain in Chapter 4.

- **Eyepiece cup.** This soft rubber frame seals out extraneous light when pressing your eye tightly up to the viewfinder, and it also protects your eyeglass lenses (if worn) from scratching.

- **Diopter-adjustment dial.** As described in Chapter 1, you can spin this to adjust the built-in diopter correction to suit your vision. Since it's right beside the viewfinder window, it's a bit difficult to change the diopter setting while your eye is at the EVF, but it's worth taking the time to adjust it.

- **Rear dial L (left)/Rear dial R (right).** This pair of dials can be used to adjust various settings. In some cases, you can use either dial to perform a function (for example, to advance from one image to the previous/next during playback). Other times they will each perform separate functions. For example, in Program, Aperture Priority, Shutter Priority, and Manual exposure modes (commonly referred to as PASM), the right rear dial is rotated to add or subtract exposure compensation. The left dial is used to adjust shutter speed, aperture, or both (depending on the exposure mode you're using.)

I will let you know when only one or the other dial is appropriate. Both dials can be defined by you to perform other specific functions, such as changing white balance or ISO, as I'll describe in Chapter 9.

- **Custom 1 button.** This button, when pressed, brings up the White Balance adjustment screen. The Custom 1 button can also be redefined to perform any of several different functions, such as metering mode, creative look, drive mode, focus mode, flash mode, flash compensation, focus area, exposure compensation, and dozens of other behaviors. You can also select Not Set to deactivate it entirely.

- **Custom 2/Delete button.** This button's dual features are not complicated. When shooting images, the C2 button enables/disables touch-screen operations, which allow you to adjust many settings, such as choosing a focus area mode or specifying a focus point. I'll touch on the LCD's tactile tactics shortly.

  When reviewing images in Playback mode, the button is used to delete an image, a group of continuous/bracketed images, or a movie. Both behaviors can be set to some other function using the Custom Key entries in the Setup menu, as described in Chapter 9.

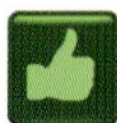

TIP As you'll learn, the control wheel, dials, and the custom buttons can be redefined to some other action, allowing you to tailor the camera's operation so it best suits your needs using the Setup > Operation Customize options. However, keep in mind that extensively customizing your camera's behavior can lead to confusion—both for you and for others you may allow to use the camera.

- **Monitor screen.** This swiveling LCD screen can be used to preview images and to view them afterward, and to display/navigate menus. The LCD monitor has 3:2 proportions, which is perfect for previewing/shooting/reviewing stills. When you're shooting movies or using the 16:9 aspect ratio for stills, black bars appear at the top and bottom of the screen.

  You can set the LCD monitor brightness with an item in the Setup menu, to be discussed in Chapter 9; there's a special feature that provides a super-bright Sunny Weather display, useful on bright days when the screen would otherwise be difficult to view. The monitor swivels outward and can be tilted up or down to provide a waist-level view or shoot images in "periscope" mode with the camera held overhead. The screen has touch functions, which I'll explain in a following section. You can also reverse the screen so it faces forward for vlogging or to provide your subject with a preview image. (See Figure 2.4.)

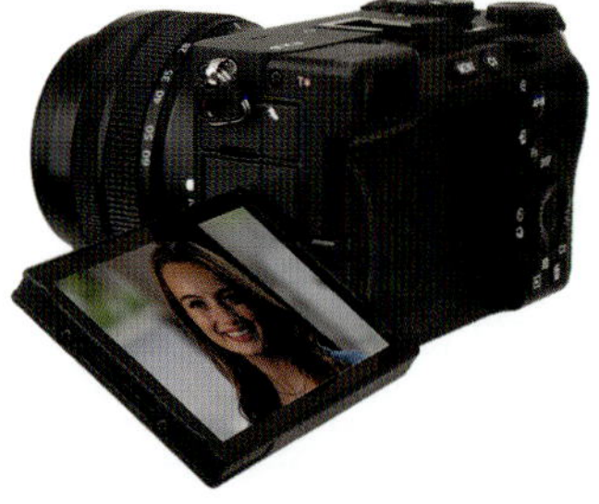
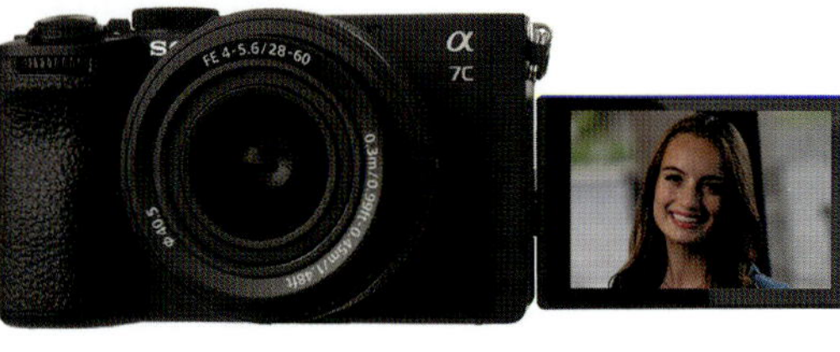

Figure 2.4 The a7C II/ a7CR's fully articulated monitor screen.

- **AF-ON/Enlarge button.** This button has two modes, depending on whether you are in shooting mode or image playback mode. It can also be redefined to perform a function of your choice.
  - **Shooting mode.** Press this button in shooting mode to commence the autofocus and tracking operations. It's especially useful when you want to use back-button focus, as described in Chapter 4. (Back-button focus separates exposure lock from autofocus, allowing you to lock the exposure by pressing the shutter release halfway or you can re-compose at will, and later start AF only when you press a button on the back of the camera.)
  - **Playback mode.** While reviewing pictures in Playback mode, pressing this button activates the zoom feature and enlarges (magnifies) the full-screen image under review. It functions as a zoom-in button. When the image is magnified, you can rotate the control wheel to zoom in and out of the image, with 30 different levels of magnification, and use the left/right/up/down directional buttons to move the magnifier frame around within the image. To exit zooming, press the MENU button.

    Three options are available for the playback zoom feature found in the Playback > Magnification menu. The first, Enlarge Image, magnifies; the Enlarge Initial Magnification entry can be set so the previous (most recent) zoom setting is used, or whether the standard magnification is applied. The third option specifies the initial position for the magnification window (as shown in the navigation box in the lower-left corner of the screen). Set Enlarge Initial Position to Focused Position to enlarge at the point used to focus the image, or set to Center to enlarge the center of the frame. For more Playback options, see Chapter 8.
- **Image Index button.** This button also has two modes, only one of which is active by default:
  - **Shooting mode.** By default, this button has no function in shooting mode. You can use Setup > Custom Operations > (Still) Custom Key/Dial Settings to change its behavior from Not Set to a function of your choice.
  - **Playback mode.** In full-frame, non-magnified view, the button shows an Index display of thumbnail images (either 9 or 30 thumbnails, depending on your selection in the Playback > Playback Option > Image Index entry). You can switch from Index to Calendar view, as explained in Chapter 1 and illustrated in Figure 1.21.

TRIPLE THREAT CUSTOM KEYS

The Setup > Operation Customize entries allow assigning separate Custom Key/Dial Settings behaviors for Shooting, Movie, and Playback modes, as outlined in Chapter 9.

- **Function/Send to Smartphone button.** In Shooting mode, press the Fn button to produce a screen with 12 shooting setting options (described in the section that follows this one). In Playback mode, pressing this button produces a Send screen that allows you to upload the current image, all images with the same date, multiple images, or images meeting criteria you specify. I'll explain the Send to Smartphone options in Chapter 9.

- **Playback button.** Displays the last picture taken. Thereafter, you can move back and forth among the available images by pressing the left/right directional buttons, or spinning the control wheel, front dial, or either rear dial to advance or reverse one image at a time. To quit playback, press this button again. The camera also exits Playback mode automatically when you press the shutter-release button halfway (so you'll never be prevented from taking a picture on the spur of the moment because you happened to be viewing an image).

- **Center button.** In shooting mode, the center button toggles the control wheel's functions between direct access functions and Focus Standard behavior (described next). When the control wheel is in either mode, pressing the button switches to the other. When viewing menus and options screens, or reviewing images during Playback, the center button functions as an Enter/OK key.

- **Control wheel buttons (Shooting mode).** This ridged dial, which surrounds the large center button, performs several important functions and is the only control on the camera that can be activated in two different ways: you can rotate the ridged part of the wheel to perform certain actions (such as navigation or setting exposure controls), and you can press in on the various edges at top, bottom, left, and right.

  The left/right/up/down edges of the wheel function as buttons, with multiple modes, which Sony dubs direct access functions and Focus Standard (focus point movement):

  - **Direct access functions.** Each directional button can serve as a direct access key to summon Display (Up button), Drive Mode (left button), or ISO (right button). The down button has no function in shooting mode until you assign one. The sidebar Direct Access Functions describes these in more detail.

  - **Focus Standard.** Those same buttons can serve as left/right/up/down directional buttons for moving the focus point/zone around within the frame when using Focus Area modes that allow repositioning the focus area (Zone, Spot, and Expand Spot).

  To toggle between direct access functions and focus point movement, press the center button. For example, if you want to move the focus point to the right and pressing the right button summons the ISO adjustment screen instead, press the center button to switch back to Focus Standard mode. When you're done moving the focus area, press the center button again to exit Focus Standard.

- **Control wheel buttons (Playback mode).** During image review, the control wheel buttons have two different functions:

  - **Image display options.** Press the right/left buttons to move to the next/previous image. The up (DISP) button cycles among the available playback informational screens: full recording data, histogram with recording data, and no recording data. When displaying a movie on the screen, the DISP button produces only two screens: with or without recording information. There is no histogram display available. During movie playback, the down button summons an adjustment screen for movie playback volume and other settings.

  - **When image is magnified.** When an image is magnified in Playback mode, all four buttons and their diagonal counterparts can be used to move the viewing area around within the magnified image and within the index screens during playback.

- **Control wheel buttons (Menu/Adjustment screen modes).** The left/right/up/down buttons function as navigation controls used to highlight entries and options, which you can then confirm using the center button.
- **Control wheel rotation.** When the camera is in Shooting mode, rotating the control wheel changes shutter speed in Manual and Shutter Priority modes, and changes the aperture in Aperture Priority mode. If you're using Program mode, the control wheel produces different combinations of shutter speed and aperture that produce the same exposure (*program shift*).

DIRECT ACCESS FUNCTIONS

Here's a summary of the behavior of the control wheel buttons in Direct Access Functions mode:

- **DISP button (Up).** The up key is labeled as DISP, for Display Contents, and it provides display-oriented functions, switching among informational screens.
- **Down button.** By default, the down key has no direct access function, but you can assign one using Setup > Custom Operation Customize > (Stills) Custom Key/Dial Settings, as described in Chapter 9.
- **Drive mode button (Left).** One press of this button leads to a series of options that let you set the self-timer, enable the camera to shoot one frame at a time or continuously at a fast or very fast rate, or set up exposure bracketing. The latter causes the camera to automatically take a series of shots, varying the exposure for each to ensure you get the best exposure possible.

  When you scroll to the Self-timer or Brackets item, you can press the right key to adjust options for those drive modes.
- **ISO button (Right).** When not helping you navigate to the right through menus and other screens, this button lets you activate the ISO screen in a compatible Shooting mode. You can then scroll up/down among the options by rotating the camera's control dial or control wheel or by pressing the control wheel's directional buttons.

Accessing Settings

The a7C II/a7CR provides several different screens that can be used to make adjustments to your camera's settings. The Function button provides quick access to some frequently used settings, using one of two modes: the For Viewfinder function menu, which appears only on the LCD monitor, and the Shooting function menu, which is displayed on the LCD monitor and viewfinder. Each of these modes offers a different set of adjustments, as I'll describe next. You can also access the Main menu, which offers 18 different adjustments. The next sections will explain all your options.

For Viewfinder Function Menu

The For Viewfinder display on the LCD monitor shows a full array of settings, and no live view of the image (see Figure 2.5, left). Press the DISP (up) button until it appears. You would most commonly display this screen when you are using the viewfinder exclusively for framing your image and want the maximum amount of data to appear on the LCD.

When this screen is shown, press the Fn button to produce what Sony formerly called the Quick Navi screen (see Figure 2.5, right). You can then use the directional controls to highlight any of the settings that are not grayed out.

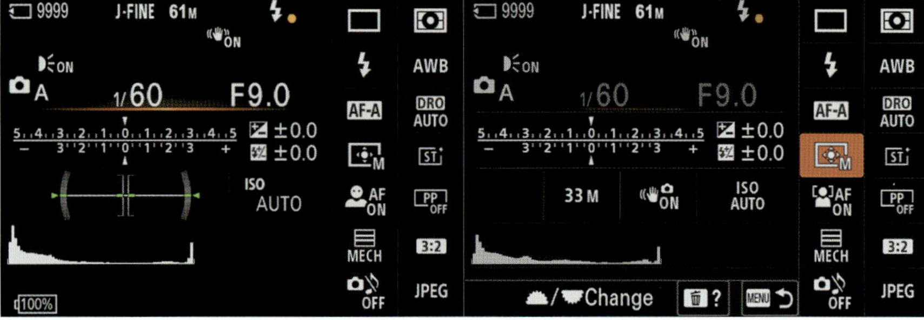

Figure 2.5 The For Viewfinder information screen is available only for the LCD monitor and is not shown in the viewfinder (left). Press the Fn button to work with the settings screen (right).

Once an option is highlighted, you can rotate the control wheel to change its settings quickly or press OK to produce a screen with all the options. Use the directional buttons and the OK button to select the setting you want. When this display is visible on the LCD monitor, you must compose images using the electronic viewfinder.

Shooting Function Menu

When you press the Fn button in shooting mode, the Function menu shown in Figure 2.6 appears in the viewfinder, and will be displayed on the LCD if the For Viewfinder screen is not shown. By default, the 12 functions shown are arrayed in two rows along the bottom. However, as I'll describe in Chapter 9, you can choose exactly which functions you'd like to display; you aren't locked into 12. If you prefer, you can define a single row of six favorite functions (choose Not Set for a given position's setting and it will appear as a blank). To adjust any of the functions, just follow these steps:

1. Press the Fn button and use the directional keys to highlight one of the setting icons.

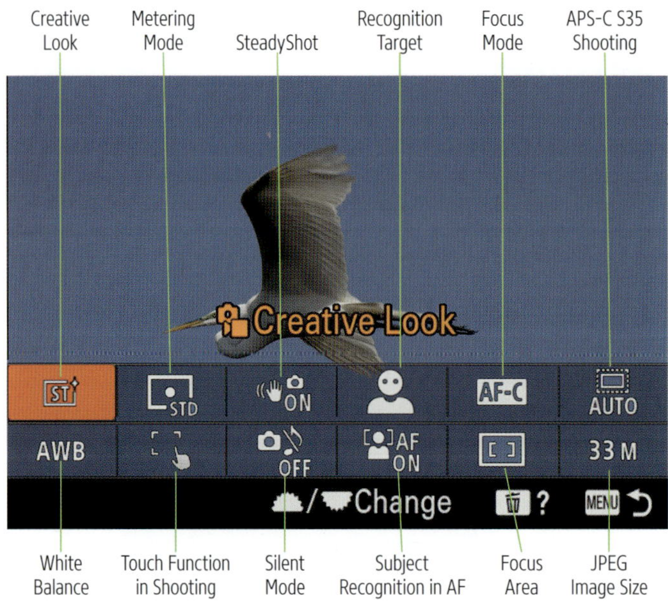

Figure 2.6 Up to 12 user-selectable choices are available in the Function menu. This is the default layout of the a7C II version; the a7CR menu is identical except that Shutter Type replaces Silent Mode.

2. When your setting is highlighted:

   - **Press the center button** to produce an adjustment screen with all the choices shown. You might need to do this as you are learning to use your camera and would like to see all your options arrayed in a vertical column. Then use the directional buttons to select the one you want. If a choice has multiple options, it will be accompanied by a right-pointing or left-pointing arrow. For example, when you choose the focus mode, you can press the left/right buttons to select from AF-S, AF-A, AF-C, DMF, and MF.

   - **Optionally, you can rotate the control wheel** *or* **the front dial** to cycle among the available choices, which will appear one by one as you spin. Some of the choices have multiple options in this mode as well, which will appear on the screen.

3. Press the center button to confirm your choice. You'll be returned to the Function menu (press MENU to exit) or exit the settings entirely.

Main Menu Adjustments

The Main menu tab has only a single screen that displays a shooting setting list. The version displayed in still photography mode is shown in Figure 2.7. A similar menu with movie shooting settings appears when the Still/Movie/S&Q dial is set to the Movie position. You can navigate to this screen when you want to be able to see at a glance the current status of your most important shooting settings. I find the display is easier to review than sorting out the cluttered icons that can populate the viewfinder or LCD screen during shooting.

You can also highlight any of the settings that are not grayed out, press the center button, and adjust that setting quickly. Note that when the shooting mode is Program Auto (P), the shutter speed and aperture value are highlighted and shown in the same area; rotate the front or rear dials to change to different combinations of shutter speed and aperture that produce the same programmed exposure (Program Shift, discussed in Chapter 3).

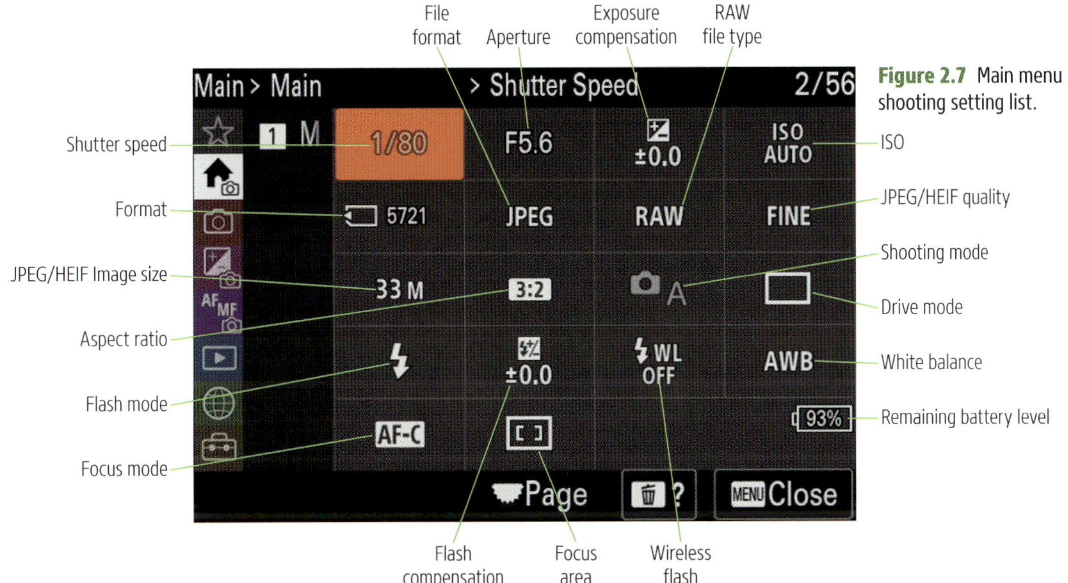

Figure 2.7 Main menu shooting setting list.

Introducing the Touch Screen/Pad

Sony has included a touch-screen/pad in the a7C II/a7CR's arsenal of tools. The dual screen/pad nomenclature is applied because the touch feature can be used in two different ways: as a touch screen when you are using the LCD monitor to compose your photos and as a touch pad that you can tap when the camera is raised to your eye and you're using the electronic viewfinder. This section explains both modes and the options available once you've set up touch operations using the step-by-step instructions in Chapter 9.

You can specify a focus point and focus tracking when shooting stills and videos. Touch focus feature is quite useful, especially when shooting movies, as it allows selecting a focus area with a gentle tap. You can choose to focus on the selected area, or focus *and* adjust exposure based on the focus position. In playback mode, you can navigate menus and select settings, scroll through images, tap to select individual images, and pinch/expand with your fingertips to zoom in and out. Here are the two modes:

- **Touch panel.** When active and you're using the LCD monitor to compose, you can select a focus point or zone anywhere that the camera is able to achieve auto-focus (that is, most of the frame other than the edges). You can tap the screen or hold down your finger and slide the focus area around. (See Figure 2.8.) A "Focus Cancel" or "Tracking Cancel" message appears; press the center button to cancel your focus selection. A quick tap may not register; this function requires a firm press. At your option, exposure can be calculated at the specified focus point. I'll explain the various AF-area modes in Chapter 4.

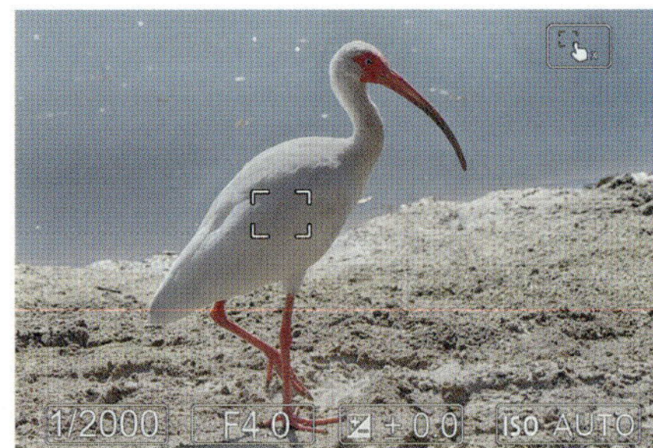

Figure 2.8 Touch the screen to indicate a focus point.

- **Touch pad.** When touch pad mode is active and you're using the electronic viewfinder to compose, you can touch the LCD monitor screen to specify the focus area. You don't have to tap the exact area (actually, that's impossible, because you're not actually looking at the LCD). Instead, when you touch the pad, a focus point appears in the viewfinder *relative to the location on the LCD*. That is, if you tap the center of the sensitive area, the focus point appears in the center; tap to the right or left, and the focus area appears to the right or left side. As I'll explain shortly, that mode is needed because you can change the size of the sensitive area of the LCD screen. Once the focus area is displayed, keep your finger on the screen and slide it around to the position you want, using your view through the EVF as your reference.

Touch Options

Three touch options are available from the Setup > Touch Operation menus. You can learn more about how to enter touch screen options in Chapter 9. Here, I'll just quickly describe the adjustments you can make, and why:

- **Touch operation.** Here you can turn touch operation on or off. If you don't want to use the touch screen you can disable it to avoid moving your focus point when you accidentally touch it.
- **Touch panel/pad.** You can define whether the LCD-oriented Touch Panel or EVF-oriented Touch Pad, or *both*, are active. Select Touch Panel Only, and the touch features operate only when you are composing using the LCD monitor; when you bring the camera up to your eye, the touch panel is disabled. Select Touch Pad Only, and touch features are disabled until you bring the camera up to your eye.
- **Touch panel settings.** This entry has three adjustments: Shooting screen (which controls options such as touch focus, touch tracking, or touch shutter) and whether or not touch functions can be used with the Playback and Menu screens, as described in Chapter 9.
- **Touch pad settings.** This entry has three adjustments:
  - **Operation in vertical orientation.** You can specify whether touch controls are available when the camera is oriented in the vertical position (On), or only when the camera is held in horizontal orientation (Off). The touch feature can be a little awkward to use when rotated vertically, so some prefer to disable touch control for that mode.
  - **Touch position mode.** Specify whether touch functions operate using the *absolute* position on your screen (tap an exact position on the screen to move the focus point to the equivalent position on the sensor) or a *relative* position (tap the screen anywhere in the sensitive area, and then slide your finger to move the focus point in that direction from its current position).
  - **Operation area.** By default, the entire touch pad is sensitive when using the EVF, and that works well for most people. However, if your left eye is dominant (i.e., you're "left-eyed"), your nose will touch the screen, and the camera registers that as a finger press. To fix that or to adjust for your personal preferences, you can limit sensitivity of the touch *pad* to the right *or* left 1/2 or 1/4 areas of the screen; or the upper-right, lower-right, upper-left, or lower-left corners. The "relative" orientation remains the same but is limited to that reduced area. (See Figure 2.9.)

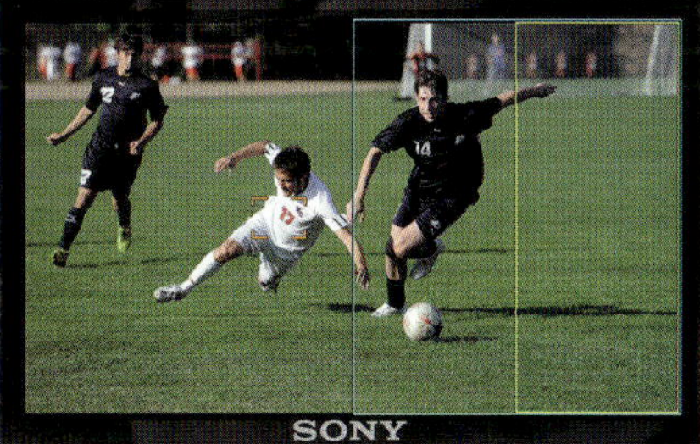

Figure 2.9 Part of the screen can be dedicated as a touch pad.

Data Displays

The Sony a7C II and a7CR each sport a tilting/swiveling 3.0-inch color LCD with 1,036,800-dot resolution and an electronic viewfinder with 2,359,296 dots. These displays show everything you need to see, from images to menu entries to a collection of informational data screens. There are different types of screens for still shooting, movie shooting, and image playback:

- **Still Shooting Mode (Monitor).** Pressing the DISP button cycles among five screens on the LCD monitor: Display All Info., No Display Info., Histogram, Level, and For Viewfinder. The first four are shown in Figure 2.10; the For Viewfinder screen was illustrated earlier in Figure 2.5, left.

- **Still Shooting Mode (Viewfinder).** The viewfinder displays are similar, with most icons relocated to black bars at the top and bottom of the screen (to reduce viewfinder clutter). Only three screens are available: No Display Info., Histogram, and Level.

- **Movie Shooting Mode (Monitor).** The screens displayed when shooting movies have black bars at top and bottom that show the 16:9 video aspect ratio used for video, with most icons overlaid on top of them. The four screens are Display All Info., No Display Info., Histogram, and Level.

- **Movie Shooting Mode (Viewfinder).** The screens displayed when shooting movies are slightly different, with black bars at top and bottom that show the 16:9 video aspect ratio, and most icons overlaid on top of them. The screens are No Display Info., Histogram, and Level.

- **Playback Mode (Monitor and Viewfinder).** Three screens are available: Display Info., a Histogram display that shows separate red, green, blue, and brightness histogram graphs, plus basic shooting information, and a blank No Display Info. screen.

Figure 2.10 Display All Info. (top left); No Display Info, (top right); Histogram (lower left); Level (lower right).

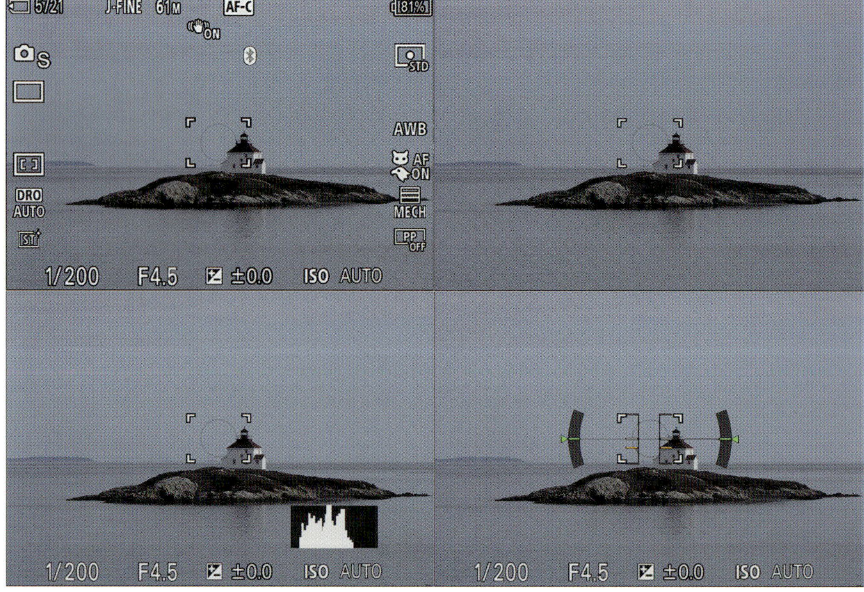

Some of the data is shown only when you are viewing the Display All Info screen, but even then, not every item of data will be available all the time. As discussed earlier, the electronic viewfinder display options provide much less data to avoid cluttering the live preview with numerals and icons during serious photography. Note that when you tilt the LCD monitor away from the camera body, the viewfinder is disabled, because the camera assumes you will be composing your image and performing other functions only with the LCD.

While it is not possible to describe all the dozens and dozens of icons available for the LCD screen (indeed, it's not possible for *all* the icons to appear simultaneously), you'll find all of them illustrated in the Sony Help Guide. The following is a description of the most important information that the camera can display in the LCD in Display All Info when it's set for P, A, S, or M mode; less data is available in other display modes and when other Shooting modes are being used:

- **Shooting mode.** Shows whether you're using Program Auto, Aperture Priority, Shutter Priority, Manual, or one of Auto/Scene modes.
- **Memory card/Uploading status.** Indicates whether a memory card is in the camera. (If you remove the card, a blinking NO CARD indicator will appear instead.) If the camera is connected using Wi-Fi, the indicator will display icons representing the upload status.
- **Exposures remaining.** Shows the approximate number of shots available to be taken on the memory card, assuming current conditions, such as image size and quality. When shooting a movie, the recordable time remaining is shown instead.
- **Image quality.** Your image quality setting (JPEG Extra Fine, JPEG Fine, JPEG Standard, JPEG Light, RAW, or RAW & JPEG) is displayed.
- **Battery status.** The remaining battery life (in percent) is indicated by this icon.
- **Metering mode.** The icons represent Multi, Center, Spot, Entire Screen Averaging, or Highlight metering. (See Chapter 3 for more detail.)
- **Flash status.** Theses icons are shown at left whenever an external flash is active to indicate the status of the flash.
- **Flash charge in progress.** This lightning bolt icon appears on the screen when the optional flash unit is active; a solid orange dot beside it indicates the flash has recycled (charged) and is ready to fire.
- **Flash mode.** Provides flash mode information when an external flash is active. The possible choices are Flash Off, Autoflash, Fill Flash, Slow Sync, Rear Curtain, and Wireless. Not all these choices are available at all times. I'll discuss flash options in more detail in Chapter 13.
- **Flash exposure compensation.** This icon is shown at right whenever an external flash is active to indicate the level of flash exposure compensation, if any, that you have set.
- **White balance.** Shows current white balance setting. The choices are Auto White Balance, Daylight, Shade, Cloudy, Incandescent, Fluorescent, Flash, Underwater Auto, Color Temperature, and Custom. I'll discuss white balance settings and adjustments in Chapter 4.
- **Shutter type.** Mechanical or Electronic shutter are displayed.
- **Dynamic Range Optimizer.** Indicates the type of dynamic range optimization (highlight/shadow detail enhancement) in use: Off, Auto DRO, and levels 1–5 of DRO.

- **Creative Look.** Indicates which of the Creative Look settings (Standard, Vivid, Neutral, Clear, Deep, Light, Portrait, Landscape, Sunset, Night Scene, Autumn Leaves, Black-and-White, or Sepia) is being applied.

- **SteadyShot indicator.** Provides information as to whether the image stabilizer is On or Off if you're using a lens with the SteadyShot mechanism and warns you that the shutter speed will be too long for the stabilizer to fully compensate for camera shake.

- **AF illuminator status.** This icon appears when conditions are dark enough that the AF Illuminator will be needed to light up the area so that the autofocus system can operate properly.

- **Drive mode.** Shows whether the camera is set for Single-shot, Continuous shooting, Self-timer, Self-timer with continuous shooting, or Exposure bracketing. There is one additional option available: Remote Commander, which sets up the camera to be controlled by an infrared remote control.

- **AE Lock.** Appears when autoexposure has been locked at the current setting.

- **ISO setting.** Indicates the sensor ISO sensitivity currently set, either Auto ISO or a numerical value. I'll discuss this camera feature in Chapter 9.

- **Exposure compensation.** This indicator shows the amount of exposure compensation, if any, currently set.

- **Aperture.** Displays the current f/stop set by the camera or, in Manual or Aperture Priority mode, as set by the user. If you're viewing the Graphic display, icons indicate that wider apertures produce less depth-of-field (a "blurry" background) while smaller apertures provide a greater range of acceptable sharpness (increasing the odds of a more distinct background).

- **Shutter speed.** Shows the current shutter speed, either as set by the camera's autoexposure system or, in Manual or Shutter Priority mode, as set by the user. If the camera's Graphic display is used, the screen illustrates that faster shutter speeds are better for action and slower speeds are fine for scenes with less movement.

- **Focus indicator.** Flashes while focus is underway, and turns a solid green when focus is confirmed.

- **Focus mode.** Shows the currently selected focus mode, such as AF-S, AF-C, DMF (Direct Manual Focus), or MF (Manual Focus), as explained in Chapter 9.

- **Focus area mode.** Displays the active focus area mode, such as Wide, Zone, Center, or Flexible Spot, as explained in Chapter 9.

- **Picture Profile.** If you've specified a picture profile image customization setting in the Exposure/Color > Color > Tone > Picture Profiles entry, your choice (from PP1 to PP11) is indicated here. I discuss picture profiles in Chapter 7.

- **Setting Effect.** Indicates whether the LCD shows the effects of any adjustments, including exposure, white balance, or Picture Effects in Shooting mode.

- **Database indicator.** This warning appears when your memory card's image database is full or has errors.

- **Shutter type.** Shows whether the mechanical shutter or electronic shutter is being used.

- **Airplane mode.** Appears when Airplane mode has disabled Wi-Fi and NFC communications.

Going Topside

The top surface of the a7C II and a7CR has several frequently accessed controls of its own. They are labeled in Figure 2.11:

- **Image sensor position mark.** Precision macro and scientific photography sometimes requires knowing exactly where the focal plane of the sensor is. The symbol etched on the top of the camera marks that plane.

- **Movie button.** This button is marked with a central red ring. When you want to make a movie, there is no need to change the Shooting mode, or to fiddle with menu systems, as with some other cameras. Simply press the Movie button; when you're finished, press it again to stop recording. I'll discuss your movie-making options in Chapters 10 and 11.

- **Multi-interface shoe.** This "standard" accessory shoe is used for electronic flash units and contains extra electrical contacts for use with Sony-brand microphones, such as the Sony ECM-XYSTM1 microphone, Sony-compatible electronic flash, and other accessories. However, it is also compatible with the ISO-518 hot shoe used by virtually all other camera manufacturers. While other flashes can be attached and fired, only Sony-compatible units can take advantage of wireless operation, through-the-lens (TTL) metering, and other options.

  The multi-interface shoe replaces the non-standard Minolta-style proprietary "iISO" shoe used by Sony for many of its cameras until about 2012. The older shoe required adapters to use non-Sony accessories. The new multi-interface connector can still be used with older Sony flash units and accessories, but it requires an adapter of its own for backward compatibility. If you own no older Sony electronic flash or accessories, you can simply move forward and purchase gear for the new, more standard hot shoe.

- **Mode dial.** Rotate this dial to select Shooting modes including Manual exposure, Shutter Priority, Aperture Priority, Program Auto, Intelligent Auto, and the Memory Recall positions, numbered 1, 2, and 3 (which each allow you to choose predefined groups of settings for each, as described in Chapter 6).

- **On/Off switch.** Rotate to the right to turn the camera on; to the left to switch it off.

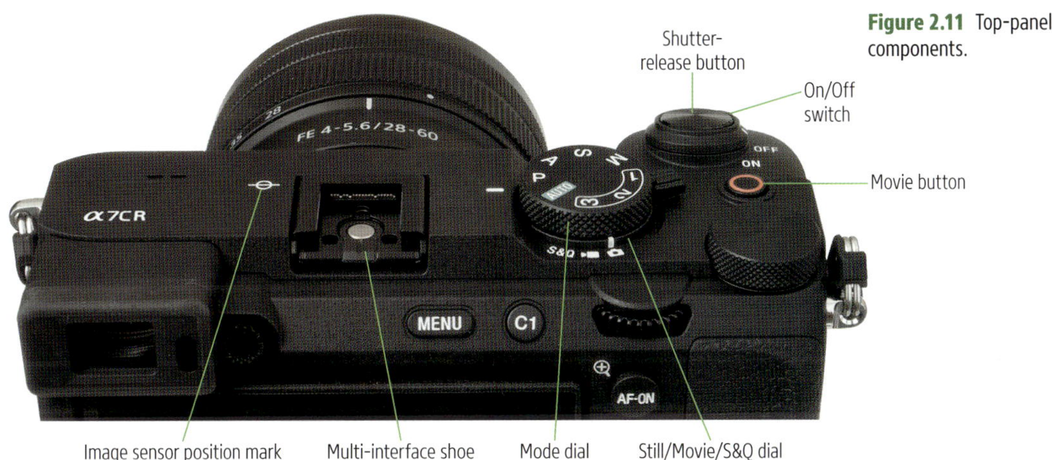

Figure 2.11 Top-panel components.

- **Shutter-release button.** Partially depress this button to lock in exposure and focus. Press it all the way to take the picture. Hold this button down to take a continuous stream of images when the drive mode is set for Continuous shooting. Tapping the shutter release when the camera's power save feature has turned off the autoexposure and autofocus mechanisms reactivates both. When a review image or menu screen is displayed on the LCD, tapping this button removes that display, returning the camera to the standard view and reactivating the autoexposure and autofocus mechanisms.

- **Still/Movie/S&Q dial.** Rotate this dial to switch from Still photography to Movie or Slow & Quick movie modes.

Underneath Your Sony a7C II/a7CR

The bottom panel of your a7C II and a7CR have only a few components, illustrated in Figure 2.12:

- **Tripod socket.** Attach the camera to the flash brackets, tripods, monopods, or other support using this standard receptacle. The socket is positioned roughly behind the optical center of the lens, a decent location when using a tripod with a pan (side rotating) movement, compared to an off-center orientation. For most accurate panning, the socket would ideally be placed a little forward (in *front* of the camera body) so the pivot point is located *under* the optical center of the lens, but you can't have everything. There are special attachments you can use to accomplish this if you like.

- **Battery compartment door.** Slide the door open to access the battery. A flip-up tab can be used to allow the exit of the optional power connector's cable.

- **Lock lever.** Slide toward the center of the camera to unlock the battery compartment door.

- **Cable port.** This door flips to allow the cable for the dummy battery of the Sony NPA-MQZ1K Multi-Battery adapter kit (or AC adapter/couplers from third parties) to exit.

- **Access lamp.** This LED flashes red when the camera is writing to the memory card.

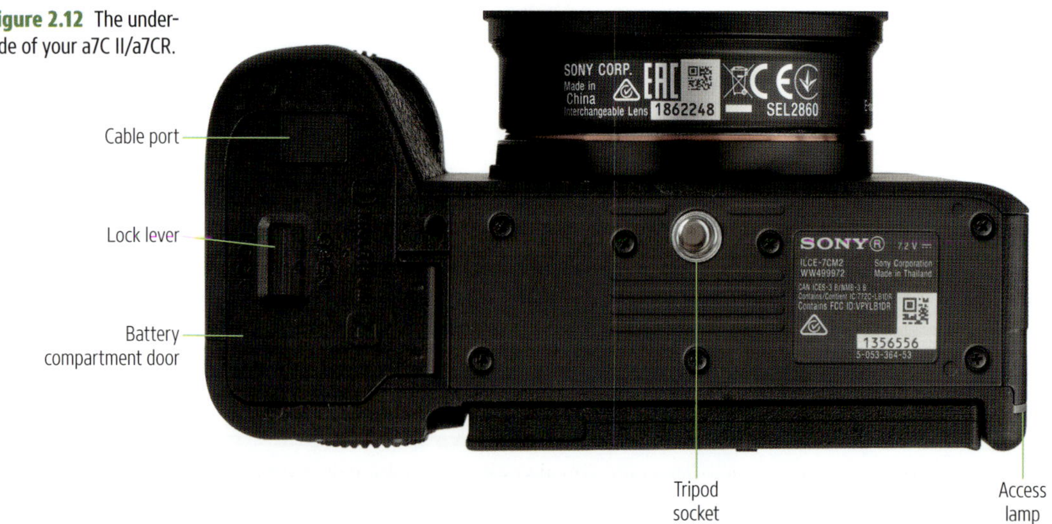

Figure 2.12 The underside of your a7C II/a7CR.

Nailing the Optimum Exposure

3

L eft to their own devices, your a7C II or a7CR can do an excellent job of providing the proper exposure for most scenes. But even a smart camera can frequently benefit from intelligent input. For example, when you shoot with the main light source behind the subject, you end up with *back-lighting*, which can result in an overexposed background and/or an underexposed subject. The camera recognizes backlit situations nicely, and, in most cases, can properly base exposure on the main subject using the default Multi metering mode, producing a decent photo.

But, as a creative photographer, there will be many instances where you would rather *not* have automatic correction for backlighting. What if you *want* to underexpose the subject, to produce a silhouette effect? The a7C II and a7CR have difficulty creating intentional silhouettes and will end up producing unwanted detail in what should have been inky black areas of your image. Fortunately, the camera has metering modes and other exposure options that allow you to produce the image you are looking for. If you're looking for an extensive exposure range, options like the camera's built-in DRO feature can adjust your exposure as you take photos, preserving detail in the highlights and shadows as required. Your Sony a7C II and a7CR also have the capability of *fine-tuning* exposure separately for each of the metering modes, so you can consistently add or subtract a little exposure to suit your creative tastes.

In the most basic sense, exposure is all about light. Exposure can make or break your photo. Correct exposure brings out the detail in the areas you want to picture, providing the range of tones and colors you need to create the desired image. Poor exposure can cloak important details in shadow or wash them out in glare-filled featureless expanses of white.

This chapter discusses using the full range of the camera's various shooting modes and exposure controls, so you'll be better equipped to override the default settings when you want to, or need to, and achieve spot-on exposures that produce the exact image you are looking for, every time.

Getting a Handle on Exposure

You're probably well aware of the traditional "exposure triangle" of aperture (quantity of light, light passed by the lens), shutter speed (the amount of time the shutter is open), and the ISO sensitivity of the sensor—all working *proportionately* and *reciprocally* to produce an exposure. The trio is itself affected by the amount of illumination that is available to work with. So, if you double the amount of light, increase the aperture by one stop, make the shutter speed twice as long, or boost the ISO setting 2X, with any one of those changes you'll get exactly twice as much exposure. Similarly, you can *increase* any of these factors while *decreasing* one of the others by a similar amount to keep the same exposure.

Working with any of the three controls involves trade-offs. Larger f/stops provide less depth-of-field, while smaller f/stops increase depth-of-field (and potentially at the same time can *decrease* sharpness through a phenomenon called *diffraction*). Shorter shutter speeds do a better job of reducing the effects of any camera/subject motion, while longer shutter speeds make that motion blur more likely. Higher ISO settings increase the amount of visual noise and artifacts in your image, while lower ISO settings reduce the effects of noise. (See Figure 3.1.)

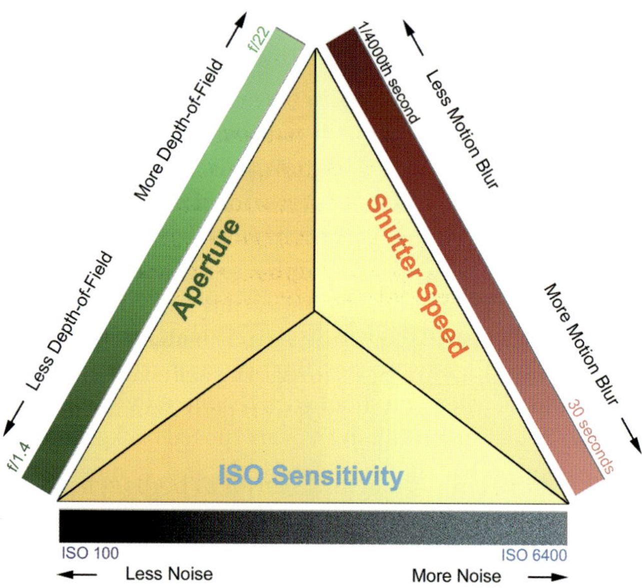

Figure 3.1 The traditional exposure triangle includes aperture, shutter speed, and ISO sensitivity.

Exposure determines the look, feel, and tone of an image, in more ways than one. Incorrect exposure can impair even the best-composed image by cloaking important tones in darkness, or by washing them out so they become featureless to the eye. On the other hand, correct exposure brings out the detail in the areas you want to picture and provides the range of tones and colors you need to create the desired image. However, getting the perfect exposure can be tricky, because digital sensors can't capture all the tones we are able to see. If the range of tones in an image is extensive, embracing both inky black shadows and bright highlights, the sensor may not be able to capture them all. Sometimes, we must settle for an exposure that renders most of those tones—but not all—in a way that best suits the photo we want to produce. You'll often need to make choices about which details are important, and which are not, so that you can grab the tones that truly matter in your image. That's part of the creativity you bring to bear in realizing your photographic vision.

For example, look at the two bracketed exposures presented in Figure 3.2. For the image at top left, the highlights are well exposed, but everything else in the shot is seriously underexposed. The version at the top right, taken an instant later with the tripod-mounted camera, shows detail in the shadow areas, but the highlights are completely washed out. The camera's sensor simply can't capture detail in both dark areas and bright areas in a single shot. With digital camera sensors, it's tricky to capture detail in both highlights and shadows in a single image, because the number of tones, the *dynamic range* of the sensor, is limited.

One solution is to resort to a technique called High Dynamic Range (HDR) photography. I produced the image shown at the bottom of the figure by merging the two original shots using a Photoshop/Photoshop Elements feature called Merge to HDR. There are also specialized software tools like Aurora H DR, Photomatix, and HDR Efex Pro (part of the Nik Collection, formerly distributed by Google, and since 2017 available from DxO).

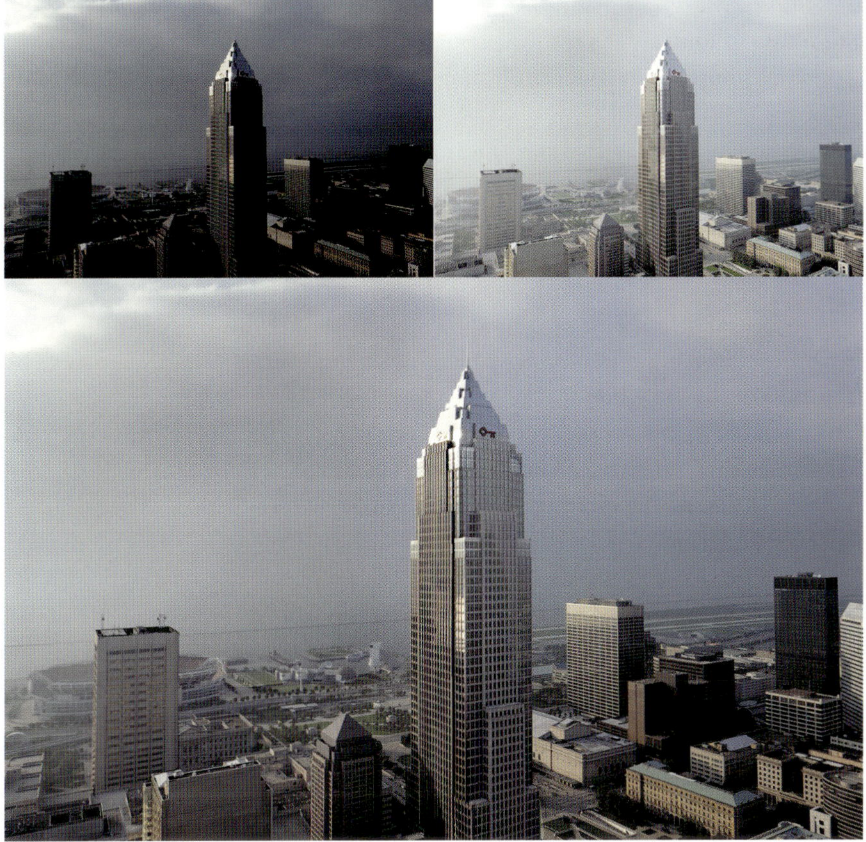

Figure 3.2 At top left, exposure for the highlights loses shadow detail. At top right, exposure for the shadows washes out the background. Bottom, combining the two exposures produces the best compromise.

I'll explain more about HDR photography, and how to explore it using the bracketing features of your camera later in this chapter. For now, though, I'm going to concentrate on showing you how to get the best exposures possible without resorting to such tools, using only the features of your camera.

To understand exposure, you need to appreciate the aspects of light that combine to produce an image. Start with a light source—the sun, a household lamp, or the glow from a campfire—and trace its path to your camera, through the lens, and finally to the sensor that captures the illumination. Here's a brief review of the things within our control that affect exposure, listed in "chronological" order (that is, as the light moves from the subject to the sensor):

- **Light at its source.** Our eyes and our cameras—film or digital—are most sensitive to that portion of the electromagnetic spectrum we call visible light. That light has several important aspects that are relevant to photography, such as color and harshness (which is determined primarily by the apparent size of the light source as it illuminates a subject). But, in terms of exposure, the important attribute of a light source is its intensity. We may have direct control over intensity, which might be the case with an interior light that can be brightened or dimmed. Or, we might have only indirect control over intensity, as with sunlight, which can be made to appear dimmer by introducing translucent light-absorbing or reflective materials in its path.

- **Light's duration.** We tend to think of most light sources as continuous. But, as you'll learn in Chapter 13, the duration of light can change quickly enough to modify the exposure, as when the main illumination in a photograph comes from an intermittent source, such as an electronic flash.

- **Light reflected, transmitted, or emitted.** Once light is produced by its source, either continuously or in a brief burst, we are able to see and photograph objects by the light that is reflected from our subjects toward the camera lens; transmitted (say, from translucent objects that are lit from behind); or emitted (by a candle or television screen). When more or less light reaches the lens from the subject, we need to adjust the exposure. This part of the equation is under our control to the extent we can increase the amount of light falling on or passing through the subject (by adding extra light sources or using reflectors), or by pumping up the light that's emitted (by increasing the brightness of the glowing object).

- **Light passed by the lens.** Not all the illumination that reaches the front of the lens makes it all the way through. Filters can remove some of the light before it enters the lens. Inside the lens barrel is a variable-sized diaphragm that dilates and contracts to produce an aperture that controls the amount of light that enters the lens. You, or the camera's autoexposure system, can vary the size of the aperture to control the amount of light that will reach the sensor. The relative size of the aperture is called the f/stop. (See Figure 3.3, which is a graphic representation of the relative size of the lens opening, not an actual photo of the aperture of a lens.)

- **Light passing through the shutter.** Once light passes through the lens, the amount of time the sensor receives it is determined by the camera's shutter; this mechanism can remain open for as long as 30 seconds (or even longer if you use the camera's Bulb or Bulb Timer settings) or as briefly as 1/8000th second (when the electronic shutter is active).

- **Light captured by the sensor.** Not all the light falling onto the sensor is captured. If the number of photons reaching a particular photosite doesn't pass a set threshold, no information is recorded. Similarly, if too much light illuminates a pixel in the sensor, then the excess isn't recorded or, worse, spills over to contaminate adjacent pixels. We can modify the minimum and maximum number of pixels that contribute to image detail by adjusting the ISO setting. At higher ISO levels, the incoming light is amplified to boost the effective sensitivity of the sensor.

Figure 3.3 Top row (left to right): f/3.5, f/5.6, f/8; bottom row: f/11, f/16, f/22.

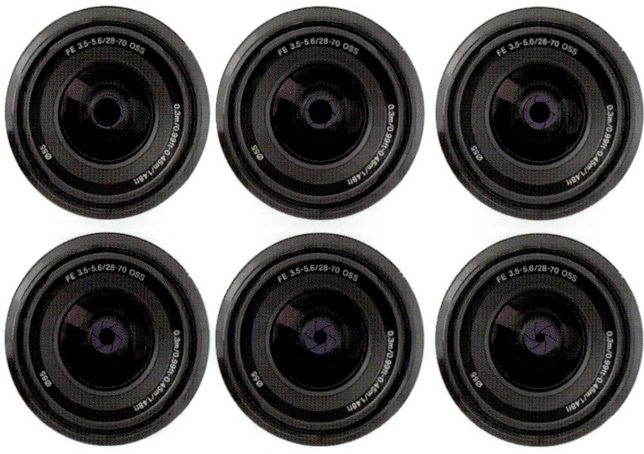

These factors all work proportionately and reciprocally to produce an exposure. That is, if you double the amount of light, increase the aperture size by one stop, make the shutter speed twice as long, or double the ISO, you'll get twice as much exposure. Similarly, you can reduce any of these and reduce the exposure when that is preferable.

As we'll see however, changing any of those aspects in P, A, or S mode does not change the actual exposure; that's because the camera also makes changes when you do so, in order to maintain the same exposure. That's why Sony provides other methods for modifying the exposure in those modes.

F/STOPS AND SHUTTER SPEEDS

Especially if you're new to advanced cameras, it's worth quickly reviewing some essential concepts. For example, the lens aperture, or f/stop, is a ratio, much like a fraction, which is why f/2 is larger than f/4, just as 1/2 is larger than 1/4. However, f/2 is actually *four times* as large as f/4. (Think back to high school geometry where we learned that to double the area of a circle, you multiply its diameter by the square root of two: 1.4.)

The full f/stops available with an f/2 lens are f/2, f/2.8, f/4, f/5.6, f/8, f/11, f/16, and f/22. Each higher number indicates an aperture that's half the size of the previous number. Hence, it admits half as much light as the one before. Figure 3.3 shows a simplified representation. (Of course, you can also set intermediate apertures with the a7C II/a7CR, such as f/6.3 and f/7.1, which are the 1/3-stop increments between f/5.6 and f/8.)

Shutter speeds are actual fractions (of a second), so that 1/60, 1/125, 1/250, 1/500, 1/1000, and so forth represent 1/60th, 1/125th, 1/250th, 1/500th, and 1/1000th second. Each higher number indicates a shutter speed that's half as long as the one before. (And yes, intermediate shutter speeds can also be used, such as 1/640th or 1/800th second.) To avoid confusion, Sony uses quotation marks to signify long exposures: 0.8", 2", 2.5", 4", and so forth; these examples represent 0.8-second, 2-second, 2.5-second, and 4-second exposures, respectively.

Equivalent Exposure

One of the most important aspects in this discussion is the concept of "equivalent exposure." This term means that exactly the same amount of light will reach the sensor at various combinations of aperture and shutter speed. Whether we use a small aperture (large f/number) with a long shutter speed or a wide aperture (small f/number) with a fast shutter speed, the amount of light reaching the sensor can be exactly the same. Table 3.1 shows equivalent exposure settings using various shutter speeds and f/stops; in other words, any of the combination of settings listed will produce exactly the same exposure.

TABLE 3.1 Equivalent Exposures

SHUTTER SPEED	F/STOP	SHUTTER SPEED	F/STOP
1/30th second	f/22	1/500th second	f/5.6
1/60th second	f/16	1/1000th second	f/4
1/125th second	f/11	1/2000th second	f/2.8
1/250th second	f/8	1/4000th second	f/2

When you set the camera to P mode, it sets both the aperture and the shutter speed that should provide a correct exposure, based on guidance from the light metering system. In P mode, you cannot change the aperture or the shutter speed individually, but you can shift among various aperture/shutter speed combinations by rotating the left rear dial, providing what is called *program shift*. (If you use program shift, an asterisk will appear next to the P on your display screens to let you know you've made an adjustment.) If you change the ISO, the camera will set a different combination automatically. As the concept of equivalent exposure indicates, the image brightness will be exactly the same in every photo you shoot with the various combinations because they all provide the same exposure.

In Aperture Priority (A) and Shutter Priority (S) modes, you can change the aperture or the shutter speed, respectively. The camera will then change the other factor to maintain the same exposure. I'll cover all of the operating modes and the important aspects of exposure with each mode in this chapter.

F/STOPS VERSUS STOPS

In photography parlance, *f/stop* always means the aperture or lens opening. However, for lack of a current commonly used word for one exposure increment, the term *stop* is often used. In the past, EV (Exposure Value) served this purpose, and was used as a measure of the total sensitivity range of a device such as a light meter, but exposure value and its abbreviation have since been inextricably intertwined with its use in describing exposure compensation. In this book, when I say "stop" by itself (no *f/*), I mean one whole unit of exposure, and am not necessarily referring to an actual f/stop or lens aperture. So, adjusting the exposure by "one stop" can mean changing to the next shutter speed increment (say, from 1/125th second to 1/250th second) or the next aperture (such as f/4 to f/5.6). Similarly, 1/3-stop or 1/2-stop increments can mean either shutter speed or aperture changes, depending on the context. Be forewarned.

Calculating Exposure

Your camera calculates exposure by measuring the light that passes through the lens and reaches the sensor, based on the assumption that each area being measured reflects about the same amount of light as a neutral gray card that reflects a "middle" gray of about 12 to 18 percent reflectance. (The photographic "gray cards" you buy at a camera store have an 18 percent gray tone; your camera is calibrated to interpret a somewhat lighter 12 percent gray. I'll explain more about this later.) That "average" 12 to 18 percent gray assumption is necessary, because different subjects reflect different amounts of light. In a photo containing, say, a white cat and a dark gray cat, the white cat might reflect five times as much light as the gray cat. An exposure based on the white cat will cause the gray cat to appear to be black, while an exposure based only on the gray cat will make the white cat appear washed out.

This is more easily understood if you look at some photos of subjects that are dark (they reflect little light), those that have predominantly middle tones, and subjects that are highly reflective. I'm not going to use actual cats but, rather, will include a more human figure in the frame (which is more common, unless you're a cat photographer), accompanied by a card with a trio of gray reference patches. The next figure shows what you would end up with if you exposed a set of photographs using a different gray patch for each.

Correctly Exposed

The image shown in Figure 3.4, left, represents how a photograph might appear if you inserted the patches shown at bottom left into the scene, and then calculated exposure by measuring the light reflecting from the middle gray patch, which, for the sake of illustration, we'll assume reflects approximately 12 to 18 percent of the light that strikes it. The exposure meter in the camera sees an object that it thinks is a middle gray (the middle patch), calculates an exposure based on that, and the patch in the center of the strip is rendered at its proper tonal value. Best of all, because the resulting exposure is correct, the black patch at left and white patch at right are rendered properly as well.

When you're shooting pictures and the meter happens to base its exposure on a subject that averages that "ideal" middle gray, then you'll end up with similar (accurate) results. The camera's exposure algorithms are concocted to ensure this kind of result as often as possible, barring any unusual subjects (that is, those that are backlit, or have uneven illumination). The camera has five different metering modes (described in an upcoming section), each of which is equipped to handle certain types of unusual subjects, as I'll outline.

Overexposed

Figure 3.4, center, shows what would happen if the exposure were calculated based on metering the leftmost, black patch. The light meter sees less light reflecting from the black square than it would see from a gray middle-tone subject, and so figures, "Aha! I need to add exposure to brighten this subject up to a middle gray!" That lightens the "black" patch, so it now appears to be gray.

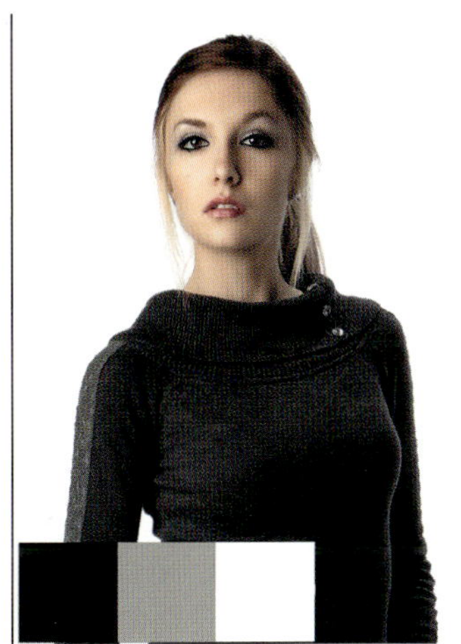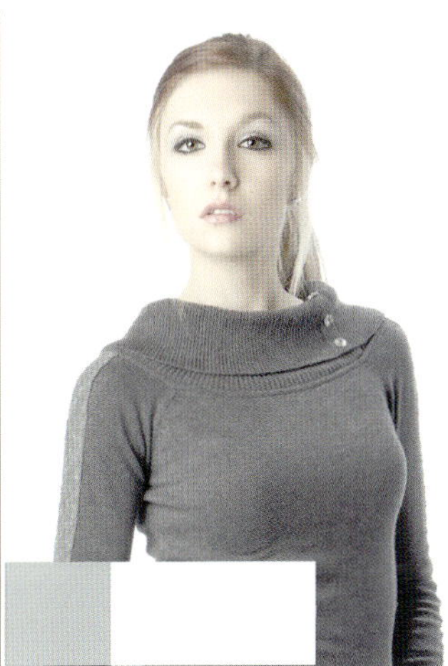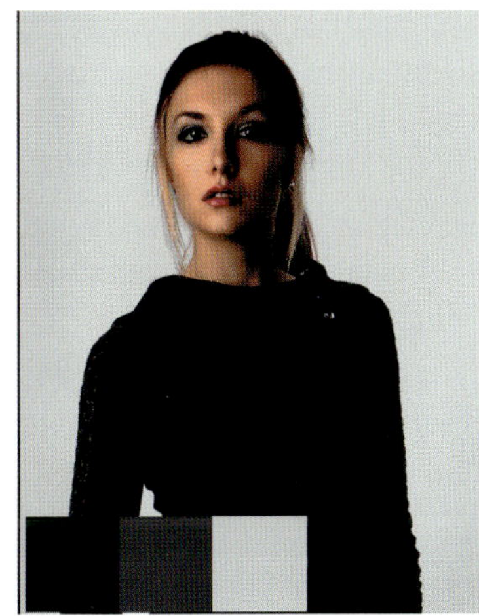

Figure 3.4 Exposure based on the middle-gray tone in the center of the card is accurate (left). Metering the black square, the black patch looks gray, the gray patch appears to be a light gray, and the white square is seriously overexposed (center). With exposure calculated from the white patch, the photo is underexposed (right).

But now the patch in the middle that was *originally* middle gray is overexposed and becomes light gray. And the white square at right is now seriously overexposed and loses detail in the highlights, which have become a featureless white. Our human subject is similarly overexposed. You should always be *aware* when overexposure occurs but note that it's not *always* a bad thing. Some slight overexposures add a dreamy look to an image; once you know how the rules are derived, you'll know how and when to break them.

Underexposed

The third possibility in this simplified scenario is that the light meter might measure the illumination bouncing off the white patch and try to render *that* tone as a middle gray. A lot of light is reflected by the white square, so the exposure is *reduced*, bringing that patch closer to a middle gray tone. The patches that were originally gray and black are now rendered too dark. Clearly, measuring the gray card—or a substitute that reflects about the same amount of light—is the only way to ensure that the exposure is precisely correct. (See Figure 3.4, right.)

As you can see, the ideal way to measure exposure is to meter from a subject that reflects 12 to 18 percent of the light that reaches it. If you want the most precise exposure calculations, the solution is to use a stand-in, such as the evenly illuminated gray card I mentioned earlier. But, because the standard Kodak gray card reflects 18 percent of the light that reaches it and, as I said, your camera is calibrated for a somewhat lighter 12 percent tone, you would need to add about one-half stop *more* exposure than the value metered from the card. Of course, in most situations, it's not necessary to do this. Your camera's light meter will do a good job of calculating the right exposure, especially if you use the exposure tips in the next section. But, I felt that explaining exactly what is going on during exposure calculation would help you understand how your camera's metering system works.

In some very bright scenes (like a snowy landscape or a lava field), you won't have a mid-tone to meter. Another substitute for a gray card is the palm of a human hand (the backside of the hand is too variable). But a human palm, regardless of ethnic group, is even brighter than a standard gray card, so instead of one-half stop more exposure, you need to add one additional stop. That is, if your meter reading is 1/500th of a second at f/11, use 1/500th second at f/8 or 1/250th second at f/11 instead. (Both exposures are equivalent.)

Small gray card versions are available that can be tucked in a camera bag. Place it in your frame near your main subject, facing the camera, and with the exact same even illumination falling on it that is falling on your subject. Then, use the Spot metering function (described soon) to calculate exposure.

In serious photography, you'll want to choose the *metering mode* (the pattern that determines how brightness is evaluated) and the *exposure mode* (determines how the appropriate shutter speed and aperture is set). I'll describe both aspects in later sections.

> **ORIGIN OF THE 18 PERCENT "MYTH"**
>
> Why are so many photographers under the impression that camera light meters are calibrated to the 18 percent "standard," rather than the true value, which may be 12 to 14 percent, depending on the vendor? You'll find this misinformation in an alarming number of places. I've seen the 18 percent "myth" taught in camera classes; I've found it in books, and even been given this wrong information from the technical staff of camera vendors. (They should know better—the same vendors' engineers who design and calibrate the cameras have the right figure.)
>
> The most common explanation is that during a revision of Kodak's instructions for its gray cards in 1977, the advice to open up an extra half stop was omitted, and a whole generation of shooters grew up thinking that a measurement off a gray card could be used as is. Kodak restored the proviso in 1997 during the next update of the instructions but by then it was too late.

The Importance of ISO

Another essential concept when discussing exposure, ISO control allows you to change the sensitivity of the camera's imaging sensor. Sometimes photographers forget about this option, because the common practice is to set the ISO once for a particular shooting session (say, at ISO 100 or 200 for bright sunlight outdoors, or ISO 800 or 1600 when shooting indoors) and then forget about ISO. Or some shooters simply leave the camera set to ISO Auto. That enables the camera to change the ISO it deems necessary, setting a low ISO in bright conditions or a higher ISO in a darker location. That's fine, but sometimes you'll want to set a specific ISO yourself. That will be essential sometimes, since ISO Auto cannot set the highest ISO levels that are available when you use manual ISO selection.

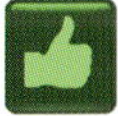

TIP When shooting in the Program (P), Aperture Priority (A), and Shutter Priority (S) modes, all discussed soon, changing the ISO does not change the exposure. If you switch from using ISO 100 to ISO 1600 in A mode, for example, the camera will simply set a different shutter speed. If you change the ISO in S mode, the camera will set a different aperture, and in P mode, it will set a different aperture and/or shutter speed. In all of these examples, the camera will maintain the same exposure. If you want to make a brighter or a darker photo in P, A, or S mode, you would need to set + or − exposure compensation, as discussed later.

However, when you use Manual (M) mode, manually changing the ISO also changes the exposure.

The camera provides the best possible image quality in the ISO 50 to 400 range. We use higher ISO levels such as ISO 1600 in low light and ISO 6400 in a very dark location because it allows us to shoot at a faster shutter speed. That's often useful for minimizing the risk of blurring caused by camera shake, which can occur even with 5-axis image stabilization in the camera body and optical image stabilization (OSS) built into many lenses. And, of course, you must also contend with movement of the subject, which no amount of image stabilization will fix.

Although you can set a desired ISO level yourself, the a7C II/a7CR also offer an ISO Auto option. When enabled, the camera will select an ISO that should be suitable for the conditions: a low ISO on a sunny day and a high ISO in a dark location. In Intelligent Auto or Scene Selection modes, ISO Auto is the only available option.

Over the past few years, there has been something of a competition among the manufacturers of digital cameras to achieve the highest ISO ratings. The highest announced ISO numbers have been rising annually, from 1600 to 3200 and 6400 and higher; a few cameras even allow you to choose a sensitivity setting that tops 1.6 *million*. Sony is a bit more conservative, but the a7C II/a7CR offer all of the ISO options you're ever likely to need, up to 104400. Obviously, the loftiest numbers come at the cost of increased contrast and grain.

Choosing a Metering Method

The Sony a7C II/a7CR has five different schemes for evaluating the light received by its exposure sensors (shown in Figure 3.5). The quickest way to choose among them is to use the Function menu, where the Metering Mode icon can be found second from left in the top row. You can also use the Exposure/Color > Metering > Metering Mode menu entry, or assign Metering Mode to a Custom Key as explained in Chapter 9.

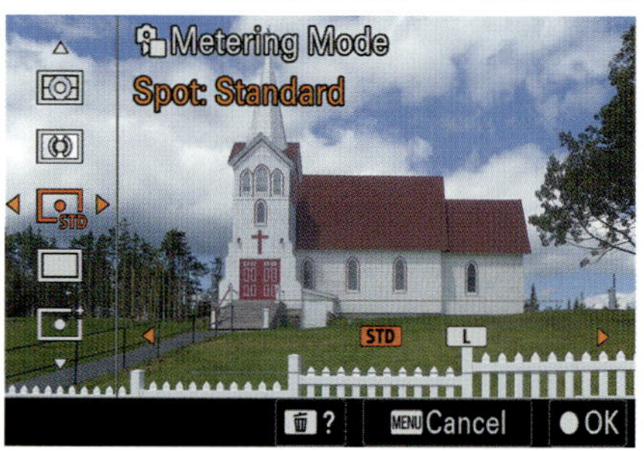

Figure 3.5 There are five options for metering mode: Multi (the default), Center Weighted, Spot (Standard or Large), Entire Screen Averaging, and Highlight Weighted (left, top to bottom).

Multi Metering

In this "intelligent" (multi-segment) metering mode, the a7C II/a7CR measures the illumination falling on all the pixels in the sensor, but slices up the frame into 1,200 different zones, as shown at left in Figure 3.6. The camera evaluates the measurements to make an educated guess about what kind of picture you're taking, based on examination of exposure data derived from thousands of different real-world photos. For example, if the top section of a picture is much lighter than the bottom portions, the algorithm can assume that the scene is a landscape photo with lots of sky. This mode is the best all-purpose metering method for most pictures. A typical scene suitable for Multi metering is shown at right in Figure 3.6.

The Multi system can recognize individual elements in a very bright scene and it can automatically increase the exposure to reduce the risk of a dark photo. This will be useful when your subject is a snow-covered landscape or a close-up of a bride in white. Granted, you may occasionally need to use a bit of exposure compensation, but often, the exposure will be close to accurate even without

Figure 3.6 Multi metering uses 1,200 zones and is suitable for complex scenes like this one.

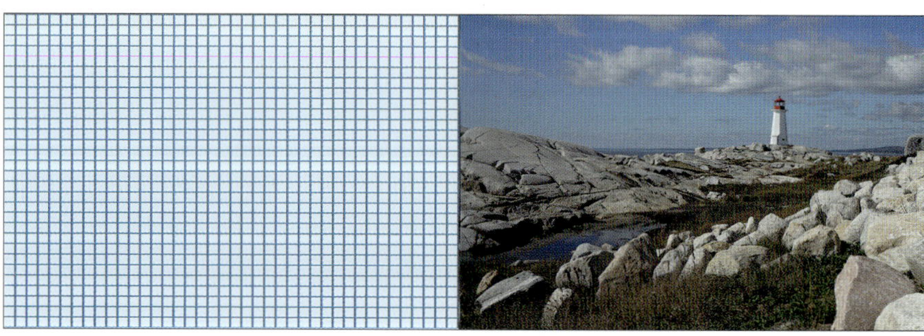

it. (In my experience, the Multi system is most successful with light-toned scenes on bright days. When shooting in dark, overcast conditions, it's more likely to underexpose a scene of that type.)

Multi-segment metering is especially suitable for people. If you activate Exposure/Color > Metering > Face Priority in Multi Metering entry, the a7C II/a7CR will use any detected faces to calculate exposure. Both sensors have enough resolution to allow detecting eyes, noses, and mouths, and thus confirm to its satisfaction that humans are in the photo (and contain detail that should be preserved, possibly at the expense of other areas, such as sky or background). If human faces are also located within the current autofocus area, the camera will consistently try to preserve detail in those faces. You can disable face detection if you're shooting landscapes.

The Multi metering mode is best for most general subjects, because it can intelligently analyze a scene and make an excellent guess of what kind of subject you're shooting a great deal of the time. The camera can tell the difference between low-contrast and high-contrast subjects by looking at the range of differences in brightness across the scene. Because once the type of subject matter is determined, the camera can underexpose slightly when appropriate to preserve highlight detail when image contrast is high. (It's often possible to pull detail out of shadows that are too dark using an image editor, but once highlights are converted to white pixels, they are gone forever.)

Center-Weighted Metering

Center-weighted metering was the only available option with cameras some decades ago. In this mode you get conventional metering without any "intelligent" scene evaluation. The light meter considers brightness in the entire frame but places the greatest emphasis on a large area in the center of the frame, as shown at left in Figure 3.7, on the theory that, for most pictures, the main subject will not be located far off-center.

Of course, Center-weighted metering is most effective when the subject in the central area is a mid-tone. Even then, if your main subject is surrounded by large, extremely bright or very dark areas, the exposure might not be exactly right. (You might need to use exposure compensation, a feature discussed shortly.) However, this scheme works well in many situations if you don't want to use one of the other modes for scenes like the one shown at right in Figure 3.7.

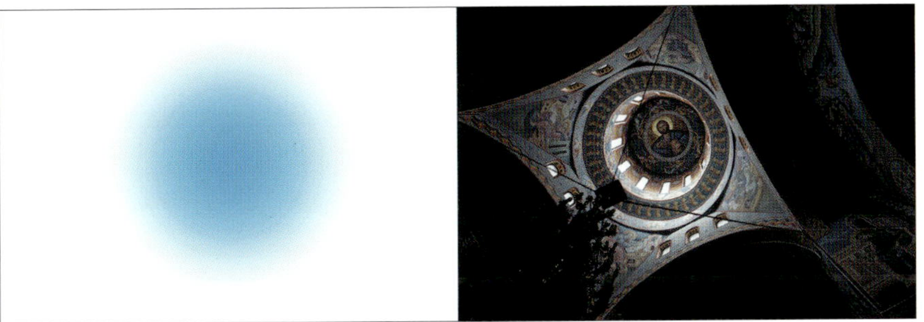

Figure 3.7 Center-weighted metering calculates exposure based on the full frame but emphasizes the center area.

Spot Metering

This mode confines the reading to a very small area in the center of the image, as shown at left in Figure 3.8, or, at your option, to coordinate with the focus spot in some Focus Area modes. When Spot is highlighted, you can press the left/right controls to choose from a standard-size spot, or a larger one. One possible source of confusion is that there are both spot *metering* options within the metering settings, and spot *focus area* options within the available Focus Area adjustments.

You can specify whether the metering spot will remain locked in the center of the frame, or whether it will coordinate with the current focus area. You might want to sync the metering and focus areas if your subject is significantly brighter or darker than the rest of your scene. If so, navigate to the Exposure/Color > Metering > Spot Metering Point and change from the default Center value to Focus Point Link. If you do that, then the metering and focus points will be synced when you use these focus areas: Spot (Small, Medium, or Large), Expand Spot, Tracking: Spot (Small, Medium, or Large), or Tracking: Expand Spot.

Even when Focus Point Link is activated, spot metering is locked to the center position when using the other Focus Areas: Wide, Zone, Center Fix, or Tracking: Wide/Zone/Center Fix.

The Spot meter does not apply any "intelligent" scene evaluation. Because the camera considers only a small target area, and completely ignores its surroundings, Spot metering is most useful when the subject is a small mid-tone area. For example, the "target" might be a tanned face, a medium red blossom, or a gray rock in a wide-angle photo; each of these is a mid-tone.

The Spot metering technique is simple if you want to Spot meter a small area that's dead center in the frame. If the "target" is off-center, you would need to point the lens at it and use the AE Lock technique discussed later in this chapter. (Lock exposure on your target before re-framing for a better composition so the exposure does not change.) For Figure 3.8, right, Spot metering was used to base the exposure on the center of the vase.

If you Spot meter a light-toned area or a dark-toned area, you will get underexposure or overexposure, respectively; you would need to use an override for more accurate results. On the other hand, you can Spot meter a small mid-tone subject surrounded by a sky with big white clouds or by an indigo blue wall and get a good exposure. (The light meter ignores the subject's surroundings so they do not affect the exposure.) That would not be possible with Center-weighted metering, which considers brightness in a much larger area.

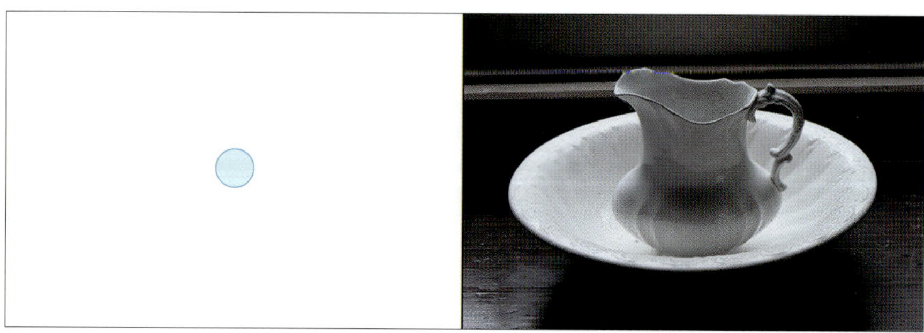

Figure 3.8 Spot metering calculates exposure based on a spot that's only a small percentage of the image area.

Entire Screen Averaging

This option simply measures all the illumination in the frame and calculates exposure based on the average value. (See Figure 3.9, left.) That may not lead to the optimal exposure for an image (if some large, very bright or very dark areas are present), but it does have one advantage: because only the average reflectance is used, the exposure will not change as your subjects move around in the frame. The woman's hands shown at right in Figure 3.9 darted back and forth as she worked, but the exposure remained constant for several successive images.

Highlight-Weighted Metering

This choice pays special attention to the highlights of an image. Figure 3.10, left, doesn't really show the active metering area, but is a graphical representation of what areas are most important in the photo at right in the figure. If your subject is surrounded by very dark areas, this metering method will help avoid overexposure.

Highlight metering is *not* a spot metering mode, despite its icon, which is the same as the Spot icon, with an asterisk added. With this mode, the camera's Exmor R processor seeks out highlight areas of your image and bases exposure on a setting that will keep those highlights from being overexposed. Less emphasis ("weight") is given to non-highlight areas.

So, if you're shooting spotlit performers on-stage at a concert or play, Jefferson Airplane/Hot Tuna bassist Jack Casady in the figure, the correct exposure can be calculated using the performers, and ignoring, for the most part, the dark surroundings. You'd have your choice of measuring exposure in Spot mode, as described in the previous section, placing the metering spot on the performer's face or shirt, or, you could select Highlight-weighted metering and allow the camera to identify the

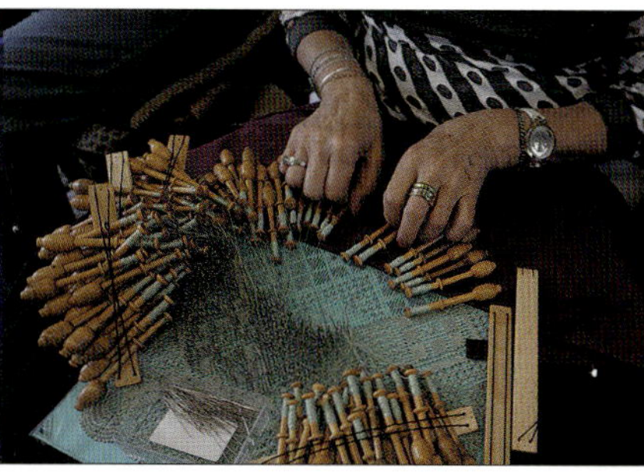

Figure 3.9 When using Entire Screen Averaging, the exposure will not change if a subject, such as this artisan's fast-moving hands, move within the frame.

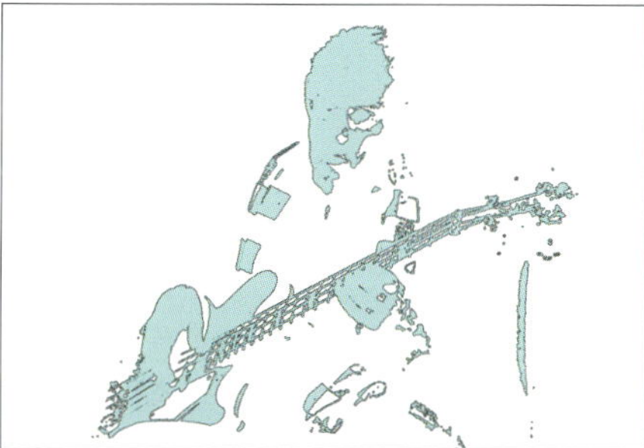
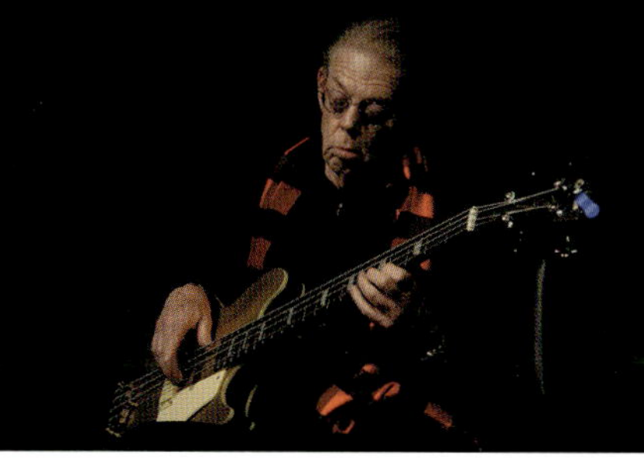

Figure 3.10 Highlight-weighted metering will help avoid overexposure of subjects surrounded by dark areas.

performer when figuring exposure. Your results might be similar with either, depending on how well you "placed" the Spot area and how cleverly the system sorts out your subject from the background. I tend to use Spot mode when the area I want to meter is clearly defined, and Highlight-weighted when there is a range of highlights.

Choosing an Exposure Mode

After you set a desired metering mode, you have several methods for choosing the appropriate shutter speed and aperture, semi-automatically or manually. Just spin the mode dial to the exposure mode that you want to use (P, A, S, or M). Your choice of which is best for a given shooting situation will depend on aspects like your need for extensive or shallow depth-of-field (the range of acceptably sharp focus in a photo) or the desire to freeze action or to allow motion blur. The semi-automatic Aperture Priority and Shutter Priority modes discussed next emphasize one aspect of image capture or another, but the following sections introduce you to all four of the modes that photographers often call "creative."

Aperture Priority (A) Mode

When using A mode, you specify the lens opening (aperture or f/stop) with the front dial or left rear dial. After you do so, the camera (guided by its light meter) will set a suitable shutter speed considering the aperture and the ISO in use. If you change the aperture, from f/5.6 to f/11, for example, the camera will automatically set a longer shutter speed to maintain the same exposure, using guidance from the built-in light meter. (I discussed the concept of equivalent exposure earlier and provided the equivalent exposure table.)

Aperture Priority is especially useful when you want to use a particular lens opening to achieve a desired effect. Perhaps you'd like to use the smallest aperture (such as f/22) to maximize depth-of-field (DOF), to keep the entire subject sharp in a close-up picture. Or, you might want to use a large aperture (small f/number, like f/4) to throw everything except your main subject out of focus, as in Figure 3.11. Maybe you'd just like to "lock in" a particular f/stop, such as f/8, because it allows your lens to provide the best optical quality. Or, you might prefer to use f/2.8

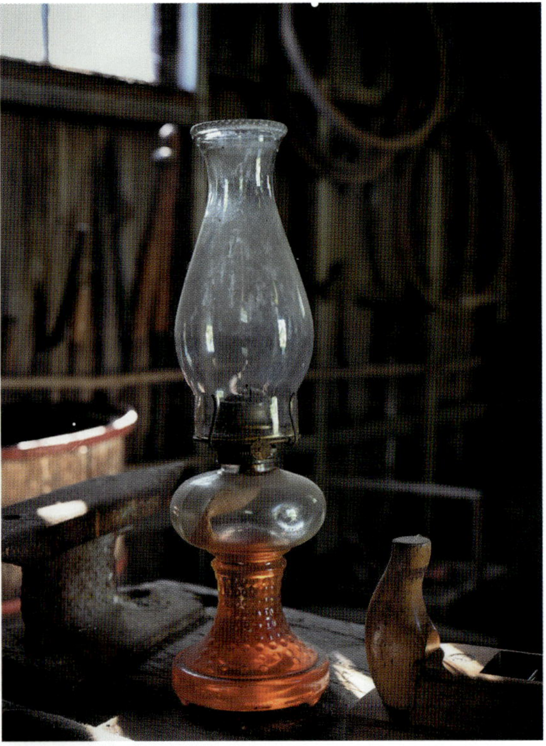

Figure 3.11 Use Aperture Priority mode to "lock in" a wide aperture (denoted by a small f/number) when you want to blur the background.

with a lens that has a maximum aperture of f/1.4, because you want the best compromise between shutter speed and optical quality.

Aperture Priority can even be used to specify a *range* of shutter speeds you want to use under varying lighting conditions, which seems almost contradictory. But think about it. You're shooting a soccer game outdoors with a telephoto and want a relatively fast shutter speed, but you don't care if the speed changes a little should the sun duck behind a cloud. Set your camera's shooting mode to A, and adjust the aperture using the front or left rear dial until a shutter speed of, say, 1/1000th second is selected at the ISO level that you're using. (In bright sunlight at ISO 400, that aperture is likely to be around f/11.) Then, go ahead and shoot, knowing that your a7C II/a7CR will maintain that f/11 aperture (for sufficient DOF as the soccer players move about the field) but will drop down to 1/800th or 1/500th second, if necessary, should a light cloud cover part of the sun.

When the camera cannot provide a good exposure at the aperture you have set, the shutter speed numeral will blink. That indicator warns that the camera is unable to find an appropriate shutter speed at the aperture you have set, considering the ISO level in use, and over- or underexposure will occur. That's the major pitfall of using Aperture Priority: you might select an f/stop that is too small or too large to allow an optimal exposure with the available shutter speeds.

Here are a couple of examples where you might encounter a problem. Let's say you set an aperture of f/2.8 while using ISO 400 on an extremely bright day (perhaps at the beach or in snow); in this situation, even your camera's fastest shutter speed might not be able to cut down the amount of light reaching the sensor to provide the right exposure. (The solution here is to set a lower ISO or a smaller aperture, or both, until the blinking stops.) Or, let's say you have set f/16 in a dark arena while using ISO 100; the camera cannot find a shutter speed long enough to provide a correct exposure so your photo will be underexposed. (In low light, the solution is to manually set a higher ISO or a wider aperture, or both, until the orange shutter speed indicator turns white again.) Aperture Priority is best used by those with a bit of experience in choosing settings. Many seasoned photographers leave their camera set on Aperture Priority all the time.

When to use Aperture Priority:

- **General landscape photography.** The a7C II and a7CR are great cameras for landscape photography, of course, because their 33- and 60-megapixel resolution allows making huge, gorgeous prints, as well as smaller prints that are filled with eye-popping detail. Aperture Priority is a good tool for ensuring that your landscape is sharp from foreground to infinity, if you select an f/stop that provides maximum depth-of-field.

  If you use A mode and select an aperture like f/11 or f/16, it's your responsibility to make sure the shutter speed selected is fast enough to avoid losing detail to camera shake, or that the camera is mounted on a tripod. One thing that new landscape photographers fail to account for is the movement of distant leaves and tree branches. When seeking the ultimate in sharpness, go ahead and use Aperture Priority, but boost ISO sensitivity a bit, if necessary, to provide a sufficiently fast shutter speed, whether shooting hand-held or with a tripod.

- **Specific landscape situations.** Aperture Priority is also useful when you have no objection to using a long shutter speed, or, particularly, *want* the camera to select one. Waterfalls are a perfect example. You can use A mode, set your camera to ISO 100, use a small f/stop, and let the camera select a longer shutter speed that will allow the water to blur as it flows. Indeed, you might need to use a neutral-density filter to get a sufficiently long shutter speed. But Aperture Priority mode is a good start.

- **Portrait photography.** Portraits are the most common applications of selective focus. A medium-large aperture (say, f/5.6 or f/8) with a longer lens/zoom setting (in the 85mm-135mm range) will allow the background behind your portrait subject to blur. A *very* large aperture (I frequently shoot wide open with my 85mm f/1.8 lens) lets you apply selective focus to your subject's *face*. With a three-quarters view of your subject, as long as her eyes are sharp, it's okay if the far ear or her hair is out of focus.

- **When you want to ensure optimal sharpness.** All lenses have an aperture or two at which they perform best, providing the level of sharpness you expect. That's usually about two stops down from wide open, and thus will vary depending on the maximum aperture of the lens. My 85mm f/1.8 is good wide open, but it's even sharper at f/2.8 or f/4; I shoot my 70-200mm f/4 wide open at concerts, but, if I can use f/5.6 instead, I'll get better results. A relatively slow lens with, say, an f/5.6 maximum aperture at the telephoto end, really needs to be set at f/11 if I crank it out to its maximum focal length. Aperture Priority allows me to use each lens at its very best f/stop.

- **Close-up/Macro photography.** Depth-of-field is typically very shallow when shooting macro photos, and you'll want to choose your f/stop carefully. Perhaps you might want to use a wider stop to emphasize your subject. Or, you might need the smallest aperture you can get away with to maximize depth-of-field. Aperture Priority mode comes in very useful when shooting close-up pictures. Because macro work is frequently done with the camera mounted on a tripod, and your close-up subjects, if not living creatures, may not be moving much, a longer shutter speed isn't a problem. Aperture Priority can be your preferred choice.

Shutter Priority (S) Mode

Shutter Priority is the inverse of Aperture Priority. You set the shutter speed you'd like, using the front dial or left rear dial, and the camera sets an appropriate f/stop considering the ISO that's in use. When you change the shutter speed, the camera will change the aperture to maintain the same (equivalent) exposure using guidance from the built-in light meter. Shutter Priority mode gives you some control over how much action-freezing capability your digital camera brings to bear in a particular situation. In other cases, you might want to use a slow shutter speed to add some blur to a sports photo that would be mundane if the action were completely frozen (see Figure 3.12).

Take care when using a slow shutter speed such as 1/8th second, because you'll potentially get blurring from camera shake unless you're using a tripod or other firm support. Of course, this applies to any mode, but in most modes the camera displays a blinking camera shake warning icon when the shutter speed is long. That indicator does not blink in S mode, however, perhaps because Sony assumes that users of Shutter Priority are aware of the potential problem caused by camera shake. The in-body 5-axis image stabilization and SteadyShot stabilizer in OSS-designated lenses are useful but they cannot work miracles.

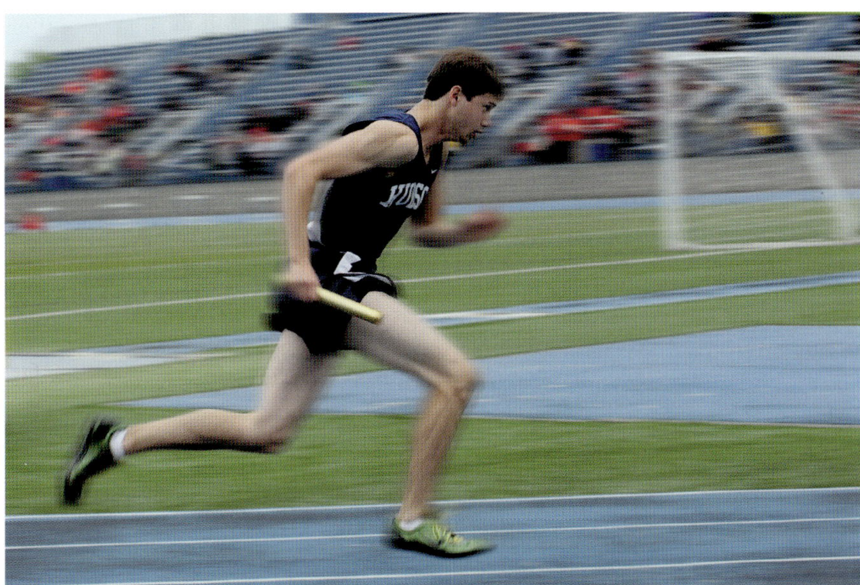

Figure 3.12 Set a slow shutter speed when you want to introduce blur into an action shot, as with this panned image of a relay runner.

As in Aperture Priority, you can encounter a problem in Shutter Priority mode; this happens when you select a shutter speed that's too long or too short for correct exposure under certain conditions. I've shot outdoor soccer games on sunny fall evenings and used Shutter Priority mode to lock in a 1/1000th-second shutter speed, only to find that my camera refused to produce the correct exposure when the sun dipped behind some trees and there was no longer enough light to shoot at that speed, even with the lens wide open.

In cases where you have set an inappropriate shutter speed, the shutter speed will blink. When might this happen? Let's say you set 1/15th second shutter speed while using ISO 400 on that extremely bright day; in this situation, even the smallest aperture available with your lens might not be able to cut down the amount of light reaching the sensor to provide a correct exposure. (The solution here is to set a lower ISO or a faster shutter speed, or both, until the blinking stops.) Or, let's say you have set 1/250th second in the arena while using ISO 100; your lens does not offer an aperture that's wide enough to enable the camera to provide a good exposure so you'll get the blinking and your photo will be underexposed. (In low light, the solution is to set a higher ISO or a longer shutter speed, or both, until the blinking stops.)

When to use Shutter Priority:

- **To reduce blur from subject motion.** Set the shutter speed to a higher value to reduce the amount of blur from subjects that are moving. The exact speed will vary depending on how fast your subject is moving and how much blur is acceptable. You might want to freeze a basketball player in mid-dunk with a 1/1000th-second shutter speed or use 1/200th second to allow the spinning wheels of a motocross racer to blur a tiny bit to add the feeling of motion.

- **To add blur from subject motion.** There are times when you want a subject to blur, say, when shooting waterfalls with the camera set for a one- or two-second exposure in Shutter Priority mode.

- **To add blur from camera motion when *you* are moving.** Say you're panning to follow a base runner. You might want to use Shutter Priority mode and 1/60th second, so that the background will blur as you pan. The shutter speed will be fast enough to provide a sharp image of the athlete, as shown in Figure 3.12.

- **To reduce blur from camera motion when *you* are moving.** In other situations, the camera may be in motion, say, because you're shooting from a moving train or auto, and you want to minimize the amount of blur caused by the motion of the camera. Shutter Priority is a good choice here, too.

- **Landscape photography hand-held.** If you can't use a tripod for your landscape shots, you'll still probably want the sharpest image possible. Shutter Priority can allow you to specify a shutter speed that's fast enough to reduce or eliminate the effects of camera shake. Just make sure that your ISO setting is high enough that the a7C II/a7CR will select an aperture with sufficient depth-of-field, too.

- **Concerts, stage performances.** I shoot a lot of concerts with my 70-200mm f/4 lens, and have discovered that, when vibration reduction is taken into account, a shutter speed of 1/160th second is fast enough to eliminate camera shake that can result from hand-holding the camera with this lens, and also to avoid blur from the movement of all but the most energetic performers. I use Shutter Priority and set the ISO so the camera will select an aperture in the f/4-5.6 range.

Program Auto (P) Mode

Program mode uses the camera's built-in smarts to set an aperture/shutter speed combination, based on information provided by the light meter. If you're using Multi metering, the combination will often provide a good exposure. Rotate the front dial or left rear dial and you can override the camera's choices and switch to other aperture/shutter speed combinations, all providing the same (equivalent) exposure. The P on the screen changes to P*. You can't use Program Shift when working with flash. To reverse Program Shift, change to another exposure mode (you can immediately switch back to P mode) or turn the camera off.

In the unlikely event that the correct exposure cannot be achieved with the wide range of shutter speeds and apertures available, the shutter speed and aperture will both blink. (The solution is to set a lower ISO in bright light and a higher ISO in dark locations until the blinking stops.) P mode is the one to use when you want to rely on the camera to make reasonable basic settings of shutter speed and aperture, but you want to retain the ability to adjust many of the camera's settings yourself. All overrides and important functions are available, including ISO, white balance, metering mode, exposure compensation, and others.

When to use Program mode:

- **When you're in a hurry to get a grab shot.** The camera will do a pretty good job of calculating an appropriate exposure for you, without any input from you.

- **When you hand your camera to a novice.** Set the mode dial to P, hand the camera to your friend, relative, or *trustworthy* stranger you meet in front of the Eiffel Tower, point to the shutter-release button and viewfinder, and say, "Look through here, and press this button."

- **When no special shutter speed or aperture settings are needed.** If your subject doesn't require special anti- or pro-blur techniques, and depth-of-field or selective focus aren't important, use P as a general-purpose setting. You can still make adjustments to increase/decrease depth-of-field or add/reduce motion blur with a minimum of fuss.

Making Exposure Value Changes

Sometimes you'll want a brighter or darker photo (more or less exposure) than you got when relying on the camera's metering system. Perhaps you want to underexpose to create a silhouette effect or overexpose to produce a high-key (very light) effect. It's easy to do so by using the exposure compensation features, available only in P, A, S, M, and Movie modes. There are several ways to set exposure compensation:

- **Exposure Compensation dial.** In PAS exposure modes, the right rear dial functions as an exposure compensation dial. It's the fastest method for adding/subtracting plus or minus five stops of exposure in one-third stop increments.

  In Manual exposure mode, by default the front dial controls aperture, the left rear dial adjusts shutter speed, and the right exposure dial is disabled. However, when ISO Auto is activated, the camera will leave your shutter speed and aperture settings undisturbed and add or subtract exposure by changing ISO sensitivity instead (effectively giving you autoexposure in Manual exposure mode). In that case, the right exposure dial *can* be rotated to add/subtract exposure compensation.

- **Exposure Compensation menu.** If you want additional exposure compensation, venture to the Exposure/Color > Exposure Compensation > Exposure Comp setting, where the Exposure Comp. entry will let you set plus or minus five stops of exposure using the front or rear dials or control wheel. This option is not available if you've made a setting with the exposure compensation dial; its menu entry will be grayed out.

- **Quick Access.** The For Viewfinder display's settings screen (which Sony previously dubbed "Quick Navi") appears when you press the Fn button in For Viewfinder mode. It can be used to set both ambient (normal) Exposure Compensation as well as Flash Exposure Compensation. When the Exposure Compensation setting is highlighted, press the up/down directional buttons to switch between Exposure Compensation and Flash Exposure Compensation. Flash Exposure Compensation is available *only* when a flash unit is mounted and powered up.

- **Define a key.** If you like, you can define a key as your exposure compensation button, using the Custom Keys feature described in Chapter 9.

In my experience, *adding* exposure compensation is the option that's most often necessary. I'll often set +2/3 when using Multi metering if the camera underexposed my first photo of a light-toned scene. With Center-weighted or Spot metering, +1.3 or an even higher level of plus compensation is almost always necessary with a light-toned subject. Since the camera provides a live preview of the scene (when Shooting > Shooting Display > Live View Display Settings is set to Setting Effect ON), it's easy to predict when the photo you'll take is likely to be obviously over- or underexposed. When the histogram display is on, you can make a more accurate prediction about the exposure; I'll discuss this feature shortly. Of course, you can also use plus compensation when you want to intentionally overexpose a scene for a creative effect.

You won't often need to use minus compensation. This feature is most likely to be useful when metering a dark-toned subject, such as close-ups of black animals or dark blue buildings, for example. Since these dark-toned subjects lead the camera to overexpose, set −2/3 or −1 compensation (when using Multi metering) for a more accurate exposure. (The amount of minus compensation that you need to set may be quite different when using the other two metering modes.) Minus compensation can also be useful for intentionally underexposing a scene for a creative effect, such as a silhouette of a sailboat or a group of friends on a beach.

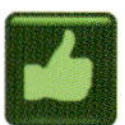

NOTE Whether you use the physical controls or one of the other options, the exposure value (EV) changes you set are synced. If you make an adjustment using one method, it will be reflected in all the other methods.

As I noted above, any exposure compensation you set will remain active for all photos you take afterward. The camera provides a reminder as to what value is currently set in some display modes. Turning the camera off and then back on does not set compensation back to zero; when you no longer need to use it, be sure to do so yourself. If you inadvertently leave it set for +1 or −1, for example, your photos taken under other circumstances will be over- or underexposed.

Manual Exposure (M) Mode

Part of being an experienced photographer comes from knowing when to rely on automation (including Intelligent Auto and P modes), when to go semi-automatic (with Shutter Priority or Aperture Priority), and when to set exposure manually (using M). Some photographers actually prefer to set their exposure manually. This is quite convenient, as the camera is happy to provide an indication of when your settings will produce over- or underexposure, based on its metering system's judgment. It can even indicate how far off the "correct" (recommended) exposure your photo will be at the settings you have made.

I often hear comments from novices first learning serious photography claiming that they must use Manual mode in order to take over control from the camera. While a back-to-basics approach does force you to learn photographic principles, it's not always necessary. For example, you can control all important aspects when using semi-automatic A or S mode as discussed in the previous sections. This allows you to control depth-of-field (the range of acceptable sharpness) or the rendition of motion (as blurred or as frozen). You can set a desired ISO level; that will not change the exposure, as the camera will adjust the aperture or f/stop to compensate. You would use exposure compensation when you want a brighter or a darker photo.

Manual mode provides an alternative that allows you to control the exposure by changing the aperture and the shutter speed. For example, when I shot the outdoor sculpture in Figure 3.13, I was not getting exactly the desired effect with A or S mode while experimenting with various levels of exposure compensation. So, I switched to M mode, set to ISO 100, and then set an aperture/shutter speed that might provide the intended exposure. After taking a test shot, I changed the aperture slightly and the next photo provided the exposure for the interpretation of the scene that I wanted.

Manual mode is also useful when working in a studio environment using multiple flash units. The additional flash units are triggered by triggering devices (gadgets that set off the flash when they sense the light from another flash or a signal from a radio or infrared remote control). In some cases, M mode is the only suitable choice. Your camera's exposure meter doesn't compensate for the extra illumination, and can't interpret the flash exposure at all, so you need to set the aperture and shutter speed manually.

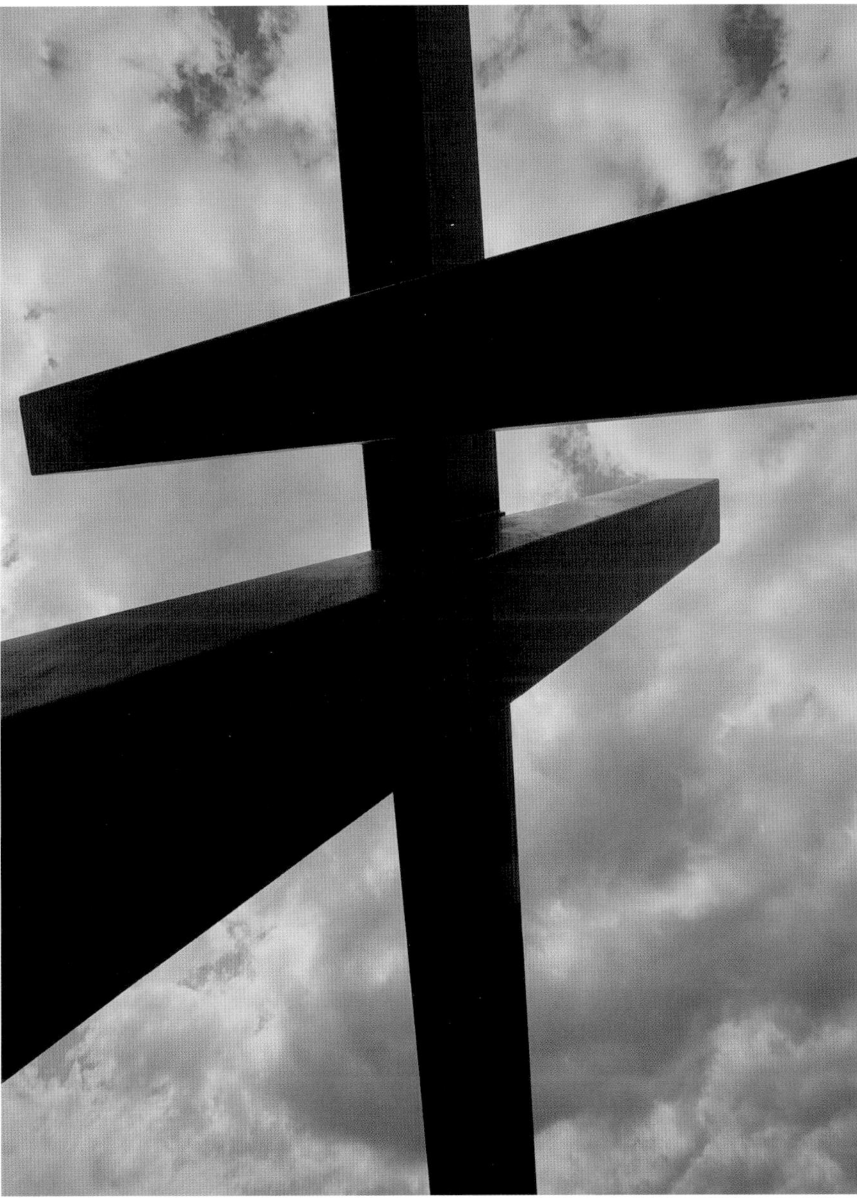

Figure 3.13 Manual mode allowed setting the exact exposure for this silhouette shot, by metering the subject and then underexposing.

The Basic M Mode Technique

Depending on your proclivities, you might not need to use M mode very often, but it's still worth understanding how it works. Here are your considerations:

- Rotate the mode dial to M.

- Use the front dial to adjust aperture and the left rear dial to adjust shutter speed (unless you've swapped their functions, as described in Chapter 9). The setting that is currently active will be highlighted in orange.

- Any change you make to either factor affects the exposure, of course. You can elect to have the camera reflect those changes in display, or to ignore them. Under most conditions, you'll want the live view to show how your exposure adjustments will affect the final image. However, under dim light or when using studio flash, you may prefer to keep the image bright. Just navigate to the Shooting > Shooting Display > Live View Display Settings entry and choose Settings Effect OFF, as described in Chapter 6.

- If the display you're viewing includes the histogram graph, that will provide an even better indication of the exposure you'll get as you set different apertures or shutter speeds. I'll explain histograms later in this chapter.

- A scale at the bottom of the viewfinder indicates exposure. To use the suggested exposure, adjust the shutter speed or f/stop until the guide is centered in the scale, or the MM guide at the bottom of the LCD monitor reads −+ 0.0.

- As I've mentioned before, automatic exposure control is still available in manual exposure mode. I'll explain that option in more detail shortly.

Long Exposures

You can specify exposures as long as 30 seconds when using P, A, or S modes. In Manual exposure mode, you can select B (for bulb exposure), located *after* the 30-second option. Bulb cannot be selected when using Silent Shooting, or when Drive mode is set to Continuous Shooting, Self-Timer Continuous, or Continuous Bracketing. If you try to shoot a bulb exposure in those modes, the a7C II/a7CR will use a 30-second exposure instead.

In Bulb mode, you can press and hold the shutter-release button, and the shutter will remain open as long as the button is depressed. Standing there with your finger on the trigger, so to speak, can produce vibration, so I prefer to use a wired release with a locking button, such as the Sony RM-VPR1 (about $60).

A final option is to use the Exposure/Color > Exposure > BULB Timer Settings feature, which allows exposures of up to 900 seconds (15 minutes). I'll provide instructions on this useful capability in Chapter 5.

Adjusting Exposure with ISO Control in M Mode

As mentioned in the previous section, changing the ISO level is another method of changing the exposure in M mode, whether you adjust it yourself manually or activate Auto ISO and let the camera do it for you when you add or subtract exposure compensation.

Most photographers control the aperture and/or shutter speed exclusively to adjust exposure, sometimes forgetting about the option to adjust ISO. The common practice is to set the ISO once for a particular shooting session (say, at ISO 100 outdoors on a bright day or ISO 1600 when shooting indoors). There is also a tendency to use the lowest ISO level possible because of a concern that high ISO levels produce images with obvious digital noise (such as a grainy effect). However, changing the ISO is a valid way of adjusting exposure in M mode, because you can usually achieve good results at relatively high ISO levels that create grainy, unusable pictures with some other camera models.

I find myself using ISO adjustment as a convenient alternate way of adding or subtracting EV (exposure values) when shooting in Manual mode. For example, if I've selected a manual exposure with both f/stop and shutter speed suitable for my image using, say, ISO 400, I can change the exposure in full-stop increments by pressing the ISO button (right directional button) and spinning the left rear dial one click at a time. The difference in image quality/noise is not much different at ISO 200 or ISO 800 than at ISO 400, and this exposure control method allows me to shoot at my preferred f/stop and shutter speed while retaining control of the exposure. Indeed, if you've activated ISO Auto (discussed next), you can specify your desired shutter speed and aperture and the a7C II/a7CR will tweak the ISO sensitivity to provide an appropriate exposure. Effectively, you've turned Manual into a semi-automatic mode, while still being able to specify the aperture and shutter speed.

Or, perhaps, I am using Shutter Priority mode and the metered exposure at ISO 400 is 1/500th second at f/11. If I decide on the spur of the moment I'd rather use 1/500th second at f/8, I can press the ISO button and quickly switch to ISO 200. Of course, it's a good idea to monitor your ISO changes, so you don't end up at ISO 6400 or above accidentally; a setting like that will result in more digital noise (graininess) in your image than you would like. Higher ISO levels are necessary only when shooting in a very dark location where a fast shutter speed is important; this might happen during a sports event in a dark arena, for example.

Using ISO Auto

ISO Auto is a powerful feature, available in PASM and Movie modes. In your camera's Fn and conventional menu settings, it's designated as ISO Auto. ISO Auto provides two major benefits. First, if the shutter speed and aperture settings in use won't provide a proper exposure, ISO Auto can adjust the ISO setting to compensate. Second, you can use ISO Auto to "lock in" a particular shutter speed or aperture (or both, in Manual mode), and use ISO sensitivity to compensate for changing or low-light conditions.

In the first case, suppose you were shooting a moving subject in Aperture Priority mode and your selected f/stop would result in a shutter speed of 1/8th second at ISO 400. All the image stabilization in the world can't protect you from blur caused by *subject* movement. If you were using ISO Auto and had specified a minimum shutter speed of 1/30th second in the Exposure/Color > Exposure > ISO Auto Minimum Shutter Speed entry (as described in Chapter 7), the camera's exposure system would automatically increase ISO from 400 to 1600. Most of us would prefer a slight increase in noise from the ISO boost than a blurry photograph.

With the a7C II/a7CR, the minimum (slowest) shutter speed allowed before ISO Auto kicks in has no effect when you're using Shutter Priority or Manual exposure, as the shutter speed you choose is locked in. But in Program and Aperture Priority modes, you can choose that minimum. If you were shooting action and wanted to ensure that P and A modes would try to use a shutter speed of 1/250th second or faster, you could select that speed as the minimum speed before ISO Auto would increase sensitivity. If you were shooting subjects with little movement, you might select 1/8th second and count on the camera and/or lens's image stabilization to give you sharp results. For most general applications, a minimum of 1/30th second should work well.

We're not done yet. ISO Auto also allows you to choose a *minimum* and *maximum* ISO speed to be used. If you want to avoid noise, you could set the Minimum ISO to 100 and the Maximum to 800, and still gain the benefits of using ISO Auto. If you wouldn't mind seeing a little noise, you could set the Maximum somewhat higher. Coupled with Minimum Shutter speed, ISO Auto gives you quite a bit of flexibility in controlling the range of shutter speeds and apertures used.

And, as I mentioned earlier, in Manual Exposure mode you can use ISO Auto in a special way. As you might expect, in Manual exposure mode, the shutter speed and aperture are selected by you and fixed at those settings until you change them. However, if ISO Auto is active, the metering system will honor your shutter speed/aperture settings, but *change the ISO sensitivity* as required to produce the metered exposure. In effect, it gives you a new exposure mode: Shutter/Aperture-priority.

Exposure Bracketing

While exposure compensation lets you adjust exposure, sometimes you'll want to quickly shoot a series of photos at various exposures in a single burst. Doing so increases the odds of getting one photo that will be exactly right for your needs and is particularly useful when assembling high dynamic range (HDR) composite images manually. This technique is called bracketing.

Years ago, before high-tech cameras became the norm, it was common to bracket exposures when shooting color slide film especially, by taking three (or more) photos at different exposures in Manual mode. Eventually, exposure compensation became a common feature as cameras gained semi-automatic modes; it was then possible to bracket exposures by setting a different compensation level for each shot in a series, such as 0, –1, and +1; or 0, –1/3, and +2/3.

Today, cameras like the a7C II/a7CR give you a lot of options for automatically bracketing exposures. When Bracket is active, you can take a series of consecutive photos: one at the metered ("correct") exposure, and others with more or less exposure. Figure 3.14 shows an image with the metered exposure (center), flanked by exposures of 2/3 stop less (left), and 2/3 stop more (right).

Bracketing cannot be performed when using Intelligent Auto mode. If flash is used, you must take the photos one at a time, manually, rather than in a continuous burst. Exposure bracketing can be used with both RAW and JPG capture. When it's set, the camera will fire the shots in a sequence if you keep the shutter-release button depressed; you can also decide to shoot the photos one at a time.

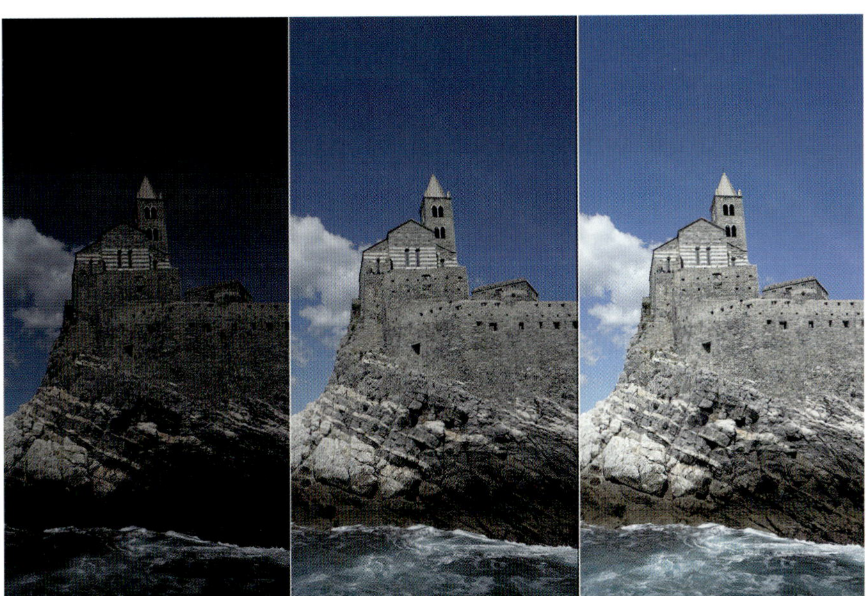

Figure 3.14 Metered exposure (center) accompanied by bracketed exposures of 2/3 stop less (left) and 2/3 stop more (right).

Bracketing is activated using the Shooting > Drive Mode > Bracket Settings menu entry, the Function menu, and summoned by pressing the left directional button or some other button you've defined as the Drive button. Four different bracketing modes can be selected: continuous bracket, single bracket, white balance bracket, and DRO (dynamic range optimizer) bracket. In the Bracket Settings entry on the same menu page, you can specify Self-Timer During Bracketing and Bracket Order, as explained in Chapter 7.

Continuous Bracketing

This mode captures 3, 5, 7, or 9 images in one burst when the shutter release is held down. You can select the size of the steps between exposures in one-third and one-half stop EV increments in the range 0.3 EV to 3.0 EV stops if you're shooting 3 or 5 exposures. If you elect to capture 7 or 9 bracketed exposures, the largest increment you can select is 2.0 EV and 1.0 EV (respectively). You also have the option of bracketing just two images over- or underexposed. The larger increments are especially useful when capturing images you'll combine later in your image editor to produce a high dynamic range (HDR) image. Use continuous bracketing when you want all the images in the set to be framed as similarly as possible, say, when you will be using them for manually assembled high dynamic range (HDR) photos.

When you highlight Cont. Bracket. in the Drive menu, the left/right buttons are used to select the increment between shots and the number of shots. In Manual Exposure (when ISO Auto is disabled), or in Aperture Priority, the shutter speed will change. If ISO Auto is set in Manual Exposure, the bracketed set will be created by changing the ISO setting. In Shutter Priority, the aperture will change. You can use flash when continuous bracketing is active, but, because of the time required for the flash to recycle, you'll need to press the shutter button each time to take subsequent images (effectively switching the camera into Single Bracket mode, described next). Continuous Bracketing (and Single Bracketing) is disabled when using Intelligent Auto.

Only the last shot in the set is displayed when using Auto Review. With all types of bracketing, the exposure/bracket scale at the bottom of the EVF or LCD monitor (in Display All Info mode) will display indicators showing the number of images shot and the relative amount of under- or overexposure.

Don't forget that you can dial in exposure compensation, and *that* will affect the amount of over-/ underexposure applied while bracketing, too. You can bracket your exposures based on something other than the base (metered) exposure value. Set any desired exposure compensation, either a plus or a minus value. Then set the Bracketing level you want to use. The camera will bracket exposures as over, under, and equal to the *compensated* value.

Single Bracketing

This mode captures one bracketed image in a series of 3, 5, 7, or 9 shots each time you press the shutter release, with the same increments available as described above. The left/right buttons are used to select the increment and number of shots. In this mode, you can separate each image by an interval of your choice. You might want to use this variation when you want the individual images to be captured at slightly different times, say, to produce a set of images that will be combined in some artistic way.

> **HDR ISN'T HARD**
>
> The 1.0 EV to 3.0 EV options are the ones you might try first when bracketing if you plan to perform High Dynamic Range magic later on in Photoshop (with Merge to HDR), Elements (with Photomerge), or with another image editor that provides an HDR feature. That will allow you to combine images with different exposures into one photo with an amazing amount of detail in both highlights and shadows. To get the best results, mount your camera on a tripod, shoot in RAW format, and use Continuous Bracket 3 EV to get three shots with 3 EV of difference in exposure.

White Balance Bracketing

In this mode, the camera shoots three images, each with a different adjustment to the color temperature. While you can't specify which direction the color bias is tilted, you can select Lo (the default) for small changes, or Hi, for larger changes using the left/right buttons. Only the last shot taken is displayed during Auto Review.

DRO Bracketing

This mode takes three images, with Lo (the default) or Hi adjustments to the dynamic range optimization. Use the left/right buttons to specify the degree of adjustment. Again, only the last shot taken is displayed during Auto Review.

Dealing with Digital Noise

Visual noise is that random grainy look with colorful speckles that some like to use as a visual effect, but most consider to be objectionable. That's because it robs your image of detail even as it adds that "interesting" texture. Noise is caused by two different phenomena: high ISO levels and long exposures, and adjustments are available to minimize both types. In Chapter 6, I'll explain how to use the Long Exposure Noise Reduction and High ISO Noise reduction entries in the Shooting > Image Quality group.

High ISO Noise

Digital noise commonly appears when you set an ISO above ISO 1600. High ISO noise appears as a result of the amplification needed to increase the effective sensitivity of the sensor. While higher ISOs do pull details out of dark areas, they also amplify non-signal information randomly, creating noise.

High ISO Noise Reduction is very useful, although, at default, it also tends to make images slightly softer as blurring the noise pattern also blurs some intricate details. The higher the ISO, the more aggressive the processing will be, depending on whether you've specified Normal or Low. The Low level for NR provides images that are more grainy but with better resolution of fine detail. Even if you've chosen Off, the camera still applies some noise reduction.

The camera does not use this feature on RAW-format photos since noise reduction—at the optimum level for any photo—can be applied in the software you'll use to modify and convert the RAW file to JPEG or TIFF. (If you shoot in RAW & JPEG, the JPEG images, but not the RAW files, will be affected by this camera feature.) I'll discuss Noise Reduction with software in more detail in the next section.

Figure 3.15 shows two pictures that I shot at ISO 6400. For the first, I used the default (Normal) High ISO NR and for the second shot, I set the NR to Off. (I've exaggerated the differences between the two slightly so the grainy/less grainy images are more evident on the printed page. The halftone screen applied to printed photos tends to mask these differences.)

Long Exposure Noise

A similar digital noise phenomenon occurs during long time exposures, which allow more photons to reach the sensor, increasing your ability to capture a picture under low-light conditions. However, the longer exposures also increase the likelihood that some pixels will register as random, "phantom," photons, often because the longer an imager collects photos during an exposure, the hotter it becomes, and that heat can be mistaken by the sensor as actual photons. The camera tries to minimize this type of noise automatically; there is no separate control you can adjust to add more or less noise reduction for long exposures.

CMOS imagers contain millions of individual amplifiers and A/D (analog to digital) converters, all working in unison though the BIONZ XR digital image processor chip. Because these circuits don't necessarily all process in precisely the same way all the time, they can introduce something called fixed-pattern noise into the image data.

Figure 3.15 The Normal level for High ISO NR (left) produces a smoother (less grainy) image than one made with High ISO NR turned off (right).

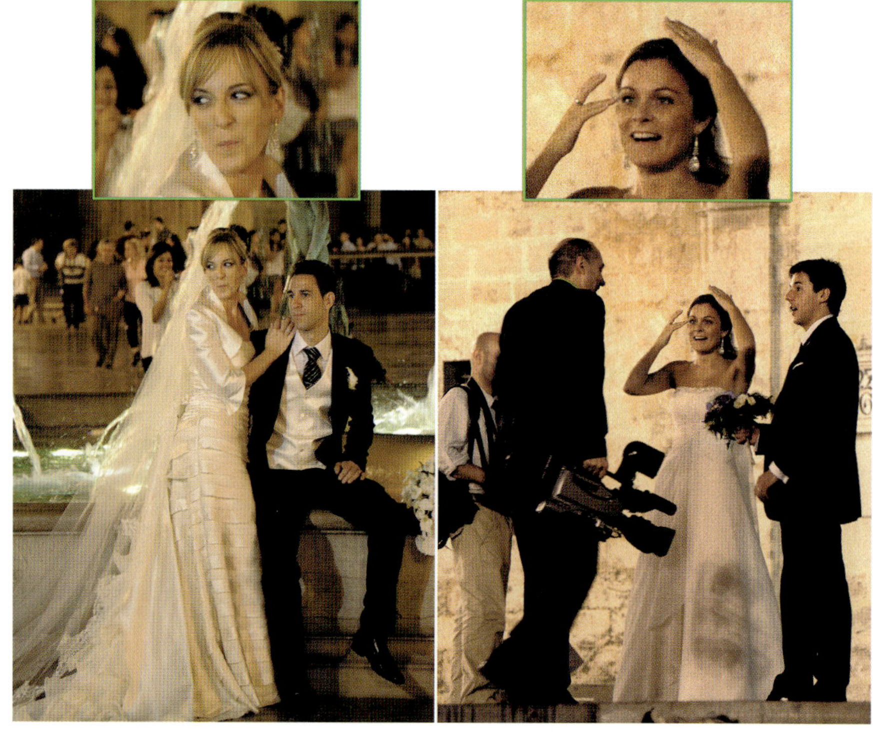

Long exposure noise reduction is used with JPEG exposures longer than 1.3 seconds. When it's active, long exposure noise reduction processing removes random pixels from your photo, but some of the image-making pixels are unavoidably vanquished at the same time.

It's possible that you prefer the version made without NR, and you can achieve that simply by shooting RAW. Indeed, noise reduction can be applied with most image-editing programs. You might get even better results with an industrial-strength product like Nik Dfine, part of the Nik collection, or Topaz DeNoise AI (www.topazlabs.com). You can apply noise reduction to RAW photos with Sony's Imaging Edge application or any other versatile converter software. Some products are optimized for NR with unusually sophisticated processing, such as Photo Ninja (www.picturecode.com) and the $129 DxO Photolab (www.dxo.com).

Using Dynamic Range Optimizer

Dynamic Range Optimizer (DRO) is a feature you can select from the Exposure/Color > Color/Tone > D-Range Optimizer menu entry, or the Function menu, as explained in Chapter 7. When enabled, the camera will examine your images as they are exposed, and, if the shadows appear to have detail even though they are too dark, will attempt to process the image so the shadows are lighter, with additional detail, without overexposing detailed highlights. The processed image is always saved as a JPEG, so if you are shooting RAW you won't notice a difference.

High dynamic range (HDR) photography, especially, is quite the rage these days, and entire books have been written on the subject. It's not really a new technique—film photographers have been combining multiple exposures for ages to produce a single image of, say, an interior room while maintaining detail in the scene visible through the windows.

Suppose you wanted to photograph a dimly lit room that had a bright window showing an outdoors scene. Proper exposure for the room might be on the order of 1/60th second at f/2.8 at ISO 200, while the outdoors scene probably would require f/11 at 1/400th second. That's almost a 7 EV step difference (approximately 7 f/stops) and well beyond the dynamic range of any digital camera, including the Sony a7C II/a7CR. (An additional problem, of course, is the mixed illumination: daylight outdoors and probably tungsten or fluorescent lamps indoors. Pro photographers sometimes gel the windows with corrective film so that inside/outside illumination matches. That's a lot of work!)

Here is how the DRO feature works:

- **D-R Off.** No optimization. You're on your own; the camera will not apply extra processing even to your JPEG photos. Of course, if you are shooting RAW (or RAW & JPEG) photos, you can apply DRO effects to your photo when converting it with the downloadable Image Data Converter SR software. (Other programs have different tools for lightening shadow areas and/or darkening highlight areas.) Use Off when shooting subjects of normal contrast, or when you want to capture an image just as you see it, without modification by the camera.

- **DRO Auto.** Press the left/right buttons after scrolling to DRO Auto and you can then set a specific intensity level for the Dynamic Range Optimizer, from Level 1 through Level 5.

  If you do not want to set a specific level, simply scroll to DRO Auto and allow the camera to decide on the amount of increased dynamic range. With the Auto setting, the camera dives into your image, looking at various small areas to examine the contrast of highlights and shadows, making modifications to each section to produce the best combination of brightness and tones with detail. In my experience, Auto provides a mid-level of DRO that's worth leaving on at all times.

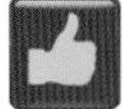

TIP   The primary method for DRO processing is lightening the dark tones and mid tones of an image. The higher the level of DRO you set, the more significantly the processor will lighten those areas; that causes digital noise to be more and more noticeable, especially in photos made at ISO 800 and at higher ISO levels. This is one reason why you would not always want to set Level 4 or 5 for DRO, particularly when using a high ISO setting. The other reason is that very high DRO produces a somewhat unnatural-looking effect with all shadow areas lighter than "normal." Auto and Levels 1 to 3 retain the most natural-looking effect.

When you activate DRO, you have your choice of specifying the aggressiveness of the processing (from Level 1 through Level 5), in which case it will *always* be applied at the level you specify. Or, you can set the feature to Auto and let the camera decide the ideal amount of optimization (or even when to apply it at all). Auto is usually your best choice, because the camera is pretty smart about choosing which images to process, and which to leave alone. Indeed, the camera's programming usually does a better job than a similar feature available in many software utilities.

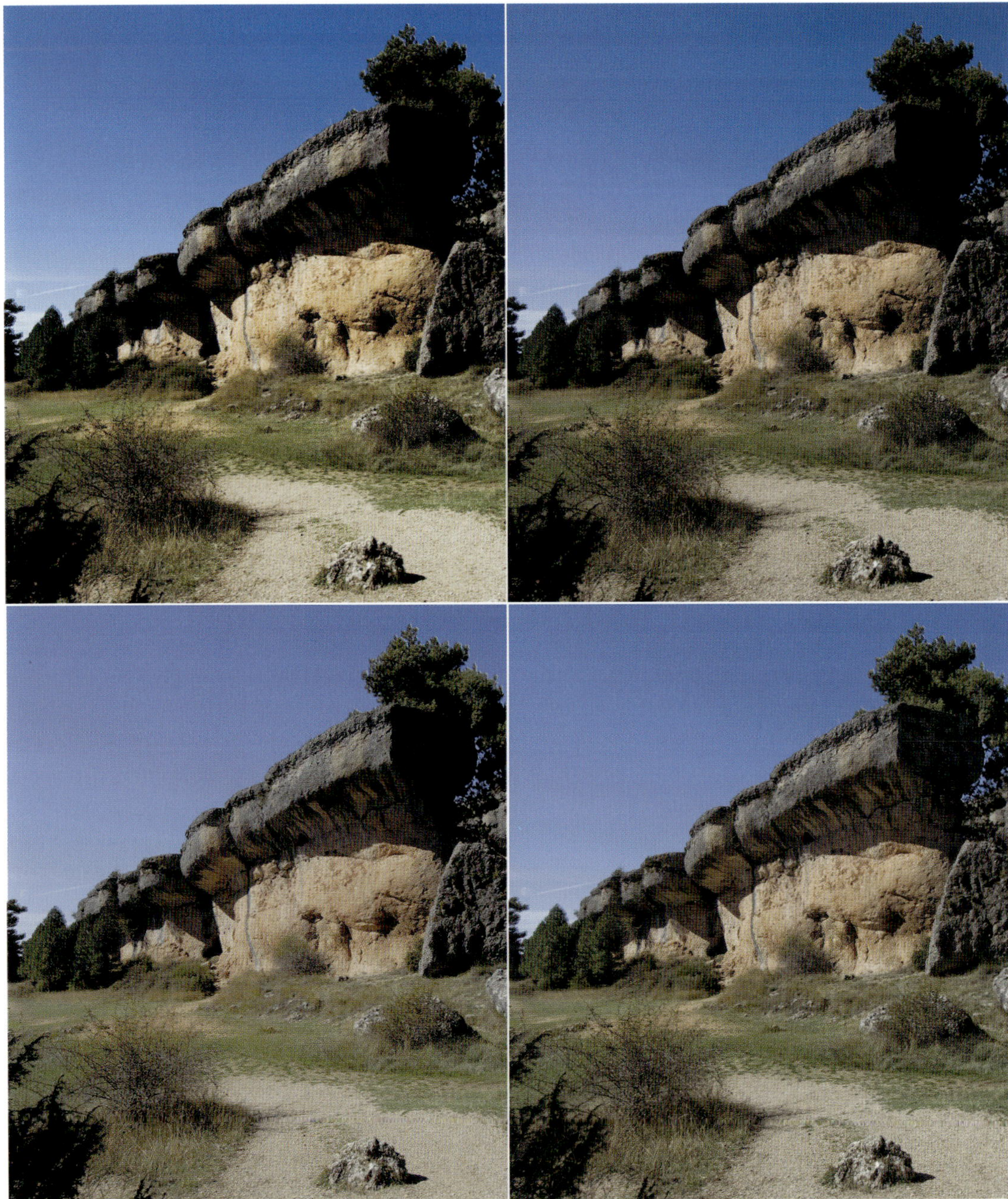

Figure 3.16 DRO Off (upper left); Level 1 (upper right); Level 3 (lower left); and Level 5 (lower right).

Figure 3.16 shows an image with DRO turned off, and using Level 1, Level 3, and Level 5 optimization. (The differences between, say, Level 1 and 2, or 2 and 3 are subtle and wouldn't show up well on the printed page, so I skipped the even-numbered levels.) The printed page also doesn't show that DRO tends to increase the amount of noise in an image as it works more aggressively; it's usually a good idea to avoid using the feature at high ISO levels where noise tends to be a real problem under any conditions.

Working with HDR

High dynamic range (HDR) photography is quite the rage these days, and entire books have been written on the subject. It's not really a new technique—film photographers have been combining multiple exposures for ages to produce a single image of, say, an interior room while maintaining detail in the scene visible through the windows.

Until camera sensors gain much higher dynamic ranges (which may not be as far into the distant future as we think), special tricks like DRO and HDR photography will remain basic tools. With the Sony a7C II and a7CR you must shoot HDR the old-fashioned way—with separate bracketed exposures that are later combined in a tool like Photomatix or Adobe's Merge to HDR image-editing feature. Auto HDR, found in some other cameras, is not supported by this one.

Bracketing and Merge to HDR

Creating HDR images manually is not difficult. You simply shoot individual images either by manually bracketing or using the camera's auto bracketing modes, described earlier in this chapter.

Although my goal in this book is to show you how to take great photos *in the camera* rather than how to fix your errors in Photoshop, the Merge to HDR Pro feature in Adobe's flagship image editor (and a variation also found in Photoshop Elements) is too cool to ignore. The ability to have a bracketed set of exposures that are identical except for exposure is key to getting good results with this Photoshop feature, which allows you to produce images with a full, rich dynamic range that includes a level of detail in the highlights and shadows that is almost impossible to achieve with digital cameras.

When you're using Merge to HDR Pro, you'd take several pictures, some exposed for the shadows, some for the middle tones, and some for the highlights. The exact number of images to combine is up to you. Four to seven is a good number. Then, you'd use the Merge to HDR Pro command to combine all of the images into one HDR image that integrates the well-exposed sections of each version. Here's how.

The images should be as identical as possible, except for exposure. So, it's a good idea to mount the camera on a tripod, use a remote release, and take all the exposures in one burst.

Just follow these steps:

1. **Set up the camera.** Mount the camera on a tripod.

2. **Set the camera to shoot a bracketed burst with an increment of at least 2 EV.** You can use auto bracketing or manually change the exposure between shots. In Manual mode, make sure Auto ISO is off, and you adjust exposures *only* by changing the shutter speed. You should be very careful when you make the adjustment to avoid jostling the camera.

3. **Choose an f/stop.** Set the camera for Aperture Priority and select an aperture that will provide a correct exposure at your initial settings for the series of manually bracketed shots. *And then leave this adjustment alone!* You don't want the aperture to change for your series, as that would change the depth-of-field and, potentially, the image size of some elements. You want the camera to adjust exposure *only* using the shutter speed.

4. **Choose manual focus.** You don't want the focus to change between shots, so set the camera to manual focus, and carefully focus your shot.

5. **Choose RAW exposures.** Set the camera to take RAW files, which will give you the widest range of tones in your images. (This is an advantage of manually creating HDR files; the camera's Auto HDR feature can't be used when RAW or RAW+JPEG is active.)

6. **Take your bracketed set.** Press the button on the remote (or carefully press the shutter release or use the self-timer) and take the set of bracketed exposures.

7. **Continue with the Merge to HDR Pro steps listed next.** You can also use a different program, such as Photomatix or Nik software, if you know how to use it.

DETERMINING THE BEST EXPOSURE DIFFERENTIAL

How do you choose the number of EV/stops to separate your exposures? You can use histograms, described at the end of this chapter, to determine the correct bracketing range. Take a test shot and examine the histogram. Reduce the exposure until dark tones are clipped off at the left of the resulting histogram. Then, increase the exposure until the lighter tones are clipped off at the right of the histogram. The number of stops between the two is the range that should be covered using your bracketed exposures. Note that if you want to override the +/− 3 stop limitation of auto bracketing, you can add or subtract exposure compensation. That will bias the exposures in the direction you choose. For example, if autobracketing in Aperture Priority mode would produce exposures of 1/125th, 1/250th, and 1/500th second, you can set EV to −2 and get 1/30th-, 1/60th-, and 1/125th-second exposures instead.

The next steps show you how to combine the separate exposures into one merged high dynamic range image:

1. **Copy your images to your computer.** If you use an application to transfer the files to your computer, make sure it does not make any adjustments to brightness, contrast, or exposure. You want the real raw information for Merge to HDR Pro to work with. Your three images might look something like the trio stacked at the left side of Figure 3.17.

2. **Activate Merge to HDR Pro.** Choose File > Automate > Merge to HDR Pro.

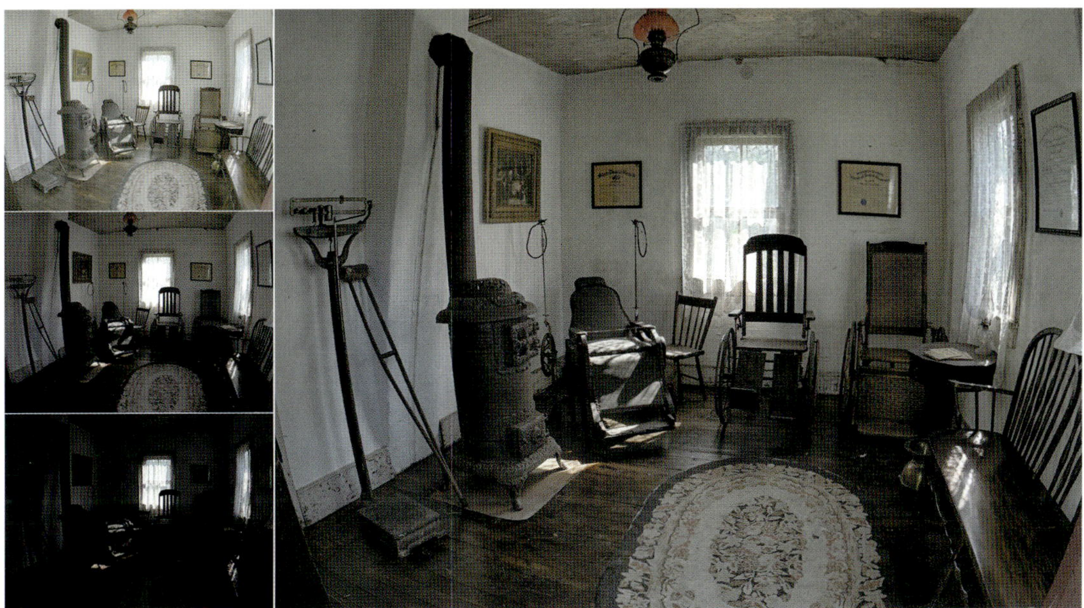

Figure 3.17 Three bracketed images (left) can be combined to produce the merged HDR image (right).

3. **Select the photos to be merged.** Use the Browse feature to locate and select your photos to be merged. You'll note a check box that can be used to automatically align the images if they were not taken with the camera mounted on a rock-steady support. This will adjust for any slight movement of the camera that might have occurred when you changed exposure settings.

4. **Choose parameters (optional).** The first time you use Merge to HDR Pro, you can let the program work with its default parameters. Once you've played with the feature a few times, you can read the Adobe Help files and learn more about the options than I can present in this non-software-oriented camera guide.

5. **Click OK.** The merger begins.

6. **Save.** Once Merge to HDR has done its thing, save the file to your computer.

If you do everything correctly, you'll end up with a full-range high dynamic range photo, like the one shown at right in Figure 3.17. What if you don't have the opportunity, inclination, or skills to create several images at different exposures, as described? If you shoot in RAW format, you can still use Merge to HDR, working with a *single* original image file. What you do is import the image into Photoshop several times, using Adobe Camera Raw to create multiple copies of the file at different exposure levels.

For example, you'd create one copy that's too dark, so the shadows lose detail, but the highlights are preserved. Create another copy with the shadows intact and allow the highlights to wash out. Then, you can use Merge to HDR to combine the two and end up with a finished image that has the extended dynamic range you're looking for. (This concludes the image-editing portion of the chapter. We now return you to our alternate sponsor: photography.)

Exposure Evaluation with Histograms

While you may be able to improve poorly exposed photos in your image-editing software or with DRO or HDR techniques, it's definitely preferable to get the exposure close to correct in the camera. This will minimize the modifications you'll need to make in post-processing, which can be very time-consuming and will degrade image quality, especially with JPEGs. A RAW photo can tolerate more significant changes with less adverse effects, but for optimum quality, it's still important to have an exposure that's close to correct.

Instead, you can use a histogram, which is a chart displayed on the camera's screen that shows the number of tones that have been captured at each brightness level. Two types of histograms are available, a "live" histogram that appears at the lower-right corner of the screen in Shooting mode, and a larger, more detailed version that appears in Histogram mode during playback. The live version can help you make exposure decisions as you shoot, whereas the playback version is useful in determining corrections to be made before you take your next shot. I'll explain both versions, but first it's useful to understand exactly what you're seeing when you view a histogram.

The Live Histogram

The camera's live histogram offers the most reliable method for judging the exposure as you shoot (although the Zebra feature described in Chapter 6 can be used to isolate specific problems involving blown highlights). A pair of live histograms are also available for display for both the viewfinder and monitor; activate both with the Setup > Operation Customize > DISP (Screen Display) Monitor or Finder entries as discussed in Chapter 9. After activating, press the DISP button a few times to reach the display that includes the histogram, which will be shown at lower right in the viewfinder and LCD monitor screens.

In Shooting mode, you'll get a luminance (brightness) histogram that shows the distribution of tones and brightness levels across the image given the current settings, including exposure compensation, Dynamic Range Optimizer (DRO) level in use, or the aperture, shutter speed, and ISO that you have set if using Manual mode. This live histogram (displayed before taking a photo) is useful for judging whether the exposure is likely to be satisfactory or whether you should use a camera feature to modify the exposure. When the histogram looks better, take the photo. I'll show you how to evaluate histograms later in this chapter.

The Playback Histograms

You can view histograms in Playback mode, too; press the DISP button until the display shown in Figure 3.18 appears. The top graph, called the luminance or brightness histogram, is conventional, showing the distribution of tones across the image. Each of the other three histograms is in a specific color: red, green, and blue. That indicates the color channel you're viewing in that histogram: red, green, or blue. These additional graphs allow you to see the distribution of tones in the three individual channels. It takes a lot

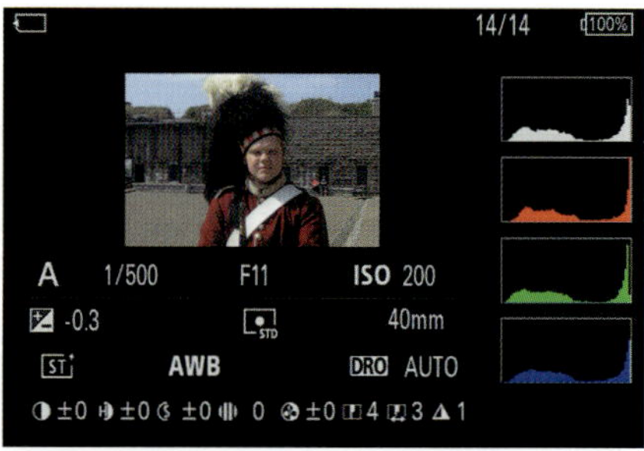

Figure 3.18 The Playback histograms show you the tonal distribution of a photo you've already taken.

of expertise to interpret those extra histograms and, frankly, the conventional luminance histogram is the only one that many photographers use.

As a bonus in Playback mode, another feature is available when the histograms are visible: any areas of the displayed image that are excessively bright, or excessively dark, will blink. This feature, often called "blinkies," warns that you may need to change your settings to avoid loss of detail in highlight areas (such as a white wedding gown) or in shadow areas (such as a black animal's fur). The camera also includes the Zebra feature to indicate overexposure, as discussed in Chapter 6. You can use the histogram information along with the flashing blinkie and Zebra alerts to guide you in modifying the exposure, and/or setting the DRO feature (discussed earlier), before taking the photo again.

Tonal Range

Histograms help you adjust the tonal range of an image, the span of dark to light tones, from a complete absence of brightness (black) to the brightest possible tone (white), and all the middle tones in between. Because all values for tones fall into a continuous spectrum between black and white, it's easiest to think of a photo's tonality in terms of a black-and-white or grayscale image, even though you're capturing those tones in three separate color layers of red, green, and blue.

Because your images are digital, the tonal "spectrum" isn't really continuous: it's divided into discrete steps that represent the different tones that can be captured. Figure 3.19 may help you understand this concept. The gray steps shown range from 100 percent gray (black) at the left, to 0 percent gray (white) at the right, with 20 gray steps in all (plus white).

Along the bottom of the chart are the digital values from 0 to 255 recorded by your sensor for an image with 8 bits per channel. (8 bits of red, 8 bits of green, and 8 bits of blue equal a 24-bit, full-color image.) Any black captured would be represented by a value of 0, the brightest white by 255, and the midtones would be clustered around the 128 marker. The actual scale may be "finer" and record say, 0 to 4,094 for an image captured when the a7C II/a7CR is capturing RAW images with 14 bits per channel.

Grayscale images (which we call black-and-white photos) are easy to understand. Or, at least, that's what we think. When we look at a black-and-white image, we think we're seeing a continuous range of tones from black to white, and all the grays in between. But, that's not exactly true. The blackest black in any photo isn't a true black, because *some* light is always reflected from the surface of

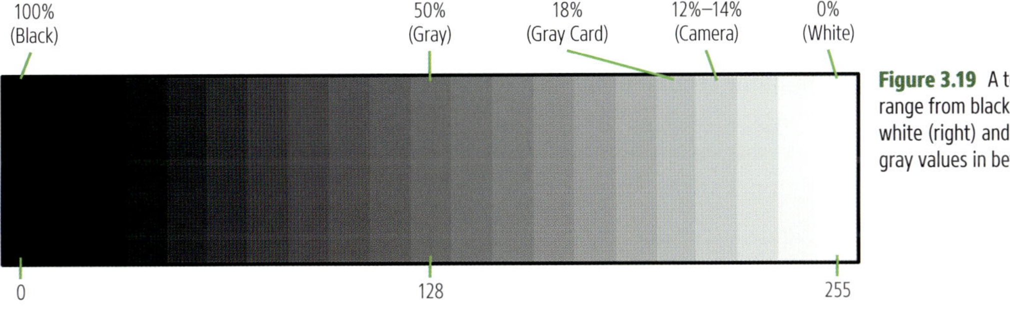

Figure 3.19 A tonal range from black (left) to white (right) and all the gray values in between.

the print, and if viewed on a screen, the deepest black is only as dark as the least-reflective area a computer monitor can produce. The whitest white isn't a true white, either, because even the lightest areas of a print absorb some light (only a mirror reflects close to all the light that strikes it), and, when viewing on a computer monitor, the whites are limited by the brightness of the display's LCD or LED picture elements. Lacking darker blacks and brighter, whiter whites, that continuous set of tones doesn't cover the full grayscale tonal range.

The full scale of tones becomes useful when you have an image that has large expanses of shades that change gradually from one level to the next, such as areas of sky, water, or walls. Think of a picture taken of a group of campers around a campfire. Since the light from the fire is striking them directly in the face, there aren't many shadows on the campers' faces. All the tones that make up the *features* of the people around the fire are compressed into one end of the brightness spectrum—the lighter end.

Yet, there's more to this scene than faces. Behind the campers are trees, rocks, and perhaps a few animals that have emerged from the shadows to see what is going on. These are illuminated by the softer light that bounces off the surrounding surfaces. If your eyes become accustomed to the reduced illumination, you'll find that there is a wealth of detail in these shadow images.

This campfire scene would be a nightmare to reproduce faithfully under any circumstances. If you are an experienced photographer, you are probably already wincing at what is called a *high-contrast* lighting situation. Some photos may be high in contrast when there are fewer tones and they are all bunched up at limited points in the scale. In a low-contrast image, there are more tones, but they are spread out so widely that the image looks flat. Your digital camera can show you the relationship between these tones using a *histogram*.

Histogram Basics

The histograms are a simplified display of the numbers of pixels at each of 256 brightness levels, producing an interesting mountain range effect. Although separate charts may be provided for brightness and the red, green, and blue channels, when you first start using histograms, you'll want to concentrate on the brightness histogram.

Each vertical line in the graph represents the allocation of pixels in the image for each brightness value, from 0 (black) on the left to 255 (white) on the right. Although histograms are most often used to fine-tune exposure, you can glean other information from them, such as the relative contrast of the image. Figure 3.20, top, is a simplified rendition of a histogram of an image having normal contrast. In such an image, most of the pixels are spread across the image, with a healthy distribution of tones throughout the midtone section of the graph. That large peak at the right side of the graph represents all those light tones in the sky. A normal-contrast image you shoot may have less sky area, and less of a peak at the right side, but notice that very few pixels hug the right edge of the histogram, indicating that the lightest tones are not being clipped because they are off the chart.

With a lower-contrast image, like the one shown in Figure 3.20, center, the basic shape of the previous histogram will remain recognizable, but gradually will be compressed together to cover a smaller

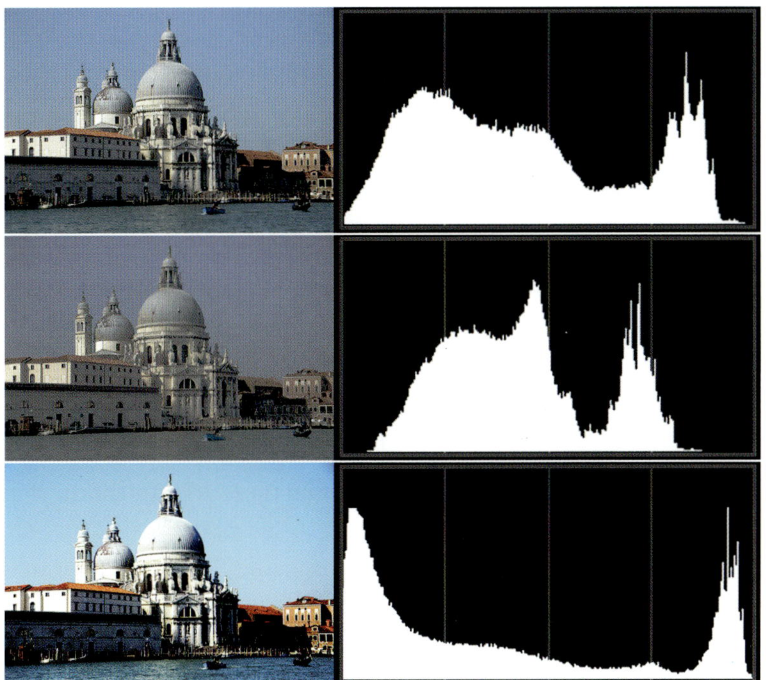

Figure 3.20 Top: This image has fairly normal contrast, even though there is a peak of light tones at the right side representing the sky. Center: This low-contrast image has all the tones squished into one section of the grayscale. Bottom: A high-contrast image produces a histogram in which the tones are spread out.

area of the gray spectrum. The squished shape of the histogram is caused by all the grays in the original image being represented by a limited number of gray tones in a smaller range of the scale.

Instead of the darkest tones of the image reaching into the black end of the spectrum and the whitest tones extending to the lightest end, the blackest areas of the scene are now represented by a light gray, and the whites by a somewhat lighter gray. The overall contrast of the image is reduced. Because all the darker tones are actually a middle gray or lighter, the scene in this version of the photo appears lighter as well.

Going in the other direction, increasing the contrast of an image produces a histogram like the one shown in Figure 3.20, bottom. In this case, the tonal range is now spread over the entire width of the chart, but, except for the bright sky, there is not much variation in the middle tones; the mountain "peaks" are not very high. When you stretch the grayscale in both directions like this, the darkest tones become darker (that may not be possible) and the lightest tones become lighter (ditto). In fact, shades that might have been gray before can change to black or white as they are moved toward either end of the scale.

The effect of increasing contrast may be to move some tones off either end of the scale altogether, while spreading the remaining grays over a smaller number of locations on the spectrum. That's exactly the case in the example shown. The number of possible tones is smaller and the image appears harsher.

Understanding Histograms

The important thing to remember when working with the histogram display is that changing the exposure does *not* change the contrast of an image. The curves illustrated in the previous three examples remain exactly the same shape when you increase or decrease exposure. I repeat: The proportional distribution of grays shown in the histogram doesn't change when exposure changes; it is neither stretched nor compressed. However, the tones as a whole are moved toward one end of the scale or the other, depending on whether you're increasing or decreasing exposure. You'll be able to see that in some illustrations that follow.

So, as you reduce exposure, tones gradually move to the black end (and off the scale), while the reverse is true when you increase exposure. The contrast within the image is changed only to the extent that some of the tones can no longer be represented when they are moved off the scale.

To change the *contrast* of an image, you must do one of four things:

- **Change the contrast setting** using the menu system. You'll find these adjustments in your camera's Creative Looks feature, as discussed in Chapter 7.
- **Use your camera's shadow-tone "booster."** As previously discussed, D-Range Optimizer can also adjust contrast.
- **Alter the contrast of the scene itself,** for example, by using a fill light or reflectors to add illumination to shadows that are too dark.
- **Attempt to adjust contrast in post-processing** using your image editor or RAW file converter. You may use features such as Levels or Curves (in Photoshop, Photoshop Elements, and many other image editors), or work with HDR software to cherry-pick the best values in shadows and highlights from multiple images.

Of the four of these, the third—changing the contrast of the scene—is the most desirable, because attempting to fix contrast by fiddling with the tonal values is unlikely to be a perfect remedy. However, adding a little contrast can be successful because you can discard some tones to make the image more contrasty. However, the opposite is much more difficult. An overly contrasty image rarely can be fixed, because you can't add information that isn't there in the first place.

What you *can* do is adjust the exposure so that the tones *that are already present in the scene* are captured correctly. Figure 3.21, top, shows the histogram for an image that is badly underexposed. You can guess from the shape of the histogram that many of the dark tones to the left of the graph have been clipped off. There's plenty of room on the right side for additional pixels to reside without having them become overexposed. So, you can increase the exposure (either by changing the f/stop or shutter speed or by adding an EV value) to produce the corrected histogram shown in Figure 3.21, center.

Conversely, if your histogram looks like the one shown in Figure 3.21, bottom, with bright tones pushed off the right edge of the chart, you have an overexposed image, and you can correct it by reducing exposure. In addition to the histogram, the a7C II/a7CR has its Highlights and Zebra options, which, when activated, shows areas that are overexposed with flashing tones (often called

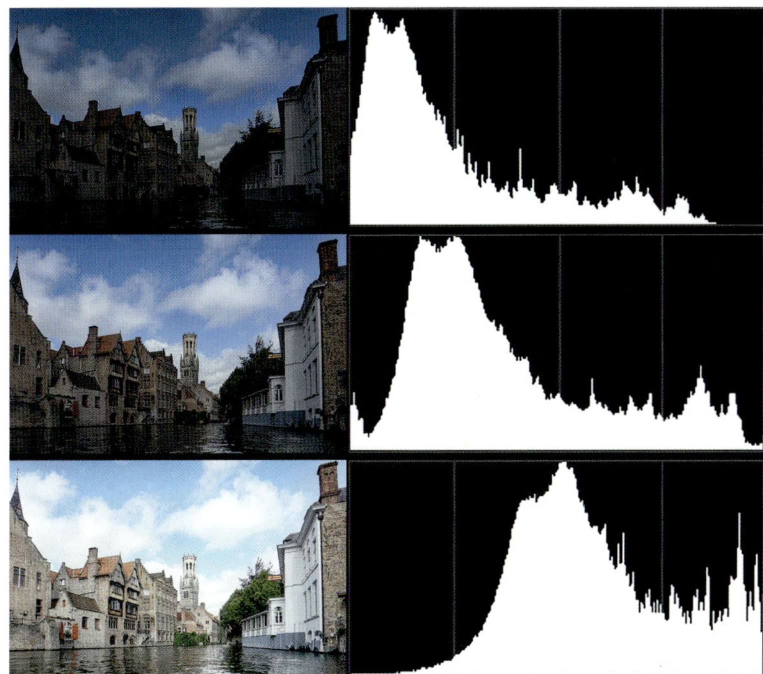

Figure 3.21 Top: A histogram of an under-exposed image may look like this. Center: Adding exposure will produce a histogram like this one. Bottom: A histogram of an overexposed image will show clipping at the right side.

"blinkies"). Depending on the importance of this "clipped" detail, you can adjust exposure or leave it alone. For example, if all the dark-coded areas in the review are in a background that you care little about, you can forget about them and not change the exposure, but if such areas appear in facial details of your subject, you may want to make some adjustments.

In working with histograms, your goal should be to have all the tones in an image spread out between the edges, with none clipped off at the left and right sides. Underexposing (to preserve highlights) should be done only as a last resort, because retrieving the underexposed shadows in your image editor will frequently increase the noise, even if you're working with RAW files. A better course of action is to expose for the highlights, but, when the subject matter makes it practical, fill in the shadows with additional light, using reflectors, fill flash, or other techniques rather than allowing them to be seriously underexposed.

A traditional technique for optimizing exposure is called "expose to the right" (ETTR), which involves adding exposure to push the histogram's curve toward the right side *but not far enough to clip off highlights.* The rationale for this method is that extra shadow detail will be produced with a minimum increase in noise, especially in the shadow areas. It's said that half of a digital sensor's response lies in the brightest areas of an image, and so require the least amount of amplification (which is one way to increase digital noise). ETTR can work, as long as you're able to capture a satisfactory amount of information in the shadows.

Exposing to the Right

It's easier to understand exposing to the right if you mentally divide the histogram into fifths (unfortunately, the histogram uses quarters instead). And, for the sake of simplicity and smaller numbers, assume you're shooting in 14-bit RAW. Any 14-bit image can record a maximum of 16,384 different tones per channel. However, each fifth of the histogram does *not* encompass 3,277 tones (one-fifth of 16,384).

Instead, the right-most fifth, the highlights, shown in Figure 3.22, accounts for fully *half*, or 50 percent of the tones; the next fifth accounts for 1/4 (25 percent); and so on, with 1/8th, 1/16th, and 1/32nd assigned to the remaining fifths. These "fifths" are fuzzy rather than hard boundaries. But note that in the left-most area, approximately only 512 different tones are captured. When processing your RAW file, there are only 512 tones to recover in the shadows, which is why boosting/amplifying them increases noise. (The effect is most noticeable in the red and blue channels; your sensor's Bayer array has twice as many green-sensitive pixels as red or blue.)

Instead, you want to add exposure—as long as you don't push highlights off the right edge of the histogram—to brighten the shadows. Because there are approximately 8,192 tones available in the highlights, even if the RAW image *looks* overexposed, it's possible to use your RAW converter's Exposure slider (such as the one found in Adobe Camera Raw) to bring back detail captured in that surplus of tones in the highlights. This procedure is the exact opposite of what was recommended for film of the transparency variety—it was fairly easy to retrieve detail from shadows by pumping more light through them when processing the image, while even small amounts of extra exposure blew out highlights. You'll often find that the range of tones in your image is so great that there is no way to keep your histogram from spilling over into the left and right edges, costing you both highlight and shadow detail. Exposing to the right may not work in such situations. A second school of thought recommends *reducing* exposure to bring back the highlights, or "exposing to the left." You would then attempt to recover shadow detail in an image editor, using tools like Adobe Camera Raw's Exposure slider. But remember, above all, that this procedure will also boost noise in the shadows, and so the technique should be used with caution. In most cases, exposing to the right is your best bet.

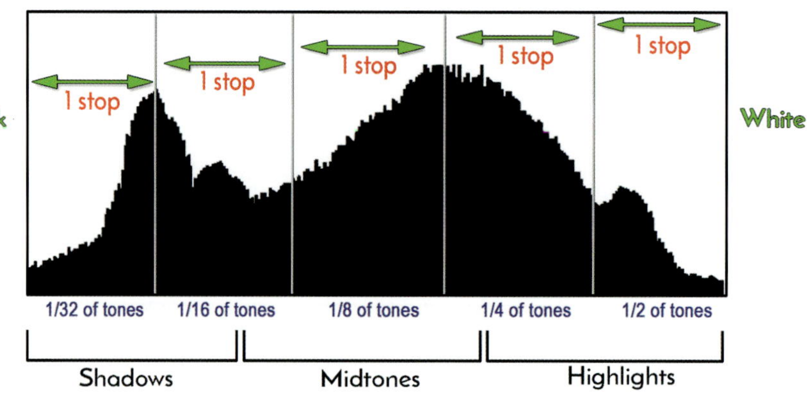

Figure 3.22 Tones are not evenly allocated throughout a histogram.

Dealing with Channels

The more you work with histograms, the more useful they become. One of the first things that histogram veterans notice is that it's possible to overexpose one channel even if the overall exposure appears to be correct. For example, flower photographers soon discover that it's really, really difficult to get a good picture of a red rose. The exposure looks okay—but there's no detail in the rose's petals. (See Figure 3.23, left.) The image's histogram will show you why: typically, you'll find a peak at the right edge that indicates that highlight information has been lost. In fact, the green channel is often blown, too, and so the green parts of the flower also lack detail. Only the blue channel's histogram may be entirely contained within the boundaries of the chart, and, on first glance, the white luminance histogram at the top of the column of graphs may appear to be fairly normal.

Any of the primary channels—red, green, or blue—can blow out all by themselves, although bright reds seem to be the most common problem area. More difficult to diagnose are overexposed tones in one of the "in-between" hues on the color wheel. Overexposed yellows (which are very common) will be shown by blowouts in *both* the red and green channels. Too-bright cyans will manifest as excessive blue and green highlights, while overexposure in the red and blue channels reduces detail in magenta colors. As you gain experience, you'll be able to see exactly how anomalies in the RGB channels translate into poor highlights and murky shadows.

The only way to correct for color channel blowouts is to reduce exposure. As I mentioned earlier, you might want to consider filling in the shadows with additional light to keep them from becoming too dark when you decrease exposure. In practice, you'll want to monitor the red channel most closely, followed by the blue channel, and slightly decrease exposure to see if that helps. Because of the way our eyes perceive color, we are more sensitive to variations in green, so green channel blowouts are

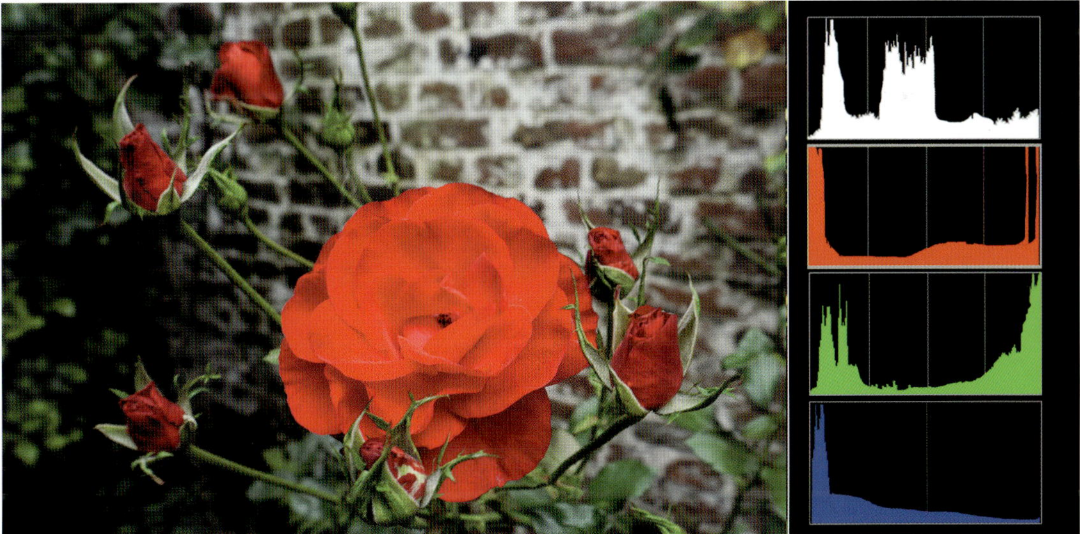

Figure 3.23 When the red channel is "blown," red portions of an image may lack detail (left), as indicated by the highlight peak in the red channel's histogram (right).

less of a problem, unless your main subject is heavily colored in that hue. If you plan on photographing a frog hopping around on your front lawn, you'll want to be extra careful to preserve detail in the green channel, using bracketing or other exposure techniques outlined in this chapter.

Fine-Tuning Exposure

When all else fails—that is, when you find your camera *consistently* over- or underexposes when using a particular exposure mode—you can recalibrate the a7C II or a7CR to produce images more to your liking. The Exposure/Color > Exposure Compensation > Exposure Standard Adjustment setting is a powerful tool that allows you to dial in a specific amount of exposure adjustment that will be applied, invisibly, to every photo you take using each of the metering modes. No more can you complain, "My camera always underexposes by 1/3 stop!" If that is actually the case, and the phenomenon is consistent, you can use the Exposure Standard Adjustment entry to compensate.

Exposure compensation is usually a better idea (does your camera *really* underexpose that consistently?), but this setting does allow you to adjust your camera's behavior yourself. Your dialed-in modifications will survive a reset. However, you have no indication that fine-tuning has been made, so you'll need to remember what you've done. After all, you someday might discover that your camera is consistently *over*exposing images by 1/3 stop, not remembering that you've made the adjustment.

In practice, it's rare that any given Sony a7C II or a7CR will *consistently* provide the wrong exposure in any of the three metering modes, especially Multi metering, which can alter exposure dramatically based on the a7C II/a7CR's internal database of typical scenes. This feature may be most useful for Spot metering, if you always take a reading off the same type of subject, such as a human face or gray card. Should you find that the gray card readings, for example, always differ from what you would prefer, go ahead and fine-tune optimal exposure for Spot metering, and use that to read your gray cards.

Mastering Autofocus Options

4

The autofocus system found in the Sony a7C II and a7CR is one of its most innovative features. The camera has the ability to lock in on subjects (what Sony now calls *recognition targets*), including people and animals (birds, dogs, and cats—using Subject Recognition), and track motion. These cameras can seamlessly switch between eye, face, and body tracking, and use these modes when shooting video, as well. And if your subject *isn't* a person or suitable animal, the camera can deploy pattern detection and use both subject color and brightness to find and lock focus.

The a7C II and a7CR are even able to focus in dimmer environments than before: down to –3 EV with a lens having an f/2 maximum aperture. For those who can't calculate EV in their head, that's equivalent to an ISO 100 exposure of 30 seconds at f/2, which is roughly the illumination you can expect at night under a full moon. This camera can now automatically focus in what you might consider to be *available darkness*.

As capable as the AF system may seem, there is still one logistical problem to overcome: no camera really knows, for certain, *what* subject *you* want to be in sharp focus. It may select an object and lock in focus with lightning speed. However, the focus plane isn't guaranteed to be your intended center of interest in your photograph. Or, the camera may lock focus too soon, or too late. This chapter will help you understand the options available with your Sony a7C II/a7CR so you can help the camera understand *what* you want to focus on, *when*, and maybe even *why*.

Getting into Focus

Simply put, focus is the process of adjusting the camera so that parts of our subject that we want to be sharp and clear are, in fact, sharp and clear. We allow the camera to focus for us, automatically, or we can rotate the lens's focus ring manually to achieve the desired focus. Manual focusing is especially problematic because our eyes and brains have poor memory for correct focus. That's why your eye doctor conducting a refraction test must shift back and forth between pairs of lenses and ask, "Does that look sharper—or was it sharper before?" in determining your correct prescription. Too often, the slight differences are such that the lens pairs must be swapped multiple times.

Similarly, manual focusing involves jogging the focus ring back and forth as you go from almost in focus, to sharp focus, to almost focused again. The little clockwise and counterclockwise arcs decrease in size until you've zeroed in on the point of correct focus. What you're looking for is the image with the most contrast between the edges of elements in the frame.

The a7C II/a7CR autofocus mechanism, like all such systems found in modern cameras, also evaluates these increases and decreases in sharpness, but it is able to remember the progression perfectly, so that autofocus can lock in much more quickly and, with an image that has sufficient contrast, more precisely. Unfortunately, while the camera's focus system finds it easy to measure degrees of apparent focus at each of the focus points in the viewfinder, it doesn't really know with any certainty *which object* should be in sharpest focus. Is it the closest object? The subject in the center? Something lurking *behind* the closest subject? A person standing over at the side of the picture? Using autofocus effectively involves telling the a7C II/a7CR exactly what it should be focusing on.

Learning to use the sophisticated autofocus system is easy, but you do need to fully understand how the technology works to get the most benefit from it. Once you're comfortable with autofocus, you'll know when it's appropriate to use the manual focus option, too.

As the camera collects focus information from the sensors, it then evaluates it to determine whether the desired sharp focus has been achieved. The calculations may include whether the subject is moving, and whether the camera needs to "predict" where the subject will be when the shutter-release button is fully depressed and the picture is taken.

The a7C II/a7CR has a hybrid autofocus system, using two technologies called contrast-detection autofocus (CDAF) and phase-detection autofocus (PDAF). I'm going to provide a quick overview of contrast detection first, and then devote much of the rest of this chapter to optimizing your camera's use of its phase-detection features.

Contrast Detection

This is a slower, but potentially more accurate mode, best suited for static subjects, and was originally the only kind of autofocus available for mirrorless cameras and for dSLRs when shooting in their live view and movie modes. The innovation of adding phase-detection abilities to the sensor itself (as I'll describe shortly) made contrast detection a fine-tuning option for hybrid autofocus systems that combined CDAF and PDAF.

Contrast detection is very easy to understand, and is illustrated by Figure 4.1, a close-up of the side of an old barn. At top in the figure, the transitions between the edges found in the siding and foundation are soft and blurred because of the low contrast between them. Whether the edges are horizontal, vertical (like the siding), or diagonal doesn't matter in the least; the focus system looks only for contrast between edges, and those edges can run in any direction.

At the bottom of Figure 4.1, the image has been brought into sharp focus, and the edges have much more contrast; the transitions are sharp and clear. Although this example

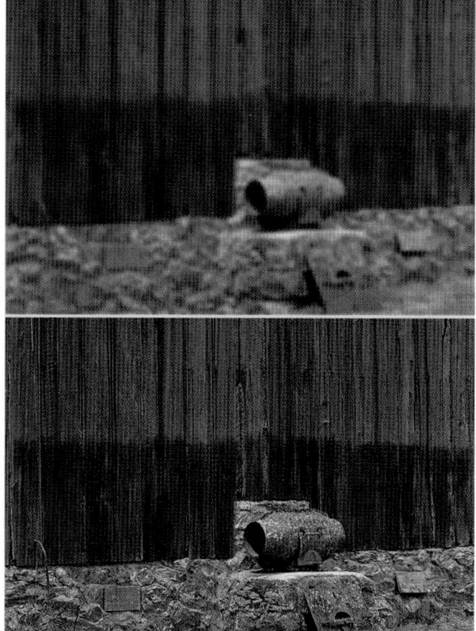

Figure 4.1 Focus in contrast-detection mode evaluates the increase in contrast in the edges of subjects, starting with a blurry image (top) and producing a sharp, contrasty image (bottom).

is a bit exaggerated so you can see the results on the printed page, it's easy to understand that when maximum contrast in a subject is achieved, it can be deemed to be in sharp focus. Although achieving focus with contrast detection is generally quite a bit slower, it can be used to fine-tune focus on a subject that has already been brought into general focus using phase detection (described next). There are several advantages—and disadvantages—to contrast detection, and I'll summarize them shortly.

Phase Detection

Phase detection is much more rapid than contrast detection. The challenge is to make its operation as accurate as possible. Digital SLRs have always used PDAF, with an array of tiny autofocus sensors, located in the "floor" of the mirror box, and a small portion of the illumination directed downward to the autofocus sensor array. With Sony mirrorless cameras, on the other hand, phase detection is built into pixels embedded in the sensor and combines with contrast detection to provide, potentially, the best of both worlds. I'll show you the location of the PDAF and CDAF areas shortly.

The phase-detection pixels in the sensor have a mask covering half of the pixel on one side, with a nearby laterally displaced phase-detection pixel masked on the opposite side. The effect is to create two different "views," each arriving from opposite sides of the lens. This pair of images functions exactly like the rangefinders used for surveying and in rangefinder-focusing cameras like the venerable Leica M series. The two images are separated when out of focus, and then gradually brought together to achieve sharp focus, as shown from top to bottom in Figure 4.2. **Note:** Using some photosites as AF sensors doesn't rob your camera of resolution; the phase-detect sensors are actually *dual-pixel* photosites and are used to collect *both* autofocus and image information. In addition, the a7C II and a7CR have *millions* of pixels available to create an image—33 and 60 million, to be exact— so assigning some to double duty has no effect on image quality.

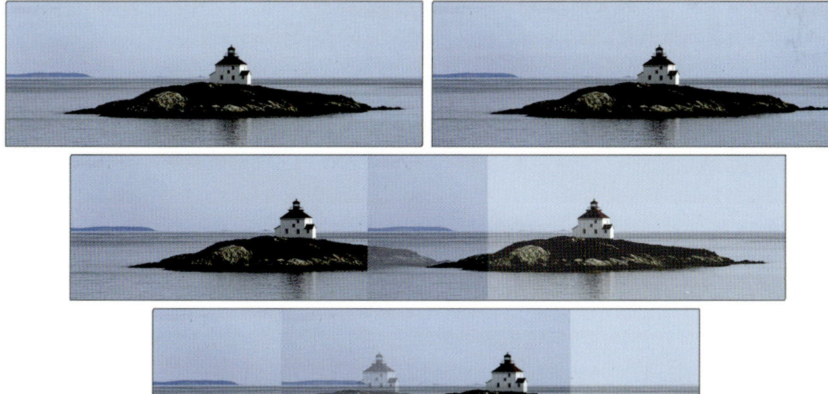

Figure 4.2 In phase detection, parts of an image are split in two and compared (top). When the image is in focus, the two halves of the image align, as with a rangefinder (bottom).

This process tells the camera when the image pair are "in phase" and aligned. The rangefinder approach of phase detection calculates exactly how out of focus the image is, and in which direction (focus is too near, or too far) thanks to the amount and direction of the displacement of the split image. The a7C II/a7CR can quickly and precisely snap the image into sharp focus and match the lines. If necessary, the contrast-detect feature can follow up to perfect the plane of focus.

The PDAF sensors are all *line sensors,* which means they work best with features that transect the sensor either perpendicularly or at an angle, as visualized in Figure 4.3, left. It's easy to detect when the two halves of the vertical lines of the weathered wood are aligned. (See Figure 4.3, center.) However, when the same sensor is asked to measure focus for, say, horizontal lines that don't split up quite so conveniently, or, in the worst case, subjects such as the sky (which may have neither vertical nor horizontal lines), focus can slow down drastically. One such scenario is pictured in Figure 4.3, right. Fortunately, as I mentioned earlier, contrast-detection AF will come to the rescue and take over where phase-detection AF is stymied.

As with any rangefinder-like function, phase-detection accuracy is better when the "base length" between the two images is larger. (Think back to your high school trigonometry; you could calculate a distance more accurately when the separation between the two points where the angles were measured was greater.) For that reason, phase-detection autofocus is more accurate with larger (wider) lens openings—especially those with maximum f/stops of f/2.8 or better—than with smaller lens openings, and may not work at all when the f/stop is smaller than f/8. As I noted, the a7C II and a7CR are able to perform these comparisons very quickly.

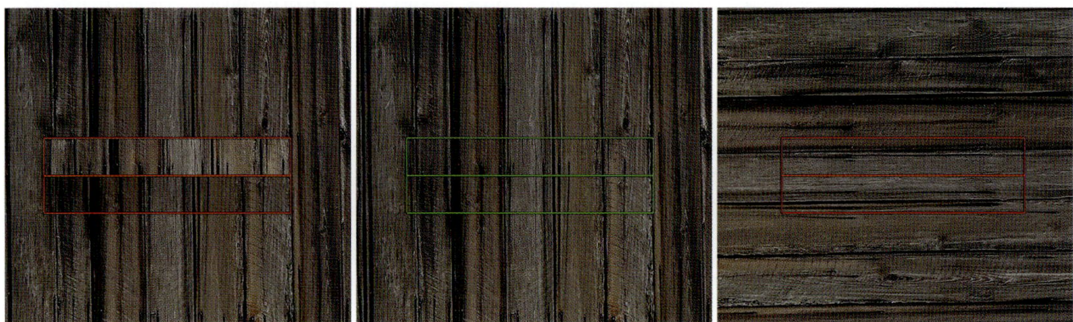

Figure 4.3 When an image is out of focus, the split lines don't align precisely (left). Using phase detection, the camera is able to align the features of the image and achieve sharp focus quickly (center). Horizontal lines aren't ideal for horizontally oriented sensors and require vertical contrast detection to achieve final focus (right).

SOLVING HORIZONTAL PROBLEMS

As I noted, each of the AF sensors consist of a tiny horizontal array of pixels and do the best job of detecting vertical or diagonal lines. The solution would be to include some vertically oriented, horizontal-line-sensitive sensors, or sensors that combine *both* orientations (called *cross sensors*), but Sony didn't need to do this, as the complementary contrast-detection fine-tuning system handles horizontal features well. However, with very difficult subjects, if you find yourself photographing something with predominantly horizontal lines, you can improve your results by rotating the camera to better align the PDAF sensors with your subject.

Comparing the Two Hybrid Components

The Sony a7C II/a7CR autofocus system uses both phase-detection autofocus (PDAF) and contrast-detection autofocus (CDAF) to provide a combination of fast and accurate AF, together covering virtually all of the frame. Figure 4.4 shows the layout of the autofocus zones used.

The hybrid autofocus system uses both types of AF. The process begins by rapidly focusing using PDAF, because the rangefinder approach always tells the camera whether to move focus closer or farther, and by approximately how much. No hunting is required, which is often the case with contrast detection, which needs to tweak the focus point until it settles on the sharpest position.

Once the PDAF has done its stuff, contrast detection kicks in, using its finicky but more accurate focusing capabilities to fine-tune focus. So, you end up with speedy initial focus (PDAF) and slightly slower final adjustments (CDAF), providing a perfect hybrid compromise. That's why Sony didn't switch to phase detection completely. Here's a quick rundown of the advantages of a hybrid system:

- **Contrast detection works with more image types.** Contrast detection doesn't require subject matter to have lines that are at angles to the PDAF points to work optimally, as phase detection does. Any subject that has edges running in any direction can be used to achieve sharp focus.

- **Contrast detection can focus on larger areas of the scene.** Whereas phase-detection focus can be achieved *only* at the points that fall on one of the special autofocus sensor pixels, with contrast detection much larger portions of the image can be used as focus zones. Focus is achieved with the actual sensor image, so focus point selection is simply a matter of choosing which part of the sensor image to use.

- **Contrast detection can be more accurate with some types of scenes.** Phase detection can fall prey to the vagaries of uncooperative subject matter: if suitable lines aren't available, the system may achieve less than optimal focus. In addition, accuracy decreases as the maximum aperture baseline used for calculations becomes smaller. A lens with a maximum aperture of f/5.6 will focus with less accuracy than one with an f/1.8 maximum aperture. Contrast-detection focus is more clear-cut. In most cases, the camera is able to determine clearly when sharp focus has been achieved.

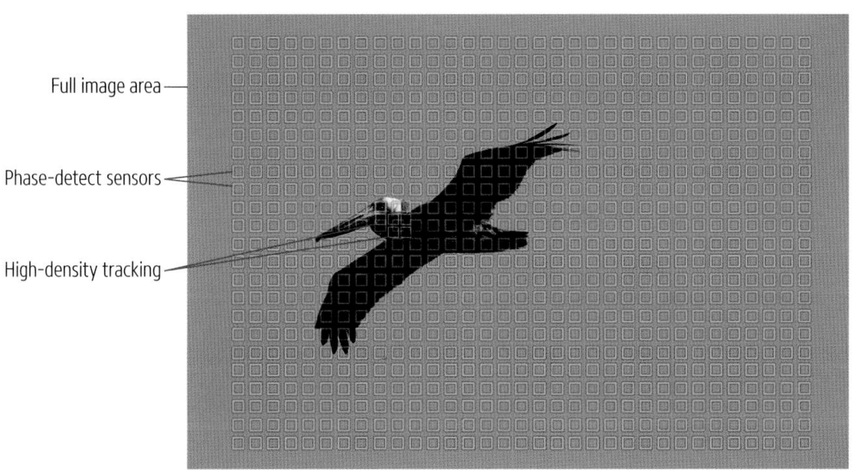

Figure 4.4 Autofocus zones for phase detection (green boxes).

- **Phase detection "knows" which direction to focus.** The split image seen by phase-detection sensors reveal instantly whether focus is too close or too far. There is no need to "hunt" for the focus point, as the AF system can immediately adjust in the proper direction. That boosts focus speed considerably.

- **Phase detection "knows" how far out of focus a subject is.** The separation between the two halves of the image let the AF system know whether the subject is grossly out of focus, or whether only a slight adjustment is needed. That means faster autofocus, too.

- **Phase detection isn't as dependent on scene brightness.** As long as the split images are illuminated well enough for the AF system to make an evaluation, greater or lesser amounts of light don't have as much of an effect on speed and accuracy. Remember, the reason phase detection systems operate less well at smaller f/stops is because the baseline diameter of the aperture is smaller.

- **Sony's 4D high-density tracking can follow moving subjects.** The phase-detection system can achieve focus quickly (even when shooting continuously at 8 to 10 frames per second), whether your subject is moving horizontally or vertically (what Sony calls *area*) or toward you or away from you (*depth* in Sony-speak). To those three dimensions, the system adds the fourth dimension of time (which the company labels as *steadfast*), so focus can be maintained as it changes position. The 4D AF also deploys *high-density* tracking to zero in on moving subjects, using focus areas that are smaller than the phase-detection sensor areas shown in Figure 4.4.

COMPATIBLE LENSES

Not all lenses are compatible with the phase-detection component. Older lenses, and lenses that need to be updated using firmware, don't support phase detection, which in turn blocks use of the Automatic AF, AF Track Duration, and AF Drive Speed features explained in Chapter 8. A-mount lenses used with the LA-EA2 or LA-EA4 adapters do not support focal plane phase detection, although most can be used with their own phase detection.

Focus Modes and Options

Now that you understand the fundamental principles of how the a7C II or a7CR achieves focus, let's discuss the practical application of these principles to your everyday picture-taking activities by setting the various modes and options available for the autofocus system. We'll also discuss the use of manual focus, and when that method might be preferable to autofocus.

As you've come to appreciate by now, the a7C II/a7CR offers many options for your photography. Focus is no exception. Of course, as with other aspects of this camera, you can set the shooting mode to Intelligent Auto or Program mode, and the camera will do just fine in most situations. But, if you want more creative control, the choices are there for you to make.

FOCUS MODES/FOCUS AREA MODES

Your camera has a lot of modes! To keep the various focus options straight, remember that *focus modes* determine *when* the camera focuses: either once or continuously using autofocus, or manually. *Focus area modes* determine *where* in the frame the camera collects the information used to achieve autofocus.

So, no matter what shooting mode you're using, your first choice is whether to use autofocus or manual focus. Yes, there's also a Direct Manual Focus (DMF) option, but that still provides autofocus, with the option of *fine-tuning* focus manually before taking the shot. Manual focus presents you with great flexibility along with the challenge of keeping the image in focus under what may be difficult conditions, such as rapid motion of the subject, darkness of the scene, and the like. Later in this chapter, I'll cover manual focus as well as DMF. For now, I'll assume you're going to rely on the camera's conventional AF mode.

The Sony a7C II and a7CR have three basic AF modes: AF-S (Single-shot autofocus) and AF-C (Continuous autofocus), as well as Automatic AF (AF-A), which switches between the two other modes as required. Once you have decided on which of these to use, you also need to tell the camera how to select the area used to measure AF. In other words, after you tell the camera *how* to autofocus, you also have to tell it *where* to direct its focusing attention. I'll explain both *AF modes* and *AF-area modes* in more detail later in this chapter.

MANUAL FOCUS

When you select manual focus (MF) in the Focus > AF/MF > Focus Mode entry, using the Function menu, the For Viewfinder screen, or by switching using a defined button, the camera lets you set the focus yourself by turning the focus ring on the lens. There are some advantages and disadvantages to this approach.

While your batteries will last slightly longer in manual focus mode, it will take you longer to focus the camera for each photo. And unlike older 35mm film SLRs, digital cameras' electronic viewfinders and LCDs are not designed for optimum manual focus. Pick up any advanced film camera and you'll see a big, bright viewfinder with a focusing screen that's a joy to focus on manually.

So, although manual focus is still an option for you to consider in certain circumstances, it's not as easy to use as it once was. I recommend trying the various AF options first and switching to manual focus only if AF is not working for you. And then be sure to take advantage of the focus peaking feature and the automatic frame enlargement (MF Assist), which can make it easier to determine when the focus is precisely on the most important subject element. And remember, if you use the DMF mode, you can fine-tune the focus after the AF system has finished its work.

Focus Pocus

Back in the pre-AF days, manual focusing was problematic because our eyes and brains have poor memory for correct focus, which you often note when you submit to that refractive test at your eye doctor that I mentioned earlier. Similarly, manual focusing involves jogging the focus ring back and forth as you go from almost in focus, to sharp focus, to almost focused again. The little clockwise and counterclockwise arcs decrease in size until you've zeroed in on the point of correct focus. What you're looking for is the image with the most contrast between the edges of elements in the image.

Adding Circles of Confusion

But there are other factors in play, as well. You know that increased depth-of-field brings more of your subject into focus. But more depth-of-field also makes autofocusing (or manual focusing) more difficult because the contrast is lower between objects at different distances. So, autofocus with a

300mm lens (or zoom setting) may be easier than at a 16mm focal length (or zoom setting) because the longer lens has less apparent depth-of-field. By the same token, a lens with a maximum aperture of f/1.8 will be easier to autofocus (or manually focus) than one of the same focal length with an f/4 maximum aperture, because the f/4 lens has more depth-of-field and a dimmer view. It's also important to note that lenses with a maximum aperture smaller than f/5.6 would give your autofocus system fits, because the smaller opening (aperture) would allow less light to enter or to reach the autofocus sensor.

Technically, there is just one plane within your picture area, parallel to the back of the camera (or sensor, in the case of a digital camera), that is in sharp focus. That's the plane in which the points of the image are rendered as precise points. At every other plane in front of or behind the focus plane, the points show up as discs that range from slightly blurry to extremely blurry. In practice, the discs in many of these planes will still be so small that we see them as points, and that's where we get depth-of-field. Depth-of-field is just the range of planes that include discs that we perceive as points rather than blurred splotches. The size of this range increases as the aperture is reduced in size and is allocated roughly one-third in front of the plane of sharpest focus, and two-thirds behind it. The range of sharp focus is always greater behind your subject than in front of it. (See Figure 4.5.)

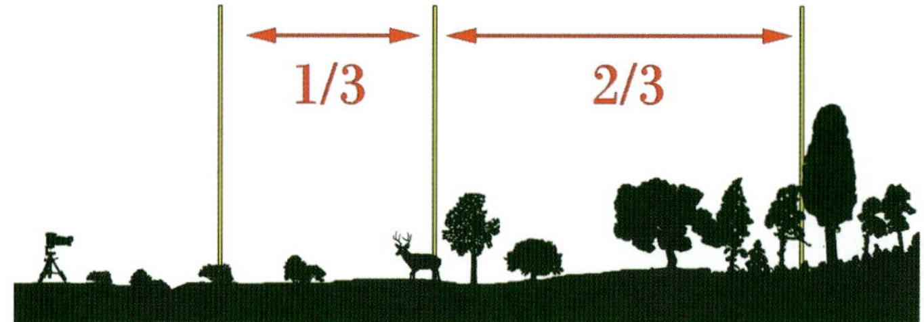

Figure 4.5 The range of sharp focus is greater behind your subject than in front of it.

To make things even more complicated, many subjects aren't polite enough to remain still. They move around in the frame, so that even if the camera's lens is sharply focused on your main subject, the subject may change position and require refocusing. An intervening subject may pop into the frame and pass between you and the subject you meant to photograph. You (or the camera) have to decide whether to focus on this new subject, or to remain focused on the original subject. Finally, there are some kinds of subjects that are difficult to bring into sharp focus because they lack enough contrast to allow the camera's AF system (or our eyes) to lock in. Blank walls, a clear blue sky, or other low-contrast subject matter may make focusing difficult even with the hybrid AF system.

If you find all these focus factors confusing, you're on the right track. Focus is, in fact, measured using something called a *circle of confusion* (see Figure 4.6). An ideal image consists of zillions of tiny little points, which, like all points, theoretically have no height or width. There is perfect contrast between the point and its surroundings. You can think of each point as a pinpoint of light in a darkened room. When

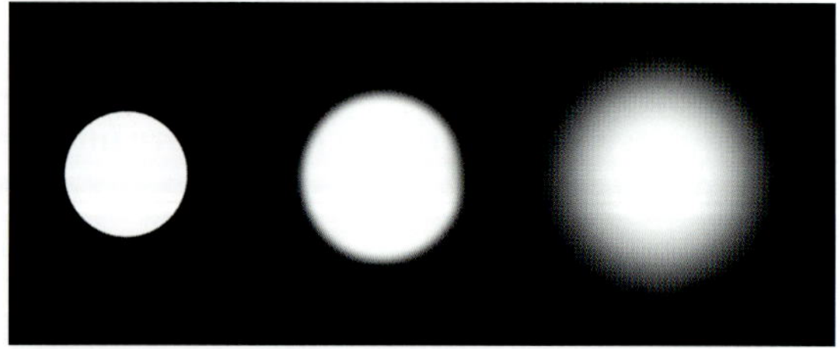

Figure 4.6 When a pinpoint of light (left) goes out of focus, its blurry edges form a circle of confusion (center and right).

a given point is out of focus, its edges decrease in contrast and it changes from a perfect point to a tiny disc with blurry edges (remember, blur is the lack of contrast between boundaries in an image).

If this blurry disc—the circle of confusion—is small enough, our eyes still perceive it as a point. It's only when the disc grows large enough that we can see it as a blur rather than as a sharp point that a given point is viewed as being out of focus. You can see, then, that enlarging an image, either by displaying it larger on your computer monitor or by making a large print, also magnifies the size of each circle of confusion. Moving closer to the image does the same thing. So, parts of an image that may look perfectly sharp in a 5 × 7–inch print viewed at arm's length, might appear blurry when blown up to 11 × 14 inches and examined at the same distance. Take a few steps back, however, and the image may look sharp again.

To a lesser extent, the viewer also affects the apparent size of these circles of confusion. Some people see details better at a given distance and may perceive smaller circles of confusion than someone standing next to them. For the most part, however, such differences are small. Truly blurry images will look blurry to just about everyone under the same conditions.

Your Focus Mode Options

Manual focus can come in handy, as I'll explain later in this chapter, but autofocus is likely to be your choice in the great majority of shooting situations. Choosing the right AF mode and the way in which focus points are selected is your key to success. Using the wrong mode for a particular type of photography can lead to a series of pictures that are all sharply focused—on the wrong subject.

But autofocus isn't some mindless beast out there snapping your pictures in and out of focus with no feedback from you. There are several settings you can modify to regain a fair amount of control. Your first decision should be which of the autofocus modes to select: Single-shot (AF-S), Continuous AF (AF-C), or Automatic AF (AF-A). DMF first uses autofocus, and then allows you to fine-tune focus manually. I recommend using the Function menu, where Focus Mode is located in the top row, second from the left.

FOCUS INDICATOR

At the lower-left corner of your screen, you'll find a green focus confirmation indicator that's active while focusing is underway. It consists of a round green disk, which may have rounded brackets at either side. If the *disk glows steadily*, the image is in focus. *Only the disk appears* when using AF-S; in AF-C mode, the *disk is surrounded by the brackets* and indicates that the focus plane may change if the subject moves. If the *brackets are flashing and no disk appears*, focusing is in progress; if the *disk is flashing*, focusing has failed. (See Figure 4.7.)

Steady: Image in focus (AF-S)

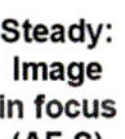
Flashing: Focus has failed

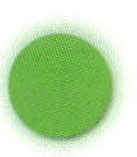
Image in focus, but focus may change (AF-C)

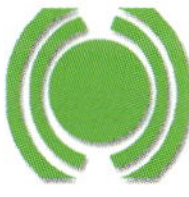
Focus in progress

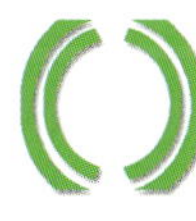

Figure 4.7 The focus indicator icon shows focus status.

In the next sections, I'm going to describe all five focus modes, so you'll understand exactly what types of subjects each is intended for. However, as you'll learn, the a7C II/a7CR's AF system is so sophisticated that you can generally set up your camera, as I'll explain later in this chapter in a section called "Magic Autofocus—Set and Forget," and then forget about twiddling with autofocus thereafter. I'll list a few settings you can make that will let the a7C II/a7CR easily nail autofocus under most conditions more than 90 percent of the time.

Single-Shot AF (AF-S) Mode

With Single-shot AF (AF-S), the camera will lock in focus when you press the shutter-release button (or an alternate button you've assigned the AF start function to) and will not adjust focus if your subject moves or you change the distance between you and your subject, as long as you hold down the button.

In AF-S mode, focus is locked. By keeping the button depressed halfway, you'll find you can reframe the image by moving the camera to aim at another angle; the focus (and exposure) will not change. Maintain pressure on the shutter-release button and focus remains locked even if you recompose, or if the subject begins running toward the camera, for example.

When sharp focus is achieved in AF-S mode, the solid green focus indicator appears in the lower-left corner of the screen and you'll hear a little beep. One or more green focus confirmation frames will also appear to indicate the area(s) of the scene that will be in sharpest focus.

For non-action photography, AF-S is usually your best choice, as it minimizes out-of-focus pictures (at the expense of spontaneity). Because of the small delay while the camera zeroes in on correct focus, you might experience slightly more shutter lag. This mode uses less battery power than Continuous AF.

If you have activated Pre-AF in the Focus > AF/MF menu (it's the last entry, and you must scroll down to see it), you may notice something that seems strange: the camera's autofocus mechanism will begin seeking focus even before you touch the shutter-release button. In this mode, no matter which AF method is selected, the camera will continually alter its focus as it is aimed at various subjects, *until* you press the shutter-release button halfway. At that point, the camera locks focus, in Single-shot AF mode.

When using AF-S or AF-C (described next), you can specify focus priority, from AF (wait until the subject is in sharp focus), Release (take the picture *now* even if not in perfect focus), and Balanced Emphasis (compromise!). I will explain setting these options in the Focus > AF/MF menu in more detail in Chapter 8.

Continuous AF (AF-C) Mode

When AF-C is active, focus is constantly readjusted as your subject (or you) move. The difference between Single-shot AF and Continuous AF comes at the point the shutter-release button (or defined focus start button) is pressed halfway. (See the discussion of *back-button focus* later in this chapter.) Switch to this mode when photographing sports, young kids at play, and other fast-moving subjects. In this mode, the camera can lock focus on a subject if it is not moving toward the camera or away from your shooting position; when it does, you'll see a green circle surrounded by brackets.

(There will be no beep.) But if the camera-to-subject distance begins changing, the camera instantly begins to adjust focus to keep it in sharp focus, making this the more suitable AF mode with moving subjects.

Automatic AF (AF-A) Mode

The camera begins using AF-S, and switches to AF-C if the subject begins moving. Use this mode when you're not certain that your subject will begin moving, and you'd like to take advantage of AF-S, as described earlier, until the subject does move. You might use AF-A to photograph a sleeping pet, which, if awakened by the activity, might respond with sudden movement.

Direct Manual Focus (DMF) Mode

The camera focuses using AF-S mode, then uncouples the focus motor so you can fine-tune focus (if necessary) manually. For best results, use this mode with focus peaking enabled to provide you with visual feedback as you adjust.

Manual Focus

No autofocus at all. You're on your own in deciding when the image is in sharp focus but provided with extra tools, such as the focus indicator in the lower-left corner, focus peaking, and the a7C II/a7CR's focus magnification features.

Focus or Release Priority?

The current focus plane is fixed and cannot be changed at a certain point in the picture-taking process. With AF-S mode, that point is when you press the shutter release halfway. As long as you keep your finger on the button, the camera will not refocus until you press down all the way, or take your finger off the release. In AF-C mode, the camera will focus, but will continue to refocus as long as the shutter release is held down halfway. Focus is *not* locked until you press down all the way to take a picture.

In either mode, when you simply press the shutter release down all the way, focus activation, locking, and picture taking take place one after the other. That's where focus/release priority come into play. When the shutter release is pressed down all the way in a continuous motion, do you want the camera to wait until sharp focus is achieved, even if that means missing the exact instant you wanted to capture? Or do you want to have the camera go ahead and take the picture anyway, even if there is a possibility that the image isn't perfectly focused? I'll explain how to set the priority options in Chapter 8, but here's a preview to using the Priority Set in AF-S/AF-C entries in the Focus > AF/MF menu:

- **AF Priority.** The shutter is not activated until sharp focus is achieved. You can choose the AF Priority option for both AF-S and AF-C modes individually. Use AF Priority for subjects that are not moving rapidly. The AF system is fast enough that the slight delay should be negligible. However, if you're using an A-mount lens that does not have a built-in AF motor with the EA-LA adapter, you can experience a significant delay. Sports shooters and others who depend on capturing the decisive moment and can countenance no delay at all generally use Release Priority, discussed next.

- **Release Priority.** When this option is selected, the shutter is activated when the release button is pushed down all the way in both AF-S and AF-C modes, even if sharp focus has not yet been achieved. I prefer this option for AF-C mode, as Continuous Focus focuses and refocuses constantly when autofocus is active, and even though an image may not quite be in sharpest focus, at least I am able to get my shot. Using Release Priority does *not* mean that your image won't be sharply focused; it just means that the camera hasn't yet *confirmed* that focus is achieved. Keep in mind that the a7C II/a7CR's AF system is *very* speedy, so your picture is likely to be in sharp focus even if the camera hasn't had quite enough time to confirm that focus is locked in. If you've been poised with the shutter release pressed halfway, the camera probably has been tracking the focus of your image.

- **Balanced Emphasis.** In this mode, the shutter is released when the button is pressed, with a slight pause if autofocus has not yet been achieved. It can be selected for both AF-S and AF-C modes, and is probably your best choice if you want a good compromise between speed of activation and sharpest focus. However, you would not want to use this setting if the highest possible continuous shooting rates are important to you.

Focus Magnified

Your a7C II/a7CR has several focusing aids that are activated when you use Manual focus. One of them is a Focus Magnifier tool, which also happens to work perfectly well in AF-S autofocus mode. The magnifier can be invoked to enlarge your image so the AF system can more easily zero in on your subject. All you need to do is create a custom key that will produce the Focus Magnifier on demand (rather than wading through the Focus > Focus Assistant > Focus Magnifier maze every time). Just follow these steps:

1. **Define a custom key** as the activating button for Focus Magnifier. You'll find instructions for creating custom keys using the Setup > Operation Customize > Custom Key/Dial Settings entry in Chapter 9. I won't repeat that information here. Select a button of your choice and choose Focus Magnifier as its custom operation.

2. **Press the Focus Magnifier custom key.** An orange box will appear on the screen. (See Figure 4.8, left.) Use the directional buttons to position the orange box over the area you want to bring into focus.

3. **Press the center button.** The Focus Magnifier will enlarge the image contained within the orange box by a factor of 6.9X. (See Figure 4.8, right.) Press the center button a second time to enlarge to 13.7X, if needed.

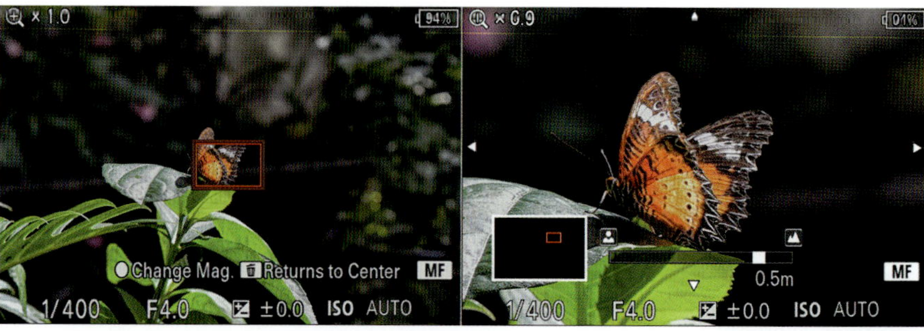

Figure 4.8 Activate focus magnifier (left) and focus on zoomed-in area (right).

4. **Rotate focus ring.** You can rotate the focus ring to focus if manual focus is enabled. If autofocus is active, continue to Step 5.

5. **Activate AF.** Press the shutter release halfway to activate autofocus (or use another key you may have defined to perform that function, say, if you're using back-button focus as described later in this chapter).

6. **AF focus commences.** The a7C II/a7CR will use the current AF settings to focus on the area you've selected with the orange box.

Choosing the AF Area

So far, you have allowed the camera to choose which part of the scene will be in the sharpest focus using its focus detection points (called *Focus areas* by Sony). However, you can also specify a single focus detection point that will be active. You can also specify the focus area using the Function menu, using the second icon from the right in the bottom row. Here is how the Focus Area options work:

- **Wide.** The camera chooses the appropriate focus area(s) in order to set focus on a certain subject in the scene. There are no focus indicators visible on the screen until you press the shutter-release button halfway. At that point, in AF-S mode, the camera displays one or more green focus indicators to show what area(s) of the image it has used to set focus on. In AF-C mode, the indicators will continue to flicker around the frame while the camera refocuses as necessary. If Subject Recognition is active, the AF system will prioritize subjects ("recognition targets" in Sony-speak) when making its decision as to where it should set focus. You'll see multiple focus indicators when several parts of the scene are at the same distance from the camera. When most of the elements of a scene are at roughly the same distance, the camera displays a single, large green focus bracket around the entire edge of the screen.

  Even if you set one of the other options, Wide is automatically selected in Intelligent Auto mode. Use this mode to give the camera complete control over where to focus. You can activate Focus > Focus Area > AF-C Area Display, as described in Chapter 8, if you want to see the focus area displayed as you use AF-C. Indeed, if you're working with AF-C, you'll see the high-density points "dance" as the a7C II/a7CR continually refocuses as your subject or camera moves.

- **Zone.** There are nine different focus zones available—three at the top left, center, and right of the frame, three in the equivalent positions at the bottom, and three in the middle. Each of those zones is populated by an array of focus points, as shown in Figure 4.9. You can move the focus array to one of the nine overlapping areas using the directional buttons while those brackets are displayed. To lock the brackets in their current position, press the center button (or other defined Focus Standard button). Press the center button again to resume moving the frames. You can also move the focusing frame quickly with the touch screen and return the zone to the center of the screen by pressing the Trash button.

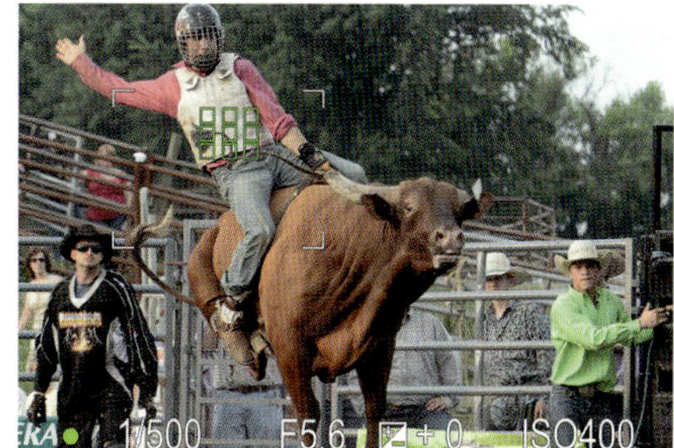

Figure 4.9 In Zone mode, brackets represent a focus zone, and you can move the zone to nine different locations on the screen. The camera selects one or more focus points within that array.

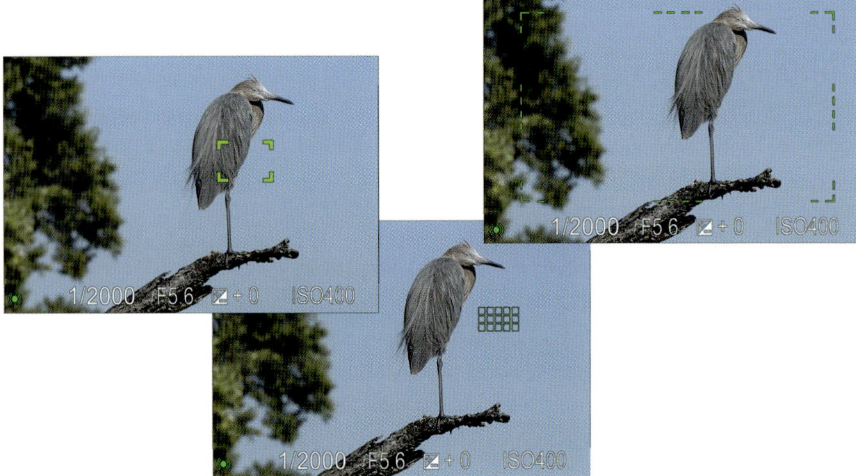

Figure 4.10 With Wide AF Area, the camera either displays a large green bracket indicating that most of the scene is at the same distance to the camera (left), or it displays one or more smaller brackets to indicate the specific area(s) of the scene that will be in sharpest focus (center). If the camera decides that all areas of the frame should be considered, a bracket around the entire focusing area is shown (right).

Press the AF-ON button or press the shutter release halfway to initiate focus. The display changes to one of the three modes described in the "Vanishing Brackets" sidebar, and the camera chooses which sections within the zone to use to calculate sharp focus. The active focus points will be highlighted in green. Use this mode when you know your subject is going to reside in a largish area of the frame and want to allow the camera to select the exact focus point within your designated zone.

■ **Center Fix.** Activate this AF area and the camera will use only a single focus detection point in the center of the frame to set focus. Initially, a pair of focus brackets appears on the screen. Touch the shutter-release button and the camera sets and locks focus on the subject in the center of the image area; the brackets then turn green to confirm the area that will be in the sharpest focus in your image. Choose this option if you want the camera to always focus on the subject in the center of the frame. (See Figure 4.11.) Center the primary subject (like a friend's face in a wide-angle landscape composition), allow the camera to focus on it, maintain slight pressure on the shutter-release button to keep focus locked, and re-frame the scene for a more effective, off-center, composition. Take the photo at any time and your friend (who is now off-center) will be in the sharpest focus.

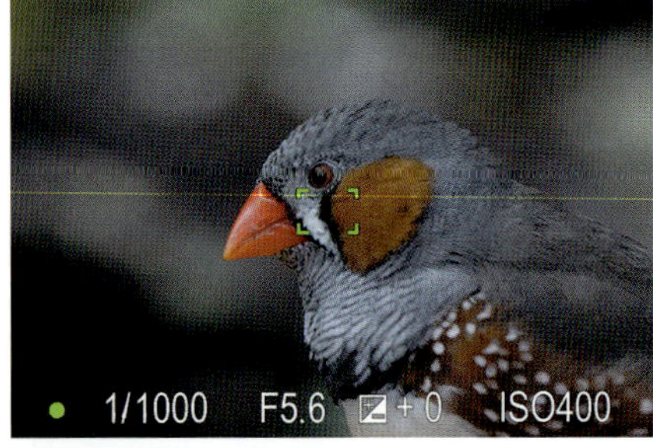

Figure 4.11 In the Center Fix Area mode, the camera displays the focus brackets in the center of the screen; the brackets turn green after focus has been set.

- **Spot.** This mode enables you to move the camera's focus detection point (focus area) around the scene to any one of multiple locations, using the directional buttons. When opting for Spot, you can use the left/right buttons to choose Small, Medium, or Large spots, which changes the size of the focus brackets in the frame. This mode can be useful when the camera is mounted on a tripod and you'll be taking photos of the same scene for a long time while the light is changing, for example. Move the focus area to cover the most important subject, and it will always focus on that point when you later take a photo.

  Use the directional buttons to move the brackets around the screen, which allows great versatility in the placement of the active focus detection point. (See Figure 4.12.) Adjust the brackets until they cover the most important subject area and touch the shutter-release button. The brackets will turn green and the camera will beep to confirm that focus has been set on the intended area.

- **Expand Spot.** If the camera is unable to lock in focus using the selected focus point, it will also use the eight adjacent points to try to achieve focus. (See Figure 4.13.)

- **Tracking AF.** In this mode, the camera locks focus onto the subject area that is under the selected focus spot when the shutter button is depressed halfway. Then, if the subject moves (or you change the framing in the camera), the camera will continue to refocus *on that subject.* You can select this mode only when the focus mode is set to Continuous AF (AF-C).

  This option is especially powerful, because you can activate it for any of the focus area options described above. That is, once you've highlighted Tracking on the selection screen, you can then press the left-right directional button and choose Wide, Zone, Center, Spot, or Expand Spot. The camera will lock on a subject, using one of those area modes to follow it. (See Figure 4.14 and the explanation which follows in the next section.)

  You cannot use this option if the Still/Movie/S&Q dial is set to Movies or S&Q quick-/slow-motion video shooting movies. I'll describe Tracking AF, along with eye/face recognition in more detail in the section that follows this one.

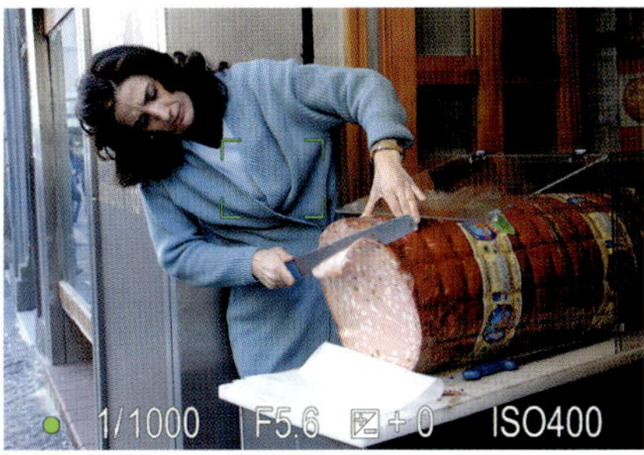

Figure 4.12 When the Spot AF Area mode is initially selected, the active focus detection point is delineated with indicators that turn green when focus is confirmed and locked. Use the directional buttons or touch screen to specify the location of the spot.

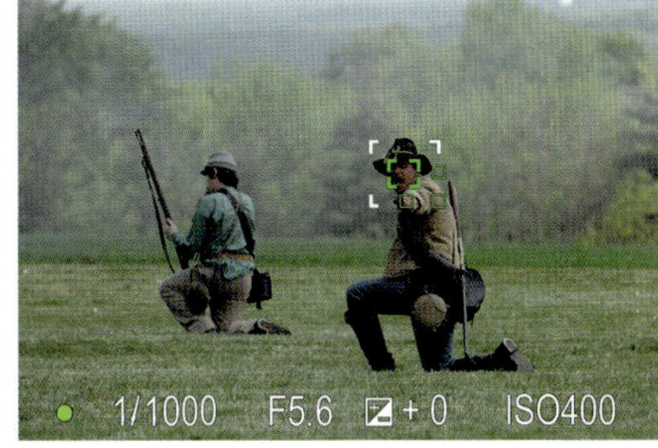

Figure 4.13 Expand Spot uses adjacent points to achieve focus.

Moving the Focus Area

When using Zone, Spot (Small/Medium/Large), or Expand Spot autofocus areas (or their Tracking counterparts), you have the option of moving the active focus frame/point to a location of your choosing with the directional controls. If touch operations (including Touch Focus) are enabled, you can alternately tap the touch screen to indicate the desired location.

Moving the focus area is available only when the a7C II/a7CR is switched to *focus point adjustment* mode from *settings mode.* You can toggle between the two modes using the center button. Here's the difference:

- **Settings mode.** The left, right, and up buttons summon settings screens for Drive mode, DISP, and ISO settings (unless you've re-defined them to some other behavior). The down button has no function in settings mode.
- **Focus point adjustment mode.** To switch into (or out of) this mode, press the center button. You can then move the focus area within the frame in any focus area mode other than Center Fix. A "Sel. Focus Point On/Off" message will appear on the screen for a few seconds to let you know you are now in focus point adjustment mode.

If you are using the Wide or Center Fix focus areas instead, you cannot move the focus area around the frame. Pressing the center button instead moves the AF focus area to the center of the screen.

Just as you're limited in the use of the AF mode in certain operating modes, there's a limitation with AF Area as well. For example, Spot is not available for selection in Intelligent Auto mode; the camera will always use Multi as the AF Area mode.

TEMPORARY TRACKING

If you find you don't need tracking (say, you're shooting landscapes or other non-active subjects) but would like to be able to turn it on quickly, just define a custom key to temporarily activate the feature. Assign the Tracking On or Tracking On + AF On behavior to the desired key, under Setup > Operation Customize > Custom Key (Shooting), as described in Chapter 9. Thereafter, if you've set, for example, the Focus Area to Wide or Spot Small, when you press the defined key, the camera will switch to Tracking: Wide or Tracking: Spot Small while the button is held down.

Tracking and Focusing on Subjects, Faces, and Eyes

The a7C II/a7CR's tracking capabilities are awesome enough on their own. The camera's upgraded face and eye detection augments the plain vanilla tracking capabilities enough that it can be considered one of the most significant improvements this camera boasts.

Tracking AF is not limited to following and focusing on faces or eyes, of course; it can track any moving subject. In general, you can turn it on and forget it. Conventional tracking does, however, only work in still photography mode; you can't use it when shooting movies. When the Still/Movie/S&Q dial is set to the Movie position, the Tracking focus area mode is not available.

However, that doesn't mean tracking is totally unavailable in Movie mode; you can still use the touch screen to specify a subject to be tracked. Navigate to Setup > Touch Operation > Touch Panel Settings > Shooting Screen > Touch Func. in Shooting > Touch Tracking and set to Touch Tracking. Or, you can access Touch Func. in Shooting from the Fn menu. Then, you can simply tap a subject on the LCD screen and the a7C II/a7CR will track it. However, if you later want to use Touch Focus in stills mode, you'll want to return to the Function of Touch Operation entry and revert to Touch Focus when you're finished shooting video.

One thing to keep in mind is that it's sometimes difficult to track subjects other than humans; if your chosen subject happens to be near a face (say, an active pet, when you have the Animal/Bird, Animal, or Bird Recognition Target [Subject Options] turned off), the AF system will sometimes jump to the face/eyes, and begin tracking it, instead. The desired subject needn't be physically near the face; proximity in two-dimensions is sufficient to fool the AF system. Perhaps you want to photograph a close-up of a bride's hand wearing her new wedding ring, with the groom smiling in the background. If the groom's face is "close" enough to the ring in the frame, instead of a sharp photo of the bride's hand and a smiling groom (who you wanted to be out of focus for creative effect), you end up with a sharp husband and blurry wedding ring.

Tracking may not work if the subject is moving too quickly, is too small or too large to be isolated effectively, has only reduced contrast against its background, or if the ambient light is too dark or changes dramatically while you're tracking. I'm going to show you how to use the basic tracking feature first, then go into detail about the new Subject Recognition features.

However, to use the full range of options available with Tracking AF, you can follow these steps, which *do* require choosing AF-C as your focus method:

1. **Choose AF-C.** Tracking works only when you are using continuous autofocus because, well, it refocuses continually.

2. **Activate Tracking AF.** Use the Function menu and choose Focus Area. Scroll down to the bottom of the list of modes and highlight Tracking.

3. **Choose Focus Area Mode.** Using Tracking does *not* mean you lose access to the AF area modes. With Tracking highlighted, use the left/right directional controls to select Wide, Zone, Center Fix, Spot (S, M, or L), or Expand Spot. That will give you both Tracking AF *and* the area mode you prefer. If you switch from AF-C to AF-S, you lose the lock-on capabilities, and the camera just reverts to whatever focus area mode you select here.

4. **Select subject to track.** Your subject will be within the selected autofocus area.
   - **Tracking: Wide.** The camera selects the focus area and subject to track.
   - **Tracking: Center Fix.** Frame the scene so the subject you want to track is under the center focus point.
   - **Tracking: Spot.** You can use the directional controls to position the Small, Medium, or Large Spot over the subject.
   - **Tracking: Expand Spot.** You can use the directional controls or touch screen to position the spot over the subject. (See Figure 4.14, left.)

Figure 4.14 Left: Place the focus point on the object the camera should track and press the shutter release to activate tracking. Right: When Tracking is active, the camera maintains focus on your preferred target, tracking it as it moves around the scene.

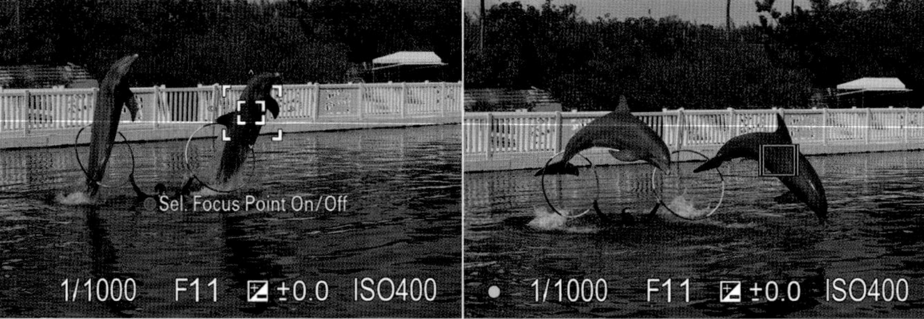

5. **Start tracking.** When you activate focus by pressing the shutter release halfway, the camera will use your selected focus area option to lock in focus, as always. However, now, once focus has been locked, the camera will *track* your subject as it roams around the screen, as long as you hold the shutter release halfway down. You'll see the green focus area box moving as your subject moves (or you reframe the image with the camera). (See Figure 4.14, right.) If a face is detected, a tracking rectangle around the face will be shown. (You'll learn more about Subject Recognition next.)

Subject Recognition Overview

As hinted already, the a7C II and a7CR have a couple more tricks for setting the AF area. The camera can detect bodies, faces, and eyes, lets you select which eye to track, and can differentiate between humans and animals—and it can do all that at high speed! You can turn Subject Recognition in AF on or off and activate visible frames around the faces the a7C II/a7CR detects. This enables the camera to attempt to identify any human faces in the scene. If it finds one or more faces, the camera will surround each one (up to eight in all) with the highest priority face outlined in white, and the others in either gray (if an unregistered face) or purple (if you have previously registered that face). In AF-S mode, an additional frame will be placed on the eyes of your subject, if detected. Press the shutter release halfway and the camera focuses on the highest priority face.

You can also specify Face Priority in Multi Metering in the Exposure/Color > Metering group, and the a7C II/a7CR will not only try to focus on faces, it will base its exposure on them as well. (It's locked to On when using Intelligent Auto.) This feature is disabled when Focus > Subject Recognition > Recognition Target is set to anything other than human.

Subject Recognition is disabled when using digital zoom features, and the focus magnifier. It's also unavailable when shooting movies with the 120p/100p Record Setting, S&Q slow-motion movies at 120/100 frames per second, or when capturing 4K movies at 30/25p 100M / 30/25p 60M.

Making Your Subject Recognition Settings

The key subject recognition settings are found in several different menus. This section will help you find and adjust all of them. I'll show you how to tell the a7C II/a7CR to base its AF decisions on subjects, give certain faces a higher priority, and explain how to switch back and forth between detecting humans and animals, birds, insects, and other "targets."

Your first stop should be the Focus > Subject Recognition group, which has seven menu entries (see Figure 4.15):

- **Subject Recognition in AF.** The entry has two choices: On or Off. When set to Off, the camera gives no special priority to subjects detected within the frame. Perhaps you're shooting landscapes or other scenes and don't want the camera to fixate on any faces it detects.

    Alternatively, choose On and the a7C II/a7CR will give a higher priority to detected faces. Up to eight faces, if present, may be detected. When autofocus is activated, the camera will attempt to focus on the eyes, if they are located within the active focus area. Note that when using Intelligent Auto, this setting is locked at On.

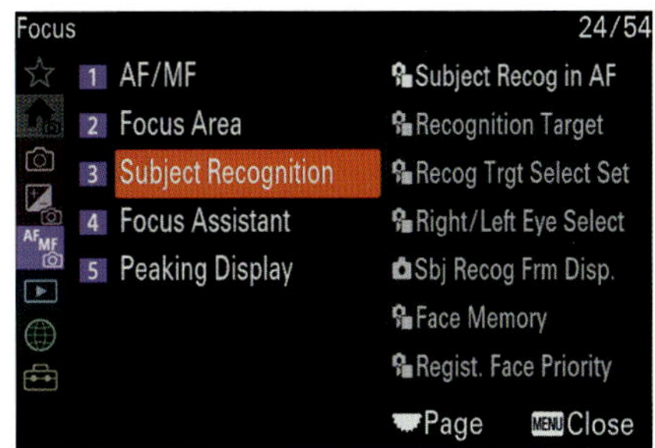

Figure 4.15 Focus > Subject Recognition group.

The Eye AF portion of Subject Recognition in AF may not function as expected with subjects which are rapidly moving, have long bangs or closed eyes, or are wearing sunglasses. Shady conditions, backlight, and low-light situations can also hinder eye detection. Keep in mind that if the camera is unable to focus on human eyes in the frame for some reason, it will fall back to focusing on the human's *face* instead. (This is useful with humans who have their eyes closed, are wearing some kinds of glasses, or who have hair that obscures their eyes. You can generally count on having to manually focus Saul "Slash" Hudson.)

A USEFUL BUG

You should keep in mind that activating Subject Recognition in Autofocus with this entry means that your a7C II/a7CR will give priority to *detecting* subjects, but doesn't guarantee that it will automatically *focus* on them! In practice, what happens is that the camera will prioritize focus on subjects found— but *only* if that particular subject resides within *the focus area you are using.* In other words, if you're using the Center Fix focus area and your human subject happens to reside outside the center area, the camera will helpfully detect a face/eye and display a frame around it, but will focus *only* on whatever is actually within the focus area. You can tell the camera to look outside the current focus area using the Tracking Shift Range setting described below.

It's easy to overlook this discrepancy, especially if the subject you want to focus on is located near to, but in front of or behind, a human. Further, most of our "people" shots have the person in the center of the frame, and, with some focus modes (such as Wide), the focus area is so large that your human may actually be in an appropriate location, anyway. However, you should be aware of this distinction.

- **Recognition Target.** When set to Human, the camera looks for human bodies, faces, and eyes. If you choose Animal/Bird, Animal, or Bird instead, it looks for animal/bird subjects only; the camera has an option to search for insects, as well, but, to date, the "faces" of other types of living creatures vary too much for existing technology to detect with any reliability. It's generally safe to leave this setting at Human, unless you happen to be at a zoo, photographing the Westminster Kennel Club show, or engaged in other animal-intensive activities. **Note:** The Animal/Bird setting looks for either type, while the separate Animal and Bird choices tell the a7C II/a7CR to detect *only* that variety.

When you highlight your subject type ("recognition target" in Sony-speak) (see Figure 4.16, left), press the right button to produce a screen of sub parameters to further refine your search. (See Figure 4.16, center.) You can then enter your preference (as in Figure 4.16, right). The available parameters differ by subject type. They include:

- **Tracking Shift Range (Human, Animal, Bird, Insect, Car/Train, Airplane).** This tells the camera how far outside the current focus frame it should search for the specified subject, in the range 1 (Narrow) to 5 (Wide). A wide setting will prompt the camera to locate a subject far outside the focus area you have selected. A narrower setting would be best if you were shooting in a crowd and wanted to confine, say, human subject detection to the focus area you've defined.

- **Tracking Persistence Level (Animal/Bird/Insect/Car/Train/Airplane only).** A detected subject may move within the frame. This setting tells the a7C II/a7CR whether it should continue tracking around where the original subject was, or to look for another, perhaps closer, subject. Select in the range 1 (Not Locked On) for fast-moving subjects that are easily lost permanently to 5 (Locked On) to keep the camera's attention on a subject that may be only temporarily hidden.

- **Recognition Sensitivity (Animal/Bird/Insect/Car/Train/Airplane only).** In the range 1 to 5 you can choose a low setting (such as 1) to counter the tendency to incorrectly identify a subject. At 5 (high sensitivity), the camera will lock on a subject only when it has high confidence.

- **Recognition Priority Settings (Animal/Bird only).** Tells the a7C II/a7CR what to do when both animals and birds are recognized in the frame. You can select Priority on Animals, Priority on Birds, or Auto to let the camera decide on its own.

- **Recognition Part (Animal/Bird, Animal, Bird only).** Allows choosing whether the a7C II/a7CR is looking for the subject's Eye/Head/Body, Eye/Head (only), Eye (only), or to follow the individual settings you've specified for that type of subject. You can choose any combination of parts to enable/disable.

- **Recognition Part Selection Settings (Animal/Bird, Animal, Bird only).** You can define the Recognition Target Select behavior to a custom button (using Setup > Operation Customize > Custom Key/Dial Settings, as described in Chapter 9.) You can press the custom button to cycle among all of the available choices. This setting lets you specify any combination of Eye/Head/Body, Eye/Head, or just Eye as available choices for the function.

- **Recognition Target Selection Setting.** This setting allows you to disable one or more of the subject possibilities, Human, Animal, or Bird. For example, if you rarely shoot birds, you can disable that choice so the a7C II/a7CR will switch only between Human or Animal subjects using the Recognition Target entry above.

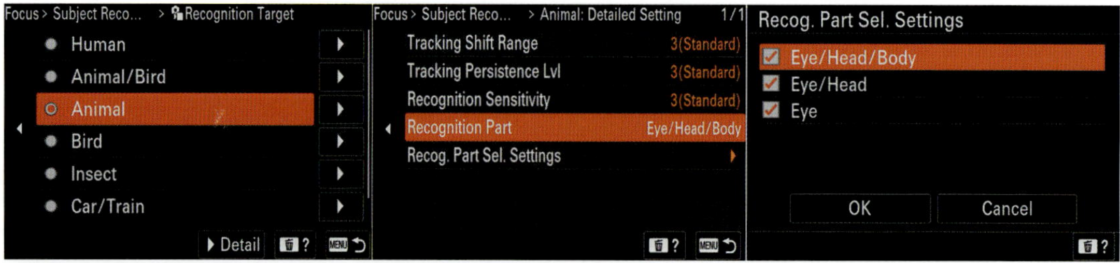

Figure 4.16 Choose Recognition Target.

- **Right/Left Eye Select.** Chooses whether to detect the left or right eye of the human subject (this option is only available when the recognition target is either Human or Animal). Note that this feature uses the *subject's* eye, which may be on the opposite side from your perspective (that is, your subject's right eye is on the left side of your frame). In general, it usually doesn't matter which eye the camera scrutinizes. If you don't care (which will usually be the case), select Auto instead of Right or Left, and the a7C II/a7CR will do a good job of finding the closest eye for you.

  One really cool thing to do (because you can!) is to assign Switch Right/Left Eye to a Custom Key in the Setup > Operation Customize > [Photo] Custom Key/Dial Set entry, just to have the power to alternate eyes on the fly if you feel the need.

- **Subject Recognition Frame Display.** The camera automatically shows a small white or gray square around an eye, face/head, or body of a human, animal, or bird it is focusing on. Only the head or entire body of insects, and front part of cars, trains, or airplanes will be given a box. (If you want the frames to display, but disappear after a time, use AF Area Auto Clear.)

  Although the eye-focus box is helpful, I find the additional box around the face very useful and leave it on at all times so I know *exactly* what face(s) have been detected. When enabled, a gray selection box appears around detected faces. The box around the face used for autofocus turns white. If there are several faces in the frame and you've registered and prioritized some or all of them, the boxes around the other faces turn reddish-purple. (I'll show you how to register faces later in this chapter.) If you find the boxes distracting, you can turn them off, and Subject Recognition, if enabled, as described earlier, will still be active.

- **Face Memory.** You can specify up to seven different registered faces to receive focusing priority. If none are recognized, the a7C II/a7CR will attempt to focus on any other faces it detects. I'll show you how to capture and prioritize faces in Chapter 8. The first face receives top priority, but you can change the preferred face at any time.

- **Register Faces Priority.** This entry lets you enable/disable use of face priority at will. If you're photographing an event and *don't* want to prioritize certain faces (say, you're at a cousin's wedding reception and would rather not highlight your immediate family who might be in some of the photos), you can disable registered face priority.

Magic Autofocus—Set and Forget

I gave this chapter the title "Mastering Autofocus Options" for a reason. Your Sony a7C II/a7CR has an incredible number of autofocus adjustments. My goal, to this point, has been to help you learn about all those options so you'll understand exactly what you can do to fine-tune the camera's incredible AF features under a variety of situations.

The good news is that your camera's AF system is so robust, you may not need to implement many features for about 90 percent of your shooting. This section will explain some basic adjustments you can set, and then forget, for most of your shooting. The a7C II/a7CR can do an excellent job of achieving focus under most conditions; my camera stumbles only under very low-light environments, insanely active sports, or with challenging subjects like birds in flight. Not that it can't perform well in those situations, but you can still benefit from the AF options described earlier in this chapter.

Here's the secret of "magic" autofocus, which I think you'll find will work very well nearly all of the time, thanks to the a7C II/a7CR's generous array of phase-detect AF points embedded in the sensor, contrast-detect zones, and the pure power of its BIONZ XR microprocessor:

- **Set your AF mode to AF-C.** Leave it there. Advanced users don't need the "automatic" AF-A mode, which is inconsistent. You might need AF-S if you want to lock focus on a particular subject. I'm going to show you how you can leave the camera set on AF-C and still temporarily switch from AF-C to AF-S when you hold down a custom key.

- **Set Focus Area mode to Tracking: Spot M.** Thereafter, you can move the box representing the focus spot around the screen with the directional buttons. Half-press the shutter-release button and the a7C II/a7CR will begin tracking whatever is under the spot location as long as you continue to hold the shutter button. Here's the cool part: if there is a human in the area you decide to track, the camera will add Subject Recognition to improve its AF performance. If the area you track does *not* have a human, the camera will track that object instead. It will continue to detect faces and eyes, but won't automatically focus on them. This is the "feature" I noted in the "A Useful Bug" sidebar earlier. Most other camera brands with Subject Recognition don't give you this flexibility. It makes it possible to track objects that are *not* human without disabling Subject Recognition—as long as the human face isn't *too* close to the tracked subject.

- **Activate Subject Recognition in AF.** I showed you how to do that in the previous section.

- **Set Recognition Target to Human and Right/Left Eye Select to Auto.** Change these only if you have a reason to switch to another type of subject.

- **Enable Subject Recognition Frame Display.** You'll appreciate the extra feedback and reassurance.

- **Begin to enjoy amazingly accurate AF.** You may find you rarely have to make most of the adjustments described earlier in this chapter—although you'll be able to once you've learned how and when to use each of them.

- **If you need to lock focus,** switch to manual focus or temporarily switch to AF-S using the technique described next.

Your AF-C to AF-S Switch

Sony doesn't offer a custom key definition to toggle between AF-C and AF-S, but you can do the next best thing—define a button so that the camera switches to AF-S *while you hold down the button* and then switches back to AF-C once you release it.

The procedure is fairly simple. Just follow these steps:

1. **Access Register Custom Shoot Set.** Navigate to Shooting > Shooting Mode > Register Custom Shooting Setting (described in more detail in Chapter 6 if you need some coaching).

2. **Select a Custom Shoot Set to register.** I selected Recall Custom Hold 1. Press the center button to enter the setup screen.

3. **Unmark all but two settings.** A wide variety of camera settings can be registered, but for this application we don't want to mess with most of your camera's settings. We only want to change the Focus Mode and Focus Area settings, and only while the defined custom key is pressed. Scroll through the list and unmark all of them except for Focus Mode and Focus Area.

4. **Specify each of the two.** Highlight Focus Mode, press the center button, and select Single-shot AF from the screen that appears. Then Highlight Focus Area, press the center button, and choose Center Fix.

5. **Select Register.** Scroll down to the bottom of the settings list and highlight Register. Press the center button to confirm your settings, and MENU to exit.

6. **Navigate to Setup >** Setup > Operation Customize > [Photo] Custom Key/Dial Set.

7. **Define the button you want to use** to switch temporarily to AF-S.

8. **When your button is highlighted** press the center button, and in the screen that appears, navigate to the Recall Custom Hold 1 option.

9. **Press enter to confirm.** Then press MENU to exit.

That's all there is to it. Henceforth, AF-C, Tracking, and Subject Recognition will, by default, be active and provide amazing AF performance under most circumstances. If you want to switch to AF-S to lock in focus on a specific subject, just press your defined custom key *and hold it down.* Then, press the shutter release halfway. The camera will use Single-shot (AF-S) to focus *and* the Focus Area will be set to the center of the screen. The camera will lock focus as long as you keep the custom key and shutter release depressed. To return to AF-C and your other previous AF settings, just release the custom key.

Understanding Aperture Drive in AF

If you used digital SLRs prior to switching to mirrorless cameras, there may be a difference in the way your new camera's aperture behaves when focusing. Single-lens reflex cameras have traditionally focused with the lens aperture set to its maximum (widest) position. That provides a big, bright image and the shallowest depth-of-field the lens is capable of at that focal length. At the moment of exposure, the lens stops down to the "taking" or *shooting* aperture (which is specified by you or the camera's autoexposure system) and the mirror flips up so the shutter can open and take the photo.

The iris of your Sony mirrorless lenses behave in a much more complicated way. That's necessary because your image preview is produced from the actual sensor image, whether you are using the viewfinder or LCD monitor, and the image you see is affected by how large or how small the current aperture is. The camera's designers made some trade-offs in how the aperture opens and closes before and during exposure. Here's a quick description:

- **AF-S mode.** When using Single-shot AF, the camera has plenty of time to achieve focus, so in what Sony calls Standard mode, AF is achieved with the aperture set to wide open (but *not* wider than f/2, if you happen to be using, say, a lens with an f/1.4 maximum aperture).

- **AF-C mode.** When using Continuous AF, in Standard mode, the iris remains closed down during focus. The camera's AF mechanism has a dimmer view (but can brighten the display for your benefit). However, by retaining the shooting aperture during the constant focusing and refocusing that happens during Continuous AF, your a7C II/a7CR avoids the rapid opening/closing of the iris, and its attendant noise. The downside is that under low-light conditions or when the shooting aperture is small, both the CDAF and PDAF systems are handicapped.

The Focus > AF/MF > Aperture Drive in AF entry provides a partial solution. Sony retains the Standard aperture drive system I just described, but adds new Focus Priority and Silent Priority modes you can select. Here are the differences:

- **Standard.** This default mode performs as I've described above. Most people will want to retain this setting under most circumstances.

- **Focus Priority.** At this setting, AF-S functions as before, but AF-C mode is forced to focus *nominally* wide open (and never wider than f/2). In practice, the camera doesn't necessarily dilate the iris all the way; it partially opens, depending on light levels. That means in bright daylight the aperture may not open much at all, because the camera has enough illumination to focus quickly without resorting to a wider f/stop. Under darker conditions, the iris tends to open much wider for focusing, which means AF can be significantly faster under low-light conditions.

  Unfortunately, while AF is faster, this Focus Priority setting introduces a certain amount of shutter lag—the time between when you press the shutter down all the way, and when the picture is actually taken. If you want to improve AF under low light and can accept some shutter lag, give this setting a try.

- **Silent Priority.** The a7C II/a7CR *always* focuses at the shooting aperture, in both AF-S and AF-C focus modes, avoiding the noise of the iris opening and closing repeatedly.

Using Manual Focus

Manual focus is not as straightforward as with an older manual focus 35mm SLR equipped with a focusing screen optimized for this purpose and a readily visible focusing aid. But Sony's designers have done a good job of letting you exercise your initiative in the focusing realm, with features that make it easy to determine whether you have achieved precise focus. It's worth becoming familiar with the techniques for those occasions when it makes sense to take control in this area.

Here are the basic steps for quick and convenient setting of focus:

- **Select Manual Focus.** After you do so using the Fn menu or Focus > AF/MF > Focus Mode entries, the letters MF will appear in the LCD display when you're viewing the default display that includes a lot of data. (You can change display modes by pressing the DISP button.)

- **Aim at your subject and turn the focusing ring on the lens.** As soon as you start turning the focusing ring, the image on the LCD is enlarged (magnified) to help you assess whether the center of interest of your composition is in focus. (That is, unless you turned off this feature using the Focus > Focus Assistant > Auto Magnifier in MF entry.) Use the up/down/left/right directional controls to move around the magnified image area until you're viewing the most important subject element, such as a person's eyes. Turn the focusing ring until that appears to be in the sharpest possible focus.

  The enlargement lasts two seconds before the display returns to normal; you can increase that to five seconds or No Limit with the Focus Magnification Time entry in the same Focus Assistant group.

- **If you have difficulty focusing, zoom in if possible and focus at the longest available focal length.** If you're using a zoom lens, you may find it easier to see the exact effect of slight changes in focus while zoomed in. Even if you plan to take a wide-angle photo, zoom to telephoto and rotate the ring to set precise focus on the most important subject element. When you zoom back out to take the picture, the center of interest will still be in sharp focus.

- **Use Peaking of a suitable color.** On by default in Shooting mode, focus peaking provides a colored overlay around edges that are sharply focused; this makes it easier to determine when your subject is precisely focused. The overlay is white, but you can change that to another color when necessary. The alternate hue may be needed to provide a strong contrast between the peaking highlights and the color of your subject. Access Focus > Peaking Display to adjust the color. To make the overlay even more visible, select High in the Peaking Level item. You can also turn peaking Off using Focus > Peaking Display > Peaking Display, if desired. You'll find more on Peaking in Chapter 8.

- **Consider using the DMF option.** Another option is DMF, or Direct Manual Focus. Activate it and the camera will autofocus with Single-shot AF and lock focus when you press the shutter-release button halfway. As soon as focus is confirmed, you can turn the focusing ring to make fine-tuning adjustments, as long as you maintain slight pressure on the shutter-release button. The MF Assist magnification will be activated immediately.

This method gives you the benefit of autofocus but gives you the chance to change the exact point of focus, to a person's eyes instead of the tip of the nose, for example. This option is useful in particularly critical focusing situations, when the precise focus is essential, as in extremely close focusing on a three-dimensional subject. Because depth-of-field is very shallow in such work, you'll definitely want to focus on the most important subject element, such as the pistil or stamen inside a large blossom. This will ensure that it will be the sharpest part of the image.

Back-Button Focus

Back-button focus is a tool you can use to separate two functions that are commonly locked together—exposure and autofocus—so that you can lock in exposure while allowing focus to be attained at a later point, or vice versa. It's a *good* thing, although using back-button focus effectively may require you to unlearn some habits and acquire new ways of coordinating the action of your fingers.

As you have learned, the default behavior of your camera is to set both exposure and focus when you press the shutter release down halfway when using AF-S mode. Both exposure and focus are locked and will not change until you release the shutter button or press it all the way down to take a picture and then release it for the next shot.

What back-button focus does is *decouple* or separate the two actions when you are using AF-S mode. You can retain the exposure lock feature of AF-S mode when the shutter is pressed halfway, but assign autofocus *start* and/or autofocus *lock* to a different button. So, in practice, you can press the shutter button halfway, locking exposure, and reframe the image if you like (perhaps you're photographing a backlit subject and want to lock in exposure on the foreground, and then reframe to include a very bright background as well).

But, in this same scenario, you *don't* want autofocus locked at the same time. Indeed, you may not want to start AF until you're good and ready, say, at a sports venue as you wait for a ballplayer to streak into view in your viewfinder. With back-button focus, you can lock exposure on the spot where you expect the athlete to be and activate AF at the moment your subject appears. The a7C II/a7CR gives you a great deal of flexibility, both in the choice of which button to use for AF, and the behavior of that button. You can *start* autofocus, *lock* autofocus at a button press, or *lock it while holding the button.* That's where the learning of new habits and mind-finger coordination comes in. You need to learn which back-button focus techniques work for you, and when to use them.

Back-button focus lets you avoid the need to switch from AF-S to AF-C when your subject begins moving unexpectedly. Nor do you need to use AF-A and *hope* the camera switches when appropriate. You retain complete control. It's great for sports photography when you want to activate autofocus precisely based on the action in front of you. It also works for static shots. You can press and release your designated focus button, and then take a series of shots using the same focus point. Focus will not change until you once again press your defined back button.

Want to focus on a spot that doesn't reside under one of the a7C II/a7CR's focus areas? Use back-button focus to zero in focus on that location, then reframe. Focus will not change. Don't want to miss an important shot at a wedding or a photojournalism assignment? If you're set to *focus priority,* your camera may delay taking a picture until the focus is optimum; in *release priority* there may still be a slight delay. With back-button focus you can focus first and wait until the decisive moment to press the shutter release and take your picture. The a7C II/a7CR will respond immediately and not bother with focusing at all.

Activating Back-Button Focus

Here's a simplified way to set up back-button focus. Follow these steps to decouple autofocus from the shutter release and assign it to just the center button:

1. **Switch to AF-S mode.** You want to start and lock in focus once, rather than have the camera continually re-focus, so you don't want to use AF-C or AF-S mode. Set the camera to AF-S mode instead.

2. **Set Focus Area to Spot.** Back-button focus works best using a relatively small focus area (rather than a larger zone). Use the Fn menu to set the Focus Area to Spot: Medium.

3. **Turn off shutter button AF Activation.** Navigate to Focus > AF/MF > AF with Shutter and set to Off. To disable back-button focus, change it back to On.

4. **Select an AF-ON button.** The a7C II/a7CR's built-in AF-ON button performs this function by default and adds tracking. For back-button focus, I assign the AF-ON function (only) to the center button. Navigate to Setup > Operation Custom > (Photo) Custom Key/Dial Settings > Rear 2 > Option 1 (center button) and choose AF ON.

5. **Confirm.** Press MENU to confirm and exit.

That's all there is to it. Henceforth, pressing the shutter release will *not* activate autofocus. Auto-exposure metering will still be initiated by pressing the button halfway, as long as Exposure/Color > Metering > AEL w/Shutter is set to Auto or On (and not Off) and pressing it all the way takes a picture. Autofocus will commence only when you press the center button.

Advanced Techniques 5

Of the primary foundations of great photography, only one of them—the ability to capture a compelling image with a pleasing composition—takes a lifetime (or longer) to master. The art of *making* a photograph, rather than just *taking* a photograph, requires an aesthetic eye that sees the right angle for the shot, as well as a sense of what should be included or excluded in the frame; a knowledge of what has been done in the medium before (and where photography can be taken in the future); and a willingness to explore new areas. The more you pursue photography, the more you will learn about visualization and composition. When all is said and done, this is what photography is all about.

The other basics of photography—equally essential—involve more technical aspects: the ability to use your camera's features to produce an image with good tonal and color values; to achieve sharpness (where required) or unsharpness (when you're using selective focus); and to master appropriate white/color balance. It's practical to learn these technical skills in a time frame that's much less than a lifetime, although most of us find there is always room for improvement. You'll find the basic information you need to become proficient in each of these technical areas in this book.

The final and most rewarding stage comes when you begin exploring advanced techniques that enable you to get stunning shots that will have your family, friends, and colleagues asking you, "How did you *do* that?" These more advanced techniques deserve an entire book of their own, but there is plenty of room in this chapter to introduce you to some clever things you can do with your a7C II or a7CR, such as focus stacking (which Sony calls Focus Bracketing), and Pixel Shift Multi Shooting (available with the a7CR only), which allows you to capture amazing 240-megapixel super-high -resolution images.

Exploring Ultra-Fast Exposures

Fast shutter speeds (such as 1/1000th second) can stop action because they capture only a tiny slice of time: a high-jumper frozen in mid-air, perhaps. The Sony a7C II/a7CR has a top shutter speed of 1/8000th second for ambient-light exposures (when the electronic shutter is used). Electronic flash can also freeze motion by virtue of its extremely short duration—as brief as 1/50000th second or less, depending on the flash unit you're using. When you're using flash, the short duration of the actual burst of light can freeze a moving subject; that can also give you an ultra-quick glimpse of a moving subject when the scene is illuminated only by flash.

> **TOP SPEED**
>
> Keep in mind that the a7C II/a7CR's highest shutter speed of 1/8000th second is available only when Shooting > Shutter/Silent > Shutter Type is set to Electronic Shutter, as explained in Chapter 6. When the mechanical shutter is enabled, your camera's top speed is 1/4000th second.

The a7C II/a7CR is fully capable of immobilizing all but the very fastest movement if you use a shutter speed of 1/8000th second (without flash). The top speeds are generally overkill when it comes to stopping action; I can rarely find a situation where even 1/4000th second is required to freeze high-speed motion. For example, the image shown in Figure 5.1 required a shutter speed of just 1/2000th second to freeze everything but the bull's tail.

Virtually all sports motion can be frozen at 1/2000th second or a slower shutter speed, and for many sports a shutter speed of 1/500th of a second or even much slower is actually preferable—for example, to allow the wheels of a racing automobile or motorcycle, or the propeller on a classic aircraft, to blur realistically.

There may be a few situations where a shutter speed faster than 1/4000th second is required. If you wanted to use an aperture of f/1.8 at ISO 100 outdoors in bright sunlight, say, to throw a background out of focus with the shallow depth-of-field available at f/1.8, a shutter speed of 1/4000th second would more than do the job. You'd need a faster shutter speed only if you set a higher ISO, and you probably wouldn't do that if your goal were to use the widest aperture possible. Under *less* than full sunlight, I doubt you'd even need to use a shutter speed of 1/4000th second in any situations you're likely to encounter.

Electronic flash works well for freezing the motion of a nearby subject when flash is the only source of illumination. Since the subject is illuminated for only a split second, you get the effect that would be provided by a very fast shutter speed and also the high level of light needed for an exposure. This feature can be useful for stopping the motion of a nearby subject.

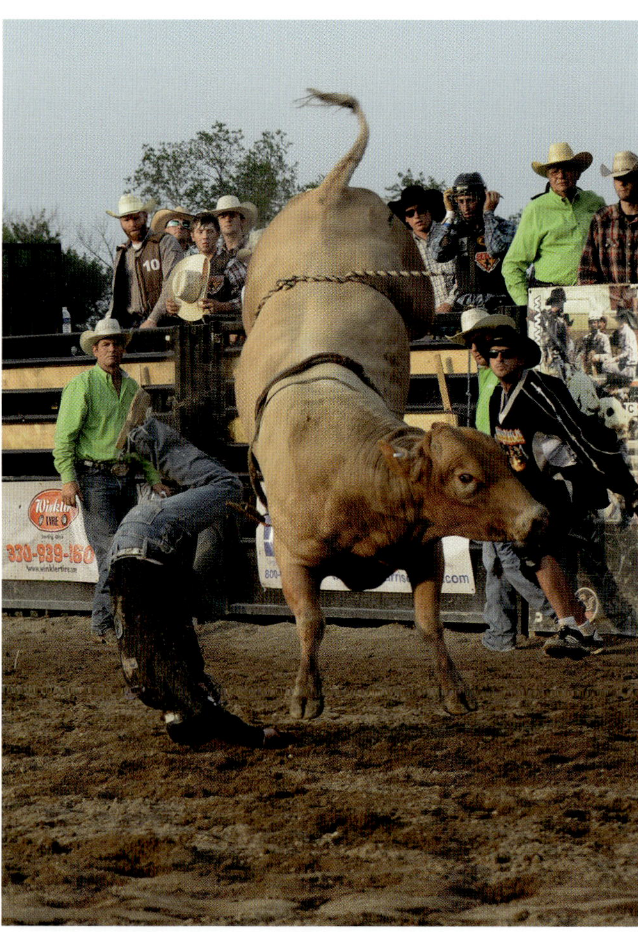

Figure 5.1 A shutter speed of 1/2000th second will freeze most action.

Of course, as you'll see in Chapter 13, the tiny slices of time extracted by the millisecond duration of an electronic flash exact a penalty. To use flash, the camera employs a shutter speed no faster than 1/160th second (or 1/200th second in APS-C mode), which are the fastest shutter speeds—called sync speed—in conventional flash photography when not using high-speed sync.

You can have a lot of fun exploring the kinds of pictures you can take using very brief exposure times, whether you decide to take advantage of the action-stopping shutter speeds (between 1/1000th and 1/8000th second) or the brief burst of light from flash that can freeze the motion of a nearby subject. Here are a few ideas to get you started:

- **Take revealing images.** Fast shutter speeds can help you reveal the real subject behind the façade, by freezing constant motion to capture an enlightening moment in time. Legendary fashion/portrait photographer Philippe Halsman used leaping photos of famous people, such as the Duke and Duchess of Windsor, Richard Nixon, and Salvador Dali, to illuminate their real selves. Halsman said, *"When you ask a person to jump, his attention is mostly directed toward the act of jumping and the mask falls so that the real person appears."* Try some high-speed portraits of people you know in motion to see how they appear when concentrating on something other than the portrait. (See Figure 5.2.)

- **Create unreal images.** High-speed photography can also produce photographs that show your subjects in ways that are quite unreal. A helicopter in mid-air with its rotors frozen or a motocross cyclist leaping over a ramp, but with all motion stopped so that the rider and machine look as if they were frozen in mid-air, makes for an unusual picture. (See the frozen rotors at top in Figure 5.3.) When we're accustomed to seeing subjects in motion, seeing them stopped in time can verge on the surreal.

- **Capture unseen perspectives.** Some things are *never* seen in real life, except when viewed in a stop-action photograph. MIT professor Dr. Harold Edgerton's famous balloon-burst photographs were only a starting point for the inventor of the electronic flash unit. Freeze a hummingbird in flight for a view of wings that never seem to stop. Or, capture the splashes as liquid falls into a bowl, as shown in Figure 5.4. No electronic flash was required for this image (and wouldn't have illuminated the water in the bowl as evenly). Instead, a clutch of high-intensity lamps bounced off a blue card and an ISO setting of 1600 allowed the camera to capture this image at 1/2000th second.

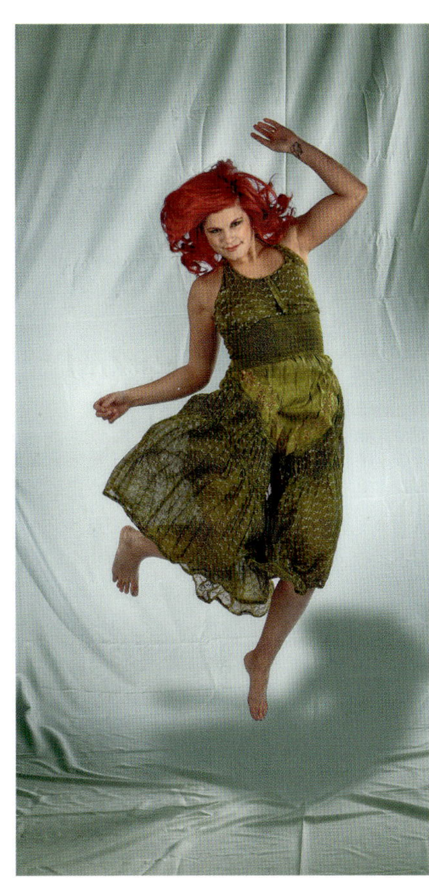

Figure 5.2 Fast shutter speeds can freeze your subject at the top of a jump.

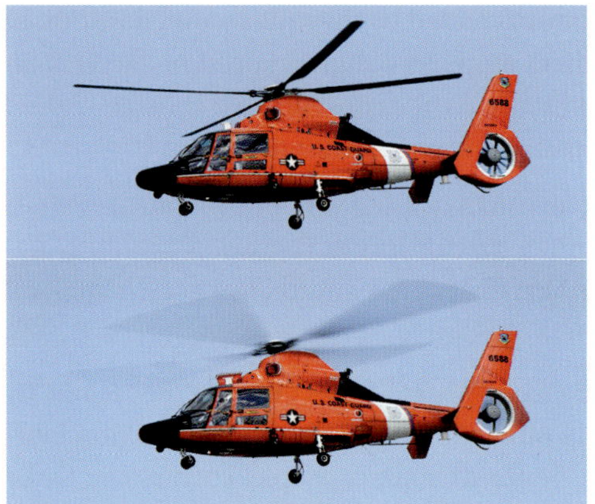

Figure 5.3 Freezing a helicopter's rotors with a fast shutter speed makes for an image that doesn't look natural (top); a little blur helps convey a feeling of motion (bottom).

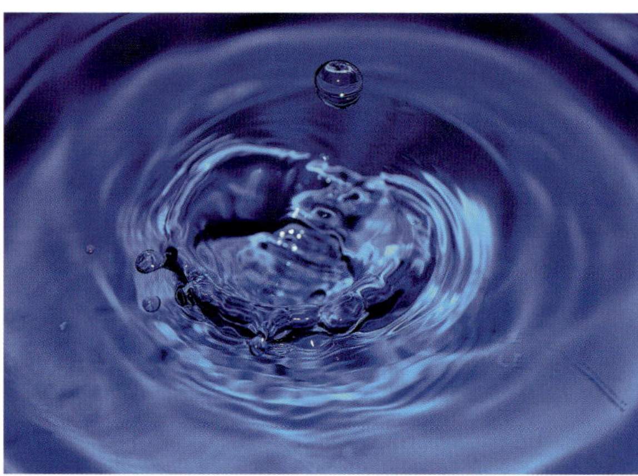

Figure 5.4 A large amount of artificial illumination and an ISO 1600 setting made it possible to capture this shot at 1/2000th second without use of electronic flash.

Long Exposures

Longer exposures are a doorway into another world, showing us how even familiar scenes can look much different when photographed over periods measured in seconds. At night, long exposures produce streaks of light from moving, illuminated subjects like automobiles or amusement park rides, or fireworks, as you can see in Figure 5.5. Or, you can move the camera or zoom the lens to get interesting streaks from non-moving light sources, such as holiday lights. Extra-long exposures of seemingly pitch-dark subjects can reveal interesting views using light levels barely bright enough to see by. At any time of day, including daytime (in which case you'll often need the help of neutral-density filters

Figure 5.5 Long exposures can produce interesting streaks of light.

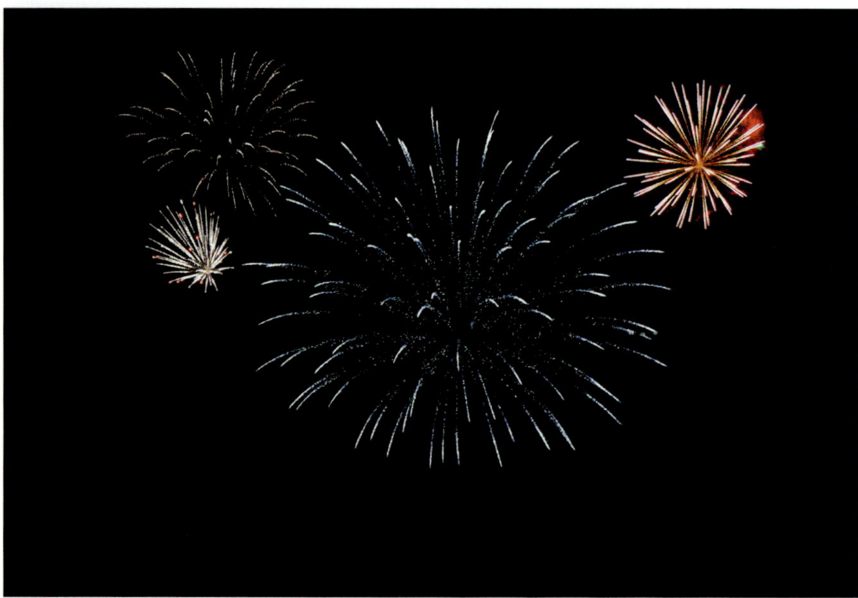

to make the long exposure practical), long exposures can cause moving objects to vanish entirely, because they don't remain stationary long enough to register in a photograph.

Because the a7C II/a7CR produces such good images at longer exposures (and at even more lengthy Bulb Timer exposures), and there are so many creative things you can do with long-exposure techniques, you'll want to do some experimenting. Get yourself a tripod or another firm support and take some test shots with long exposure noise reduction both enabled and disabled in the Setup menu (to see whether you prefer low noise or high detail) and get started. Your camera has three different ways of achieving long exposures:

- **Timed Exposure.** The camera can automatically take exposures as long as 30 seconds in P, A, S, and M modes. In Program and Aperture Priority modes, the camera selects the shutter speed, but you can specify a speed up to 30 seconds in Shutter Priority and Manual exposure mode.

- **Bulb Exposure.** In Shutter Priority and Manual exposure modes, rotate the rear dial past the 30" mark to Bulb. Then, hold down the shutter release and then release it at the end of the desired exposure time. The camera helpfully displays the current length of the exposure so you don't have to count it off yourself. If noise reduction is being applied, a Processing... message appears on the display to indicate that a second "blank" exposure is being made, which will be used to apply a *dark-frame subtraction* algorithm, as described in Chapter 6. This type of exposure can be inconvenient for long exposures, because, if you're not using a remote control with a locking button, such as the Sony RM-VPR1 ($60), you must physically hold down the shutter button for the duration. The Bulb option is not available if you're using Silent Shooting, or any mode that captures multiple images with the single press of the shutter release, such as continuous shooting, self-timer (continuous), or continuous bracketing.

- **Bulb Timer.** This setting allows you to pre-set one specific length of time. Then, in bulb mode, the camera will open the shutter and close it after the interval you've selected has elapsed. A countdown is displayed showing you the time remaining. You must turn the Bulb Timer on using the Exposure/Color > Exposure > BULB Timer Settings entry, and then choose the length of the exposure from 2 to 900 seconds. It's a shame Sony doesn't let you dial in specific long exposure times on the fly, say, for bracketing purposes, but at least your single setting isn't limited to specific exposure times. A 123-second exposure is entirely possible.

If you want to experiment with long exposures, here are some things to try:

- **Make people invisible.** One very cool thing about long exposures is that objects that move rapidly enough won't register at all in a photograph, whereas the subjects that remain stationary are portrayed in the normal way. That makes it easy to produce people-free landscape photos and architectural photos at night, or even in full daylight if you use one or more dark neutral-density filters to allow an exposure of at least a few seconds. At ISO 100 and f/16, for example, a pair of 8X (three-stop) neutral-density filters will allow you to make an exposure of nearly two seconds on a sunny day. Overcast days and/or even more neutral-density filtration would work even better if daylight people-vanishing is your goal. They'll have to be walking *very* briskly and across the field of view (rather than directly toward the camera) for this to work. At night, it's much easier to achieve this effect with the 20- to 30-second exposures that are possible in low light without any filter.

- **Create streaks.** If you aren't shooting for total invisibility, long exposures with the camera on a tripod can produce some interesting streaky effects. Even a single 8X ND filter will let you shoot at f/22 and 1/6th second in daylight. Indoors, you can achieve interesting streaks with slow shutter speeds, which is a technique I often use when photographing ballet dancers.

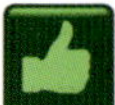 **TIP** Neutral-density filters are gray (non-colored) filters that reduce the amount of light passing through the lens, without adding any color or effect of their own.

- **Produce light trails.** At night, car headlights, taillights, and other moving sources of illumination can generate interesting light trails. Your camera doesn't even need to be mounted on a tripod; hand-holding the camera for longer exposures adds movement and patterns to your trails. If you're shooting fireworks, a longer exposure—with the camera on a tripod—may allow you to combine several bursts into one picture, as you can see in Figure 5.5.

- **Blur waterfalls, etc.** You'll find that waterfalls and other sources of moving liquid produce a special type of long-exposure blur, because the water merges into a fantasy-like veil that looks different at different exposure times, and with different waterfalls. Cascades with turbulent flow produce a rougher look at a given longer exposure than falls that flow smoothly. Although blurred waterfalls and rapids have become almost a cliché, there are still plenty of variations for a creative photographer to explore.

- **Show total darkness in new ways.** Even on the darkest, moonless nights, there is enough starlight or glow from distant illumination sources to see by, and, if you use a long exposure, there is enough light to take a picture, too. I was visiting a Great Lakes park hours after sunset but found that a several-second exposure revealed the skyline scene shown in Figure 5.6, even though, in real life, there was barely enough light to make out the boats in the distance. Although the photo appears as if it were taken at twilight or sunset, in fact the shot was made at 10 p.m.

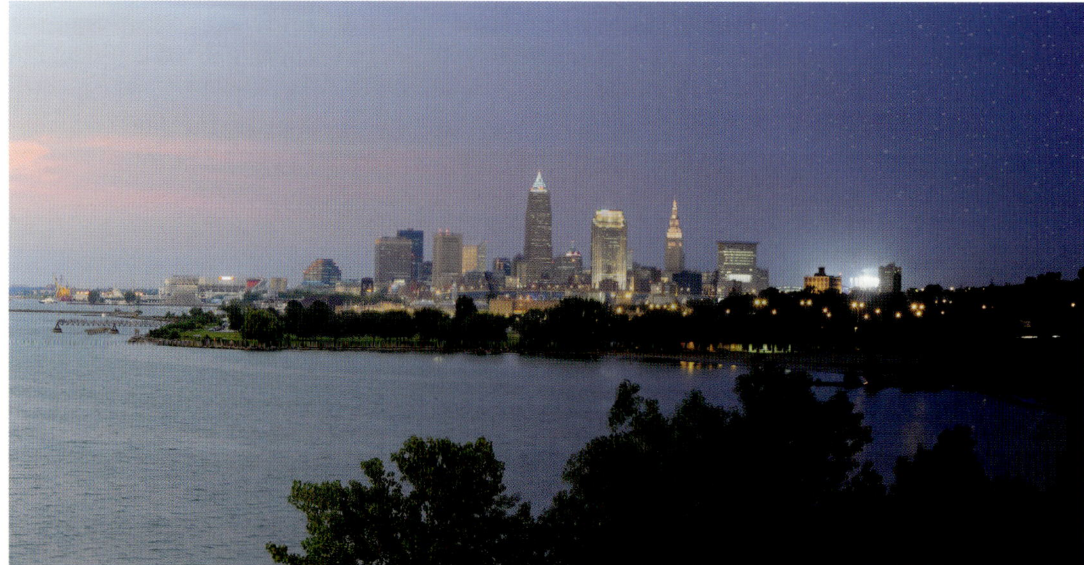

Figure 5.6 A long exposure transformed this night scene into a picture apparently taken at dusk.

Continuous Shooting

The a7C II and a7CR's continuous shooting modes are indispensable for the sports photographer, and useful for anyone photographing an event in which, even if you have lightning-fast reflexes, a decisive moment may occur a fraction of a second after you've completed an exposure. The a7C II is capable of capturing images continuously at *up to* (and note that qualification) 10 frames per second 8 frames per second with the a7CR), so you can shoot consecutive images non-stop until the camera's buffer fills. At an air show I covered earlier this year, I took more than 7,000 images in a couple hours. I was able to cram hundreds of Large/Fine JPEGs on a single memory card. That's a lot of shooting. Given an average burst of about eight images per sequence at the camera's highest frame (nobody really takes 15 to 20 shots or more of one pass, even with a slow-moving biplane as shown in Figure 5.7), I was able to capture more than 100 different sequences like the one shown before I needed to swap cards. For some types of action (such as soccer), even longer bursts come in handy, because exciting running, dribbling, and passing sequences often last 5 to 10 seconds. (See Figure 5.8.)

To use the a7C II/a7CR's continuous advance mode, press the drive button (left directional button), access the Function menu, or navigate to the Shooting > Drive Mode > Drive Mode entry. Press the left/right buttons to select Hi+, Hi, Mid, or Lo frame rates. The camera takes advantage of the

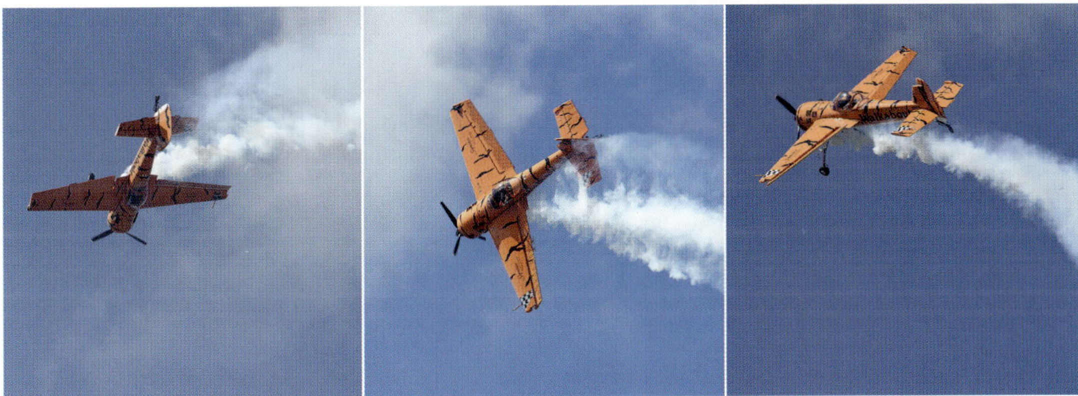

Figure 5.7 Air shows make a perfect subject for continuous bursts.

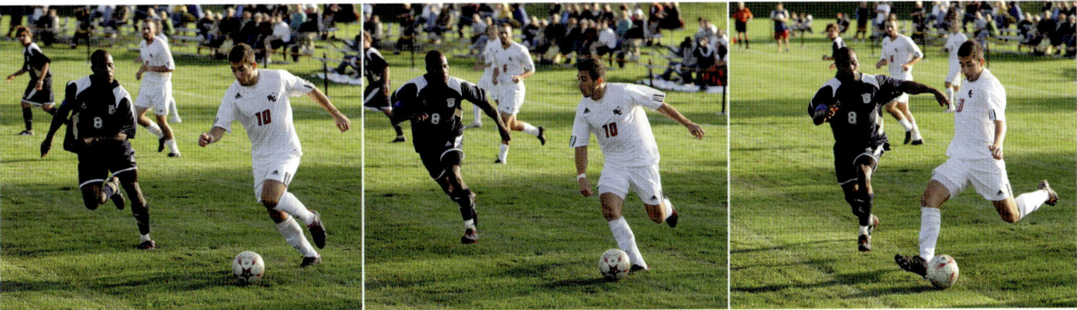

Figure 5.8 Continuous shooting allows you to capture an entire sequence of exciting moments as they unfold.

electronic front-curtain shutter to produce the highest frame rates, and actually slows down in Hi+, Hi, Mid, or Lo modes if you have turned it off. The available rates vary between the a7C II and a7CR:

Shooting Speeds:	Hi+	Hi	Mid	Lo
a7C II	10 fps	8 fps	6 fps	3 fps
a7CR	8 fps	6 fps	5 fps	2.5 fps

If you set the focus mode (in the Function submenu) to AF-C (Continuous autofocus) and Exposure/ Color > Metering > AEL w/Shutter to Off or Auto, then autofocus will be available in all continuous drive modes, but only as long as the subject is covered by the active focus detection point(s). This feature is useful when a moving subject is approaching the camera or moving away from it; the camera will continuously adjust to focus on the subject as the distance changes, so the entire set of photos should be sharply focused.

When using Hi+, Hi, or Mid, and an f/stop smaller than f/22, the a7C II/a7CR focuses for the first image in a burst, then keeps that focus point for subsequent shots. Moreover, in Hi+ mode, the image is not displayed in real time (you see the last picture taken). Even the speedy BIONZ XR processor isn't fast enough to keep up with that clip, a speed at which you probably won't even notice the difference. However, in H, Mid, or Lo modes, you'll be looking at the actual image as it is captured.

Surprise! Your a7C II/a7CR is fast enough to shoot continuously even when capturing RAW, although the shooting speed will be slower if you're grabbing uncompressed RAW images. In addition, at the Hi+ setting, the camera captures 12-bit RAW rather than full-range 14-bit RAW files to reduce the size of the files it must write to the memory card. Continuous images are first shuttled into the camera's internal memory buffer, then doled out to the memory card as quickly as the card can write the data. Technically, the camera takes the data received from the digital image processor and converts it to the output format you've selected—JPEG, RAW, or both—and deposits it in the buffer ready to store on the card.

The internal "smart" buffer can suck up photos much more quickly than the memory card and, indeed, some memory cards are significantly faster or slower than others. When the buffer begins to fill, the framing speed may slow significantly; eventually the buffer fills and then you can't take any more continuous shots until the a7C II/a7CR has dumped some of them to the card, making more room in the buffer.

The exact number of images you can capture depends on whether you're using the a7CR or a7C II. Obviously, the a7CR's huge 60MP images slow down the continuous shooting rate significantly, especially when you are capturing RAW images. For example, at the top speed of 8 frames per second (H+), the a7CR's buffer fills when it has sucked up 320 JPEG images, while the a7C II's buffer can accommodate 1000-plus JPEG shots before the shooting rate slows down.

Capturing RAW images slows things down even more, whether you're using the Compressed RAW, Uncompressed RAW, or Lossless Compression options. Table 5.1 provides a comparison of the number of images you can expect from your buffer with both the a7CR and a7C II. **Note:** The Number of Images columns include both RAW and either JPEG or HEIF files for the modes that capture both RAW and JPEG/HEIF simultaneously.

TABLE 5.1 Recordable Images Using Continuous Shooting: H+

	A7CR		A7C II	
FILE FORMAT	**NUMBER OF IMAGES (JPEG)**	**NUMBER OF IMAGES (HEIF)**	**NUMBER OF IMAGES (JPEG)**	**NUMBER OF IMAGES (HEIF)**
JPEG/HEIF (Fine)	320	1,000	1,000+	1,000+
RAW (Compressed RAW)	36	36	44	44
RAW & JPEG or HEIF (Compressed RAW)	32	33	35	38
RAW (Uncompressed RAW)	14	14	18	18
RAW & JPEG or HEIF (Uncompressed RAW)	13	13	16	16
RAW (Lossless Compression RAW: L)	16	16	27	27
RAW & JPEG or HEIF (Lossless Compression RAW: L)	15	15	20	22

If you need a reminder of how much space remains in your buffer, you can opt to display the Continuous shooting length indicator using the entry in the Setup > Display Option > Remaining Shooting Display option, which I'll explain in Chapter 9. Continuous shooting may be disabled if your battery level is low.

Customizing White Balance

Back in the film days, both color transparency and color negative ("print") films were standardized, or balanced, for a particular "color" of light. Most were balanced for daylight but you could also buy "tungsten" balanced color negative and transparency film for shooting under incandescent lamps that produced light of an amber color, or use conversion filters. This type of film had a bluish color balance, intended to moderate the effect produced by light that was amber. Digital cameras like the Sony a7C II and a7CR can be adjusted for specific white balance options suitable for particular types of illumination.

This is important because various light sources produce illumination of different "colors," although sometimes we are not aware of the difference. Indoor illumination tends to be somewhat amber when using light bulbs that are not daylight balanced, while noonday light outdoors is close to white, and the light early and late in the day is somewhat red/yellow.

White balance is measured using a scale called color temperature. Color temperatures were assigned by heating a theoretical "black body radiator" (which doesn't reflect any light; all illumination comes from its radiance alone) and recording the spectrum of light it emitted at a given temperature in degrees Kelvin. So, daylight at noon has a color temperature in the 5,500- to 6,000-degree range. Indoor illumination is around 3,400 degrees. Hotter temperatures produce bluer images (think blue-white hot) while cooler temperatures produce redder images (think of a dull-red glowing ember). Because of human nature, though, bluer images are actually called "cool" (think wintry day) and redder images are called "warm" (think ruddy sunset), even though their color temperatures are reversed.

Take a photo indoors under warm illumination with a digital camera sensor balanced for cooler daylight and the image will appear much too red/yellow. An image exposed outdoors with the white balance set for incandescent (tungsten) illumination will seem much too blue. These color casts may be too strong to remove in an image editor from JPEG files. Of course, if you shoot RAW photos, you can later change the WB setting to the desired value in RAW converter software; this is a completely "non-destructive" process so full image quality will be maintained.

Mismatched white balance settings are easier to achieve accidentally than you might think, even for experienced photographers. I'd just arrived at a Dwight Yoakam concert after shooting some photos indoors with electronic flash and had manually set WB for Flash. Then, as the concert began, I resumed shooting using the incandescent stage lighting—which looked white to the eye—and ended up with a few shots like Figure 5.9, left. Fortunately, the live view image looked a little weird, which

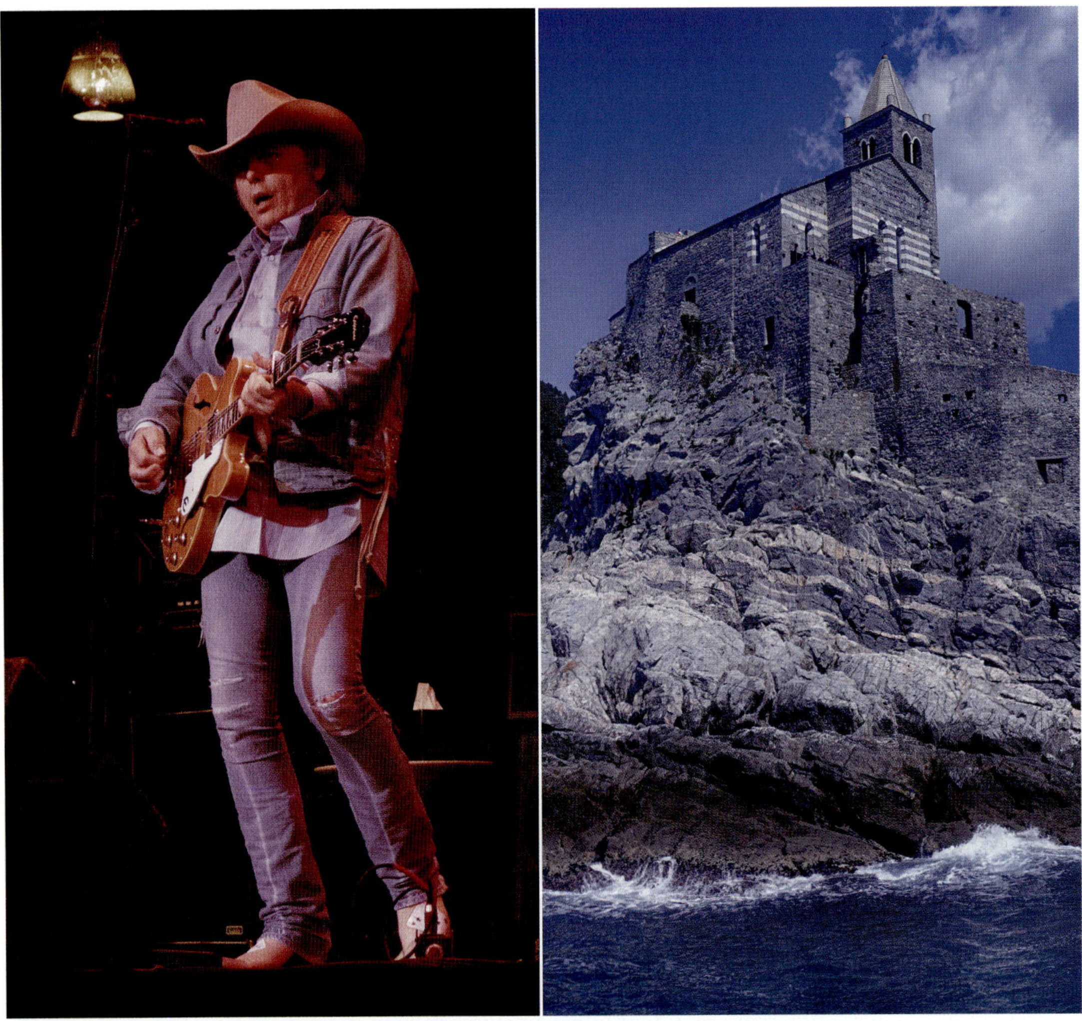

Figure 5.9 An image exposed indoors with the WB set for electronic flash will appear too reddish (left); using the incandescent setting outdoors makes an image too blue (right).

I confirmed during picture review. I changed my white balance and captured the rest of the concert with better color. Another time, I was shooting outdoors, but had the camera white balance still set for incandescent illumination. The excessively blue image is shown in Figure 5.9, right.

The Auto White Balance (AWB) setting is available in the Exposure/Color > White Balance > White Balance menu, from the Function menu, or from a key defined with that function. It examines your scene and chooses an appropriate value based on its perception of the color of the illumination and even the colors in the scene. However, the process is not foolproof (with any camera). Under bright lighting conditions, it may evaluate the colors in the image and still assume the light source is daylight and balance the picture accordingly, even though, in fact, you may be shooting under extremely bright incandescent illumination. In dimmer light, the camera's electronics may assume that the illumination is tungsten, and if there are lots of reddish colors present, set color balance for that type of lighting. With mercury vapor or sodium lamps, correct white balance may be virtually impossible to achieve with any of the so-called presets. In those cases, you should use flash instead, or Custom WB with JPEGs, or shoot in RAW format and make your corrections after importing the file into your image editor with a RAW converter.

Shockless White Balance

Still photographers new to video will soon notice that unwanted changes in exposure, focus, or white balance that occur while the video is being captured can be disconcerting. Sony takes care of the shifting white balance problem by providing a setting called Shockless White Balance, which is available only when the Still/Movie/S&Q dial is set to one of the two movie positions.

This setting determines how quickly white balance switches during movie shooting. You can choose:

- **Off.** White balance switches immediately if you change the WB setting during movie shooting.
- **1 (Fast), 2 (Medium), 3 (Slow).** The white balance shifts more smoothly, depending on the speed you select. Note that Auto White Balance (AWB) is not affected by this option, nor are changes to white balance specified using the Color Temperature/Filter setting.

The a7C II and a7CR provide many WB presets, each intended for use in specific lighting conditions. You can choose from Daylight, Shade, Cloudy, Incandescent (often called Tungsten by photographers), four types of Fluorescent (Warm White, Cool White, Day White, and Daylight), Underwater Auto, and Flash. However, the camera also offers a method for setting a desired color temperature/filter as well as a custom WB feature.

The Daylight preset provides WB at 5,200K, while the Shade preset uses 7,000K to give you a warming effect that's useful in the bluish light of a deeply shaded area. The chief difference between direct sun and an area in shade, or even incandescent light sources, is nothing more than the proportions of red and blue light. The spectrum of colors used by the a7C II/a7CR is continuous, but it is biased toward one end or the other, depending on the white balance setting you make.

However, some types of fluorescent lights produce illumination that has a severe deficit in certain colors, such as only particular shades of red. If you looked at the spectrum or rainbow of colors encompassed by such a light source, it would have black bands in it, representing particular wavelengths of light that are absent. You can't compensate for this deficiency by adding all tones of red.

That's why the fluorescent setting of your camera may provide less than satisfactory results with some kinds of fluorescent bulbs. If you take many photographs under a particular kind of non-compatible fluorescent light, you might want to investigate specialized filters intended to be mounted on your lens for use under various types of fluorescent light, available from camera stores, or develop skills in white balance adjustment using an image editor or RAW converter software program. However, you do get four presets for fluorescent WB and one of these should provide close to accurate white balance with the common types of lights.

It's when you find that AWB and the various presets simply cannot produce pleasing white balance in certain lighting conditions that you'll need the other options (discussed shortly): use the white balance adjustment feature, set a specific color temperature, or calibrate the WB system to set a custom white balance.

Fine-Tuning Preset White Balance

After you scroll to any of the WB options (AWB, Daylight, Shade, etc.), pressing the right directional button reveals the White Balance Adjustment screen, with a grid, shown in Figure 5.10. This feature allows you to fine-tune the white balance by biasing it toward certain colors. Use any of the four directional keys to move the orange dot (cursor) from the center of the grid: upward to bias the WB toward green (G), downward toward magenta (M), right toward amber (A), or left toward blue (B). You can move the cursor seven increments (although Sony doesn't reveal exactly what those increments are) in any of the four directions.

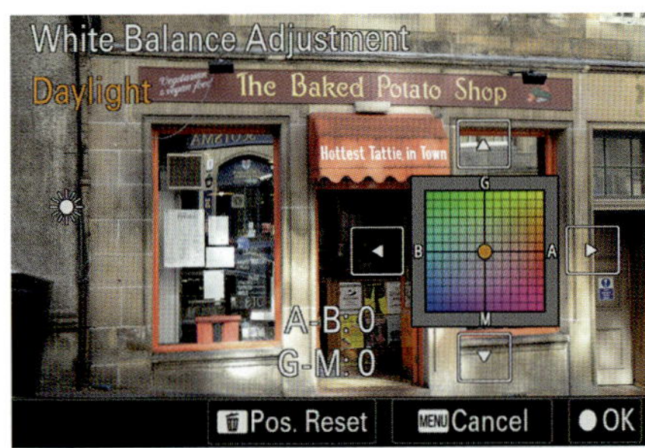

Figure 5.10 Use this feature when you want to fine-tune white balance when using AWB or any of the presets.

Naturally, you can also move the orange dot to any point within the grid: toward amber/magenta, for example. While biasing the WB, examine the scene in the LCD or viewfinder preview display; stop making adjustments when the white balance looks fine. Tap the shutter release to escape from the WB settings adjustments. Let's look at the options in more detail:

- **Cooler or warmer.** Pressing the left/right directional buttons changes the white balance to cooler (left) or warmer (right) along the blue/amber scale. There are seven increments, and the value you "dial in" will be shown in the lower-right corner of the screen as an A-B value (yes, the labels are *reversed* from the actual scale at the right side of the screen). The red dot will move along the scale to show the value you've selected. Typically, blue/amber adjustments are what we think of as "color temperature" changes, or, "cooler" and "warmer." These correspond to the way in which daylight illumination changes: warm at sunrise and sunset, very cool in the shade (because most of the illumination comes from reflections of the blue sky), and at high noon. Indoor light sources can also be cooler or warmer, depending on the kind of light they emit.

- **Green/magenta bias.** Press the up/down buttons to change the color balance along the green (upward) or magenta (downward) directions. Seven increments are provided here, too, and shown as vertical movement in the color balance matrix at the right of the screen. Color changes of this type tend to reflect special characteristics of the light source; certain fluorescent lights have a "green" cast, for example.

- **Either or both.** Because the blue/amber and green/magenta adjustments can be made independently, you're free to choose just one of them, or both if your fine-tuning requires it.

- **Never mind.** If you want to cancel all fine-tuning and shift back to neutral, just press the Trash button to cancel. The orange dot in the color chart will be restored to the center position. Press the OK button to confirm the changes you've made, or the MENU button to cancel any changes and exit.

Setting a Custom White Balance

If you often shoot in locations that are illuminated by artificial light of unusual colors, the best bet is to set a custom white balance. This calls for teaching (calibrating) the WB system to render white as white under a specific type of illumination. When white is accurately rendered, other colors will look accurate as well. You can use this feature under more common types of lighting too; it's very useful under tungsten lamps, for example, when the Incandescent WB option does not adequately correct for the amber color of the light. Custom WB is the most accurate way of getting the right color balance, short of having a special meter that gives you a precise reading of color temperature. It's easy to do; just follow these steps:

1. Navigate to Exposure/Color > White Balance > White Balance or use the Function menu.

2. Use the directional buttons or the control wheel to scroll up/down through the list of white balance options until you reach Custom 1, Custom 2, or Custom 3 registers. Highlight the custom white balance register you want to use and press the right directional control.

3. Select the Set icon, as shown in Figure 5.11, left. These are white balance memory register "slots" you can use to store customized white balance settings.

4. Press the center button. The display shown in Figure 5.11, center, appears. Point the camera at a white or gray object (such as a sheet of white paper or a gray card) large enough to fill the small orange square that's displayed in the center of the frame. Your target must be in the same light as the subject you plan to photograph, not in some entirely different part of the scene where the illumination is different.

5. Press the center button. The target (such as the sheet of white paper) that you had aimed at, as well as the custom white balance data, appears on the LCD or EVF screen. (The image is not recorded to the memory card.)

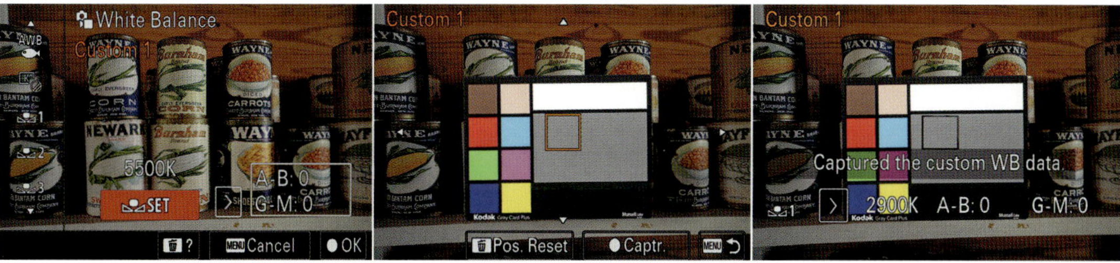

Figure 5.11 Choose a Custom register (left); point the camera at a white or gray area (center); press the center button to capture the white balance (right).

6. The white balance of the target you photographed will appear at the bottom of the screen. (See Figure 5.11, right.) You can press the right directional control to adjust the white balance further using the screen shown earlier in Figure 5.10.

7. Press the center button to confirm and return to the live view on the LCD. Henceforth, you can select that Custom register to load a particular set of white balance parameters. You can use the White Balance Adjustment screen at any time to further fine-tune the balance.

Setting White Balance by Color Temperature

If you want to set a specific white balance based on color temperature, choose C. Temp/Filter in the White Balance menu, and press the right button. You'll next see a display of color temperatures arrayed along the bottom of the screen. Press the right button a second time to view an adjustment screen similar to the one shown in Figure 5.11, but with a scrolling list of color temperatures displayed. Here's how to use this feature:

- **Change color temperature.** Rotate the control wheel on the camera's backside to select a specific color temperature in 100K increments, from 2,500K (a level that makes your image much bluer, to compensate for amber illumination) to 9,900K (a level that makes images much redder to correct for light that is extremely blue in color). The live preview changes as you scroll to give you an indication as to the white balance you can expect at any K level. If you have a color temperature meter accessory, or reliable tips that guide you in making the optimal setting, this WB feature will be particularly useful. Even if you don't have that accessory or useful information, you may want to experiment with this setting using the live preview, especially if you are trying to achieve creative effects with color casts along the spectrum from blue to red.

- **Fine-tune the color temperature.** In addition to color temperature, you can press the right directional button to access the screen that allows you to change the blue/amber or green/magenta bias, exactly as described earlier and shown in Figure 5.10; move the cursor in any direction with the directional keys: left/right for blue/amber and up/down for green/magenta bias. If you change your mind, press the MENU button to cancel the bias adjustments you've made.

  This feature corresponds to the use of CC (Color Compensation) filters that were used to compensate for various types of lighting when shooting film. When you use C. Temp/Filter, the color filter value you set takes effect in conjunction with the color temperature you set. In other words, both of these settings work together to give you very precise control over the degree of color correction you are using.

Note that the color temperature you set here is not affected by the Shockless White Balance option discussed earlier.

Interval Shooting

With some earlier Sony cameras, this very popular feature has previously required a special app or external device to trigger successive shots over a specific period of time. Today, interval shooting is built right into your a7C II/a7CR's capabilities (and has been added to some earlier Sony models via a firmware upgrade).

This section will help you get the most from this capability, and provide some ideas for setting up and capturing your own sequences. There is a lot more to interval shooting than you might think. Here are a few ideas to get you started:

- **Time-lapse nature movies.** Although interval shooting captures a series of *still* images, which you can view one at a time, it's easy to combine a set of consecutive exposures to create a time-lapse movie. This technique is often used to good effect in nature films, such as Walt Disney's pioneering *The Living Desert*. I'll show you how to create a time-lapse movie later in this chapter.

- **Star trails.** You don't need interval shooting to capture images of the heavens—a long exposure will suffice. However, still photos of the sky longer than a certain length produce blurry images (even if the camera is mounted on a tripod), due to the rotation of the Earth and the apparent "movement" of the stars. You can, however, use interval photography to capture a series of sharp star images over a period of time and combine them into a sweeping star trail image. I'll show you how to do that later in this chapter, as well.

- **Sunsets.** I shoot plenty of sunset photos, particularly in Florida during the winter, and find that images taken at different times as the sun sinks below the horizon often look dramatically different. Interval shooting is particularly useful for capturing the elusive "green flash," a phenomenon in which the sun changes color (usually green, but other colors are possible) for one or two seconds. If you take one photo every second or two for a long enough period, you have a better chance of capturing the green flash—if it happens at all. (It doesn't always appear.)

  The green flash is caused by the separation of the light into different colors as it is refracted through the thickest section of atmosphere (much like the way prisms or raindrops create a rainbow). The shorter wavelengths of blue, indigo, and violet are scattered by the atmosphere, while the longer red, orange, and yellow colors are absorbed, making the "middle" color, green, most visible for a few seconds. (I *knew* that the mnemonic ROY G. BIV would come in handy after elementary school!)

- **Capture the decisive moment.** You know deer and other wildlife wander into your backyard to munch on the delectables in your garden during the daytime. It would almost be worth the loss of lettuce to capture a few images of them—but you don't have four or five hours to waste waiting for them to show up. (I know erecting a "Deer Crossing" sign doesn't work; it appears the animals either can't read or ignore them.) Instead, set up your camera (indoors, and shoot through a window if you wish), take a series of photos, and then review them to find your prize photo.

- **Documentation.** Use your imagination, and you'll discover dozens of ways to document things using sequences of photos taken at intervals. Wondering how hard your friends worked at helping you re-roof your garage? You can capture an entire workday with shots taken every ten minutes or so to create a hilarious series showing who spent the most time hammering, and who took the most frequent beer breaks (and ended up hammered). How often do you toss and turn at night? A dim nightlight can provide enough illumination to capture images at intervals and see if you slept like a log, or rolled like one.

- **Self-portraits.** You can use your self-timer to take a self-portrait or two—but what if you wanted to shoot 30 or 40 shots of you mugging for the camera or assuming different poses? Choose an interval of 10 seconds or more, and you can take as many consecutive photos of yourself—or someone else—without the need to press the shutter button each time.

Interval Shooting Checklist

Interval photography is not a technique where you can get your best shots by winging it. The shooting process can be—and usually is—lengthy, so you don't want to spend two hours driving to a location, then 10 minutes or 10 hours capturing a sequence to discover poor planning has ruined your final results. The following section provides some tips for preparing for your interval or time-lapse shooting session:

- **Know your subject.** If you plan to shoot a sunset, make sure you know exactly *when* the sun will set, so you can arrive early enough to set up your equipment and adjust your camera. You can Google the necessary information, but apps for Android and iOS devices called PhotoPills and The Photographer's Ephemeris can tell you exactly when a celestial event will occur, and even provide you with a map that will help you calculate your best location. If, say, you want to shoot the sun setting behind a lighthouse, the app will tell you the precise spot to stand, and when. If you're capturing the ebb and flow of tides, you'll need to know the time of high and/or low tides at a specific location. Don't forget to scout the location ahead of time, too.

- **Use a sturdy tripod.** If you don't have a sturdy tripod, take along an empty sack (I use the lightweight mesh bags that oranges come in), fill it with rocks when you arrive at your location, and hang it from the center column of your tripod to add ground-hugging weight. Successful interval photography calls for a camera that doesn't move between shots so the successive images show what has changed between intervals. That's not to say that some interesting photos can't be taken by panning and/or moving the camera between intervals. You want to avoid *unwanted* movement, and save intentional movement for experimental photography.

- **Have a fully charged battery or another power source.** Interval photography drains the batteries at an alarming pace. For long sequences, you'll want to use a charged battery or external power. Turn off picture review to reduce power consumption.

- **Make sure the camera is protected** from the elements, accidents, and theft.

- **Disable Long Exposure Noise Reduction.** When Long Exposure NR is enabled, the camera takes an additional dark "comparison" frame using the same exposure time so sensor noise can be removed. Long Exposure NR is disabled during interval shooting.

  Think about it. If you're taking a 20-second exposure at intervals of less than 40 seconds, you would *not* want the camera to follow the original shot with an additional 20-second dark frame. That's true whenever the total time required for the original/dark frame exposures is longer than your interval. So with Long Exposure NR disabled, you'll have to accept a little noise to maintain your shooting rate.

- **Focus manually.** There aren't many common interval-shooting situations in which I'd want to have focus change from shot to shot. Perhaps you're expecting a herd of deer to cavort through your garden and would like the camera to attempt to focus on the nearest beast. Most of the time, however, consistent manual focus is best. Choose whether you want to focus on the foreground, middle range, or background, and set your focus point there. If you're capturing photos of, say, a flower opening, use the Focus Magnifier to help you choose the precise plane of focus. Depth-of-field can be used creatively with small apertures (to increase the range of sharpness) or large f/stops (to allow selective focus).

- **Manual exposure—or not?** If you set exposure manually, each picture you take will use the same ISO, f/stop, and shutter speed setting. If the light remains even during the sequence, that can be a good thing. If the light changes (say, throughout a day), that can be bad, or distracting, or, in some cases, add a certain desirable look. The Shooting > Drive Mode > Interval Shooting Functions > AE Tracking Sensitivity option can be used to fine-tune exposure. If autoexposure is active, you can specify a fast response to changes (High), or opt for slower adjustments using the Medium or Low sensitivity settings. Know that quick changes in exposure can be distracting, especially when combining shots into a time-lapse movie. If you *want* to see dramatic light shifts as your scene lightens or darkens, use Manual Exposure and set the shutter speed, ISO, and aperture to give the correct "normal" exposure.

- **Choose an interval.** The time *between* each shot can be important. If you wait too long, you may miss an important event; choose a very brief interval, and you can end up with too many photos that are almost identical and lacking in the time-lapse effect. The interval is especially important if you intend to combine your shots into a time-lapse movie. With, say, slow-moving clouds, one shot every 10 seconds may produce a majestic march across the sky; fast-moving clouds can require taking one picture every three to five seconds. Sunsets work best with 30-second intervals; I get good results using 60-second gaps between shots when shooting the stars.

  To add Charlie Chaplin–like movement to pedestrians, one shot every second or two does the job. (**Fun fact:** The cameras used for Chaplin's comedies were hand-cranked at frame rates of around 14 to 16 frames per second; when projected at the eventual standard of 24 fps, the motion was sped up. To compensate, Chaplin later had some frames duplicated in printing to simulate the 24 fps rate—while the motion was less frenetic, it became jerkier in the process.)

- **Choose number of shots to capture.** For practical reasons, you need to know how long it will take to capture your sequence. When you've chosen an interval and number of shots, the camera displays the total elapsed time, but common sense will tell you that if you are shooting one frame every 10 seconds (six per minute), and if you want to capture 60 minutes' worth of action, you'll need to take 360 shots. Conversely, if you plan to convert your images into a movie, you'll know that at, say, 30 frames per second, your 360 images will provide a movie only 12 seconds in length! Obviously, for time-lapse movies, you'll probably be capturing a lot more than 360 images; up to 9,999 frames can be captured—about 5.5 minutes' worth at 30 fps.

- **Choose your start time.** Use this setting to delay the start of image capture, from 0 minutes, 0 seconds (begin immediately) to 99 minutes, 59 seconds. While you may want to begin shooting immediately, you should still set a short delay (say, 20 seconds) as a start time so the camera can settle down in its tripod perch. If you want to begin capturing an event, say, a sunset, in 10 minutes, you can specify that much of a delay, and spend the intervening time setting up other cameras, performing other tasks, or chatting with your companions about how great your photos are going to be.

A REMINDER

The interval should not be shorter than the shutter speed; for example, it's not smart to set one second as the interval if the images will be taken at two seconds or longer. Fortunately, you can set the Shooting Interval Priority, which tells the camera what to do when the shooting time is longer than the interval.

Settings Recap

I detail all major settings for the Interval Shooting Functions in Chapter 6. Here's a quick preview:

- **Interval shooting.** Choose On or Off to enable/disable the feature. You'll want to keep this setting at Off until you are ready to begin interval shooting.

- **Shooting start time.** Use this setting to delay the start of image capture, from 0 minutes, 0 seconds (begin immediately) to 99 minutes, 59 seconds.

- **Shooting interval.** Specify how often an image should be captured. If you need an interval longer than 60 seconds, you'll need to purchase an external intervalometer.

- **Number of shots.** This setting determines the total number of exposures in a time-lapse sequence. You can choose from 1 to 9,999 shots. A message at the bottom of the screen will display how long it will take to capture the number of shots you specify using the shooting interval you've chosen.

- **Autoexposure Tracking Sensitivity.** Select from High, Mid (Medium), or Low sensitivity.

- **Shutter Type in Interval.** Choose On or Off. If you select On, the a7C II or a7CR will operate silently, which allows capturing your sequence in "stealth" mode if you need it. Shutter type is set to Electronic Shutter by default.

- **Shoot Interval Priority.** When shooting sequences using Program or Aperture Priority modes, the shutter speed will be adjusted to provide the correct exposure. That may result in a shutter speed that is longer than the specified interval. Choose Off for this setting and the a7C II/a7CR will go ahead and expose for the correct amount of time, skipping the shot that would have taken place.

  Choose On, and when another interval exposure is due, the camera will terminate the previous shot (underexposing it) and begin the next one on schedule. You might use the On option if you feel that just dropping the poorly exposed image from the sequence produces the best series. You may be able to avoid the underexposure by activating Auto ISO Sensitivity, and selecting a minimum shutter speed that is shorter than the interval time. In that case, the camera will increase the ISO setting (if necessary) to produce the correct exposure using the automatically selected shutter speed. The chief drawback is that increasing the ISO automatically may also increase the amount of noise in your image. Significant changes in graininess may detract from your sequence or time-lapse movie.

After you've made your settings, double-check to make sure the Interval Shooting entry is set to On, then exit the menu. When you're ready to begin, press the shutter-release button down all the way. You'll see a message that the camera is in Standby mode, and be notified when the first and all subsequent images are captured. A display at the lower-left corner of the screen shows the interval and number of shots taken in the series. Auto Review is disabled, so you will not see each picture as it is captured.

Take care, because with short intervals, the camera can get hot over an extended period of time. As shooting begins, you can use a previously defined function key to activate one of the following functions: Autoexposure Hold, Spot Autoexposure Hold, Register AF Area Hold, or Auto White Balance Hold. The function invoked will remain active during your sequence. You can cancel an interval sequence by pressing the shutter release again.

Viewing Your Interval Sequences

You can view your sequences as if they were a time-lapse movie in the camera. You can also create an actual time-lapse movie from your photos; I'll describe that in the section following this one. To view your sequence as a movie in the camera, just follow these steps:

1. **Choose speed.** In the Playback > Viewing group, you can choose Play Speed for Interval and choose a speed from 1 (slow) to 9 (fast).

   - **At the slowest speed,** each frame you took one after the other will be displayed, so you'll see every image captured. The apparent speed of motion will be determined by length of the interval between each frame, and, to a certain extent, the size of the image file. That is, motion captured with larger intervals will appear to be moving faster, so sequences shot at 10-second intervals will seem "slower" than those taken at 20-second intervals. In addition, you may need to take into account how many images can fit into the camera's buffer as they are displayed. Images captured in Large JPEG Extra Fine format may take longer to display than those captured in Small JPEG Standard format. In most cases, the difference in speed will be much less than the difference caused by the interval.

   - **At faster speeds,** frames are "skipped," so only every second, third, fourth, etc., image is displayed, producing faster apparent motion, but also resulting in a jerkier appearance. In effect, faster playback speeds decrease the interval between shots.

2. **Select Continuous Playback.** First scroll to the group of continuous shots you want to view, then navigate to Playback > Viewing > Continuous Playback. Press the center button. The camera will display the images in order quickly, at the speed you've specified.

Time-Lapse Movies

Your a7C II/a7CR actually has *two* ways of capturing time-lapse movies. The most versatile method is using the Shooting > Drive Mode > Interval Shooting Functions options described in the previous section. Sony also has included a convenient, more automated version you can find in the Shooting > Image Quality/Recording > Time-lapse Settings entry. It's easy to get them confused. I'll show you how to use the latter in Chapter 6. Here's a comparison:

- **Interval Shooting Functions.** This entry is available *only* when the Still/Movie/S&Q dial is set to the Still position. As you've learned, interval shooting captures a series of frames, which can be assembled into a finished movie, as I'll show you shortly. While more time consuming, you gain more control, as you can choose more parameters, including shooting start time, shooting interval, number of shots taken, autoexposure adjustments, whether to use the electronic or mechanical shutter, and the interval priority.

- **Time-lapse settings.** This more automated option is available *only* when the Still/Movie/S&Q dial is set to the Movie or S&Q position. It only allows you to choose a frame rate, interval between shots, record setting, and video light setting. It captures a series of frames and then assembles them into a time-lapse movie automatically with no further input required from you.

If you want to go the do-it-yourself route. It's easy to convert your Interval Shooting sequence of images into a time-lapse movie. All you need is the Viewer module from the free Imaging Edge software suite. It can quickly convert your individual frames into a Full HD (1920 × 1080) or Ultra HD (3840 × 2160) MP4 video clip. Just follow these steps:

1. **Deposit sequence in a folder.** Copy all the frames you want to use to a new folder on your computer. You'll find it easier to select them if they are located in their own folder. Your images can be RAW or JPEG files.

2. **Launch Viewer.** The left-hand panel displays your computer's directory tree. Select the drive and folder that contain your files.

3. **Sort files.** In the Viewer's Tools menu, choose Sort > Sort by Date and Time Taken.

4. **Select All.** Press Control-A (Command-A on a Mac) to select all the files in the folder. Note that you must have at least 15 images to create a time-lapse movie.

5. **Commence processing.** In the Tools menu, choose Create Time Lapse Movie (see Figure 5.12, left).

6. **Select options.** The screen shown at right in Figure 5.12 appears. There are four adjustments you can make:

   - **Output method.** In general, you can leave the Apply Each RAW File's own settings to each RAW file marked. The app will use the parameters you specified in the camera for white balance, etc. If, for some reason, the RAW settings differ among your files, you can apply the parameters for an image you select (say, the first one in a sequence) and apply them to all subsequent frames.

   - **Save Format.** Here you can choose a color space and/or compression level for your video. I recommend going with the defaults. If you needed an extra-high-quality movie, you could change to Compression Level 1.

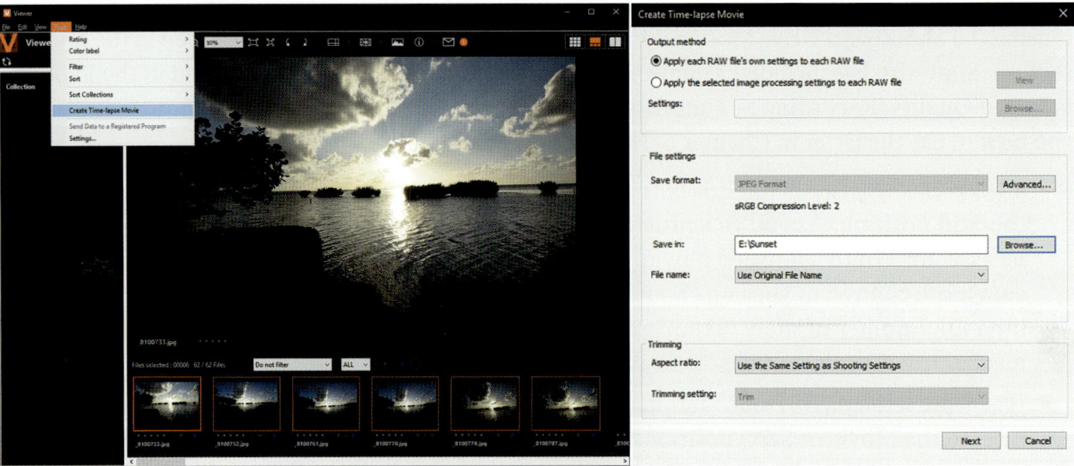

Figure 5.12 Select images and start the process (left). Select options (right).

- **Save To.** Select a folder to save your video to, and specify a filename. You can use the original filename or select various combinations of Date Taken, Date and Time Taken, and a 5-digit number generated by the program.

- **Trimming.** Here you can specify the aspect ratio of your movie. For greatest compatibility with other videos you may want to add or intercut, choose the 16:9 ratio standard for HD movies. You can also select 4:3, 3:2, or 1:1 aspect ratios, or tell the program to use whatever proportions the a7C II/a7CR was set to when the stills were captured.

7. **Click Next.** If you're working with JPEG still photos instead of RAW images, the program will suddenly come to the conclusion that no further processing (adjusting white balance and so forth) is required, and tell you "Some of the selected images will not be processed because they do not have to be developed or are in unsupported formats." Ignore this message if Sony's programmers haven't corrected this bug in your current release of the Imaging Edge software. The program will tell you which files it skipped (basically, all your JPEG images), and invite you to click Next once again to proceed.

8. **Edit settings.** The Edit screen, shown at left in Figure 5.13, appears. It has several options that you can reveal from drop-down lists:

- **Time Lapse Setting.** This panel is shown at far left in Figure 5.13. You can adjust playback speed from 1X to 16X, and view the total time recorded, although with the most recent copy of Viewer that I used, the speed didn't seem to vary as described. Look for a fix in a future update of the software.

- **Music.** Allows you to select music tracks on your computer, and to download additional music from Sony's website (see Figure 5.13, center right).

- **Music Settings.** Here you can balance the volume of the music you added with the soundtrack already recorded on your video. That allows you to have the music predominate, fade in, fade out, and/or loop continuously during playback (see Figure 5.13, far right).

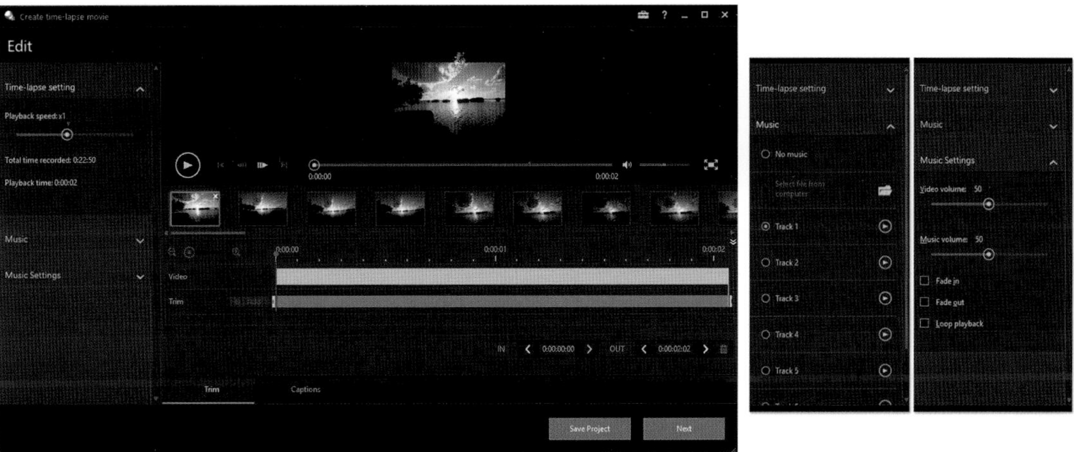

Figure 5.13 Edit time-lapse settings (left); add music (center right); select music settings (far right).

9. **Save your work or produce a movie.** You can stop working at this point and return to this point by clicking Save Project. It's a good idea to do this, just in case your final video needs to be tweaked and redone. When you're ready to produce your time-lapse clip, click Next.

10. **Specify filename, folder, and format.** When the Save screen shown in Figure 5.14 appears, you can type in a new filename for your movie, specify a different directory to save your file in, or choose one of three movie formats:

    - **4K.** This choice produces a 2160p/30 fps MP4 video clip in XAVC S format. (You can read about various video formats and parameters in Chapter 10.) You'll need a 4K-compatible display to view this UHD movie.

    - **Good for Viewing on a TV or Computer.** This is usually your best choice, as it delivers a 1080p/30 fps MP4 file in AVC format, viewable on any HDTV or modern-day computer screen that can handle Full HD.

    - **Smaller Size for Easier Uploading.** Choose this to create a Standard HD 720p/30 fps MP4 clip in AVC format. This creates a much smaller file that can be transferred over the Internet, and uploaded to YouTube more easily.

11. **Click Save.** The program will create your video clip and store it in the specified folder. The process may take some time, but a progress bar (seen at center in Figure 5.14) will keep you updated.

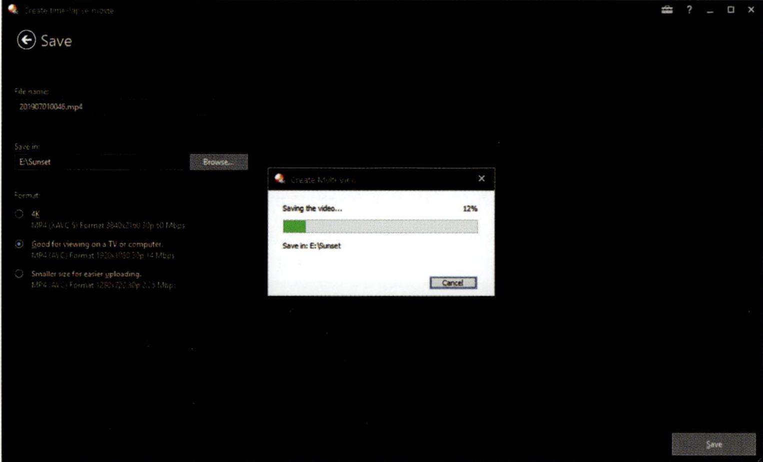

Figure 5.14 Choose filename, folder, and movie format.

Star Trails

Star trails are another great application for interval shooting. As I noted earlier, you can shoot the night sky using long exposures with your camera mounted on a tripod. However, because of the rotation of the Earth, longer exposures will record the apparent motion of the celestial objects through the sky, producing a light trail. If you use a very, very long exposure, the light trail will record as continuous streaks, centered around the Polaris (the North Star) in the northern hemisphere and Sigma Octantis (which is, unfortunately, too dim to be easily seen with the naked eye) in the southern hemisphere.

Such long exposures can result in excessive noise and sensor overheating, so it's more common for photographers to take a series of individual exposures and combine them to produce a single star trail image. If you want your stars to appear as reasonably sharp points, you'll need to keep the exposure short enough that their movement in the sky isn't apparent. Fortunately, there's a simple formula you can use to calculate that exposure time, the "500 Rule." Divide 500 by the focal length of your lens to determine the longest exposure (in seconds) before stars start to produce a blurred trail. For example, with a 50mm lens, the longest exposure would be 10 seconds (500 divided by 50). Capturing the complete canopy of stars generally requires a wider viewing perspective. With a 16mm wide-angle setting, exposures could be as long as roughly 30 seconds.

For Figure 5.15, I set my camera to ISO 200, and used a basic exposure of 30 seconds at f/5.6. I selected an interval of 32 seconds and 170 total exposures, which totals about 90 minutes. Then, I followed these steps, using Photoshop:

1. **Transfer files to a folder.** Select a folder on your computer, and copy all your files to that location.
2. **In Photoshop.** Choose Files > Scripts > Load Files into Stack.
3. **Browse to folder.** Click the Browse button and navigate to the folder where your images are stored.
4. **Click OK.** Photoshop will create a file with one layer for each of your captured images.
5. **Select All layers.** Then click Layer Blending Options from the Layers palette, and choose Lighten.
6. **Flatten image.** You'll want to flatten your image (the multi-layer file will be huge!). You'll end up with an impressive star trail image.

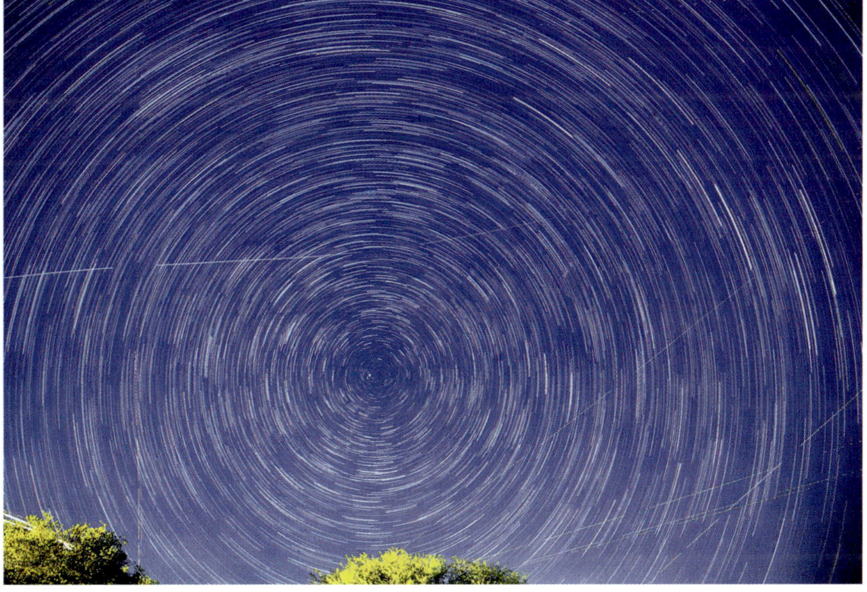

Figure 5.15 Capturing a star trail.

Focus Bracketing

Focus stacking—which Sony calls Focus Bracketing—is commonly used as a way of increasing the narrow depth-of-field commonly encountered when doing macro (close-up) photography of flowers or other small objects at short distances. In some cases, depth-of-field will be so narrow that it's impossible to keep the entire subject in focus. Although having part of the image out of focus can be a pleasing effect for a portrait of a person, it is likely to be a hindrance when you are trying to make an accurate photographic record of a flower, or small piece of precision equipment.

In a sense, Focus Bracket shooting can be considered like HDR translated for the world of focus—taking multiple shots with different settings, and, using software, combining the in-focus areas of each image in order to make a whole that is better than the sum of the parts. Focus stacking requires a non-moving object, so some subjects, such as flowers, are best photographed in a breeze-less environment, such as indoors. You can do focus stacking outdoors, and it can be a useful tool for deep-focus landscape images with important content much closer to the camera than conventional depth-of-field constraints would accommodate.

To use the feature, you must choose Focus Bracketing from the Drive mode options, then make a series of settings, which I'll describe in a how-to shortly. With the Focus Bracket option, the camera takes a series of pictures starting at a focus point you specify. The camera then adjusts the focus slightly between each image, refocusing from closest to your subject to infinity. You end up with a series of images that can be combined using two simple Photoshop commands, which I will describe shortly. Figure 5.16 can help you visualize what's going on. At left in the figure is a close-up of a box of crayons captured at f/2.8 and focused on the front rows. The center image shows the same crayons, but with the focus on the back rows. Focus Bracket takes as many as 299 separate exposures at different focus points in-between, and then merges them in a way that uses only the *sharpest* pixels in each individual image, as seen at right in the figure.

It's a shame, but most of the discussions you see about focus bracketing don't really explain the full potential and advantages of this powerful technique.

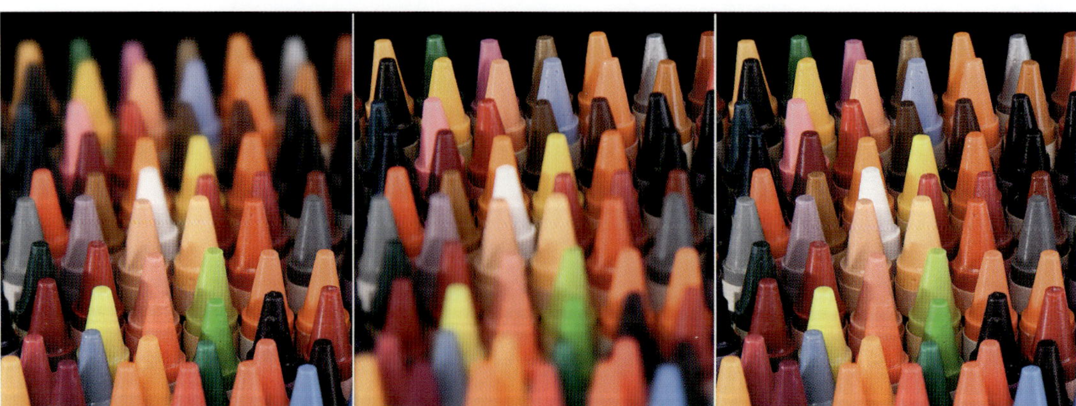

Figure 5.16 Images focused at the nearest focus planes (left) are combined with others at increasing distances, to a most distant point (center), and then merged to produce an image with extreme depth-of-field (right).

Here's a summary:

- **Focus bracketing increases depth-of-field.** Everybody knows this; it's the first thing associated with the technique. The second thing they think of is macro photography. But the process can be used for many other types of static subjects, including landscape and architectural photography.

- **Focus bracketing makes the best use of your lens' sharpness.** Yes, you can increase DOF without focus bracketing just by stopping down your lens to a smaller aperture. However, every lens has an optimum, sharpest, aperture. If you use a smaller f/stop you will lose sharpness due to *diffraction effects*. So, the increased *range* of sharpness comes at the cost of some definition. Apertures *wider* than a given lens' best f/stop will be less sharp due to uncorrected aberrations and other effects that are reduced at the optimum aperture.

  But with focus bracketing, each and every exposure in the stack can be made using the *sharpest* aperture setting available with that lens.

- **Focus bracketing can alleviate image noise effects.** You don't always have absolute control over the lighting you use, especially if you're working with electronic flash. So, if you shoot at f/32 to get maximum depth-of-field you may have to boost the ISO sensitivity to compensate, potentially to the point of increasing noise levels in your image. A single image shot at f/32 and ISO 1000 might have depth-of-field similar to a stack-focus image exposed at f/5.6 and ISO 100, but pixel-peepers may find the sharpness and noise qualities to be very different.

- **Focus bracketing provides unprecedented control over focus range.** You can choose exactly what areas of your image are in sharp focus, including some ways I discovered that are impossible to achieve under normal conditions.

  With focus shift shooting, you have dozens or hundreds of individual images to work with, each with a narrow plane of focus. You can, then, pick and choose exactly where your depth-of-field begins and ends with remarkable precision. If, for creative reasons, you want everything a millimeter in front of your main subject to be blurry, and everything a millimeter or more behind it to blur, you can do that, while keeping your subject tack sharp. When stacking your final image, all you have to do is not merge any of the frames in the area you want to be out of focus. This can lead to the extraordinary effect I describe in the next section.

Freaky Focus

I'd never seen this effect until I figured out how to do it, and it tends to blow people's minds at presentations I give. The three images shown in Figure 5.17 were all extracted from the same series of 100 shots created with a Focus Bracket sequence. Not all the results are what you might expect to see:

- At top is an image of some pottery, created using 100 images in a Focus Bracket sequence. As you can see, each of the pieces is in sharp focus. I discarded the shots focused behind and in front of the pottery, so those areas of the seamless background are blurred. The green arrows point to components that are in focus.

- For the center image, I discarded the frames shot of the bowl in the rear, so it ended up out of focus, while the four pieces in front of it are sharp. This demonstrates one way to control the extent of the sharply focused area.

- I got a little weird for the image at the bottom of the figure, discarding all the well-focused shots for the two pieces in the middle. This is a view you'll never, ever see in real life: a tableau of five elements with the *front* and *rear* pieces sharply focused, while the pieces in the middle are blurry. While you can do some nifty tricks with shift/tilt lenses, the only way you can achieve this particular effect (outside of tedious compositing) is by creatively manipulating sets of focus-stacked images.

I plan on playing with this some more. My next project is to set up some chess pieces so that alternating rows are in focus, while the rest of the rows are sharp.

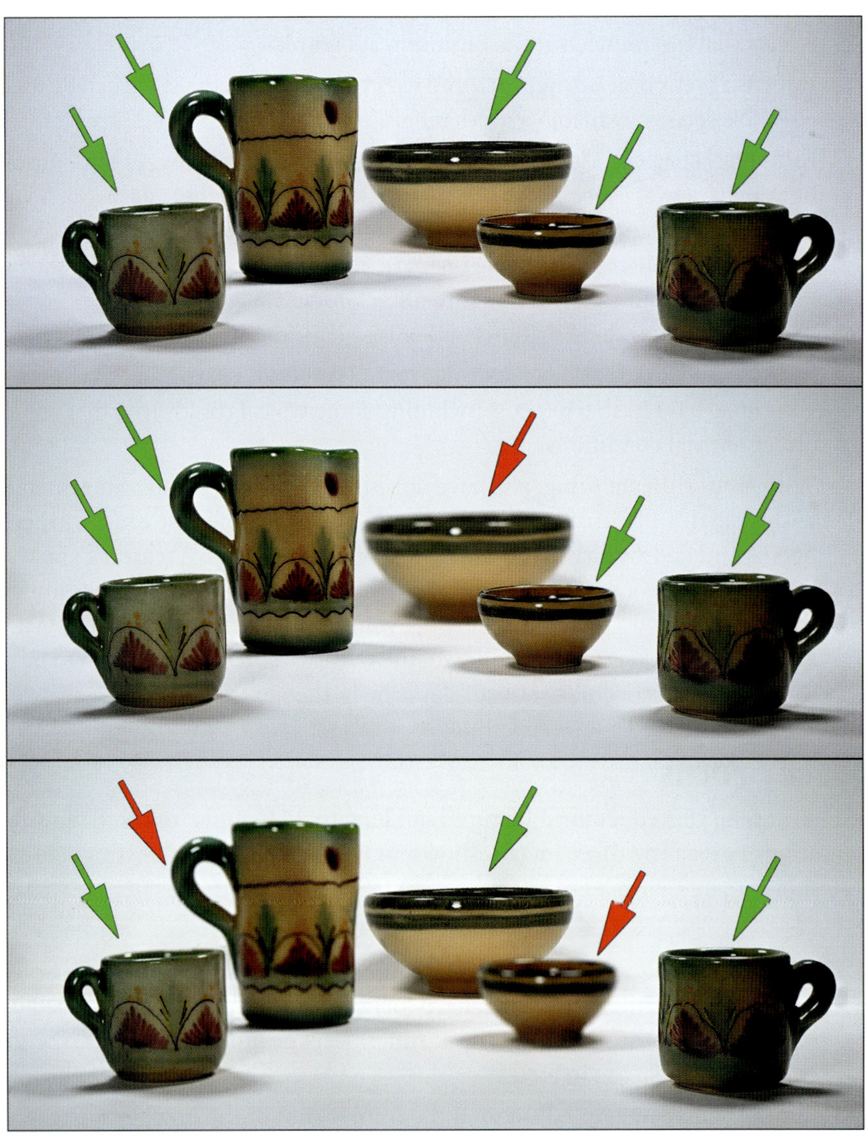

Figure 5.17 Freaky fun with Focus Bracket.

Focus Bracket How-To

Fortunately, producing a conventional focus-stacked image doesn't require my variety of unhinged thinking if all you want is enhanced depth-of-field. Here are the detailed steps you can take to use Focus Bracket shooting for your own deep-focus images:

1. **Set the camera firmly on a solid tripod.** A tripod or other equally firm support is absolutely essential for this procedure. You don't want the camera (or the subject) to move at all during the exposures.

2. **Use a remote release, if desired.** It's probably best if you trigger the camera without moving it. However, the procedure does pause for a short period of time once you activate it, perhaps giving your tripod/camera time to settle down.

3. **Attach a lens with an appropriate focus range.** Focus Bracket Shooting uses the lens's built-in autofocus motor, and so will not work with lenses that do not autofocus, including adapted lenses. Your lens must be one that focuses to the required distance, obviously.

4. **Set the focus modes.** Choose AF-S (single-shot) focus mode and Center Fix focus area.

5. **Set the quality of the images to JPEG Extra Fine.** You'll want the best-quality images for merging later on.

6. **Set the exposure, ISO, and white balance manually.** Use test shots, if necessary, to determine the best values.

   - **Maintain exposure.** Indoors, when lighting conditions are stable, by turning off autoexposure, Auto ISO, and Auto White Balance, you can prevent visible variations from arising among the multiple shots that you'll be taking. When shooting indoors, you don't want the camera to change exposure, the ISO setting, or white balance between shots. However, if you're *outdoors* where lighting may change, you may need to use Aperture Priority to keep a constant exposure.

   - **Avoid wide apertures, too.** As I said above, even though you'll be effectively increasing depth-of-field through focus bracketing, you should still avoid the *widest* apertures of your lens, as well as the smallest, as they are rarely the sharpest f/stops. In addition, because wide apertures do have less DOF, if you shoot at f/2.8, say, instead of f/5.6, the camera will need to capture more shots.

   - **Close down a few stops.** I always close down at least 1.5 f/stops. Shutter speed is not as important (and less so if you're using flash). Since the camera is on a tripod, ambient-light exposures won't add any blur from camera movement, but I tend to avoid very slow speeds anyway to keep the process speedy and efficient. You can manually set a slightly higher ISO sensitivity, if needed, to obtain the shutter speed/aperture combination you want to use.

7. **Avoid conflicting features.** Disable your camera's image stabilization features, including SteadyShot (in the camera body) and Optical SteadyShot (OSS, built into the lens), even when you are using lenses that can detect being mounted on a tripod.

8. **Set focus point to nearest point.** Use the directional buttons to position the focus point on the subject nearest the camera lens that you want to include. The less of the foreground you include in your set, the fewer shots you'll need to complete your sequence. Focus *slightly in front of that subject*. It's safer to include some of the out-of-focus foreground and discard those images.

9. **Access the Focus Bracket options.** Navigate to Shooting > Drive Mode > Drive Mode and press the right directional button to view the Drive Mode screen and scroll down to Focus Bracket. There, you can set:

   - **Step Width.** You can specify values from 1 (a narrow slice per adjustment) to 10 (a much wider focus change). (See Figure 5.18, left.) Sony does not specify how much each increment changes the focus, for a very good reason: it *can't*. Depending on the focal length of your lens and your f/stop, the effective plane of apparent focus may vary from narrow, to very narrow, to super-narrow in macro shooting environments. (If you're confused, see "Circles of Confusion" in Chapter 4.)

     You may need some trial-and-error to choose the correct number of shots and focus step width. For example, with 50 shots and a wide focus step, the first 10 may encompass your entire subject and the last 40 may be wasted on completely out-of-focus images. It's often worthwhile to take a test shot, view a slide show of all your images, and decide whether to increase/decrease the number of shots and/or focus step width.

     As a guideline, you should consider using a step width of 4 or 5 for distant subjects (e.g., landscapes) and smaller steps (1 or 2) for macro photos, because the changes in focus are large between steps with close-ups.

   - **Number of Shots.** You can choose from 0 to 299 individually refocused shots (see Figure 5.18, right). The number of images captured will depend on how finely you want to have the camera change focus between shots (and you'll combine this with the step-width option described next). For a subject with a lot of fine detail and depth (such as a macro shot of an insect), you'll want lots of images, a hundred or more, to record focus at many different planes. For architectural or landscape scenes taken with a wide-angle lens, you'll need fewer.

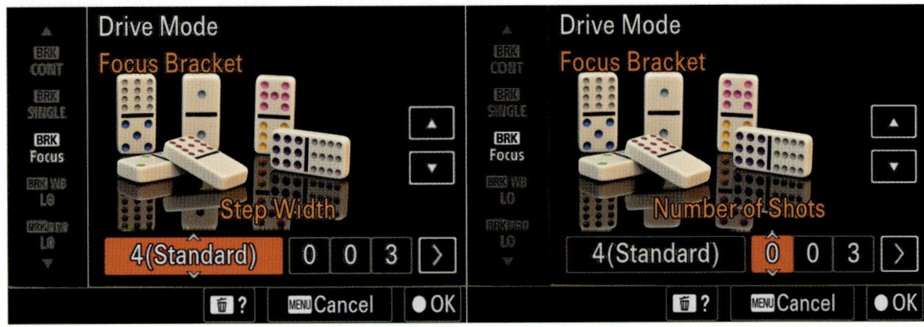

Figure 5.18 Specify width of steps (left) and number of shots to be captured (right).

10. **Advance to Focus Bracket Settings.** When finished, press the right directional button to view the next setting screen, shown in Figure 5.19. There, you can set:

    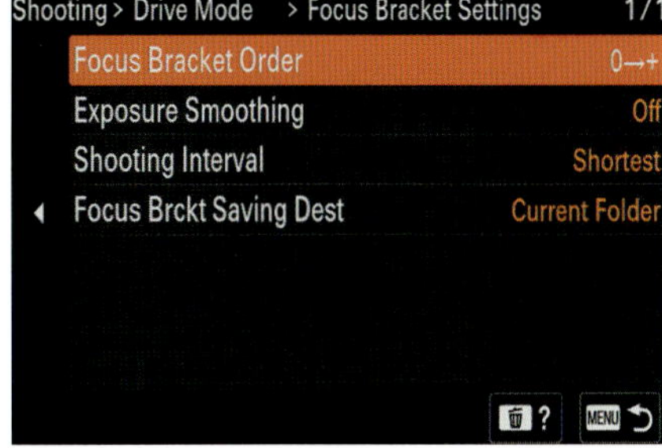

    Figure 5.19 Focus Bracket Shooting options.

    - **Focus Bracket Order.** Be careful with this one; it doesn't work like the bracket order command. It has two options:

        - **0 > +.** With this default setting, the camera starts the sequence at the closest focusing distance, and then takes a series of shots at increasing distances using the relative width you specified above until focus reaches infinity. The number of shots you requested will be taken, but may stop short of that number if infinity is reached first.

        - **0 >> +.** This setting tells the camera to take just three shots (ignoring the number you specified). The first shot is focused at the current focus position you set to start, the second at the front of your subject matter, and the third at the farthest position. I must admit I haven't figured out a situation in which this would be useful.

    - **Exposure Smoothing.** Because both camera and subject must be immobile, most focus bracketing takes place indoors where you have control over illumination. As I noted above, it can be used for landscape and architectural shots where keeping the same lighting can be problematic. If you turn exposure smoothing on, the camera will adjust exposure as necessary to keep the same brightness throughout the sequence.

    - **Shooting Interval.** You can select the interval between shots. Ordinarily, you'd want the shortest delay possible (given variables like shutter speed). So, Shortest is the default setting; you can also choose 1, 3, 4, 5, 10, 15, or 30 seconds. The shorter settings work well when shooting by ambient light that doesn't change. However, you can use flash, too. Just specify an interval that is *greater* than the maximum recycle rate of your flash. **Note:** Also consider how much your flash heats up when fired at brief intervals, particularly when the full power of the flash is needed for each shot. Multiple shots at close range in macro mode can work fine, because only a fraction of the flash's power is used for each exposure.

    - **Focus Bracket Saving Destination.** Choose Current Folder or New Folder to deposit your images in a new folder you specify. I can't think of a reason you would not want to do that. You could also reset file numbers to make it easier to differentiate between the first, last, and in-between images of your set.

11. **Capture images.** When all the parameters are locked in, start your exposure, by pressing the shutter release down all the way. The sequence ends when the number of shots you requested has been taken *or* focus reaches infinity. So, you may end up with many "extra" shots—or not—depending on your settings.

12. **Combine your images.** I'll describe the steps for that next.

The next step is to process the images you've taken in Photoshop. Transfer the images to your computer, and then follow these steps:

1. In Photoshop, select File > Scripts > Load Files into Stack. In the dialog box that then appears, navigate on your computer to find the files for the photographs you have taken and highlight them all.

2. At the bottom of the next dialog box that appears, check the box that says, "Attempt to Automatically Align Source Images," then click OK. The images will load; it may take several minutes for the program to load the images and attempt to arrange them into layers that are aligned based on their content.

3. Once the program has finished processing the images, go to the Layers panel and select all the layers. You can do this by clicking on the top layer and then Shift-clicking on the bottom one.

4. While the layers are all selected, in Photoshop go to Edit > Auto-Blend Layers. In the dialog box that appears, select the two options, Stack Images and Seamless Tones and Colors, then click OK. The program will process the images, possibly for a considerable length of time.

5. If the procedure worked well, the result will be a single image made up of numerous layers that have been processed to produce a sharply focused rendering of your subject. You can see the image captured at the closest focus distance, farthest distance, and the combined final image in Figure 5.20 (top, center, and bottom, respectively). If it did not work well, you may have to take additional images the next time, focusing very carefully on small slices of the subject as you move progressively farther away from the lens.

6. You'll want to flatten the final image before saving it. Given the 33- and 60-megapixel resolution of the a7C II and a7CR, the stack of individual shots will easily be more than 2GB, which exceeds the maximum file size of some older storage media and/or OS file systems. The a7CR, in particular, will produce some massive files.

Although this procedure can work very well in Photoshop, you also may want to try it with programs that were developed more specifically for Focus Bracketing and related procedures, such as Helicon Focus (www.heliconsoft.com), PhotoAcute (www.photoacute.com), or CombineZM (https://combinezm.informer.com/).

Pixel Shift (a7CR Only)

If the 60MP resolution of the a7CR isn't enough, that camera features an amazing Pixel Shift Multi Shooting capability that can mimic the amount of detail you might expect from a sensor with a whopping 240 megapixels! The limitations: the camera takes 4 or 16 separate pictures that are merged in the free Sony Imaging Edge software, and they must be captured with the a7CR rock-steady on a tripod, and I strongly recommend using a remote release.

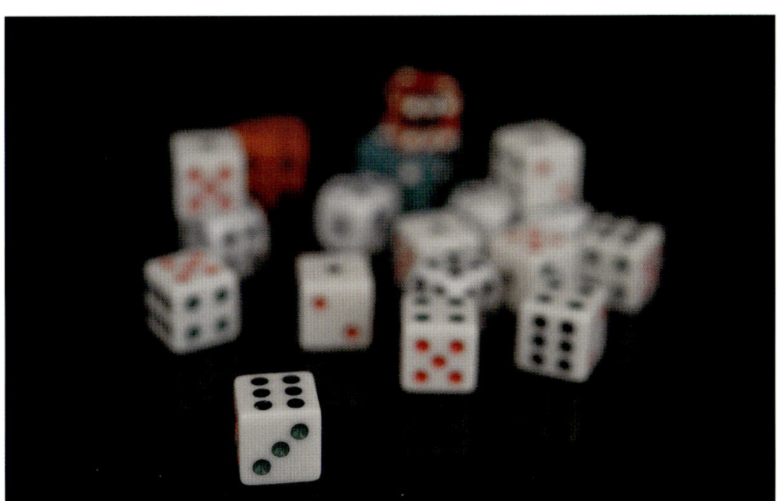
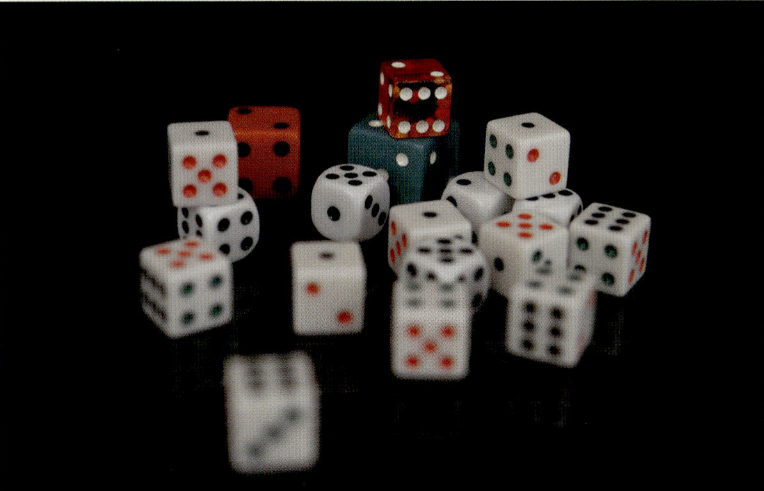
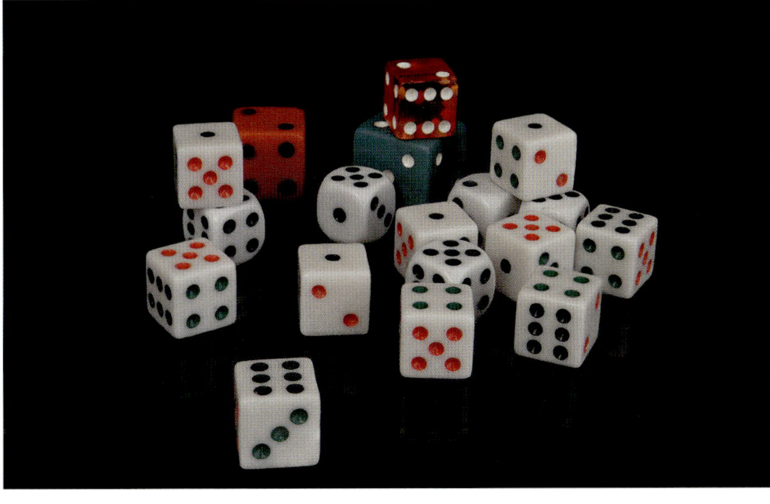

Figure 5.20 Closest point of sharp focus (top); furthest point of sharp focus (center); merged image (bottom).

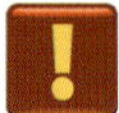

WARNING These large files can be quite taxing on your computer's resources. The 240MP test shot I use as an example in this chapter measured 19,008 × 12,672 pixels and occupied 690MB of space on my hard disk drive when converted to TIF format—almost 12X the disk real restate commanded by the same scene captured as an .ARW raw file!

If you intend to work with these massive styles frequently, it may be worth upgrading the amount of RAM in your computer. I already had Adobe Photoshop running as quickly as possible on my 2TB solid-state boot drive, so I added a second SSD internally and designated it as Photoshop's "scratch" disk. Now Photoshop is able to perform most operations on my a7CR's image files without resorting to slow magnetic memory frequently.

The secret behind the pixel-shift process is that your a7CR doesn't actually have 60MP of resolution in the first place. It does have 60MP worth of pixels, but each pixel can only detect one color—red, green, or blue. When you capture a conventional picture, about 15MP are sensitive *only* to blue light, another 15MP detect only red light, and 30MP are sensitive to green light. Even though each pixel captures only one of the three RGB colors, by examining the values of surrounding pixels, the a7CR can make a pretty good guess as to the actual color of a particular pixel through an interpolation process called *demosaicing*. The algorithms may tell the camera that a pixel captured by a green-sensitive photosite is probably red or blue instead. This works fairly well, but, as you might think, isn't perfect.

Figure 5.21 shows a small section of a Bayer array, named after Kodak scientist Dr. Bryce Bayer, who patented the technology in 1976. He specified using twice as many green elements as red or blue to simulate human vision, which, in daylight, combines two different types of cells in the retina that are most sensitive to green light. At left, I've superimposed the array's red, green, and blue microfilters over a representation of the photosensitive layer beneath, which is colored gray for the illustration. At right in the figure, I show how the pixels are arranged: every other pixel is green, and the remaining pixels are red or blue, alternating rows.

While each pixel detects only one of the primary colors in ordinary shooting, the pixel-shift process fixes this deficiency by capturing *multiple* images, shifting the sensor slightly between shots so that each photosite has the opportunity to read each of the primary colors in turn. In four-shot mode, the camera captures four separate images. The first shot produces the standard image that results from non-shift mode. Then, the sensor moves by one pixel after each of three more images to capture information such that all colors are captured by every photosite. The result is a higher degree of detail without the need to "guess" which colors each pixel represents.

Figure 5.21 A section of a Bayer array (left) and relative distribution of the red, green, and blue filters (right).

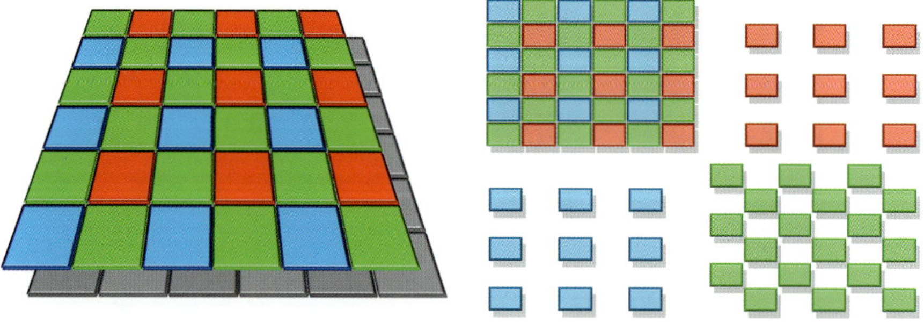

In 16-image pixel-shift mode, the a7CR also starts by shooting four images centered around one pixel. Then, the camera shifts the sensor *half a pixel* sideways and takes four more images; then half a pixel more for an additional four images. The process is done two more times, giving you 16 separate images that can be processed to provide the detail you'd get from a 240-megapixel sensor. That's a huge amount of information, prodigious enough that the camera cannot process it internally (and you wouldn't want to wait that long between shots even if it could). So, the Imaging Edge Viewer's software interprets these multiple shots for you, to produce a single image in which every pixel reflects the actual color of your subject. You get more detail and potentially more accurate color at the cost of a little post-processing.

Capturing Your Images

Pixel shift works *only* with non-moving, static subjects, and neither the camera nor subject matter can move *at all* during the sequence of exposures. For that reason, you'll get the best results shooting indoors, as there are many factors outdoors that can cause subject/camera movement, even when a tripod is used. For example, you'd need to pay special attention to foliage; if there is any breeze at all, the leaves on trees will move. Using a high shutter speed may help somewhat, but, like MPG, your actual results may vary considerably between different sets of shots when working outdoors.

The plane of focus must not change, either, so you should use manual focus. The exposure itself should be constant, so I recommend manual exposure when using ambient lighting, as long as the illumination itself remains constant. Outdoors, swiftly moving clouds can cause changes in lighting, and indoors you'll find that fluorescent and other non-incandescent sources flicker slightly. I've found that Sony's electronic flash units work well, even in automatic exposure mode, and can provide consistent illumination between shots (if you set the interval between them appropriately, as described in Step 4 below).

FLASH NOTE

When using a dedicated flash unit, the a7CR's flash sync speed (explained in Chapter 13) *is automatically fixed at 1/8th second*, because the Pixel Shift mode uses the camera's electronic shutter. If you are using a "dumb" flash, such as a studio flash unit connected through the a7CR's PC/X connection (described in Chapter 2) or with a trigger attached to the camera's flash/accessory shoe, you should set the shutter speed to 1/8th second manually.

Keep in mind that if you are using a "dumb" flash, change the Shooting > Shooting Display > Live View Display Set > Live View Display setting to Off. Otherwise, the a7CR will base the preview image on the exposure provided by the ambient light, and may produce a viewfinder/monitor image that is too dark.

To capture a pixel-shift image, just follow these steps:

1. **Activate.** In the Shooting > Drive Mode > Pixel Shift Multi Shooting entry the screen shown in Figure 5.22 appears.

2. **Select parameters.** You can choose among Off, Shoot 4 Shots, or Shoot 16 Shots.

3. **Number of shots.** I recommend starting with four-shot sequences to help you master the pixel-shift feature. The exposures are made quickly, and the files are smaller and are combined faster in Imaging Edge's Viewer module. You'll rapidly see how and where your technique can be improved.

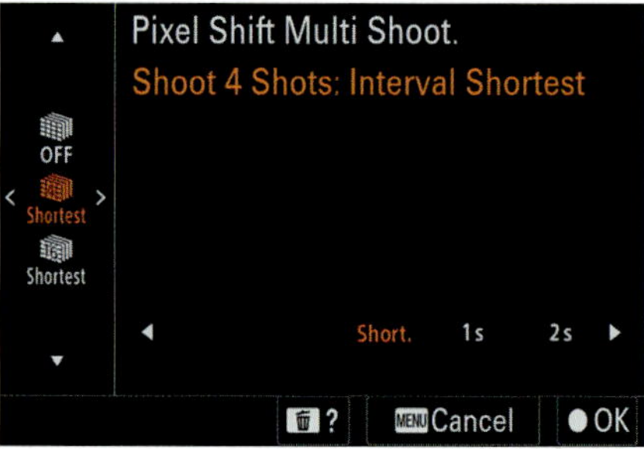

Figure 5.22 Choose Pixel Shift parameters.

4. **Interval between shots.** When your choice of 4 or 16 shots is highlighted, use the left/right controls to choose the amount of delay between shots. Your options include:

   - **Shortest.** Use this default setting to capture all the images continuously, one after another. This is usually your best choice, because it minimizes the chance of even slight movement of your subject between shots.

   - **Delays of 1–30 seconds.** You can also select specific delays of up to 30 seconds. Select a longer pause if you plan to use flash. Just set the time for the amount of time it takes for your flash to recycle; you can err on the side of caution if using battery-powered units, which may have varying recycle times.

5. **Check your lighting.** Indoors, I use incandescent light or flash instead of fluorescent illumination; the flickering fluorescent lighting can produce banding in your image. Keep in mind that softer lighting (such as that produced by umbrellas, soft boxes, diffusers, or bounce lighting) reduces glare but may mask that extra detail you're looking for. More contrasty illumination (generally, direct lighting) can emphasize detail—and also any defects in your subject matter.

6. **Set your exposure.** Manually set your exposure for ambient light and illumination from a "dumb" (say, studio-type) flash. The shutter speed should be 1/8th second or slower. If you're using a dedicated flash unit, the camera will set the shutter speed for you.

7. **Mount your camera on a rock-solid tripod.** If possible, use only the legs of the tripod to achieve the shooting elevation you want, and avoid raising the center column. Lock all the tripod's positional controls. If you're using a lightweight tripod, suspend your camera bag or another weight from the center column to steady it. In my tests I discovered that even almost imperceptible movement (which can be produced simply by pressing the a7CR's shutter release too vigorously) can ruin a series. The tip-off: a slight amount of blurring in the first shot of a series, or a "ghost" image from ambient light when using flash, compared to the additional exposures, taken after a short delay.

8. **Some settings are automatic.** You can turn SteadyShot off if you like, but when Pixel Shift is active it is automatically disabled. The a7CR also switches to silent shooting (again, to reduce camera vibrations) and uncompressed RAW, regardless of how you have the camera set. As I've noted twice before, silent shooting requires a shutter speed no faster than 1/8th second if you're using electronic flash.

9. **Manually focus to get the sharpest possible image.** Your extra resolution is wasted if you haven't focused properly. I use the Focus Magnifier to ensure tack-sharp focus.

10. **Connect the a7CR to a remote release device or cable.** You'll want to eliminate any camera shake caused by pressing the shutter release manually. I use the Sony RM-VPR1 remote control with the multi-terminal cable. Do this even if you plan to expose using electronic flash. During my tests *without* a remote release, I noticed that in the first shot of each sequence, the main exposure from the flash was augmented by some ambient-light "ghost images" (explained in Chapter 13). My solution was to use the RM-VPR1 remote *and* reduce the room's ambient light for good measure.

11. **Trigger the shutter to take your 4 or 16 images.** Don't touch the camera between shots.

Processing Your Pixel-Shift Exposures

Once you've captured your images, transfer them to your computer and launch the Imaging Edge software (which you can download from the Sony website in your country). Then, just follow these steps:

1. **In the Viewer module**, browse to your images in the panel shown at left in Figure 5.23, which features a directory/folder tree.

2. **Choose images to process.** Select one image of the 4 (or 16). The software "knows" which of the additional images belong to the complete sequence, so you don't have to select them individually. Right-click and select Create and Adjust Px. Shift Multi Shoot.

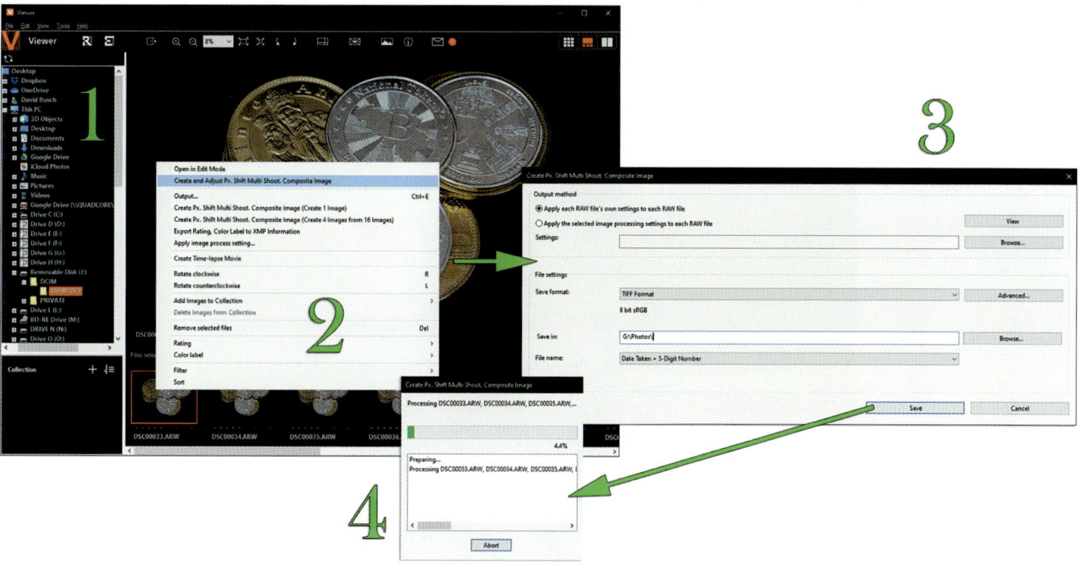

Figure 5.23 1. Navigate to the folder containing your images. 2. Choose pixel-shift processing. 3. Enter parameters. 4. Watch as images are combined.

3. **Enter parameters.** In general, you can set the parameters once and use them for future pixel-shift processing if you want to standardize:

   - **Output method.** Click Apply Each RAW File's Own Settings to Each RAW file. You'd use the alternate only if you wanted a specific set of adjustments and follow the instructions to override your original settings.

   - **File settings.** Select the Save Format for the combined image. I often use TIFF, because it can be opened by virtually all image-editing software utilities. Choose ARQ, which is Sony's proprietary pixel-shift format if you want to be able to access a full range of adjustments in Imaging Edge or Lightroom.

   - **Save In.** You can select a directory/folder to store your images, and a filename convention (either the original filename, or a combination of filename, date, and a number).

4. **Click Save.** A dialog will pop up showing you the images are being combined, and you'll be notified when the process is completed.

The software will create a composite image with the resolution shown in Figure 5.24. It's difficult to illustrate just how detailed the processed images are on the printed page, but you'll be amazed when you try this feature for yourself.

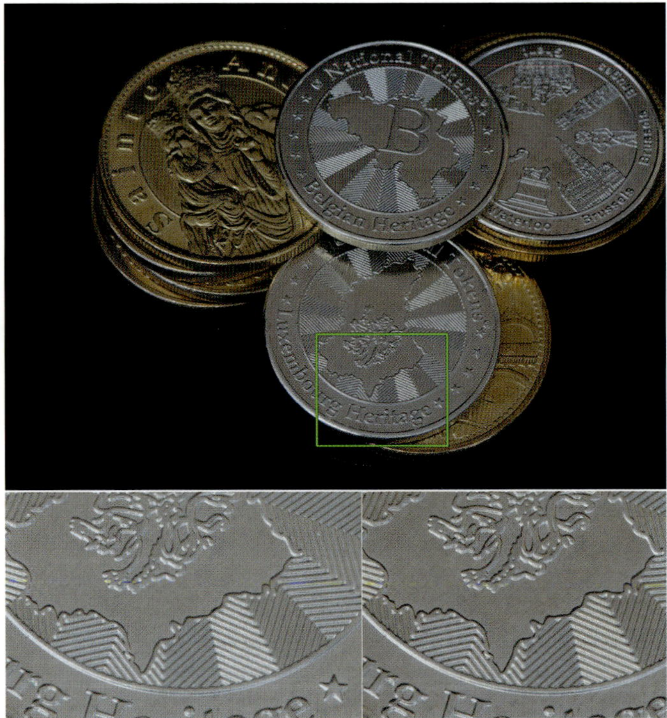

Figure 5.24 The final composite image (top); an enlargement of the original image (lower left); and the pixel-shift version (lower right).

My Menu, Main Menu, and Shooting Menu

6

This chapter and the three that follow provide in-depth coverage of all the commands and options available from the a7C II and a7CR's revamped menu system, which includes eight top-level menu *tabs*, each with multiple numbered *groups*, which contain the individual *entries* and their *options*.

Many of the explanations in these chapters expand on the descriptions found in other parts of this book. I integrate the technical discussions with the how-to instructions using cross-references. That makes it easier to absorb the important basics first, and access the menu reference chapters only when you really need to see every possible option.

Menu Navigation

I introduced you to the updated Sony menu system in Chapter 1, and labeled each of the main components of a typical menu in Figure 1.10. To recap, each menu consists of the elements shown in Figure 6.1:

- **Top-level menu tabs.** The eight top-level menu tabs are shown in the first column in Figure 6.1, left. They are the My Menu tab (represented by a star icon), followed by the Main menu tab (house), Shooting menu (camera), Exposure/Color (+/– sign), Focus (AF/MF), Playback (right arrow), Network (globe), and Setup (toolbox).
- **Numbered groups.** Also in Figure 6.1, left, you can see that the Image Quality/Rec (Recording) group is highlighted. Below it are six of the other groups in the Shooting menu tab: Media, File, Shooting Mode, Drive Mode, Shutter/Silent, and Image Stabilization. An additional three groups, Zoom, Shooting Display, and Marker Display, appear when you scroll down.

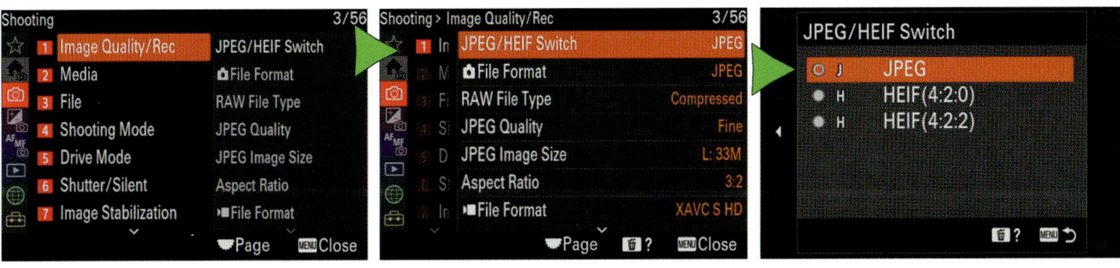

Figure 6.1 The Menu hierarchy.

- **Menu entries.** Each individual group has its own roster of entries. In Figure 6.1, center, you can see seven of the fourteen entries that reside in the Shooting > Image Quality/Rec group. The entries shown include JPEG/HEIF Switch, File Format, RAW File Type, JPEG Quality, JPEG Image Size, Aspect Ratio, and File Format. Again, you'll need to scroll down within the group to see all the entries.

- **Entry options.** When you select one of the menu entries within a numbered group, the available options for that entry appear, as shown at right in Figure 6.1. Some options screens will contain several sub-entries with choices of their own.

- **Stills/Movies.** Some menu entries can be accessed only when the Still/Movie/S&Q dial is set to the Still Photo position, or one of the two Movie positions (Movie and S&Q [Slow and Quick]). I'm going to specify whether a particular entry can be accessed from a given Still/Movie/S&Q dial position by adding (Stills) or (Stills/Movies) after the entry name. Note that while some entries can be adjusted in *all* modes (such as Shooting > Image Quality/Rec > Movie Settings), you may have to switch to the appropriate mode (e.g., Movie mode) to access all the options.

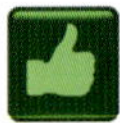

TIP I will use the menu hierarchy I just described to direct you to a specific entry, for example:

Shooting > Image Quality/Rec > JPEG/HEIF Switch > Options

or, I may use:

JPEG/HEIF Switch entry within the Shooting > Image Quality/Rec group

As you work with your a7C II/a7CR, you'll learn which menu entries reside in which tab and group. They're color-coded and arranged so that related functions are associated with an appropriate top-level tab and group within that tab. Use the up/down controls (such as the top and bottom edges of the control wheel) to move up and down within the main/primary menu tabs, groups, and options. Press the center button to select the highlighted item. Press the MENU button to back out. If you're in a hurry, the front dial can be used to move up and down main menu tabs; the rear dial will navigate up/down among or within groups.

- **My Menu (Gray).** You can set up your own customized menus to reside here, installing the entries from any of the other tabs for quick access. The tab initially has just one group, My Menu Setting, with options that allow you to add/delete, sort, and arrange pages of favorite entries. I'll explain using My Menu in this chapter.

- **Main Menu (White).** This special menu has no groups or individual entries in the conventional sense. Instead, it provides an array of 18 different settings, including exposure controls, focus settings, etc., that you can access quickly from a single screen.

- **Shooting (Red/Orange).** This tab has ten groups (you'll need to scroll down to the last three of them). The groups include commands for handling image quality, recording media and files, shooting modes, USB streaming, drive modes, shutter option, image stabilization, optical/digital zoom, and shooting display. This tab is also covered in this chapter.

- **Exposure/Color (Pink).** Includes seven groups with options for exposure, metering, flash, white balance, color rendition, and overexposure warnings. I explained about exposure and color control in Chapter 3, and will detail the menu choices available in Chapter 7.

- **AF/MF (Violet).** Here you'll find five groups with all the controls you need to set focus parameters and the aids which make focusing more accurate and convenient. Chapter 4 described the a7C II and a7CR's autofocus and manual focus systems, and I'll explain focus setting options in Chapter 8.
- **Playback (Blue).** This tab has seven groups of entries that will enable you to review, manage, edit, and delete the photos you've taken. These are all explained in Chapter 8.
- **Network (Green).** The a7C II and a7CR include a broad range of Wi-Fi, Bluetooth, and wired LAN options, all controlled through the eight groups of entries within this tab. You'll find what you need to know in Chapter 9.
- **Setup (Yellow).** These highly customizable cameras have a host of options you may not use on an everyday basis, such as Area/Date settings, custom control definitions for various dials and buttons, USB connectivity, and output to external monitors and recorders. You'll need to scroll down to access all 13 groups found in this tab. I'll explain Setup options in Chapter 9.

My Menu Tab

Options: Add Item, Sort Item, Delete Item, Delete Page, Delete All, Display From My Menu
My preference: N/A

The My Menu feature lets you create your own customized menu containing the entries you use most often, which can save you a lot of time wading through the many pages of menu tabs and entries. You can create up to six My Menu screens, each with as many as seven menu items, for a total of 42 My Menu entries. So, you can find you've created *your own* maze of entries—but, at least, it is *your* maze.

Virtually any menu entry from the other main menu tabs (except for the Playback menu) can be added to your personalized menu. You can even specify that your custom My Menu will appear first when you press the MENU button.

The first time you access My Menu, no custom pages will exist, so you'll see a screen similar to the one shown at upper left in Figure 6.2, except all the entries apart from Add Item will be grayed out. Press the center button, and you'll be shown a screen with a list of menu entries (see Figure 6.2, upper right). Use the directional controls to scroll among available menu pages, and highlight a particular entry you want to add. (See Figure 6.2, center left.) Press the center button and you'll be given the opportunity to choose which page to add it to, numbered from 1 through 6, and its position within that page. (See Figure 6.2, center right.)

You don't need to fill up one page before starting another one. Conceivably, you could have six My Menu pages, each with a single entry. After you've created a new My Menu page, the My Menu Setting command function page (Add, Sort, etc.) moves to the end of the line. Each newborn My Menu page will look something like Figure 6.2 (bottom), but with your personal entries included. My only beef with Sony is that all your custom pages are named My Menu 1, My Menu 2, etc. It would be really cool to assign them specific appropriate names, such as Sports or Landscapes (say, to group all settings you use frequently when shooting sports or landscapes).

Figure 6.2 Adding My Menu functions.

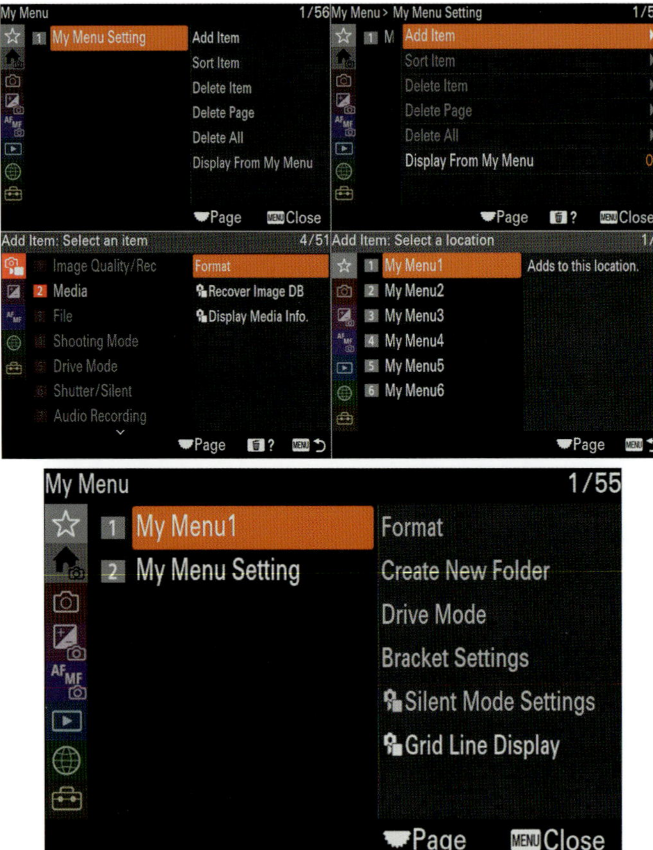

The additional options available include:

- **Sort Item.** Highlight a My Menu item and press the center button. You can then use the up/down controls to move it within its current menu, or the left/right controls to transport it to a different My Menu page.

- **Delete Item/Delete Page/Delete All.** Highlight an entry or page and press the center button to remove that item or page from My Menu. Delete All will remove all your My Menu items so you can start from scratch.

- **Display From My Menu.** This setting is Off by default. When enabled, pressing the MENU button will produce the My Menu entry you last accessed. For example, if you change shutter types frequently, a press of the MENU button would take you to that setting immediately.

Main Menu Tab

This menu tab is the only one that has no groups or individual entries. Instead, it provides a screen of 18 adjustable settings, as if it were an expanded Function (Fn) or For Viewfinder menu. (See Figure 6.3.) When the Main menu is displayed, you can tap the icon of a setting to produce the adjustment screen for that setting. (Setup > Touch Operation > Touch Operation must be set to On.) Alternatively, you can highlight the setting and press OK to invoke the settings screen.

Although the Main menu tab offers more choices than the Fn menu, it cannot be customized, nor set to display on the LCD screen all the time while you use the viewfinder to compose (which is one of my favorite uses of the For Viewfinder display).

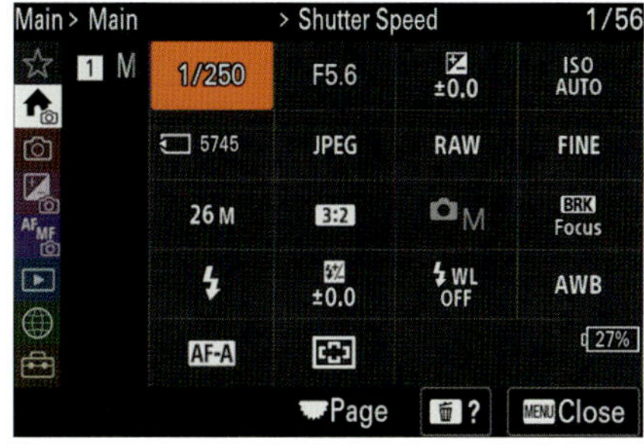

Figure 6.3 The Main menu offers 18 different settings that can be accessed quickly.

Shooting Menu Tab

The Sony a7C II/a7CR's red-coded Shooting tab menus have 10 groups when the Still/Movie/S&Q dial is set to the Still Photography position. Each group is devoted to specific adjustments that are most likely to be made during a given session. They are as follows:

1. Image Quality/Recording
2. Media
3. File
4. Shooting Mode
5. Drive Mode
6. Shutter/Silent
7. Image Stabilization
8. Zoom
9. Shooting Display
10. Marker Display

The first four groups in the Movie-oriented tabs have exactly the same names and numbers. This chapter covers all the menu entries shared in common by the Still Photography and the two video modes, Movie and S&Q. However, when the Still/Movie/S&Q dial is set to the Movie or S&Q positions, the numbering changes and there are additional groups shown. The Movie-only entries are boldfaced below. I'm going to save descriptions of the Audio Recording, TC/UB, Marker Display, and Shooting Option groups for Chapters 10 and 11, which are dedicated to movie topics.

1. Image Quality/Recording
2. Media
3. File
4. Shooting Mode
5. Shutter/Silent
6. **Audio Recording (Movie-only entry)**
7. **TC/UB (Movie-only entry)**
8. Image Stabilization
9. Zoom
10. Shooting Display
11. Marker Display
12. **Shooting Option (Movie-only entry)**

1. Image Quality

Here you'll find 14 entries (see Figure 6.4). These entries allow you to choose parameters that directly affect image quality, including image file format, aspect ratio, two types of noise reduction, HLG settings, color space, and lens aberration compensation. In the listings that follow, default values are indicated in bold with an asterisk before the option name. Note that some entries have additional sub-entries; in those cases, I'll list only the top-level choices and not show default values for the multiple entries in the extra screens. The Image Quality entries in Still mode are:

- JPEG/HEIF Switch
- (Still) File Format
- RAW File Type
- JPEG Quality
- JPEG Image Size
- Aspect Ratio
- (Movie) File Format
- (Movie) Movie Settings
- APS-C Super 35 Shooting
- Long Exposure NR
- High ISO NR
- HLG Still Image
- Color Space
- Lens Compensation

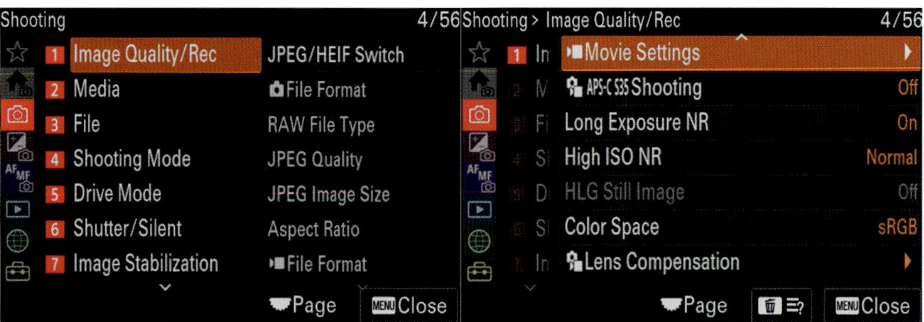

Figure 6.4 Image Quality settings.

JPEG/HEIF Switch 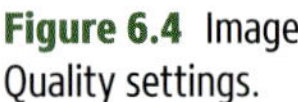

Options: *JPEG, HEIF (4:2:0), HEIF (4:2:2)
My preference: JPEG

For most users, I recommend sticking with the default value, JPEG, unless you have a special need for the features of HEIF (high-efficiency image file) format, such as creating still images that will match HLG (hybrid-log gamma) video (discussed later in this chapter). In this book I will, for the most part, use JPEG as an example for most functions. You can assume that in nearly all cases HEIF can be substituted for JPEG even if I don't use "JPEG/HEIF" terminology every time. If JPEG or HEIF *only* apply, I will point that out.

Apple's iOS 11 operating system for its smart devices was the first consumer product to use the HEIF format. In a nutshell, HEIF images use an advanced compression scheme to produce files with higher image quality that may be only half the size of JPEGs, and have more features, including transparency and 16-bit color. The downside is that, as I write this, only Apple's Safari browser supports it natively, and many software applications as well as operating systems like Windows and Android need updates to accommodate HEIF. For example, Photoshop CC releases have required HEIF Image Extensions and HEVC Video Extensions support tools from the Microsoft Store, and had a tendency to recognize these files only if the extension is .HEIF (not the .HIF Sony uses). Macs need macOS High Sierra or later to interpret HEIF images.

If you're using a recent iPhone with HEIF, it can convert your images to JPEG automatically when you export them but will use the format to deploy special features internally (say, for live images). Sony has integrated its free HEIF Converter (which can create both JPEG and TIFF images from HEIF files) into the functionality of Imaging Edge software for both Windows and macOS. So, while HEIF may eventually replace JPEG (last updated in 1994), the transition will take many years. The good news is that, if you need HEIF files, you can create them now with your Sony a7C II or a7CR.

This entry, shown earlier in Figure 6.1, center and right, gives you three choices:

- **JPEG.** This option creates highly compressed 8-bit images using 4:2:0 color (described next). Some image quality is lost, but virtually all applications are compatible with the files produced. On average, a JPEG file is about 28MB in size.

- **HEIF (4:2:0).** You end up with 10-bit images using 4:2:0 color, also highly compressed, but typically about a third the size of your average JPEG file. The image is *encoded* using a procedure called *chroma subsampling,* which does reduce the amount of information that needs to be transferred.

  Chroma subsampling takes advantage of the fact that human beings don't detect changes in color (chroma) as easily as they do for brightness (luma). The designation 4:2:0 simply indicates that the full amount of brightness information is passed along ("4") while half the information ("2") is sampled in the horizontal direction, and the vertical information is ignored entirely ("0").

- **HEIF (4:2:2).** Also creates highly compressed 10-bit files using 4:2:2 encoding in which every other horizontal pixel and every other vertical row are sampled. Subsampling in this way reduces the size of the otherwise uncompressed image (which would be expressed "4:4:4"), with virtually no visual difference. You'll end up with files that are even smaller than their JPEG counterparts.

Just remember that HEIF images may not be viewable or editable by everyone if their equipment or software don't support it. Note that, by default, HEIF images are always recorded using the sRGB color space, except when the Shooting > Image Quality > HLG Still Image setting is set to On, in which case the BT.2020 color gamut is used. I'll explain HLG and Color Spaces later in this chapter.

File Format

Options: RAW, RAW & JPEG/(HEIF), ***JPEG**/(HEIF)
My preference: RAW & JPEG

Should you select RAW, JPEG (or its HEIF alternative), or both? You can elect to store only JPEG versions of the images you shoot, or you can save your photos as "unprocessed" RAW files, which consume several times as much space on your memory card. Or, you can store both file types at once as you shoot. Note that to open a RAW file, you must have an image editor or RAW processor capable of converting the RAW file to editable form. The free Sony Imaging Edge software can do this for you; Photoshop, Lightroom, Photoshop Elements, and other programs compatible with Adobe Camera Raw (ACR) can also make the conversion for you.

Many photographers elect, as I do, to shoot *both* a JPEG and a RAW file (RAW & JPEG), so they'll have a JPEG version that might be usable as is, as well as the original "digital negative" RAW file in case they will later want to make some serious editing of the photo with imaging software for reasons discussed shortly. If you use the RAW & JPEG option, the camera will save two different versions of the same file to the memory card: one with a .JPG extension, and one with the .ARW extension that signifies Sony's proprietary ARW RAW format that consists of raw data.

The RAW Deal

You'll sometimes be told that RAW files are the "unprocessed" image information your camera produces before it's been modified. That's nonsense. RAW files are no more unprocessed than old-school camera film is after it's been through the chemicals to produce a negative or transparency. A lot can happen in the developer that can affect the quality of a film image—positively and negatively—and, similarly, your digital image undergoes a *significant* amount of processing before it is saved as a RAW file. Sony even applies a name (BIONZ XR) to the digital image processor used to perform this magic in its latest Sony cameras.

A RAW file is closer in concept to a film camera's processed negative. It contains all the information, with no compression (in the Uncompressed RAW version), no sharpening, and no application of any special filters or other settings you might have specified when you took the picture. Those settings are stored with the RAW file, so they can be applied when the image is converted to JPEG, HEIF, TIFF, or another format. However, using RAW converter software such as Adobe Camera Raw (in Photoshop, Elements, or Lightroom) or Sony's Imaging Edge software (available for download from various Sony websites worldwide), you can override a RAW photo's settings (such as White Balance and Saturation) by applying other settings in the software. You can make essentially the same changes there that you might have specified in your camera before taking a photo.

Making changes to settings such as White Balance is a non-destructive process in a RAW converter since the changes are made before the photo is fully processed by the software program. Adjusting settings does not affect image quality, except for changes to exposure, highlight or shadow detail, and saturation; the loss of quality is minimal however, unless the changes you make for these aspects are significant. The RAW format exists because sometimes we want to have access to all the information captured by the camera before the camera's internal logic has processed it and converted the image to a standard file format.

A RAW photo does take up more space than a JPEG and, in uncompressed or lossless compressed modes, preserves all the information captured by your camera after it's been converted from analog to digital form. Since we can make changes to settings after the fact while retaining optimal image quality, errors in the settings we made in-camera are much less of a concern than in JPEG (or HEIF) capture. When you shoot in these formats, any modification you make in software is a destructive process; there is always some loss of image quality, although that can be minimal if you make only small changes or are skilled with the use of adjustment layers.

JPEG/HEIF formats provide smaller files by compressing the information in a way that loses some image data. The lost data is reconstructed when you open the file in a computer, but this is not a perfect process. If you shoot at the highest quality (Extra Fine) level (Quality choices are explained below), the compression (and loss of data) is minimal; you might not be able to tell the difference between a photo made with RAW capture and a Large/Extra Fine image. If you use the lower quality level, you'll usually notice a quality loss when making big enlargements or after cropping your image extensively.

So, why don't we always use RAW? Although some photographers do save only in RAW format, it's more common to use either RAW plus the JPEG/HEIF option or to just shoot JPEG/HEIF and eschew RAW altogether. While RAW is overwhelmingly helpful when an image needs to be modified, working with a RAW file can slow you down significantly. The RAW images take longer to store on the memory card, so you cannot shoot as many in a single burst. Also, after you shoot a series, the camera must pause to write them to the memory card, so you may not be able to take any shots for a while (or only one or two at a time) until the RAW files have been written to the memory card. When you come home from a trip with numerous RAW files, you'll find they require more post-processing time and effort in the RAW converter, whether you elect to go with the default settings in force when the picture was taken or make minor adjustments.

Those who often shoot long series of photos in one session, or want to spend less time at a computer, may prefer JPEG over RAW. Wedding photographers, for example, might expose several thousand photos during a bridal affair and offer hundreds to clients as electronic proofs on a flash drive, their websites, or an old-school DVD (for those still using those legacy media). Wedding shooters take the time to make sure that their in-camera settings are correct, minimizing the need to post-process photos after the event. Given that their JPEGs are so good, there is little need for them to get bogged down working with RAW files in a computer. Sports photographers also avoid RAW files because of the extra time required for the camera to record a series of shots to a memory card and because they don't want to spend hours in extra post-processing. As a bonus, JPEG files consume a lot less memory in a hard drive.

My recommendation: When shooting sports, I'll switch to shooting Large/Extra Fine JPEGs (with no RAW file) to minimize the time it takes for the camera to write a series of photos to the card; it's great to be able to take another burst of photos at any time, with little or no delay. I also appreciate the fact that I won't need to wade through long series of photos taken in RAW format.

In most situations however, I shoot virtually everything as RAW & JPEG. Most of the time, I'm not concerned about filling up my memory cards, as I usually carry at least three 128GB memory cards with me. If I know I may fill up all those cards (say, on a long trip), I'll also carry a notebook computer and an external 4 terabyte hard drive to back up my files.

RAW File Type

Options: Uncompressed, Lossless Compressed (Large, Medium, Small), *****Compressed**
My preference: Compressed

This option allows selecting Uncompressed; Lossless Compressed (in Large, Medium, or Small resolutions); or Compressed. The Lossless Compressed (Large) setting is available only when shooting full frame (rather than APS-C/Super 35 mode). All RAW files are typically extended dynamic range 14-bit files. During Continuous Shooting, if RAW file type is set to Compressed, the camera stores 12-bit files instead.

Note that RAW files are always saved in the 3:2 aspect ratio. If you are shooting RAW & JPEG/HEIF, only the JPEG or HEIF version will be saved in a different aspect ratio selected with the Aspect Ratio entry discussed shortly.

Increased file size translates into less storage space on your memory card (and computer), and a longer wait while your camera's buffer clears after a continuous sequence. (Using a faster UHS-II memory card instead of a slower UHS-I card can make your buffer last longer.) I recommend using Compressed because it's almost impossible to detect differences between Compressed and Uncompressed files.

JPEG Quality

Options: Extra Fine, *Fine, Standard, Light

My preference: Extra Fine

To reduce the size of your image files and allow more photos to be stored on a given memory card, the camera's processor uses JPEG compression to squeeze the images down to a smaller size. This compacting reduces the image quality a little, so you're offered your choice of Extra Fine, Fine, and Standard compression. Standard compression is quite aggressive; the camera discards a lot of data. While Fine is, well, just fine, you'll find that Extra Fine provides even better results, so it should really be your *standard* when shooting JPEG photos. The more compressed versions lose detail, forever, that you can never regain—the price you pay for saving some storage space. The Light option produces files that may be 1/10th the size of their Extra Fine counterparts. Unless your final images are only going to be emailed over a wireless connection as, say, documentation (rather than edited or printed), it's not worth it.

For most work, extra compression (or lower resolution, described next) is false economy. You never know when you might need that extra bit of picture detail. Your best bet is to have enough memory cards to handle all the shooting you want to do until you have the chance to transfer your photos to your computer or a personal storage device. In my tests, the actual file size for a JPEG file can vary quite a bit, depending on the content of the image (large areas, such as sky, with little detail compress more efficiently). The typical JPEG Extra Fine, Fine, Standard, and Light files were 14MB, 5.2MB, 3.1MB, and 2.1MB, respectively.

If you're using HEIF format instead of JPEG, the same choices are available, and the file sizes are typically 1/4th to 1/5th the size.

JPEG/HEIF Image Size

Options (a7C II). *Large: 33M, Medium: 14M, Small: 8.2M

Options (a7CR). *Large: 60M, Medium: 26M, Small: 152M

My preference: Large

Here you can choose between the a7C II/a7CR's Large, Medium, and Small settings for JPEG still pictures. The larger the size that's selected, the higher the resolution: the images are composed of more megapixels. As you scroll among the options, you'll note that the size for Large, Medium, and Small is displayed in megapixels, as shown for the a7C II/a7CR in Tables 6.1 and 6.2. The number of pixels will vary, depending on the *aspect ratio* you've chosen, as illustrated in the tables. (I'll explain aspect ratios next.)

TABLE 6.1 Image Sizes Available (a7C II)

IMAGE SIZE	MEGAPIXELS 3:2 ASPECT RATIO	RESOLUTION 3:2 ASPECT RATIO	MEGAPIXELS 4:3 ASPECT RATIO	RESOLUTION 4:3 ASPECT RATIO	MEGAPIXELS 16:9 ASPECT RATIO	RESOLUTION 16:9 ASPECT RATIO	MEGAPIXELS 1:1 ASPECT RATIO	RESOLUTION 1:1 ASPECT RATIO
FULL FRAME								
Large (L)	33MP	7008 × 4672 pixels	29MP	6224 × 4672 pixels	28MP	7008 × 3944 pixels	22MP	4672 × 4672 pixels
Medium (M)	14MP	4608 × 3072 pixels	13MP	4096 × 3072 pixels	12MP	4608 × 2582 pixels	9.4MP	3072 × 3072 pixels
Small (S)	8.2MP	3504 × 2336 pixels	7.3MP	3120 × 2336 pixels	6.9MP	3504 × 1968 pixels	5.5MP	2336 × 2336 pixels

TABLE 6.2 Image Sizes Available (a7CR)

IMAGE SIZE	MEGAPIXELS 3:2 ASPECT RATIO	RESOLUTION 3:2 ASPECT RATIO	MEGAPIXELS 4:3 ASPECT RATIO	RESOLUTION 4:3 ASPECT RATIO	MEGAPIXELS 16:9 ASPECT RATIO	RESOLUTION 16:9 ASPECT RATIO	MEGAPIXELS 1:1 ASPECT RATIO	RESOLUTION 1:1 ASPECT RATIO
Large (L)	60MP	9504 × 6336 pixels	54MP	8448 × 6336 pixels	51MP	9504 × 5344 pixels	40MP	6336 × 6336 pixels
Medium (M)	26MP	6240 × 4160 pixels	23MP	5552 × 4160 pixels	22MP	6240 × 3512 pixels	17MP	4160 × 4160 pixels
Small (S)	15MP	4752 × 3168 pixels	13MP	4224 × 3168 pixels	13MP	4752 × 2672 pixels	10MP	3168 × 3168 pixels

There are some limited advantages to using the Medium and Small resolution settings, and similar space-saving benefits accrue to the Standard JPEG compression setting. All these options help stretch the capacity of your memory card, so you can shoehorn quite a few more pictures onto a single card. That can be useful when you're away from home and are running out of storage, or when you're shooting non-critical work that doesn't require full resolution (such as photos taken for real estate listings, web page display, photo ID cards, or similar applications).

Navigate to the Shooting > Image Quality/Rec > JPEG (or HEIF) Image Size menu item, press the center button, and scroll to the desired option: L, M, or S. Then press the center button to confirm your choice. As I noted, the actual size of the image depends on the aspect ratio you have chosen in the subsequent menu item (discussed below).

There are few reasons to use a size other than Large with either camera, even if reduced resolution is sufficient for your application, such as photo ID cards or web display. Starting with a full-size image gives you greater freedom for cropping and fixing problems with your image editor. An 800 × 600–pixel web image created from a full-resolution (large) original can end up better than one that started out as a small JPEG.

Of course, the Medium and Small settings make it possible to squeeze more pictures onto your memory card. The smaller image sizes might come in handy in situations where your memory cards are almost full, and/or you don't have the opportunity to offload the pictures you've taken to your computer. For example, if you're on vacation and plan to make only 4 × 6–inch snapshot prints of the photos you shoot, setting a lower resolution will stretch your memory card's capacity. Even then, it makes more sense to simply buy and carry memory cards with higher capacity and use your a7C II/ a7CR camera at its maximum resolution. The most compelling reason to shoot at a lower resolution is if you need to post-process a large number of images with a slower computer (including one with limited RAM) and find that the a7CR's 60MP files require more computing resources than your system has.

Aspect Ratio

Options: *3:2, 4:3, 16:9, and 1:1 aspect ratios

My preference: 3:2; you can always crop to any of the others in your image editor

The aspect ratio is simply the proportions of your image as stored in your image file. The standard aspect ratio for digital photography is approximately 3:2; the image is two-thirds as tall as it is wide, as shown at upper left in Figure 6.5. These proportions conform to those of the most common snap-shot size in the USA, 4 × 6 inches. Of course, if you want to make a standard 8 × 10–inch enlarge-ment, you'll need to trim some of the length of the image area since this format is closer to square; you (or a lab) would need 8 × 12–inch paper to print the full image area. The 3:2 aspect ratio was also the norm in photography with 35mm film. The a7C II and a7CR also support the 4:3 ratio used in Panasonic and OM System (Olympus) Micro Four Thirds cameras (see Figure 6.5, upper right).

If you're looking for images that will "fit" a wide-screen computer display, or a high-definition televi-sion screen, you can use this menu item to switch to a 16:9 aspect ratio, which is much wider than it is tall. (See Figure 6.5, lower left.) The camera performs this magic by cutting off the top and bottom of the frame, and storing a reduced-resolution image (see Table 6.1 and 6.2). If you need the wide-screen look, this menu option will save you some time in image editing, but you can achieve the same proportions (or any other aspect ratio) by trimming a full-resolution image with your software. The 16:9 option is most useful if you plan to take a *lot* of photos that will work best in that format. For example, if you're creating a storyboard for a video production, still images taken in this format will match the proportions of 4K and HD movies. As I noted earlier, only the JPEG/HEIF version

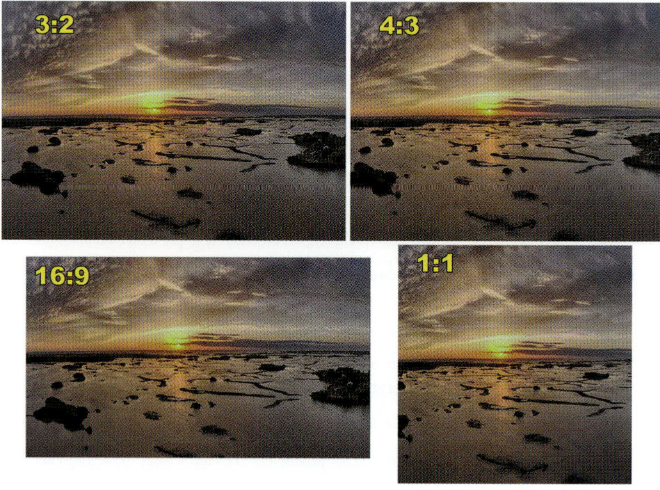

Figure 6.5 Available aspect ratios for still photos: 3:2 (upper left); 4:3 (upper right); 16:9 (lower left); 1:1 (lower right).

of a shot is cropped; the RAW file retains its full image area, which can be trimmed by your RAW converter when you import the image into your image editor.

You can also choose the square 1:1 aspect ratio, shown in Figure 6.5, lower right. Although the square format was popular during the film era for twin-lens reflexes and many professional cameras like early Hasselblads, it enjoyed a resurgence thanks to the popularity of Instagram. Although Instagram now supports both vertical and horizontal formats, the traditional square format remains popular. It's been calculated that more square Instagram photos are taken each day than for all other formats *combined*.

(Movie) File Format

Options: XAVC HS 4K, XAVC S 4K, *XAVC S HD*, XAVC-I 4K, XAVC-I HD
My preference: XAVC S HD

The a7C II and a7CR offer 4K UHD and Full HD (high-definition) video recording in several formats. The camera will display a warning that this is a basic movie setting if the Still/Movie/S&Q switch is in the Still position. Press OK to continue. By default, movies are recorded in XAVC S HD, but this menu item allows you to choose other formats. I'm going to save most of the technical details for the movie chapters (Chapters 10 and 11), but there are three major differences between the choices offered in this menu entry:

- **Codec.** The 4K HS format uses the HEVC (High-Efficiency Video Coding) codec (coder/decoder). Also known as H.265, this software produces higher image quality with the same size files as the other settings, which use the less-efficient H.264 (Advanced Video Coding) codec. The HEIC still photo format is based on HEVC, which is why images captured in that format will better match video captured using the HEVC codec.

- **Resolution.** The 4K and full HD formats provide 3840 × 2160 and 1920 × 1080 pixel resolution, respectively.

- **Movie compression format.** The first three file formats offered use long GOP (group of pictures) interframe compression. The last two, XAVC-I 4K and XAVC S-I HD, use All-I compression.

  With long GOP compression, one I-frame (intraframe) is recorded that contains all the information for a frame, minimally compressed. The next frame after this *key frame* is called a B-frame, and it stores *only the changes* from the I-frame, which greatly reduces the amount of information that must be kept. It may be followed by another B-frame, and then a P-frame, which just predicts what the actual frame should look like based on the information from the previous frames, and, eventually, the next I-frame. This type of compression is sometimes called IPB Compression, after the Intra, Predictive, and Bidirectional frame types.

  The XAVC-I 4K and XAVC S-I HD formats use All-I compression, in which each frame is an Intra or key frame. All-I compression produces larger files and the capability of the camera to support the higher transfer rate they demand, but they are more friendly for editing, particularly for those who are doing tight, frame-by-frame editing. For example, if you are capturing a video at a wedding and a still photography flash burst occurs at an inopportune time, you can edit out that particular frame.

Movie Settings

Options: Recording Frame Rate: ***60p/50p**, 30/25p, 24p, 120/100p; Record Setting: Bit rate, Color Sampling, Bit Depth.

My preference: XAVC S HD: 60p 50M 4:2:2 8 bit

The camera will display a warning that this is a basic movie setting if the Still/Movie/S&Q switch is in the Still position. Press OK to continue. This item allows you to choose from various parameters including:

- **Recording Frame Rate.** Choose from 60p, 30p, 24p, or 120p. Note that the frame rates differ between countries using the NTSC system, such as the US, Japan, and some other countries, and those using PAL. In locations using the PAL system, 25, 50, and 100 frame rates replace 30, 60, and 120 fps, respectively. I'll explain frame rates, scanning, and bit rates in Chapters 10 and 11.

- **Record Setting.** Select from a broad range of combinations of bit rates, color sampling, and bit depths, shown in five tables starting on page 278 of the Sony Help Guide. The three parameters, from left to right are:
  - **Bit rate.** This is the rate at which your video is transferred to the memory card or recorder. Faster transfer rates generally correspond to higher quality, depending on the amount/type of compression, and also place more demands on your camera and storage.
  - **Color sampling.** I described the difference between 4:4:2 and 4:4:0 color sampling earlier in this chapter, under the JPEG/HEIF Switch entry. It applies here, too.
  - **Bit depth.** This describes the number of bits used to record information. Formats using 4:4:2 color sampling use 10 bits of data per frame, for up to 1,024 tone levels (gradation) per channel possible. The assumption is made that the video will be displayed and/or edited on a computer that can handle that depth. In contrast, 8-bit video can capture only 256 levels per channel, but it is compatible with a wide variety of playback options.

S&Q Settings

Options: Record Frame Rate: ***60p**, 30p, 24p, 120p (NTSC); Frame Rate: 240, ***120**, 60, 30, 15, 8, 4, 2, 1 frames per second; Record Setting: Bit Rate, Color Sampling, Bit Depth

My preference: N/A

This entry is available only when the Still/Movie/S&Q dial is in one of the two movie positions. It is a great feature if you want to shoot some slow motion movies as a special effect, analyze the dynamics of a particular motion, or speed up a sequence to provide a humorous herky-jerky appearance. Sony's implementation of high/slow frame rate photography, which it now calls slow-motion/quick-motion, allows you to capture a *silent* (no sound) slow-motion video at up to 120 frames-per-second rate (100 fps for PAL). It will play back 4X or 5X slower, depending on whether you select 30p/25p or 24p as your Record Setting option within this menu entry. You can also record at slower speeds (down to 1 frame per second) for speeded-up, Charlie Chaplinesque footage.

Here are your options (shown in Figure 6.6), and how it works:

- **Record Frame Rate (Playback rate).** This parameter is labeled a bit misleadingly. It determines the *playback* speed of your video clip and, therefore, how much of a slow-motion/fast-motion effect you will see when viewing the movie. Your choices are 120p, 60p, 30p, or 24p when using the NTSC television system. Think of this setting as a *factor,* which, when dividing the Frame Rate, determines the motion effect you get. All will become clear in a moment.

- **Frame Rate (Capture rate).** Here you select the number of frames per second captured in S&Q mode. You can select 120, 60, 30, 15, 8, 4, 2, and 1 frames per second. (Scroll down to find the last two options.) When the frames per second is divided by the record setting, you will arrive at the slow-motion effect or speed factor. I'll show you some typical results next.

- **Record Setting.** Choose the bit rate, color sampling, and bit depth of your S&Q recording.

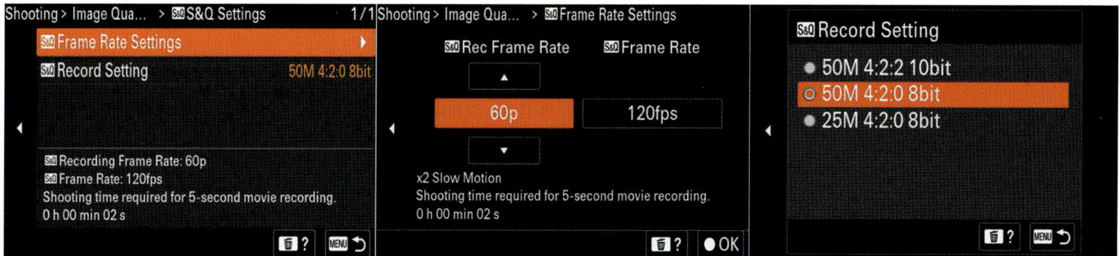

Figure 6.6 S&Q Options.

OH SHOOT!

By default, when the Still/Movie/S&Q dial is set to S&Q, you can choose this entry to capture slow-motion or quick-motion effects. Sony gives you the option of changing the behavior of the entry so that time-lapse photography (discussed next) is performed instead. To toggle between the two, use Shooting > Shooting Mode > Shoot Mode when the Still/Movie/S&Q dial is in the S&Q position, as described later in this chapter.

Slow-Motion

When you capture video at any frame rate and then play it back at a *slower* frame rate, the result is slow-motion. For example, if you choose 120 fps for the frame rate, a 10-second video will include 1,200 individual frames (120 fps × 10). If you've chosen 30 fps for your Record Setting, those frames will require 40 seconds to play back (1,200 frames divided by 30). The playback time is increased 4X. Other playback times involve different amounts of slow-motion: 24 fps gives you 5X playback. Table 6.3 shows the amount of slow-motion or quick-motion you get with each combination of capture frame rates from 1 to 120 frames per second, and playback settings of 120, 60, 30, and 24 frames per second.

Quick-Motion

Frame rates *slower* than 30 fps give you speeded-up quick-motion instead of slow-motion. For example, with a frame rate of 4 frames per second you'll capture just 40 frames in 10 seconds. When viewed at a record setting of, say, 24 fps, that 10-second clip will be compressed into only 1.7 seconds of viewing time. Obviously, because of the speed-up factor, you'll get the maximum effect when you shoot longer sequences that can be displayed very, very quickly. Look over Table 6.3, and the explanation that follows, to calculate your own slow-/quick-motion effects. For clarity, I've labeled what Sony calls Record Frame Rate as Playback.

TABLE 6.3 Slow-Motion/Quick-Motion Effects

CAPTURE FRAME RATES	120P PLAYBACK RATE	60P PLAYBACK RATE	30P PLAYBACK RATE	24P PLAYBACK RATE
120 fps	1X standard speed	2X slow-motion	4X slow-motion	5X slow-motion
60 fps	2X quick-motion	1X standard speed	2X slow-motion	2.5X slow-motion
30 fps	4X quick-motion	2X quick-motion	1X standard speed	1.25X quick-motion
15 fps	8X quick-motion	4X quick-motion	2X quick-motion	1.6X quick-motion
8 fps	15X quick-motion	7.5X quick-motion	3.75X quick-motion	3X quick-motion
4 fps	30X quick-motion	15X quick-motion	7.5X quick-motion	6X quick-motion
2 fps	60X quick-motion	30X quick-motion	15X quick-motion	12X quick-motion
1 fps	120X quick-motion	60X quick-motion	30X quick-motion	24X quick-motion

To calculate the *slow-motion* effects you can look forward to, multiply any of the figures labeled "slow-motion" by the number of seconds captured in your original clip. For example, if you shot a two-minute, 120 fps sequence and played it back at 30p (4X slow-motion), you'd need 8 minutes to watch the whole thing. Going the other way, a two-minute clip captured at 4 fps and played back at 30p, would zip by in four seconds of frantic action.

Obviously, in real life you probably won't be shooting slow-motion video for two whole minutes (a golf swing or sports action sequence can be captured in a few seconds) and will be shooting quick-motion, time-lapse-like clips (such as a blooming flower or the march of the stars across the night sky) for longer periods so you'll have time to enjoy what you see. As you work with this cool feature, you may have to experiment to see which combination of frame rate capture speeds and the three possible playback speeds that work best for you in a given situation. Also, keep in mind that many video-editing programs can handle clips captured at various frame rates and output them at a different rate for playback.

When shooting slow-motion video, TC Run and TC Output (under TC/UB Settings, described later) are disabled. And, obviously, fast frame rates require shorter shutter speeds, so be ready to boost your ISO settings, if necessary, to cope.

Time-lapse Settings

Options: Frame Rate: ***60p/50p**, 30/25p, 24p; Interval Time: ***1 second**, 2–10 seconds, 20, 30, 40, 50, 60 seconds; Record Setting: Bit Rate, Color Sampling, Bit Depth; Video Light Setting: ***Off**, 2, 5, 10 seconds

My preference: N/A

Time-lapse shooting has had the distinction of long being one of the most desired features for Sony's E-mount mirrorless cameras. Until recently, you needed an external intervalometer device or a special app to capture individual shots at regular intervals—say, to take progressive photographs of a flower opening. Now, Sony has gifted us with *two* different ways of capturing time-lapse video, using this entry, and one called Interval Shooting Functions, described later in this chapter. Here's the difference between them:

- **Time-lapse settings.** This entry is available *only* when the Still/Movie/S&Q dial is set to the Movie or S&Q position. It allows you to choose a frame rate, interval between shots, record setting, and video light setting. It captures a series of frames and then assembles them into a time-lapse movie automatically.

- **Interval Shooting Functions.** This entry is available *only* when the Still/Movie/S&Q dial is set to the Still position. Sony considers this to be a still photo function, and deposits the entry in the Shooting > Drive Mode group along with continuous shooting and bracketing. Interval shooting captures a series of frames that you must assemble yourself into a finished movie, using the steps described in Chapter 5. This version is more versatile; you can also choose a shooting start time, number of shots taken, autoexposure adjustments, whether to use the electronic or mechanical shutter, and the interval priority. (I'll detail these options later in this chapter.)

Here are the parameters you can specify for time-lapse movies (see Figure 6.7 upper left):

- **Frame Rate Settings.** Here you can choose the frame rates, from 24p to 30/25p to the default 60/50p. You can also choose the amount of time elapsed between individual frames. The default value is one second, but you can choose 2 to 10 seconds, plus 20-, 30-, 40-, 50-, and 60-second intervals. (See Figure 6.7, upper right.) Note that the full range of times is available only for HD recordings; intervals longer than 5 seconds cannot be selected when shooting 4K time-lapse movies.

- **Record Setting.** Choose the bit rate, color sampling, and bit depth of your time-lapse recording. (See Figure 6.7, lower left.)

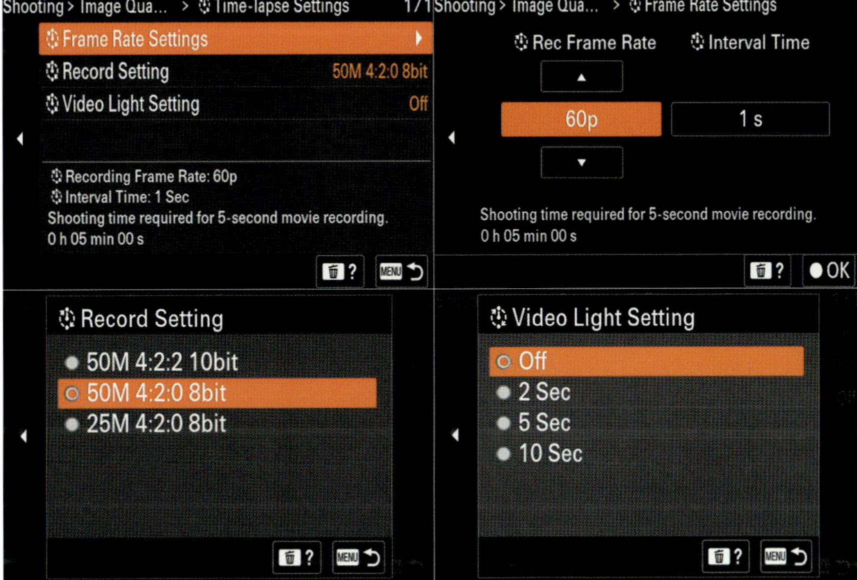

Figure 6.7 Time-lapse settings.

- **Video Light Setting.** You may want to illuminate your scene with an optional compatible video light, such as the Sony HVL-LBPC LED light. That may be a good idea indoors or in any environment in which the light changes—and you don't want to record the light transitions in your time-lapse movie. (Dawn-to-dusk videos are especially dramatic and you *want* to include the progression throughout the day.)

  If you do use a video light, you can control when it turns on or off or remains dim during shooting (see Figure 6.7, lower right):

  - **Off.** The video light is not controlled and will remain on at all times during shooting, even when the camera is on Standby.
  - **2/5/10 Seconds.** The video light is illuminated when the camera is on standby and is turned off when not recording. However, it will light up 2, 5, or 10 seconds before recording begins after each interval. This ensures the light is on during every exposure. **Note:** If Setup > Setup Option > Video Light Mode is set to REC Link&STBY, the light will dim rather than shut off completely. I'll explain video light modes in more detail in Chapter 9.

Keep in mind that the camera will become warm during long recording periods, especially when ambient temperatures are high. Heat buildup can occur even when the interval between recording is fairly long. You can reduce the amount of heat generated by reversing the LCD monitor so it faces the camera back and will thus be automatically disabled, and navigating to Network > Network Option > Airplane Mode, which disables Wi-Fi. You can then expect to record for as long as 120 minutes using XAVC S HD video formats or only 60 minutes with XAVC S 4K video. When Setup > Power Setting Option > Auto Power OFF Temperature is set to High, recording time may be increased. For long recordings, an external power source may be necessary.

Log Shooting Setting

Options: Log Shooting: ***Off**, On (Flexible ISO); Color Gamut: ***S-Gamut3.Cine/S-Log3**, S-Gamut3/S-Log3; Embed LUT File: ***On**, Off

My preference: N/A

I discuss Log shooting and LUTs in a little more depth in Chapters 7 and 11, and won't go into detail here. Your choices are:

- **Log Shooting.** When set to Off, the a7C II/a7CR uses Picture Profiles or Look-Up Tables (LUTs). Choose On (Flexible ISO) to use one of the two Log types, as described next. The Flexible ISO notation is a reminder that ISO sensitivity can be changed from the Base 800 (which is not the case with some Log formats not available for the a7C II/a7CR).
- **Color Gamut.** Select either S-Gamut3.Cine/S-Log3 or S-Gamut3/S-Log3.
- **Embed LUT File.** If you choose On, then the Look-Up Table selected in Exposure/Color > Color/Tone > Select LUT will be used during playback (as described in Chapter 7).

Proxy Settings ▣ ▣ S&Q

Options: Proxy Recording: On, *Off; Proxy File Format: XAVC HS HD, **XAVC S HD**; Proxy Recording Settings: 16M 4:2:0 10 bit, **9M 4:2:0 10 bit**

My preference: On, XAVC S HD

If you like, you can record a compact, low-bit-rate version of your XAVC S movies simultaneously while capturing your main movie. Although lower in quality, these "proxy" recordings are suitable for emailing, display on a smartphone or tablet, or uploading online. Your choices include:

- **Proxy Recording.** Select On or Off, depending on whether you feel you need that second, compact copy.

- **Proxy File Format.** Choose higher quality XAVC HS HD to save a proxy video file at full HD (1920 × 1080) resolution or XAVC S HD standard HD (1280 × 720). The same frame rate selected for the main video will be used (that is, 60/50p, 30/25p, or 24p). You cannot create a proxy video file when using the 120/100p frame rate.

- **Proxy Recording Settings.** If you choose the Full HD 1920 × 1080 resolution option under Proxy File Format, you can specify either 16M 4:2:0 10-bit video or extra-compressed 9M 4:2:0 10-bit video. The standard HD proxy uses a 6M 4:2:0 8-bit transfer rate.

The proxy recordings are tucked away under the PRIVATE\M4ROOT\SUB folder on your memory card. A "Px" label appears over a main movie's icon during image review to indicate that a proxy movie was recorded at the same time (the proxy itself cannot be displayed or edited in-camera). Any time you delete the main movie from your memory card the proxy is erased, too.

APS-C/S35mm Shooting ▣ ▣ S&Q

Options: On, **Auto**, Off

My preference: Auto

This entry tells the a7C II or a7CR whether to automatically switch to the APS-C/Super 35mm "crop" mode when a lens not designed for full-frame coverage is mounted on the camera. (APS-C is a still-image format; Super 35mm is a movie format.) In Chapter 12, I'll fully explain crop mode, which effectively captures pictures using only the center portion of the image, corresponding to the APS-C area used by Sony cameras that are *not* full-frame models and for Super 35mm film mode. There are three options within this menu entry:

- **On.** The camera *always* captures only the APS-C size area. If you're using a non-FE E-mount lens, then the image will correspond to what you'd see with an ASP-C camera, such as the Sony a6700. The cropped image will have the same field of view as a lens with 1.5X the actual focal length. That is, if you're using the Sony 16-55mm f/2.8 "kit" lens often supplied with the a6700 and other models, the effective focal length will be 24-82.5mm, and the cropped image will have a resolution of 14MP on the a7C II and 26MP with the a7CR. Because the On setting always activates the cropping effect, even if you're using a full-frame FE lens (such as the Sony FE 70-200mm f/2.8 lens), the effective focal length will be 105-300mm. This APS-C crop "boost" works well with either camera, because their 14/26MP images in crop mode in the 3:2 aspect ratio are still reasonable.

Some sports photographers force use of the crop with FE lenses to get some extra "reach" without the need to crop later in an image editor. I generally don't do that; when shooting sports, it's helpful to have the full frame available so you can "see" your subject moving toward the center of the frame, while retaining the option of positioning the crop closer to the right and left edges.

- **Auto.** When you use this setting, the camera will (often) detect whether you've mounted an FE or APS-C E-mount lens, and either crop or not crop as appropriate. It may not detect *all* APS-C E-mount lenses, particularly those from third-party vendors, so it's often safest to use the On option when you know you will be using an APS-C-type lens and want to avoid vignetting.

- **Off.** With this setting, the camera *never* crops the image. If you are using a non-FE, non-full-frame lens, you'll probably end up with severe vignetting in the corners. (I'll show you this effect in Chapter 12.) I sometimes use this setting when working with lenses intended for APS-C cameras, because some lenses *do* cover the full frame (even if just barely) at some focal lengths. Off is not available when shooting 4K 120p/100p video.

Long Exposure NR/High ISO NR

Long Exposure NR: Options: *On, Off

High ISO NR: Options: *Normal, Low, Off

My preference: Long Exposure NR: On; High ISO NR: Off

I've grouped these two menu options together because they provide similar adjustments, each under slightly different circumstances. Moreover, the causes and cures for noise involve some overlapping processes. Digital noise is that awful graininess that shows up as multicolored specks in images, and these menu items help you manage it. In some ways, noise is like the excessive grain found in some high-speed photographic films. However, while photographic grain is sometimes used as a special effect, it's rarely desirable in a digital photograph.

The visual noise-producing process is something like listening to music in your car, and then rolling down all the windows. You're adding sonic noise to the audio signal, and while increasing the volume may help a bit, you're still contending with an unfavorable signal-to-noise ratio that probably mutes tones (especially higher treble notes) that you really want to hear.

The same thing happens when the analog signal is amplified: You're increasing the image information in the signal but boosting the background fuzziness at the same time. Tune in a very faint or distant AM radio station on your car stereo. Then turn up the volume. After a certain point, turning up the volume further no longer helps you hear better. There's a similar point of diminishing returns for digital sensor ISO increases and signal amplification as well.

Your a7C II and a7CR can reduce the amount of grainy visual noise in your photo with noise-reduction processing. That's useful for a smoother look, but NR processing does blur some of the very fine detail in an image along with blurring the digital noise pattern. These two menu items let you choose whether to apply noise reduction to exposures of one second or longer and how much noise reduction to apply (Normal or Low) when shooting at a high ISO level (at roughly ISO 1600 and above).

Digital noise is also created during very long exposures. Extended exposure times allow more photons to reach the sensor but increase the likelihood that some photosites will react randomly even though not struck by a particle of light. Moreover, as the sensor remains switched on for the longer exposure, it heats up, and this heat can be mistakenly recorded as if it were a barrage of photons. To minimize the digital noise that can occur during long exposures, the a7C II and a7CR use a process called "dark frame subtraction." After you take the photo, the camera fires another shot at the same shutter speed, with the shutter closed to make the so-called dark frame. The processor compares the original photo and the dark frame photo and identifies the colorful noise speckles and "hot" pixels. It then removes (subtracts) them so the final image saved to the memory card will be quite "clean."

EXCEPTIONS

Long Exposure NR is always enabled when using Intelligent Auto. It is not available with the electronic shutter and is deactivated when using continuous shooting or continuous bracketing. High ISO NR is fixed at Normal when using Intelligent Auto and is not applied to RAW images.

The reason the a7C II/a7CR does not use this feature on RAW-format photos is that noise reduction—at the optimum level for any photo—can be applied in the software you'll use to modify and convert the RAW file to JPEG or TIFF. (If you shoot in RAW & JPEG, the JPEG images, but not the RAW files, will be affected by this camera feature.)

Context-Sensitive

The a7C II and a7CR have a "context-sensitive" noise-reduction algorithm that examines the image to identify smooth tones, subject edges, and textures, and apply different NR to each. This processing works best with areas with continuous tones and subtle gradations and does a good job of reducing noise while preserving detail. Because the BIONZ XR digital processing chip is doing so much work, you may see a message on the screen while NR is underway. You cannot take another photo until the processing is done and the message disappears. If you want to give greater priority to shooting, set Long Exposure NR and High ISO NR to Off.

Long Exposure NR works well, but it causes a delay; roughly the same amount of time as the exposure itself. During that interval, the camera takes a second exposure used to apply *dark frame subtraction*, which isolates the natural sensor noise so it can be compared with the noise added by the long exposure. That process would be an excruciating long 30 seconds after a 30-second exposure. During this delay the camera locks up, so you cannot take another shot. You may want to turn this feature off to eliminate that delay when you need to be able to take a shot at any time.

You might want to turn off Long Exposure noise reduction and set High ISO NR to a weak level to preserve image detail. (NR processing blurs the digital noise pattern, but it can also blur fine details in your images.) Or, you simply may not need NR in some situations. For example, you might be shooting waves crashing into the shore at ISO 200 with the camera mounted on a tripod, using a neutral-density filter and long exposure to cause the pounding water to blur slightly. To maximize detail in the non-moving portions of your photos, you can switch off long exposure noise reduction.

It's also important to turn off noise reduction when taking interval photos. But don't worry about that—the a7C II/a7CR does it for you when you use the Interval Shooting Function. For example, the long exposures needed to record star trails would trigger the dark frame subtraction process, producing a 30-second delay following each 30-second exposure in a continuous sequence. So noise reduction is disabled to allow shooting long exposures, one after another, to capture your star trails.

HLG Still Image

Options: On, *Off

My preference: Off

A relatively new wrinkle in the Sony toolkit is the addition of HLG (Hybrid-Log Gamma) output, which can be applied to still photos when working in HEIF mode. You can consider it a type of HDR shooting, without the need to capture and combine multiple images. Instead, all you need to do is activate HEIF shooting, using either 4:4:2 or 4:4:0 color sampling, and then enable HLG capture with this entry. You'll then be able to capture still photos with the extended dynamic range and wide color gamut offered using this gamma setting.

As with HDR video, HLG still images may not be rendered accurately on the camera's display or on an external monitor. For best results, set Setup > Display Option > Gamma Display Assist to On, and Setup > Display Option > Gamma Display Assist Type to Auto or HLG (BT.2020). When directing your camera's output to an external monitor, you'll want to use an HLG-compatible television or monitor and choose Setup > External Output > HDMI Resolution to anything other than 2160p.

Two of the biggest gorillas in the broadcast industry, BBC and NHK, developed Hybrid-Log Gamma, which produces video that can show HDR content on non-HDR displays. But when you direct the same image or video to a 4K television with HLG/HDR support, it will play back with the increased contrast, brighter highlights, and the larger color gamut possible with high dynamic range video.

For HLG to be activated, the JPEG/HEIF Switch in the Shooting > Image Quality/Rec menu must be set to HEIF (alone), rather than RAW or RAW & HEIF; shooting mode must be P, A, S, or M. D-Range Optimizer, Creative Look, DRO Bracketing, and Picture Profile are deactivated, and the available ISO range changes.

Color Space

Options: *sRGB, Adobe RGB

My preference: sRGB

The Color Space option gives you two different color spaces (also called *color gamuts*), named Adobe RGB (because it was developed by Adobe Systems in 1998), and sRGB (supposedly because it is the *standard* RGB color space). These two color gamuts define a specific set of colors that can be applied to the images your a7C II/a7CR captures. Note that when you're shooting HLG, a third color space, BT.2020 is used instead.

You're probably surprised that the Sony a7C II and a7CR cameras don't automatically capture *all* the colors we see. Unfortunately, that's impossible because of the limitations of the sensor and the filters used to capture the fundamental red, green, and blue colors, as well as that of the phosphors used to display those colors on the LEDs in your camera and computer monitors. Nor is it possible to *print* every color our eyes detect, because the inks or pigments used don't absorb and reflect colors perfectly.

On the other hand, the cameras do capture quite a few more colors than we need. A 14-bit RAW image contains a possible 4 *trillion* different hues (16,384 colors per red, green, or blue channel), which are condensed down to a mere 16.8 million possible colors when converted to a 24-bit (eight bits per channel) image.

The set of colors, or gamut, that can be reproduced or captured by a given device (scanner, digital camera, monitor, printer, or some other piece of equipment) is represented as a color space that exists within the larger full range of colors. That full range is represented by the odd-shaped splotch of color shown in Figure 6.8, as defined by scientists at an international organization back in 1931. The colors possible with Adobe RGB are represented by the black triangle in the figure, while the sRGB gamut is represented by the smaller white triangle. The location of the corners of each triangle represent the position of the primary red, green, and blue colors in the gamut.

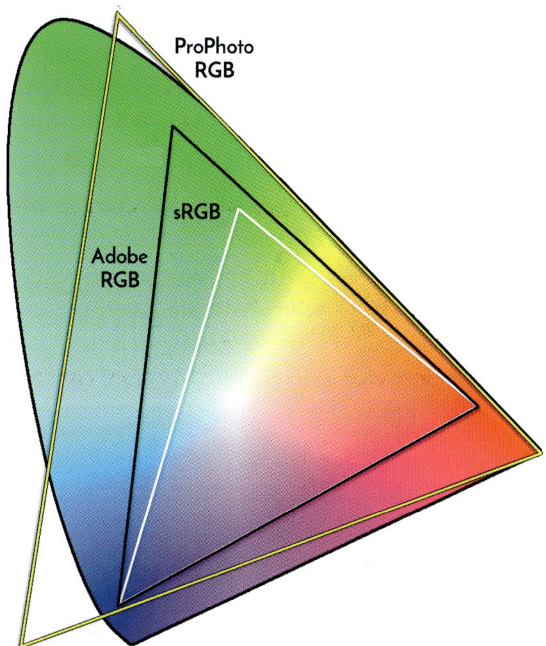

Figure 6.8 The outer curved figure shows all the colors we can see; the outlines show the boundaries of Adobe RGB (black triangle), sRGB (white triangle), and ProPhoto RGB (yellow triangle).

A third color space, ProPhoto RGB, represented by the yellow triangle in the figure, has become more popular among professional photographers as more and more color printing labs support it. While you cannot *save* images using the ProPhoto gamut with your a7C II/a7CR, you can convert your photos to 16-bit ProPhoto format using Adobe Camera RAW when you import RAW photos into an image editor. ProPhoto encompasses virtually all the colors we can see (and some we can't), giving advanced photographers better tools to work with in processing their photos. It has richer reds, greens, and blues, although, as you can see from the figure, its green and blue primaries are imaginary (they extend outside the visible color gamut). Those with exacting standards need not use a commercial printing service if they want to explore ProPhoto RGB: many inkjet printers can handle cyans, magentas, and yellows that extend outside the Adobe RGB gamut.

Regardless of which triangle—or color space—is used by the a7C II and a7CR, you end up with some combination of 16.8 million different colors that can be used in your photograph. (No one image will contain all 16.8 million!) But, as you can see from the figure, the colors available will be *different*.

Adobe RGB, like ProPhoto RGB, is an expanded color space useful for commercial and professional printing, and it can reproduce a wider range of colors. It can also come in useful if an image is going to be extensively retouched, especially within an advanced image editor, like Adobe Photoshop, which has sophisticated color management capabilities that can be tailored to specific color spaces. As an advanced user, you don't need to automatically "upgrade" your a7C II/a7CR to Adobe RGB, because images tend to look less saturated on your monitor and, it is likely, significantly different from what you will get if you output the photo to your personal inkjet. (You can *profile* your monitor for the Adobe RGB color space to improve your on-screen rendition using widely available color-calibrating hardware and software.) Note that HEIF doesn't support AdobeRGB, and you can't select it in HEIF mode. It's another reason why sticking to JPEG is a good idea.

While both Adobe RGB and sRGB can reproduce the exact same 16.8 million absolute colors, Adobe RGB spreads those colors over a larger portion of the visible spectrum. Think of a box of crayons (the jumbo 16.8 million crayon variety). Some of the basic crayons from the original sRGB set have been removed and replaced with new hues not contained in the original box. Your "new" box contains colors that can't be reproduced by your computer monitor, but which work just fine with a commercial printing press. For example, Adobe RGB has more "crayons" available in the cyan-green portion of the box, compared to sRGB, which is unlikely to be an advantage unless your image's final destination are the cyan, magenta, yellow, and black inks of a printing press.

The other color space, sRGB, is recommended for images that will be output locally on the user's own printer, as this color space matches that of the typical inkjet printer fairly closely. You might prefer sRGB, which is the default for the Sony a7C II/a7CR and most other cameras, as it is well suited for the range of colors that can be displayed on a computer screen and viewed over the Internet. If you plan to take your image file to a retailer's kiosk for printing, sRGB is your best choice, because those automated output devices are calibrated for the sRGB color space that consumers use.

Of course, choosing the right color space doesn't solve the problems that result from having each device in the image chain manipulating or producing a slightly different set of colors. To that end, you'll need to investigate the wonderful world of *color management*, which uses hardware and software tools to match or *calibrate* all your devices, as closely as possible, so that what you see more closely resembles what you capture, what you see on your computer display, and what ends up on a printed hardcopy. Entire books have been devoted to color management, and most of what you need to know doesn't directly involve your Sony a7C II or a7CR, so I won't detail the nuts and bolts here.

To manage your color, you'll need, at the bare minimum, some sort of calibration system for your computer display, so that your monitor can be adjusted to show a standardized set of colors that is repeatable over time. (What you see on the screen can vary as the monitor ages, or even when the room light changes.) I use the SpyderX Pro monitor color correction system from Datacolor (www.datacolor.com) for my computer's 32-inch main monitor, flanked by two 26-inch wide-screen LCD displays. The unit checks room light levels every five minutes and reminds me to recalibrate every week or two using a small sensor device, which attaches temporarily to the front of the screen and interprets test patches that the software displays during calibration. The rest of the time, the sensor sits in its stand, measuring the room illumination, and adjusting my monitors for higher or lower ambient light levels.

Lens Compensation

Options: Shading Compensation, Chromatic Aberration Compensation, Distortion Compensation, (Default for each is ***Auto**), Breathing Compensation (Default is ***Off**) (Movies Only)

My preference: Auto for all three; set to Off if you want to preserve a lens's distortion effects.

This trio of submenus optimizes lens performance by compensating for optical defects; they're useful because very few lenses in the world are even close to perfect in all aspects. All three items work only with lens-compensation-compatible E-mount lenses and not when using A-mount lenses with an adapter accessory.

Shading Compensation

One key defect is caused by a phenomenon called *vignetting*, which is a darkening of the four corners of the frame because of a slight amount of fall-off in illumination at those nether regions. This menu option allows you to activate built-in "shading" compensation, which partially (or fully) compensates for this effect. Depending on the f/stop you use, the lens mounted on the camera, and the focal length setting, vignetting can be non-existent, slight, or may be so strong that it appears you've used a too-small hood on your camera. (Indeed, the wrong lens hood can produce a vignette effect of its own.)

Vignetting, even if pronounced, may not be much of a problem for you. I actually *add* vignetting, sometimes, in my image editor when shooting portraits and some other subjects. Slightly dark corners tend to focus attention on a subject in the middle of the frame. On the other hand, vignetting with subjects that are supposed to be evenly illuminated, such as landscapes, is seldom a benefit. Figure 6.9, left, shows an image without shading correction at top, and a corrected image at the bottom. I've exaggerated the vignetting a little to make it more evident on the printed page. Note that this effect is applied to both RAW and JPEG images.

Chromatic Aberration Compensation

The second defect involves fringes of color around backlit objects, produced by *chromatic aberration*, which comes in two forms: *longitudinal/axial,* in which all the colors of light don't focus in the same plane, and *lateral/transverse,* in which the colors are shifted in one direction. (See Figure 6.9, top right.) When this feature is enabled, the camera will automatically correct images taken with one of the supported lenses to reduce or eliminate the amount of color fringing seen in the final photograph. (See Figure 6.9, bottom right.)

Distortion Compensation

Distortion is the tendency of some lenses to bow outward (most often wide-angle lenses) or curve inward (found in some telephoto lenses). Figure 6.10, left, shows an exaggerated version of the outward-curving variety, called *barrel distortion,* exhibited by many wide-angle lenses—especially in fisheye optics, where the distortion is magically transformed into a feature. This feature works with most E-mount lenses, but not with all.

In Figure 6.10, right, you can see inward bowing, or *pincushion distortion,* as found in many telephoto lenses. Both types can be partially fixed using Photoshop's Lens Correction or Photoshop Elements' Correct Camera Distortion filters. Or, you can apply this in-camera feature to fix mild distortion. You should realize that correcting lens distortion involves warping pixels, mostly at the

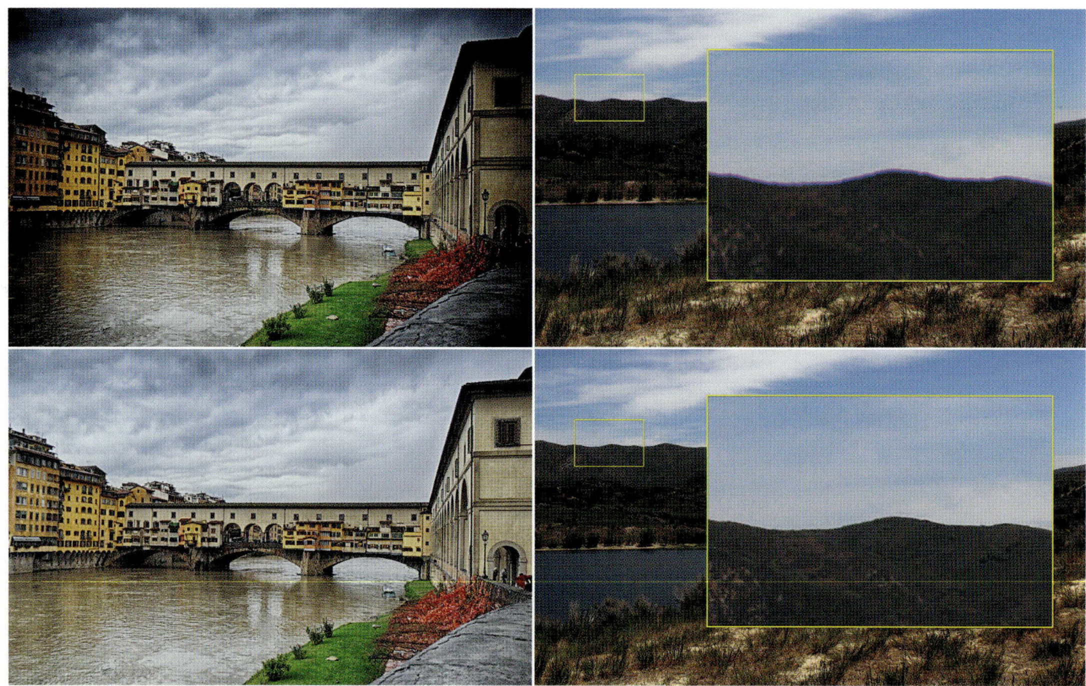

Figure 6.9 Vignetting (top left) is undesirable in a landscape photo, but the camera's shading correction feature can fix dark corners (bottom left). Lateral chromatic aberration, which shows as color fringes (top right), can also be corrected (bottom right).

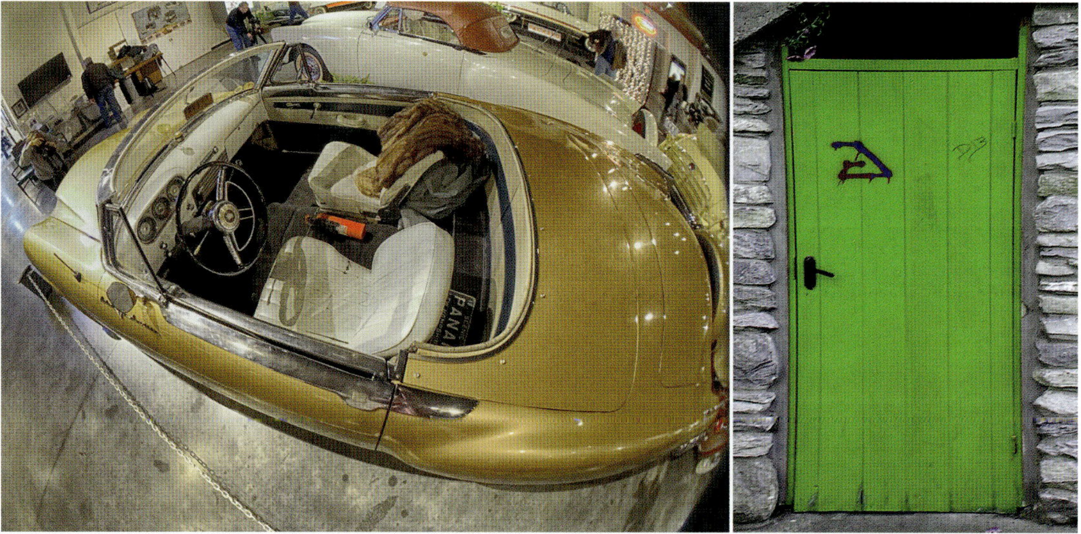

Figure 6.10 Left: Barrel distortion in wide-angle lenses becomes a useful feature with fisheye lenses. Right: Pincushion distortion causes straight lines at the edges of the frame to curve inward.

edges of the frame, providing a little less sharpness in those areas. The image area of your final picture will be slightly smaller than the frame you composed, and, during playback, the active focus point is not shown in the review image.

In addition, applying distortion correction involves extra processing, which can reduce the number of consecutive shots possible. Because the correction is applied *after* you take the picture, the effect is not displayed on the screen when shooting in live view, even if Shooting > Shooting Display > Live View Display Settings > Live View Display > Setting Effect is set to On.

Breathing Compensation

This option appears only when the Still/Movie/S&Q dial is set to either Movie position. Some lenses effectively change their magnification (and thus their field of view) slightly, depending on the focusing distance. This is commonly referred to as *breathing,* and can actually refer to two different phenomena, a change in the angle of view or of the effective focal length of a lens. For example, a subject captured at a distance of five feet with a 100mm lens subject to breathing might actually appear to be slightly smaller, as if photographed with a 90 or 95mm optic.

In still photography, you ordinarily wouldn't notice this change without comparing images taken with a lens that exhibits less breathing. When shooting movies, breathing can interfere with rack focus or follow focus (when you deliberately change the focus plane for dramatic effect or to track a moving subject). If you use such techniques, enable Breathing Compensation to reduce unwanted changes in your composition as you change focus. Although breathing effects are reduced, they may not be entirely eliminated. The list of compatible lenses includes:

Sony E 11mm f/1.8	Sony FE 100mm f/2.8 GM
Sony FE 14mm f/1.8 GM	Sony FE 135mm f/1.8 GM
Sony E 15mm f/1.4 G	Sony FE 12-24mm f/2.8 GM
Sony FE 20mm f/1.8 G	Sony FE 16-35mm f/2.8 GM/GM II
Sony FE 24mm f/2.8 G	Sony FE 24-70mm f/2.8 GM/GM II
Sony FE 24mm f/1.4 GM	Sony FE 20-70mm f/4 G
Sony FE 35mm f/1.4 GM	Sony FE 24-105mm f/4 G
Sony FE 35mm f/1.8	Sony FE 24-135mm f/4 G
Sony FE 40mm f/2.5 G	Sony FE PZ 28-135mm f/4 G OSS
Sony FE 50mm f/1.2 GM	Sony FE 300mm f/2.8 GM
Sony FE 50mm f/1.4 GM	Sony FE 70-200mm f/2.8 GM
Sony FE Planar T* 50mm f/1.4 ZA	Sony FE 70-200mm f/2.8 GM II
Sony FE 50mm f/2.5 G	Sony E 10-20mm f/4 PZ G
Sony FE 85mm f/1.4 GM	Sony FE 12-24mm f/2.8 GM
Sony FE 85mm f/1.8	Sony FE 12-24mm f/4 G

EXCEPTIONS

These functions can operate only when a lens with automatic compensation data available in firmware is mounted on the camera. Distortion compensation may be locked at Auto when Movie SteadyShot is set to Active in movie recording mode, and also with certain lenses (not specified by Sony).

2. Media

The Media group has just three entries (shown in Figure 6.11) allowing you to choose parameters that apply to media. The first, Format, is used to apply the correct format to a blank memory card, or to reformat one that you want to erase and reuse. Entries are also offered for recovering a damaged image database file, and to view information about the media currently in either of the two slots.

- Format
- Recover Image Database
- Display Media Information

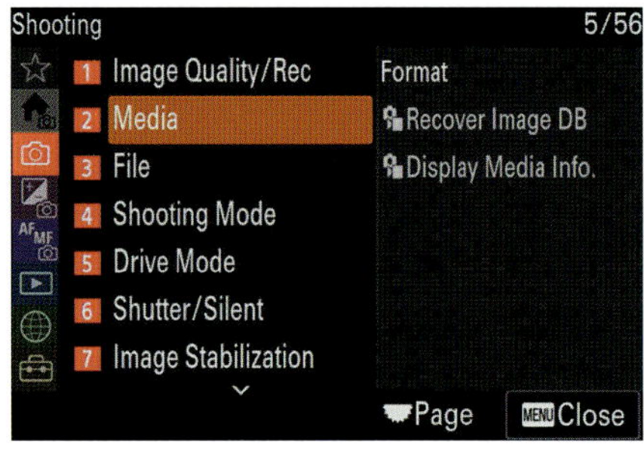

Figure 6.11 Media settings.

Format

Options: Select Media; *__Quick Format__, Full Format

My preference: Quick Format

As you'd guess, you'll use Format to re-format your memory card while it's in your camera. If you want to apply a "Quick" format, select OK and press the center button to confirm. If you want to perform a more thorough "Full" format, press the trash button, then OK to receive a message about the full format process, and then press the center button to confirm. In either case, you can highlight Cancel and press the center button to chicken out.

Use the Format command to erase everything on your memory card and to set up a fresh file system ready for use. The Quick format simply zeroes out the addresses in the file system and creates new folders for storing your images, without actually removing all the previous information. This process takes only a few seconds, but theoretically can often be reversed (as long as you haven't written anything new to the card) using file recovery software.

A "Full" format, on the other hand, removes all data that was on the memory card and reinitializes the card's file system by defining anew the areas of the card available for image storage, locking out defective areas, and creating new folders in which to deposit your images. The Full format takes much longer, is more secure, and helps lengthen the useful life of your card by locking out those bad areas.

It's usually a good idea to reformat your memory card in the camera, at least with a Quick format (and not in your camera's card reader using your computer's operating system), before each use. Formatting is generally much quicker than deleting images one by one. Before formatting the card, however, make sure that you have saved all your images and videos to another device; formatting will remove images that were marked with the Protect command.

Recover Image Database 📷 🎬 S&Q

Options: Select Media; *Enter, Cancel
My preference: N/A

The Recover Image DB function is provided in case errors crop up in the camera's database that records information about your movies. According to Sony, this situation may develop if you have processed or edited movies on a computer and then re-saved them to the memory card that's in your camera. I have never had this problem, so I'm not sure exactly what it would look like. But, if you find that your movies are not playing correctly in the camera, or the camera reports that the image database is corrupt, try this operation. Highlight this menu option and press the center button, and the camera will prompt you, "Check Image Database File?" Press the center button to confirm, or the MENU button to cancel. The camera will create/recover a database or report that no errors were found in an existing database. You may also encounter this if using a card that includes images recorded using another camera, as it will not contain a Sony image database.

Display Media Information 📷 🎬 S&Q

Options: Select Media
My preference: N/A

This entry gives you a report of *approximately* how many still images and how much movie time remains on the memory card that's in the camera, given the current shooting settings. This can be useful, but that information is already displayed on the screen when the camera is being used to shoot still photos (unless you have cycled to a display with less information), and the information about minutes remaining for movie recording is displayed on the screen as soon as you press the Record button. But, if you want confirmation of this information, this menu option is available.

3. File

This group has six entries used for creating or selecting folders, and embedding shooting, copyright, or serial number information in the file. See Figure 6.12.

- File/Folder Settings
- Select Recording Folder
- Create New Folder
- IPTC Information
- Copyright Info
- Write Serial Number

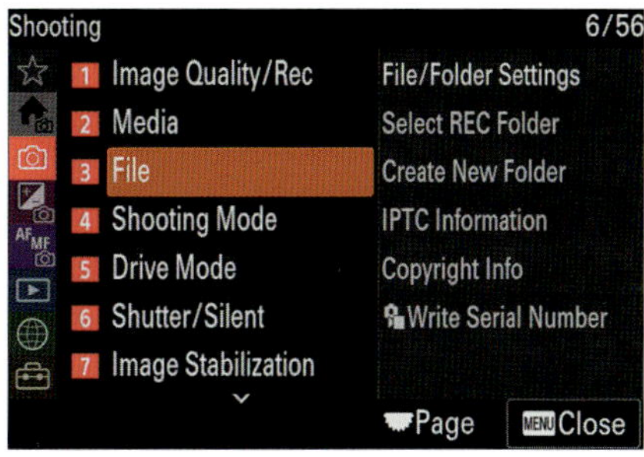

Figure 6.12 The File group.

Sony has organized all the commands you need to organize the file system of your a7C II/a7CR in one location.

File/Folder Settings 📷 🎬 S&Q /File 📷 🎬 S&Q

Options (Stills): File Number (*****Series**, Reset); Forced File Number Reset (*****OK**, Change Folder Name); Set File Name (*****DSC**, User Entry); Folder Name: (*****Standard Form**, Date Form)

Options (Movies): File Number (*****Series**, Reset); Series Counter Reset; File Name Format (*****Standard**, Title, Date+Title, Title+Date); Title Name Settings

My preference: See below

This entry allows you to specify when file numbers are reset to zero, choose the first three letters of your camera's file names, create a new folder, and select the format for your folders. Figure 6.13, upper left, shows the array of options in the File/Folder Settings submenu. I'll explain each of them separately.

Although your camera will create new folders automatically as needed, you can create a new folder at any time, and switch among available folders already created on your memory card. (Of course, a memory card must be installed in the camera.) This is an easy way to segregate photos by folder. For example, if you're on vacation, you can change the Folder Name convention to Date Form (described next). Then, each day, create a new folder (with that date as its name), and then deposit that day's photos and video clips into it. A highlighted bar appears; press the up/down buttons to select the folder you want to use and press the center button.

File Number 📷 🎬 S&Q

Options: *****Series**, Reset

My preference: Series

The default for the File Number item is Series, indicating that the a7C II/a7CR will automatically apply a file number to each picture that you take, using consecutive numbering; this will continue over a long period of time, spanning many different memory cards, and even if you reformat a card. Numbers are applied from 0001 to 9999; when you reach the limit, the camera starts back at 0001. The camera keeps track of the last number used in its internal memory. So, you could take pictures numbered as high as 100-0240 on one card, remove the card, insert another, and the next picture will be numbered 100-0241 on the new card. Reformat either card, take a picture, and the next image will be numbered 100-0242. Use the Series option when you want all the photos you take to have consecutive numbers (at least until your camera exceeds 9999 shots taken).

If you want to restart numbering back at 0001 frequently, use the Reset option. In that case, the file number will be reset to 0001 *each* time you format a memory card or delete all the images in a folder, insert a different memory card, create a new folder, or change the folder name format (as described in the next menu entry). I do not recommend this since you will soon have several images with exactly the same file number. However, if you import your images to your computer using a utility that renames the files as they are copied, you won't have duplicate file number/names if you specify a unique prefix each time you transfer.

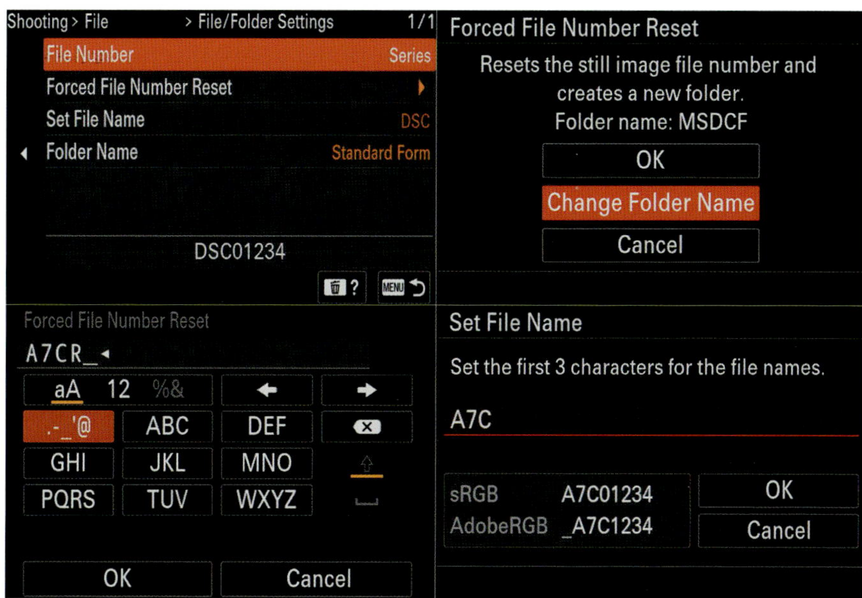

Figure 6.13 File/Folder Settings.

Forced File Number Reset ▢▦S&Q */Series Counter Reset* ▢▦S&Q

Options: *OK, Change Folder Name, Cancel

My preference: Folder Name: A7CII/A7CR_

If you choose Reset with the File Number entry described above, the reset will happen only when a new folder is created. However, you can also force a reset any time you want and, optionally, change the name applied to new folders. (See Figure 6.13, upper right.) In Movie mode, only the Series Counter is reset. If you select Change Folder Name, the screen shown in Figure 6.13, lower left, appears, giving you the opportunity to replace the default MSDCF prefix with five characters of your choice (uppercase alpha plus numbers and spaces). If you do that, numbering restarts automatically. Note that entry uses the archaic multi-tap text-entry system used by your parents and grandparents decades ago. For example, to enter the letter C, you must tap ABC three times. When finished, highlight OK and press the center button.

Set File Name ▢▦S&Q

Options: Up to three characters

My preference: A7C

This entry allows you to specify the first three characters in the file name applied to your images. The a7C II/a7CR, like other cameras in the Sony product line, automatically applies a name like _ DSC0001.jpg or DSC00001.arw to your image files as they are created. You can use this menu option to change the names applied to your photos, but only within certain strict limitations. In practice, you can change only three of the eight characters, the *DSC* portion of the file name. The other five are mandated either by the Design Rule for Camera File System (DCF) specification that all digital camera makers adhere to or to industry conventions.

DCF limits file names created by conforming digital cameras to a maximum of eight characters, plus a three-character extension (such as .jpg, .nef, or .wav in the case of audio files) that represents the format of the file. The eight-plus-three (usually called 8.3) length limitation dates back to an evil and frustrating computer operating system that we older photographers would like to forget (its initials are D.O.S.), but which, unhappily, lives on as the wraith of a file-naming convention.

Of the eight available characters, four are used to represent, in a general sense, the type of camera used to create the image. By convention, one of those characters is an underscore, placed in the first position (as in _DSCxxxx.xxx) when the image uses the Adobe RGB color space, and a zero in the fourth position (as in DSC0xxxx.xxx) for sRGB and RAW files. That leaves just three characters for the manufacturer (and you) to use. The remaining four characters are used for numbers from 0000 to 9999, which is why your a7C II/a7CR "rolls over" to DSC_0000 again when the 9999-number limitation is reached.

Because the default DSC characters don't tell you much, don't hesitate to change them to something else. I use A7C for my a7C II/a7CR. (See Figure 6.13, lower right.) You can change the three characters to anything else that suits your purposes. You must use capital letters, numbers, or underscores, with the exception that you cannot use an underscore as the *first* character in your file name; it's reserved for AdobeRGB files. You could not use _R4, for example.

You might prefer to use your initials (DDB– or JFK–, for example), or even customize for particular shooting sessions (EUR–, GER–, FRA–, and JAP– when taking vacation trips). You can also use the file name flexibility to partially overcome the 9999 numbering limitation. You could use the template A71_ to represent the first 10,000 pictures you take with your a7C II or a7CR, and then A72_ for the next 10,000, and A73_ for the 10,000 after that.

This capability is especially useful for those who own more than one camera, whether it's a Sony model or another brand that also defaults to the DSC nomenclature. It's often important to know exactly *which* camera produced a given image, particularly when you discover some sort of problem in your photos and would like to pin down which camera is the culprit.

This file-renaming feature assumes that you don't rename your image files in your computer. In a way, file naming verges on a moot consideration, because, they apply *only* to the images as they exist in your camera. After (or during) transfer to your computer, you can change the names to anything you want, completely disregarding the 8.3 limitations (although it's a good idea to retain the default extensions). If you shot an image file named DSC_4832.jpg in your camera, you could change it to Paris_EiffelTower_32.jpg later.

In Movie mode, the equivalent setting is Title Name Settings.

Folder Name/File Name Format

Options: *Standard Form, Date Form
My preference: N/A

If you have viewed one of your memory card's contents on a computer, you noticed that the top-level folder on the card is always named DCIM. Inside it, there's another folder created by your camera. Different cameras use different folder names, and they can co-exist on the same card. For example, if your memory card is removed from your Sony camera and used in, say, a camera from another vendor that also accepts the same memory cards, the other camera will create a new folder using a different folder name within the DCIM directory.

By default, the a7C II and a7CR create folders using a three-number prefix (starting with 100), followed by MSDCF. As each folder fills up with 9999 images, a new folder with a prefix that's one higher (say, 101) is used. So, with the "Standard Form," the folders on your memory card will be named 100MSDCF, 101MSDCF, and so forth. As I noted earlier, the camera *must* be set to Standard Form if you want to be able to specify a folder using the Select Recording Folder entry described next.

However, you can also select Date Form instead, and the a7C II/a7CR will use a *xxxymmdd* format, such as 10051009, where the initial *100* is the folder number, the following *1009* representing the month and day (10/09), and the 5 is the last digit of the year (2025). If you want the folder names to be date-oriented, rather than generic, use the Date Form option instead of Standard Form. This entry allows you to switch back and forth between them for folder creation.

In Movie mode, the equivalent setting is called File Name Format.

CAUTION Whoa! Sony has thrown you a curveball in this folder-switching business. Note that if you are using Date Form naming, you can *create* folders using the date convention, but you can't switch among them when Date Form is active. The Shooting > File > Select Recording Folder entry is grayed out.

   If you *do* want to switch among folders named using the date convention, you can do it. But you have to switch from Date Form back to Standard Form. *Then* you can change to any of the available folders (of either naming format). So, if you're on that vacation, you can select Date Form, and then choose New Folder each day of your trip, if you like. But if, for some reason, you want to put some additional pictures in a different folder (say, you're revisiting a city and want the new shots to go in the same folder as those taken a few days earlier), you'll need to change to Standard Form, switch folders, and then resume shooting. Sony probably did this to preserve the "integrity" of the date/folder system, but it can be annoying.

Select Recording Folder

Options: Choose from among available folders
My preference: N/A

This entry allows you to choose which of the folders *that have already been created* within the *currently selected slot* is used to store images as you create them. You can select the recording folder only if Folder Name is set to Standard Form. When you access this entry a list of the available folders and the number of images currently in each one is displayed for your selection.

I like to use this capability to keep various images separate while they still reside on my memory card. For example, if I am working on two different projects, I can store images for one project in a particular folder, switch to a different folder for the second project, and switch back to the original one at any time. When traveling, I may spend a few hours shooting wildlife, then spend some time photographing landscapes before moving on to a different location to continue taking wildlife photos. I assign the Select Recording Folder to a custom key, and can switch back and forth more quickly than alternate methods, such as swapping memory cards in and out.

Create New Folder

Options: N/A
My preference: N/A

This item will enable you to create a brand-new folder. Press the center button, and a message like "102MSDCF folder created" (if Standard Form is enabled) or "10220225 folder created" (if Date Form is enabled instead) appears. The alphanumeric format will be determined by the Folder Name option you've selected and either Standard Form or Date Form.

This entry allows you to create a new storage folder in the currently selected slot. Although your camera will create new folders automatically as needed, you can create a new folder at any time, and switch among available folders already created on your memory card, using the Select Recording Folder entry described above.

As I mentioned earlier, using multiple folders is an easy way to segregate photos. For example, if you're on vacation, you can change the Folder Name convention to Date Form. Then, each day, create a new folder (with that date as its name), and then deposit that day's photos and video clips into it. A highlighted bar appears; press the up/down buttons to select the folder you want to use and then press the center button.

IPTC Information

Options: Write IPTC Info, Register IPTC Info
My preference: N/A

This entry allows you to enable or disable embedding of IPTC (International Press Telecommunications Council) metadata in your JPEG and RAW files. The IPTC standard is used by news and photo agencies, photojournalists, libraries, and museums. You can load, edit, save, and register specifications using a free utility available from Sony, the IPTC Metadata Preset (https://www.sony.net/iptc/help/). Professional journalists should investigate Sony's Transfer and Tagging Add-On, a smart device app available for both iOS and Android that works in conjunction with Creators' App to streamline transfer of images and IPTC information to your smart device as you shoot. It operates with both Wi-Fi and transfer using a special USB cable connecting the camera and your device.

To embed IPTC information, just follow these steps:

1. **Launch the IPTC Metadata Preset.** Your computer will display a screen something like the one shown in Figure 6.14.

2. **Enter your default information.** For general use, you will want to enter information only for the fields shown at the bottom of the figure, under Image Rights. These include photographer's name, title, URL, copyright notice, and credit line. You can embed this information in all the photos you take.

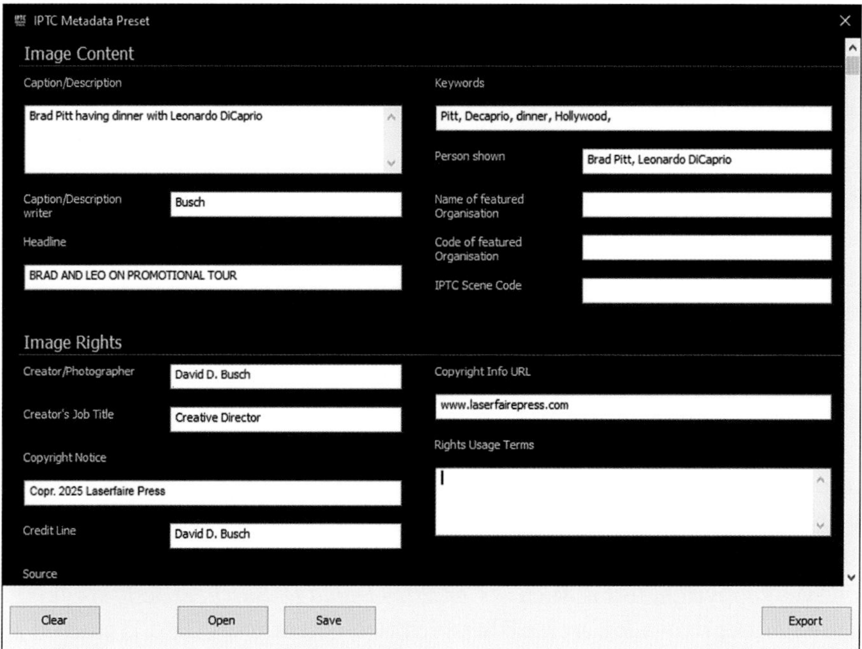

Figure 6.14 Sony IPTC Metadata Preset utility.

3. **Enter shoot-specific data (optional).** If you will be taking many pictures for a particular project, you can optionally add more information about a specific series or individual image. Photojournalists might find this especially useful, but most of us can skip entering these minutiae.

4. **Save preset.** You'll need to save the information entered to your computer, a memory card, or both:

   - Click Save in the utility and specify a storage location on your computer. You can later retrieve your settings using the Open command in the utility to revise, edit, or create a new version.

   - Click Export to store the metadata on a memory card. Insert the card into a card reader, first. A dialog box will appear allowing to select the drive representing your memory card. (The card will usually appear as a USB card in your file manager.)

5. **Copy to camera.** You'll next need to transfer the information to the camera in order to make it available for embedding in your photos. With a memory card containing the information loaded into one of the camera's slots, navigate to the IPTC Information entry and choose Register IPTC Info.

6. **Store data.** The data will be recorded in the camera's memory, *overwriting any existing IPTC data* that may already have been there. Note that you can store separate IPTC data on different memory cards and choose which one to write to the camera's register.

7. **Highlight Write IPTC Info.** Select On to enable embedding the IPTC data you have just registered to your images.

Copyright Info 📷 🎬 S&Q

Options: *Off, Write Copyright Info, Set Photographer, Set Copyright, Display Copyright Info
My preference: Add all information

Your choices include:

- **Write Copyright Info.** Turn On to embed copyright information in your image file; Off to disable this feature. If you choose On, a copyright symbol will appear on the shooting screen to indicate that copyright data is being written to the image file.

- **Set Photographer.** Enter the name of the photographer. Highlight this and press the center button to move to the next screen, where a blank line appears. Highlight that and press the center button, and the text-entry screen appears. As I mentioned earlier, the screen functions much like the multi-tap cell phone keypads in the primordial pre-smartphone era: highlight a button and press the center button multiple times to enter a particular character. For example, if you highlight the "abc" button, pressing once inserts an a, twice a b, and three times a c. When finished, highlight OK and press the center button to return to the initial screen, where you can highlight OK again and press the center button a last time to confirm.

- **Set Copyright.** Define your copyright terms, such as *Cpr. 2025 David D. Busch*. Strictly speaking, "Cpr." should be used rather than a lowercase c between two parentheses. Text is entered as described above.

- **Disp. Copyright Info.** Displays whatever copyright information you've specified.

Write Serial Number 📷 🎬 S&Q

Options: On, *Off
My preference: On—but you probably will prefer Off

When enabled, the a7C II or a7CR will embed your camera's unique serial number in the EXIF data for a particular image. That will help you identify which camera was used to capture a particular image. Back in the days when news organizations had large photo staffs and a pool of equipment that was sometimes (or often) shared among photographers, this would have been a killer feature (along with IPTC info) for providing a digital photo trail. Today, while equipment pools still exist (according to legend), it is more likely to be used by individual shooters who own more than one a7C II or a7CR (or other Sony cameras with the Write Serial Number feature). I happen to be one of them: it's also available with my Sony a9 III and a1.

4. Shooting Mode

This group has entries that are used to store settings that you can access by turning the mode dial to the 1, 2, or 3 numbered positions. Figure 6.15 shows the entries in the Shooting > Shooting Mode group. The Stills version is at left, and the Movie mode at right.

- Exposure Control Type (Movies)
- Recall Camera Setting
- Camera Settings Memory
- S&Q Shoot Mode (Movies)
- Auto/Scene Selection (Stills)
- Register Custom Shooting Set (Stills)

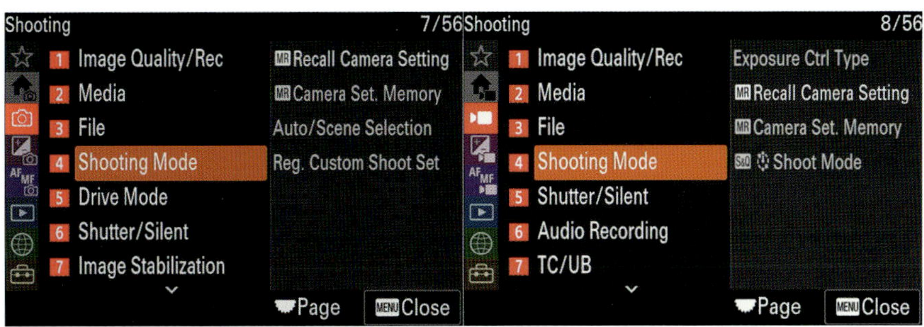

Figure 6.15 The Shooting Mode group: Stills (left) and Movie version (right).

Exposure Control Type

Options: *P/A/S/M Mode, Flexible Exposure Mode

My preference: N/A

This menu item appears only when the Still/Movie/S&Q dial is set to either Movie position. (See Figure 6.16.) It provides a flexible exposure mode in which you can choose whether aperture, shutter speed, or ISO individually are set manually or automatically. When enabled, a movie camera and an F icon appear in the upper-left corner of the screen indicating that Flexible mode is active.

When Flexible Exposure is enabled, each of the three exposure controls (Aperture, Shutter Speed, and ISO Sensitivity) can be individually locked or adjustable using one of three defined camera controls:

- **C1 button/Front Dial (Aperture Value).** You'll recall the C1 button is located on the back panel, just to the right of the MENU button. In Flexible mode, when you press this button, the camera toggles between locked (the camera sets the aperture) and manual (you set the aperture) using the front dial.

- **AF-ON button/Rear Left Dial (ISO Sensitivity).** Press the AF-ON button to toggle between locked and manual adjustment using Rear Dial L.

- **C2 button/Control Wheel (Time Value/Shutter Speed).** The C2 button doubles as the Trash/Delete button. Press it to toggle between locked and being able to make shutter speed adjustments with the control wheel.

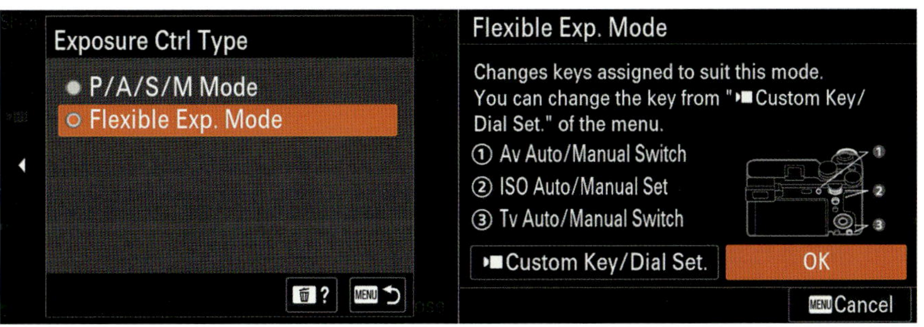

Figure 6.16 Flexible Exposure mode allows choosing aperture, ISO, or shutter speed manually or automatically.

As I noted, this menu option is only available when the Still/Movie/S&Q dial is in a Movie position. If the Still/Movie/S&Q dial is set for Still photos, and you press the Movie button to begin video capture, the Flexible Exposure Mode, if set, will be ignored. The camera will use whichever mode (P, S, A, or M) you've already selected.

Introduction to Memory Registers

The next three entries involve the Sony a7C II/a7CR's memory features, which allow you to save almost all the settings that you use for a particular shooting situation, including shutter speed and aperture (but *not* Program Shift adjustments), and then recall them quickly. The settings you can store include most of the entries in the Shooting, Exposure/Color, and Focus tabs.

Sony has done its best to make the Memory features as confusing as possible, but I'll straighten everything out for you. The first thing to understand is the difference between the a7C II/a7CR's numbered physical positions on the mode dial (1, 2, or 3) that retain settings within the camera's internal memory, and the numbered registers that store settings on your memory cards. Here's an overview:

- **Physical registers/slots.** There are three numbered positions on the mode dial labeled 1, 2, and 3. You can store groups of settings in any or all of these registers, and once stored they do not change until you overwrite them with a new set. All you need to do to recall the settings you want is to rotate the mode dial to the 1, 2, or 3 position. **Remember:** *These are stored in the camera itself.*

- **Memory card registers.** There are *four* of these, also numbered and assigned labels M1, M2, M3, and M4. These settings are stored on the memory card. Because they reside on the card itself, they become unavailable if you reformat the card, remove the card, or switch to a different memory card. **Remember:** *These are stored on your memory card.*

- **Using settings.** When the mode dial is in the 1, 2, or 3 position, you can use whatever settings are currently stored in those physical registers, *or* you can use the settings in the M1, M2, M3, or M4 memory registers on your card. I'll explain how to do this shortly.

- **Adjusting settings.** Once you've loaded settings into the camera, you can adjust them and your new settings are "sticky." However, any changes you make don't affect the memory registers. You can reload your saved settings at any time. Think of the memory registers as a sort of bookmark; you're free to use different settings but can return to your "bookmarked" values any time you want.

- **Settings library.** The settings you've stored in the three physical slots, plus four more in the M1, M2, M3, and M4 registers on the card give you seven groups of settings in all. If you like, you can store additional M1–M4 settings on as many different memory cards as you like, and they will remain until you reformat that card. The settings are stored in a folder on the card labeled /PRIVATE/SONY/SETTING with a subfolder for each different camera you use. The file names end in .DAT. The Memory feature lets you save custom-crafted sets that you can activate at any time. Simply activate the set that fits your current needs. For example, you might set up Register 1 with the settings you use while shooting volleyball in an indoor arena, Register 2 for use in landscape photography outdoors, and Register 3 for street photography. Whenever you encounter any of those three types of scenes, activate the memory channel with the suitable settings for that situation. You can then begin shooting immediately.

Recall Camera Setting

Options: Select memory register to use: Current numbered physical slot (1, 2, 3); or M1, M2, M3, M4 on memory card

My preference: N/A

This setting is only available when you've rotated the mode dial to the 1, 2, or 3 position. It enables you to choose which group of settings that have already been stored in your camera or on your memory card. Choose one of the three dial positions, access Shooting > Shooting Mode > Recall Camera Setting, and a screen similar to the one shown at left in Figure 6.17 appears. The selected slot/register is highlighted in the top line and the stored settings shown in the panel below. Only some of the registered settings are visible; you can scroll down to see the additional values.

You can scroll to the right in the top line to highlight M1, M2, M3, or M4. Press the center button, and the values in the selected register will be loaded into the current physical slot. These settings will remain in that slot until you return to this screen and choose a different group of settings. As I noted earlier, you can *change* the camera settings as you take pictures, but the values stored in the memory registers remain the same until you adjust them using the Camera Settings Memory entry, described next.

Note that you can *store* sets of settings when using any shooting modes (using the MR Memory entry). But to *recall* a set of stored settings, you *must* rotate the mode dial to one of the three Memory positions, marked with a 1, 2, or 3 on the dial and then either use the settings already stored or, optionally, use this menu entry to load the additional settings saved in M1, M2, M3, or M4 files on your memory card. I'll explain recalling settings here and show you how to store them under the next menu entry, Camera Settings Memory.

To recap, there are two ways to activate saved settings:

- **Mode dial.** Simply rotate the mode dial to the 1, 2, or 3 position. A set of settings for each of those positions is stored internally in the camera. When the mode dial is switched to 1, 2, or 3, the settings already loaded into that camera register automatically become active.

- **MR Recall.** This menu entry allows you to recall *additional* memory settings, numbered M1, M2, M3, and M4, which are stored on the memory card currently in the camera. You can load the M1, M2, M3, or M4 settings into the 1, 2, or 3 mode dial position. That may be confusing at first, but the bottom line is that the a7C II/a7CR can use *any of three memory registers* (1, 2, and 3), but any of those three physical registers can be loaded with each of four sets of settings *on your current memory card*. Remove your card (or reformat it), and those extra four settings are lost! (Smart move, Sony.)

To recall settings previously stored on your memory card using MR Recall, just follow these steps:

1. **Rotate the mode dial to the 1, 2, or 3 position.** Select the position you want to load settings into.
2. **Access the MR Recall entry.** Navigate to this menu entry. When you press the center button, a screen like the one shown at left in Figure 6.17 appears.

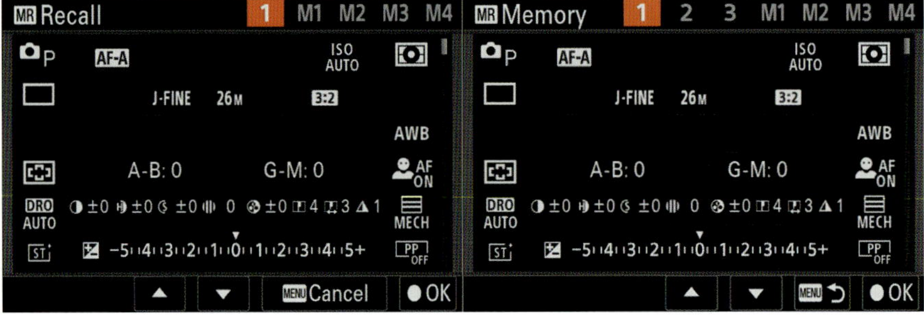

Figure 6.17 Recall settings stored on your memory card (left). Store settings in the 1, 2, or 3 mode dial positions, or as M1, M2, M3, or M4 on your memory card (right).

3. **Review your stored settings.** The 1 highlighted in orange at right in Figure 6.17 indicates that the mode dial currently has been set to the 1 position, and the settings displayed show the values currently stored for that slot. While the 1 is highlighted, you can scroll down the list with the up/down controls and review all the settings that have been stored.

4. **Change to settings on memory card.** If you want to use settings stored on your memory card instead, highlight any of the M1, M2, M3, and M4 entries, which represent four different sets of settings registered to your card. You can review the M1 to M4 settings by scrolling, as described in Step 3. If no settings have been stored for a particular M1 to M4 register, the message No File appears.

5. **Confirm.** If a selected set is satisfactory, press the center button to confirm your choice and exit. Your settings are now active in the camera.

Camera Settings Memory

Options: Store settings on your memory card

My preference: N/A

This entry registers your camera's current settings, either to one of the three physical memory registers (1, 2, or 3) within your a7C II/a7CR or to one of the card-based M1 to M4 files. The power of the memory feature stems from the fact that so many shooting settings can be saved for instant recall in any memory register.

Before you access the Camera Settings Memory item in the menu, make sure the mode dial is *not* rotated to the 1, 2, or 3 positions. Instead, the dial should be moved to the shooting mode you want to store, P, S, A, M, or Auto. Then make your desired settings in terms of camera operating mode, drive mode, ISO, white balance, exposure compensation, metering mode, focus mode, and so forth. Then, to save your current settings on your memory card to one of the physical slots in your camera, or in one of the M1, M2, M3, or M4 card-based sets, just follow these steps:

1. **Set up your camera.** Set your camera to shooting mode and adjust the camera to use the settings you'd like to store.

2. **Navigate to this entry.** Select Shooting > Shooting Mode > Camera Settings Memory and press the center button. A screen like the one shown in Figure 6.17, right, appears.

3. **Review settings.** Use the up/down buttons to scroll through the current settings to make sure they are satisfactory. A great deal more information is available than is shown in the figure (note the scroll bar at right). You can press the up/down buttons to view additional screens with detailed listings of your current settings. Exit and change desired settings, then start again at Step 2.

4. **Choose Register.** Press the left/right buttons to select which of the memory locations you'd like to store your current settings in:

   - If you choose 1, 2, or 3, the settings will be loaded into the camera's physical memory and will be available regardless of which card is in the camera.

   - If you choose M1, M2, M3, or M4, the settings will be stored *on the memory card* and will be available *only* when that memory card resides in the camera.

5. **Proceed or cancel.** Press the center button to confirm and store your settings, or the MENU button to cancel.

6. **Activate register.** To use your stored settings, rotate the mode dial to Register 1, Register 2, or Register 3 (1, 2, or 3 on the mode dial).

Auto/Scene Selection

Options: *Intelligent Auto*, Scene Selection
My preference: N/A

This menu item appears only when the Still/Movie/S&Q dial is in the Still position. It allows you to specify whether Intelligent Auto or a specific Scene selection is the default when the mode dial is set to the green Auto position in still mode. Your choices are as follows:

- **Intelligent Auto.** When this is set, each time the mode dial is rotated to the Auto position, Intelligent Auto will be active. You can still switch to Scene Selection using the directional controls. Only the default mode is set.

- **Scene Selection.** Choose this option instead, and you can use the left/right buttons to choose a specific Scene mode, such as Portrait, Landscape, Macro, etc. Then when the mode dial is set at the Auto position, that particular Scene mode will be active. You can still choose other Scene modes or Intelligent Auto; only the default Scene is specified. Use this if you find yourself frequently using a particular Scene mode.

Shoot Mode

Options: *S&Q Motion*, Time-lapse Photography
My preference: N/A

This is a function similar to Auto/Scene Selection, but for Movie mode. You can select whether S&Q Motion or Time-lapse Photography are the default modes when the Still/Movie/S&Q dial is rotated to the S&Q position.

Register Custom Shooting Set

Options: Recall **Custom Hold 1*, 2, or 3

My preference: N/A

This function is an expansion of the Camera Settings Memory feature and available when using PASM exposure modes. It allows storing sets of settings for *temporary* recall at the press of a custom key, and lets you choose to store *some* settings and ignore others. You can register three groups of settings but can assign only one at a time to your defined key. The Custom Shooting set is active only while you are holding down the defined key; when you release it the a7C II/a7CR returns to its previous settings. You might want to use this feature to switch quickly and temporarily from one set of registered settings to another. Perhaps you're shooting landscapes and unexpectedly spy a rare raptor swooping by. If you've registered a set of parameters for "birds in flight" you can press your custom button, capture the bird, then release it and continue with your landscape shooting.

There are three available slots (Recall Custom Hold 1–3) and you can assign each of the three to a different button, giving you three settings available at the press of a defined button, three settings available from the 1, 2, and 3 physical mode dial positions, and four settings stored as M1 to M4 on your current memory card. Here's how to use this feature, which is available only when PASM modes are active:

1. **Access this setting from Shooting > Shooting Mode > Register Custom Shooting Settings.** The screen shown in Figure 6.18, left, appears.

2. **Choose the registration number in which to store your settings.** Select from Recall Custom Hold 1 to Recall Custom Hold 3.

3. **Check current settings.** You can view the current settings of the camera. Only the settings that can be registered are shown. Use the up/down controls to scroll.

4. **Adjust or disable settings.** There are two columns in the settings display: enabled/disabled check-boxes and a setting name/current setting listing. (See Figure 6.18, center.) Use the left/right controls to switch columns.

5. **To disable registration of a setting.** Highlight the left column of a setting listing and press the center button to add/remove the checkmark.

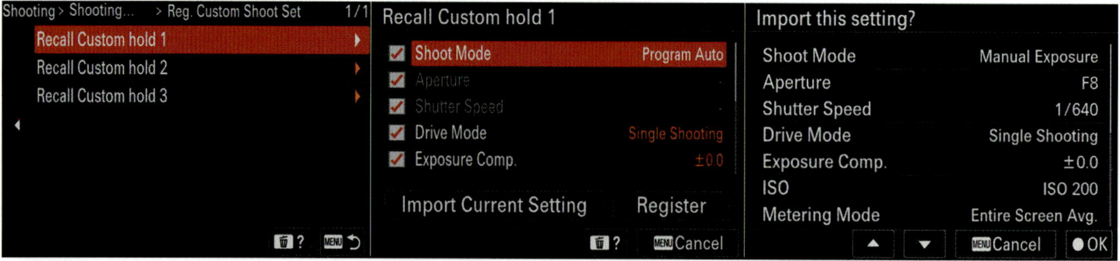

Figure 6.18 Select a Custom Hold register number (left). Review settings (center). Register settings (right).

6. **To change a setting.** Highlight the right column of a setting listing and press the center button. A screen will appear with the available options. For example, for Shoot Mode you can switch from the current mode to Program Auto, Aperture Priority, Shutter Priority, or Manual exposure.

7. **Store settings.** Scroll down to the bottom of the screen and highlight Import Current Setting. Press the center button. The screen shown in Figure 6.18, right, appears.

8. **Register additional numbers.** Highlight Register to return to the screen seen in Figure 6.18, left, to register additional groups of settings.

9. **Assign a custom key.** To use this feature, you must assign a button to the Recall Custom Hold *x* (1, 2, or 3) behavior. Use the Custom Key/Dial Settings (Stills) entry in the Setup > Operation Customize group, which I'll describe in Chapter 9. Note that you can define settings for all three Custom Hold registration numbers and can *define separate buttons* for each one. That means you can instantly (and temporarily) recall three additional sets of memory settings using custom keys, if you can spare that many from other duties.

10. **Use Custom Shooting Set.** Press the defined key to activate the Custom Hold settings assigned to that key, then press the shutter release down all the way to take a picture using those settings. When you release the custom key, your a7C II/a7CR will return to its previous settings.

5. Drive Mode

The Drive Mode group is visible only when the Still/Movie/S&Q dial is set to Still photos. (See Figure 6.19.) It has four entries:

- Drive Mode
- Bracket Settings
- Interval Shooting Functions
- Pixel Shift Multi Shooting (a7CR Only)

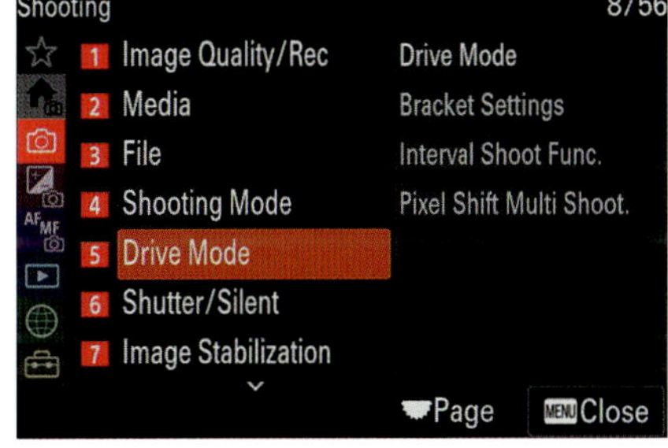

Figure 6.19 Drive Mode group.

Drive Mode

Options: **Single Shooting*; Cont. Shooting (Hi+, Hi, Mid, Lo); Self-timer (Single) (2/5/10 seconds); Self-timer Continuous (2/5/10 seconds with 3 or 5 shots); Continuous Bracket/Single Bracket (2, 3, 5, 7, or 9 images at 0.3 to 3.0 EV increments); Focus Bracket (Step Width, Number of Shots, Focus Bracket Order, Exposure Smoothing, Shooting Interval, Focus Bracket Saving Destination); White Balance Bracket (Lo/Hi); DRO Bracket (Lo/Hi)

My preference: N/A

Just as with the Drive (left directional) button on the back of the camera, there are several choices available through this single menu item. Your choices include:

- **Single shooting.** Takes one shot each time you press the shutter-release button. You must use this mode or one of the self-timer modes (described shortly) if you want to take a Bulb or Bulb Timer (long exposure) setting when working with Manual exposure.

- **Continuous shooting.** Captures images at rates that vary, depending on whether you're using the a7C II or a7CR. When this option is highlighted, press the left/right directional buttons to switch among Hi+ (10/8 fps—a7C II/a7CR, respectively), Hi (up to 8/6 fps, respectively), Mid (up to 6/5 fps), or Lo (up to 3/2.5 fps). The continuous speed will slow down if you're shooting uncompressed RAW. The Hi+ speed is maintained, but the viewfinder/LCD monitor doesn't display the image in real time. You'll be viewing a slightly delayed image as the camera churns away capturing high-speed images.

  Focus and exposure can adjust during the burst if you set Focus Mode to Continuous AF and AEL w/Shutter to Off or Auto. However, when an f/stop smaller than f/8 is in use, focus is set for the first shot, and retained for subsequent images as long as you hold down the shutter button. Continuous shooting becomes slower when using flash, when the RAW file type is set to Uncompressed.

  If you want to keep track of your remaining shots, the Continuous Shooting Length indicator can be activated using the Setup > Display Option > Remain Shoot Display entry, as described in Chapter 9.

- **Self-Timer (2 sec./5 sec./10 sec.).** Takes a single picture after two, five, or ten seconds have elapsed. When this choice is highlighted, press the left/right buttons to switch among the three durations.

- **Self-Timer Continuous.** The self-timer counts down, and then takes either 3 or 5 images, after delays of 2, 5, or 10 seconds. The left/right buttons cycle among the choices. You can cancel the timer by pressing the Drive button and selecting Single Shooting, or by tapping the shutter button a second time. Note that if you're using any of the continuous self-timer, continuous shooting, or continuous bracketing options, manual Bulb exposures produce an exposure time of 1/30th second.

- **Continuous Bracket.** Captures 2, 3, 5, 7, or 9 images in one burst when the shutter release is held down. You have a 2 Images (+) and 2 Images (–) choice which takes two shots biased toward over- and underexposure (respectively). Bracketing increments of 0.3, 0.5, 0.7, 1.0, 1.3, 1.5, 1.7, 2.0, 2.3, 2.5, 2.7, and 3.0 EV can be specified. Use the directional buttons to select the increment and number of shots.

  In Manual exposure (when ISO Auto is disabled), or in Aperture Priority, the shutter speed will change. If ISO Auto is set in Manual exposure, the bracketed set will be created by changing the ISO setting. In Shutter Priority, the aperture will change. Use continuous mode when you want all the images in the set to be framed as similarly as possible, say, when you will be using them for manually assembled high dynamic range (HDR) photos. You can use an external flash when continuous bracketing is active, but, because of the time required for the flash to recycle, you'll need to press the shutter button each time to take subsequent images (effectively switching the camera into Single Bracket mode, described next).

  Only the last shot in the set is displayed when using Auto Review. With all types of bracketing, the exposure/bracket scale at the bottom of the EVF or LCD monitor (in Display All Info mode) will display indicators showing the number of images shot and the relative amount of under-/overexposure. Don't forget that you can dial in exposure compensation, and *that* will affect the amount of over/underexposure applied while bracketing. Continuous bracketing (and Single Bracketing) is disabled when using Intelligent Auto.

- **Single Bracket.** Captures one bracketed image in a set, using the number of shots and increments available as described with Continuous Bracketing, above. In this mode, you can separate each image by an interval of your choice. You might want to use this variation when you want the individual images to be captured at slightly different times, say, to produce a set of images that will be combined in some artistic way.
- **Focus Bracket.** Choose Step Width from 1 (Narrow) to 4 (Standard) to 10 (Wide); Number of shots (1 to 299); plus Choose Focus Bracket Order, Exposure Smoothing, Shooting Interval, and Focus Bracket Saving Destination. I showed you how to perform focus bracketing in Chapter 5.

SELF-TIMER IN BRACKET MODES

You can set continuous and single bracket modes, and still make use of the self-timer. Access Bracket Settings (discussed next) and activate Self-Timer During Bracketing.

- **White Balance Bracket.** Three images are produced, each with adjustments to the color temperature. While you can't specify which direction the color bias is tilted, you can select Lo (the default) for small changes, or Hi, for larger changes using the left/right buttons. Only the last shot taken is displayed during Auto Review.
- **DRO Bracket.** Produces three image adjustments using dynamic range optimization. You can't specify the amount of optimization, but you can select Lo (the default) for small changes, or Hi, for larger changes, using the left/right buttons. Again, only the last shot taken is displayed during Auto Review.

Bracket Settings

Options: Self-timer During Bracketing: *Off, 2 sec., 5 sec., 10 sec.; Bracket Order: *0-+, -0+; Focus Bracket Settings: Focus Bracket Order: *0-+, -0+, Exposure Smoothing: *Off, On, Shooting Interval: *Shortest, 1–30 seconds; Focus Bracket Saving Destination: *Current Folder, New Folder

My preference: N/A

This item has three entries that let you customize how bracketing is applied. I described focus bracketing in detail in Chapter 5 and will not repeat that information here.

- **Self-timer During Bracketing.** You can choose delays of 2, 5, or 10 seconds before bracketing begins, or disable the self-timer during bracketing. This clever option solves a problem: how to use the self-timer (say, to avoid shaking a camera mounted on a tripod) when bracketing (which resides in the same Drive menu). With continuous bracketing, all exposures will be taken after the self-timer delay; if you're using single bracketing, the delay takes place before each shot in the bracket set is exposed.
- **Bracket Order.** The default is metered exposure > underexposure > overexposure. However, if you're shooting photos that will later be manually assembled into an HDR photo, you might find it more convenient to expose in order of progressively more exposure: underexposure > metered exposure > overexposure. The order you choose will also be applied to white balance bracketing.
- **Focus Bracket Settings.** You can choose Focus Bracket Order, Exposure Smoothing, Shooting Interval, and Focus Bracket Saving Destination, as described in Chapter 5.

Interval Shooting Functions

Options: Interval Shooting, Shooting Start Time, Shooting Interval, Number of Shots, AE Tracking Sensitivity, Shutter Type in Interval, Shoot Interval Priority

My preference: N/A

This is the a7C II and a7CR's "manual" time-lapse movie feature, which captures still images that can be assembled into a finished video. Your a7C II/a7CR can now capture a series of shots of the moon marching across the sky or compile one of those extreme time-lapse picture sets showing something that takes a very, very long time, such as a building under construction.

You probably won't be shooting such construction shots, unless you have a spare camera you don't need for a few months (or are willing to go through the rigmarole of figuring out how to set up your camera in precisely the same position using the same lens settings to shoot a series of pictures at intervals). However, other kinds of interval and time-lapse photography are entirely within reach. Best of all, with Sony's free Imaging Edge software, you can turn a series of time-lapse stills into a movie! I provided step-by-step instructions for capturing interval stills and time-lapse video in Chapter 5, and included tips on recommended intervals between shots. There are seven major settings you have to work with. The first five are shown at upper left in Figure 6.20. The remaining two, shown at upper right, can be viewed by scrolling down.

- **Interval Shooting.** Choose On or Off to enable/disable the feature. You'll want to keep this setting at Off until you are ready to begin interval shooting.

Figure 6.20 Interval Shooting options.

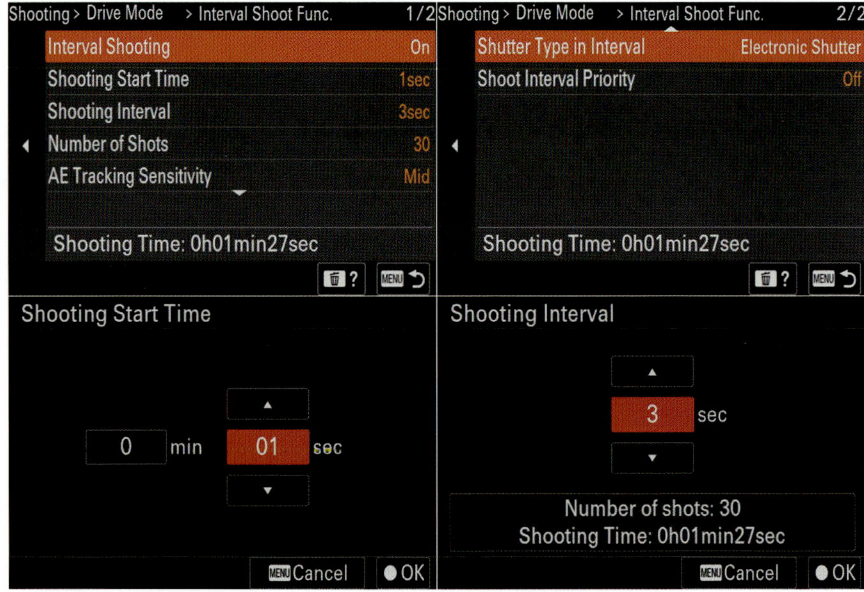

- **Shooting Start Time.** Use this setting to delay the start of image capture, from 0 minutes 0 seconds (begin immediately) to 99 minutes, 59 seconds. Say you're planning on capturing a sunset and know that the best time to begin shooting will be in one hour. Specify 60 minutes and 0 seconds, set up your camera, and the a7C II/a7CR will begin taking your sequence at the designated time. You're free to do other things in the interim. (See Figure 6.20, lower left.)

- **Shooting Interval.** Specify how often an image should be captured. You might need an interval of 3 to 4 seconds to capture the march of fast-moving clouds across the sky, or prefer a more relaxed 10 to 12 seconds to shoot clouds with a slower pace. Intervals can range from 1 to 60 seconds between shots. (See Figure 6.20, lower right.)

- **Number of Shots.** This setting determines the total number of exposures in a time-lapse sequence. You can choose from 1 to 9999 shots. A message at the bottom of the screen will display how long it will take to capture the number of shots you specify using the shooting interval you've chosen. If you select the maximum 60-second interval and 9999 shots, your sequence will take almost one week to capture (166 hours and 36 minutes). See Figure 6.21, upper left.

- **Autoexposure Tracking Sensitivity.** When the light levels are changing—say when capturing an entire day's activity, or something that happens fairly quickly, such as a sunset—you can specify whether the a7C II/a7CR adjusts exposure quickly, or slowly. Select from High, Mid (Medium), or Low sensitivity. Quick changes in exposure can be jarring, especially when combining shots into a time-lapse movie. You may want to experiment to see what works for your particular sequence, but the Mid setting should work for most projects. Note that if you *want* to see dramatic light shifts as your scene lightens or darkens, use Manual Exposure, and set the shutter speed, ISO, and aperture to give the correct "normal" exposure (say, for mid-day when shooting a day-long series). The dawn/early morning and dusk/night exposures will have different degrees of underexposure—probably for a more dramatic effect. (See Figure 6.21, upper right.)

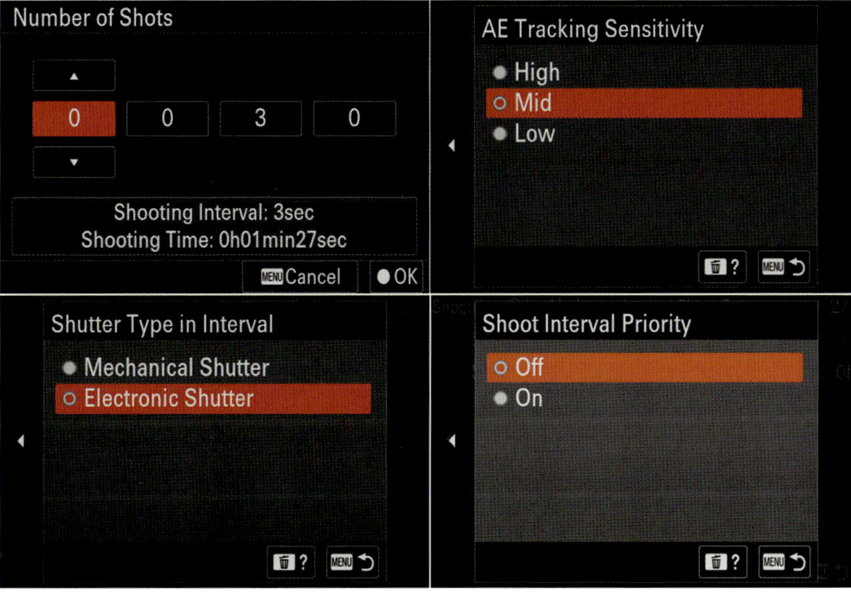

Figure 6.21 More Interval Shooting options.

- **Shutter Type in Interval.** Choose Mechanical Shutter or Electronic Shutter. If you select Electronic Shutter, the a7C II/a7CR will operate silently, which allows capturing your sequence in "stealth" mode if you need it. Silent shooting also makes the series of shots less intrusive in environments where low noise levels are prized—such as religious ceremonies, concerts, college libraries prior to finals week, or capturing a sleeping baby without interrupting parents' "quiet time." (See Figure 6.21, lower left.)

- **Shoot Interval Priority.** When shooting sequences using Program or Aperture Priority modes, the camera will adjust the shutter speed to provide the correct exposure. Unfortunately, when light levels are low, that may result in a shutter speed that is longer than the specified interval. That is, you may want to take a photo every two seconds, but the camera calculates that a four-second exposure is required. (See Figure 6.21, lower right.)

If you select Off for this setting, when the a7C II/a7CR encounters a conflict, it will go ahead and expose for the correct amount of time, skipping the shot that would have taken place. This is the default behavior and often the best choice. In most cases, there is not enough subject motion between frames to result in a jarring effect. You're more likely to dislike having that conflicting image underexposed, which is what happens when this setting is On. When another interval exposure is due, the a7C II/a7CR will terminate the previous shot (underexposing it) and begin the next one on schedule. You might use the On option if you feel that just dropping the poorly exposed image from the sequence produces the best series.

Pixel Shift Multi Shooting ▣ ▣ ▣ (a7CR Only)

Options: *Off, Shoot 4 Shots, Interval; Shoot 16 Shots, Interval
My preference: N/A

If the a7CR's 60-megapixel resolution isn't enough for you, you can use this facility to capture images with up to 240MP of awesome detail. I explained how to do Pixel Shift Multi Shooting in Chapter 5, and won't repeat that information here.

6. Shutter/Silent

This group has five settings that control how your physical and electronic shutters operate. (See Figure 6.22.)

- Silent Mode Settings
- Shutter Type
- Release without Lens
- Release without Card
- Anti-Flicker Settings

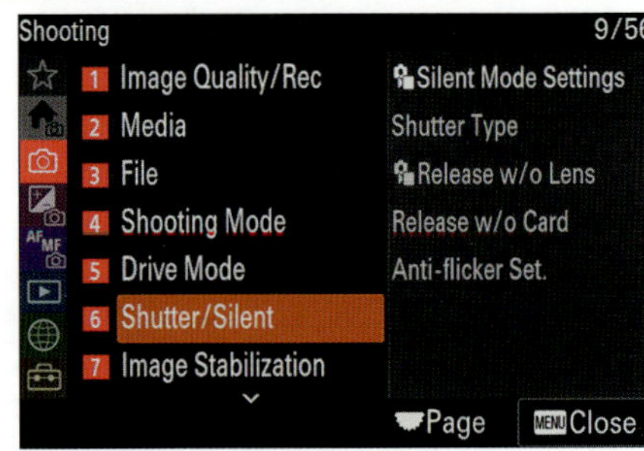

Figure 6.22 Shutter/Silent group entries.

Silent Mode Settings

Options: Silent Mode: (On, ***Off**); Target Function Settings: Aperture Drive in AF: Not Target, **Standard**, Silent Priority); Shutter When Power OFF: *Off, Not Target; Auto Pixel Mapping: ***Off**, Not Target

My preference: N/A

If you shoot acoustic concerts, stage performances, weddings, or stealth street photography, you'll want to explore this option, which lets you *almost* silence your a7C II/a7CR by reducing shutter sounds. You may still hear noise as the lens aperture changes, autofocus operates, you use Face Memory to register a face, and when functions including anti-dust and pixel-mapping kick in as the camera is powered down. Fortunately, this entry, available in P, S, A, and M modes, has options that help improve your chances of silent operation. If you navigate to Shooting > Shutter/Silent > Silent Mode Settings, you see the following two entries, shown at left in Figure 6.23:

- **Silent Mode.** Silent mode is Off by default. If you enable it by selecting On, the a7C II/a7CR *always* uses the electronic shutter, which doesn't emit a sound. The Setup > Sound Option > Audio Signals entry is switched to Off, and the camera will not beep when it achieves focus in Continuous AF mode. The Shutter Type in Interval setting is locked at Electronic Shutter.

  Keep in mind that in Silent mode, flash and Bulb exposures are disabled, along with the e-Front Curtain Shutter and long exposure noise reduction.

- **Target Function Settings.** This option has sub-entries, seen at right in Figure 6.23. They determine whether the a7C II/a7CR should simultaneously change your current values of three *other* settings that can cause noise when the camera has been switched to Silent mode.

  - **Aperture Drive in AF.** The default setting is Standard, which means the camera may emit noise as the AF mechanism operates, even when Silent mode is active. You may also choose Silent Priority, which tends to slow the focusing speed, making it quieter, but also possibly making focus more difficult (depending on the performance of the lens you are using).

    Select Not Target instead, and the a7C II/a7CR will retain whatever setting you have specified in the Focus > AF/MF > Aperture Drive in AF entry (which I'll explain in Chapter 8). Don't confuse this sub-entry with the Aperture Drive in AF entry found in the AF/MF group. The latter entry globally sets the aperture drive system used for *both* the Mechanical and Electronic shutters. This one is used to override the basic setting and applies *only* when the electronic shutter is active.

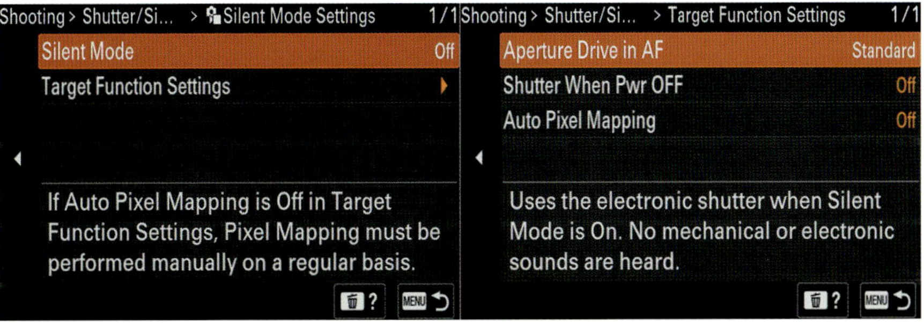

Figure 6.23 Silent Mode Settings.

- **Shutter When Power OFF.** Specifies whether the shutter is closed when you power down the camera, making a sound that may be unwanted and can be disabled here by choosing Not Target.
- **Auto Pixel Mapping.** If you have turned on Auto Pixel Mapping, you'll find that it too sometimes makes a slight sound when the camera is powered down. The default, Off, eliminates this noise, while selecting Not Target allows it.

Shutter Type

Options: *Mechanical Shutter*, Electronic Shutter

My preference: Mechanical Shutter

Here you can choose whether the a7C II/a7CR uses its conventional mechanical shutter or its silent electronic shutter. Under very bright conditions, such as snow or beach scenes, if a very high shutter speed is required, the camera may switch to electronic shutter even if you've specified mechanical shutter here. In addition, this setting is only available in P, S, A, and M modes. I tend to reserve the electronic shutter for stealthy and sound-sensitive environments, partially because of the electronic shutter's limitations on flash shooting and long Bulb exposures.

But the most important limitation of the electronic shutter is the effects of its "rolling shutter," which can be problematic both in still and video shooting. The camera records each line one line after another. That may produce distortion with moving subjects, because as a subject crosses the frame, the portion at the top of the frame will be in a different position from the part of the subject at the bottom of the frame. For stills, this "Jell-o effect" may be most noticeable when shooting uncompressed RAW images. To reduce the distortion, change the RAW file type to Compressed, and use continuous shooting. You'll get the best results, however, capturing in JPEG mode.

Of course the electronic shutter is also used for video. Even though a video frame is cropped at top and bottom so that fewer rows of pixels have to be captured, your subject, or even the camera, may be moving as well, which makes the Jell-o distortion even more objectionable.

Release w/o Lens

Options: Disable, *Enable*

My preference: Enable

By default, the camera will open its shutter when you depress the shutter-release button when no lens is mounted. This option will be useful if you attach the camera to some accessory such as a telescope or a third-party optic that's not recognized as a lens. I prefer to select Enable, because I frequently use oddball third-party and "foreign" lenses on my camera, such as my favorite Lensbaby distortion lens or a fisheye lens designed with a different camera mount. Select Disable instead, and the a7C II/a7CR will refuse to try to take a photo when a lens is not mounted on the camera. This is a logical setting only for easily distracted folks who fail to notice that they have a lens-less camera body hanging around their necks.

Release w/o Card

Options: Disable, *****Enable**
My preference: Disable

The ability to trip the shutter without having a memory card installed is not especially useful unless you want to hand your camera to someone for demonstration purposes and do not want to give them the capability of actually taking a picture. This happens frequently at trade shows, where vendors want you to try out their equipment, but would prefer you not leave the premises with any evidence/image samples, especially if the memory card in question belongs to the vendor rather than you.

On the contrary, it's more likely that you'd prefer to have your own camera inoperable if you've forgotten to insert a memory card. It's easy to miss the orange No Card warning that flashes when the non-picture is taken. Disabling release when a card is absent can help you avoid losing a card (you removed it to load some pictures onto someone else's computer) or having to sheepishly ask the bride and groom if they would be willing to re-stage their wedding.

Anti-Flicker Settings

Options: Anti-Flicker Shooting (On, *****Off**); Variable Shutter (On, *****Off**); Variable Shutter Settings
My preference: Off, unless shooting under flickering light source

Novice sports photographers often ask me why shots they take in certain gymnasiums or arenas have inconsistent exposure, wildly varying color, or banding. The answer is that certain types of artificial lighting actually have a blinking cycle that is imperceptible to the eye, but which the camera can capture. This setting, when enabled, detects the frequency (it's optimized for 100 Hz to 120 Hz illumination) of the light source that is blinking, and takes the picture at the moment when the flicker has the least effect on the final image.

Sony gives you two different tools for reducing or eliminating these problems, both available within this Anti-Flicker Settings entry. They are Anti-Flicker Shooting and Variable Shutter. Anti-Flicker intelligently examines the sensor's Live View feed and determines the frequency, or flicker rate. When you press the shutter release down all the way to take an image, the camera introduces a slight delay before the capture begins (up to 1/120th second) until the darkest part of the illumination's cycle has passed. As a result, the image brightness is consistent as the sensor scans the frame from top to bottom.

Variable Shutter provides an alternate/additional way of combating flicker/banding. When active, in Manual and Shutter Priority modes you can specify fractional shutter speeds (e.g., 1/270.3 second) to better synchronize capture with the flickering cycle of the light source.

Anti-flicker cannot be used with the electronic shutter, with Bulb exposures, or during movie shooting. *However,* even if anti-flicker is turned off, you can *still* use the variable shutter feature described shortly with the mechanical *or electronic shutter* and during video capture. Although they are adjusted within the same entry, anti-flicker and variable shutter *are two different functions.* You can use the Anti-Flicker Shooting and Variable Shutter features described below individually or together. The options available are shown at left in Figure 6.24.

Figure 6.24 Anti-Flicker Settings (left). Set a variable shutter speed (right).

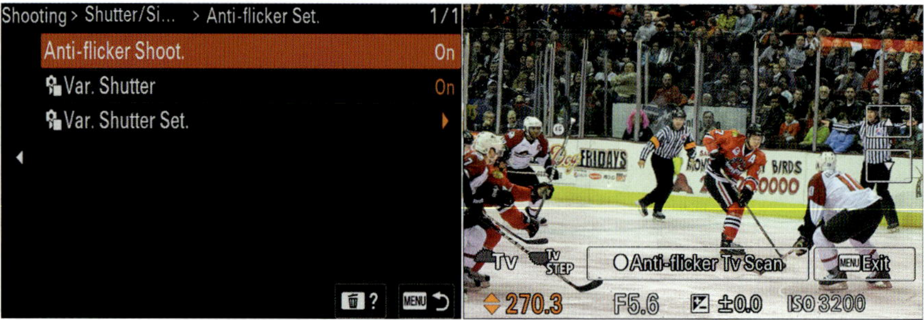

Anti-Flicker Shooting

This stills-only option allows you to turn the fully automated Anti-Flicker feature on or off. It can be used with any of the PASM exposure modes, and is available *only* when using the mechanical shutter.

When anti-flicker is enabled, you should press the shutter release down halfway so the a7C II/a7CR can detect the frequency of the flicker, and then press it the rest of the way when the Flicker icon is displayed. You can also use the AF-ON button to tell the camera to measure flicker. This can be especially useful when focusing manually.

You may experience a slight shutter release time lag as the camera "waits" for the proper instant, and your continuous shooting speed may be reduced, which makes this setting a necessary evil for sports and other activities involving action. Your results may vary when using P or A modes, because the shutter speed can change between shots as proper exposure requires, so color tones can vary. You're better off using S or M mode, so the shutter speed remains constant.

A handy Flicker warning will appear, alerting you that the feature is enabled, except in Intelligent Auto mode. This feature may not work as well with dark backgrounds, a bright light within the image area, when using wireless flash, and under other shooting conditions. I recommend taking test shots to see how effective the feature is under the light source you are working with. The feature is not available at all when using Bulb exposures or shooting movies. If you have Priority Set in AF-S, or AF-C set to Release or Balanced Emphasis, the camera will focus and shoot immediately when you press the shutter release down all the way. You'll need to use a half-press first to give Anti-Flicker a chance to do its thing.

Variable Shutter

This entry lets you turn Variable Shutter on or off. You might want to use this option if effects continue when using the automated Anti-Flicker Shooting feature. It lets you fine-tune the actual shutter speed that will be used in Shutter Priority and Manual exposure mode in 1/4-stop increments. This feature is available in stills and movie mode and can be used with the mechanical and electronic shutters. Moreover, while anti-flicker works *only* with 100 Hz to 120 Hz illumination frequencies, the variable shutter can prove helpful even if some higher frequencies are present. When you later turn this variable shutter feature off, the camera will switch to the closest conventional shutter speed.

Variable Shutter Settings

Here you use the up/down buttons or front dial to change the actual shutter speed in small increments of 1/4 stop, or the rear dial to use larger increments. The available range of speeds is 1/48.0 second to 1/4098.4th second with the mechanical shutter (or 1/8064.5th second with the electronic shutter). (Sony dubs this "high-resolution shutter speed.") When you access this option, a live view image like the one shown at right in Figure 6.24 appears. Use the controls to make fractional adjustments to the shutter speed until the monitor view looks okay. Press MENU to confirm and exit.

Once you've locked in a frequency by pressing the center button, the a7C II/a7CR will make matching adjustments in multiples (i.e., 2X, 4X, 1/2X, etc.) when you rotate the front dial to adjust the shutter speed in small increments, and the left rear dial for larger whole-stop increments. However, you should be aware that even with anti-flicker compensation, color tones may vary if a different shutter speed is used.

You'll want to double-check during image review to make sure flickering effects have been reduced. As shutter speeds grow shorter, there may be more of a difference between the preview and the actual image, so you may have to adjust. For faster access, some like to assign the Anti-Flicker TV Scan function to a custom key using Setup > Operation Customize > Custom Key/Dial Setup, as described in Chapter 9.

Movie Settings

When the Still/Movie/S&Q dial is set to the Movie position, two additional groups that pertain exclusively to video functions appear between Shutter/Silent and Image Stabilization. They are:

- **Audio Recording.** Five additional entries that deal with audio recording, audio levels and display, along with wind noise reduction.
- **TC/UB.** This group has six entries used when setting Time Codes for video capture.

Since this long list of entries apply only to movie making, rather than bury them in a chapter that covers features that apply either to still photography, or to both still photography and movie making, I'm going to relegate those settings to Chapter 11. There, I'll cover the basics of movie making, and discuss the hows and whys of these particular parameters in more detail.

7. Image Stabilization

This group has three settings for controlling how your a7C II/a7CR applies image stabilization as images are captured, shown at left in Figure 6.25:

- SteadyShot
- SteadyShot Adjustment
- Focal Length

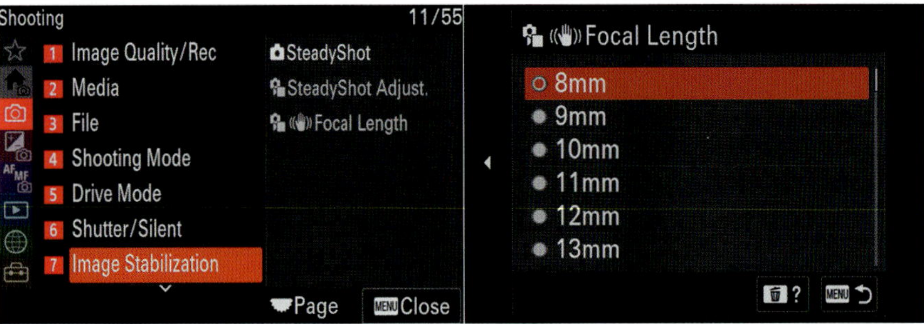

Figure 6.25 Image Stabilization settings (left). Focal length adjustments (right).

SteadyShot 📷 🎬 S&Q

Options: *On, Off

My preference: On

The a7C II/a7CR has both in-body image stabilization (the awesome 5-axis SteadyShot that so many of us are crazy about), and the ability to use optical image stabilization (Optical SteadyShot or OSS) built into certain lenses. Both systems work well with each other and can be used simultaneously. If for some reason you want to disable SteadyShot, you can use this menu entry. Some lenses, like the Sony FE 24-105mm f/4 G OSS, have an Optical SteadyShot On/Off Switch. If so, this menu setting is not available.

SteadyShot is on by default to help counteract image blur that is caused by camera shake, but you should turn it off when the camera is mounted on a tripod, as the additional anti-shake feature is not needed, and slight movements of the tripod can sometimes "confuse" the system. In other situations, however, I recommend leaving SteadyShot turned on at all times.

(Movies) SteadyShot 📷 🎬 S&Q

Options: Active, *Standard, Off

My preference: Standard

This is the Movie version of the SteadyShot entry. Instead of just on or off, you can choose Standard mode, which deploys the same IBIS and OSS anti-shake process used in still photography mode; or select Active (to counter continuous, extreme movement). In Active mode, often referred to as *electronic image stabilization*, the camera compares each video frame with the one just before it, and can then can crop and rotate each image to keep the pixels in alignment despite camera movement. The actual image area may be slightly smaller because of the need to crop slightly; the frame size in Active mode is roughly 87 percent that of Standard mode. Active mode is not available at 120/100 fps rates. Sony does not recommend using it when working with lenses with focal lengths of 200mm or more. Both modes also embed additional information in the video file that can be used with Sony's optional extra-cost Catalyst Prepare software.

SteadyShot Adjustments 📷🎥🆂&🆀

Options: *__Auto__, Manual

My preference: Auto

This setting allows the camera to adjust the behavior of SteadyShot, based on the amount of image stabilization typically required at particular focal lengths. That is, telephoto lenses "magnify" camera shake and thus can benefit from more aggressive image stabilization. Indeed, this aspect is one reason why in-lens is often touted as superior to in-body stabilization. Your a7C II and a7CR give you the opportunity to benefit from both! This setting is not available if you have disabled Steady-Shot using the entry above. If your lens has Optical SteadyShot, settings can only be changed using the control on the lens. When the default Auto setting is enabled, the camera receives focal length information electronically from the lens and can activate the appropriate amount of SteadyShot anti-shake.

Focal Length 📷🎥🆂&🆀

Options: 8mm–1000mm

My preference: N/A

You can enter the focal length of the lens or the zoom position from the range 8mm to 1000mm. This is especially useful if you're working with a teleconverter, which produces magnification beyond that which the camera can detect from the supplied lens data alone. It's also a good option if you are using a lens (possibly a "foreign" lens with an adapter) that cannot communicate focal length to the a7C II/a7CR. (See Figure 6.25, right.)

8. Zoom

This group has four entries for the a7C II/a7CR's digital zoom features, which include a facility for adding an ersatz "power" zoom to many of your lenses. The entries are shown in Figure 6.26, left:

- Zoom
- Zoom Range
- Custom Key Zoom Speed
- Remote Zoom Speed

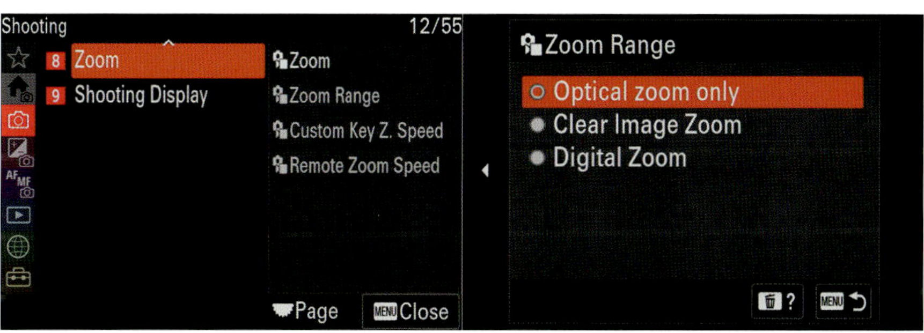

Figure 6.26 Zoom group (left). Setting Zoom Range (right).

Zoom

Options: Smart or Clear Image Zooming in shooting mode

My preference: None

This feature adds an ersatz "power zoom" physical control to the a7C II/a7CR, which otherwise lacks one. It's useful once you understand what it does and how it works, but Sony has done its best to make the feature as confusing as possible. This entry is available only when you have a power zoom lens attached to the camera, or have chosen either Clear Image Zoom or Digital Zoom in the Zoom Range entry that follows this one.

Some other cameras in the Sony mirrorless lineup have a physical zoom lever located concentrically with the shutter release. The a7C II/a7CR does not have this feature. But, in effect, you still have *five* different ways to zoom while you're taking still photographs or movies. This list will sort out the options for you:

- **Optical zoom with zoom ring.** Zoom lenses always have a ring around their barrel that can be rotated back and forth to zoom in or out on your subject. The sole exception might be a few lenses that have a power zoom lever that takes the place of the zoom ring.

- **Optical Power Zoom.** Certain E-mount lenses include a PZ (power zoom) designation in their name. These include several APS-C-format Sony lenses for the a7C II/a7CR, and the Sony FE 28-135mm PZ F4 G OSS full-frame E-mount power zoom lens. They all have a zooming motor built in that can be activated by sliding a switch on the lens barrel itself.

- **Smart Zoom.** This is one of three zoom options that take you beyond the true optical zoom range of your lens into the realm of digitized zooming, which produces a zoom *effect* by taking the pixels in the center of the original image and filling the frame with them.

  Smart Zoom is available *only* for JPEG/HEIF images when you have set the camera to M (medium) or S (small) image size. It provides a limited amount of zooming, but, technically, requires no quality-reducing interpolation. The camera simply produces each "zoomed" image by cropping the photo to the zoomed size. The resolution of your final image corresponds to the resolution of the Medium or Small image size. When using Smart Zoom, an S label appears in the viewfinder or LCD monitor zoom scale to indicate that the feature is in effect.

- **Clear Image Zoom.** This option is available when Zoom Range is set to Clear Image Zoom or Digital Zoom. When using this feature, some quality is lost, as this kind of zooming doesn't produce any actual additional information; it just *interpolates* the pixels captured optically to simulate a zoomed-in perspective. Pixels are created to fill the frame at the resolution of the given Image Size setting (Large, Medium, or Small). Clear Image Zoom has many options, and I'll explain them later in this chapter. When a zoom scale is shown in the viewfinder or on the LCD monitor, a C label appears whenever you leave optical zooming behind and enter the Clear Image realm. When Clear Image Zoom is used alone, you'll typically achieve 1X to 2X magnifications *over and above* whatever optical zoom setting you've used. At Medium and Small image size settings, you can zoom up to 3X and 4X, respectively.

■ **Digital Zoom.** This option, only available when Zoom range is set to Digital Zoom, gives you even higher magnifications than Clear Image Zoom, with an additional decrease in image quality. When a zoom scale is shown in the viewfinder or on the LCD monitor a D label appears when you are using digital zoom. I'll explain the options later in the chapter. When Digital Zoom is active, it takes up where Clear Image Zoom leaves off, giving you up to 4X magnification *beyond* the optical zoom focal length you've selected when using Large image size. At Medium image size, you can zoom up to 6.1X; with Small image size, up to 8X.

Zoom Range ◻ ◻ S&Q

Options: Optical Zoom Only, ***Clear Image Zoom***, Digital Zoom
My preference: None

Here you choose how the zoom features are applied (see Figure 6.26, right):

■ **Optical Zoom Only.** The a7C II/a7CR will only use the zoom range available from the mounted zoom lens. However, you can still use Smart Zoom if your JPEG/HEIF Image Size is set to Medium or Small.

■ **Clear Image Zoom.** The image will be magnified using the Clear Image Zoom feature described above.

■ **Digital Zoom.** Once you zoom beyond the range of Clear Image Zoom, Digital Zoom kicks in, producing the maximum amount of image degradation. Use this setting with caution.

Custom Key Zoom Speed ◻ ◻ S&Q

Options: Fixed Speed STBY (Standby): 1 (Slow), 2, ***3***, 4, 5, 6, 7, 8 (Fast); Fixed Speed REC (Record): 1 (Slow), 2, ***3***, 4, 5, 6, 7, 8 (Fast)
My preference: None

Sony has added a handy function that lets you specify how fast zooming takes place if you use the controls on the a7C II/a7CR. You can also specify the zoom speed on the + and – buttons on the remote commander, or the remote shooting function with a smart phone, using the Remote Zoom Speed entry, described next. This feature does not affect zooming with any lens's zoom ring, or zoom lever of a power zoom lens. Specifying a speed here insures that zooming will be smooth, which may not be the case when you just press the buttons.

You can assign the Zoom function to a custom key using the Custom Key/Dial Set (Stills) or Custom Key/Dial Set entries of the Setup > Operation Customize group. Pressing the assigned key of your choice summons the Zoom feature, which you then invoke using the directional controls. This entry allows you to set separate fixed zoom speeds when the camera is in standby (STBY) mode or recording (REC) modes. You can choose from 1 (Slow) to 8 (Fast).

Sony offers a clever suggestion: Set the STBY speed to fast so you can quickly zoom to set up a shot. Choose a slow speed for REC, so you can fine-tune during the shot and avoid distracting fast zooms (like you see in kung-fu movies of the '70s).

Remote Zoom Speed

Options: Speed Type: *Variable, Fix; Fixed Speed STBY (Standby): 1 (Slow), 2, *3, 4, 5, 6, 7, 8 (Fast); Fixed Speed REC (Record): 1 (Slow), 2, *3, 4, 5, 6, 7, 8 (Fast)

My preference: None

This is a separate entry for assigning a zoom speed to the +/− buttons on a remote. An additional option, Speed Type, which controls the relative speed of the STBY and REC options is available. When Speed Type is set to Variable, pressing the zoom controls on compatible remotes will gradually increase the zoom speed. Choose Fix instead, and the Fixed Speed (STBY) setting will invoke a fast zoom speed so you can set up your shot while in standby mode, while Fixed Speed (REC) will produce a slower zoom to change smoothly as you record.

Using Zoom

My basic recommendation is to use optical zoom only most of the time, and this feature might not be available. If you've set the camera for Optical Zoom Only in the Zoom Settings entry, then this Zoom feature is not available at all if Image Size is set to Large. If Clear Image Zoom is set to On, you can use Clear Image Zoom; if Digital Zoom is set to On, you can use both. When Image Size is set to Medium or Small, then Smart Zoom is also available for all three Zoom Range options. After you've sorted out which of the zoom methods you want to use, using the Zoom feature while shooting is fairly easy. Just follow these steps:

1. **Navigate to Shooting > Zoom > Zoom.** You can assign this function to a custom key and skip the menu if you like, as I noted. A live view of your sensor image appears in the EVF and LCD monitor, with a zoom scale at lower right, as shown in Figure 6.27.

2. **Zoom in or out.** You can rotate the control wheel, front/rear dials, or use the left/right directional controls to zoom in or out.

3. **Change zoom steps.** Press the up/down controls to change the size of the zoom increment, from 1X to 1.4X and thence all the way up to 8X, depending on whether you've selected Large, Medium, or Small as your image size.

4. **Confirm or cancel.** When you're satisfied with the zoom level, press the center button to confirm, or the MENU button to cancel. You can then continue to shoot at the new zoomed magnification.

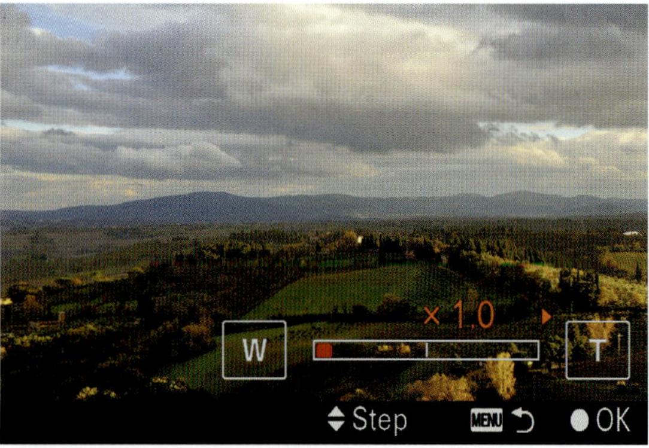

Figure 6.27 The zoom scale shows the amount of magnification and type of zoom in use.

9. Shooting Display

This group has three entries in both Still and Movie modes. The Grid Line Display and Grid Line type are common to both; each mode sports a different third entry. Figure 6.28 shows the Still version:

- Grid Line Display
- Grid Line Type
- Live View Display Settings (Stills)
- Emphasized REC Display (Movies)

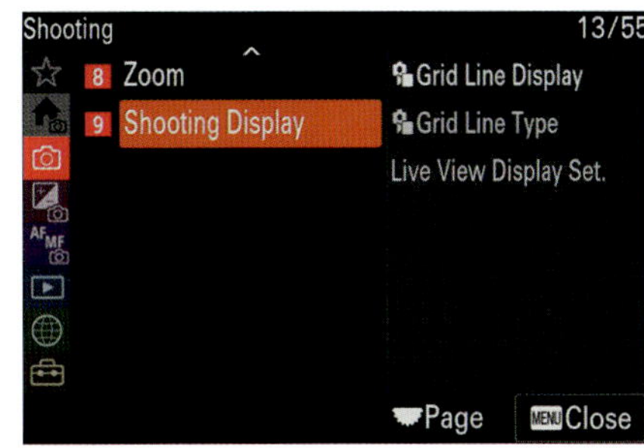

Figure 6.28 Shooting Display group for Still mode.

Grid Line Display/Grid Line Type 📷 🎬 S&Q

Grid Line Display Options: On, *Off

Grid Line Type Options: *Rule of 3rds Grid, Square Grid, Diag.+Square Grid

My preference: Off, Rule of 3rds

These two entries allow you to activate one of three optional grids, so it's superimposed on the LCD or EVF display. The grid pattern can help you with composition while you are shooting architecture or similar subjects. I sometimes use the Rule of Thirds grid to help with composition, but you might want to activate another option when composing images of scenes that include diagonal, horizontal, and perpendicular lines. Figure 6.29 shows the three types of grids available.

Live View Display Settings 📷 🎬 S&Q

Options: Live View Display: Setting Effect (*On, Off); Exposure Effect (*Exposure Setting & Flash, Exposure Setting Only); Frame Rate Low Limit (On, *Off)

My preference: Setting Effect ON, unless using flash in manual mode

Mirrorless cameras are always in a so-called "live view" mode, showing you what the sensor sees. This entry lets you specify whether the camera should apply any exposure settings or effects that you've selected to the image before presenting it to you as a preview.

There are times when you don't want to see the effects of the settings you've made on the screen/ EVF. For example, when you are using flash in manual mode, the camera has no way of knowing exactly how much light will be illuminating your scene. That f/16 aperture may be ideal for a shot exposed by your studio strobes, but the camera will, when Setting Effect is set to ON, show you a preview based on the ambient light, rather than the flash. The result? Your viewfinder or LCD monitor image is very, very dim. You'll want to select Setting Effect OFF so the camera will boost the electronic image to viewable levels.

Figure 6.29 Grid lines can help you align your images on the LCD monitor or EVF.

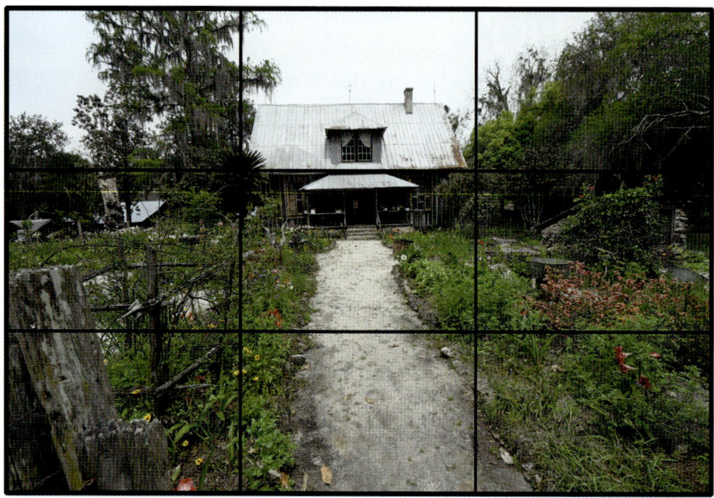

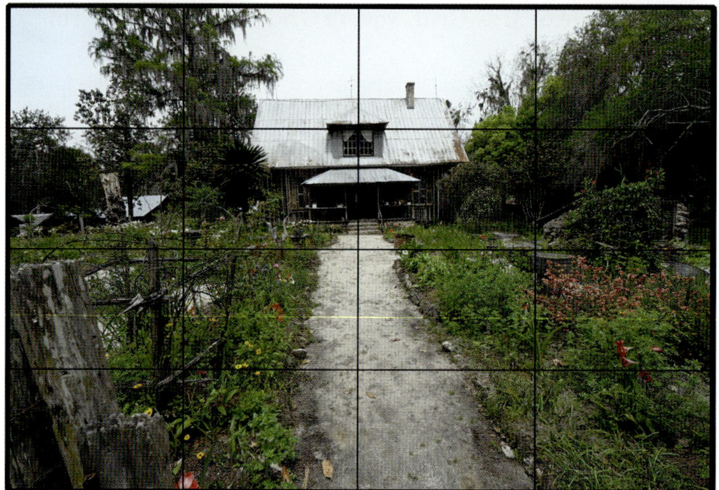

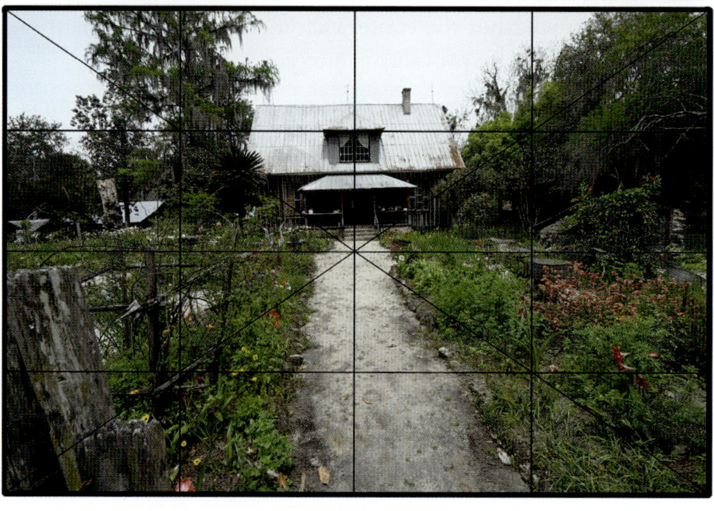

When Setting Effects are active, the live view display in the EVF or the LCD reflects the *exact* effects of any camera features that you're using to modify the view, including as exposure compensation and white balance. In that mode, this allows for an accurate evaluation of what the photo will look like and enables you to determine whether the current settings will provide the effects you want.

The ON option can be especially helpful when you're using any of the Creative Look effects because you can preview the exact rendition that the selected effect and its overrides will provide. It's also very useful when you're setting some exposure compensation, as you can visually determine how much lighter or darker each adjustment makes the image. And when you're trying to achieve correct color balance, it's useful to be able to preview the effect of your white balance setting.

If you'd like to preview the image without the effect of settings visible, you can set this feature to OFF. Naturally, the display will no longer accurately depict what your photo will look like when it's taken. So, for most users, ON is the most suitable option. Unfortunately, this setting has caused more than a few minutes of head-scratching among new users who switch to Manual exposure mode and find themselves with a completely black (or utterly white) screen. The black screen, especially, may fool you into thinking your camera has malfunctioned.

There are three options:

- **Live View Display.** Choose Setting Effect On to have all shooting settings applied to the display on the monitor or electronic viewfinder. Set to Off, the display may be easier to view in darker conditions, especially when shooting in Manual exposure mode. The camera will show a VIEW icon to remind you that the display no longer reflects what the image will look like with settings applied. Off is not available when using Intelligent Auto, Movie, or S&Q Motion modes.
- **Exposure Effect.** You can choose from Exposure Setting & Flash or Exposure Setting Only. The Exposure Setting & Flash option tells the a7C II/a7CR to take into account exposure from a Sony-brand electronic flash when Setting Effect is On. (Non-Sony flashes are not supported.) If you're basing exposure on ambient light only and using flash, choose Exposure Setting only.
- **Frame Rate Low Limit.** With the default Off setting, under dim conditions, the display's frame rate will slow down in order to provide a brighter, more easily seen view. You might want to choose On when using shutter speeds slower than 1/60th second or panning when you want to be able to preserve the normal display frame rate. However, the image will become darker, and may even black out.

Emphasized Record Display

Options: On, *Off
My recommendation: N/A

This is a handy feature that places a red frame around the edge of the monitor display when the a7C II/a7CR is actively recording video. Akin to the light indicator on the front of conventional movie cameras and webcams, it's a quick way to know whether the camera is in standby or recording mode. If you've set Setup > External Output > HDMI Information Display to On (as described in Chapter 9), the frame will show on an external monitor linked with an HDMI cable as well.

10. Marker Display (Stills/Movies)

This group has four entries in Movie mode, and for movies only (three for Stills Only), and one that applies to both Stills and Movies. The Stills choices are shown in Figure 6.30 (I'll describe the Movie options in detail in Chapter 11):

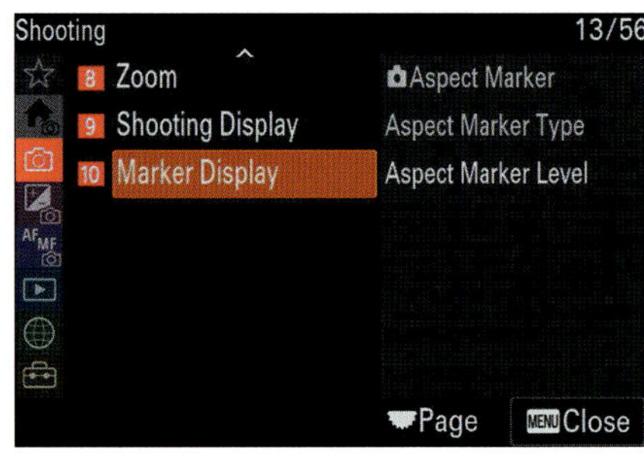

Figure 6.30 The Marker Display group.

- Marker Display (Movies Only)
- Center Marker (Movies Only)
- Aspect Marker (Stills/Movies)
- Aspect Marker Type (Stills Only)
- Aspect Marker Level (Stills Only)
- Safety Zone (Movies Only)
- Guideframe (Movies Only

Aspect Marker

Options: On, *Off

My recommendation: N/A

Your a7C II and a7CR give you two different ways of framing images using proportions other than the default 3:2 aspect ratio of your sensor. You can lock in a specific cropping using the Shooting > Image Quality/Rec > Aspect Ratio entry described earlier in this chapter; or you can capture the full frame but *preview* what a particular aspect ratio would produce using this entry to enable or disable Aspect Markers during shooting. Here's the difference:

- **Aspect Ratio setting.** If you select a particular aspect ratio (3:2, 4:3, 16:9, or 1:1) as described earlier, the camera applies the specific crop to the picture and does not capture any image information outside the selected aspect ratio.

- **Aspect Marker.** If you enable Aspect Marker here, no actual cropping of your image is performed. Instead, a translucent gray overlay is applied over the display, masking off the area that lies outside the selected proportions. In addition, you can specify proportions not available with the Aspect Ratio entry: 1.91:1 and 2:35:1, which are motion-picture formats. *Star Wars*, for example, was filmed in CinemaScope, with a 2.35:1 aspect ratio. See the Aspect Marker Type entry, described next

In Stills mode, Aspect Markers (enabled or disabled using this entry) use a mask overlay on the area that would be included in images captured using a particular aspect ratio. As described earlier in the chapter, you can specify 3:2, 4:3, 16:9, and 1:1 proportions using the Aspect Ratio entry in the Shooting > Image Quality/Recording group.

You can use Aspect Markers *and* Grid Lines (described earlier) at the same time, and specify that the marker seen during shooting be shown during playback (using the Playback > Playback Option >Aspect Marker Display entry explained in Chapter 8. Aspect markers rotate vertically when the camera is rotated 90 degrees. The Crop command in the Playback menu can be used to crop the images using the aspect marker you set here. If you're directing the output of the a7C II or a7CR to an external monitor, display, or recorder through the HDMI port, aspect markers are not shown.

Aspect Marker Type

Options: ***1:1**, 5:4, 4:3, 16:9, 1.91:1, 2.35:1
My recommendation: N/A

Here you can choose the aspect ratio of the mask that will be overlaid on the display.

Aspect Marker Level

Options: Transparency: 16 levels from 0 to 15, ***12** (default)
My recommendation: N/A

When you access this entry, a scale appears on the screen with increments from 0 to 15. At the zero setting there is no darkening, but lines appear to frame the aspect ratio on the display. At the maximum 15 setting, the mask is opaque black.

Shooting Option (Movies)

This group appears only when the Still/Movie/S&Q dial is set to a movie position. It has two movie-only entries:

- Self-timer
- Auto Framing Settings

Self-timer

Options: On: Repetition: ***Only Once**, Repeat, Recording Start Delay (***3 seconds**, 5 seconds, 10 seconds); ***Off**
My recommendation: N/A

This useful feature lets you use the camera's self-timer to start video capture, giving your subjects/actors/victims time to get ready. You can set it up to function every time you start shooting, or just once, with delays of 3, 5, and 10 seconds available.

Auto Framing Settings

Options: Auto Framing: *Off, On; Framing Operation Mode: Start When Tracking, ***Auto Start**, Auto Start (15 sec. switch), Auto Start (30 sec. switch); Crop Level: Large, Medium, Small; Framing Track Speed: Slow (1, 2) Normal **(*3)**, Fast (4, 5); Movie Recording/Streaming: ***Crop**, Do Not Crop; HDMI Output: ***Crop**, Do Not Crop

My recommendation: N/A

This is a feature vloggers or any one-person videography producer will love for its ability to follow the "talking head" around just as if a camera operator were there framing the scene. I'll explain how to use this feature in Chapter 10.

7

Exposure/Color Menu

You learned the most basic elements of exposure in Chapter 3. In this chapter, I'm going to lead you through the seven menu groups (shown in Figure 7.1) you'll need to master to calculate ambient and flash exposure, and fine-tune both white balance and color tone.

1. Exposure

The Exposure group includes these entries:

- BULB Timer Settings (Stills)
- Auto Slow Shutter (Movies)
- ISO
- ISO Range Limit
- ISO Auto Minimum Shutter Speed
- Auto/Manual Switch Settings (Movies)

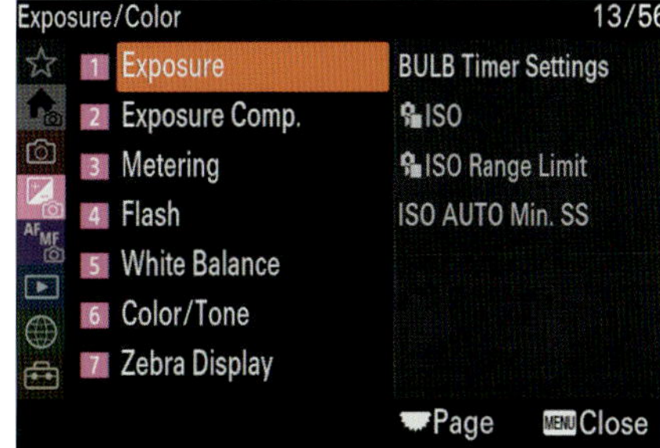

Figure 7.1 Exposure/Color menu.

BULB Timer Settings

Options: On, *Off; Exposure Time: 2 to 900 seconds, *60 seconds (default)

My preference: N/A

This setting allows extra-long-timed shutter speeds, up to 900 seconds (15 minutes), which are available when the mode dial is set to Manual and you've chosen Bulb as your exposure. It's useful for all kinds of long exposures, including star trails. Simply turn the feature on or off here, and specify the length of the exposure, from 2 to 900 seconds. Thereafter, when you choose Bulb in Manual mode, the a7C II or a7CR will dutifully open the shutter and close it after the requested interval.

This Bulb Timer setting makes up for, in part, the camera's lack of the Time Exposure setting found in other cameras. Here's the difference between the three types of long exposures:

- **Time Exposure.** With a timed exposure invoked by cameras that have the feature, you press the shutter release once and release it, then press it again to end the exposure. You'll generally have to count off or measure the interval yourself and control the length of the exposure manually. The amount of time the shutter remains open is limited only by your patience and battery power.
- **Bulb Exposure.** The basic bulb exposure requires you to hold down the shutter release for the duration of the exposure. Sony's implementation is better than most, as the camera shows the

current length of the exposure on the display so you don't have to count it off yourself. Exposure ends when you release the button. If long exposure noise reduction is being applied after the exposure, a Processing... message appears on the display. The length of the exposure is limited in practice by how long your index finger can hold out (unless you use a remote control to keep the shutter open).

- **Bulb Timer.** This setting allows you to choose a specific length of time. When enabled, in bulb mode, the camera will open the shutter and close it after the interval you've selected has elapsed. A countdown is displayed showing you the time remaining. You must turn the Bulb Timer on here, then choose the length of the exposure from 2 to 900 seconds. Sony's approach is not the most versatile; I would have preferred simply activating extended shutter speeds here, and selecting a specific exposure time (such as 60, 90, 120, 180, 240, 300, 480... seconds using a dial). Doing it this way means you're not limited to specific time increments; if you want a 47-second exposure for some reason, you can have one.

  Sony's implementation means it's not easy to do extended exposure "bracketing," say, to capture a trio of 60-, 90-, and 120-second exposures. You'd have to return to this menu repeatedly. In all cases, I recommend you use a remote or the 2-second self-timer to eliminate camera shake from "punching" the shutter release. The resulting blur is not likely to be dramatic over the course of a very long exposure, but, for best results, erring on the side of caution is always a good idea.

Auto Slow Shutter

Options: *On, Off

My preference: Off

When shooting movies in very dark locations, the best way to ensure that the video clips are bright and with less noise is to use a slow shutter speed. When this menu item is On, the camera can automatically switch to a slower shutter speed than its default. There's no need to use Shutter-priority mode and set a slow shutter speed yourself in dark locations. I like to leave it off, because when I am capturing video with a slow shutter speed, I want to make sure I have the camera mounted on a tripod, and the need to activate this feature manually is a reminder to me that I need to do so. To use it, the camera should be using Aperture Priority, with ISO set to ISO Auto.

ISO

Options: Fixed settings: ISO 50 to 102400; ISO Auto

My preference: N/A

When you select Exposure/Color > Exposure > ISO, you can adjust the ISO sensitivity of the camera. I'll address each of the sub-screens separately. This menu item can also be accessed by pressing the right (ISO) button on the control wheel and from the Function menu.

It allows you to specify the ISO setting (sensor sensitivity) in one of two ways:

- **ISO Auto.** The Auto ISO setting is at the top of the scrolling list. When it's highlighted, press the right button and choose a minimum ISO to be used as well as the maximum ISO applied (which prevents the camera from taking a clutch of pictures at, say, ISO 25600, unbeknownst to you).

For general shooting, I use ISO 100 and ISO 3200 for my limits, as I mentioned. I sometimes lower the upper limit to ISO 1600 when I especially want to minimize noise, and raise the upper end to ISO 6400 or higher for indoor subjects (especially sports, which can benefit from faster shutter speeds and/or smaller f/stops). (See Figure 7.2.)

The ISO Auto label will appear at lower right of the viewfinder or LCD monitor screen, warning you that sensitivity is being set automatically. When you depress the shutter button halfway, the ISO that has been set will appear.

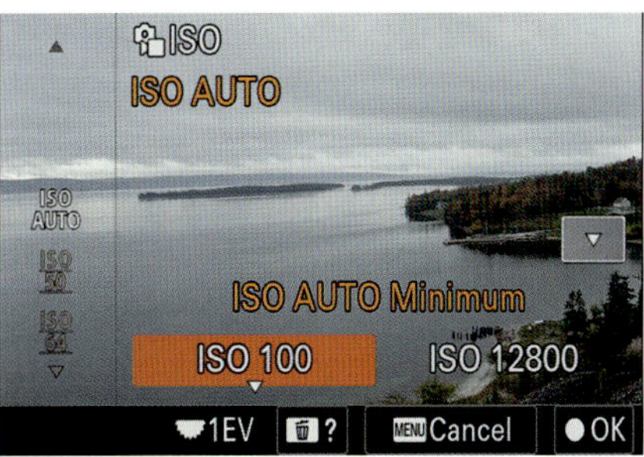

Figure 7.2 ISO Auto allows specifying minimum and maximum ISO sensitivity.

- **Fixed ISO settings.** You can Select ISO settings from 50 to 102400 (or between 100 to 32000 in Movie mode), and the camera will take all its shots at that sensitivity. Strictly speaking, ISO 100 is the lowest real sensitivity the camera can produce; that's the "native" sensitivity of the sensor. The 50/64/80 settings are "interpolated" and produce slightly higher contrast and lower quality. The a7C II/a7CR places horizontal bars above and below the number for those values as a "warning." Similarly, the same bars sandwich ISO settings above 32000 to let you know that quality is reduced at the loftier settings.

I recommend using the interpolated lower values only when you really need a lower sensitivity, say, to use a wider f/stop in very bright conditions, or when you want to use a slower shutter speed to intentionally produce blur of, perhaps, a waterfall. A neutral-density filter attached to your lens can also reduce the amount of light reaching the sensor. The upper extended settings are best reserved for situations where you really need high ISO sensitivity and are willing to accept the visual noise that results.

> **FAST FORWARD**
>
> If you're choosing fixed ISO settings and want to move quickly down the list, use the rear dial—which tells the a7C II/a7CR to jump in whole-stop leaps (i.e., from ISO 100 to 200 to 400) rather than the intermediate settings.

When making fixed ISO adjustments, you can scroll up and down the list in 1/3-stop increments with the up/down directional controls, and by rotating the control wheel or front dial. Rotate either rear dial to make adjustments in full EV steps.

Your choices are restricted when you're using movies or S&Q video. The a7C II allows ISO settings between ISO 100 and 102400 when shooting movies, while the a7CR is limited to the range ISO 100 to ISO 32000. In either case, if you choose a lower or higher ISO setting, the camera will revert to its minimum or maximum values while recording a movie, then return to its original setting when shooting stops. ISO Auto is also available and is set automatically when using Intelligent Auto. The available range may also change when using Picture Profiles, which mandate the use of higher ISO settings in order to capture an extended tonal range.

Surprise! You can use ISO Auto in Manual exposure mode, giving you an "automatic" exposure mode. You still select the shutter speed and aperture and the a7C II/a7CR will increase or decrease ISO sensitivity to produce an appropriate metered exposure within the Minimum ISO and Maximum ISO settings you specify. You'll know your manual exposure is being "corrected" when you see the ISO Auto label at lower right of the viewfinder or LCD monitor screen. When you depress the shutter button halfway, the actual ISO that has been set will appear.

ISO Range Limit

Options: ISO 50 to 102400

My preference: Minimum: ISO 50, Maximum: ISO 12800

This setting works exactly like the ISO Auto range settings shown in Figure 7.2, except that it limits the ISO settings you can choose manually. Use this option if you want to intentionally restrict the ISO settings that are available (say, to avoid accidentally using settings you find are not usable from a quality standpoint). You can specify the minimum and maximum available ISO settings from 50 to 102400. The a7C II and a7CR do let you set the minimum and maximum to the *same* figure, which is a minimum of ISO 100 and a maximum of ISO 100 (thus locking you into a single ISO sensitivity), but it is intelligent enough to keep you from setting a maximum that is lower than your minimum.

Auto/Manual Switch Setting

Options: Av Auto/Manual Switch; Tv Auto/Manual Switch; ISO Auto/Manual Setting

My preference: N/A

This entry appears only when the Still/Movie/S&Q dial is set to either Movie position, and works in conjunction with a setting that Sony, in its wisdom, decided to locate in the Shooting menu (Shooting > Shooting Mode > Exposure Control Type, discussed in Chapter 6), instead of here under Exposure/Color. This option can be accessed only if the Exposure Control Type has been set to Flexible Exposure Mode.

This entry allows you to specify whether each setting (Av, Tv, or ISO) starts out in locked (Auto) or Manual setting mode. You can choose any combination of Auto or Manual here.

ISO Auto Minimum Shutter Speed

Options: Fixed: 1/8000th to 30 seconds; Slow, Slower, *Standard, Fast, Faster

My preference: 1/30th second

Use this entry to specify the shutter speed that activates the ISO Auto feature described above. You'll want to use ISO Auto most frequently to avoid having the camera select a blur-inducing slow shutter speed when using P (Program Auto) or A (Aperture Priority) modes. (*You* always select the shutter speed yourself in S and M modes.) Depending on how well you can hand-hold the camera, or your level of trust for the lens and/or in-body image stabilization, you can choose which shutter speed you deem "too slow," and your camera will boost the ISO sensitivity as required when ISO Auto is active. You can choose from values that the camera calculates, or supply a specific shutter speed, below which Auto ISO will start to do its stuff.

The camera-calculated minimum speeds are very cool because they are based on the focal length of your lens, giving you faster minimum speeds with telephoto lenses, and longer minimum speeds with wide angles. The Fast and Faster settings increase the minimum shutter speed by 1 and 2 stops (respectively) from the standard setting for a particular focal length. The Slow and Slower settings lower the minimum shutter speed for that focal length by 1 and 2 stops (respectively).

- **Faster/Fast.** When you highlight this entry, you can press the left/right directional buttons to choose among Faster and Fast, STD (Standard), Slow, or Slower. The a7C II/a7CR will activate ISO Auto at shutter speeds that are faster than the "standard" setting (which is calculated individually based on the focal length or zoom setting of your lens). This is a more conservative setting.

- **STD (Standard).** At this default value, the camera detects the current focal length/zoom setting and selects a minimum shutter speed that takes into account the effect the focal length has in magnifying the degree of blur. That is, a 200mm lens calls for higher shutter speeds than, say, a 50mm lens.

- **Slow/Slower.** This is a more liberal setting that allows slightly slower shutter speeds than specified by STD before ISO Auto kicks in. Use if you have an extraordinarily steady hand.

- **1/8000th–30 seconds.** You can bypass the camera's internal algorithm mumbo-jumbo and directly select a shutter speed that you want to use to activate ISO Auto. If you choose 1/8000th second, ISO Auto will effectively be active all the time (except when 1/8000th second is used as the shutter speed). Select 30 seconds, and ISO Auto will not activate at all.

2. Exposure Compensation

There are three entries in the Exposure Compensation group. (See Figure 7.3.)

- Exposure Compensation
- Exposure Step
- Exposure Standard Adjustment

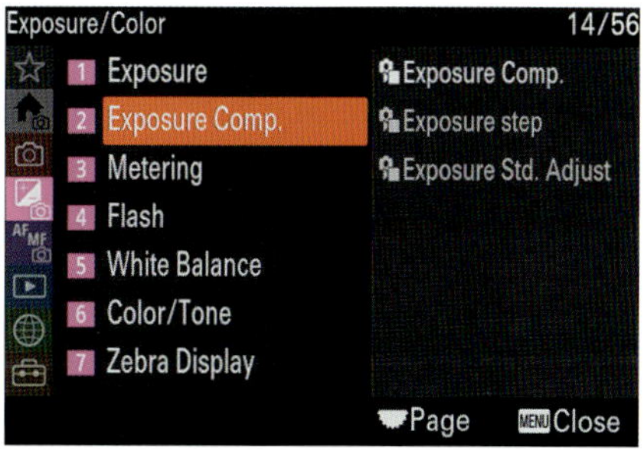

Exposure Compensation

Options: From +5 to –5, (Default: *0.0)
My preference: N/A

There are two ways to specify exposure compensation:

- **This menu entry.** Here you can adjust EV values from +5 to –5 using the directional buttons or by rotating the control wheel, either rear dial, or front dial. (See Figure 7.4.)

- **Rear Dial R.** Rotate the right rear dial to choose values from +5 to –5. This is the fastest option.

Figure 7.3 Exposure Compensation group.

Adjust until you reach the value for the amount of compensation you want to set to make your shots lighter (with positive values) or darker (with negative values). Note that only values between –3 and +3 will be reflected by a decrease or increase in brightness in the screen display; higher or lower exposure compensation settings will apply only to the recorded image. When shooting movies, only +2 to –2 values are valid.

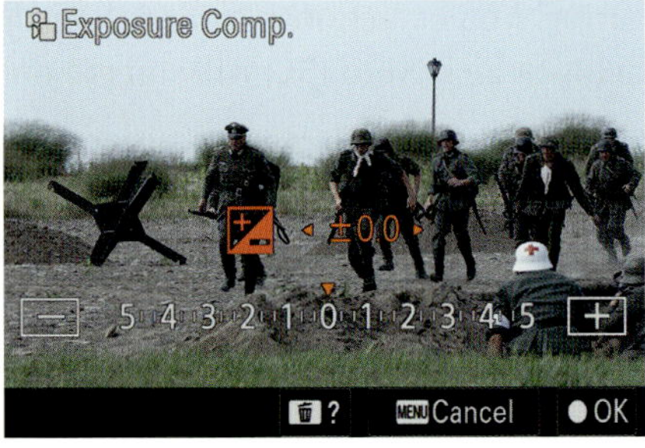

Figure 7.4 Using Exposure Compensation.

Remember that any compensation you set will stay in place until you change it, even if the camera has been powered off in the meantime. It's worth developing a habit of checking your display to see if any positive or negative exposure compensation is still in effect; return to 0.0 before you start shooting.

Exposure compensation cannot be used when the camera is set to Intelligent Auto. In Manual exposure mode, the EV settings only apply if ISO has been set to ISO Auto. The EV changes you make with the menus will be in either 1/3 or 1/2 EV increments, depending on the step size you specify in the Exposure Step entry, which I'll explain next.

Exposure Step

Options: *0.3EV, 0.5EV
My preference: 0.3EV

This setting specifies the size of the exposure change for both exposure compensation and flash exposure compensation. The 0.3EV (1/3 stop) default allows fine-tuning exposure more precisely, while selecting 0.5EV (1/2 stop) lets you make larger adjustments more quickly, which is useful when you are trying to capture more dramatic exposure changes. The actual difference between 1/3-stop and 1/2-stop changes is relatively small, so this setting is primarily a convenience feature that's most useful when you plan to, say, use exposure compensation and want to move from 0.0 to plus or minus several whole stops in bigger jumps. I'm never in that much of a hurry, so I opt for the greater precision of the 1/3 EV steps.

Exposure Standard Adjustment

Options: Adjust Multi, Center, Spot, Entire Screen Averaging, or Highlight Metering
My preference: Zero values for each

This setting is a powerful adjustment that allows you to dial in a specific amount of exposure compensation that will be applied to every photo you take using each of the five metering modes. No more can you complain, "My camera *always* underexposes by 1/3 stop!" If that is the case, and the phenomenon is consistent, you can use this menu adjustment to compensate.

Exposure compensation is usually a better idea (does your camera *really* underexpose that consistently?), but this setting does allow you to "recalibrate" your camera yourself. You can fine-tune exposure separately for each of the metering modes. However, you have no indication that fine-tuning has been made, so you'll need to remember what you've done. After all, you someday might discover that your camera is consistently *over*exposing images by 1/3 stop, not realizing that your Exposure Standard Adjustment setting is the culprit.

In practice, it's rare that the exposure system will *consistently* provide the wrong exposure in any of the five metering modes, especially Multi metering, which can alter exposure dramatically based on the camera's internal database of typical scenes. This feature may be most useful for Spot metering, if you always take a reading off the same type of subject, such as a human face or 18 percent gray card. Should you find that the gray card readings, for example, always differ from what you would prefer, go ahead and fine-tune optimal exposure for Spot metering, and use that to read your gray cards. To use this feature:

1. **Select Exposure Standard Adjustment.** Select this menu entry from the Exposure/Color > Exposure Compensation group.

2. **Consider yourself warned.** In the screen that appears, choose OK after carefully reading the warning that Sony insists on showing you every time this option is activated.

3. **Select metering mode to correct.** Choose Multi metering, Center, Spot, Entire Screen Averaging, or Highlight-weighted metering in the screen that follows by highlighting your choice and pressing the center button. You can set the standard adjustment separately for each exposure mode. (See Figure 7.5.)

4. **Specify amount of correction.** Press the up/down buttons to dial in the exposure compensation you want to apply. You can specify compensation up to +1 or −1 stops in increments of 1/6 stop, half as large a change as conventional exposure compensation. This is truly *fine-tuning.*

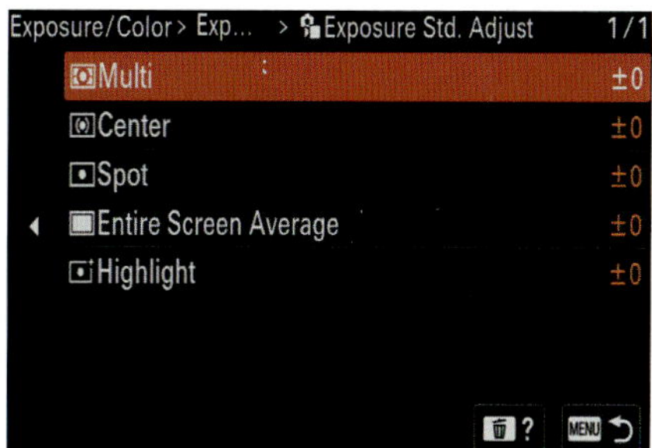

Figure 7.5 Changing the standard exposure adjustment.

5. **Confirm your change.** Press the center button when finished to return to the previous menu. You can repeat the action to fine-tune the other exposure modes if necessary. When finished, press MENU to exit. Note that the values you set will survive using the Reset option of the Setting Reset entry in the Setup menu but will be canceled if you choose Initialize instead.

3. Metering

There are four entries in the Metering group in Stills mode, shown in Figure 7.6.

- Metering Mode
- Face Priority in Multi Metering
- Spot Metering Point
- AEL with Shutter (Stills)

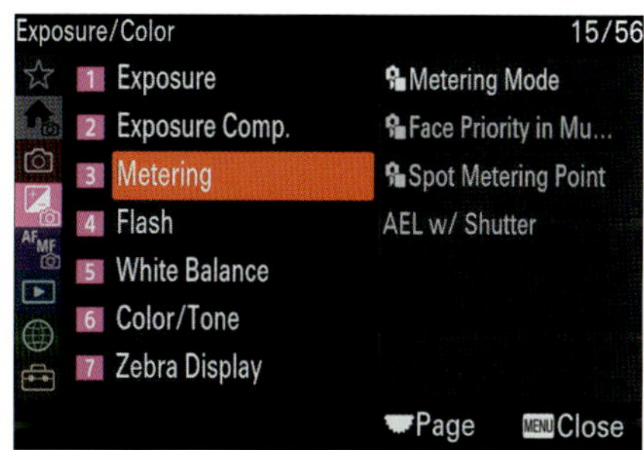

Figure 7.6 The Metering group.

Metering Mode

Options: *Multi, Center, Spot (Standard, Large), Entire Screen Averaging, Highlight
My preference: Multi

The metering mode determines how the camera will calculate the exposure for any scene. The camera is set by default to Multi, which is a multi-zone or multi-segment metering approach. No other options are available in Intelligent Auto mode or when you're using digital zoom. You'll find more information on these modes in Chapter 3, where exposure considerations are discussed in detail.

- **Multi.** Evaluates 1,200 individual segments of the scene using advanced algorithms; often, it will be able to ignore a very bright area or a very dark area that would affect the overall exposure. It's also likely to produce a decent (if not ideal) exposure with a light-toned scene such as a snowy landscape, especially on a sunny day. While it's not foolproof, Multi is the most suitable when you must shoot quickly and don't have time for serious exposure considerations. Note that when Face Priority in Multi Metering (discussed shortly) is On, this metering mode will base exposure on faces detected, if any.

- **Center.** Center-weighted metering primarily considers the brightness in a large central area of the scene, while still taking into account the average value of the rest of the frame. This approach ensures that a bright sky that's high in the frame, for example, will not severely affect the exposure. However, if the central area is very light or very dark in tone, your photo is likely to be too dark or too bright (unless you use exposure compensation).

- **Spot.** When using Spot metering, the camera measures only the brightness in a very small central area of the scene; again, if that area is very light or very dark in tone, your exposure will not be satisfactory. It's important to spot meter an area of a medium tone. Use this mode to zero in on a specific area of your image, such as a performer on a darkened stage.

  - **Size of spot.** When Spot is highlighted, press the left/right controls to change from a standard-size spot to a larger spot.

  - **Position of spot.** By default, the metering spot is placed in the center of the frame. You can optionally link the spot to the current focus point using the Spot Metering Point entry, discussed shortly.

- **Entire Screen Averaging.** The exposure is calculated based on the average brightness of the entire frame. This setting is useful if the overall scene has similar brightness values throughout; you can recompose slightly, or your subject can move within the frame and the exposure will not change.

- **Highlight.** In this mode, the camera adjusts the exposure to avoid blowing out the highlights, if at all possible. Use this setting if the highlights of a scene are the most important and you don't care if some shadow detail is lost. You can give Highlight metering some extra muscle by activating D-Range Optimizer. The a7C II/a7CR will segment the image into small areas and analyze the difference between the light and dark areas, preserving the highlights but also keeping as much shadow detail as possible.

Face Priority in Multi Metering

Options: *On, Off

My preference: Off

When you choose On, this setting tells the a7C II/a7CR to adjust its Multi metering to prioritize exposure for any faces in the scene. Select Off, and the standard 1,200-zone evaluative metering system is used without looking for faces. For most shooting I disable this feature, as Multi metering does a good job of exposing so that faces and other parts of the image are well exposed. I turn it on when I am photographing individuals or groups and their surroundings are extra bright or dark and I want to make sure the faces receive optimal exposure.

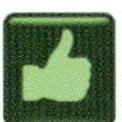 **NOTE** This option works only when Focus > Subject Recognition > Recognition Target (as described in Chapter 8) is set to Human. If you choose Animal/Bird, Animal, Bird, Insect, Car/Train, or Airplane, the feature is disabled.

Spot Metering Point

Options: *Center, Focus Point Link

My preference: Focus Point Link

If Focus Area is set to Spot (Small, Medium, or Large) or Expand Spot, and Spot metering is selected as the metering mode, then the Spot metering area can be linked to the focus point, rather than locked in the center. Just choose Focus Point Link here. If Center is selected instead, the focus point is locked in the center of the frame.

Note that Focus Point Link also works when Focus Area is set to Tracking: Spot or Tracking: Expand Spot, but the spot metering area is moved to the starting area and does not move once tracking begins. In Wide, Zone, Center Fix, or Tracking: Wide/Zone/Center Fix, the spot metering is locked to the center.

Autoexposure Lock with Shutter

Options: *Auto, On, Off

My preference: On

This item allows locking the exposure (as well as the focus in AF-S mode) when you apply light pressure to the shutter-release button. Point the camera at your primary subject and maintain contact with the button while re-framing for a better composition. This technique will ensure that both focus and exposure are optimized for the primary subject. There are three modes to choose from:

- **Auto.** Adjusts focus and then locks in exposure in AF-S mode when you press the shutter release down halfway. In AF-A mode, the camera will do the same thing if the subject is stationary. If the subject is moving (that is, the camera switches to AF-C mode) or you are shooting continuously in burst mode, exposure is *not* locked. However, even if Auto is activated, pressing the AEL lock button overrides this behavior.
- **On.** Exposure is locked when you press the shutter release halfway.

- **Off.** Pressing the shutter release halfway locks only focus. Exposure is not locked when you press the shutter release halfway, and exposure will be adjusted automatically during continuous shooting. Exposure isn't locked until you press the shutter release down all the way to take the photo, or you press the AEL lock button. Use this setting when you prefer to lock exposure manually using the AEL button or when taking the actual picture.

You might want to choose the Off option to lock focus on one subject in the scene while locking the exposure for an entirely different part of the scene. To use this technique, focus on the most important subject and keep the focus locked by keeping your finger on the shutter-release button while you recompose. You can then point the lens at an entirely different area of the scene to read the exposure, and lock in the exposure with pressure on the AEL button. Finally, reframe for the most pleasing composition and take the photo.

In your image, the primary subject will be in sharpest focus while the exposure will be optimized for the area that you metered. This technique makes the most sense when your primary subject is very light in tone like a snowman or very dark in tone like a black Lab dog. Subjects of that type can lead to exposure errors, so you might want to expose for an area that's a middle tone, such as grass.

4. Flash

The Flash group, which is visible only in Still mode, has seven entries, shown in Figure 7.7:

- Flash Mode
- Flash Compensation
- Exposure Compensation Settings
- Wireless Flash
- Red Eye Reduction
- External Flash Settings
- Register Flash Shooting Set

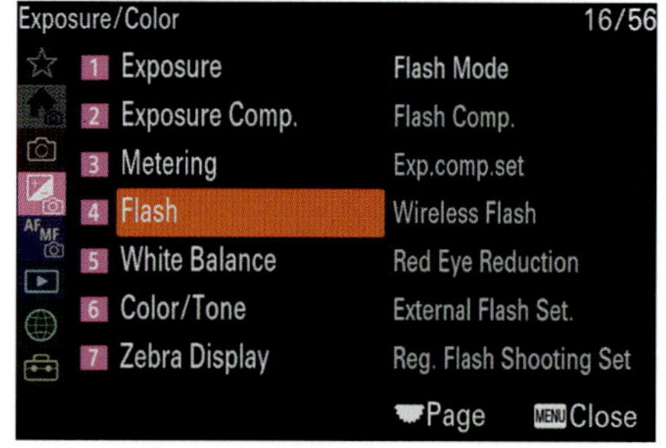

Figure 7.7 The Flash group.

Flash Mode

Options: Flash Off, Auto Flash, Fill Flash, Slow Sync., *Rear Sync.

My preference: N/A

This item offers options for the several flash modes that are available. Not all the modes can be selected at all times, as shown in Table 7.1. I'll describe what these modes do, and the use of flash in detail, in Chapter 13.

TABLE 7.1 Flash Modes

EXPOSURE MODE	FLASH OFF	AUTO FLASH	FILL FLASH	SLOW SYNC.	REAR SYNC.	WIRELESS	FLASH EXPOSURE COMPENSATION	RED-EYE REDUCTION
Intelligent Auto	✓	✓	✓					✓
Program Auto			✓	✓	✓	✓	✓	✓
Aperture Priority			✓	✓	✓	✓	✓	✓
Shutter Priority			✓	✓	✓	✓	✓	✓
Manual Exposure			✓	✓	✓	✓	✓	✓

Flash Compensation

Options: –3 to +3 in 1/3 or 1/2 EV steps

My preference: N/A

This feature controls the flash output. It allows you to dial in plus compensation for a brighter flash effect or minus compensation for a subtler flash effect. If you take a flash photo and it's too dark or too light, access this menu item. Scroll up/down to set a value that will increase flash intensity (plus setting) or reduce the flash output (minus setting) by up to three EV (exposure value) steps. You can select between 1/3 and 1/2 EV increments in the Exposure Compensation Step entry described earlier in this chapter. Flash compensation is "sticky," so be sure to set it back to zero after you finish shooting. This feature is not available when you're using Intelligent Auto mode. I'll discuss this and many other flash-related topics in detail in Chapter 13.

Exposure Compensation Settings

Options: Ambient & Flash, **Ambient Only*

My preference: Ambient & Flash

I prefer using the Ambient & Flash option, so that any exposure compensation value set will apply to both the ambient light exposure and to the flash exposure when using flash. You'd want to stick to this option in flash photography when you find that both the available-light exposure and the flash exposure produce an image that's too dark or too light. Setting plus or minus exposure compensation will affect both. However, in another situation when using flash, you might want to control only the brightness of the ambient-light exposure and not the flash exposure.

The Ambient Only option allows you to control only the brightness of the background, such as a city skyline behind a friend when you're taking flash photos at night in a scene of this type. Setting exposure compensation will now allow you to get a brighter or a darker background (at a + and – setting, respectively) without affecting the brightness of your primary subject, who will be exposed by the light from the flash. (Any exposure compensation you set will have no effect on the flash intensity.)

Wireless Flash

Options: ***Off**, On

My preference: N/A

Sony is still playing catch-up in the electronic flash arena, having supported only optically triggered wireless flash until relatively recently, but now offers radio-controlled wireless flash using the Sony AF-WRC1M/FA-WRR1 wireless radio commander/receiver combination or radio-compatible external flash units like the Sony HVL-F60RM/RM2, HVL-F46M, HVL-F45RM, and HVL-F28RM. This entry allows you to enable/disable both optical and radio wireless modes. I'll explain these and other flash options in Chapter 13.

Red Eye Reduction

Options: On, ***Off**

My preference: Off

When flash is used in a dark location, red-eye is common in pictures of people, and especially of animals. Unfortunately, your camera is unable, on its own, to totally *eliminate* the red-eye effects that occur when an electronic flash bounces off the retinas of your subject's eyes and into the camera lens. The effect is worst under low-light conditions (exactly when you might be using a flash) as the pupils expand to allow more light to reach the retinas. The best you can hope for with this option is to *reduce* or minimize the red-eye effect. After all, the feature is called red-eye *reduction,* not red-eye *elimination.*

It's fairly easy to remove red-eye effects in an image editor (some image importing programs will do it for you automatically as the pictures are transferred from your camera or memory card to your computer). But, it's better not to have glowing red eyes in your photos in the first place.

To use this feature, you first have to attach an external flash to the multi-interface shoe. When Red Eye Reduction is turned on through this menu item, the flash issues a few brief bursts prior to taking the photo, theoretically causing your subjects' pupils to contract, reducing the red-eye syndrome. It works best if your subject is looking toward the flash. Like any such system, its success ratio is not great. This feature is not available when using wireless flash, as described in Chapter 13.

External Flash Settings

Options: External Flash Firing Settings, External Flash Custom Settings

My preference: N/A

This setting allows you to make adjustments to compatible flash units attached to the camera's multi-interface shoe (currently Sony's radio-controlled units), as described in Chapter 13. Unlike other Sony flash units, these can be adjusted right from the menus, instead of the controls on the back panel of the flash itself. The options include:

- **Flash Control Mode.** Choose TTL Flash Firing for automatic flash metering, Manual Flash Firing, Multi Flash Firing (for "stroboscopic" effects), and Group Flash Firing (when using more than one flash in Wireless mode).

- **Memory Recall.** Recalls M1 and M2 Custom Settings registered to your particular flash and stored in your camera.
- **Zoom.** Changes the coverage area of flash units that have Zoom features.
- **CMD.** Used to set a flash to either Commander (to trigger other flash units, if the unit has that capability) or Receiver mode (to respond to a commander). You can also turn the wireless features off here.
- **High-Speed Sync.** Allows using flash at a shutter speed higher than the a7C II/a7CR's sync rate of 1/250th second (full frame) or 1/320th second (APS-C mode).
- **CMD Flash Firing.** Available only with units that have both optical and radio wireless capabilities. It disables the optical protocol, which prevents your flash from being triggered by any Sony flash units used in optical wireless mode by others in your surroundings.
- **Flash Compensation.** Flash exposure can be adjusted in the range of –3 to +3, duplicating the Exposure/Color > Flash > Flash Compensation setting.
- **Ratio Control.** Allows you to set output levels for as many as three flash groups. I'll tell you about groups, channels, and other wireless concepts in Chapter 13.
- **External Flash Custom Settings.** This entry has three tabs used to create custom settings that can be stored in your flash's memory, select a communication channel, and make other adjustments, including power saving.

Register Flash Shooting Settings ⊡ ▸ ⌕

Options: Shutter Speed Range, ISO

My preference: Shutter Speed Range: 1/15th–1/160th second; ISO: 400

This handy option allows you to specify the shutter speed range and ISO sensitivity to use when a compatible flash is mounted on the a7C II/a7CR and powered up. When enabled, the camera will detect when the flash is turned on and switch from your current shutter speed range and/or ISO setting to the one you indicate here. To use this feature, just follow these steps:

1. **Access this entry.** Navigate to Exposure/Color > Flash > Reg. Flash Shooting Set. The screen shown at left in Figure 7.8 appears.
2. **Choose Flash Shutter Speed Range.** If you want to specify a shutter speed range for flash, highlight this option and press the right directional button. The screen shown at upper right will be displayed.
3. **Select Minimum Speed.** Use the up/down directional buttons to choose the slowest speed that can be used for flash, in the range of 30 seconds to 1/8000th second. **Note:** If the minimum speed you select is faster than the maximum sync speed (1/160th second), you'll need to use high-speed sync, as described in Chapter 13.
4. **Select Maximum Speed.** Sync Speed (1/160th second) is displayed by default. If you want to enable a faster speed (because you'll be using high-speed sync), you can select a maximum speed between 30 seconds and 1/8000th second.

Note: The Minimum and Maximum speeds interact. If you choose a minimum speed faster than Sync speed, then the maximum cannot be set lower than that value. If you set a maximum speed

Figure 7.8 Registering flash shooting settings.

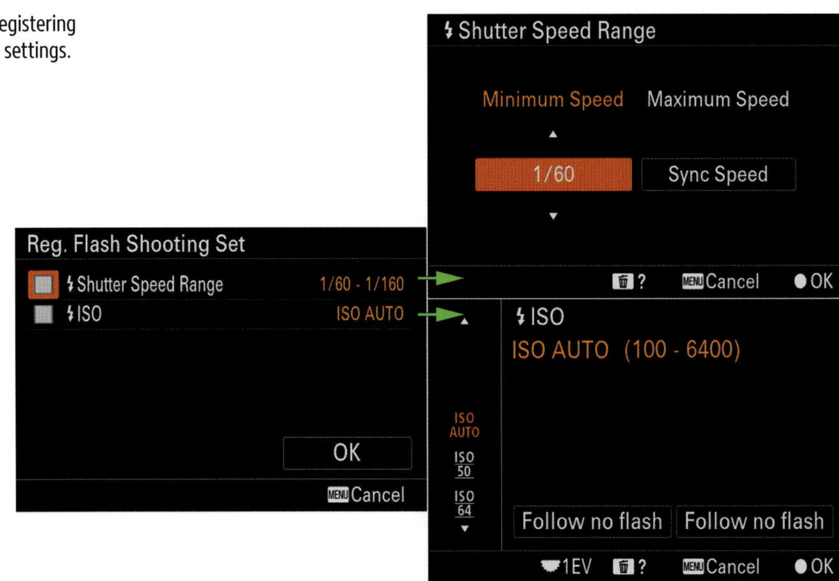

lower than the minimum speed, the minimum speed is adjusted downward. In other words, you can't have a minimum speed that is faster than the maximum setting, nor a maximum that is lower than the minimum.

5. **Confirm.** Press OK to return to the previous screen or MENU to cancel.

6. **Highlight ISO option.** If you want to specify an ISO or ISO range, highlight the ISO option and press the right directional button. **Note:** You can set Flash Shutter Speed Range or ISO or *both*, as you prefer.

7. **Set specific ISO or Auto ISO Range.** You can choose to select a specific ISO for flash shooting, or choose an Auto ISO range:

   - **Specific ISO.** Choose a fixed ISO setting between ISO 50 and ISO 102400 from the scrolling list at the left side of the screen seen at lower right in Figure 7.8. Use the up/down directional buttons to scroll through individual settings, or use the rear dial to jump in whole EV steps.

   - **Choose ISO Auto Range.** If you don't want to lock in a fixed ISO sensitivity setting, you can choose ISO Auto instead from the scrolling list, and then specify lower and upper ISO limits. The default setting is to use the exact same ISO upper and lower range specified in Exposure/Color > Exposure > ISO Range Limit, as described earlier. The setting Follow No Flash will appear for both options, as seen in Figure 7.8, lower right.

   You can change the Minimum, Maximum, or both. Press the right directional button to highlight the Minimum and Maximum settings and use the up/down buttons to select a new minimum and/or maximum value. You can use the rear dial to change the values in whole EV steps.

8. **Confirm.** Press OK to confirm and return to the previous screen, or MENU to cancel.

9. **Enable/Disable the Settings.** There are check boxes next to the Shutter Speed Range and ISO options. Highlight either box (not the entry label) and press the center button to mark/enable or unmark/disable that setting. Press OK when finished to confirm and exit.

5. White Balance

The White Balance group has three entries in Stills mode, shown in Figure 7.9, plus Shockless White Balance, available only in Movie mode:

- White Balance
- Priority Settings in Auto White Balance
- Shutter Auto White Balance Lock (Stills)
- Shockless White Balance (Movies)

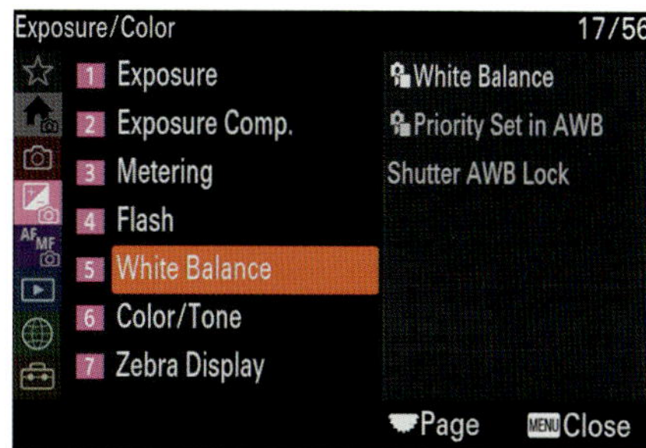

Figure 7.9 White Balance group.

White Balance

Options: *Auto WB, Daylight, Shade, Cloudy, Incandescent, Fluorescent (4 options), Flash, Underwater Auto, C.Temp/Filter, Custom 1–3

My preference: AWB

The various light sources that can illuminate a scene have light that's of different colors. A household lamp using an old-type (not Daylight Balanced) bulb, for example, produces light that's quite amber in color. Sunlight around noon is close to white but it's quite red at sunrise and sunset; on cloudy days, the light has a bluish bias. The light from fluorescents can vary widely, depending on the type of tube or bulb you're using. Some lamps, including sodium vapor and mercury vapor, produce light of unusual colors.

The Auto White Balance feature works well, particularly outdoors and under artificial lighting that's daylight balanced. Even under lamps that produce light with a slight color cast such as green or blue, you should often get a pleasing overall color balance. One advantage of using AWB is that you don't have to worry about changing it for your next shooting session; there's no risk of having the camera set for, say, incandescent light, when you're shooting outdoors on a sunny day.

The a7C II/a7CR also lets you choose a specific white balance option—often called a preset—that's appropriate for various typical lighting conditions, because the AWB feature does not always succeed in providing an accurate or the most pleasing overall color balance. Your choices include:

- **Daylight.** Sets white balance for average daylight.
- **Shade.** Compensates for the slightly bluer tones encountered in open shade conditions.
- **Cloudy.** Adjusts for the colder tones of a cloudy day.
- **Incandescent.** Indoor illumination is typically much warmer than daylight, so this setting compensates for the excessive red bias.
- **Fluorescent (four types).** You can choose from Warm White, Cool White, Day White, and Daylight fluorescent lighting.
- **Flash.** Suitable for shooting with an external electronic flash unit.

- **Underwater Auto.** Although you may find a third-party vendor offering an underwater housing for your camera, it's more likely that your "underwater" shooting will involve photographing fish and other sea life through the glass of an aquarium of the commercial variety. This setting partially tames the blue-green tones you can encounter in such environments, producing a warmer tone that some (but not all) may prefer.

- **C.Temp/Filter/Custom/Custom Setup.** These advanced features provide even better results once you've learned how to fine-tune color balance settings, which was explained in Chapter 5.

When any of the presets are selected, you can press the right button to produce a feature that allows you to adjust the color along the amber (yellow)/blue axis, the green/magenta axis, or both, to fine-tune color rendition even more precisely. The screen shown in Figure 7.10 will appear, and you can use the up/down and left/right controls to move the origin point in the chart shown at lower right to any bias you want. The amount of your amber/blue and/or green/magenta bias are shown numerically to the left of the chart. Return the origin point to the center by pressing the Trash button. You'll find more information about setting White Balance in Chapter 5.

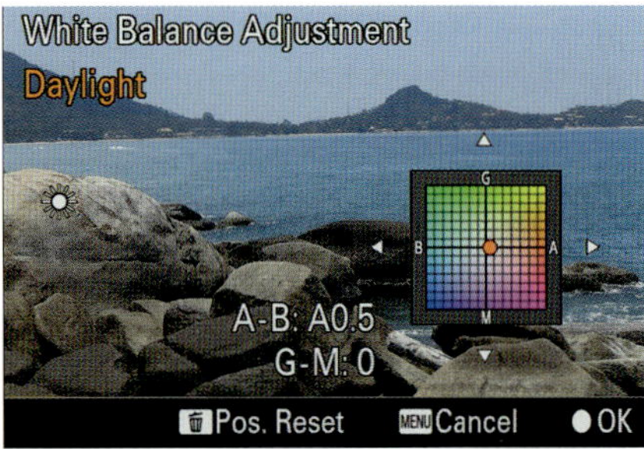

Figure 7.10 Fine-tune the color bias of your images using this feature.

My recommendation: If you shoot in RAW capture, though, you don't have to be quite as concerned about white balance, because you can easily adjust it in your software after the fact. Here again, as with ISO and exposure compensation, the white balance item is not available in Intelligent Auto mode; the camera defaults to Auto White Balance.

Priority Settings in AWB

Options: *Standard, Ambience, White

My preference: Standard

You can finally exercise some control over Auto White Balance. This setting allows you to fine-tune how AWB works, producing "automatic" color balance that may more closely suit your personal taste than the default balance the a7C II/a7CR is initially set for. You have three choices:

- **Standard.** The camera makes its own adjustments for white balance, based on its interpretation of the colors it sees in your scenes. The a7C II and a7CR do a pretty good job of telling daylight from incandescent illumination and responding accordingly, and a fair job with other forms of illumination. This will work for you most of the time, although you'll want to use one of the presets or other white balance customizing features described above when appropriate.

- **Ambience.** Detects the light source and, if a naturally warm source is identified, will bias the color to keep warmer tones. Your interior photos, fireside chats, and similar scenes can keep their rosy colors. An indicator on your shooting settings screens will indicate that Ambience (or White) bias is being used.

- **White.** The reverse of Ambience, this setting tries to preserve whites in scenes with warm color temperatures.

Shutter AWB Lock

Options: Shutter Half Press, Continuous Shooting, *****Off**
My preference: Off

As described earlier, your a7C II or a7CR actually have *two* Auto White Balance controls—the standard AWB setting and Underwater Auto. Each selects the appropriate white balance for their respective conditions. However, neither auto white balance option is perfect; you may find that white balance adjustments may occur as you hold the shutter release down halfway, or during continuous shooting. If color consistency between individual shots is important, you can tell the camera to *lock* color balance temporarily. These are the settings:

- **Shutter Half Press.** If you choose this setting, the camera will always lock the white balance at its current setting whenever AWB or Underwater Auto are active and the shutter release is half-pressed. If the Drive mode is Continuous, when you press the shutter release down all the way and hold it down, the white balance is locked for the entire sequence.

- **Continuous Shooting.** White balance is locked to the white balance of the first frame *only* during continuous shooting. Either Auto WB setting may continue to make adjustments when the shutter release is half-pressed.

- **Off.** White balance may change during a half-press or continuous shooting when either of the two Auto white balance presets are enabled. (The non-auto fixed presets, of course, do not change until you adjust them.) Be sure to set to Off when using flash.

Shockless White Balance

Options: Off, *****1 (Fast)**, 2, 3 (Slow)
My preference: 1

When capturing video, abrupt changes in white balance can be disconcerting. This setting allows you to specify how quickly the camera adjusts the white balance when you make a manual change to a different setting. It has no effect when Auto White Balance is set for video. You can choose 1 (fastest) to 3 (slowest), or disable the feature entirely.

6. Color/Tone

The Color/Tone group has six entries. Four of them are available in Still photography mode, as shown in Figure 7.11, while two additional entries for working with Look-Up tables (LUTs) appear in Movie mode:

- D-Range Optimizer
- Creative Look
- Picture Profile
- Select LUT (Movies)
- Manage User LUTs (Movies)
- Soft Skin Effect

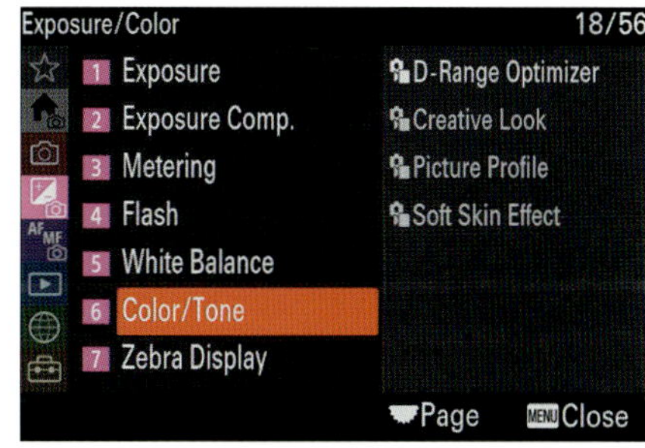

Figure 7.11 Color/Tone group for Still photography.

D-Range Optimizer

Options: DRO Off; DRO *Auto, Levels 1–5

My preference: Auto

The brightness/darkness range of many images is so broad that the sensor has difficulty capturing detail in both bright highlight areas and dark shadow areas. That's because a sensor has a limited dynamic range. However, the a7C II and a7CR are able to expand the dynamic range using extra processing when dynamic range optimization (DRO) is active. It's on by default at the Auto level where the camera evaluates the scene contrast and decides how much extra processing to apply; this is the only available setting in Intelligent Auto mode. In other modes, you can turn DRO off, or set it manually to one of five intensity levels.

When the DRO Auto option is highlighted, you can press the left/right controls to set the DRO to a specific level of processing, from 1 (weakest) to 5 (strongest). You'll find that DRO can lighten shadow areas; it may darken bright highlight areas too, but not to the same extent. By level 3, the photos you take will exhibit much lighter shadow areas for an obviously wide dynamic range; DRO Auto will never provide such an intense increase in shadow detail. There is no effect on RAW files, whether captured alone or as part of a RAW + JPEG duo.

Creative Look

Options: *ST, PT, NT, VV1, VV2, FL, IN, SH, BW, SE

My preference: N/A

This JPEG/HEIF-only option is an evolution and improvement over Sony's previous Creative Styles presets, now offering the ability to make many more adjustments. The older Creative Styles let you tweak Sharpness, Saturation, and Contrast only. With these new "looks," you can also adjust Highlights, Shadows, Fade, Sharpness Range, and Clarity. The available Creative Looks include:

- **ST (Standard).** This is, as you might expect, your default setting, with a good compromise of sharpness, color saturation, contrast, and the other parameters. Choose this, and your photos will have excellent colors, a broad range of tonal values, and standard sharpness that avoids the "over-sharpened" look that some digital pictures acquire.

- **PT (Portrait).** You'll get reduced saturation, contrast, and sharpness for a more "gentle" rendition that often works well for people pictures, especially skin tones. This style is a good choice if you're planning on fine-tuning those aspects of your JPEG photos in your computer and don't want the camera to overdo any of them.

- **NT (Neutral).** Reduces saturation and sharpness to produce images with more subdued tones. Use this if you plan on tweaking your photos in an image editor and you want a basic image without any of the enhancements of the other styles.

- **VV1 (Vivid 1).** If you want more punch in your images, with richer colors, heightened contrast that makes those colors stand out, and standard sharpness, this setting is for you. It's good for flowers, seaside photos, any picture with expanses of blue sky, and on overcast days where a punchier image can relieve the dullness.

- **VV2 (Vivid 2).** Provides even brighter and more saturated colors. You may find this preset to be too much for your taste, so use it with caution.

- **FL.** Sony claims this setting will give you a "moody" look with sharp contrast and impressive colors in the sky and greens. Reds and blues seem to be suppressed while greens are enhanced. The shifted colors remind me of some fluorescent lighting effects, which may be where the FL designation came from.

- **IN.** This one should give you a flatter look, compared to NT (Neutral) thanks to reduced contrast and color saturation.

- **SH.** Sony describes this one as "bright, transparent, soft, and vivid." Ordinarily, "soft" and "vivid" are contradictory terms, especially since this setting reduces color saturation. However, the reduced saturation isn't applied evenly. Reds are muted to orange, while greens and blues are affected less. Blacks are lightened. Overall color changes do give you a dreamy look.

- **BW (Black-and-white).** This is useful if you want to shoot monochrome photos in the camera, so you won't need to modify color photos in software. This style will allow you to change the contrast and sharpness, but not the saturation (because there are no colors to saturate).

- **SE (Sepia).** A monochrome image with an overall sepia tone.

- **Numbered Versions.** You'll find a second version of the ST, FL, IN, SH, SE, and BW "looks" (in that order), prefixed by a number. That gives you a total of 16 available "looks" to work with.

Each of the Creative Looks has its own "base" level of each of the adjustable parameters. That is, sharpness, saturation, contrast, and the other settings for the Standard preset are different from those for, say, the Neutral "look." When a particular look is highlighted (as in Figure 7.12, left), press the left/right directional controls to scroll among the available adjustments, and then use the up/down controls to change a highlighted parameter (Figure 7.12, right). Press the center button to confirm. You can press the Trash button to return a particular Creative Look's values to their defaults. Although the looks are applied only to the JPEG/HEIF files, the settings are embedded in the RAW files so your image editor can apply them during the conversion process if you like. Here is a summary of how changing the parameters in a Creative Style will affect your images:

- **Contrast (+/−9).** Compresses the range of tones in an image (increase contrast from 0 to +9) or expands the range of tones (from 0 to −9) to decrease contrast. Higher-contrast images tend to lose detail in both shadows and highlights, whereas lower-contrast images retain the detail but appear more flat and dull, without any snap.

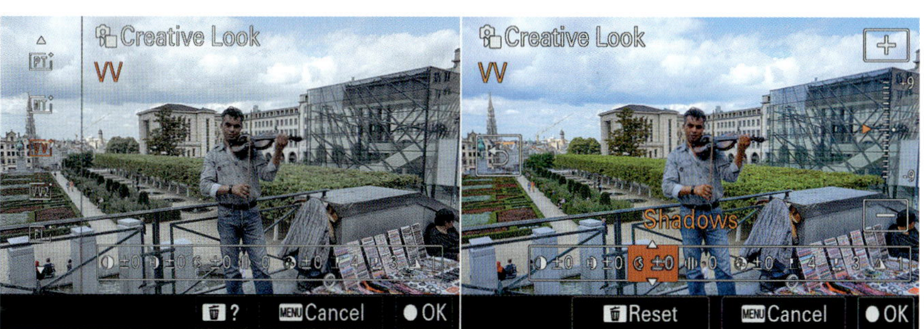

Figure 7.12 Choosing a Creative Look (left). Adjusting parameters (right).

- **Highlights (+/−9).** Increases or decreases the brightness of the lightest areas of your image without affecting the shadows.
- **Shadows (+/−9).** Increases or decreases the brightness of the darkest areas of your image without affecting the highlights.
- **Fade (0−9).** Determines the effect of the Creative Look, from imperceptible (0) to strongest (9).
- **Saturation (+/−9).** You can adjust the richness of the color from low saturation (0) to high saturation (9). Lower saturation produces a muted look that can be more realistic for certain kinds of subjects, such as humans. Higher saturation produces a more vibrant appearance but can be garish and unrealistic if carried too far. Boost your saturation if you want a vivid image, or to brighten up pictures taken on overcast days. Saturation cannot be changed for the Black & White Creative Look.
- **Sharpness (0−9).** Increases or decreases the contrast of the edge outlines in your image, making the photo appear more or less sharp, depending on whether you've selected 0 (no sharpening), to 9 (extra sharpening). Remember that boosting sharpness also increases the overall contrast of an image, so you'll want to use this parameter in conjunction with the contrast parameter with caution.
- **Sharpness Range (1−5).** Determines the range of the outlines affected by the Sharpness parameter. A setting of 5 applies sharpness to finer outlines, which can cause unwanted halo effects.
- **Clarity (0−9).** Increases the sharpness of the middle tones of an image, avoiding adjusting the dark and light tones, adding "punch" to your image while avoiding an unnatural look that can result from oversharpening.

Note that Creative Looks and Picture Profiles (discussed next) cannot be used at the same time.

Picture Profile

Options: Picture Profiles PP1–PP11, ***Off**

My preference: Off

Picture Profiles are a great tool for advanced movie shooters. You can customize the picture quality, including color and gradation of your movies, by defining the parameters included in each of 8 different Picture Profiles. (Profiles 7–9, although listed and described in the manual, are not available.) To make these adjustments, connect the camera to a TV or monitor using the HDMI port, and use the picture on the screen as a guide while making your changes. After connecting the camera to your HDTV/monitor, navigate to this menu entry and select which Picture Profile you want to modify. Press the right button to access the index screen, then press the up/down buttons to select the parameter to be changed. Then make your adjustments and press the center button to confirm.

Even a short course in how each of the parameters affects video images, and a discussion of how to select the best settings would require a chapter or two of technical discussion and is thus beyond the scope of this book. I'm going to provide a quick listing of each type of setting for a reminder; your Sony manual provides more information about each of these.

The Picture Profile presets already have default values that correspond to the settings normally used for those profiles:

- **PP1:** Example setting using [Movie] gamma
- **PP2:** Example setting using [Still] gamma
- **PP3:** Example setting of natural color tone using the [ITU709] gamma
- **PP4:** Example setting of a color tone faithful to the [ITU709] standard
- **PP5:** Example setting using [Cine1] gamma
- **PP6:** Example setting using [Cine2] gamma
- **PP7:** Example setting using [S-Log2] gamma
- **PP8:** Example setting using [S-Log3] gamma with the Picture Profile's Color Mode set to [S-Gamut3.Cine]
- **PP9:** Example setting using [S-Log3] gamma with the Picture Profile's Color Mode set to [S-Gamut3]
- **PP10:** Example setting for HDR Movies using [HLG2] gamma
- **PP11:** Example setting using [S-Cinetone] gamma

The list that follows is not for the faint-of-heart. As I noted, you can find entire books and motion-picture school classes on color grading and adjusting these parameters:

- **Black Level.** Sets the black level (–15 to +15). Black level is the level of brightness at which no light is emitted from a screen, resulting in a pure black screen. Adjustment of this parameter ensures that blacks are seen as black, and not a dark shade of gray.
- **Gamma.** Selects a gamma curve, a formula which corrects for the nonlinear relationship between the brightness (*luminance*) captured by a sensor and the brightness of the image as it's displayed on a monitor. In other words, correction is needed to make what you see on a screen more closely resemble what the camera captured in real life. You can choose from 13 different gamma curves.
- **Black Gamma.** Corrects gamma in low-intensity areas, using Range and Level controls.
- **Knee.** Sets "knee point" and slope for video signal compression to prevent overexposure by limiting signals in high-intensity areas of the subject to the dynamic range of your camera. In short, a higher knee level produces more detail in the highlights; a lower knee level produces fewer details in the highlights. Your adjustments include:
  - **Mode.** In Auto mode, the knee point and slope are set automatically; in Manual mode, they are set manually.
  - **Auto Set.** Even when the mode is set to Auto, you can still choose maximum point for the knee point, from 90 to 100 percent, and Sensitivity, from High, Medium, or Low.
  - **Manual Set.** When mode is set to Manual, you specify a knee point (75 to 105 percent), and Slope from gentle (–5) to steep (+5).
- **Color Mode.** Sets type and level of colors, from among Movie, Still, S-Sinetone, Cinema, Pro, ITU709 Matrix, Black & White, and S-Gamut3.Cine, S-Gamut3, BT-2020, and 709.
- **Saturation.** Sets the color saturation, from –32 to +32 values.

- **Color Phase.** Sets the color phase (–7 to +7).
- **Color Depth.** Sets the color depth for each color phase.
- **Detail.** Sets parameters including Level, and Detail adjustments including Mode, Vertical/Horizontal Balance, B/W Balance, Limit, Crispening, and Hi-Light Detail.
- **Copy.** Copies the settings of the Picture Profile to another Picture Profile number.
- **Reset.** Resets the Picture Profile to the default setting. You cannot reset all Picture Profile settings at once.

Select LUT

Options: S-Log3, s709, 709 (800%), User 1–16

My preference: N/A

Look-up Tables (LUTs) are a way of remapping the (typically low-contrast, prior to grading) colors captured during video shooting using a format such as S-Log3, so the footage can be viewed on a standard monitor before color grading has been applied. This entry allows you to choose one of three built-in LUTs, or apply any of 16 different LUTs that you upload to the camera. Of the three built-in LUTs, S-Log3 is the most commonly used; s709 corresponds to the BT.709 specification used with high-definition televisions, and 709 (800%) is an older standard not frequently used. As I noted above, this is an advanced capability beyond the scope of this book, and I won't be showing you how to adjust or create Look-up Tables.

Sony, in its wisdom, has scattered all the entries that manage LUTs among various different menus:

- **Log Shooting.** Navigate to the Shooting > Image Quality > Log Shooting Setting entry to enable access to this entry. When you do, Picture Profiles, described above, will be disabled.
- **Select LUT.** This entry will allow you to choose one of the three canned LUTs or one you have uploaded.
- **Manage User LUTs.** That's the entry that follows this one, used to import, edit, or delete customized LUTs.
- **Display LUT.** Navigate to Setup > Display Option > Display LUT to enable playback of video footage in the camera using the active LUT.

Manage User LUTs

Options: Import/Edit, Delete All

My preference: N/A

Videographers have access to a wide variety of LUT files that can be found on the Internet, both free and with price tags attached. Once downloaded, they can be placed in the /Private/Sony/PRO/LUT folder of your memory card where the a7C II/a7CR can find them when you access this menu entry. They will be loaded into the camera's menu and can be erased from the memory card after they've been imported.

Soft Skin Effect 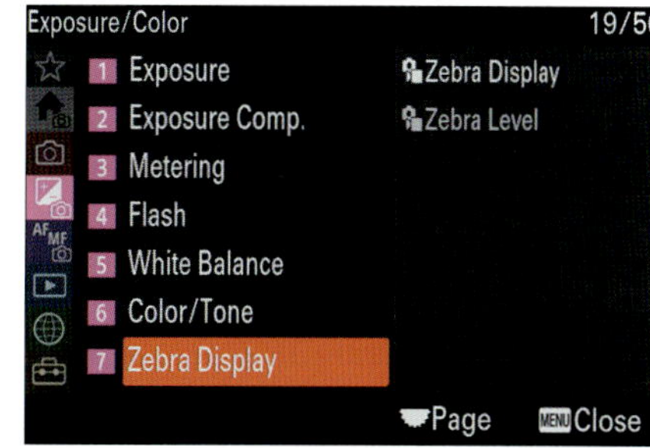

Options: *Off, On: Low, Mid, High

My preference: Off

If you want to shoot portraits that you can use straight out of the camera (SOOC), this setting tells the a7C II/a7CR to smooth skin tones when using the Face Detection feature. It tends to smooth out skin while retaining detail in the eyes and other high-contrast parts of the face. If you plan on editing your photos, you should leave it turned off. When you highlight On, you can use the left/right directional controls to choose Low, Medium, or High levels. This setting is not available when shooting only RAW, or RAW & JPEG/HEIF. It is also unavailable when using digital zoom.

7. Zebra Display

There are just two entries in the Zebra Display group, seen in Figure 7.13:

- Zebra Display
- Zebra Level

Zebra Display

Options: On, *Off

My preference: Off

Figure 7.13 The Zebra group.

The Zebra warns you when highlight levels in your image are brighter than a setting you specify in the Zebra Level entry, discussed next. This entry allows you to turn the effect on and off. Sony has made it a separate entry so you can assign the on/off function to a custom key and not have to return to this menu entry to enable/disable it.

Zebra Level

Options: IRE *70, 75, 80, 85, 90, 95, 100, 100+

My preference: 80

The Zebra display is a useful warning, especially when shooting movies, as it clearly shows when highlight levels in your image are brighter than a setting you specify here. It's somewhat comparable to the flashing "blinkies" that digital cameras have long used during image review to tell us, after the fact, which highlight areas of the image we just took are blown out.

Zebra patterns are a much more useful tool because you are given an alert *before* you take the picture and can specify exactly how bright *too bright* is. Even better, the Zebra stripes tell you *exactly where* the overexposure is taking place. Live histograms, as discussed in Chapter 3, only show that your tones are crowding the right side of the graph or spilling over. There may be parts of the frame where overexposure is acceptable as long as the main subject is properly exposed. The Zebra feature gives you that information. The stripes appear only when portions of the scene equal the setting you choose.

The Zebra feature has been a staple of professional video shooting for a long time, as you might guess from the moniker assigned to the unit used to specify brightness: IRE, a measure of video signal level, which stands for *Institute of Radio Engineers.*

When you want to use Zebra pattern warnings, access this menu entry, and specify an IRE value from 70 to 100, and 100+. Once you've been notified, you can adjust your exposure settings to reduce the brightness of the highlights, as I described in Chapter 3.

So, exactly how bright *is* too bright? A value of 100 IRE indicates pure white, so any Zebra pattern visible when using this setting (or 100+) indicates that your image is extremely overexposed. Any details in the highlights are gone and cannot be retrieved. Settings from 70 to 90 can be used to make sure facial tones are not overexposed. Generally, Caucasian skin falls in the 80 IRE range, with darker skin tones registering as low as 70, and very fair skin or lighter areas of your subject edging closer to 90 IRE. Once you've decided the approximate range of tones that you want to make sure do *not* blow out, you can set the camera's Zebra pattern sensitivity appropriately and receive the flashing striped warning on the LCD of your camera. (See Figure 7.14.) The pattern does not appear in output to a device through the HDMI port, nor in your final image, of course—it's just an aid to keep you from blowing it, so to speak.

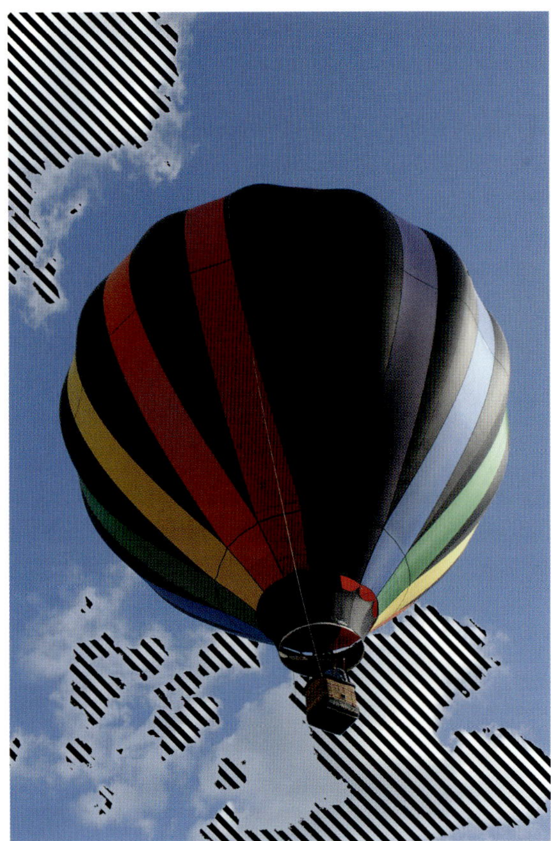

Figure 7.14 The flashing stripes can show an area is going to be overexposed, or set to signal when a human face is properly exposed.

Focus and Playback Menus | 8

This chapter focuses (ahem) on the features found in the Focus tab and Playback tab. I'm going to emphasize the entries available in still photography mode or in both still photography and movie (Movie and S&Q Movie) modes. Several of the tabs described in this chapter have a few slightly different entries when the Still/Movie/S&Q dial is set to either movie position. I'll explain those extra features in Chapter 10.

Focus Menu Tab

The Focus menu tab has five groups that adjust settings for autofocus, manual focus, and focus assistance aids. (See Figure 8.1.)

- AF/MF
- Focus Area
- Subject Recognition
- Focus Assistant
- Peaking Display

1. AF/MF

These are the entries in the AF/MF group. Figure 8.2 shows the entries available when Still/Movie/S&Q dial is set to Still mode. The entries marked (Movies) appear only when the Still/Movie/S&Q dial is set to either Movie position.

- Focus Mode
- Priority Setting in AF-S
- Priority Setting in AF-C
- AF Tracking Sensitivity
- AF Transition Speed (Movies)
- AF Subject Shift Sensitivity (Movies)
- AF Assist (Movies)
- AF Illuminator
- Aperture Drive in AF
- AF with Shutter
- Full Time DMF
- Pre-AF

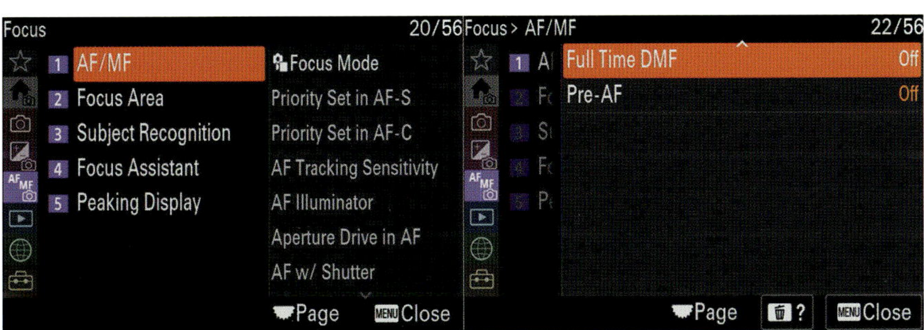

Figure 8.1 Focus tab.

Figure 8.2 AF/MF group.

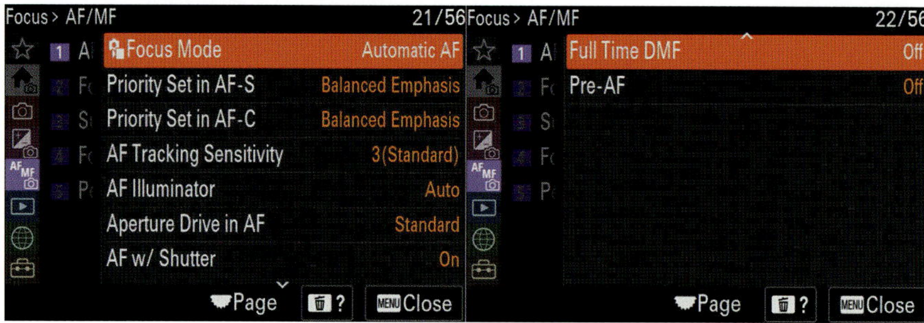

Focus Mode

Options: *Single-shot AF (AF-S)*, Automatic AF (AF-A), Continuous AF (AF-C), DMF (Direct Manual Focus), MF (Manual Focus)

My preference: Continuous AF (AF-C)

This menu item can be used to set the way in which the camera focuses. I discussed focus options in detail in Chapter 4.

- **Single-shot AF (AF-S).** With this default setting, the camera will set focus and it will keep that focus locked as long as you maintain slight pressure on the shutter-release button; even if the subject moves before you take the photo, the focus will stay where it was set. If you use this setting for still photos and then switch to Movie mode, the camera switches temporarily to AF-C.

- **Automatic AF (AF-A).** Begins to focus using AF-S but will switch to continuous autofocus (AF-C) if your subject is moving. This is a good all-purpose setting when you aren't sure whether your subject will suddenly begin moving around as you shoot.

- **Continuous AF (AF-C).** The camera will continue to adjust the focus if the camera-to-subject distance changes, as when a cyclist approaches your shooting position. The camera will constantly adjust focus to keep the subject sharply rendered. It uses predictive AF to predict the moving subject's position at the time you'll take the next shot and focuses at that distance. This option is useful when you're photographing sports, active children, animals, or other moving subjects, making it possible to get a series of sharply focused shots.

- **Direct Manual Focus (DMF).** Press the shutter button halfway down to let the camera start the focusing process in AF-S mode; then, keeping the button pressed halfway, turn the focusing ring to fine-tune the focus manually. You might want to use DMF when you are focusing from a short distance on a small object and want to make sure the focus point is exactly where you want it. It's good for close-up/macro photography, especially if you use Peaking Display (discussed later in this chapter) to outline the in-focus areas in a contrasting color. If you use this setting for still photos and then switch to Movie mode, the camera switches temporarily to AF-C.

- **Manual Focus (MF).** If you select Manual Focus, you turn the focusing ring on the lens to achieve the sharpest possible focus. With both DMF and Manual Focus, the camera will show you an enlarged image to help with the focusing process, if you have the Focus Magnifier option enabled in the Focus > Focus Assistant group.

Priority Set in AF-S/Priority Set in AF-C

Options: AF, Release, ***Balanced Emphasis**
My preference: AF for AF-S mode; Release for AF-C mode

These are two separate entries, one for AF-S and one for AF-C autofocus, but functionally they are identical, differing only in the autofocus mode they are applied to. It makes sense to describe them together.

These features let you specify whether the camera *waits* to actually take the picture until it has achieved sharp focus (when using an autofocus mode, not manual focus mode); whether it takes the picture immediately, even if sharp focus is not guaranteed; or whether it uses a balanced approach somewhere between the two. For most kinds of candid photography, sports, or photojournalism, most of us would rather get the shot rather than lose a fleeting moment, and so Release is often your best choice. If you have a little more time, and the shot won't be affected by a short delay (less than half a second, on average), Balanced Emphasis, the default, will do the job. If you're looking for the best sharpness your camera can provide, the AF choice might be your best option. The choices are as follows:

- **AF.** The shutter is not activated until sharp focus is achieved. This is best for subjects that are not moving rapidly.
    - **AF-S.** When using AF-S, most prefer to set this to AF, because in this focus mode the subject is usually not moving rapidly, and it makes sense to allow a slight extra delay to get the best focus possible. However, I find that with the a7C II/a7CR, when equipped with a lens having a fast built-in focus motor, in combination with the hybrid AF system, focus is fast enough that I can choose Release instead. If your camera/lens combination is slower to focus, you'll want to stick with the AF setting that I recommend for general use. The Priority setting you specify here is also applied to DMF mode.
    - **AF-C.** When working in AF-C focus mode, if you select AF, the camera will continue to track your subjects' movement, but the camera won't take a picture until focus is locked in. An indicator in the viewing screen will flash green until focus can be achieved. You might miss a few shots, but you will have fewer out-of-focus images. Sports shooters probably won't choose AF priority for AF-C. Instead, they'll select Release priority, discussed next.
- **Release.** When this option is selected, the shutter is activated when the release button is pushed down all the way, even if sharp focus has not yet been achieved. As I noted, I prefer this option for AF-C mode, as continuous focus focuses and refocuses constantly when autofocus is active, and even though an image may not quite be in sharpest focus, at least I got the shot. Use this option when taking a picture is more important than absolute best focus, such as fast action or photojournalism applications. (You don't want to miss that record-setting home run, or the protestor's pie smashing into the governor's face.) Using this setting doesn't mean that your image won't be sharply focused; it just means that you'll get a picture even if autofocusing isn't *quite* complete. If you've been poised with the shutter release pressed halfway, the camera probably has been tracking the focus of your image.

- **Balanced Emphasis.** In this mode, the shutter is released when the button is pressed, with a slight pause if autofocus has not yet been achieved. It can be selected for both AF-S and AF-C modes and may be your best choice if you want a good compromise between speed of activation and sharpest focus. I don't use this setting much because I prefer a predictable response from the camera. In addition, you would not want to use this setting if the highest possible continuous shooting rates are important to you.

AF Tracking Sensitivity

Options: 5 (Responsive) to 1 (Locked On); *3 (Standard) (default)

My preference: 1 (Locked On) for sports

This feature determines how quickly the camera unlocks focus from the subject it is currently tracking and focuses instead on another subject that intervenes. For example, if you're shooting a football game as a running back is breaking through the line and a referee bolts along the sideline in front of you. With this feature set to Responsive, the camera will very quickly switch to the ref, and then should return its attention to the running back—but often, not quickly enough. A better choice would be to use Locked On, so that the camera briefly ignores the referee, who is likely to have moved on in a second or two. Focus tracking will remain on your running back.

Note that this setting applies *only* to still photos; the equivalent setting for movies is AF Transition Speed, discussed next. Your options include:

- **Responsive.** At the 4 and 5 settings, the camera quickly responds to new subjects that cross the frame. This is the best setting to use for fast-moving subjects, such as sports or frenetic children, *as long as you don't expect intervening subjects.* The camera will smoothly follow your subjects. It works well when subjects within the frame are at significantly different distances.

- **Standard.** At the 3 setting, response to movement is a bit slower, so that the camera doesn't constantly refocus as subjects move about the frame. This is the default and should be used when there is only moderate movement, and especially if the movement is across the width or height of the frame (rather than coming toward you or away from you), and when you're using a small f/stop, because the increased depth-of-field will eliminate the need for most re-focusing.

- **Locked On.** At the 1 and 2 settings, the autofocus system will lock onto the initial subject and follow it until it leaves the frame. Use this setting when you know you'll have intervening subjects often and are certain that you want to ignore them. Many sports events, including football, soccer, and baseball, fall into this category.

AF Transition Speed

Options: Fast (7), Normal (4), Slow (1); *5 (default)

My preference: Normal for most scenes, Fast for sports and action

This is a movies-only setting that, like other video-exclusive commands, appears only when the Still/Movie/S&Q dial is set to one of the movie positions. It is used to adjust how quickly the camera focuses while capturing video using an integer scale from Fast (7) to Slow (1). It's used in conjunction with AF Subject Shift Sensitivity, described next. Unlike stills, when focus changes while shooting movies it is apparent in the clip and can be undesirable.

Your three options are as follows:

- **Fast (5, 6, or 7).** The camera focuses as quickly as possible, but with slightly less precision. This setting is good for sports, action, photojournalism, and street photography, and any situation where it's important to keep the main subjects in focus as they move around. In such situations, the automatic focus adjustments add to the feeling of following the action; any delay in refocusing would be disconcerting.
- **Normal (4).** The AF responds smoothly to subject movement by refocusing gradually. With scenes that are not filled with constant action, this mode may be the least noticeable to the viewer.
- **Slow (3, 2, or 1).** Focusing is much less speedy and is a good choice if your subjects are moving at a constant rate of speed and direction. This setting will allow the camera to smoothly follow focus. Choose Slow to be on the safe side, in such situations, particularly when using older lenses that are themselves somewhat pokey in achieving focus.

AF Subject Shift Sensitivity

Options: Scale from 1 (Locked On) to *5 **(Responsive)**

My preference: 3 (Standard)

This entry, also available only when the Still/Movie/S&Q dial is set to one of the two movie positions, works hand-in-hand with the AF Transition Speed entry above and uses a scale from 1 (Locked On) to 5 (Responsive). It is another movies-only setting and determines how quickly the camera unlocks focus from the subject it is currently tracking and focuses instead on another subject that intervenes. For example, if you're shooting a video of a child or grandchild enjoying a playground and another kid unexpectedly darts between you and your youngster, you don't want the camera to switch to the intervening subject. With this feature set to the Responsive end of the scale, the camera will very quickly switch to the other youth, and then should return its attention to your child—but often, not quickly enough. A better choice would be to use Standard, so that the camera briefly ignores the other kid, who is likely to have moved on. Focus tracking will remain on the intended "star" of your video. Your options include:

- **Responsive (4 or 5).** The camera quickly responds to new subjects that cross the frame. This is the best setting to use for fast-moving subjects, such as sports or frenetic children, *as long as you don't expect intervening subjects*. The camera will smoothly follow your subjects, especially if AF Transition Speed has been set to Fast, too.
- **Standard (3).** Response to movement is a bit slower, so that the camera doesn't constantly refocus as subjects move about the frame. It should be used when there is only moderate movement, and especially if the movement is across the width or height of the frame (rather than coming toward you or away from you), and when you're using a small f/stop, because the increased depth-of-field will eliminate the need for most re-focusing.
- **Locked On (2 or 1).** Use either of these settings if you want to keep the camera focused on the same subject, despite intervening subjects that might appear. I use the Locked On setting when I want to emphasize a particular subject (often a person) using selective focus and a large aperture.

AF Assist

Options: On, *Off
My preference: Off

This is a handy feature that lets you manually choose the autofocus target while capturing video. When enabled, all you need to do is use the lens's focus ring to focus on your desired subject, then release the ring. The a7C II or a7CR will now continue to focus on that target with no further intervention needed. This is one instance where the Peaking Display feature described later in this chapter can be a useful indicator that your intended subject is, in fact, in focus. This feature does not work with the Sony 16-50mm and 18-200mm APS-C lenses.

AF Illuminator

Options: *Auto, Off
My preference: Auto

The AF illuminator is light activated when there is insufficient light for the camera's autofocus mechanism to zero in on the subject. This light emanates from the same lamp on the front of the camera that provides the indicator for the self-timer (and which may be blocked by lens hoods or stray fingers). The extra blast from the AF illuminator provides a bright target for the AF system to help the camera set focus for subjects roughly no farther away than 10 feet. When you're shooting in environments so dark that conventional focusing is difficult, the a7C II/a7CR will ignore the focus area you've specified and instead focus on whatever the AF assist lamp is able to illuminate. This menu item is a still-photos-only option, as the illuminator does not operate while shooting conventional or S&Q motion movies.

The default setting, Auto, allows the AF illuminator to work any time the camera judges that it is necessary. Turn it off when you would prefer not to use this feature, such as when you don't want to disturb the people around you or call attention to your photographic endeavors. Disabling the lamp is virtually mandatory when shooting stage performances, especially ballet. The illuminator is ineffective at such distances anyway, and can be particularly distracting to dancers, according to one choreographer, who told me they partially orient their pirouettes based on light fixtures they see in the auditorium as they spin.

The AF illuminator doesn't work when the camera is set for manual focus or when using AF-C or AF-A while the subject is moving. It is also disabled when using the Focus Magnifier, or one of the EA-LA adapters (which allow using A-mount lenses).

Note that some Sony flash units (such as the HVL-F45RM) include a white LED video light that the a7C will use as an AF illuminator lamp if the flash is mounted on the camera and powered up.

Aperture Drive in AF

Options: Focus Priority, *Standard, Silent Priority
My preference: N/A

This setting determines whether and how much the aperture opens between shots, allowing you to choose whether you want the camera to operate more quietly or focus more accurately. Why is that even necessary? Well, if you're a photography veteran, you may wonder why Sony cameras don't have a depth-of-field preview button. The short answer is that they don't need one, because, unlike most other models, these cameras always focus with the lens stopped down to the working f/stop ("taking aperture" in photo jargon) used to expose the picture.

When using cameras that keep the aperture wide open until the moment of exposure (when it stops down to take the picture), it's useful to have a depth-of-field preview that temporarily closes the aperture to the working f/stop. With the lens stopped down, you can see (more or less) exactly how much is in focus, and how much is not.

There are some advantages and disadvantages to having the lens already set to the taking aperture while composing your images. You *always* get to see the current depth-of-field; the live view is automatically brightened on the LCD or electronic viewfinder to compensate. (However, *exposure adjustments* do change the brightness of the display when Shooting > Shooting Display > Live View Display Setting is set to On. In addition, because the camera doesn't have to keep opening and closing the aperture between shots, faster continuous shooting speeds are possible.

The downside is that it's more difficult to focus at smaller f/stops, even with your camera's hybrid phase detect/contrast detect AF system. At f/stops smaller than f/11, autofocus is not used between continuous shots when using the electronic shutter (to achieve the high Hi+ speed of 8 frames per second). Instead, in that mode focus is fixed at that determined for the first shot. This entry offers three options for specifying exactly how the camera adjusts the aperture while shooting. Your choices are as follows:

- **Focus Priority.** When shooting continuously with the electronic shutter (but *not* Mechanical Shutter or Auto chosen for Shutter Type), the aperture will open slightly. Sony doesn't specify how much, but in my tests the lens does not necessarily open to its maximum aperture. With the wider aperture, the AF system can focus more quickly and accurately.

  There is a slight increase in noise with this setting because the camera is not silent due to the movement of the iris; the display may flicker, and the aperture level may not be displayed on the screen. The camera uses Standard instead of Focus Priority when not using continuous shooting, even if Focus Priority is set here.

- **Standard.** The a7C II and a7CR use the working aperture to focus, and lock the aperture to the working f/stop of the first shot for subsequent continuous shots with the electronic shutter.

- **Silent Priority.** The f/stop doesn't change, even when an f/stop smaller than f/11 is set. Focusing may be slower, but the audible noise is less than both Focus Priority and Standard settings. This option is available only when certain lenses are mounted on the camera. (Check with Sony for compatible optics. No list is available as I write this.)

AF with Shutter

Options: *On, Off

My preference: N/A

As you know, a gentle touch on the shutter-release button causes the camera to begin focusing when using an autofocus mode. There may be some situations in which you prefer that the camera not re-focus every time you touch the shutter-release button, such as when you want to work with *back-button focus*, which I explained in detail in Chapter 4.

Let's say you are taking multiple pictures in a laboratory or studio with the subject at the same distance; you have no need to refocus constantly, and there is no need to put an extra burden on the autofocus mechanism and on the battery. But you don't want to switch to manual focus. Instead, you can set AF w/Shutter to Off. From then on, the camera will never begin to autofocus, or to change the focus when the shutter release is pressed. You can still initiate autofocus by pressing the AF-ON button or another key that you've assigned the AF-ON function (as I'll describe later under Custom Keys). The AF-ON button will start autofocus at any point, independent of the shutter release. Pressing the shutter release still locks *exposure,* unless you've disabled that function, too, using the Exposure/Color > Metering > AEL w/Shutter entry discussed in Chapter 7.

Full Time DMF

Options: *Off, On

My preference: On

This setting allows you to fine-tune focus manually even when the camera is set to autofocus (when set to On). With the default Off setting, the focus ring is disabled while using autofocus. Note that this setting is disabled when using the 16-50mm Power Zoom and 18-200mm f/3.5-6.3 or the Sony FE 70-200mm F/2.8GM OSS lens when Focus Mode is set to Continuous AF. It is also disabled with Sony A-mount lenses attached with an adapter and during continuous shooting in other than Low speed mode.

Pre-AF

Options: *Off, On

My preference: Off, On when shooting rambunctious pets or kids

This setting tells the camera to attempt to adjust the focus even before you press the shutter button halfway, giving you a head start that's useful for grab shots. When an image you want to capture appears, you can press the shutter release and take the picture a bit more quickly. However, this pre-focus process uses a lot of juice, depleting your battery more quickly, which is why it is turned off by default. Reserve it for short-term use during quickly unfolding situations where the slight advantage can be useful.

In my tests with the a7C II and a7CR and various lenses, Pre-AF can be a little slow to respond sometimes, but it does work with all autofocus modes and E-mount optics. If you find Pre-AF to be sluggish, say, under low-light conditions, just press the shutter release halfway to commence autofocus manually.

2. Focus Area

The Focus Area tab has 12 groups in Still Photography mode, covering almost two menu pages, with options for specifying, adjusting, and displaying the areas used to achieve autofocus. (See Figure 8.3.) In either Movie mode, only five of these appear in the tab.

- Focus Area
- Focus Area Limit
- Switch Vertical/Horizontal AF Area (Stills)
- Focus Area Color
- AF Area Registration (Stills)
- Delete Registered AF Area (Stills)
- AF Area Auto Clear (Stills)
- Area Display During Tracking (Stills)
- AF-C Area Display (Stills)
- Phase Detection Area (Stills)
- Circulation of Focus Point
- AF Frame Movement Amount

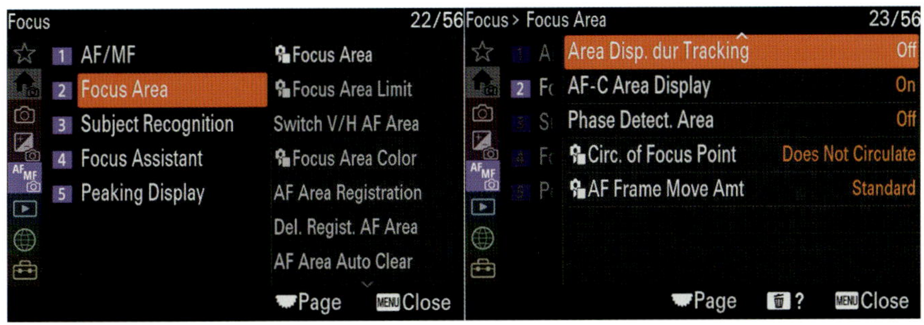

Figure 8.3 Focus Area group.

Focus Area

Options: *__Wide__, Zone, Center Fix, Spot (Small, Medium, Large), Expand Spot, Tracking: Wide, Zone, Center Fix, Spot (Small, Medium, Large), Expand Spot

My preference: Wide for general use; Tracking: Wide for sports and action

When the camera is set to Autofocus, use this menu option to specify where in the frame the camera will focus when you compose a scene in still photo mode, using the focus area selection you specify. I explained these options in Chapter 4.

- **Wide.** The camera uses its own electronic intelligence to determine what part of the scene should be in sharpest focus, providing automatic focus point selection. A green frame is displayed around the area that is in focus. Even if you set one of the other options, Wide is automatically selected in certain shooting modes, including both Intelligent Auto and all Scene modes.

- **Zone.** Select one of nine focus areas (described in Chapter 4), and the camera chooses which section of that zone to use to calculate sharp focus. You can move the focus zone with the directional buttons.

- **Center Fix.** Choose this option if you want the camera to always focus on the subject in the center of the frame. It covers the same area as Expand Spot (discussed shortly), but is locked into the middle of the frame. Center the primary subject (like a friend's face in a wide-angle landscape composition); allow the camera to focus on it; maintain slight pressure on the shutter-release button to keep focus locked; and re-frame the scene for a more effective, off-center, composition. Take the photo at any time and your friend (who is now off-center) will be in the sharpest focus. Use this option instead of manually selecting a focus point to quickly lock focus on the center of the frame, then press the defined AF lock button to fix the focus at that point so you can recompose the image as you prefer.

- **Spot (Small, Medium, Large).** This mode allows you to move the camera's focus detection point (focus area) around the scene to any one of multiple locations using the directional buttons. When this option is highlighted, use the left/right directional buttons or control wheel to change the size range of the spot among Small (S), Medium (M), and Large (L).

  This mode can be useful when the camera is mounted on a tripod and you'll be taking photos of the same scene for a long time, while the light is changing, for example. Move the focus area to cover the most important subject, and it will always focus on that point when you later take a photo.

- **Expand Spot.** If the camera is unable to lock in focus using the selected focus point, it will also use the eight adjacent points to try to achieve focus. You can move the spot using the directional buttons.

- **Tracking (Wide, Zone, Center Fix, Spot [Small, Medium, Large], Expand Spot).** In this mode, available only in Still mode, the camera locks focus onto the subject area that is under the selected focus spot when the shutter button is depressed halfway. Then, if the subject moves (or you change the framing in the camera), the camera will continue to refocus *on that subject*. You can select this mode only when the focus mode is set to Continuous AF (AF-C).

  This option is especially powerful because you can activate it for any of the five focus area options described above. That is, once you've highlighted Tracking on the selection screen, you can then press the left/right directional buttons and choose Wide, Zone, Center Fix, Spot (Small, Medium, Large), or Expand Spot.

Focus Area Limit 📷 🎥 S&Q

Options: Wide, Zone, Center, Spot (Small, Medium, Large), Expand Spot, Tracking; ***All Available***
My preference: Deactivate little-used focus area choices

Experiencing too much of a good thing? This entry allows you to deactivate focus options that you rarely (or never) use, so that they don't appear when you select a focus area using the Focus Area entry, or use the Function menu's Focus Area option. Only the choices you enable will be shown; the others will be grayed out.

When you select this entry, the screen shown in Figure 8.4 appears. The check marks above each focus area indicates the option is available. To disable/enable a particular focus area choice, highlight it using the directional buttons and press the center button to remove/add the check mark. The top row shows the non-tracking options (left to right): Wide, Zone, Center, Spot (Small), Spot (Medium), Spot

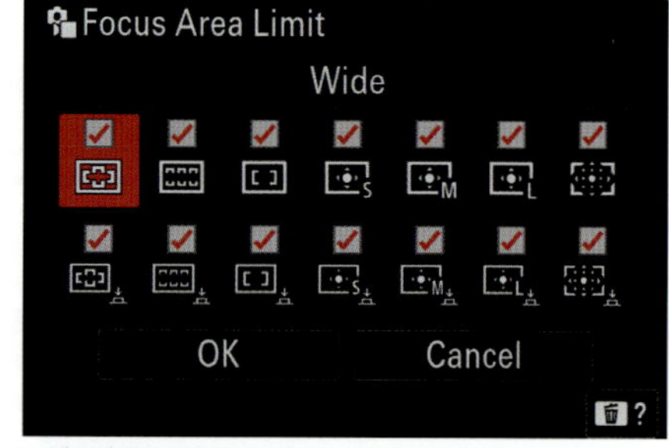

Figure 8.4 Focus Area Limit options.

(Large), and Expand Spot. The bottom row includes the Tracking counterparts of the exact same choices.

That configuration gives you a great deal of flexibility. You can have one set of focus areas enabled for general use, and choose a different set when using the Tracking capabilities. In my case, I use the Spot (Small) focus area frequently, but disable the Medium and Large options. However, when shooting sports and action, I use Tracking almost exclusively, so I disable *all* the Tracking choices except for Spot (Small), (Medium), and (Large). As you'll learn in Chapter 4, you can assign the Switch Focus Area function to a custom key, using the Setup > Operation Customize > Custom Key/Dial Settings entry. So, I can cycle among those that remain simply by pressing the assigned function key. Fast and easy.

Alternatively, you can just press the Fn button, highlight Focus Area, and select Tracking. You can then switch among Small, Medium, or Large by pressing the left/right directional buttons, or among the roster of focus areas you choose to enable using this menu entry.

Switch Vertical/Horizontal AF Area

Options: *****Off**, AF Point Only, AF Point+AF Area

My preference: Depends on subject

Here you can choose whether the Focus Area mode and the location of the focusing area within the frame adjusts when you change the camera's orientation from horizontal to vertical. It's especially useful when you want to change orientation frequently for the same type of subject matter. For example, when I am photographing family and individual portraits, I might shoot one set of images with the camera held horizontally to capture several members of a group, then rotate to use a vertical frame to capture a head-and-shoulders image of an individual. Many sports, such as basketball, involve the same sort of adjustment—a horizontal photo showing two or three players fighting for the ball, followed by a vertically oriented picture of a pair of roundballers going after a rebound off the boards.

Here are some things to consider:

- **You can/must set the Focus Area mode and/or focus point for each orientation individually.** That is, you must choose a Focus Area mode/focus point for horizontal orientation, then shift to each of the two vertical orientations and select a different location for either/both. If you don't specify a new location, the Focus Area and focus point remain where they were.

  You are free to change the preferred position for any orientation by rotating the camera to that orientation and moving the focus point. To cancel out any changes, just turn this feature off.

- **Only three orientations available.** They are horizontal, rotated 90-degrees clockwise with the shutter release on the lower half of the camera, and rotated 90 degrees from horizontal with the shutter release on the upper half of the camera. The horizontal/upside down orientation is the same as the conventional horizontal orientation. When the camera is pointed straight up (toward the sky) or straight down (toward your feet), it has no idea about the orientation.

- **AF Area mode/Focus Point Switching disabled.** Changes in orientation are ignored if you are using Intelligent Auto, Movie, or S&Q Motion shooting modes. The feature is also temporarily disabled if you press the shutter halfway down (and then change orientations), and during auto-focus, continuous shooting, self-timer countdown, or Focus Settings adjustments. Using the Focus Magnifier also disables the feature.

You have three options for this feature:

- **Off.** The Focus Area mode and Focus Point (Frame) remain the same regardless of camera orientation. If you've selected a particular Focus Area mode and you've placed the focus at the lower-left area of the frame when shooting horizontally (as seen in Figure 8.5, top center), it will remain in the equivalent position when you rotate the camera 90-degrees counterclockwise (see Figure 8.5, top left), or 90-degrees clockwise. (See Figure 8.5, top right.)
- **AF Point Only.** The Focus Area mode remains the same while the Focus Point adjusts to the camera orientation. (See Figure 8.5, bottom.)
- **AF Point+AF Area.** Both the Focus Area mode and Focus Point adjust, so you can use a different Focus Area mode for each orientation in addition to the position of the focus point.

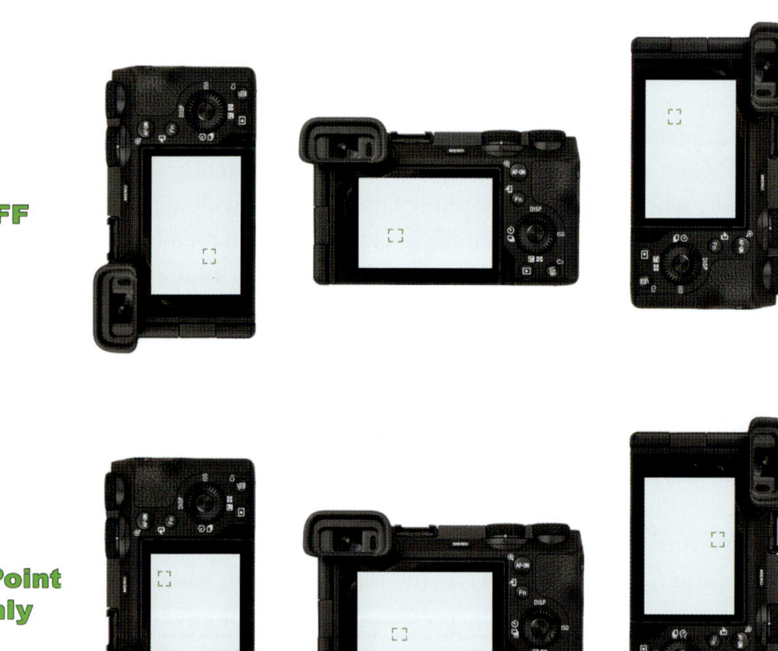

Figure 8.5 When the feature is turned off, the focus points remain in the same relative position as the camera is rotated (top). When switching is enabled, you can position the focus points in different locations within the frame for each of the three orientations (bottom). You can also optionally specify a different Focus Area mode for each presentation.

Focus Area Color 📷 🎥 S&Q

Options: *White, Red
My preference: Red

By default, with each Focus Area other than Wide, the a7C II/a7CR shows the current focus frame in white, displaying the active points in green when focus is achieved. Many (including me) find the white frame difficult to discern with many subjects, particularly those that are bright or light in color. I prefer to see the frame highlighted in red, which seems more natural and provides a strong contrast.

AF Area Registration 📷 🎥 S&Q

Options: *Off, On
My preference: On

This is an absolute killer feature for sports photographers, as it allows you to switch from your current focus point to a pre-registered point—and then back to your original point—just by pressing a custom key. Say you're covering a baseball game and frequently alternate between photographing the batter or some other position and first base, where a lot of action takes place. If you've registered first base (as I'll describe shortly), you're free to focus elsewhere and then, when the batter makes contact and begins running toward first (or the pitcher decides to throw to first to cut off a base runner who's taken a lead), you can press the defined key and the focus point will instantly move back to the registered first-base location within the frame.

To use this feature, just follow these steps:

1. **Activate AF Area Registration.** Navigate to this menu entry and choose On, then press the center button to confirm. A message will appear reminding you to register a specific focus area. I'll explain how to do that shortly. Press the center button again to exit to the menu.

2. **Register a Focus Area.** Move the focus point to the location you want to register. Press the Fn button and hold it down until the message Registered the Focus Area appears (it will take about three seconds).

3. **Access Setup > Operation Customize > Custom Key/Dial Settings (Stills).** To relocate the focus point to a registered position, you'll need to define a custom button to do that. Select a button within the Custom Key/Dial Settings entry and navigate to one of the three registration variations listed below. You'll find them in the Focus > Focus Area group.

   - **Registered AF Area Hold.** Pressing the button switches to the registered location *only* while you hold the button down. When you release the custom key the focus point returns to your previous focus point. This option is useful if you want to be able to switch to the registered area only temporarily. If you find it awkward to manipulate two buttons at once (holding down your custom key, plus pressing the shutter release to take the picture), you may be better off switching back and forth using the toggle option described next.

   - **Registered AF Area Toggle.** Press and release the button to switch to the registered location and press it a second time to return to your previous focus point. Use this if you think you'll need to take several consecutive images using the registered point. Toggle is the only available option for the left, right, and down keys.

- **Registered AF Area+AF On.** When the custom key is pressed, the focus point switches to the registered area and autofocus is initiated. When you release the custom key, the focus point returns to its previous location. If you've registered first base you can then move the focus point to home plate and continue to capture the batter's efforts. Then, if action unfolds at first base, press the defined button and the a7C II or a7CR will switch to your registered focus point and focus. You can then continue to hold the key while pressing the shutter release down to take the picture. Release the button and the focus point returns to home plate. (You can avoid the need to hold down the button if you're using back-button focus, which decouples the AF activation feature from the shutter release.) This *sounds* complicated if you don't know how back-button focus works, but I explained it in more detail in Chapter 4.

4. **Registered focus frame appears.** When the defined custom key is pressed, the focus frame and points will flash in the viewfinder and on the LCD monitor. It may also appear in some of your live view displays as a reminder.

AF Area Registration cannot be used when shooting movies or S&Q video, when using digital zoom, while tracking, while focus is locked, or when you are focusing using the lens's focus ring or the Touch Focus feature.

Delete Registered AF Area

Options: Delete, ***Cancel**

My preference: N/A

Use this to delete a registered focus area. That prevents the camera from shifting to the previously defined area if you accidentally press the defined custom key.

AF Area Auto Clear

Options: ***Off**, On

My preference: Off

This setting controls whether the focus area is shown all the time as you shoot, or whether it disappears a short time after focus is achieved in AF-S mode. Choose On if you prefer having an uncluttered screen while you shoot. I prefer to have focus information available at all times, so I leave this setting at its default Off value.

Area Display During Tracking

Options: ***Off**, On

My preference: Off

This is a similar de-cluttering tool that can be applied when using the AF-C autofocus mode and any of the Tracking AF focus areas other than Wide. When enabled, the frame used for the current focus area is displayed to help you locate the focus point over the desired subject when you activate tracking. When disabled, the focus area frame is displayed for just a moment, and then vanishes. I prefer to leave this setting on Off to declutter the screen after tracking begins.

AF-C Area Display

Options: Off, *On

My preference: On

This item determines whether the previewing display on the monitor or EVF shows the active Wide or Zone focus areas when you're using Continuous AF. It has no effect on their display if you're using Center Fix, Spot, or Expand Spot or any Tracking option in Continuous AF area modes, or autofocus modes other than AF-C.

Sometimes too much information can be distracting. That's especially true in AF-C mode, because if you've framed a moving subject, the camera can continue to change the active focus areas if your subject is moving. In Wide mode, you may be treated to a dancing array of green rectangles squirming around on your screen as the a7C II or a7CR focuses and refocuses in anticipation of you eventually pressing the shutter release all the way down and taking a picture. I think that the constantly shifting focus requires less continual feedback about what focus areas are being used, so you may want to switch the feature off. In my case, I don't mind the display, and I tend to leave it on most of the time, even though it consumes a little more battery power. **Note:** When Focus Area is set to Center Fix, Spot, or Expand Spot, the focus area turns green.

Phase Detection Area 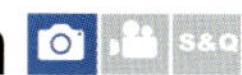

Options: On, *Off

My preference: Off

Ostensibly, this feature, when activated, will display vertical bars on the screen representing the sensor area covered by the embedded phase detection points. It works only with certain APS-C lenses designed for cameras like the Sony a6700. If you don't own any APS-C lenses, you can safely leave this setting at its default (Off) and then forget about it for the rest of your life. You'd think it would be useful when you've activated the a7C II or a7CR's APS-C/Super 35 mode in the Shooting > Image Quality/Recording menu, *but it does not work* with any full-frame lens, even in APS-C mode.

Sony cautions that the feature is enabled only with certain compatible APS-C lenses, assuming their firmware has been properly updated (if an update is available). I tried eight different official Sony APS-C lenses in my arsenal, and they worked just fine. None of my non-Sony lenses triggered the display. The bars are also disabled when recording movies.

Circulation of Focus Point

Options: *Does Not Circulate, Circulate

My preference: N/A

This setting simply determines whether you can only move the focus point within the image frame, or whether, when it reaches left, right, top, or bottom edges it wraps around to the opposite side. A lot of people like this feature quite a bit, but unless you played too much *Pac-Man* in your youth, you will probably prefer Does Not Circulate. It is loved by those who tend to scoot the focus point around the frame frantically, as you can move from one edge of the frame to the opposite edge quite quickly.

AF Frame Movement Amount

Options: *Standard, Large

My preference: Standard

This setting adjusts how rapidly a movable focus spot can be relocated using the directional controls. Sony shooters can sometimes be divided into two camps. On the one hand, you have those who like to keep the Zone or Spot/Expand Spot focus areas in one position, often the center of the frame. They typically point the camera at the subject they want to focus on, and lock focus (in AF-S).

Others prefer to relocate the Zone or Spot focus areas to suit the subject they're working with, especially if that subject will likely be out of the center of the frame. If you're one of the latter, you may find this setting handy. You can choose whether the movement is in smaller or larger increments, based on the focus area you choose. The distance doesn't change much for Zone and Spot-Small Focus Areas, but the focus point moves twice as fast when using Spot-Medium, Spot-Large, or Expand Spot.

3. Subject Recognition

The Subject Recognition group (which Sony called the Face/Eye AF group in previous cameras) has seven entries you can use to customize the a7C II or a7CR's remarkable subject detection features, which are no longer limited to just faces and eyes and now includes birds, pets, insects, cars, trains, and airplanes. (See Figure 8.6.) All these entries are available in both Still and Movie modes.

> **SUBJECT RECOGNITION IN DEPTH**
>
> I'm going to describe the major menu entries dealing with subject recognition in the sections that follow. For more information on what they do and how to use them, refer to Chapter 4. Sony's subject recognition and tracking capabilities are too robust to describe fully in this menu guide.

- Subject Recognition in Autofocus
- Recognition Target
- Recognition Target Selection Setting
- Right/Left Eye Selection
- Subject Recognition Frame Display
- Face Memory
- Registered Face Priority

When you're photographing people, the a7C II and a7CR can optionally look for faces, and can base autofocus decisions on the human subjects located. Even better, you can give certain countenances a higher priority than others by registering them with the camera, so, say, if your significant other is ensconced in the frame, the camera will favor that person as its AF focus (so to speak) over other humans in the frame. Further, the camera can locate human or animal eyes within your frame, plus targets like insects, cars, trains, and airplanes, and focus on them.

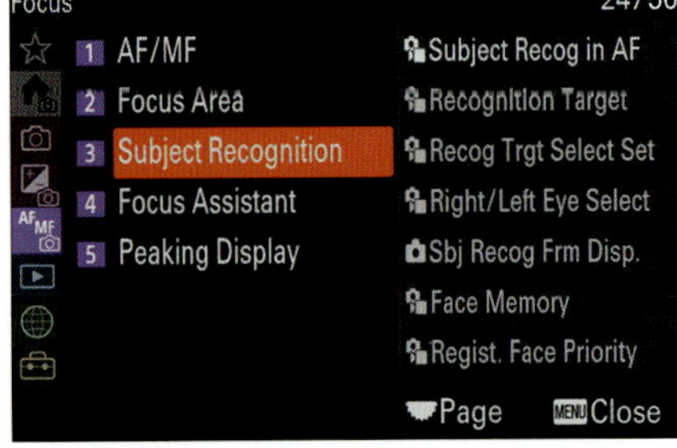

Figure 8.6 The Subject Recognition AF group.

Subject Recognition in Autofocus

Options: **On*, Off

My preference: On

Choose On and the a7C II/a7CR can give a higher priority to detected subjects. Select Off and AF will proceed without looking for faces. When autofocus is activated, the camera will attempt to focus on the eyes or face, *if they are located within the active focus area*. This can cause problems if the face(s) involved are not your main subject. Perhaps you want to focus on an object in the foreground, and not onlookers in the background. In that case, press the center button to temporarily switch to Center Fix and AF-S.

Face detection may be stymied if your subjects are rapidly moving, have long bangs, closed eyes, or are wearing sunglasses. Shady conditions, backlight, and low-light situations can also hinder eye detection. Note that when using Intelligent Auto, Subject Recognition is locked at On.

Recognition Target

Options: **Human*, Animal/Bird, Animal, Bird, Insect, Car/Train, Airplane

My preference: Human

As I noted above, you can tell the camera to look for a variety of different subjects. Note that you can choose Animal/Bird (in which case the camera looks for either) instead of Animal *or* Bird, in which case it looks only for the type you select. (See Figure 8.7, left.) When you highlight your subject type ("recognition target" in Sony-speak), press the right button to produce a screen of subparameters to further refine your search. (See Figure 8.7, right.) The available parameters differ by subject type, and I explained what they are and how to use them in Chapter 4, and will not repeat that information here.

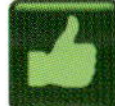

TIP If you define the Recognition Target Select behavior to a custom button (using Setup > Operation Customize > Custom Key/Dial Settings, as described in Chapter 9), you can press the custom button to cycle among all of the available choices.

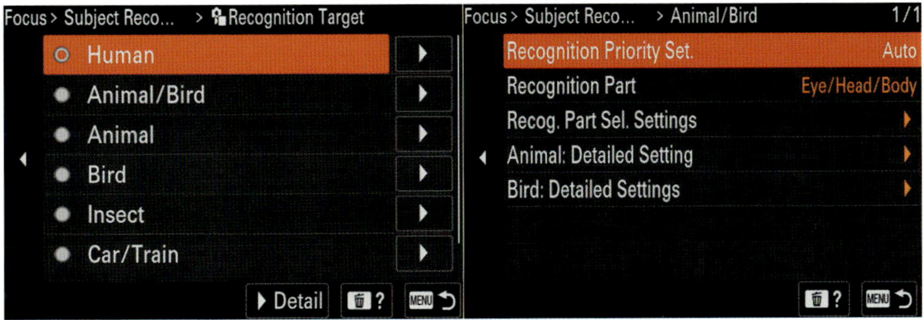

Figure 8.7 Choose subject type (left) and parameters for each (right).

Recognition Target Selection Setting 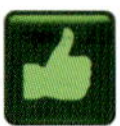

Options: *Human, *Animal/Bird, *Animal, *Bird, *Insect, *Car/Train, *Airplane

My preference: All selected (the default)

This setting allows you to disable the availability of one or more of the seven options, depending on your shooting preferences. For example, if you generally take photos only of humans and birds (especially those in flight), you can disable the subjects you rarely shoot. A scrollable screen with all the subject types appears. Highlight each option you want to remove and mark or unmark the types of subjects you want to look for. If you assign Subject Select Setting to a custom key, pressing the defined button will cycle among the active choices and show the current subject type on the display.

> **TIP** If you define the Recognition Target Select behavior to a custom button (as recommended above) you can disable the choices you do not use here, and thus cycle *only* among your preferred subjects with the custom button.

Right/Left Eye Selection

Options: *Auto, Left, Right

My preference: Auto

This entry is available *only* if your recognition target/subject selection is either Human or Animal, based on the assumption that birds (non-owls, at least), insects, cars, trains, and airplanes do not have right or left eyes. You can use this option to choose whether to detect the left or right eye of the subject when both are visible. Note that this feature uses the *subject's* eye, which may be on the opposite side from your perspective (that is, your subject's right eye is on the left side of your frame). (See Figure 8.8.)

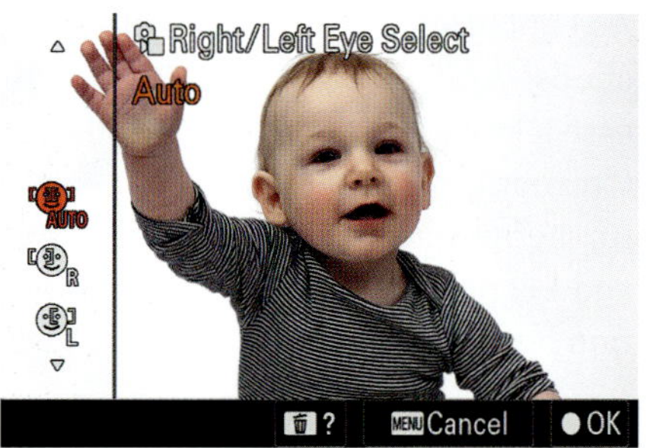

Figure 8.8 You can switch to focus on the left or right eye.

Subject Recognition Frame Display

Options: *Off, On

My preference: On

The camera automatically shows a small white or gray square around an eye, face/head, or body of a human, animal, or bird it is focusing on. Only the head or entire body of insects, and front part of cars, trains, or airplanes will be given a box. (If you want the frames to display, but disappear after a time, use AF Area Auto Clear, described earlier in this chapter.)

Although the eye-focus box is particularly helpful, I find the additional box around the face very useful and prefer to have it available at all times so I know *exactly* what face(s) have been detected. When enabled, a gray selection box appears around detected faces. The box around the face used for autofocus turns white. If there are several faces in the frame and you've registered and prioritized them, the boxes around the other faces turn reddish-purple. (I'll show you how to register faces later in this chapter.) If you find the boxes distracting, you can turn them off, and face detection, if enabled as described earlier, will still be active.

> 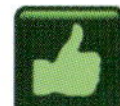 **TIP** Use Setup > Operation Customize > Custom Key/Dial Settings to assign Select Face to Track to a custom key. Then, if several faces are detected—say, at a wedding reception or in a group photo—an orange bar will appear below the white box around the face to be tracked and gray boxes around the other faces. Rotate the control wheel and press the center button to select a different face.

Face Memory

Options: New Registration, Order Exchanging, Delete, Delete All

My preference: N/A

You can specify up to seven different registered faces to receive focusing priority. If none are recognized, the camera will attempt to focus on any other faces it detects. When you access this entry, the screen shown at upper left in Figure 8.9 appears. Seven boxes are available to register individual faces. To capture and store faces, just follow these steps:

1. **New Registration.** When the box with the plus sign is highlighted with a red frame, press the center button to begin a new registration.

2. **Capture face.** For best results, line up your victim (subject) using a bright area as a background to allow easier detection of the face. A white box appears that you can use to frame the face. (See Figure 8.9, upper right.) Press the center button to capture.

3. **Confirm.** A Register? Confirmation message appears (see Figure 8.9, lower left). Alternatively, a Could Not Register, Try Again warning is shown instead, usually because you need to frame the face better.

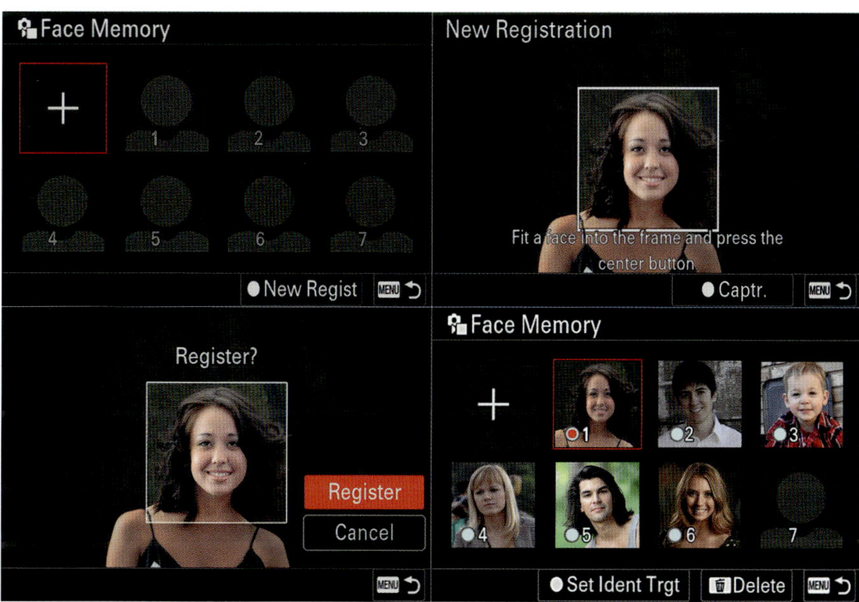

Figure 8.9 Adding faces to Face Memory.

4. **Register.** With the orange Register option highlighted, press the center button once more. You can also highlight Cancel to start over.

5. **Add faces.** You can repeat Steps 1–4 to add additional faces, as shown in Figure 8.9, lower right.

6. **Change Priority.** By default, the first face you captured will receive top priority if you've activated Registered Face Priority in the menu entry discussed next. The prioritized face will have an orange radio button overlaid as an indicator. You can select any other face as the target by highlighting it and pressing the center button. For example, at the wedding you'd want the a7C II/a7CR to zero in on the bride, rather than that annoying brother-in-law.

7. **Delete faces.** You can also select a specific face and delete it from the registry (say, you broke up with your significant other!) or delete *all* faces from the registry (your SO got custody of the camera). Face data remains in the camera when you delete individual faces but is totally erased when you select Delete All.

This is another feature that lends itself to custom key definitions for those who use it frequently. For example, if you assign Switch Identification Target to a key, you can cycle among the registered faces by pressing the defined custom button.

Registered Face Priority

Options: *On, Off

My preference: On

If I've gone to the trouble of registering important faces, I will generally want to give those faces priority. However, you might want to give all faces equal priority, say, if you're at a wedding reception that includes your family members, but other guests and/or the bride and groom are more/just as important. In that case, turn this option off.

4. Focus Assistant

This group has five entries that are aids in focusing in still photography mode, particularly when you're using manual focus. (See Figure 8.10.) Two additional entries, Focus Map and Initial Focus Magnification (Movies), apply only to video. The entries explained here include:

- Focus Map (Movies)
- Auto Magnifier in Manual Focus
- Focus Magnifier
- Focus Magnifier Time
- Initial Focus Magnification (Stills)
- [Movie] Initial Focus Magnification (Movies)
- Autofocus in Focus Magnification

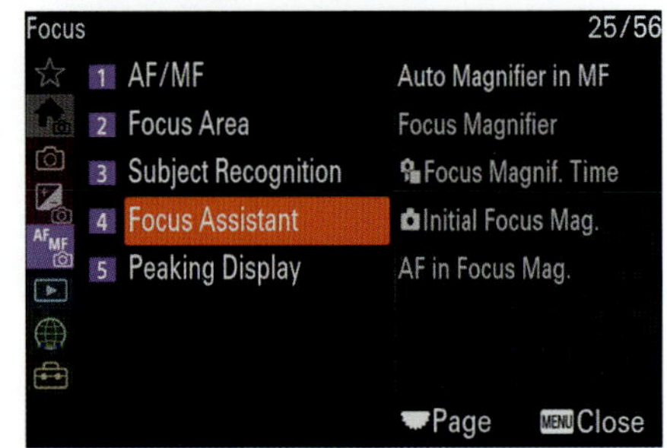

Figure 8.10 Focus Assistant group.

Focus Map ⬚ ▣ S&Q

Options: *On, Off

My preference: Off

It's become common to refer to use "on steroids" as a superlative when describing virtually any feature except an athlete's performance. Sony's new Focus Map feature might better be described as Focus Peaking on Valium. It provides an interesting depth map in very low resolution by using a blocky overlay that shows you roughly what is in focus, and what is not. Blocks in a blue color indicate what's behind the plane of focus, and those in a warm color show what's in front. Areas that are in focus are not overlaid. This feature doesn't work when using digital zoom, USB streaming, mount adapters, certain older lenses, and when using the Focus Magnifier. See Figure 8.11 for a simulation of this hard-to-like feature.

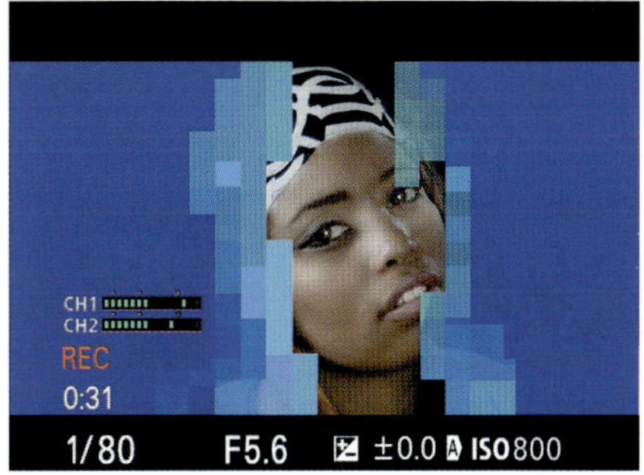

Figure 8.11 Focus Map, a less effective tool than Peaking (at the moment).

Auto Magnifier in Manual Focus ▣ ▣ S&Q

Options: *On, Off

My preference: N/A

This entry is rightfully activated by default, so that as you rotate the focus ring in manual focus mode the center of the focus area is automatically enlarged so you can focus more precisely. You can use the directional buttons to move the magnified area around within the frame. This is the most useful focusing aid your a7C II or a7CR provides. It's available only with native E-mount lenses; for others, you'll want to use the plain Focus Magnifier feature, described next. **Note:** Sony uses the oddball X 1.0, X 4.7, and similar notation to describe magnification in its menus and displays. I will conform to the more common 1.0X (or 1X), 4.7X, etc., convention for clarity.

1. **Switch to manual focus.** You can use the AF/MF switch on your lens, if present, or by pressing the Fn button and using the Function menu to choose MF from among the focus mode choices. Manual focus can also be chosen by accessing the Focus Mode entry in the menu system, described earlier in this chapter.

2. **Access Focus Magnifier.** If this entry is enabled, it should activate automatically as you rotate the focusing ring in Manual focus mode. When activated, the image will be shown within a screen like the one shown in Figure 8.12.

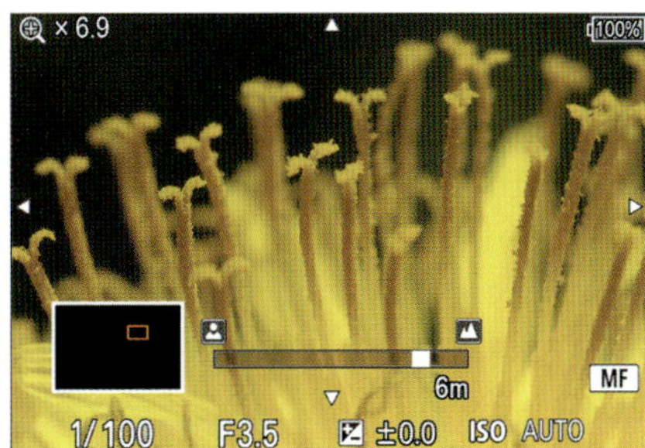

Figure 8.12 The Focus Magnifier can be zoomed from 6.9X to 13.7X.

3. **Rotate the focus ring.** The image is first enlarged to 6.9X and then to 13.7X (4.5X and 9.0X in APS-C mode). A third press cycles back to the original magnification. A navigation window appears at lower left showing an orange rectangle that represents the current location of the blown-up section (as seen in Figure 8.12). You can also use the control wheel's center button to zoom in.

4. **Adjust the magnified area.** A quartet of triangles surrounds the image, indicating that you can move the enlarged window around with the frame. Use the left/right/up/down directional controls to move the enlarged area.

5. **Center the magnifier.** You can press the Trash button to center the magnified section back in the center of the frame.

6. **Manually focus.** Rotate the lens's focus ring to achieve sharp focus. A scale along the bottom of the screen shows the approximate focus distance.

7. **Take the picture.** Press the shutter release down all the way to take the picture.

8. **(Optional) Return to autofocus.** Remember to return to autofocus when you no longer want to focus on your subject manually.

Focus Magnifier

Options: Activate

My preference: N/A

This entry allows accessing the Focus Magnifier manually, without needing to rotate the focus ring. Why would you bypass automatic invoking in favor of manual operation? The main reason is that some lenses don't automatically trigger the Focus Magnifier, so you must invoke it manually. This entry has several superpowers:

- **Works in Movie mode.** You can use the Focus Magnifier in movie mode, although it offers only a single 4X magnification.
- **More lenses.** Certain lenses, particularly non-Sony or adapted optics, may not automatically trigger the Auto Magnifier in Manual Focus feature. If so, you can manually initiate the magnifier with this entry, or invoke it by assigning the function to a custom key, as described in Chapter 9.
- **Works with Autofocus.** You can use it in both manual focus and AF-S/AF-A autofocus modes. Magnification with autofocus is great for fast, highly accurate focus on the fly.

Note that this menu item is grayed out if the camera is not in Manual Focus (MF) or Direct Manual Focus (DMF) focus modes. If you use this feature a lot, it's a good idea to assign it to a custom key to avoid a trip to the menu each time you invoke it. It operates similarly to the Auto Magnifier in MF feature above, but you must summon it from this menu or a custom key defined to produce it, and the available magnifications differ. There's one extra step: an orange rectangle appears in the middle of the screen that you can relocate to define the area you want to magnify. Press the center button to change magnification from 1X to 4.7X to 9.3X. The Trash button returns the box to the center of the screen. Press the Fn button to toggle between keeping the Focus Magnifier active after you've taken your shot, or returning to unmagnified view. That function is available when using Single-shot AF, Direct Manual Focus, or Manual Focus—as long as Setup > Display Option > Auto Review is Off. A message alerting you that focus magnification ends/continues after shooting appears when you press the Fn button.

> **TOUCH FOCUS**
>
> Your a7C II or a7CR's touch screen may be a faster way to invoke the Focus Magnifier when the camera is set to manual focus. You'll need to enable Touch Operation, which is in the Setup > Touch Operation > Touch Operation menu entry, as described in Chapter 9. When enabled, simply double tap the LCD monitor to select the area to focus on. You can then use a finger on the monitor screen to drag the focused area around. Double tap the monitor again to exit.

Focus Magnifier Time

Options: 2 sec., 5 sec., *No Limit
My preference: 5 sec.

This entry can be used to specify the length of time that the Focus Magnifier will magnify the image during manual focusing. If you find that it takes you longer than two seconds to manually focus using MF Assist, you can change the time to five seconds, or to No Limit; the latter will cause the image to remain magnified until you tap the shutter-release button (you don't need to actually take a picture), press the center button again to return to full frame, or double tap the LCD monitor if you have enabled Touch Operation. Don't use No Limit with DMF, as one of two things will happen, both bad. If you keep the shutter release pressed halfway after you've focused, the magnification will remain until you press the shutter release down all the way. That's a lousy way to compose an image. If you release the shutter button or tap the shutter button to cancel the magnification, when you press down the button again to actually take a picture, the a7C II/a7CR will refocus.

(Stills) Initial Focus Magnification

Options: *1.0X, 4.7X
My preference: 4.7X

You can specify the initial magnification presented when the Focus Magnifier is invoked. The default is 1.0X (no magnification), which is fine if your first step is frequently to move the magnification window around in the frame before zooming in. At 1.0X, you see the entire frame and can position the window anywhere you like. I prefer to skip that step and jump right in at 4.7X, which usually positions the window close enough that I can go ahead and move it within the frame if I want. The 4.7X magnification is automatically used if you have enabled Touch Operation and double tap the LCD monitor to zoom in.

(Movie) Initial Focus Magnification

Options: *1.0X, 4X

My preference: 4X

This menu item is visible only when the a7C II/a7CR's Still/Movie/S&Q dial is in either Movie position. It's similar to the Stills version, described above, but the magnification choices are 1.0X and 4.0X.

AF in Focus Magnification

Options: *On, Off

My preference: Off when not shooting macro/close-up images

As I mentioned earlier, the Focus Magnifier works just fine in autofocus mode. You can use it to view an enlarged image to confirm that correct focus has been achieved automatically, or to fine-tune focus when working with Direct Manual Focus (DMF) mode.

Once you've enabled the AF focus magnification option, activate the Focus Magnifier as described earlier, and adjust the enlarged area using the directional controls and the navigation box. Avoid positioning the enlarged area at the edges of the frame, as the camera may be unable to focus at those positions. When you're ready, press the shutter release halfway. In any AF mode or DMF, the a7C II/a7CR will focus on the center of the enlarged area. If you're using DMF, you can fine-tune focus with the lens's focus ring. Then press the shutter release down all the way to take the photo.

Focus magnification cannot be used with autofocus when shooting movies; when the Focus mode is set to AF-C; or when using AF-A and continuous shooting or a shooting mode other than P, A, S, or M. The feature is also disabled when using one of the EA-LA mount adapters. Certain autofocus features are disabled when using the focus magnifier, including Subject Recognition AF, Pre-AF, and Subject Recognition in AF.

5. Peaking Display

The Peaking Display group has three entries used to activate and adjust your Peaking settings during manual focus. (See Figure 8.13.)

- Peaking Display
- Peaking Level
- Peaking Color

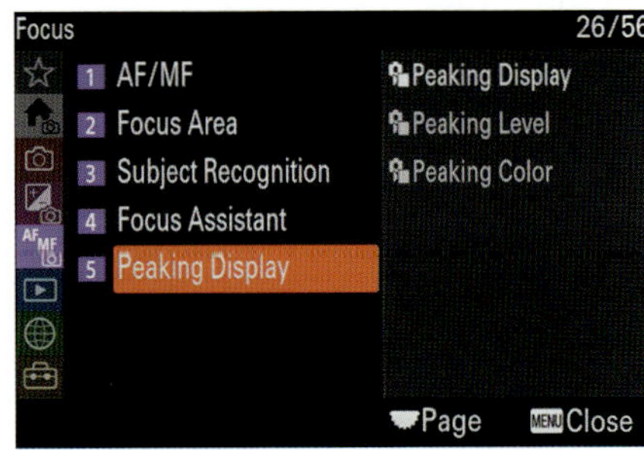

Figure 8.13 Peaking Display group.

Peaking Display

Options: **Off*, On

My preference: On

This is a useful manual focusing aid (available only when focusing in Manual and Direct Manual modes) that's difficult to describe and to illustrate. You're going to have to try this feature for yourself to see exactly what it does. *Focus peaking* is a technique that outlines the area in sharpest focus with a color—as discussed below, that can be red, yellow, blue, or white. The colored area shows you at a glance what will be very sharp if you take the photo at that moment. If you're not satisfied, simply change the focused distance (with manual focus). As the focus gets closer to ideal for a specific part of the image, the color outline develops around hard edges that are in focus. You can choose how much peaking is applied (High, Middle, or Low), select a specific accent color (Red, Yellow, Blue, or White), or turn the feature off. Peaking is available in movie mode—even when you're using AF-C autofocus. **Note:** If you're using an external monitor or video recorder through the HDMI port, the Peaking Display highlighting will not appear. That's a shame, because it would be even more useful for precision focusing on a larger display, but, of course, you wouldn't want peaking to appear in video footage output to an external recorder through an HDMI connection.

Peaking Level

Options: High, **Mid*, Low

My preference: High

This setting allows you to choose how strong the contrasting highlights are. I find a maximum application of color works the best for most subjects that have strong colors.

Peaking Color

Options: Red, Yellow, Blue, **White*

My preference: Red

Peaking Color allows you to specify which color is used to indicate peaking when you use manual focus. White is the default value, but if that color doesn't provide enough contrast with a similarly hued subject, you can switch to a more contrasting color, such as red or yellow. (See Figure 8.14.)

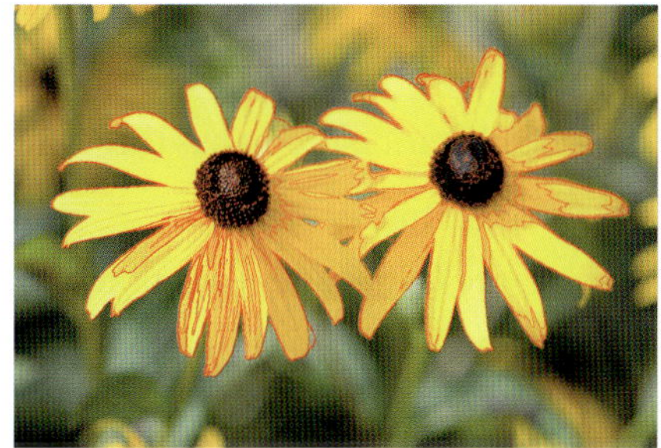

Figure 8.14 You can choose any of four colors for peaking color (for manual focus), but only if you have activated the Peaking Level item. For these blossoms, red was a better choice than blue, white, or yellow.

Playback Tab

The Playback tab has seven groups with a wide selection of options for reviewing your images. (See Figure 8.15.) Most of these are functions that you select as needed rather than settings, so my preferences don't apply, and I won't be providing any. They include:

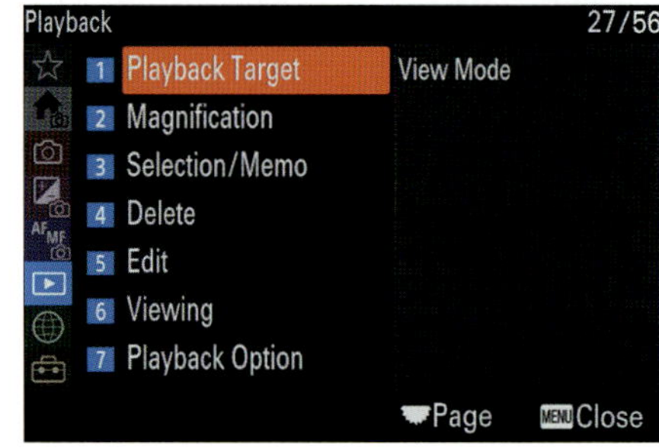

Figure 8.15 Playback tab.

- Playback Target
- Magnification
- Selection/Memo
- Delete
- Edit
- Viewing
- Playback Option

1. Playback Target

This group has just one entry, shown in Figure 8.15:

- View Mode

View Mode

Options: *Date View*, Folder View (Still), Movie View

Adjusts the way the camera displays image/movie files, which is useful for reviewing only certain types of files, or for deleting only particular types. You can elect to display files by Date View, Folder View (still photos only), or Movie View. Date View can come in handy, particularly on trips, when you want to see your images in reverse chronological order.

2. Magnification

The Magnification group has three entries, shown at left in Figure 8.16:

- Enlarge Image
- Enlarge Initial Magnification
- Enlarge Initial Position

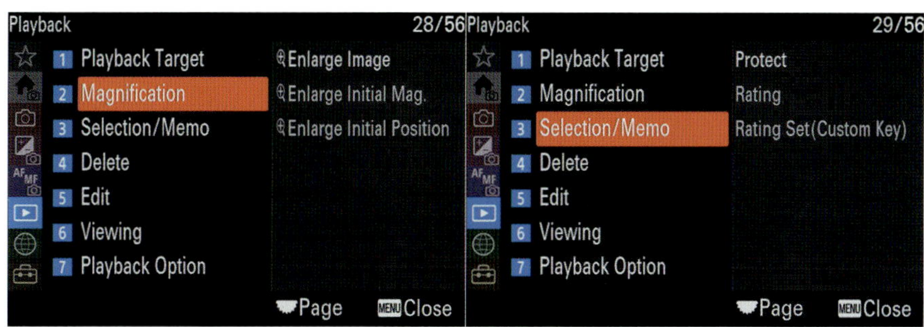

Figure 8.16 Magnification group (left); Selection/Memo group (right).

Enlarge Image

Options: Zoom In, Zoom Out

Whenever you are playing back still images (not movies), you can use this menu entry to magnify the image. (You can also double tap the touch screen to zoom in or press the AF-ON/Magnify button.) The a7C II or a7CR will try to zoom in on the point used to focus the image, if possible, and will zoom into the center of the frame if not. Use the control wheel to zoom in and out, and you can scroll around inside the enlarged image using the control wheel's directional controls. Rotate the front or rear dials to view the next or previous image (respectively) at the same magnification. Press MENU or the center button to exit. The initial magnification of the image is set using the entry that follows.

Enlarge Initial Magnification

Options: *Standard Magnification*, Previous Magnification

Here you can choose the initial magnification used by the Enlarge Image entry. Use Standard Magnification to always see any image you magnify at the same zoom level. This is a good choice if you magnify from time to time to closely examine an image and may want to zoom in or out to view more or less of your subject matter. When you select Previous Magnification, the enlargement resumes at the most recent level used. For example, if you are checking focus of your images as you shoot and zoom in tightly, it's convenient to return to the same zoom level for each successive image.

Enlarge Initial Position

Options: *Focused Position*, Center

By default, whenever you magnify an image during playback, the a7C II or a7CR centers the enlargement around the area in the frame where focus was achieved. That's often the best choice, because when evaluating an image during playback, focus is the parameter most often checked. However, I prefer the enlargement positioned in the center of the frame, so I can move the magnifying window around anywhere I like. That setting potentially minimizes the amount of "travel" if the previous area I examined is located some distance in the frame from my new area of interest.

3. Selection/Memo

The Selection/Memo group has three entries, shown at right in Figure 8.16. If you're wondering about the Selection/Memo nomenclature, the Sony a1, a9 II, and a9 III have a voice memo feature with two entries that inhabit this group. My guess is that Sony has no intention of adding it to the a7C II or a7CR in the future through a firmware update, but decided to keep the same group title across all its products.

- Protect
- Rating
- Rating Settings (Custom Key)

Protect

Options: *****Multiple Images**, All with [Current View Mode: Folder, Date], Cancel All [This Folder, Date]

You might want to protect certain images or movie clips on your memory card from accidental erasure, either by you or by others who may use your camera from time to time. This menu item enables you to tag one or more images or movies for protection, so a delete command will not delete it. (Formatting a memory card deletes everything, including protected content.) A white key ("locked") icon will appear above the image. This menu item also enables you to cancel the protection from all tagged photos or movies. If all you want to do is protect/unprotect the image currently on the screen, and you do this frequently, consider assigning a custom key to the Protect function, as described in Chapter 9.

To use this feature, make sure to specify whether you want to do so for stills or movies; use the View Mode item in the Playback Target group to designate the desired view mode. There, you can select from Date View, Folder View (Still), or Movie View to see only items matching that parameter.

Then, access the Protect menu item, choose Multiple Images, and press the center button. An image (or thumbnail of a movie) will appear; scroll among the photos or videos using the control wheel to reach the photo you want to tag for protection; press the center button to tag it with an orange check mark at the left of the image. (If it's already tagged, pressing the button will remove the tag, eliminating the protection you had previously provided.)

After you have marked all the items you want to protect, press the MENU button to confirm your choice. A screen will appear asking you to confirm that you want to protect the marked images; highlight OK and press the center button to do so. Later, if you want, you can go back and select the Cancel All Images option to unprotect all the tagged photos or movies.

Rating ⬛ 🎦 S&Q

Options: One to five stars, Off

This setting lets you apply a quality rating to still images (but not movies) you've shot. You can also use the rating system to represent some other criteria. Simply select this menu item (or define a custom key as a dedicated Rating button, as described next). You can use this entry to give images one, two, three, four, or five stars, or turn the rating off. The Image Jump function (described later in this chapter) can display only images that have been given a specific rating, or any rating at all. Suppose you were photographing a track meet with multiple events. You could apply a one-star rating to jumping events, two stars to relays, three stars to throwing events, four stars to hurdles, and five stars to dashes. Then, using the Image Jump feature, you could review only images of one type. I personally find this type of use more helpful than simply critiquing my own work.

With a little imagination, you can apply the rating system to all sorts of categories. At a wedding, you could classify pictures of the bride, the groom, guests, attendants, and parents of the couple. If you were shooting school portraits, one rating could apply to first grade, another to second grade, and so on. Given a little thought, this feature has many more applications than you might think. Ratings can be used to specify images for a slide show, too.

To use the Ratings menu entry, follow these steps:

1. Choose the Rating menu item.
2. The most recently viewed image appears.
3. Press the center button, and an icon appears, flanked by left/right triangles. (See Figure 8.17, left.)
4. Use the left/right controls to scroll among Off, and the individual star settings available. (You can specify which ratings can be applied, as I'll describe shortly.)
5. Press MENU to confirm and exit.
6. The star rating (if any) that you've applied will henceforth be overlaid on the image each time you review it.

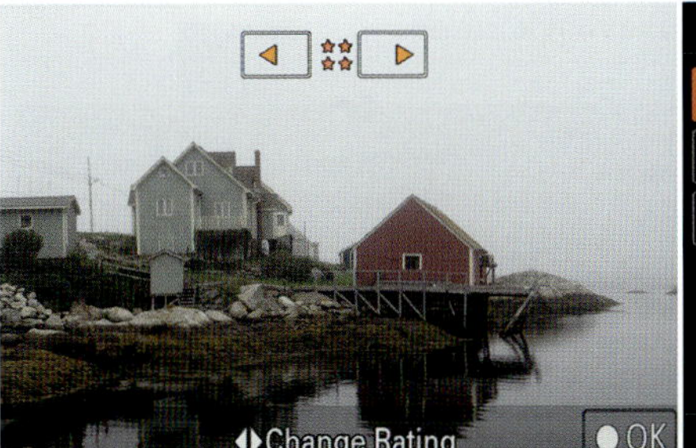

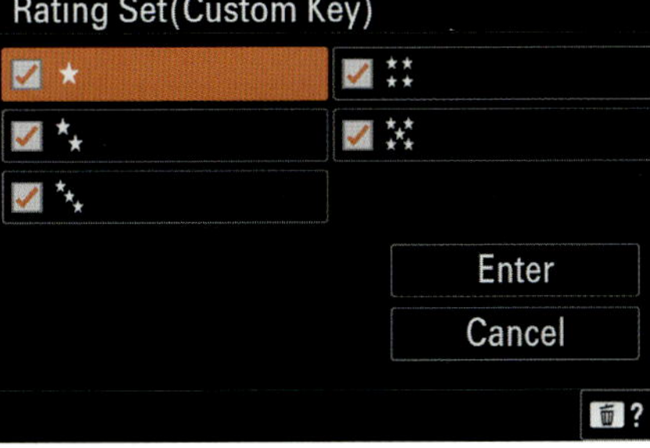

Figure 8.17 You can apply one to five stars or turn ratings off (left). If you rarely use a particular star value, you can deactivate it when using a custom key.

Rating Settings (Custom Key)

Options: Activate any (or all) star ratings

This is a clever option that allows you to specify *which* star ratings can be applied when rating images using a defined custom key for the Rating function. For example, if you're rating by quality and don't deign to mark your really bad images, you can disable the * or ** star values. Thereafter, you'll only need to consider ***, ****, or ***** ratings.

For this to work, you must apply the Rating behavior to a custom key of your choice. After that, you can visit this menu entry, shown in Figure 8.17, right, and highlight individual star values. Press the center button to mark/unmark them, then highlight Enter and press the center button again to confirm and exit. When rating an image using the custom key, just press the key multiple times. The ratings change to the next available value each time you press the key. (This should be your default way of applying ratings!)

4. Delete

The Delete group has three entries, seen at left in Figure 8.18:

- Delete
- (Trash) Delete Pressing Twice
- Delete Confirmation

Delete

Options: *Multiple Img.*, All with [Current View Mode]

Sometimes we take pictures or video clips that we know should never see the light of day. Maybe you were looking into the lens and accidentally tripped the shutter. Perhaps you really goofed up your settings. You want to erase that photo *now,* before it does permanent damage to your reputation as a good photographer. Unless you have turned Auto Review off, you can delete a photo immediately after you take it by pressing the Trash key (Delete button). Also, you can use that method to delete any individual image that's being displayed on the screen in Playback mode.

Figure 8.18 Delete group (left); Edit group (right).

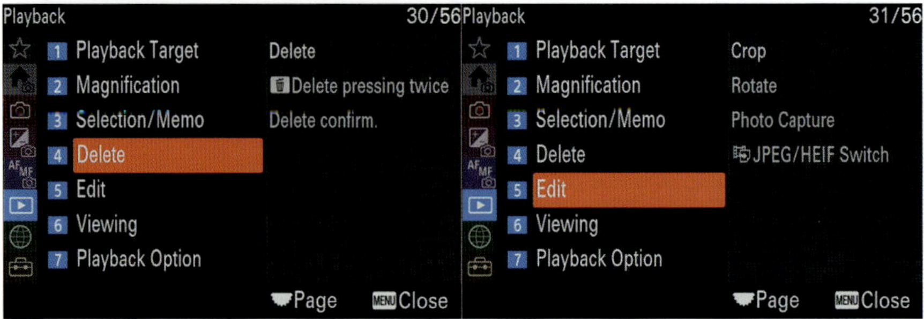

However, sometimes you need to wait for an idle moment to erase all pictures that are obviously not "keepers." I sometimes do this during halftime when shooting sports, to eliminate a series of continuous shots I know were a waste of storage space. This menu item makes it easy to remove selected photos or video clips (Multiple Images), or to erase all the photos or video clips taken, sorted by your currently active view mode (such as folder or date). (Change the type of view using the View Mode option, described earlier in this chapter.) Note that there is no delete method that will remove images tagged as Protected.

To remove one or more images (or movie files), select the Delete menu item, and use the up/down directional buttons, front dial, rear dial, or the control wheel to choose the Multiple Images option. Press the center button, and the most recent image *using your currently active view* (Date View, Folder View [Still], or Movie View) will be displayed on the LCD.

Scroll left/right through your images and press the center button when you reach the image you want to tag for deletion; a check mark then appears beside it and an orange check mark appears in the left of the screen. You can press the DISP button to see more information about a particular image. You can also press the Thumbnail button to view thumbnails of multiple images and select them in that mode.

The number of images marked for deletion is incremented in the indicator at the lower-right corner of the LCD, next to a trash can icon. When you're satisfied (or have expressed your dissatisfaction with the really bad images), press the MENU button, and you will be asked if you're sure you want to proceed. To confirm your decision, highlight OK and press the center button. The images (or video clips) you had tagged will now be deleted. If you want to delete *everything* on the memory card, it's quicker to do so by using the Format item in the Setup menu, as discussed in Chapter 9.

Delete Pressing Twice 📷 🎬 S&Q

Options: On, *Off

With the default Off setting, when you press the Trash/Delete button, a screen pops up requiring you to select DELETE and the center button to confirm. It's a safety measure to help prevent accidental deletions. You can switch to a *different* safety measure by setting this entry to On. Thereafter, all you have to do is press Delete twice to remove an image.

Delete Confirmation 📷 🎬 S&Q

Options: *"Delete" First, "Cancel" First

Sony, in its wisdom, gives you yet a third way to confirm you really, really want to delete an image. You can choose whether Delete or Cancel is the default value that pops up when you press the Delete key. That's a bit faster than needing to manually switch from Cancel to Delete, but supposedly less dangerous than pressing the Delete button twice in a row. Note that if you've activated the Delete/Twice option, this setting is not available.

5. Edit

The Edit group has four entries. See Figure 8.18, right.

- Crop
- Rotate
- Photo Capture
- JPEG/HEIF Switch

Crop

Options: Crop, Aspect Ratio: 3:2, 4:3, 16:9, 1:1, 2:3, 3:4, 9:16

You may find it convenient to crop your images in your camera without needing to import them into your laptop or computer first. That's likely to happen while traveling, when you want to post an image with an improved composition on social media, or to send by email. Since it's easy to upload photos from your camera to your smartphone, this cropping capability can be very handy. Just follow these steps:

1. **Select image to crop.** When you first access this entry, you can scroll around among your images to locate the one you want to crop. Then, press the center button to begin your edit.

2. **Adjust aspect ratio.** As you begin, the screen shown in Figure 8.19 appears. Rotate either rear dial to choose from 3:2, 4:3, 16:9, 1:1, 2:3, 3:4, or 9:16 aspect ratios, which give you a selection of portrait and landscape orientations.

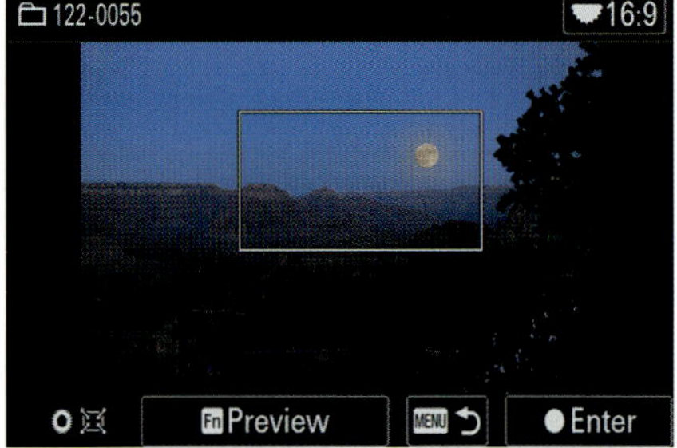

Figure 8.19 Cropping an image in the camera.

3. **Choose crop size.** Rotate the front dial or control wheel to adjust this size of the rectangle/square used to specify the area cropped. You can also use pinch and zoom out gestures on an active touch screen.

4. **Position cropping frame.** The directional buttons can be used to move the cropping frame around the screen.

5. **Preview your image.** Press the Fn button to view the cropped image; press again to return to full-screen mode.

6. **Save.** When you're satisfied, press the center button to confirm and exit. A new file will be saved with the next image number applied, leaving your original image intact.

Rotate 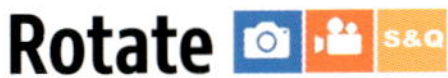

Options: None

When you select this menu item, you are immediately presented with a new screen showing the current or most recently reviewed image along with an indication that the center button can be used to rotate the image. (While you can rotate movies with this entry, they will still be played back horizontally on the camera.) Scroll left/right to reach the image you want to rotate. Successive presses of the center button will now rotate the image 90 degrees at a time. The camera will remember whatever rotation setting you apply here. You can use this function to rotate an image that was taken with the camera held vertically when you have set Display Rotation to Manual or Auto. Press the MENU button to exit.

Photo Capture

Options: Capture video frame

This menu entry can be accessed only when you're playing back a video clip. You can use it to extract a still frame from a movie you've captured. Just follow these steps:

1. **Select the movie.** In Playback mode, navigate to the movie you want to clip from.

2. **Press MENU.** Choose Photo Capture. The first frame of the video will appear, along with a display offering playback controls. (See Figure 8.20.)

3. **Play video.** Press the center button to start playback of the video at normal speed.

4. **Pause.** Press the center button again to pause playback when you reach the approximate location containing the desired frame.

5. **Select frame.** Use one of the following controls to navigate to the exact frame you want to extract:

   - **Up button.** Plays back slowly so you can monitor the action easily.

   - **Forward/Reverse.** Press the left/right buttons to move to next frame/previous frame.

   - **Down button.** Saves the currently displayed frame to your memory card.

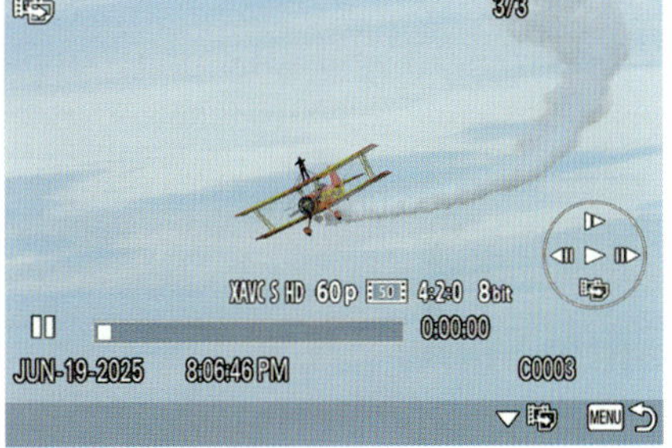

Figure 8.20 Photo Capture can extract a single frame from a movie.

JPEG/HEIF Switch

Options: *JPEG, HEIF (4:2:0), HEIF (4:2:2)

This menu entry specifies the file format to be used for photos captured using the Photo Capture facility. I explained the differences between JPEG and HEIF image files in Chapter 6.

6. Viewing

The Viewing group has three entries, shown in Figure 8.21, left:

- Continuous Play for Interval
- Play Speed for Interval
- Slide Show

Continuous Playback for Interval

Options: Plays back interval shots

Use this setting to play back a sequence of images you captured using the Interval feature described in Chapter 9, or when shooting with the Continuous drive mode. Select the image or image group you want to view, and then press the center button to display the images. Press the center button again to pause during playback, or to resume playback. Change the playback speed by rotating the control wheel while you are watching. You can also adjust playback speed using the menu entry described next. If you want to create a movie from the sequence, use the Imaging Edge software, as outlined in Chapter 5.

Playback Speed for Interval

Options: Playback speeds from 1 (Slow) to 9 (Fast)

While you can adjust the speed of playback for interval sequences while viewing them, you can also set a value to be used automatically. You can still speed up or slow down while watching your sequence. The camera accomplishes playback speed by skipping frames, depending on the speed requested. The faster playback goes, the jerkier the motion will appear.

Slide Show

Options: Repeat (On/Off), Interval: 1 second, 3 seconds, 5 seconds, 10 seconds, 30 seconds

Use this menu option when you want to display all the still images on your memory card in a continuous show. You can display still images in a continuous series, with each one displayed for the amount of time that you set. Choose the Repeat option to make the show repeat in a continuous loop. After

Figure 8.21 Viewing group (left), Playback Option group (right).

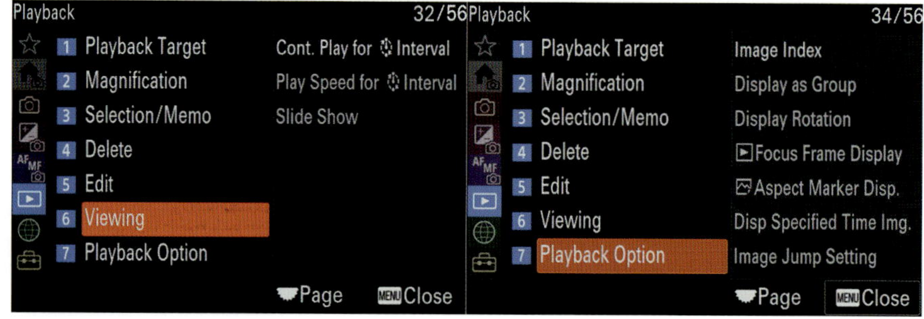

making your settings, press the center button and the slide show will begin. You can scroll left or right to go back to a previous image or go forward to the next image immediately, but that will stop the slide show. The show cannot be paused, but you can exit by pressing the MENU button. If you're displaying your images on an external monitor using an HDMI cable, you'll want to make sure the Display Rotation entry, discussed shortly, is set to Auto so the photos will be shown in the correct orientation.

7. Playback Option

The Playback Option group has seven entries, seen at right in Figure 8.21:

- Image Index
- Display as Group
- Display Rotation
- [Playback] Focus Frame Display
- Aspect Marker Display
- Display Specified Time Image
- Image Jump Setting

Image Index

Options: *9, 30

You can view an index screen of your images on the camera's LCD by pressing the down directional button while in Playback mode. By default, that screen shows up to 9 thumbnails of photos or movies; you can change that value to 30 using this menu item. Remember to use the View Mode menu item first, to identify the folder that the index display should access; by default, it will show thumbnails of still photos, but you might want to view thumbnails of your movie clips instead. When viewing an index, highlight the bar at the left side of the screen and use the directional controls to move quickly among available thumbnails. Press the center button to switch view mode quickly.

Display as Group

Options: On, *Off

If you shoot sports, you'll love this feature. The a7C II and a7CR are smart enough to know that when you shoot a burst of images in continuous shooting mode it would be helpful to group them all together. That makes it easy to evaluate the first shot in a particular set of images captured sequentially, without having to wade through all of them. When set to On, the camera groups images in a burst together, and overlays a "stack" icon on the group, so you'll know you are viewing/evaluating only the first image in that burst. The view mode must be set to Date View to use this feature. Set this option to Off and you'll be shown every picture you captured, one by one, during image review.

Display Rotation 📷 🎬 S&Q

Options: *Auto, Manual, Off

You can use this function to determine whether a vertical image is rotated automatically during picture review. If you want to rotate the image more, use the Rotate entry, described earlier in this chapter.

- **Auto.** The image will be shown in the orientation indicated by information in the image, no matter how the camera itself is rotated during picture review. For example, a vertical image will be shown in the correct orientation, as shown at top left in Figure 8.22, when the camera is held horizontally. It will be shown smaller in size to fit the long dimension of the image into the short dimension of the screen. Rotate the camera 90 degrees, and the camera will automatically rotate the photo so it's *still* shown in the correct orientation, but it will now fill the LCD screen, as you can see in Figure 8.22, top right. This is the best setting when displaying your images on an external monitor.

Figure 8.22 Display Rotation configurations.

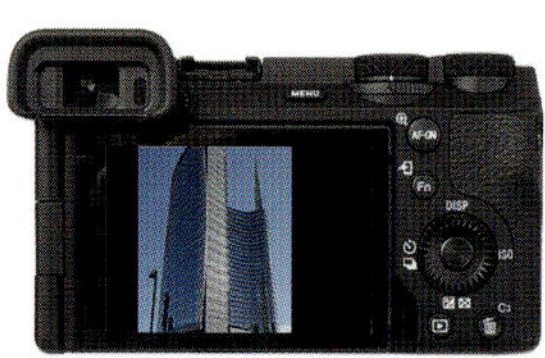
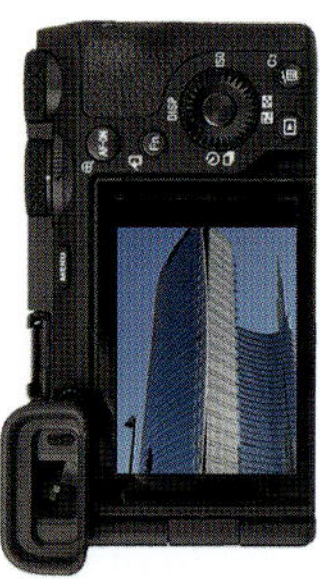

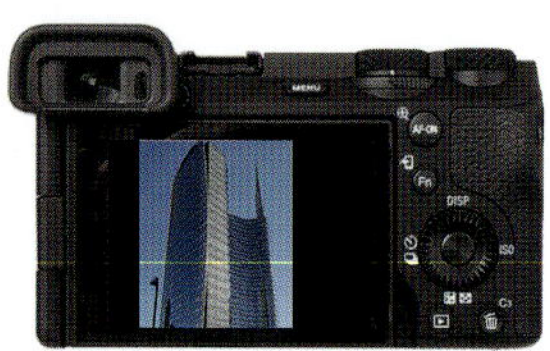
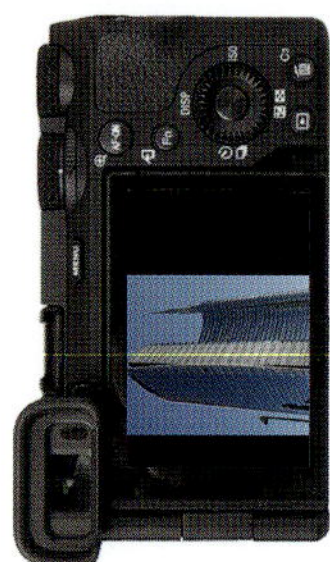

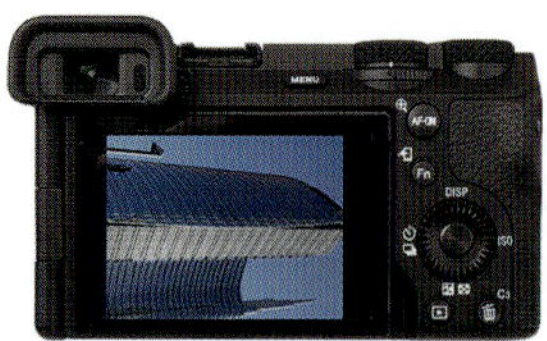
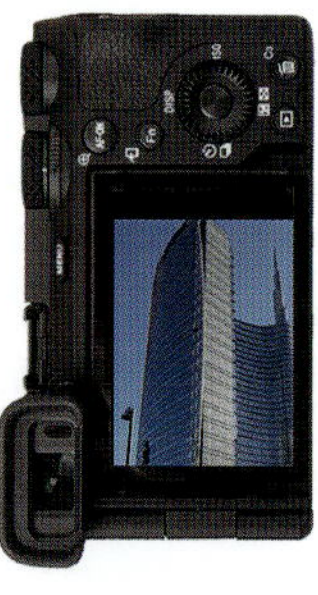

- **Manual.** With this setting, the image is always displayed on the LCD in the same orientation it was taken. That is, a vertically oriented photo will be displayed in a smaller size, just as it is when using Auto, as shown at center left in Figure 8.22. However, when you rotate the camera during picture review, the a7C II or a7CR do *not* automatically rotate the image at the same time, so it will be shown with an incorrect orientation (see Figure 8.22, center right).

- **Off.** With this setting, both vertical and horizontal images are displayed to fill the screen as much as possible with the image. Vertical shots are larger, as shown at bottom left in Figure 8.22, but the camera must be rotated to view them in the correct orientation. (See Figure 8.22, bottom right).

[Playback] Focus Frame Display

Options: *****Off**, On

When activated, during playback the a7C II/a7CR will display a green box that indicates the focus point used to achieve focus. It's useful for confirming that the camera actually focused where you intended. If not, you can make adjustments for your next photo.

Aspect Marker Display

Options: *****On**, Off; Aspect Marker Level: 0 to 15 (*****8** default)

As described in Chapter 6, you can select an aspect ratio for still images other than the default 3:2 proportions. This entry affects how those images are displayed during playback. By default, the a7C II and a7CR darken the frame outside the area of the aspect ratio you chose in the Shooting > Marker Display entry. When enabled, you can specify the level of darkness from 0 (none) to 15 (quite dark). The default setting is 8, which applies a moderate amount of darkening.

Display Specified Time Image

Options: Time

This is a clever feature that lets you locate images on your memory card based on the date and time when they were taken. Say, after a full day's shooting, you want to review all those photos you took of your exotic lunch in a local bistro. Access this entry, enter the approximate time and date, and the a7C II/a7CR will jump to still photos and movies taken at approximately that time, either before or after.

Image Jump Setting

Options: Select Dial, Image Jump Method

Sony obviously expects you'll be taking a lot of photos, because it provides you with a multitude of ways to filter them and jump among them during playback. This clever setting lets you specify which of three dials (front dial or left and right rear dials)—or all three—can be used to scroll among your images. (See Figure 8.23, left.) Best of all, you can choose a *different* selection method for each dial. You can select One by One for the front dial, or By 10 Images for the rear dial if you want.

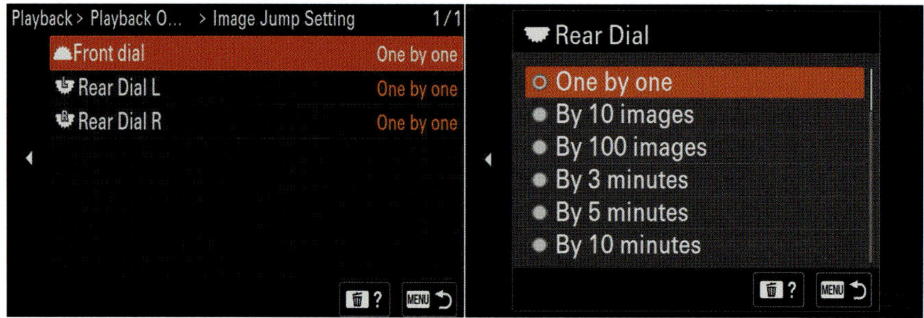

Figure 8.23 Choose a dial to use for Image Jump (left). Then, specify the jump method for that dial (right).

But when I said multitude, I wasn't kidding (almost). Figure 8.23, right, shows six of the choices; you must scroll down to view the entire multitude:

- **Numerically.** You can choose One by One, By 10 Images, or By 100 images.
- **By Minutes.** Select from 3-, 5-, 10-, or 30-minute jumps.
- **By Hours.** Choose 1-, 3-, 6-, 12-, or 24-hour intervals.
- **By Status.** Protected Only, Rated Only, or those with a specific Rating (1 to 5 stars), or no stars.
- **Shot Mark.** All with Shot Marks, or with Mark 1 or Mark 2 Only, or No Shot Mark. Shot marks are the marking tool you can add to videos while recording them or playing them back. To add or delete a Shot Mark, you must define a key to perform that function, using Setup > Operation Customize > (Playback) Custom Key Setting, as discussed in Chapter 9.
- **Divider Frame.** Only those with a divider frame, or the first image *after* a divider frame. Divider frames are markers you can insert as separators between sequences of images. It beats taking a picture of your hand, as I used to do, and lets you find particular sequences more quickly.
- **Image After Divider.** Jumps to images next to divider frames.

Network and Setup Menus

The Network menu, which controls setting up and using the a7C II and a7CR's wireless communications features, and the Setup menu, used to adjust key operational controls of the camera, are the last two configuration components you'll need to master. Each provides a broad range of options.

Network Menu Tab

There are eight groups in the Network tab. Seven are shown in Figure 9.1, left. The eighth, Network Options, will be illustrated and explained later in this chapter. Don't confuse your camera's wireless Wi-Fi and Bluetooth capabilities with the a7C II and a7CR's wireless *flash* features, discussed in Chapter 13. Both can use radio transmission/reception, but of differing varieties and frequency bands.

I'm going to help you get started using the communications features, but I need to emphasize that all the heavy-duty information and technology gobble-de-gook is beyond the scope of this book, which is primarily a still photography guide that also explores movie making. We won't be going down the IT rabbit hole in this book. It's unlikely that the majority of you will be using the most advanced connection technology Sony has to offer.

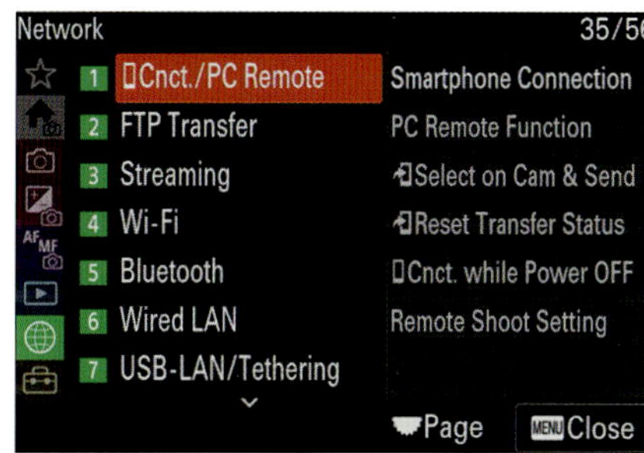

Figure 9.1 The Network groups (left), and Smartphone Connect entries (right).

1. Smartphone Connect/PC Remote

There are six entries in the Smartphone Connect group. (See Figure 9.1, right.) They allow you to control the camera remotely with a live preview on your phone and move images from your camera to your smartphone so you can post photos on your Instagram, Facebook, or other accounts—even if the camera happens to be powered down when you decide to make the transfer. The camera-to-smartphone features are the capabilities most likely to be of use to most Sony photo enthusiasts.

- Smartphone Connection
- PC Remote Function
- Select On Camera and Send
- Reset Transfer Status
- Connect While Power Off
- Remote Shooting Settings

Smartphone Connection

Options: Pair your smart device and camera

Working with the new Creators' App (which replaces the Imaging Edge Mobile app you may have used with your previous Sony camera) on your smart device, you can transfer images from your a7C II or a7CR to your smartphone, and thence to email, social media, or a cloud service, like the Creators' Cloud platform Sony offers. You can even use the app to wake up the camera when it's turned off (if it's within Wi-Fi range) when you want to transfer those images. Best of all, you can operate your camera remotely in a wireless tethering mode, using a live preview on your smartphone's screen to frame, focus, adjust settings, take a photo, and then review the image you captured.

This entry lets you register your smartphone to the camera so you can connect to it as needed. Go to the Apple App store or Google Play store (depending on whether you use iOS or Android) and install the Sony Creators' app. Then activate Bluetooth on your phone and camera (visit Network > Bluetooth > Bluetooth Function). When you access this entry, you'll see basic instructions, like those shown at top in Figure 9.2. You'll be prompted to then launch Creators' App on your smartphone, select your camera, and follow the instructions shown on the screens seen in the bottom two-thirds of Figure 9.2. Depending on your device, you may see additional slightly different screens and prompts, such as reminders to activate Bluetooth, to allow the app to find devices on your network, or permit it to use your location. Once you're connected, you should not have to repeat this process. Should you switch to a different smartphone (I'm talking to you yearly upgraders!), use Network > Bluetooth > Manage Paired Device (described shortly) to "forget" your old phone.

PC Remote Function

Options: PC Remote: (On, Off); Pairing, Wi-Fi Direct Information
My preference: N/A

This entry allows you to take control of your camera for tethered shooting from a computer. If you're using a computer to connect to your camera, the PC Remote function is the easiest, fastest way to shoot tethered. The file-saving options are similar to those listed later in this chapter for the Remote Shooting Settings entry. You'll need to connect using one of these methods and the Remote module of Sony's Imaging Edge Desktop software for your PC or Mac:

- **USB cable link.** This type of connection is usually most convenient, easiest to set up, and is fast. This is the one I strongly recommend, and which I'll describe shortly.
- **Ethernet.** You'll need a USB-C port and Ethernet adapter for this direct link.
- **Wi-Fi.** This is a wireless connection, which can use an access point.

While the camera-to-PC option seems complex, getting connected is the most difficult part because of the variety of options that must be set elsewhere in the Network tab. Once you've linked successfully, it's not hard to use. That's especially true if you are able to use a USB cable connection rather than Wi-Fi link, which I recommend. The USB connection is much easier to set up and is typically faster, although it requires using a computer instead of your smart device. This section will show you everything you need to know to begin shooting your camera by remote control using the PC Remote entry. After you've downloaded, installed, and launched Imaging Edge Desktop, you're ready to go.

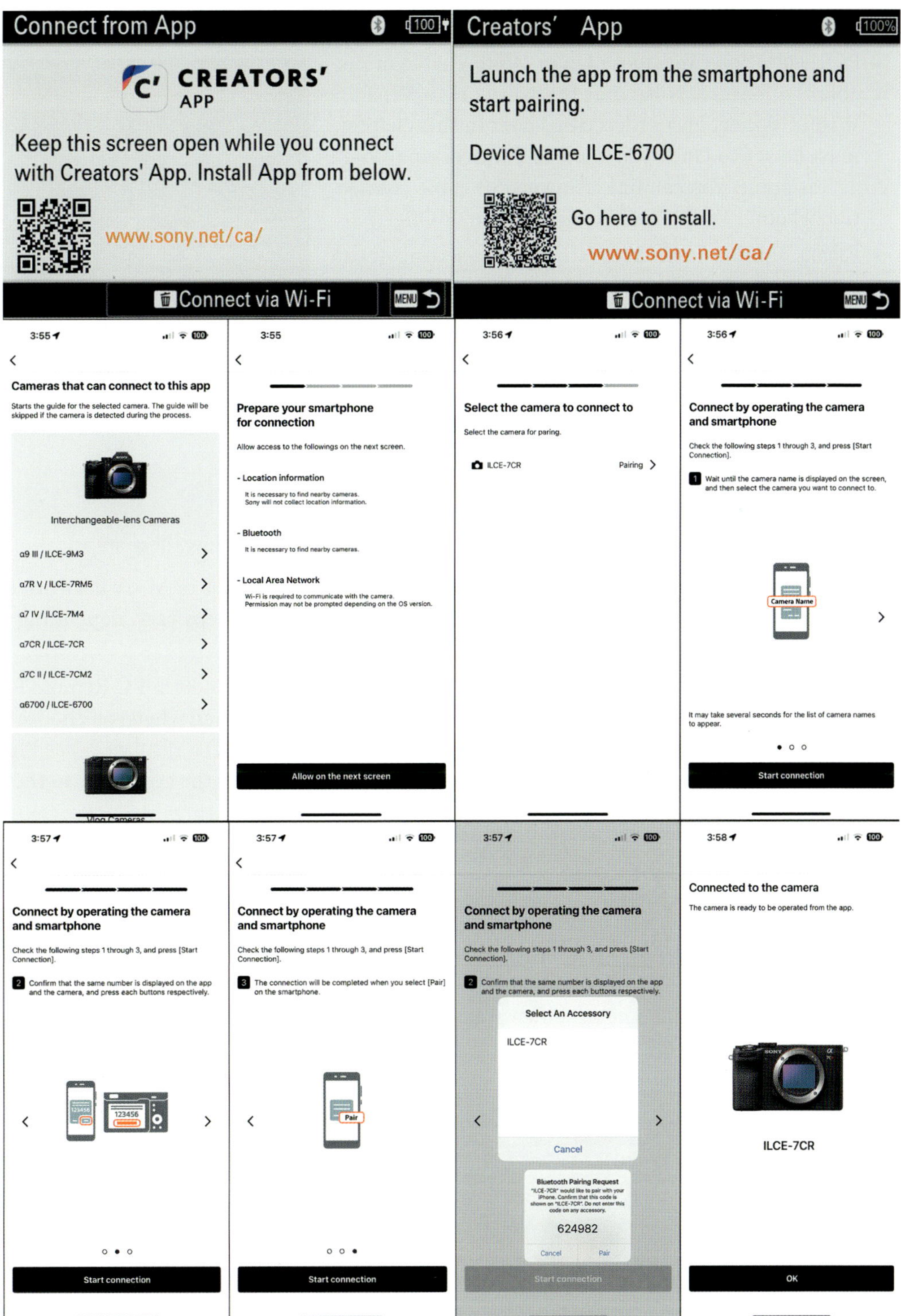

Figure 9.2 Sending images to your smartphone.

There are three options available with this entry, shown in Figure 9.3:

- **PC Remote.** You can choose On or Off to enable or disable the feature. Note that the Network > Wi-Fi > Wi-Fi Connect entry (described later in this chapter) must be set to On if you want to connect to a Wi-Fi access point. You can link using a USB cable connection whether Wi-Fi Connect is set to On or Off.

- **Pairing.** This is a command, rather than a setting. It can be invoked when Network > Network Option > Access Authentication Settings is Off if you want to connect without the extra protection of authentication and encryption.

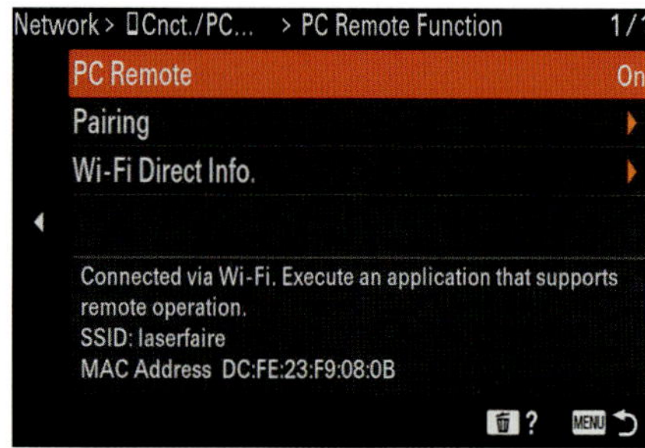

Figure 9.3 PC Remote Function options.

- **Wi-Fi Direct Information.** This screen provides connection information when Wi-Fi Access Point is the PC Remote Connection Method.

Connecting with Wi-Fi Direct

To connect your camera to your computer using Wi-Fi Direct, just follow these steps:

1. **Use the a7C II/a7CR's built-in access point.** You'll need to use your PC's or Mac's network facilities to connect to the access point built into the camera. The exact steps vary, depending on your computer's operating system.

2. **Display connection information.** Navigate to Network > Cnct/PC Remote > PC Remote Function > Wi-Fi Direct Info. The screen seen at left in Figure 9.4 pops up, and when you choose OK, the Wi-Fi connection information (SSID and password for the camera) is displayed (see Figure 9.4, right). Then use your computer's network commands to connect the computer to the camera using the Wi-Fi information displayed on the camera.

Connecting Using a USB-C Cable

To connect your camera to the computer using a USB-C cable link, just follow these steps:

1. **Attach cable.** Plug a USB-C to USB-C cable into your computer's USB-C port at one end, and the camera's USB-C port with the other end.

2. **Specify connection.** The screen shown at left in Figure 9.5 appears. Highlight Remote Shoot (PC Remote) and press OK.

Figure 9.4 Connect using Wi-Fi Direct.

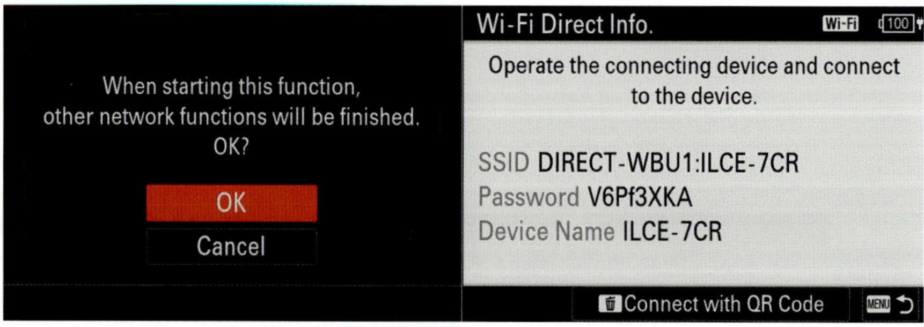

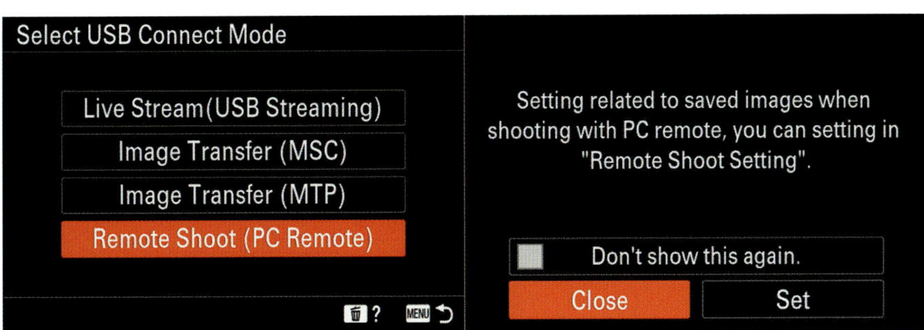

Figure 9.5 Connect using a USB-C cable.

3. **Choose Image Saving Settings (optional).** The screen seen at right in the figure appears. If you choose Set, you can specify Remote Shooting Settings, which include destination, image size, and whether to save RAW, JPEG, or both. The Remote Shooting Settings options are described later in this chapter, and I won't repeat that information here.

   If you've already made those settings, you can highlight Close and press OK. The screen can be permanently hidden (if you don't want to be offered this choice each time you tether) by checking the Don't Show This Again box.

4. **Launch Imaging Edge Desktop.** The screen seen at left in Figure 9.6 appears, with the options to start the Remote, Viewer, or Edit modules of the program. Highlight the Start box next to Remote and click to launch the Remote module.

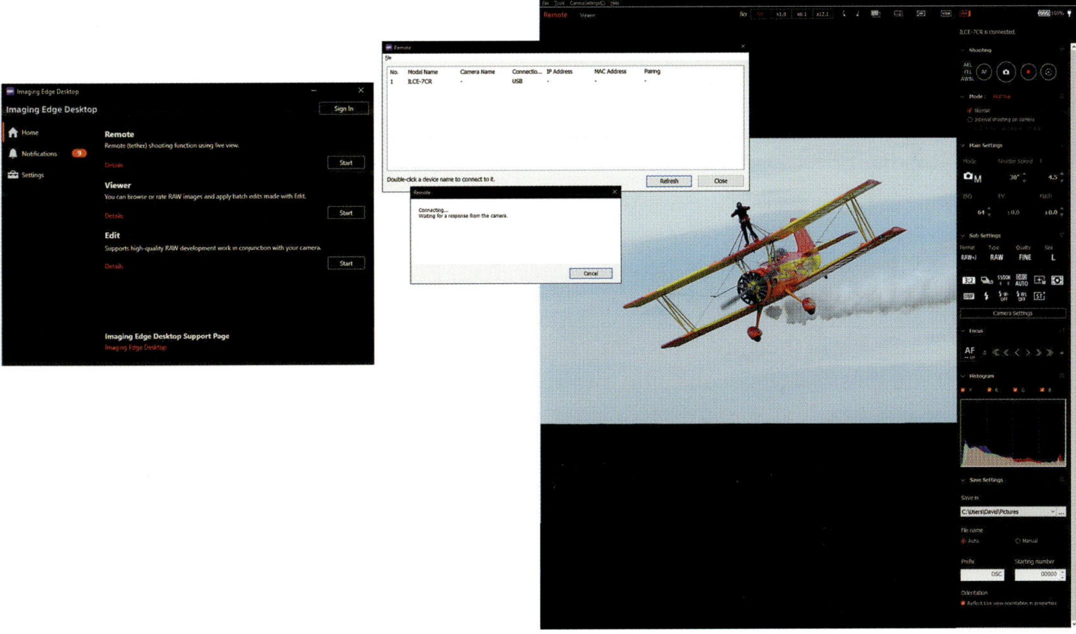

Figure 9.6 Working with Imaging Edge Remote.

5. **Select your camera.** The Remote app will look for your connected camera and display its name. Double-click it when it appears, and a Connecting... message appears (as shown upper center in the figure).

6. **You're tethered!** Imaging Edge Remote will display your camera's live view image and a full array of camera controls and displays, as seen at right in Figure 9.6.

Select on Camera and Send 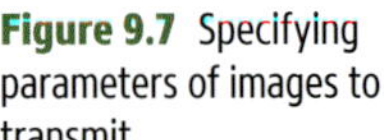

Options: Send, Size of Sending Image, RAW+JPEG/HEIF Send Target, Proxy Sending Target, Movie with Shot Mark

My preference: N/A

With this entry you can select and send images to your smartphone, and select the size, type, and other parameters. Your choices are shown in Figure 9.7, left:

- **Send.** You can direct the camera to send This Image, All with This Date, Filtered Images, or Multiple Images, as seen in Figure 9.7, right. If you press the Fn button while a still image or movie is displayed, that same Send to Smartphone screen appears, bypassing this menu. See the Transmitted Filtered Images section that follows for more information on selecting certain types of pictures.

- **Size of Sending Image.** Choose to send the original size to preserve the image's quality and resolution, or select a more compact 2M (2MB) image for uploading to social media or transmitting by email.

- **RAW+J/H Send Target.** Here you can choose whether to send JPEG & HEIF, RAW only, or RAW+JPEG & RAW+HEIF. Your phone may only be able to handle JPEG images once they've been received.

- **Px Sending Target.** Select whether you want to transmit the original, full-resolution movie file, or only the smaller proxy clip instead. If transmission times/speeds aren't a concern, you can send both.

- **Movie with Shot Mark.** Sometimes it makes sense to just send a "preview" to your phone. This setting can create a brief preview clip from any movie that has a Shot Mark embedded. Your choices are Cut to 60 Seconds, Cut to 30 Seconds, Cut to 15 Seconds, and Don't Cut.

  The a7C II/a7CR will then produce a clip of the desired length with the Shot Mark in the center. That is, if you specify a 60-second clip, the preview will include 30 seconds *before* the Shot Mark and 30 seconds *after* the Shot Mark.

Figure 9.7 Specifying parameters of images to transmit.

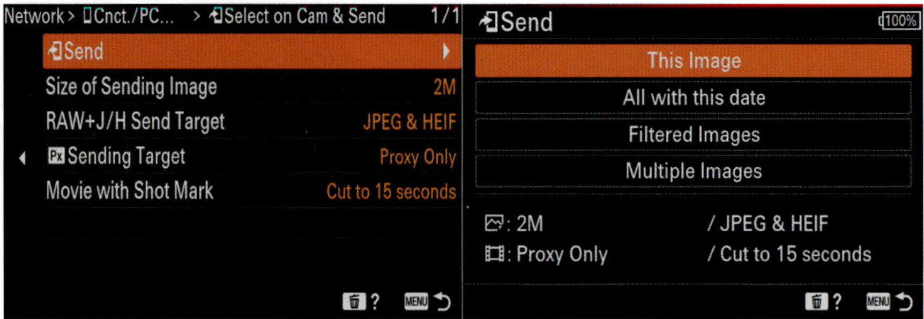

Transmitting Filtered Images

Search filters are a powerful capability that allows you to quickly select certain images or movies to transmit, without needing to select them one by one. The This Image, All with This Date, and Multiple Images selection options available during Playback mode (as described in Chapter 8) are available here, too. When you choose Filtered Images from the screen at right in Figure 9.7, the choices shown in Figure 9.8 appear. The available filters include:

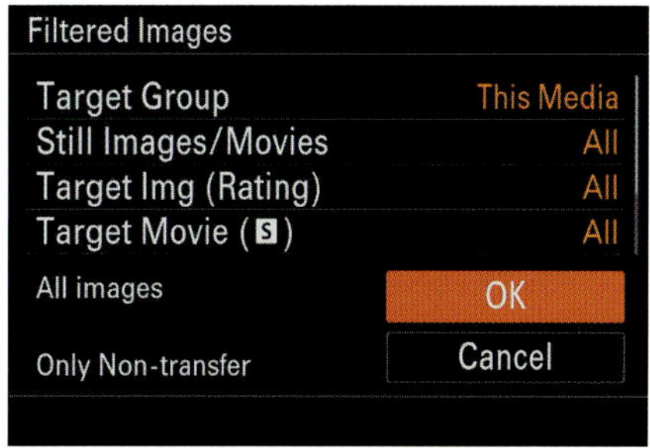

Figure 9.8 Select which images to transfer.

- **Target Group.** Choose either all the images/movies captured on the current date or everything on your memory card, both stills and movies.

- **Still Images/Movies.** Choose All (still images and movies), Only Still Images, or Only Movies.

- **Target Image (Rating).** Choose images or movies assigned zero (Off) to five stars, or any combination of those.

- **Target Movie (S).** Select All movies, or only those containing Shot Marks (those files will have an S overlay on their preview image).

- **Target Img (Protect).** Choose All images, or only Protected images.

- **Transfer Status.** Transfer all images, or only those that have not already been transferred.

Reset Transfer Status 

Options: None
My preference: N/A

This entry resets the transfer status of the image sent to the smartphone and sets all images to non-transfer status. You can use this facility when you want to retransmit images that have already been transferred and, accordingly, marked as such in the camera. Once you reset, you can reselect images from the full complement on your memory card.

Connect While Power Off

Options: On, *Off
My preference: N/A

Your smartphone can download images from your previously paired a7C II or a7CR, even if it is ostensibly powered down. When you enable the feature, a warning screen appears noting that Bluetooth pairing is required, giving you the choice of using the currently paired device or to perform a new pairing. Once activated, the camera will keep its Bluetooth *receiver* active even when it's powered down. Your smartphone can then wake up your camera remotely to allow the app to download thumbnails of the images on the card, in date order. You can view indexes of the images and tap the images you want to import. Follow the instructions to begin transferring the selected images to your phone. Make sure Airplane Mode (discussed shortly) is not set to On, or that your camera is not already connected to another device. If you turn on your camera while transfer is taking place, the connection will be terminated. This feature does consume a small amount of battery power, so use it judiciously.

Remote Shooting Settings 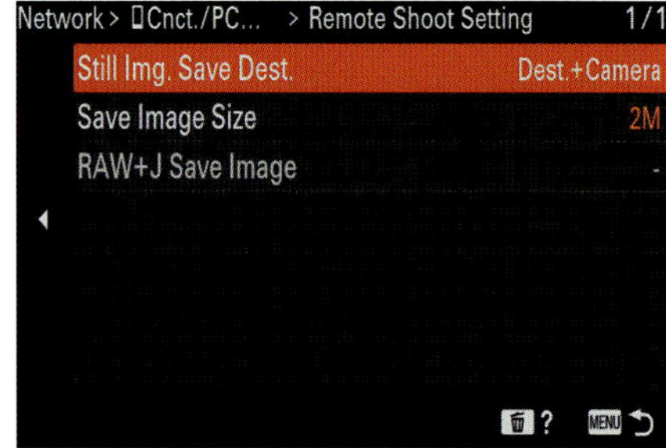

Options: Still Image Save Destination: Destination Only, *Destination+Camera, Camera Only; Save Image Size: Original, *2M; RAW+JPEG/HEIF Save Image: RAW & JPEG, *JPEG Only, RAW Only

My preference: N/A

This entry lets you set the parameters for controlling your camera remotely from your smartphone (or from your computer using the PC Remote Function entry described earlier). There are three settings you can make (see Figure 9.9):

- **Still Image Save Destination.** Choose Smartphone Only, Smartphone+Camera, or Camera Only to specify where the a7C II/a7CR should store the images it captures during remote shooting.

- **Save Image Size.** Choose Original size, or, for much faster transfer, 2M to transmit only a small 2MB version suitable for social media or email.

Figure 9.9 Remote Shooting Settings.

- **RAW+JPEG/HEIF Save Image.** This entry is not available if your still image quality is set to JPEG/HEIF. If you've chosen RAW & JPEG (or HEIF), you can select whether you want remote shooting to save only RAW, only JPEG (or HEIF), or both. You may want to shoot both conventionally, but prefer to save only one or the other when shooting remotely because of the extra time required for transmission of both formats.

When shooting remotely with the Creators' App, you'll see the camera's live view image on your phone, as shown at left in Figure 9.10. You have access to a full roster of features, some of which are shown at center and right in the figure.

Figure 9.10 Controlling your camera from your phone.

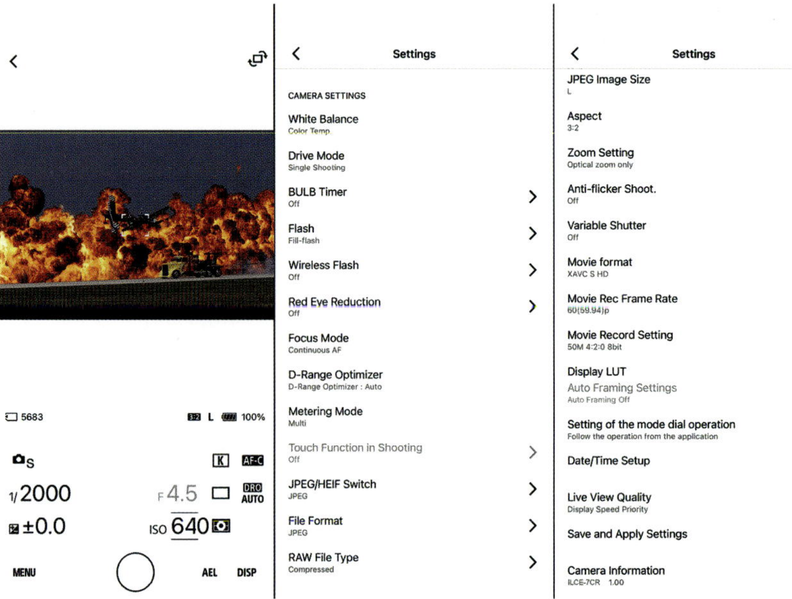

2. FTP Transfer

There is only one entry in the FTP Transfer group. (Not shown in a figure.)

■ FTP Transfer Function

FTP Transfer Function 📷 🎬 S&Q

Options: FTP Function, Server Setting, Save/Load FPT Settings, FTP Transfer

My preference: N/A

Techies who understand FTP server functions can transfer images from the camera to a networked FTP (File Transfer Protocol) server, view the results, select which server to send to, and define up to three different FTP servers. Only JPEG and RAW files can be transferred using FTP. Sony offers a detailed FTP Help Guide (at 124 pages it's much too long to summarize here!) through its website: https://helpguide.sony.net/di/ftp/v1/en/index.html. Readers who use these functions definitely don't need coaching from me, so I am not going to divert pages in this book to discussions of information technology that I could devote to photography-oriented topics.

3. Streaming

Why use the webcam built into your laptop, or a $100 camera plugged into a USB port on your desktop computer when you can use your a7C II or a7CR instead with either type? One key advantage is that the larger sensor of your camera (compared to that of the typical webcam) provides less depth-of-field (as discussed in Chapter 12), so your background can be pleasantly out-of-focus. The autofocus and auto framing features are more sophisticated than what you find with a typical webcam, too.

However, while your a7C II and a7CR are versatile for streaming, setup can be somewhat complex, with best results requiring visits to several different menu tabs, as outlined below. Only one of them—this one—is found in the Network menu. I'll describe how to use the USB Streaming entry and the other required settings next. (See Figure 9.11, left.)

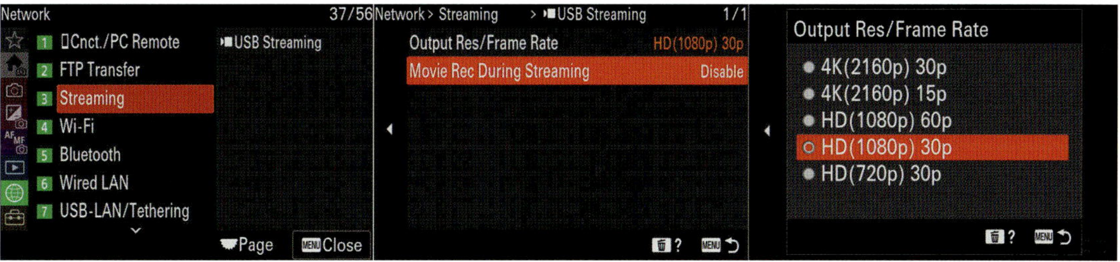

Figure 9.11 Live streaming options.

USB Streaming

Options: Output Resolution/Frame Rate: 4K (2160p) 30p, 4K (2160p) 15p, HD (1080p) 60p, ***HD (1080p) 30p**, HD (720p) 30p; Movie Recording During Streaming

My preference: HD (1080p) 30p; Disable recording

This entry allows you to select the resolution of your video stream and whether or not your stream is recorded to your memory card or external recorder. (See Figure 9.11, center.) You have two options to set:

- **Output Res/Frame Rate.** You can select among 4K (at 30p or 15p), Full HD (at 60p or 30p), or standard HD (at 30p), as shown in Figure 9.11, right. Your choice should be based on how good you want/need your stream to look, and whether or not your streaming service (such as You-Tube, Twitch, Zoom, or Hitbox) and Internet connection can handle it. Some services have a maximum transfer bit rate they accept, and higher resolutions and frame rates obviously call for faster transfer speeds. If you really need 4K streams you may have to experiment. As a fallback, the lowest resolution 720p setting works just about anywhere. Just keep in mind that anything other than the HD (1080p) 30p setting I recommend may not be visibly different to those view-ing your stream. The chief advantage of higher resolutions is to have better quality video if you choose to record your stream, as described next.

  Note that Sony's Imaging Edge Webcam software is limited to 1024 × 576 resolution.

- **Movie Recording During Streaming.** Just enable or disable this capability. Capturing your stream can be handy, especially if you do online workshops or classes and want to retain your presentation for later review or use. Fortunately, you have full control of *how much* of your stream is recorded. For example, you might not want to record introductions, intermissions, Q&A sessions, etc. When movie recording is enabled, when the stream is underway, press the Movie button to start the actual recording process.

As I mentioned, several other settings must be made to use USB streaming using utilities, such as Zoom or the free Imaging Edge Webcam utility. The utility is available from the Sony support site for your country. URLs can change, but at the time I wrote this, the link for the USA was https://imagingedge.sony.net/en-us/ie-webcam.html. Be sure to take care of these settings:

- **Disable other connections.** The Webcam utility, in particular, will not work if your camera is linked to your smartphone or tablet or if you are using Imaging Edge Remote. All network functions are disabled during streaming.

- **Disable sleep mode.** If your computer is set to go to sleep after a period of inactivity, you should disable that function. To keep your camera awake as well, visit Setup > Power Setting Option and adjust your settings, as described later in this chapter. Power Save Start Time and Auto Monitor Off are automatically disabled.

- **Enable USB Power Supply.** Operating your camera as a webcam for extended periods uses a lot of battery power, and may cause overheating when higher resolutions and frame rates are enabled. You'll want to navigate to Setup > USB > USB Power Supply, and choose On if power consump-tion and overheating are not concerns. That will allow you to (potentially) stream for hours.

However, if you are using a laptop running on its own battery power, you may want to choose Off instead. The duration of your stream will be limited by the amount of juice your a7C II or a7CR and your laptop have in their batteries.

- **Specify USB Streaming.** Navigate to Setup > USB > USB Connection Mode and choose USB Streaming. The additional options available for that entry are explained later in this chapter.

Once you're ready to go, follow these steps:

1. **Connect to computer.** Connect your camera to your computer using a USB Type-C cable. Make sure your cable supports SuperSpeed USB 5 Gbps (USB 3.2). Otherwise, you'll be limited to HD (720p) 30p.

2. **Enable/Adjust microphone.** The Sony Webcam utility and other apps do not capture sound from the a7C II/a7CR's microphones; you'll need to use the microphone built into or attached to your computer or an external microphone. Note that settings such as shutter speed or ISO cannot be adjusted during live streaming if you don't assign them to a dial or control wheel or register the settings to the function menu.

3. **Launch streaming service.** After performing steps 1 and 2, I loaded my desktop Zoom application, which immediately recognized my Sony as its camera, with no additional steps required. If you are using a different service you may have to specifically enable the a7C II or a7CR, or switch from any other camera connected to your computer.

4. **Activate streaming.** When using some services, a message: USB Streaming: Standby may appear on the display. If Setup > USB > USB Connection Mode has been set to Select When Connected *instead of* USB Streaming (as advised above), you can now choose Live Stream (USB Streaming). Then, a USB Streaming: Output message will appear.

   If you *haven't* specified USB streaming, as described above, and chose Select When Connected instead, you may see a screen that asks you to choose between Live Stream (USB Streaming) and other USB modes. Select Live Stream.

4. Wi-Fi

There are six entries in the Wi-Fi group. (See Figure 9.12.)

- Wi-Fi Connect
- WPS Push
- Access Point Settings
- Wi-Fi Frequency Band
- Display Wi-Fi Info
- SSID/PW Reset

This group includes features for connecting the a7C II or a7CR to a Wi-Fi access point, either semi-automatically using WPS Push or by manually registering by entering the SSID name of the access point and entering security information. You can choose whether to use your Wi-Fi network's standard 2.4GHz band, or the faster 5GHz band (if available from your router). You can also view the device's detailed information, including IP address, DNS server, and MAC Address.

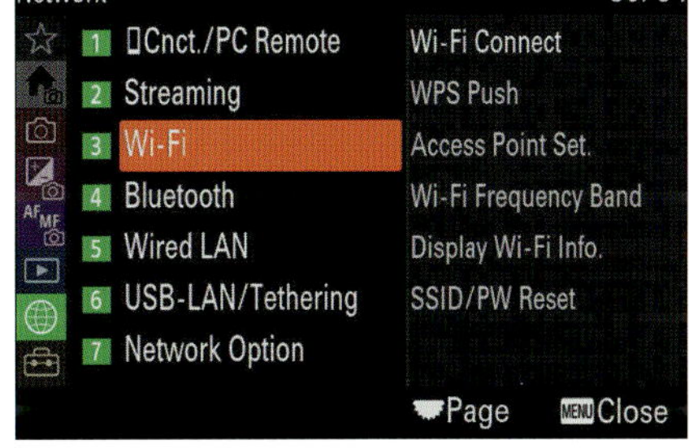

Figure 9.12 Wi-Fi group.

SSID/PW Reset deletes the current SSID and password. You might want to do this for security reasons (say, you loan/give/sell your a7C II/a7CR to someone else) or if you need to start over in registering your camera with a network. Reset Network Settings removes all network settings from the camera. As I mentioned earlier, detailed IT technology for connecting through LANs is beyond the scope of this book, as I've discovered that those who end up needing to use all these features already understand the concepts, and nearly all my readers are happy just knowing how to link their smartphones to their cameras, or the procedure for doing fast tethering using the USB-C cable connection described earlier. So, as Sony provides a comprehensive Help Guide (available online), I'm going to provide just an overview.

Wi-Fi Connect

Options: On, *Off

My preference: N/A

This setting simply turns an existing Wi-Fi connection to an access point on or off. When enabled, the a7C II/a7CR will search for an access point you have already registered, using Network > Wi-Fi > Access Point Settings, described next.

WPS Push/Access Point Settings

Options: Set up an access point using WPS or manually

This pair of entries allow you to configure an access point automatically using the WPS button on your router (WPS Push) or by entering the SSID (Service Set Identifier) and password manually. Wi-Fi Protected Setup (WPS) works only when you're in range of a network provided by a wireless router that is equipped with a WPS button. Not all are. Examine your router and look for a button labeled WPS, or with a ⟳ symbol. Or, find the owner's manual for your router or use a Google search (try "*routername* manual PDF") to locate the WPS button, if one is available. Some routers that support WPS provide it with software instead of a physical button; in that case, you'll need to access the router's control panel using a computer and then click the button on the WPS page. The WPS Push tactic is great, but it would not work at a Wi-Fi hotspot in a supermarket, for instance, since the network owner is unlikely to use the WPS feature for hundreds of customers.

WHAT'S WPS?

The abbreviation WPS indicates Wi-Fi Protected Setup. This is a security standard that makes it easier and quicker to connect a device, including your a7C II/a7CR, to a wireless home network. It eliminates the need to key in the password. Because it's possible for an aggressive hacker to recover the WPS PIN number, some experts suggest turning the router's WPS feature off when you're not actually using it; this may not be possible with all router models but check the owner's manual for the one you own.

Just follow these steps:

1. **Access Network > Wi-Fi > WPS Push.** If your router provides WPS, scroll to the WPS Push item in the camera's Wi-Fi settings menu and press the center button.

2. **Press the router's WPS button.** A screen will appear advising you to press the router's WPS button within 2 minutes. When you press the button (or use the software to do so), the camera should be able to establish connectivity.

3. **Confirm registration.** Once the connection is established, a screen reporting "Registered. SSID *network name*" appears. Press the center button to confirm.

Registering Manually

You can also select an access point manually when within range of a wireless network; you'll need to know the network password, if one is in place, to do so. Just follow these steps:

1. **Scroll to Access Point Set.** Press the center button. A Wi-Fi Standby screen will appear confirming that the camera is searching for available access points.

2. **Wait for the camera to find your network.** The a7C II or a7CR will find the nearby access points (networks) in less than a minute. If there is more than one network or available access point, all of those found will be shown. If your smartphone has a hotspot feature and it's turned on, that "network" may appear as well. (See Figure 9.13, upper left.)

   When several networks are displayed, some may belong to nearby businesses or your neighbors, and you can ignore them (their signal strength is probably weaker than your own network in any case, even if your neighbor's network is not protected by a password). In my case, my wireless router resides in my office; in other, more distant rooms is a wired access point, and, on the second floor, a wireless repeater.

Figure 9.13 Wi-Fi settings.

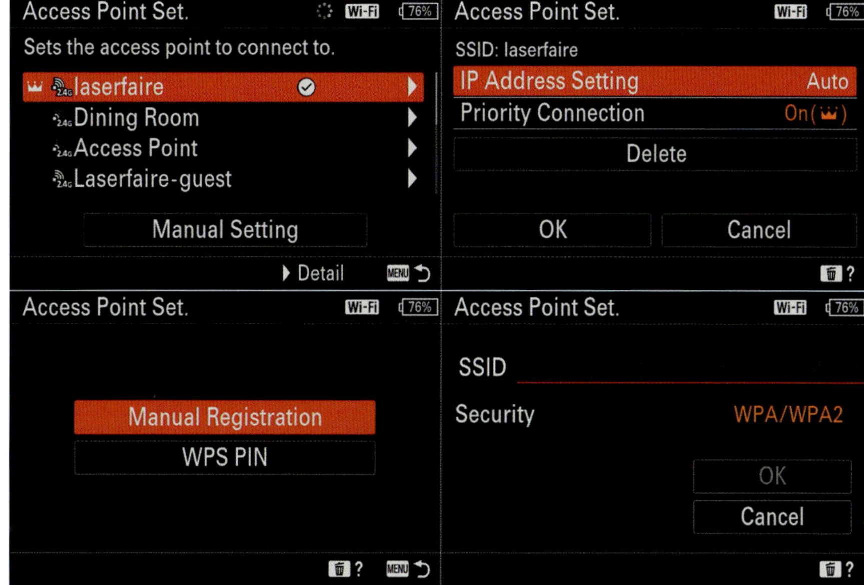

3a. Select and confirm. Scroll to the one you intend to use and press the center button to confirm. A message will appear: Completed. (Priority Connection: On) indicating this access point is prioritized when connecting by Wi-Fi. A tiny crown emblem appears to the left of the access point SSID. Alternatively, you can press the right directional button to view the additional screen shown at upper right in Figure 9.13, and switch from Auto IP if the Auto IP Address Setting option does not work. If you have some networking expertise, change from Auto to Manual, and a screen appears that allows you to enter the IP address, Subnet Mark, and Default Gateway. You can safely leave the Priority Connection parameter set to Off. Fortunately, you probably won't have to resort to these additional steps. (Non-IT types will have fallen asleep by this point.)

3b. Or specify parameters manually. Alternatively, you can scroll down to Manual Setting at the bottom of the screen, press OK, and proceed with manual registration instead. (See Figure 9.13, bottom left and right.) I'll show you how to select an access point manual in the section that follows this one.

4. Input the password (if necessary). You may see a screen with a field for entering your network password, if your router/access point is set up to require one. If not, proceed to Step 5. Otherwise, press the center button and a virtual keyboard will appear. Using this keyboard, enter the password for your network. The keyboard works a bit like the physical multi-tap keyboard found on some (older) cell phones. Use the directional buttons to highlight a letter group, such as abc, def, ghi, and press the center button once to enter the first character in the group, twice for the second character, three times for the third character, and four times for the fourth. Some of the virtual keys allow you to backspace, delete characters, and toggle between uppercase and lowercase. When finished, highlight OK and press the center button.

5. Confirm connectivity. After the Wi-Fi connectivity has been made, a screen will appear confirming that your network has been registered, with an orange dot next to the connected network. If you get a screen with a note stating *cannot authenticate*, or that the *input value is invalid*, you'll need to start again at step 1; make sure you have the correct password for the network and be extra careful when keying it in. Remember that when a capital letter is required, you must use the shift feature (an arrow pointing upward) on the virtual keyboard.

6. Try it again later. After you have established Wi-Fi connectivity, you can revert to using the a7C II or a7CR as usual; a touch of the shutter-release button returns it to shooting mode. The camera will retain the connection to the network until you turn it off or it goes into power-saving sleep mode; Wi-Fi is then temporarily disconnected. When you're ready to use Wi-Fi again, activate the a7C II/a7CR while in range of the same network, scroll to Access Point Settings in the Wireless menu, and press the center button. The camera will quickly find your network to re-establish Wi-Fi connectivity.

If you're connecting to a public Wi-Fi hotspot, the steps should be the same, but you'll most likely find a screen that requires you to agree to the hotspot's terms and conditions. Some hotspots may not require you to enter a password.

Selecting an Access Point Manually

If the desired access point (network) is not displayed on the screen as described in Step 2 above, you may need to enter it yourself. Just follow these steps:

1. **Choose Manual Setting.** Scroll down to Manual Setting and press the center button.
2. **Select Manual Registration.** Press the center button to begin the manual registration process.
3. **Enter SSID.** On the Manual Registration screen, there's a field for entering the SSID name of the access point (network) you plan to use. Press the center button when this field is visible, and the virtual keyboard appears. Enter the data. When you're finished press the center button.
4. **Change Security (if necessary).** Again, if you have some networking expertise, you'll know if the security setting on your router is WPA (Wi-Fi Protected Access, the default), WEP (Wired Equivalent Privacy, an older, easily "hacked" protection scheme), or None (effectively, no security). If you want to change the Security setting, highlight that field and press the center button. Select your choice and press the MENU button to return.
5. **Enter password.** The next screen will ask for your password, which you can enter using the virtual keyboard.
6. **Enter WPS PIN (if necessary).** If your WPS connection requires a PIN, you can enter it.

Take care not to lose the network connection by inadvertently using the Initialize or the Reset Network Settings item of the Wireless menu. If you do so, the camera will eliminate all your network settings and you'll need to repeat the steps in this section.

Wi-Fi Frequency Band 📷 🎥 S&Q

Options: *2.4GHz, 5GHz
My preference: N/A

Select the frequency band used by your router.

Display Wi-Fi Information 📷 🎥 S&Q

Options: Informational screen
My preference: N/A

This entry displays your Wi-Fi network's information, including IP Address, Subnet Mask, Default Gateway, DNS servers, Mac Address, and Wi-Fi Frequency Band.

SSID/PW Reset 📷 🎥 S&Q

Options: Reset
My preference: N/A

Resets the SSID and password used when using your a7C II or a7CR as the access point. If you do this and later want to re-establish the same connection, you'll need to delete the original access point connection completely, and then either use WPS or manual SSID/PW entry again.

5. Bluetooth

There are five entries in the Bluetooth group. (See Figure 9.14.)

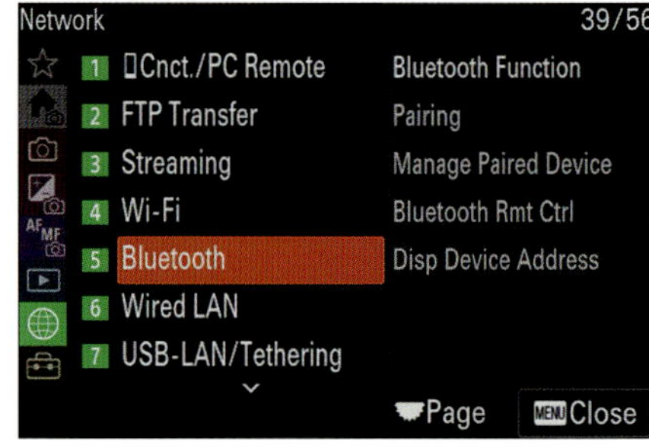

Figure 9.14 Bluetooth group.

- Bluetooth Function
- Pairing
- Manage Paired Device
- Bluetooth Remote Control
- Display Device Address

Bluetooth Settings

Options: Bluetooth Function (On, *****Off**); Pairing; Display Device Address

Your a7C II or a7CR can access the GPS information available from your smartphone and embed that data in your image files using low-energy Bluetooth connectivity. Use this, and you no longer have to wonder where you took a photo; the GPS data can be displayed by many applications, including Lightroom's Map tab. This entry allows you to turn off Bluetooth sharing, pair your phone with your camera, and display the device's address. Keep in mind that when you initialize your camera, as described in this chapter, pairing settings are canceled as well.

Pairing

Options: Pairs Bluetooth

My preference: N/A

Use this entry to pair your camera with another device, such as your smartphone; the camera's Device Name is ILCE-7CM2 or ILCE-7CR.

Manage Paired Device

Options: Delete Paired Devices

My preference: N/A

This entry shows you a list of paired devices. You can select one or more to delete. The a7C II and a7CR can each be paired with only two devices simultaneously, so if you want to connect to a third device, you'll have to delete one of the others.

Bluetooth Remote Control

Options: On, *****Off**

My preference: N/A

This entry lets you enable or disable the Bluetooth connection to the Sony RMT-P1BT wireless remote control. It allows zooming (with a Power Zoom lens attached), autofocus adjustments, access to a custom C1 button, and the ability to stop and start movie shooting.

Display Device Address

Options: Displays MAC address

My preference: N/A

This is an informational screen that shows the MAC address of your camera.

6. Wired LAN

There are just two entries in the Wired LAN group. (See Figure 9.15, left.)

- LAN IP Address Settings
- Display Wired LAN Information

(LAN) IP Address Setting

Options: *Auto, Manual

My preference: N/A

You can specify an IP address manually if you're into that sort of thing, or allow the camera to specify one automatically using the DHCP protocol.

Display Wired LAN Info

Options: Informational screen

My preference: N/A

Displays an informational screen similar to the Display Wi-Fi Information entry described earlier.

7. USB-LAN Tethering

There are two entries in the USB-LAN Tethering group. (See Figure 9.15, right.)

- USB-LAN Connection
- Tethering Connection

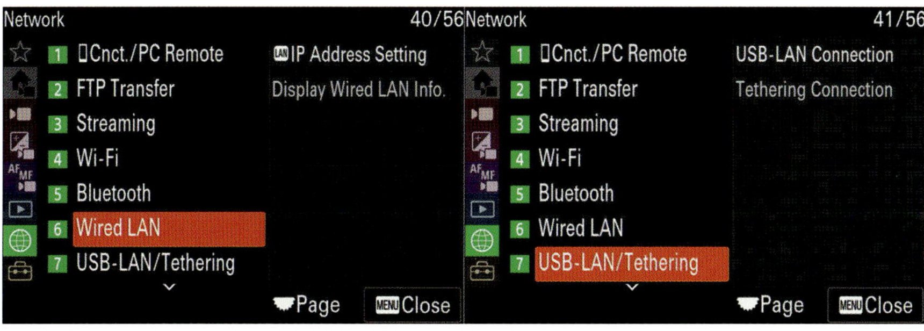

Figure 9.15 Wired LAN group (left). USB-LAN Tethering (right).

USB-LAN Connection/Disconnection 📷 🎥 S&Q

Options: Connect to or disconnect from an Ethernet network

My preference: N/A

Earlier, I showed you how to control your camera and shoot tethered using your smartphone (with the Creators' App) and with your computer (Using Imaging Edge Desktop and a USB-C cable connection). If you have a USB-to-Ethernet (LAN) adapter you can also tether your camera over a wired Ethernet link. This entry prepares the camera for connection to the adapter.

Tethering Connection 📷 🎥 S&Q

Options: Connects to the network using your device's tethering connection

My preference: N/A

This entry is similar to the one above, except that instead of a connection made using a USB to Ethernet (LAN) adapter, the connection is to your device's software. When you invoke this entry, a processing screen appears, followed by a message that the camera has completed preparations for connection, and you can now connect the USB tethering device, using software like Capture One.

8. Network Option

There are six entries in the Network Option group. (See Figure 9.16.)

- Airplane Mode
- Edit Device Name
- Import Root Certificate
- Access Authentication Settings
- Access Authentication Information
- Reset Network Settings

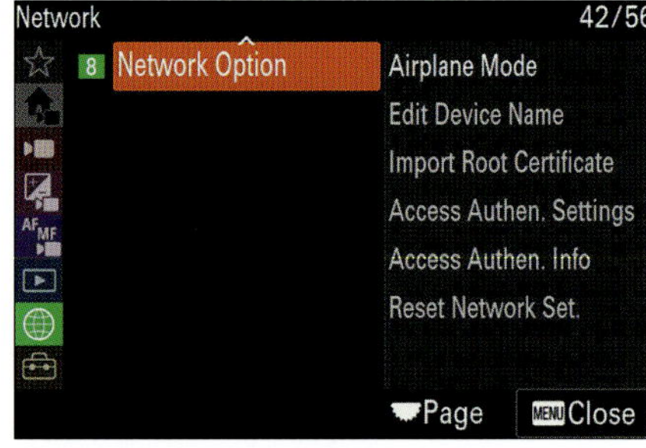

Figure 9.16 Network Option group.

Airplane Mode 📷 🎥 S&Q

Options: On, *Off

My preference: N/A

This setting enables/disables wireless functions. You could use this to save power, or when theoretically required (as when boarding an airplane, although that is rarely enforced these days). Note that Bluetooth, if active, uses negligible power and that Wi-Fi connections consume power only while the camera is connected to a network, so that ordinarily you do not need to use Airplane mode.

Edit Device Name

Options: Change Device Name

My preference: N/A

By default, the label applied to your camera is ILCE-7CM2 or ILCE-7CR. You can change it to something else, if, say, you own or have access to three or four of these cameras and want to differentiate between them—or simply want to personalize your camera's "name."

Import Root Certificate

Options: Import certificate

My preference: N/A

Encrypted communications with an FTP server may require verification using a root certificate. This entry allows you to import that certificate, which you have stored on a memory card. You'll find detailed instructions on using this FTP function in the Sony FTP Help Guide, described earlier.

Access Authenticity Settings

Options: On, *Off; Enter User name, Password

My preference: N/A

This entry allows you to enable/disable encryption of the data shared between your camera and the Creators' App. It is only available when the PC Remote feature is turned off. Most a7C II/a7CR owners will have no need for this extra layer of security. Are you really concerned about someone stealing your information when you transfer your photos to your laptop while relaxing at Starbucks? If that's the case, you need to implement even more layers of security, because if a hacker tries to access your computer, safeguarding the photos therein are the least of your worries.

When you enable this feature, a screen appears that allows you to enter a user name, password, or generate a password. (See Figure 9.17.) These can be set up in the Creators' App.

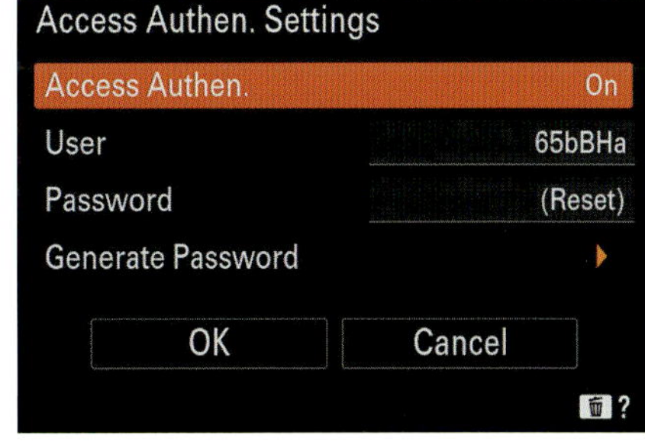

Figure 9.17 Authenticity information.

Access Authenticity Information

Options: Informational screen

My preference: N/A

This entry allows you to view the authenticity information, by entering the username and password.

Reset Network Settings 📷 🎥 S&Q

Options: Reset Network settings

My preference: N/A

Changes all network settings to their factory defaults and reboots your a7C II or a7CR. This entry is necessary because the Setup > Reset/Save Settings > Setting Reset > Initialize entry does not erase any existing SSID or passwords. It is not available when PC Remote is On.

Setup Menu Tab

The Sony a7C II and a7CR's yellow-coded Setup tab menu has 13 groups, each devoted to specific adjustments that are most likely to be set once and changed only when you need a new camera configuration. (See Figure 9.18.) They are as follows:

1. Area/Date
2. Reset/Save Settings
3. Operation Customize
4. Dial Customize
5. Touch Operation
6. Accessibility
7. Finder/Monitor
8. Display Option
9. Power Setting Option
10. Sound Option
11. USB
12. External Output
13. Setup Option

1. Area/Date (Stills/Movies)

The Area/Date group has three localization settings that let you specify the language, time parameters, and video system used where you live and work. (See Figure 9.18, left)

- Language
- Area/Date/Time Setting
- NTSC/Pal Selector

Language 📷 🎥 S&Q

Options: English, French, Italian, Spanish, Japanese, Chinese languages

My preference: English; improving in Spanish; the French have urged me to give up.

If you accidentally set a language you cannot read and find yourself with incomprehensible menus, don't panic. Just find the Setup tab, the one with the yellow toolbox for its icon, and choose the entry with an icon that looks like an alphabet block "A" to the left of the item's heading. No matter which

Figure 9.18 Setup menu groups.

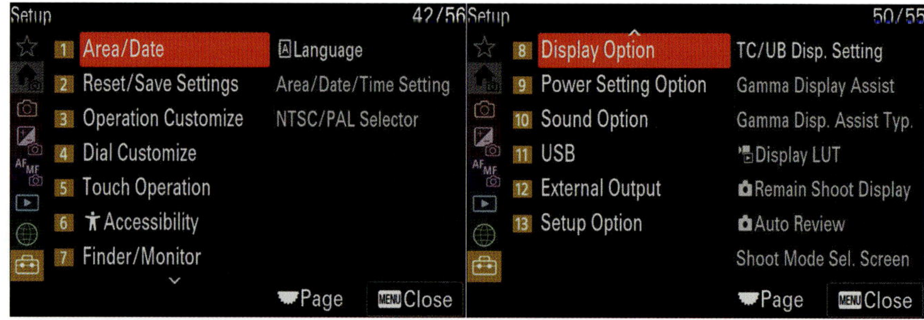

language has been selected, you can recognize this menu item by the "A" icon. Scroll to it, press the center button to select this item, and scroll up/down among the options and choose a language, langue, lingua, or idioma, you can read.

Area/Date/Time Setting 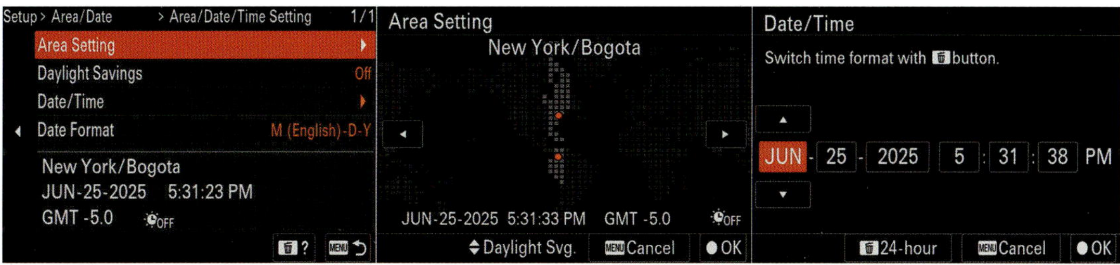

Options: Area Setting, Daylight Saving, Date/Time, Date Format

My preference: N/A

Use this option to specify your preferred localization, which will be displayed by the a7C II or a7CR, and embedded in the image file's EXIF metadata along with exposure information and other information. Having the date set accurately is also important for selecting movies for viewing by date. You set these values the first time you operated your camera, but may need to re-enter the information if your battery goes dead long enough for the camera's internal clock/CMOS battery to discharge. You can choose the parameters shown at left in Figure 9.19:

- **Area Setting.** The left/right controls will take you through a world tour map. Settle on your current location. While viewing the map, you can use the up/down controls to turn Daylight Saving time on or off (a Sun icon at bottom right indicates your current status). You can also switch using the entry described next. (See Figure 9.19, center.)

- **Daylight Saving (sic).** Apparently, those who designed your camera didn't realize the correct English term for summer hours is *Daylight Saving Time.* They got the French, Italian, and Spanish versions correct however: *Heure d'été, Ora Legale,* and *Horario verano.* I can neither confirm nor deny the accuracy of the Japanese and Chinese renditions.

- **Date/Time.** Here you can enter the current month, day, year, hour, minute, and second. You can't directly change the AM/PM setting; you need to scroll the hours past midnight or noon to change that setting. Use the up/down directional buttons or rotate the control wheel to change each value as needed. (See Figure 9.19, right.)

- **Date Format.** Select from Y-M-D, M-D-Y (English), M-D-Y, or D-M-Y. The difference between M-D-Y (English) and M-D-Y is that the English version starts with the English abbreviation for the month. The M-D-Y rendition substitutes the month's numeric value instead, for the benefit of those who speak other than English but want to use the insane system favored almost exclusively by the USA (and protectorates), Canada, and Micronesia. Virtually everyone else uses D-M-Y.

Figure 9.19 Localization settings.

NTSC/PAL Selector 📷 🎥 S&Q

Options: NTSC, PAL

My preference: N/A

Allows you to switch the camera between the two major television video systems, NTSC (used in North and South America, Korea, Japan, and some other Pacific countries), and PAL, which is used in Europe, the Middle East, and elsewhere. Your camera will be set up at the factory to default to the video system used in your country. If you switch to the alternate system, the start-up screen will display a message "Running on NTSC" or "Running on PAL" to make sure you're aware of the change. Note that a few countries in South America (Brazil, Argentina, Paraguay, and Uruguay) use a modified PAL system, while others, including Bulgaria, France, Greece, Guiana, Iran, Iraq, Monaco, Russia, and Ukraine use a third system, called SECAM.

2. Reset/Save Settings

The Reset/Save Settings group has two settings. (See Figure 9.20, left.)

- Setting Reset
- Save/Load Settings

Setting Reset 📷 🎥 S&Q

Options: Camera Settings Reset, Initialize

My preference: N/A

If you've made a lot of changes to your camera's settings, you may want to return the features to their defaults, so you can start over without manually going back through the menus and restoring everything. This menu item lets you do that. Your choices, shown in Figure 9.20, right, are as follows:

- **Camera Settings Reset.** Resets the main shooting parameters for both still and movies in the Shooting, Exposure/Color, and AF/MF tabs to their default values. Note that Fn settings and those for Picture Profiles or Different Settings for Still/Movies are not reset.

- **Initialize.** Resets virtually *all* settings to their default values, except for including the time/date and Wi-Fi settings, but *not* including any Picture Profile adjustments or Different Settings for Still/Movies (discussed later in this chapter).

Figure 9.20 Reset/ Save Settings group (left). Setting Reset options (right).

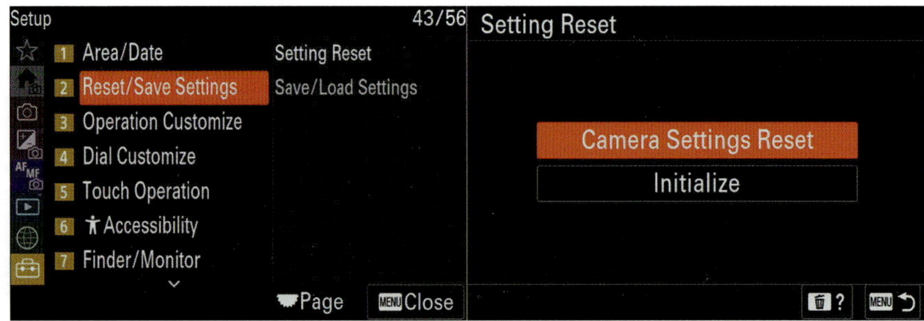

Save/Load Settings 📷🎬 S&Q

Options: Load, Save, Delete
My preference: N/A

Consider this entry an extension of the Memory Recall feature. It allows you to save current camera settings to a memory card. You can save up to 10 settings, named, by default, CAMSET01.DAT through CAMSET10.DAT. You have the option of choosing a name that's different from the default, to help you remember a particular group of settings. However, the 10-setting limit applies no matter what nomenclature you choose.

The files are stored on your memory card in a folder named PRIVATE > SONY > SETTING > 7CM2/7CR > CAMSET and are, of course, removed when you reformat the card. (Note that this particular folder is created only after you save your first setting on that card.) At some later time, you can load them back into the camera, choosing from a scrolling list of all the settings files available on that card. From there, you can store the settings in the camera's Memory Recall registers if you like. In effect, you can have many, many more stored settings than is available with the Memory Recall feature (described in Chapter 6). You could dedicate several memory cards just to store your settings if you like. (If you use low-capacity memory cards, it would cost you very little to use them for nothing else.)

There are some limitations, of course. Settings that have no parameters, such as Focus Magnifier, cannot be saved. You cannot load or save settings when the camera's mode dial is set to the 1, 2, or 3 Memory positions. In addition, there are some settings that cannot be saved (in other words, the camera retains those settings even when the new ones are loaded). They include Copyright Information, External Flash Settings, White Balance Custom Settings, Face Memory, WPS Push, Access Point Settings, Wi-Fi Frequency Band, LAN IP Address Setting, Edit Device Name, Access Authenticity Settings, and Area/Date/Time Setting.

3. Operation Customize

The Operation Customize group has eight entries for customizing the way your camera responds to button and dial controls, rotation of the focusing ring, and display of shooting information on your LCD monitor and electronic viewfinder. The first seven are shown in Figure 9.21, right; scroll down to see the eighth, Zoom Ring Rotate.

- Custom Key/Dial Settings (Stills)
- Custom Key/Dial Settings (Movies)
- Custom Key Settings (Playback)
- Function Menu Settings
- Different Settings for Stills/Movies
- DISP (Screen Display) Settings
- (Movie) Record with Shutter
- Zoom Ring Rotate

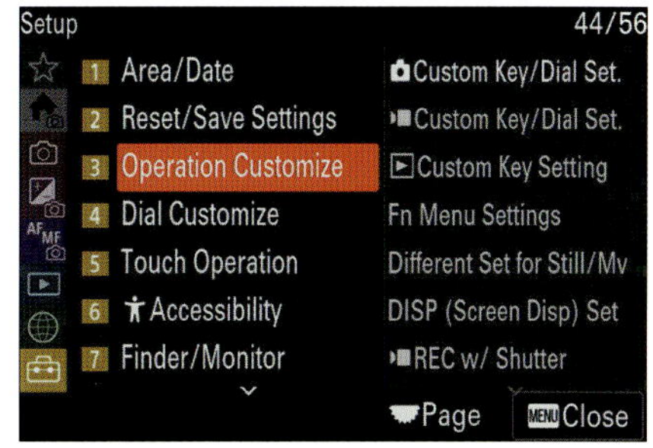

Figure 9.21 Operation Customize group.

Your a7C II/a7CR has a mind-boggling array of customization features. I covered the ways you can create your own My Menu system and store custom arrays of settings using the 1, 2, and 3 Memory Recall positions on the mode dial in Chapter 6.

In addition, you can assign more than 100 different functions listed in the Shooting, Exposure/Color, Focus, Playback, Network, and Setup tabs to buttons and dials of your choice. Some choices enable you to invoke features, such as Zoom, with a button-press that would otherwise require a visit to the menu system. Others allow you to turn features, like Eye AF, on or off as needed. While not all functions can be assigned to every control, you'll find that you should be able to configure your camera to operate exactly the way you need it to. Keep in mind that once you've reassigned the controls of your camera, anyone else operating it (and sometimes yourself) may find the new function assignments confusing.

Custom Key/Dial Settings

Options: Definitions for buttons including AF-ON, Custom C1–C2, Center, Left, Right, Down, Movie Shooting, Focus Hold (on lens), plus Control Wheel, Front Dial, and Rear Dial Left, Rear Dial Right
My preference: N/A

This entry can be accessed in both Stills and Movie modes, but its settings are applied only in Still mode. It allows customization of as many as 8 buttons on the camera, Focus Hold (found on some lenses), and front/rear dials (both left and right) and control wheel. You can access each of these using five pages of options, shown in Figure 9.22. (The bottom two images in the figure show two different ways of defining the dial/wheel controls and are not separate pages.) Indeed, the following is a list of the only buttons on the camera that you *cannot* redefine to perform some other function:

- **Shutter release.** It is always used to take a picture and will initiate autofocus if you haven't assigned AF-ON and other AF functions to a different key.
- **Up directional button.** It is used to change your information display in shooting and Playback modes, and as a directional button in menus.
- **Playback button.** Activates picture review.
- **Fn (Function) button.** (Almost) always summons the Function menu, and in Playback mode sends the current image to a smart device. However, you *can* redefine the Fn button to several functions when in Playback mode (only), as I'll describe shortly.

Your custom key definitions override any default definitions for those buttons when in Shooting mode; they retain their original functions in Movie and Playback mode (unless you redefine them, as I'll describe shortly). Because button definition is such a personal choice, I steer away from recommending particular definitions for each of the buttons, even though certain functions can be accessed *only* by assigning them to a custom key setting. Our fingers and agility vary, so, while buttons like the AF-ON button are traditionally used for something like back-button focus, you may prefer to assign that function to a different key.

When assigning definitions to keys, keep in mind that certain behaviors can be used *only if* you have made them available using a custom key definition. For example, if you want to use the Bright Monitoring feature, which temporarily turns the Live View Setting Effect to Off to increase the brightness level of the screen in dark locations, you must assign it to a key.

Figure 9.22 Default values of assignable controls.

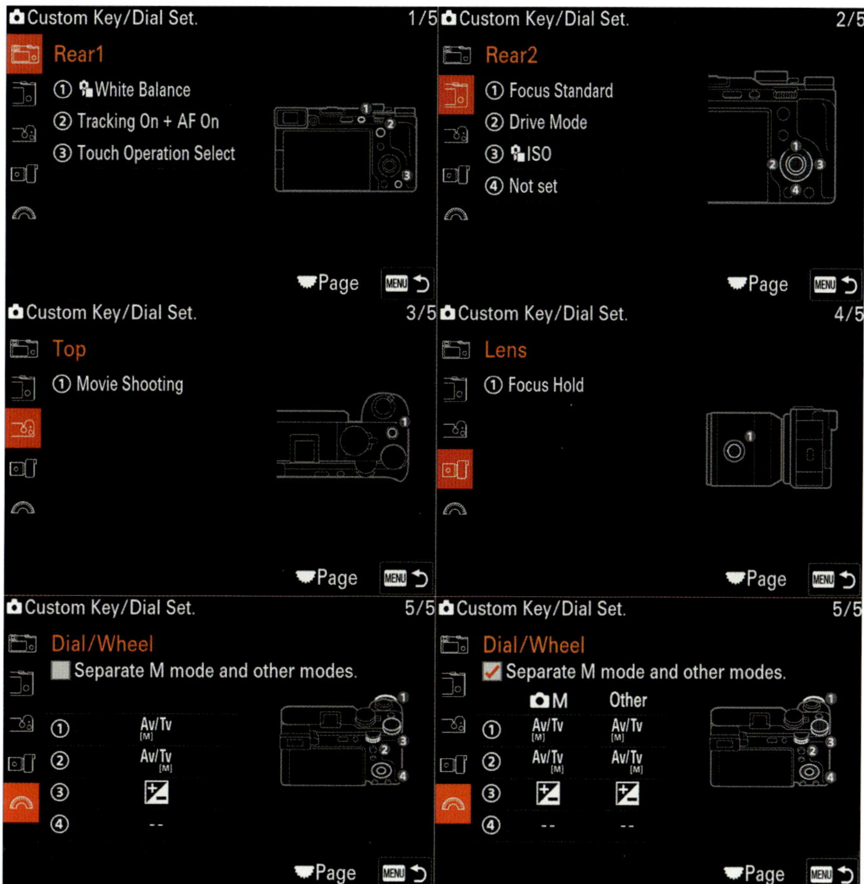

Each of the customizable controls, except the down button and control wheel, have a default behavior assigned for shooting mode, listed below. In Movie mode, these buttons have the exact same behavior, unless you choose a different option. In Playback mode, only Movie, Fn button, and C1–C2 buttons can be redefined. The Fn and Custom 2 (C2) controls have the only default behavior (Send and Delete, respectively), while the Movie and Custom 1 (C1) buttons keep the same definitions assigned to Still and Movie modes until you reassign them. The default actions for the controls in Still mode are:

- Custom 1 button: White Balance
- Custom 2 button: Touch Operation Select (On/Off)
- AF-ON button: Tracking On+AF On
- Control Wheel: Not Set
- Control Wheel Center button: Focus Standard
- Left button: Drive Mode
- Right button: ISO
- Down button: Not Set
- Up button: DISP (Not customizable)
- Focus Hold (on lens): Focus Hold
- Movie Button: Shoot Movies
- Front Dial: Av/Tv (Av in Manual mode)
- Rear Dial Left: Av/Tv (Tv in Manual mode)
- Rear Dial Right: Exposure Compensation

> **DIFFERENT STROKES**
>
> As I noted earlier, the bottom two screens in Figure 9.21 show that you can assign one set of defini-
> tions to the front/rear dials and control wheel (bottom left), and separate functions for each in Shoot-
> ing/Movie and Manual exposure modes (bottom right). Just mark the Separate M Mode and Other
> Modes box, and a new column of choices appears.

Useful Assignable Functions

Here's a list of useful functions you can assign to a control:

- **Interval Shooting.** If you find yourself using the Interval Shooting feature frequently, and think it's a pain to navigate to the Shooting menu every time, you can assign a custom key of your choice to jump immediately to the interval photography settings.

- **Subject Recognition in AF.** Assign this function to one of the available keys to enable/disable giving higher priority to detected faces or other targets. You'll find this capability especially useful to turn the feature off when your subjects include faces that may be difficult for the a7C II/a7CR to detect (often people with long bangs or wearing sunglasses) or in difficult lighting conditions (shade, backlight, or low-light scenes).

- **Subject Detection.** If pet or animal photography is a big part of your shooting, you switch back and forth among Human, Animal, and Bird detection more frequently than your average photographer. Visit Focus > Subject Recognition > Recognition Target Selection Set, as described in Chapter 8, and disable any of the subjects you *don't* frequently shoot. Then, assign a custom key to Recognition Target Selection Set, and you can cycle among the remaining modes with multiple presses of a button. Or assign Eye AF, Right/Left Eye Selection, or invoke Focus Magnifier to let you focus on a particular part of your subject.

- **AF Tracking Sensitivity.** Sports photographers will like the ability to change how quickly the camera responds to new subjects entering the frame. Assign the function to a custom key, and you can switch to responsive, standard, or locked-on settings.

- **Aperture Drive in AF.** If you need quiet operation in certain environments, you can assign a key to enable or disable this feature, described earlier in this chapter.

- **FINDER/MONITOR switch.** If you turn off automatic switching between finder and monitor, you'll want to have a button that will quickly toggle between the two. Just assign Finder/Monitor Select to a button.

- **Fast ISO change.** Assign ISO to the control wheel, and as you shoot you can spin the wheel to adjust your ISO setting on the fly without venturing to a menu or pressing the right directional button. While the Auto ISO feature works well (especially when you're shooting fast and quickly), at times the photographer can do a better job of adjusting sensitivity to suit the task at hand.

- **More pairs.** The control wheel and its center button can also be assigned pairs of related functions. For example, if you've set the control wheel to change ISO sensitivity, the center button can be used to specify ISO Auto Minimum Shutter Speed when you select ISO Auto with the wheel. Image Size/Quality is another good pair for the wheel/center button combination.

- **Freed-up keys.** Once you assign ISO to the control wheel, that leaves the right button, formerly used to set ISO, free for a new definition. You could assign it to Metering Mode or another function.

- **MENU.** I find the MENU button easy to find, even in the dark, as it's located to the immediate left of the viewfinder. If you often make adjustments while viewing through the viewfinder, you might prefer having a second menu button that can be accessed with the camera up to your eye.

- **My Dial Assignments.** You can assign up to three different behaviors to the control wheel and/or control dial, and return them to their default functions quickly. The custom functions let you activate the alternate behavior by holding the button down, switching among the three dial assignments by spinning a control, and toggling one of the three on or off. I'll explain this feature later in the chapter.

One cool thing about custom keys is that certain functions can be assigned that are not available from the menu system. The list is surprisingly extensive, and includes:

- **Move AF Frame Left/Right or Up/Down.** Moves the focus area left/right or up/down when the control wheel is rotated in Zone, Spot, or Expand Spot focus modes. Standard and Large versions are available for Left/Right and Up/Down.

- **HLG Still Image.** When shooting HEIF, pressing the defined button applies HLG gamma to the image.

- **Switch Silent Mode.** Toggles between silent mode and normal audio feedback. If the mechanical shutter is being used, the electronic shutter is activated along with silent mode.

- **Zoom Operation (T), (W).** Assigns the tele and wide functions to buttons for use when using the Zoom feature.

- **Add Rating (1–5 Stars).** Assign a specific Star rating to the last image captured. You can choose any one rating, from 1 to 5 stars.

- **Create Divider Frame.** It's often useful to separate one set of images from another. Perhaps you're shooting photos at a track event and would like to insert a marker to indicate where one heat ended and another began. The camera can insert a divider frame (a blank JPEG with a right-pointing arrow) that you can easily use to mark where one set of images stops and the next one begins.

- **Aperture Preview.** This option tells the camera to stop down the lens to the currently specified "taking" aperture, acting as a depth-of-field preview.

- **Shot Result Preview.** Think of this as a depth-of-field preview to see the effects of dynamic range optimization (DRO), shutter speeds, aperture, and ISO sensitivity settings. You can even see the blurring effects caused by slow shutter speeds.

- **Bright Monitoring.** This option makes it easier to compose and focus scenes that are extremely dark, by making the live view image brighter.

- **In-Camera Guide.** When you press the button (by default, the Trash key), a brief reminder of what a menu item, setting, or Fn (Function) does appears. This is mostly of use to absolute beginners; by the time you've finished this book you will rarely need it.

- **Hold/Toggle Functions.** Sony offers a series of button definitions that invoke a function any time you either press the button down and *hold* it, or which *toggle* the function on or off each time the button is pressed and released. They are listed as *function* Hold or *function* Toggle. The available Hold/Toggle functions include:

AEL	Spot (Metering) AEL	FEL Lock
FEL-AEL	AWB	AF/MF Selector
Register AF Area	Tracking Off	Tracking (and) (Subject) Recognition Off

- **Register AF Area + AF On.** Recalls the registered AF Area and initiates autofocus when pressed.

- **AF On.** Initiates autofocus, but *does not* lock exposure, as contrasted with the AF-ON button's default behavior of initiating AF *and* locking exposure when it is pressed. It's useful when you want to separate the two functions, say, to lock exposure with the shutter release (only) and initiate AF with the AF-ON button (only).

- **Focus Hold.** When the defined button is pressed, the camera will cease autofocus activity. Think of it as a reverse AF-ON button.

- **Tracking On.** Allows you to activate tracking when the Focus Area is not set to any of the Tracking variations. For example, if you're using Wide, Spot (Small, Medium, or Large), or Expand Spot and press the defined button, the Focus Area will switch to the Tracking version while the button is held down. It will return to the non-tracking Focus Area when the button is released.

- **Tracking + AF On.** Identical to Tracking On, except it also initiates autofocus while the button is held down.

- **Switch AF Frame Move Hold.** Adjusts speed of Spot or Expand Spot focus area when the defined button is pressed and held down.

- **Switch Identification Target.** Cycles among the available faces registered using Face Memory.

- **Wireless Test Flash.** Performs a test flash of a connected wireless electronic flash.

- **Menu.** If reaching the default MENU button with a finger is a stretch for you, you can use a different defined button to access it instead.

- **Switch Monitor when Flip Display.** When the defined button is pressed, the LCD display cycles through its Auto, Horizontal Flip, or No Flip behaviors, as described in Setup > Finder/Monitor > Monitor Flip direction later in this chapter.

Custom Key/Dial Settings

Options: Definitions for buttons including AF-ON, Custom C1–C2, Center, Left, Right, Down, Movie Shooting, Focus Hold (on lens), plus Control Wheel, Front Dial, and Rear Dial Left, Rear Dial Right

My preference: N/A

The same buttons used for still photography can be redefined for different behaviors while shooting movies—or, you can tell the a7C II or a7CR to just apply whatever setting you've specified for stills to movie shooting. Note that this menu entry can be *accessed* in both Still and Movie modes, but its adjustments are applied only when you are using Movie mode.

You can assign *different* functions to each of the customizable controls when shooting movies, assuming you have such a need and an excellent memory. The default definition for most of those controls is Follow Custom (Stills), which uses whichever behaviors you have assigned using the Custom Key (Stills) entry. Keep in mind that in Movie mode, the Drive (left) button is used only to activate the self-timer.

Custom Key Settings (Playback)

Options: Definitions for Custom Buttons C1 and C2, plus Movie and Fn/Send to Smartphone buttons
My preference: N/A

Only a limited number of controls and functions are available using this entry. The front dial, both rear dials, and control wheel cannot be redefined. The Custom 1 (C1) and Custom 2 (C2) buttons can be assigned behaviors during Playback, most of them options from the Playback tab itself, plus some from the Network and Setup tabs. C1 and C2 follow the setting made for Stills/Movie mode (unless you choose another behavior). The Fn button, which, by default, sends the displayed image to your smartphone, can also be defined to switch to FTP settings, and a few Setup functions.

The most important function to make available during Playback is the ability to add or delete *Shot Marks* to movies. You can define two different buttons, one to Add/Delete Shot Mark 1 and a second to Add/Delete Shot Mark 2, using Setup > Operation Customize > (Playback) Custom Key Setting, as discussed in Chapter 9. Then, just press the defined button when the movie you want to mark or unmark is displayed on the Playback screen.

The Shot Marks you embed in your movie files have two functions:

- **Filtered Playback.** You can select which movies to review using the Playback > Playback Option > Image Jump Setting entry. You can choose to see only those given a Shot Mark, only those *without* a Shot Mark, plus additional criteria listed in Chapter 8.
- **Create preview clip.** As I described earlier, the Select on Camera and Send entry can create a 60-, 30-, or 15-second preview clip centered around a Shot Mark you have defined.

Function Menu Settings

Options (Stills) Defaults: Top Row: Creative Look, Metering Mode, SteadyShot, Recognition Target, Focus Mode, APS-C Super35 Shooting; Bottom Row: White Balance, Touch Function in Shooting, Silent Mode (a7C II)/Shutter Type (a7CR), Subject Recognition in Autofocus, Focus Area, JPEG Image Size
Options (Movies) Defaults: Top Row: Picture Profile, Audio Recording Level, SteadyShot, Recognition Target, Focus Mode, Zebra Display; Bottom Row: White Balance, Touch Function in Shooting, Focus Map, Subject Recognition in Autofocus, Focus Area, Zebra Level
My preference: N/A

When you select this entry, a screen appears like the one shown in Figure 9.23. It displays the icons available in both still and movie modes. Still functions are shown at top, and Movie functions are shown in the bottom half of the figure. Each version has six settings each in two rows arrayed along the bottom. The default options are illustrated.

> **MORE DIFFERENT STROKES**
>
> Note that in the Movie version, the Focus Mode, Focus Area, White Balance, Touch Function in Shooting, and Subject Recognition in Autofocus include a small camera symbol which indicates that those settings are the same as the settings you make for their Stills counterparts. If you change the Stills version, that change will be reflected in the Movie Function menu as well. You are free to change any of those to a different value if you want something different from what you've specified in the Stills Function menu. By default, however, the SteadyShot setting will include a movie camera symbol, indicating that a different adjustment is made for movie shooting.

This entry allows you to change the function of any of the 12 positions in either Function menu, so you can display only those you use most, and arrange them in the order that best suits you. There are 55 different functions available, plus Not Set. Browse through the lists and decide which 12 you want to display on the Function menu.

When you highlight Function Menu Set. and press OK, the screen shown in Figure 9.23 appears. The screen has an entry for each of the positions in the top row and bottom row, along with the current function with the still photo version at the top and movie Function menu at the bottom.

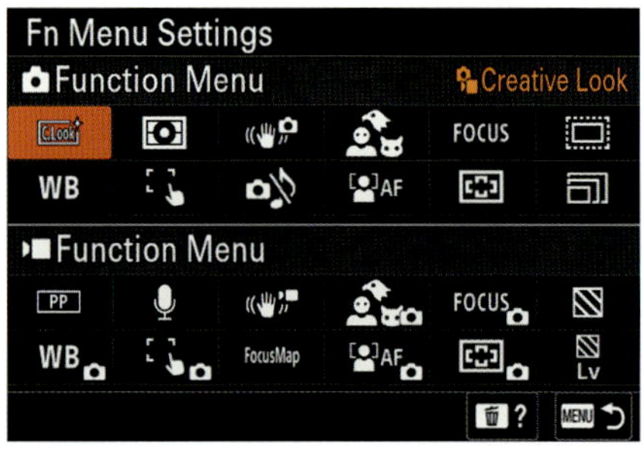

Figure 9.23 Function menu default settings.

Highlight the position you want to modify and press OK. All the available options are explained in detail elsewhere in this book.

Note that you can select Not Set to leave a position blank if you want to unclutter your screen, or even duplicate an entry in multiple positions, accidentally or on purpose. Don't underestimate the power of this function. You can, in effect, create your own pop-up Function menu using any of more than four *dozen* different functions.

Different Settings for Stills/Movies

Options: Enable: Aperture, Shutter Speed, ISO, Exposure Compensation, Metering Mode, White Balance, Picture Profile, Focus Mode

My preference: Enable all

Veteran still photographers moving into video soon discover that shooting movies requires a whole 'nother skill set. As you'll learn in Chapter 10, choice of shutter speed can be critical for different reasons when capturing video; focus modes and even white balance may be selected in different ways when shooting stills and movies. Sony gives your a7C II/a7CR the ability to use the same settings for stills and movies, or mandate different settings for your choice of parameters. The setting screen shown in Figure 9.24 displays a scrollable column listing Aperture, Shutter Speed, ISO, Exposure Compensation, Metering Mode,

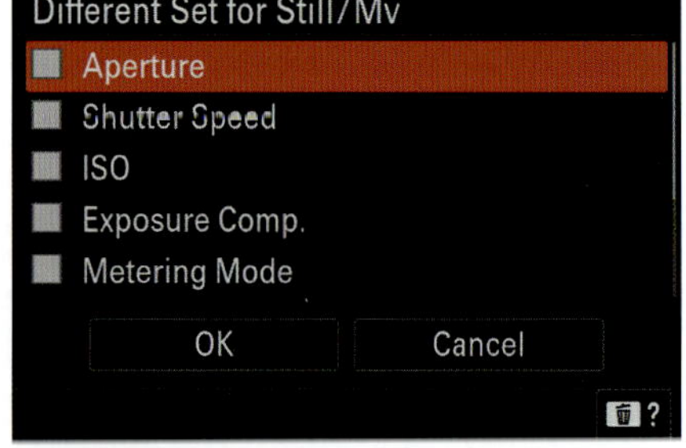

Figure 9.24 Different settings for still and movie shooting.

White Balance, Picture Profile, and Focus Mode, with a check box next to each. Highlight the setting you want to specify and press the center button to add or subtract a check mark. Then highlight OK to confirm, or Cancel to chicken out and press the center button again.

Display (Screen Display) Settings

Options (Monitor): Display All Info., No Disp. Info. (Exposure: On, Exposure: TimeOut), Histogram, Level, For Viewfinder, Monitor Off

Options (Viewfinder): Display All Info., No Disp. Info., Histogram, Level

My preference: Activate all

Use this item to specify which of the available display options will—and will not—be available in Shooting mode when you use the LCD or viewfinder and press the DISP button to cycle through the various modes. Choose from Monitor or Viewfinder and mark or unmark the screens you want to enable or disable. The Monitor selection includes a For Viewfinder option that displays a text/graphic display of your current settings on the back-panel LCD. (See Figure 9.25.)

You can use this menu item to deselect one or more of the display options, so it/they will never appear on the LCD when you press the DISP button. To make that change, scroll to an option and press the center button to add or remove the check mark beside it. A preview of the display screen is shown as a thumbnail. Naturally, at least one display option must remain selected. If you de-select all of them, the camera will warn you about this and it will not return to Shooting mode until you add a check mark to one of the options. If you turn the camera off while none are selected, the camera will interpret this as a Cancel command and return to your most recent display settings.

The viewfinder versions have some slight differences; for example, at the bottom of the viewfinder version is an analog exposure indicator. You can select a different set of displays for the viewfinder and monitor. That is, you can choose to view the plain-vanilla No Display Info view in the EVF and Display All Info on the LCD monitor. Here's a recap of the available display options for the monitor:

- **Display All Info.** The default screen when you first turn the camera on, this option displays data about current settings for a complete overview of recording information. Not all the information in the figure may be displayed at one time, and there are additional icons not shown because they occupy the same space on the screen as another indicator.

- **No Disp. Info.** Despite its name, this display option provides the basic exposure information settings, in a conventional size. Select Exposure: On and the exposure information will remain

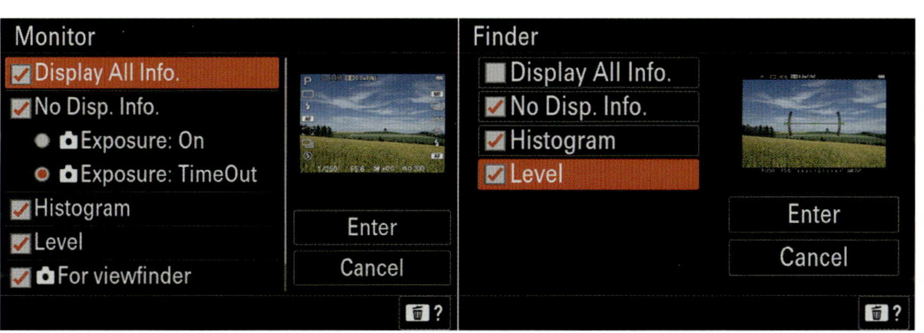

Figure 9.25 Display Screen settings for Monitor (left) and Finder (right).

visible; with the Exposure: TimeOut choice, the exposure information will vanish after a few seconds.

- **Histogram.** Activate this option if you want to be able to view a live luminance histogram to assist you in evaluating the exposure before taking a photo. The basic shooting data will appear in addition to the histogram.

- **Level.** This display shows how much the camera is rotated around the lens axis (horizontal tilt) as well as how far it is adjusted forward and backward (vertical tilt). When the camera is not perfectly level, orange indicators show the amount of vertical (forward/backward) and horizontal tilt. (See Figure 9.26, left.) When the camera is level in both directions, the indicators turn green. (See Figure 9.26, right.)

- **For Viewfinder.** This display can be shown only on the LCD monitor. When visible, you can press the Fn button to produce the For Viewfinder's "Quick Navi" settings screen, as explained in Chapter 2.

- **Monitor Off.** You must scroll down to see this choice. When this option is selected, pressing the DISP button eventually takes you to a blank monitor screen, which you might need to use when a brightly lit LCD is distracting or intrusive.

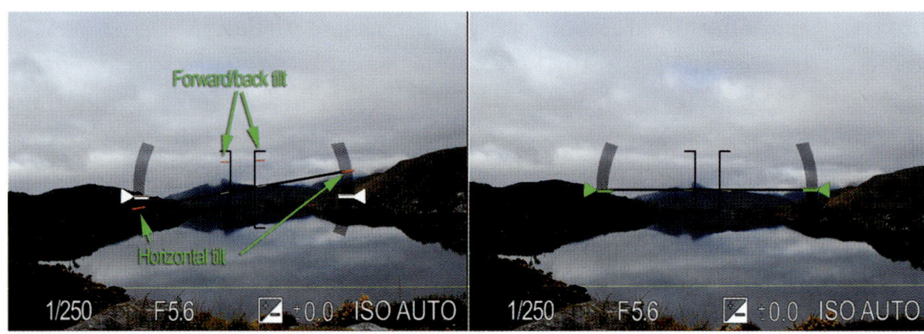

Figure 9.26 The Level display shows how much the camera is rotated around the lens axis.

(Movie) Record with Shutter

Options: On, *Off
My preference: Off

Your a7C II and a7CR give you the option of using the shutter release to start and stop shooting movies as an alternate to the Movie button located to the right of the viewfinder. Select On, and either button can be used; choose Off, and only the movie button will activate/stop movie capture. It's usually easier to find the shutter release, which is larger and located on top of the camera, when your eye is up to the viewfinder. It's easy to press the AF-ON button by mistake. If your current session will be confined to video capture, you'll probably decide that using the shutter button will be more convenient.

I like this option when I am capturing movies hand-held. If the camera is mounted on a tripod and I am generally framing, composing, or focusing using the LCD monitor, I'll usually use either the Movie button or a remote release to stop/start video capture. (The latter helps avoid camera motion from "stabbing" the Movie button with a finger.)

Zoom Ring Rotate 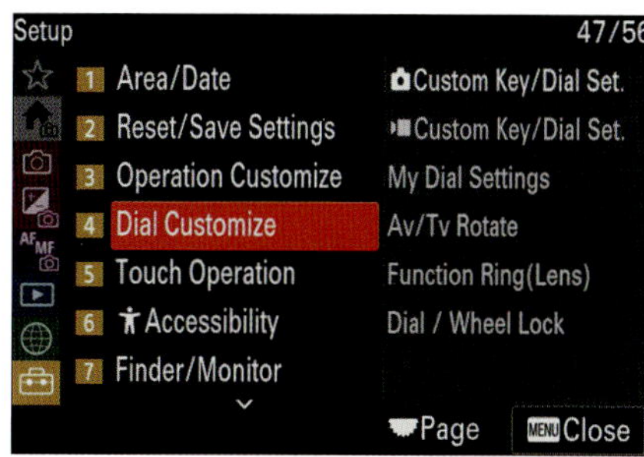

Options: *Left/Right (Wide-Tele)**, Right/Left (Wide-Tele)

My preference: N/A

This setting controls whether power zooming (with PZ-designated lenses that have a power zoom feature) proceeds from wide-angle to telephoto settings when the zoom control is pressed from left to right, or in the reverse direction, from right to left. The setting is compatible only with power zoom lenses that support this feature.

4. Dial Customize

The Dial Customize group has six settings that let you specify settings for the front dial, rear dials, and the control wheel. (See Figure 9.27.)

- Custom Key/Dial Settings (Stills)
- Custom Key/Dial Settings (Movies)
- My Dial Settings
- Av/Tv Rotate
- Function Ring (Lens)
- Dial/Wheel Lock

Figure 9.27 The Dial Customize group.

(Stills) Custom Key/Dial Settings /
(Movies)Custom Key/Dial Settings

Options: Define custom keys and dials

My preference: N/A

These two entries more or less duplicate the Custom Key/Dial Settings entries described above, except that summoning either takes you directly to the stills and movie versions of the Dial/Wheel setting screen with the settings for the front dial, both rear dials, and control wheel.

My Dial Settings

Options: Allows temporarily changing the functions of the control dials or control wheel.

My preference: N/A

This is an extremely versatile feature, which allows you to *temporarily* assign a different behavior to the control wheel and/or front and rear control dials, and still return them to their default functions easily. You can register three different sets of definitions.

Most of the time in shooting mode, you'll want to use the wheel/dial to control shutter speed or aperture. But a quick spin of the dial/wheel can be convenient for making other settings, such as ISO or white balance adjustments. You can assign that alternate function to one of those controls here in registers called My Dial 1, My Dial 2, and My Dial 3, and then recall any of those by pressing a custom key that you've defined using the Operation Customize features described earlier.

When you access this entry, a screen similar to the one shown in Figure 9.28 appears. The left column shows the front dial, rear dial left, rear dial right, and control wheel. The right-most three columns show the current values for the three definitions for My Dial 1, My Dial 2, or My Dial 3. Before you have added any definitions, each of the current settings will be Not Set, represented by double-dashes like the ones in the right-most column in the figure.

Note that each of the three My Dial settings can define actions for the front dial, two rear dials, and control wheel,

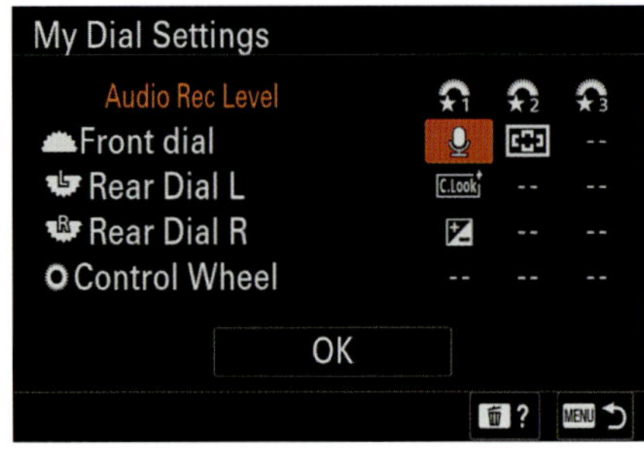

Figure 9.28 My Dial Settings.

but you do not have to define a function for all four. For example, you could use My Dial 1 to assign a particular function to the control wheel, but leave the front and rear dials at Not Set (which means they would retain their default behaviors).

To assign a definition, just follow these steps:

1. **Access Setup > Dial Customize > My Dial Settings.** The settings screen appears.
2. **Choose Select My Dial 1, 2, or 3 registers.** Use the left/right directional buttons to highlight the My Dial 1, My Dial 2, or My Dial 3 columns.
3. **Select Control to Define.** Use the up/down directional buttons to choose from Front Dial, Rear Dial L, Rear Dial R, or Control Wheel within the My Dial column you've selected.
4. **Press the center button.** A set of screens will appear with seven pages that encompass the 16 possible functions (plus Not Set) that can be assigned to the control you've highlighted:

   Shooting Tab
   - Audio Recording Level

   Exposure Tab
   - Av/Tv (Av in M mode)
   - Av/Tv (Tv in M mode)
   - Aperture
   - Shutter Speed
   - Shutter Speed (Step)
   - ISO
   - Exposure Compensation
   - White Balance
   - White Balance (Color Temperature)
   - Creative Look

   Focus Tab
   - Focus Area
   - Move AF Frame Left/Right (Standard)
   - Move AF Frame Left/Right (Large)
   - Move AF Frame Up/Down (Standard)
   - Move AF Frame Up/Down (Large)

   Setup Tab
   - Operation Customize: Not Set

5. **Press the center button to confirm.** You can then repeat steps 2 to 4 to define additional My Dial registers.
6. **Highlight OK.** Press OK to exit.

7. **Assign My Dial 1, 2, or 3 to a custom key.** Use the Custom Key/Dial Settings (Stills) entry described earlier to assign the temporary behavior to the button you will use to switch to the alternate function. You have three different modes for activating the feature:

- **My Dial 1 (or 2, or 3) During Hold.** When you press the assigned custom key, the alternate function for the specified My Dial register is active. As soon as you release it, the wheel/dial resumes its default function.

- **My Dial 1-> 2-> 3.** When you press and hold the Custom Key, rotating that control switches among each of the registers in turn, and then wraps around to the first. Think of this as a meta-control: instead of activating a particular My Dial register and its settings, it allows you to quickly cycle among all three of them, each with their own set of settings. I suspect only those who truly need a larger number of alternate actions for the control wheel and control dial will really need this (and I don't envy them the learning curve required to remember which My Dial settings contain which customized functions).

- **Toggle My Dial 1 (or 2, or 3).** The specified My Dial register is activated when the custom key is pressed, and deactivated when the custom key is pressed again. Use this if you need to turn on particular features for a period of time, and then return to the controls' default operation with a second key press.

Av/Tv Rotate 📷 🎬 S&Q

Options: *Normal, Reverse
My preference: N/A

This entry lets you specify the direction of rotation of the front dial, rear dials, plus the control wheel when using them to adjust the aperture or shutter speed. When the default Normal is in effect, rotating the appropriate dial clockwise produces a smaller f/stop or faster shutter speed; rotating counterclockwise sets a larger f/stop or slower shutter speed. Choose Reverse, and clockwise rotation sets a larger f/stop or slower shutter speed, while counterclockwise produces a smaller f/stop or faster shutter speed. This is a personal preference setting, often invoked by those who are migrating to the Sony world from another platform that defaults dial rotation to the opposite direction.

Function Ring (Lens) 📷 🎬 S&Q

Options: Power Focus, APS-C/Super 35–Full frame Select
My preference: N/A

Sony has begun introducing lenses with an additional "Function" control ring, including the FE 400mm f/2.8 GM (SEL400F28GM) and FE 600mm f/4 GM OSS, which ring in at roughly $12,000 and $13,000, respectively. The more affordable FE 100-400 f/4-5.6 GM OSS also comes with a function ring. An accompanying select switch on these lenses has three positions: Preset, Function, and Off. This entry specifies what will happen when the Function control ring is set to the Function position. (It has no effect when Preset or Off settings are chosen.)

Here's a quick explanation of all three positions, and the two options available with this entry:

- **Preset.** In this position, pressing the SET button on the lens memorizes a desired focus point. The present focus plane can be recalled instantly using the function ring. That's an important feature for sports photography and other scenes with rapid movement. Importantly, the preset focus point can be specified and recalled whether the photographer is using autofocus or manual focus, and can be outside any focus limit range currently active.

- **Function.** In this position, the function ring can be assigned a specific function.
  - The Power Focus function uses focus-by-wire technology to move the focusing plane toward infinity when the function ring is rotated to the right, and closer when the function ring is rotated to the left. However, the speed at which focus is adjusted is determined by the amount of function ring rotation. This allows smooth focus shift for movies. Think of it as power "zoom" for focusing.
  - The APS-C/Super 35–Full Frame Select function switches quickly between cropped and full-frame modes, allowing you to make the adjustment using a lens control rather than using the menus or a custom-defined key on the camera body.

- **Off.** The function ring does nothing.

Dial/Wheel Lock

Options: *Unlock, Lock

My preference: Unlock

If you want to avoid accidentally changing settings by inadvertently using the front dial, either rear dial, or control wheel, you can implement this locking option. Choose Lock and the specified controls are frozen whenever the Fn button is pressed and held down for three seconds. A "Locked" indicator appears on the screen. If the default Unlock option is selected, pressing the Fn button has no effect on the controls. **Note:** You can also lock all buttons, dials, and wheels (except for the shutter release) by holding down the MENU and Fn buttons for five seconds. Hold them down again for five seconds to unlock the controls.

5. Touch Operation

The Touch Operation group has four settings that let you specify how your back-panel LCD monitor responds to touch gestures. (See Figure 9.29.)

- Touch Operation
- Touch Panel/Pad
- Touch Panel Settings
- Touch Pad Settings

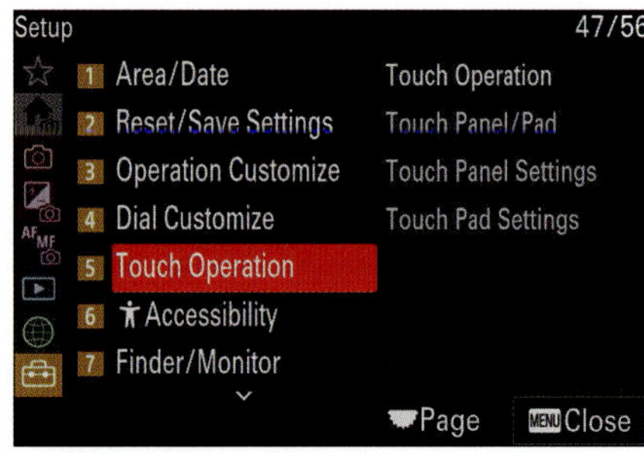

Figure 9.29 Touch Operation group.

Touch Operation 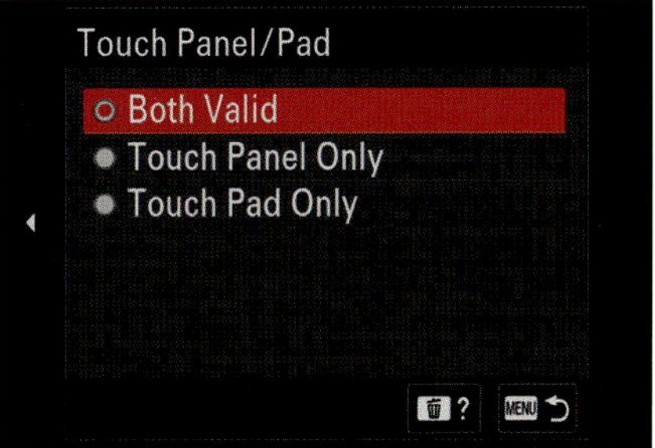

Options: *On, Off

My preference: On

This entry allows you to enable/disable the touch functions of the LCD monitor. Choose On if you plan on using the spot focusing and tracking features, particularly for video.

Touch Panel/Pad

Options: Both Valid, *Touch Panel Only, Touch Pad Only

My preference: Both Valid

As I described in Chapter 2, the a7C II and a7CR have a touch-sensitive LCD. With this setting, you can define whether the LCD-oriented Touch Panel or EVF-oriented Touch Pad, or *both* are active. The dual screen/pad modes are used because the touch feature can be used in two different ways: as a touch *screen* or *panel* when you are using the LCD monitor to compose your photos, and as a touch *pad* that you can tap when the camera is raised to your eye and you're using the electronic viewfinder. (See Figure 9.30.)

Figure 9.30 Choose the touch-sensitive area of the LCD monitor.

Unfortunately, the touch features are limited to the ability to specify a focus *point* when shooting stills and videos. You still have to press the shutter release halfway or the AF-ON button (or other defined key) to initiate focus. You can't select menu entries, type in text, scroll through playback views, or pinch/expand with your fingertips to zoom in and out during image review. However, the touch focus feature is quite useful, especially when shooting movies, as it allows selecting a focus area with a gentle tap. There are two modes:

- **Touch screen.** When active and you're using the LCD monitor to compose, you can select a focus point or zone anywhere that the a7C II or a7CR is able to achieve autofocus (that is, most of the frame other than the edges). You can tap the screen or hold down your finger and slide the focus area around. Cancel your focus selection by pressing the center button. A quick tap may not register; this function requires a firm press. I'll explain the various AF-area modes in Chapter 8.

- **Touch pad.** When touch pad mode is active and you're using the electronic viewfinder to compose, you can touch the LCD monitor screen to specify the focus area. You don't have to tap the exact area (actually, that's impossible, because you're not actually looking at the LCD). Instead, when you touch the pad, a focus point appears in the viewfinder *relative to the location on the LCD.* That is, if you tap the center of the sensitive area, the focus point appears in the center; tap to the right or left, and the focus area appears to the right or left side. As I'll explain shortly, that mode is needed because you can change the size of the sensitive area of the LCD screen. Once the focus area is displayed, keep your finger on the screen and slide it around to the position you want, using your view through the EVF as your reference.

Select whether you want the touch screen *and* touch pad, or only one to be used, depending on your preference.

Touch Panel Settings 📷 🎬 S&Q

Options: Shooting Screen, Footer Icon Touch, Swipe Right, Swipe Left, Swipe Up, Touch Functions in Shooting, Icon When Monitor Flipped; Playback Screen: *On, Off; Menu Screen: *On, Off

My preference: N/A

Sony has added some options you can select when using the rear LCD screen as a touch panel. See Figure 9.31, left. Note that these settings are ignored when Touch Operation (described above) is set to Off, or when Touch Panel/Pad is set to Touch Pad Only. In other words, don't expect your touch panel settings to be in force when the touch panel itself is not available.

Figure 9.31 Touch panel settings.

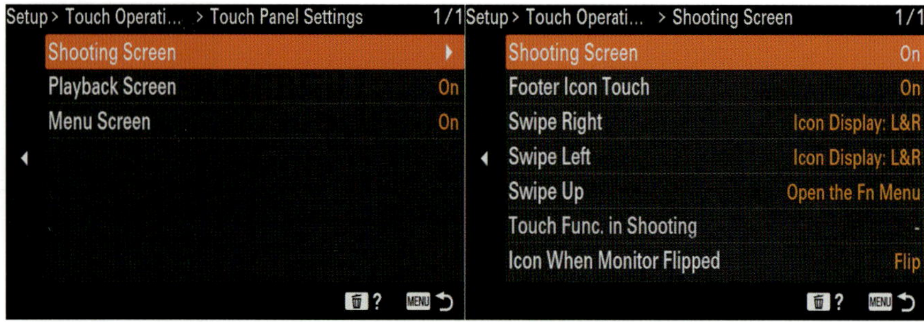

There are separate settings for Shooting Screen, Playback Screen, and Menu Screen. The seven options for the Shooting screen are shown at right in Figure 9.31:

- **Shooting Screen.** Enables/disables touch operations on the shooting screen for stills and movies.
- **Footer Icon Touch.** Enables/disables touch operations for the exposure control footer icons that appear at the bottom of some shooting screens.
- **Swipe Right.** Determines which icons appear when you use the swipe-right gesture. Select from Icon Display: Left, Icon Display: Left/Right, and Off.
- **Swipe Left.** Determines which icons appear when you use the swipe-left gesture. Select from Icon Display: Right, Icon Display: Left/Right, and Off.
- **Swipe Up.** Determines whether you can summon the Function menu by swiping up. Select from Open the Fn Menu or Off.
- **Touch Function in Shooting.** Determines what happens when you touch a subject on the screen. A screen appears with a scrolling list of five options:
  - **Touch Focus/Touch Focus+AE.** When the Touch Focus icon is highlighted, you can press the left/right directional buttons to toggle between Touch Focus (only) or Touch Focus+AE, which combines touch focus and automatic exposure lock. An adjustment bar will appear that allows you to fine-tune brightness.

When either Touch Focus option is enabled, you can tap the LCD screen and select a focus point or zone. The camera will focus at that point. Or slide your finger around the screen to move the focus area around within the frame. You can do this whether composing on the LCD monitor or looking through the viewfinder. In manual focus mode, a double-tap on the LCD activates the focus magnifier.

In autofocus mode, the a7C II/a7CR will focus when you press the shutter release down halfway. You can deactivate touch focus by pressing the center button, or by tapping the "cancel focus" icon (a pointing finger with an X next to it) that appears at upper right on the screen. A quick tap may not register; this function requires a firm press.

This mode is not available for autofocus activation when Focus Area is set to Flexible Spot or Expand Flexible Spot, but you can still move the focus frame around. In Movie mode, Spot Focus can be used with the LCD only. Touch Focus is not available when using Digital Zoom or with A-mount lenses when using the LA-EA2 or LA-EA4 adapters.

- **Touch tracking/Touch Tracking+AE.** When the Touch Tracking icon is highlighted, you can press the left/right directional buttons to toggle between simple Touch Tracking or Touch Tracking+AE, which combines the two. In this mode, you can specify a subject that will be tracked by tapping the LCD monitor. Tracking will start and continue until you press the center button or tap the Cancel Tracking icon in the upper-right corner of the LCD monitor. The camera will focus on the tracked subject when you press the shutter release down halfway. Note that this feature is not available in Manual Focus modes; with Smart, Clear Image, or Digital zoom features; and when using the LA-EA2 or LA-EA4 lens adapters. It is also disabled in Movie mode when Record Setting is set to 120p/100p.

- **Touch Shutter/Touch Shutter+AE.** When the Touch Shutter icon is highlighted, you can press the left/right directional buttons to toggle between simple Touch Tracking or Touch Tracking+AE, which combines the two. If you select this mode, touching the LCD screen takes a picture, *or* uses Spot metering to calculate and lock exposure and then take a picture. It's not available when Spot, Flexible Spot, Expand Flexible Spot, or their Tracking counterpart focus areas are enabled.

- **Touch AE.** Touch the screen to calculate exposure using Spot metering at the position you tapped.

- **Off.** Disables all Touch Function in Shooting options.

- **Icon When Monitor Flipped.** When the monitor is flipped forward ("selfie mode") the LCD image is reversed, so you appear to yourself as you do in a mirror. Choose Flip or Do Not Flip to specify whether the touch function icons are swapped as well. As I write this, the screen doesn't always conform to the setting. Look for a firmware update to fix it.

The Playback Screen and Menu Screen options have only On and Off choices, allowing you to enable or disable touch operations on the Playback and Menu screens, respectively. I ordinarily allow touch operations to remain enabled for both; the ability to zoom in on an image during review and move around within the frame is useful, and touch gestures can significantly speed up menu navigation. Note that turning touch operations off for the Menu screen *does not* disable touch control on the Fn menu.

Touch Pad Settings

Options: Operation in Vertical Orientation: ***On**, Off; Touch Position Mode: ***Absolute Position**, Relative Position; Operation Area: Whole screen, ***Right half**, Right quarter, Upper right, Lower right, Left half, Left quarter, Upper left, Lower left

My preference: N/A

Additional settings that relate only to the touch pad configuration can be selected from this menu entry:

- **Operation in Vertical Orientation.** Here you can specify whether touch controls are available when the camera is oriented in the vertical position (On), or only when the camera is held in horizontal orientation (Off).

- **Touch Position Mode.** Choose Absolute Position, to allow you to quickly move the focusing frame to a distant position on the LCD. This setting automatically changes the Operation Area (described next) to encompass the full screen. Use Relative Position to move the focus point relative to the location on the LCD.

- **Operation Area.** By default, the entire touch pad is sensitive when using the EVF. However, if your *ocular dominance* favors your left eye (i.e., you're "left-eyed"), you may be more comfortable choosing an active area on the left side of the screen that avoids contact with your nose. The "relative" orientation remains the same, but is limited to that reduced area. However, if you selected Absolute Position for the Touch Position Mode above, the entire screen is used, regardless of your setting here. (See Figure 9.32.)

Figure 9.32 Choose the touch-sensitive area of the LCD monitor.

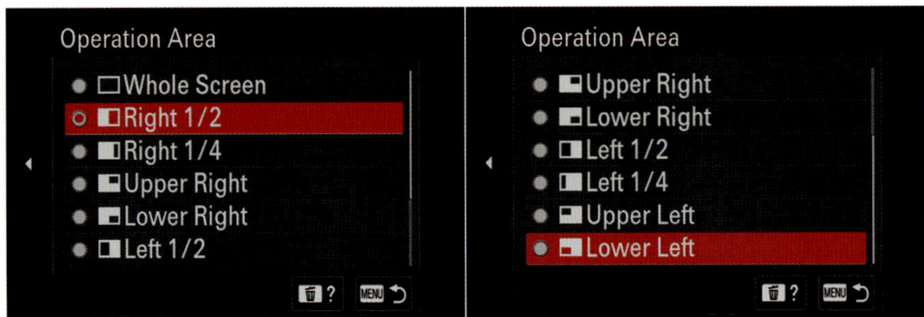

6. Accessibility

The Accessibility group has only two entries: Screen Reader and Enlarge Screen. The former is a doozy if you happen to have an application that involves having your camera read menu settings to you and the feature's limitations don't bother you.

- Screen Reader
- Enlarge Screen

Screen Reader 📷 🎥 S&Q

Options: Screen Reader: On, ***Off**; Speed: Fast 1–3, ***Standard**, Slow 1–2; Volume (0–15), MENU Long Press to Switch: ***Off**, On

My preference: N/A

You can bring your camera to life, like Frosty the Snowman, and you don't need a magic hat. However, you must have an a7C II or a7CR sold in North America and set to English. With that combination, set your camera to read menu listings to you in a clear voice provided by Siri and Alexa's third cousin. I suspect this entry is an exploration into additional accessibility options to come, as it needs a bit of work. Not all screens and menus—such as the Fn menu—are read out. Those who are visually impaired to the extent that reading the camera's menus is difficult may find this feature useful. When activated, a pleasant female voice will track your navigation through the menu system by telling you where you are and the parameters of each setting that you make.

You can turn the feature on or off, adjust the reading speed, and set the volume. (See Figure 9.33.)

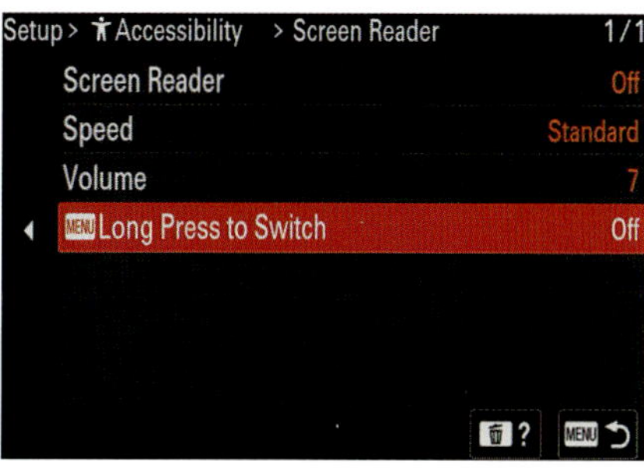

Figure 9.33 Settings for the Screen Reader feature.

Enlarge Screen 📷 🎥 S&Q

Options: Enlarge Menu Screen: ***Off**, On (Custom Button 1); Magnification: ***1.5X**, 2.0X, ***2.5X**

My preference: N/A

Those who have difficulty seeing menu entries on the rear LCD monitor can have the camera provide 1.5X, 2.0X, or 2.5X enlarged views at the press of a custom button. Use this entry to turn the feature on or off, and choose the combination of magnifications you want available. By default, 1.5X and 2.5X magnifications will be activated, but you can specify all three, or any combination thereof.

Once activated, you can cycle through menu magnifications and back to the original 1X view by pressing the C1 button, which is redefined to the Enlarge Screen function when the feature is enabled. While the menu is enlarged you can scroll around within the menu's contents using the front dial/control wheel to move left or right and either rear dial to move up or down. The up/down/left/right directional buttons navigate among entries, when Setup > Touch Operation and Setup > Touch Operation > Touch Panel Settings are both set to On. If you find yourself needing to get close to the LCD monitor to review the menus, you'll want to adjust Setup > Finder/Monitor > Select Finder/Monitor to Monitor (Manual) to avoid having the screen switch to the viewfinder as your face approaches. The camera will offer to make this setting for you, set it later, or stop reminding you.

7. Finder/Monitor

The Finder/Monitor group has seven settings that let you specify the characteristics and selection of your viewfinder and LCD monitor displays. (See Figure 9.34.)

- Select Finder/Monitor
- Monitor Brightness
- Viewfinder Brightness
- Finder Color Temperature
- Display Quality
- Finder Frame Rate
- Monitor Flip Direction

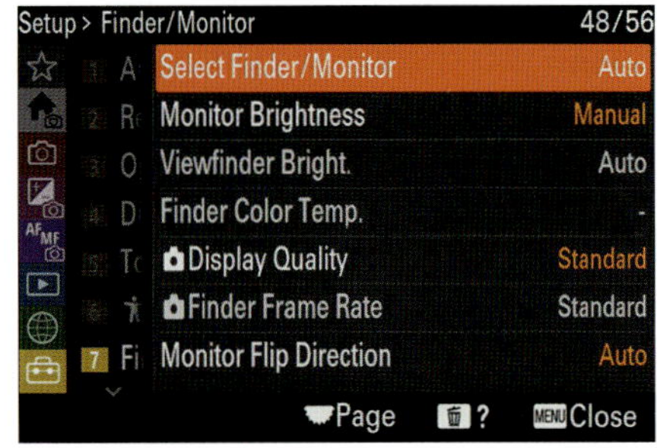

Figure 9.34 Finder/Monitor group.

Select Finder/Monitor

Options: *****Auto**, Viewfinder (Manual), Monitor (Manual)

My preference: Auto; then define a Custom Key to perform Monitor Off

This uses the infrared eye sensor located to the right of the viewfinder window, but it controls only whether the camera turns off the LCD and switches the view to the viewfinder when your eye comes near the EVF. With the default setting of Auto, the screen goes blank and the viewfinder activates when your eye (or any other object) approaches the Eye-Start sensor. The eye sensor is *disabled* when you tilt the LCD monitor away from the camera body, presumably because in that mode you'll be working exclusively with the LCD and do not want the a7C II or a7CR to switch to viewfinder mode if your hand (or any other object) passes in front of the sensor.

Switch to the Viewfinder (Manual) or Monitor (Manual) options and the eye sensor no longer initiates a switch from one display to the other. The display is then *always* sent to the viewing device you selected, and the other one is turned off. You might want to use the Monitor (Manual) option if you are doing work involving critical focusing using the LCD, and as you examine the screen closely, your face will frequently be close to the back of the camera where the sensor might detect it. Or, perhaps, you are shooting at a concert or other venue where the bright LCD can be distracting to others. Choose Viewfinder (Manual), and the shooting preview, menus, photos displayed for review during playback, and so forth will be shown only in the EVF. The Viewfinder (Manual) mode has a useful power-saving feature: the viewfinder actually illuminates *only* when the eye sensor detects your face (or anything else) approaches the viewfinder. So, even if you leave your camera turned on for long periods (say, when shooting intermittently or during a long interval photography sequence), the viewfinder draws juice *only* when you're actually peering at the EVF.

Most of the time, however, it's easier to leave this setting on Auto, and use the Operations Customize functions explained earlier in this chapter to assign Finder/Monitor Selection to a Custom Key. Alternatively, you can activate the Monitor Off setting in Setup > Operation Customize > DISP (Screen Display) Settings > Monitor, and use the DISP button to cycle the LCD monitor off.

Monitor Brightness

Options: **Manual*, Sunny Weather

My preference: Manual

When you access this menu item, two controls appear. The first is a Brightness bar (shown just above the grayscale/color patches in Figure 9.35). It's set to Manual adjustment by default but press the center button and you can change it to Sunny Weather for a brighter display. You might resort to this setting if you're shooting outdoors in bright sun and find it hard to view the LCD even when shading it with your hand.

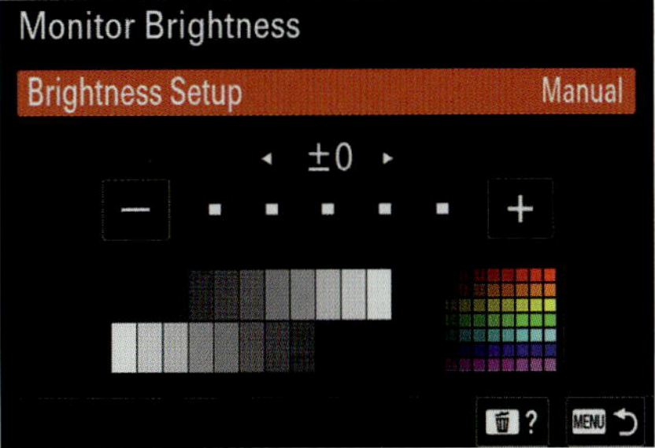

Figure 9.35 Adjust monitor brightness.

If you set it to Sunny Weather, the LCD brightness will automatically increase, making the display easier to view in very bright light. This makes the display unusually bright and less suitable for judging exposure and color, so use it only when it's really necessary. In such bright conditions, you're usually better off using the electronic viewfinder. Remember too that it will consume a lot more battery power, so have a spare battery available.

The grayscale steps and color patches can be used as you manually adjust the screen brightness using the left/right directional buttons. Scroll to the right to make the LCD display brighter or scroll to the left to make the LCD display darker, in a range of plus and minus 2 (arbitrary) increments. As you change the brightness, keep an eye on the grayscale and color chart to visualize the effect your setting will have on various tones and hues. The zero setting is the default and it provides the most accurate display in terms of exposure and color, but you might want to dim it when the bright display is distracting while shooting in a dark theater, perhaps. A minus setting also reduces battery consumption but makes your photos appear to be underexposed (too dark).

I prefer to choose Manual but then leave the display at the zero setting. This ensures the most accurate view of scene brightness on the LCD for the best evaluation of exposure while previewing the scene before taking a photo. When shooting 4K video or 120/100 fps video, the Monitor Brightness setting is ignored.

Viewfinder Brightness

Options: **Auto*, Manual

My preference: Manual+1

This entry is similar to the Monitor Brightness control but adds an Auto setting that adjusts the viewfinder's output based on the camera's reading of the ambient light falling on the full-frame sensor. No Sunny Weather option is available, but I still like a slightly brighter viewfinder, so I prefer Manual with a +1 boost. A notice will appear on the LCD monitor advising you to look through the viewfinder and make your settings. When shooting 4K video or 120/100 fps video, the Monitor Brightness setting is ignored.

Finder Color Temperature 📷 🎥 S&Q

Options: +2 to –2 ; Default: **0**

My preference: N/A

While looking through the viewfinder, press the left/right buttons to adjust the color balance of the finder to make it appear warmer (using the left button) or colder/bluer (using the right button), according to your preference. This setting affects only what you see; it does not change the color balance of the captured photo or video.

Display Quality 📷 🎥 S&Q

Options: **Standard*, High

My preference: Standard

Two parameters determine the quality of the image you see through the viewfinder. This one determines the resolution of the image, while the one that follows, Finder Frame Rate, determines how many frames per second are displayed. I prefer Standard, because it uses a *lot* less battery power and the difference between Standard Quality and High Quality is hard to spot. Note that this entry is available *only* when the Finder Frame Rate is set to Standard.

Finder Frame Rate 📷 🎥 S&Q

Options: **Standard*, High

My preference: Standard

To reduce a slight jerkiness in the EVF when shooting action, you can switch from the default Standard (60 fps) frame rate to a blistering High (120 fps) rate that displays fast-moving subjects more smoothly. The tradeoff is a reduced resolution view at the highest frame rate. That's because at the High setting, Display Quality is forced to Standard. Standard is also automatically invoked when reviewing images or video in playback mode, when viewing using an HDMI connection, or when the temperature inside the camera body is high. I tend to stick with the higher-resolution Standard frame rate, except when tracking sports or action subjects.

Monitor Flip Direction 📷 🎥 S&Q

Options: **Auto*, Horizontal Flip, 180 Degree Flip, No Flip

My preference: Auto

The a7C II/a7CR's accommodation for using the LCD monitor in front-facing ("selfie") mode is not as straight-forward as you might think. When the monitor is reversed, the image is flipped side-to-side. The net result is that the display shows you as you normally see yourself in a mirror. The photos you take are not affected in any way; only the displayed image. In practice, however, you may want some other orientation. For example, words within the frame (on signs and such) are reversed in selfie mode, making them difficult to read for some (me). At times you may need to have the camera at an odd orientation, such as upside down, for a particular reason. While the Auto setting works most of the time, you can choose Horizontal Flip (the LCD is *always* in "mirror" mode), 180 Degree Flip (the image is always inverted but shown in non-mirror mode), or No Flip (the display remains the same regardless of how you rotate or flip the LCD).

8. Display Option

The Display Option group has three settings that let you specify parameters for Time Code/User Bits, and how the display handles gamma settings specified using Picture Profiles. Three additional settings control useful displays while shooting or using image review features. (See Figure 9.36.)

- TC/UB Display Settings
- Gamma Display Assist
- Gamma Display Assist Type
- Display LUT
- Remaining Shooting Display
- (Images) Auto Review
- Shooting Mode Selection Screen

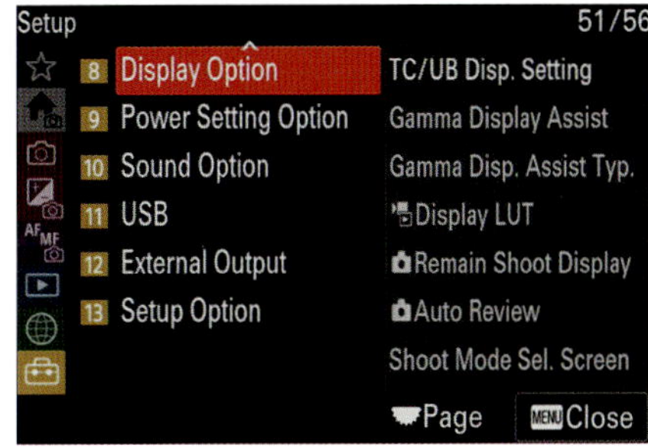

Figure 9.36 Display Option group.

TC/UB Display Settings

Options: *Counter, TC, U-Bit

My preference: N/A

The Time Code (TC) and User Bit (U-Bit) settings are information that can be embedded and used to sync clips and sound when editing movies, especially those captured by multiple cameras. I'll describe this advanced feature in a little more detail in Chapter 11, including what each of the options do. This entry has nothing to do with what actually is *recorded* onto the Time Code track; it determines how the information is displayed during review.

- **Counter.** When this default value is chosen, the display will include the time counter, which starts at zero and is shown as H:MM:SS (hours, minutes, seconds).
- **TC.** The SMPTE (Society of Motion Picture and Television Engineers) time code is displayed as HH:MM:SS:00 (hours, minutes, seconds, frames, but the frames are always shown as 00).
- **U-Bit.** A system used in the past to embed a four-character string ("Userbit") on the video track used to identify the particular camera used to capture the video.

Gamma Display Assist

Options: *Off, On

My preference: N/A

As you'll learn in Chapter 10, the a7C II and a7CR are capable of recording movies using Picture Profiles. These profiles can use gamma correction to extend the dynamic range (range of tones from black to white) recorded during video capture. Movies captured using gamma profiles appear to be very low in contrast until processed using software on your computer. As a result, reviewing these clips in the camera can be difficult. This menu entry allows selecting options that will adjust the display of extended dynamic range clips so they appear *in the camera* with a more normal look, which is useful if you use live view to evaluate your captures. The display is not changed if you're viewing through a device such as an external monitor plugged into the HDMI port, and you'll still need to process the video in your video-editing software. With this entry, you can turn Gamma Display Assist off. This entry is not available if (Movie) Shooting > Image Quality/Recording > Log Shooting Setting is set to On.

Gamma Display Assist Type

Options: ***Auto**, S-Log3->709 (800%), HLG (BT.2020), HLG (709)
My preference: N/A

Specifies the type of gamma for which correction needs to be applied to correct for the low-contrast image that would be displayed without correction. Your options are:

- **Auto.** The a7C II and a7CR analyze the video and decide how to make the adjustment.
- **S-Log3->709 (800%).** An inverse gamma curve is applied.
- **HLG (BT.2020)/HLG (709).** A pair of high-dynamic-range standards created to allow display on HDR television displays.

Display LUT

Options: ***Off**, On
My preference: On

Tells the a7C II/a7CR to apply the current LUT (Look-up Table) in effect to provide a corrected preview of the video being displayed on the camera. You'll find discussions of LUTs in Chapters 10 and 11.

(Images) Remaining Shooting Display

Options: Always Display, Shoot-Only Display, ***Not Displayed**
My preference: Not displayed

This setting enables a remaining-shots indicator during continuous shooting, represented by a vertical bar on the left side of the display. Ostensibly, it will warn you when the buffer fills and continuous shooting will begin to slow down. It's mainly of use to rapid-fire sports photographers who capture long sequences. Most plays last only a few seconds, but I've encountered a few situations in football and soccer where exciting action can stretch out and tax the capabilities of even the speedy BIONZ XR processor and UHS-II storage with a fast memory card.

If you feel you need this capability, you can choose Always Display or Shoot-Only Display, in which the remaining shots bar appears only when the shutter release is pressed down halfway or all the way. When the buffer begins to fill, a SLOW icon will eventually be displayed on certain screens as the frame rate slows.

Auto Review 📷 🎬 S&Q

Options: 10 seconds, 5 seconds, 2 seconds, *Off
My preference: 2 seconds

In prehistoric times (pre–live view), it was necessary to review your photos from time to time to confirm that you were getting the images you wanted. All mirrorless cameras produce a WYSIWYG (what you see is what you get) view unless Setting Effect is turned off. So, there is much less need to review your images. Even so, I frequently set Auto Review to 2 seconds, so I can double-check my settings and framing. You can select reviews up to 10 seconds if you like. I sometimes use the longer review setting if I am taking shots of several groups in quick succession, so I can check to see if anyone had their eyes closed, and capture another shot before the next group moves in. The a7C II and a7CR automatically terminate the review of a given image when you press the shutter release to begin to focus or take the next picture, so you will never miss a shot. If given a more leisurely pace, however, it's more efficient to manually review my images, without any auto review.

Shooting Mode Selection Screen 📷 🎬 S&Q

Options: *Display, Not Displayed
My preference: Display

This setting determines whether a screen appears to allow you to select either Intelligent Auto or Scene Selection (when the mode dial is set to the Auto position), or whether a screen appears that allows you to choose between S&Q Motion or Time-lapse, when the Still/Movie/S&Qs dial is set to the S&Q position.

If you frequently use both Intelligent Auto or Scene modes, or find yourself working with both S&Q Motion and Time-lapse photography, retain the default Display setting so you can switch on the fly.

9. Power Setting Option

The Power Setting Option group has four settings that let you set parameters for certain features that can help make your battery last longer. (See Figure 9.37.)

- Auto Monitor OFF
- Power Save Start Time
- Power Save by Monitor
- Auto Power OFF Temperature

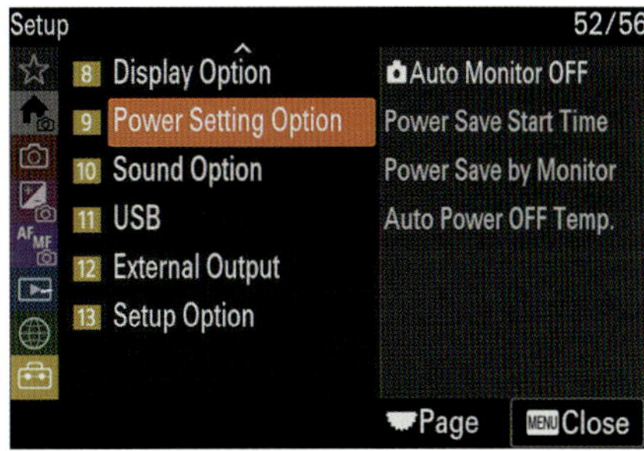

Figure 9.37 Power Setting Option group.

Auto Monitor Off

Options: *Does not turn off*, 2 seconds, 5 seconds, 10 seconds, 1 minute

My preference: 5 seconds; Does not turn off setting for macro photography

Although the NP-FZ100 battery is more powerful than the one Sony used in its first interchangeable-lens mirrorless cameras, you'll still want to avoid wasting juice. You can use this setting and the one that follows to control how your camera conserves power. This one specifies how long the back-panel LCD monitor stays illuminated while the camera is idle (it does not affect the viewfinder display). The setting does not affect the monitor when the Still/Movie/S&Q dial is set to the Movie or S&Q positions.

I generally leave this at 5 seconds for most shooting; conceivably if your battery is running low you might want to use the 2-second setting. Of course, because I always carry plenty of extra batteries with me, the only time I end up working with a nearly exhausted battery is when swapping would be badly timed (something important/crucial is about to happen), or I'm capturing a long video sequence. Keep in mind that only the monitor is turned off; the camera doesn't "go to sleep" until the Power Save Start Time, described next, has elapsed. So, if your monitor takes a break, you can revive it instantly by tapping the shutter-release button.

I find the best use of the Does Not Turn Off setting is when doing macro photography, because I typically use the LCD monitor for composing and focusing close-ups. It's convenient to have the monitor active for the entire time I am setting up my shot.

Power Save Start Time

Options: 30 minutes, 5 minutes, 2 minutes, *1 minute*, 10 seconds

My preference: 5 minutes

This item lets you specify the exact amount of time that should pass before the camera goes to "sleep" when the eye sensor under the viewfinder window, and a lack of recent button/dial activity, indicates you're not taking photos. The default of 1 minute is a short time, useful to minimize battery consumption. You can select a much longer time before the camera will power down, or a much shorter time. I use 5 minutes most of the time to avoid having to "waken" the camera frequently. Keep in mind that a lot of the idle power demand comes from the LCD monitor, so if you've used the entry above to specify a 2-, 5-, or 10-second shutoff time you can safely set a longer interval here.

If I'm wandering around with long periods of time between shots or the camera is mounted on a tripod, I may set it to 2 or 5 minutes. In street photography or sports mode, I use 30 minutes to make sure my camera will always be ready for action. But, of course, I tend to carry at least two spare batteries with me at all times, and in a pinch will use my RavPower 16,750 mAh power pack linked to the camera with a USB-C cable for long-term non-stop shooting.

You'll need to keep in mind that this setting will be ignored if the camera is linked to an external monitor or video recorder through the HDMI port, and shutoff will be postponed while you are uploading images over a Wi-Fi connection.

Power Save By Monitor

Options: *Both Linked*, Open: Return, Close: Power Save, Does Not Link

My preference: Close: Power Save

This item lets you send the a7C II or a7CR into power-save mode when the LCD monitor is closed. You have four options:

- **Both Linked.** The screen turns off when the monitor is closed facing inward (say, for protection). The monitor turns back on when you reverse it and open it again.
- **Open: Return.** The camera exits power-saving mode when the monitor is opened again.
- **Close: Power Save.** Close the monitor facing inward and the a7C II/a7CR automatically enters power-saving mode.
- **Does Not Link.** Power saving is not affected by the position of the monitor.

Auto Power Off Temperature

Options: *Standard*, High

My preference: High

Don't panic! Your a7C II or a7CR will not spontaneously combust. However, it *may* overheat if operated continuously (as when shooting 4K movies or you are using the High finder frame rate) for periods of time or with extended continued use. The a7C II/a7CR can turn itself off when its internal temperature gets too high, which is particularly useful if the camera is mounted on a tripod so that your hands don't feel the increasing warmth. Shooting 4K video, for example, can generate a lot of heat and deplete your battery rather quickly. This option allows you to stretch the safe operating time by switching from the default Standard mode to High (which allows operation when the camera is hotter than normal). Sony recommends not holding the camera in your hands when you've activated the High setting.

Sony says you should be able to shoot 4K video for up to two hours with the High setting, or 10 minutes with Standard. In practice, you generally won't exceed 10 minutes for most individual shots, but an unwanted cutoff can be annoying or disruptive, so I leave this setting on High for the most part.

10. Sound Option

The Sound Option group has four settings that let you specify how your camera emits sound during video playback. (See Figure 9.38, left.)

- Volume Settings
- 4 Channel Audio Monitoring
- Audio Signal (Shooting)
- Audio Signal (Start/End)

Figure 9.38 Sound Options Group (left); 4 Channel Auto Monitoring (right).

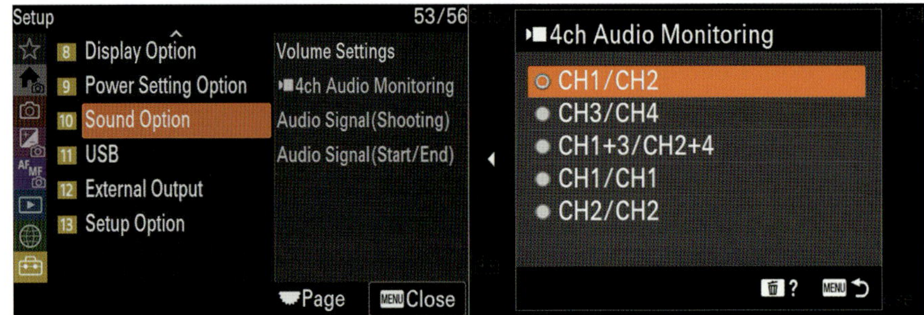

Volume Settings

Options: 0–15

My preference: 15

This menu item affects only the audio volume of movies that are being played back in the camera (and not the beeps or other noises the camera emits). When you select Volume Settings, the camera displays a scale of loudness from 0 to 15; scroll up/down to the value you want to set, and it will remain in effect until changed.

You might want to use this menu item to pre-set a volume level that you generally prefer. However, you can also adjust the volume whenever you're displaying a movie clip, to set it to just the right level. To do so, press the down directional button and use the up/down directional buttons to raise or lower the volume.

4 Channel Audio Monitoring

Options: *CH1/CH2, CH3/CH4, CH1+3/CH2+4, CH1/CH1, CH2/CH2

My preference: CH1+3/CH2+4

The Sony XLR-K3M audio kit is a pricey ($599) adapter that slides right into the multi-interface shoe so you can capture pro-quality sound. It includes a Sony ECM-XM1 stereo microphone (it *should* for that price), but if you *really* want to go pro, it also has two XLR-1/4-inch combination mic/line inputs so you can record quadraphonic sound. Your camera, however, can only play back two-channel, stereophonic sound through the headphone jack, so you'll need to decide which channels to play back to get the full audio picture. Channels 1 and 3 are considered the *left* side, while Channels 2 and 4 are considered the *right* side for headphones/speakers.

You can choose Channels 1/2 (left/right side), Channels 3/4 (left/right side), or listen only to either Channels 1 or 2 to provide monophonic playback. Your best bet is to combine Channels 1 and 3 (the two left sides) together, and merge Channels 2 and 4 (the two right sides) so, at least, you'll get a stereo version of all four channels captured. Obviously, if you're shooting stereo instead of quadraphonic, you don't need this feature. (See Figure 9.38, right.)

Audio Signal (Shooting)/Audio Signal (Start/End) 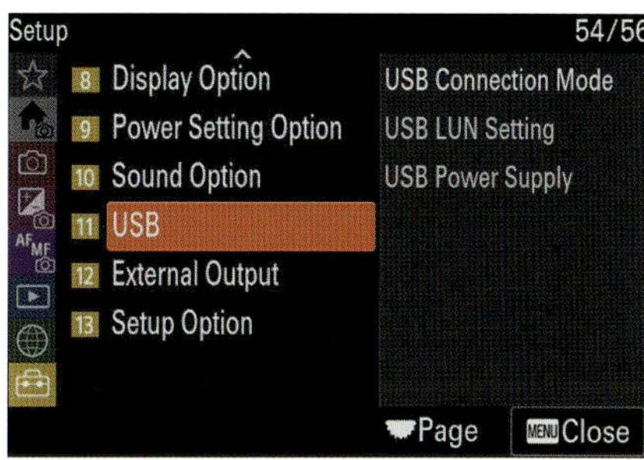

Options: *On, Off

My preference: Off for both.

These two entries enable and disable the beeping/chirping sounds the camera makes when various operations happen, such as achieving autofocus, during the self-timer countdown, or when the camera powers on or off. If the focus mode is set to Continuous AF, the camera will not beep when it has focused on a subject. Most of the time I don't require the feedback and, on the contrary, want to blend in without calling attention to myself, so I disable the noises. The self-timer countdown is especially noticeable, even in environments with a moderate amount of noise. Couple this setting with Silent Shooting (which automatically sets both to Off) and you can often take pictures virtually unnoticed. If you rely on beep in Continuous AF, consider leaving the Audio Signal (Shooting) entry set to On.

11. USB

The USB group has three settings that let you specify how the camera's USB port functions. (See Figure 9.39.)

- USB Connection Mode
- USB LUN Setting
- USB Power Supply

Figure 9.39 USB group.

USB Connection Mode

Options: *Select when connected, USB Streaming, Mass Storage (MSC), MTP, PC Remote

My preference: Select when connected

This entry allows you to select the type of USB connection protocol between your camera and computer.

- **Select when connected.** This setting lets you choose which of the following protocols to use each time you link your camera to the computer. Unless you typically perform only one function, you'll want to use this selection.
- **USB Streaming.** This is a new option, which enables your camera to perform video streaming using Imaging Edge Webcam and the streaming software of your choice.
- **Mass Storage (MSC).** In this mode, your camera appears to the computer as just another storage device, like a disk drive. You can drag and drop files between them. Lightroom workers will use this when transferring photos.

- **MTP.** This mode is short for Media Transfer Protocol, a slow system that is not used much today. It's a version of the PTP (Picture Transfer Protocol) that was standard in earlier cameras. It allowed better two-way communication between the camera and the computer.
- **PC Remote.** This setting is used with Sony's Imaging Edge software to adjust shooting functions and take pictures from a linked computer.

USB LUN Setting

Options: *Multi, Single

My preference: Multi, Single for Macs

This setting specifies how the camera selects a Logical Unit Number when connecting to a computer through the USB port. Normally, you'd use Multi with the USB Connection set to MTP; the camera will adjust the LUN automatically as necessary. If you've set USB Connection Mode (above) to Mass Storage, your memory in your camera will appear on your computer as an individual device, and a third "drive" will appear named PMHOME, a vestigial folder used only by the camera itself. Use Single to lock in a LUN if you have trouble making a connection between your camera and a particular computer or device. But don't worry, Single is generally required only for Macs.

USB Power Supply

Options: *On, Off

My preference: On

When set to On, the camera receives charging power from a connected computer or other device through the USB-C cable link. Use this setting if you want to charge the battery when connected to a computer or other device. Set to Off, and power is not supplied, except when using the AC Adapter furnished with your camera.

If you choose On and are connected to a computer, the USB Mode Mass Storage screen appears, with a Playback icon in the lower-right corner. If you ignore the prompt, the Playback icon will disappear after about five seconds and charging will *not* take place; your batteries are being depleted. If you *do* press the Playback button, followed by the center button, you'll be able to operate the camera while charging takes place.

You can set it to Off to completely avoid draining power from the computer host. Although I frequently connect my camera to a desktop computer, if I am using a laptop, I set this to Off, as I have plenty of NP-FZ100 batteries and recharging the laptop is sometimes inconvenient. You'll want to leave this On if you're using an external power pack or power source, but only if the source can supply sufficient juice to fully recharge (rather than trickle charge). Modern USB-C chargers are specifically designed to do this and may offer 100W of power, unlike chargers designed for most smartphones and tablets.

12. External Output

The External Output group has four settings that let you specify how your HDMI connection operates. (See Figure 9.40, left.)

- HDMI Resolution
- HDMI Output Settings
- HDMI Information Display
- Control For HDMI

HDMI Resolution

Options: *Auto, 2160p, 1080p, 1080i

My preference: Auto

The camera can direct its output to an external monitor or recorder, or for display on a high-definition television. This setting determines the resolution of that output when shooting still photos, or reviewing them during Playback. There is a separate resolution entry for movies within the HDMI Output Settings entry, described next.

The Auto setting will work about 99 percent of the time, as the a7C II and a7CR do a good job of identifying the HDMI specifications your external device needs. I formerly used an older BlackMagic Intensity Shuttle capture device to grab camera menu and screen displays. Some cameras I work with seem unable to detect in Auto mode that the BlackMagic device requires 1080i (interlaced) output, so I am glad I can specify it manually. I'm now using a Rybozen 4K Audio/Video USB 3.0 HDMI capture device and OBS Studio, a combination that works with every device I've tried it with.

But if you, too, sometimes have trouble getting the image to display correctly, try setting the resolution manually here to 2160p or 1080p (for 4K and Full HD), or 1080i. (See Figure 9.40, right.) If you do resort to setting the resolution manually, keep in mind that if you Reset or Initialize your camera, it will default back to Auto and you'll need to return here to restore your desired setting.

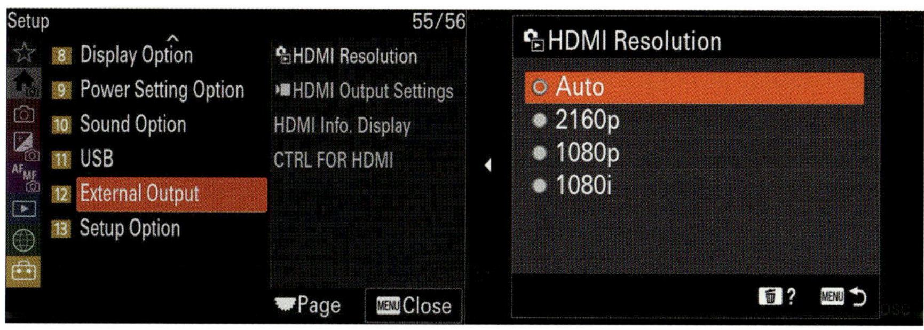

Figure 9.40 External Output group entries (left). HDMI Resolution (right).

HDMI Output Settings 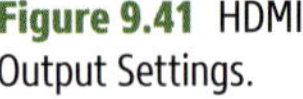

Options: Recording Media During HDMI Output, Output Resolution, 4K Output Settings (HDMI Only), RAW Output, RAW Output Setting, Time Code Output, Recording Control, 4ch Audio Output

My preference: N/A

This is a separate entry that determines how video output is directed to an external device. You can choose from eight parameters, but you probably won't need to use all of them. (See Figure 9.41.) Your options include:

- **Recording Media During HDMI Output.** Choose On (the default), and the camera will record video to your internal memory cards and also direct output to the HDMI port, to which you can connect a recorder or monitor. If you don't want/need backup, you can choose Off (HDMI Only) and output to the HDMI port and an attached recorder only. In that case, the HDMI Information Display setting, described shortly, becomes unavailable, and the in-camera counter of the actual recording time is not incremented.

- **Output Resolution.** Sets output resolution *only* when Recording Media During HDMI Output is set to On. This is otherwise a duplicate of the Stills/Playback version described above. You can choose from Auto (the default), 2160p, 1080p, or 1080i.

- **4K Output Settings (HDMI Only).** Determines the frame rate and depth of HDMI output when Recording Media During HDMI Output is set to Off (HDMI Only). You can select 60p/10-bit, 30p/10-bit, or 24p/10-bit when recording in 4K mode.

- **RAW Output.** You can choose On or Off to specify whether RAW movies are output to a RAW-compatible external device (such as a recorder) connected to the HDMI port.

- **RAW Output Setting.** Specifies the frame rate for RAW movies output through the HDMI port. You can choose 60/50p, 30/25p, or 24p.

- **Time Code Output.** Choose on or off to enable/disable including time code in the HDMI output signal. Use On if you are outputting to professional video equipment and want to include the time code information. Note that the time code is *data* and will not actually appear on the screen. If this setting is on and you are sending the signal to a television or some other device, the image may not appear properly. Change this setting to off when outputting to devices not equipped to handle TC information.

Figure 9.41 HDMI Output Settings.

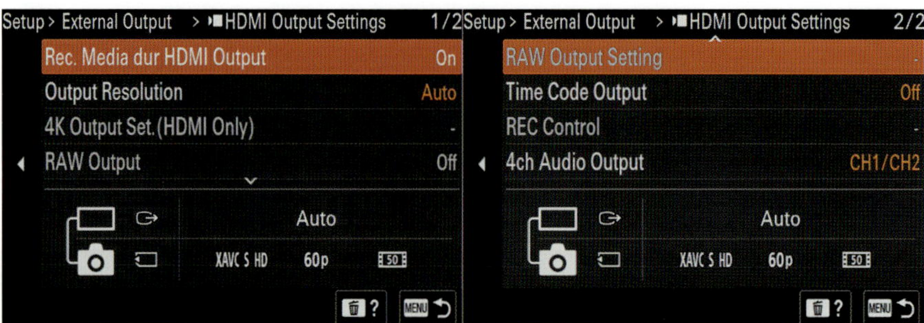

- **REC Control.** This setting is available only when TC Output is set to on. Choose on or off. The setting allows you to start and stop REC Control–compatible external video recorders connected to the camera. A REC or STBY icon will be displayed on the camera's screen as appropriate.

- **4ch Audio Output.** You can choose either CH1/CH2 or CH3/CH4. I described quadraphonic sound earlier within the 4 Channel Audio Monitoring entry.

HDMI Information Display

Options: *On, Off

My preference: On

Choose On if you want the shooting information to display when the camera is connected to an HDTV television/monitor or other device using an HDMI cable. For example, I left this setting On when capturing screenshots of live view images, so all the overlaid icons appear. Select Off if you don't want to show the shooting information on the display.

CTRL FOR HDMI

Options: *On, Off

My preference: Off

This option can be useful when you have connected the camera to a non-Sony HDTV and find that the TV's remote control produces unintended results with the camera. If that happens, try turning this option Off, and see if the problem is resolved. If you later connect the camera to a Sony Bravia sync-compliant HDTV (vendors other than Sony also use it), set this menu item back to On. Be aware that not all so-called Bravia-friendly devices conform completely, so you should be prepared to turn the function off if necessary.

13. Setup Option

The Setup Option group has settings that let you specify a few crucial setup parameters. (See Figure 9.42.)

- Video Light Mode
- Anti-dust Function
- Auto Pixel Mapping
- Pixel Mapping
- Version
- Display Serial Number
- Privacy Notice

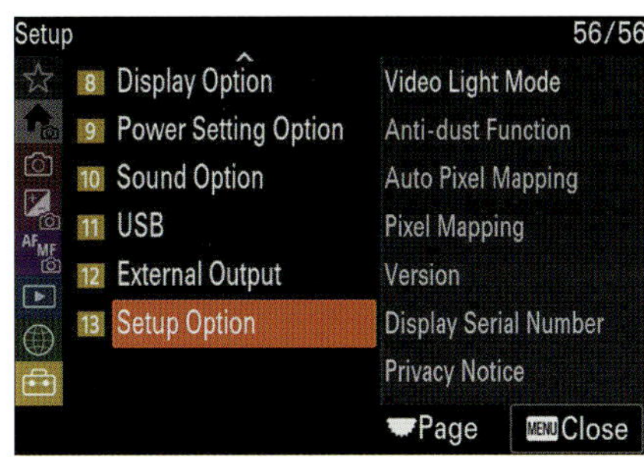

Figure 9.42 Setup Option group.

Video Light Mode 📷 🎥 S&Q

Options: ***Power Link**, REC Link, REC Link & Standby, Auto

My preference: Auto

Sony offers video lighting units for its camcorders and digital cameras, such as the HVL-LE1 (about $250), which is a battery-operated LED video light. This menu entry allows you to control when the light illuminates. Your choice is a matter of personal preference, depending on how you operate. Your choices are as follows:

- **Power Link.** Turns on when the camera is powered up, and off when the camera is powered down. Use this if you'll be shooting more or less continually and don't need to save battery power between sequences. Pro videographers will usually want to use this setting.

- **REC Link.** Video light turns on when movie recording starts, and off when you stop capture. This setting will preserve your battery. I like to use it when I definitely want to use the video light at all times during movie capture, such as when I am shooting exclusively indoors, or am outdoors and want some fill light to illuminate shadows for close-ups.

- **REC Link & STBY.** Illuminates when movie capture is underway and dims at other times. Operates like the previous choice but stretches the life of your battery.

- **Auto.** The video light turns on under dim lighting conditions. You might want to use this if you intend to shoot movies under both dim and bright lighting conditions (say, indoors and out) and want the light to come on only under reduced illumination.

Anti-dust Function 📷 🎥 S&Q

Options: Sensor Cleaning, Shutter When Power Off: On, ***Off**

My preference: N/A

Access the Sensor Cleaning option when you want to use the camera's auto image sensor cleaning feature. You'll hear a buzzing sound as the camera gives the sensor a good shake. Your tip-off that the sensor needs cleaning will be blurry spots and artifacts that show up in less detailed areas of the image (such as the sky) in photos taken at small f/stops (the extra depth-of-focus makes them more obvious).

If the camera's own sensor cleaning isn't sufficient, you can use a "rocket"-style blower, special sensor cleaning brushers, or wet-wipe swabs available online and from photo retailers. Use care; while the sensor surface is reasonably well-protected, the carriage for the SteadyShot image stabilizer can be damaged with rough treatment.

Auto Pixel Mapping/Pixel Mapping

Options: Auto Pixel Mapping: *On, Off

Options: Pixel Mapping: None

My preference: Auto Pixel Mapping: On

I've combined the descriptions of these two entries, because they perform similar functions. Even with the most sophisticated manufacturing techniques and quality-control measures, producing a sensor with absolutely no defects among 33 or 60 million individual photosites is quite a challenge. Sometimes a pixel "dies" and becomes permanently dark or, worse, becomes stuck or "hot" so that it will shine through brightly in areas that should be dark or even black. Pixel mapping provides a way to detect those defective pixels and automatically map them, so they no longer contribute to your images. Instead, information from surrounding pixels will be used to determine how that photosite appears in your image.

If you notice what appears to be a bad pixel, compare several different shots to see if it appears in the same place. Keep in mind that some "bad" pixels can be caused by overheating and will return to normal once your camera has been powered down for a short period. Sony gives you two separate entries:

- **Auto Pixel Mapping.** Set to On, and the camera will periodically analyze the sensor and, if a stuck pixel is discovered, will map it out. That's accomplished by ignoring the value of that particular pixel when an image is captured, and substituting the average of all the surrounding pixels instead.

  The process requires a "dark frame," that is, one that receives no light at all, so that any stuck pixels will stand out like a sore thumb, er...pixel. So the shutter closes and the self-test/mapping takes about 10 seconds. Then, the camera reboots. The process is unobtrusive, so I leave the Auto Pixel Mapping entry set to On.

- **Pixel Mapping.** You can also perform pixel mapping manually if you've turned the Auto feature off. Indeed, Sony recommends performing the function once every three days. Don't worry, you won't be losing pixels at that pace, but it's always better to be safe than sorry about all the retouching you need to do in Photoshop.

Version

Options: Display Version, Software Update

My preference: N/A

Select this menu option to display the version number of the firmware (internal operating software) installed in your camera. From time to time, Sony updates the original firmware with a newer version that adds or enhances features or corrects operational bugs. When a new version is released, it will be accompanied by instructions, which generally involve downloading the update to your computer and then connecting your camera to the computer with the USB cable to apply the update. It's a good idea to check occasionally at the Sony website, www.esupport.sony.com, to see if a new version of the camera's firmware is available for download. (You can also go to that site to download updates to the software that came with the camera, and to get general support.)

Certification Logo (Non-US/Canada Models Only)

Options: None

This information-only entry displays various certification logos indicating the camera has met specifications mandated by other countries. It's included in cameras intended for non-US/Canada sales so that the logos can be tailored for specific areas through firmware updates, rather than printed notices on the bottom of the cameras themselves.

Display Serial Number

Options: None

This is another information-only entry display, which shows the serial number also imprinted on the bottom of the camera.

Privacy Notice

Options: None

The final informational entry is simply a warning that use of the a7C II or a7CR may involve "biometric" data that you are responsible for. A QR code and URL are displayed for you to view additional information. Apparently, this notice is required because the Face Memory registration feature is considered to be storing biometric information, and Sony wants you to know that the facial features are retained *only* on the camera itself and not collected by Sony for other purposes. You are reminded that you can delete the facial recognition data at any time if requested by your subject.

Movie-Making Basics

As we've seen during our exploration of its features so far, the a7C II and a7CR are superbly equipped for taking still photographs of very high quality in a wide variety of shooting environments. But their superior level of performance is not limited to stills. Both are highly capable in the movie-making arena as well and can shoot Full HD (high-definition) and 4K (ultra-high-definition) clips. Sony has also provided overrides for controlling all important aspects of a video clip.

So, even though you may have bought your camera primarily for shooting stationary scenes, you acquired a device that's also great for recording high-quality video clips. Whether you're looking to record informal clips of the family on vacation, the latest viral video for YouTube, or a set of scenes that will be painstakingly crafted into a cinematic masterpiece using editing software, the a7C II or a7CR will perform admirably. This chapter and the next deal with conventional video; S&Q (slow- and quick-motion video) settings were explained in Chapter 6.

The a7C II/a7CR can shoot HD video in the XAVC S format at 120/100p, 60/50p, 30/25p, and 24p with Full HD 1920 × 1080–pixel resolution, and, optionally, a "proxy" copy recorded simultaneously. The a7C II/a7CR adds the ability to capture superior 4K video *internally* using XAVC S 4K at 60/50p and 30/25p. Good news for vloggers and those who need to shoot long-form video (such as presentations or concerts) is that the 29-minute recording limitation has been eliminated; you can capture as much video as your memory card (or attached video recorder) can hold—subject only to possible overheating that can occur in warm environments or when recording 4K video at the fastest transfer speeds.

The a7C II and a7CR offer Standard and Active image stabilization; Standard takes advantage of the camera's in-body stabilization (and that of a lens with built-in Optical Image Stabilization), while the Active mode uses electronic stabilization as well, with a small 1.13x crop used to trim the borders as the frames are realigned to account for blur. If, like most amateur videographers, you capture most of your video with the camera not locked down to a tripod, you'll especially appreciate the a7C II/a7CR's Active image stabilization mode, which keeps the non-moving pixels aligned, even when hand-held shooting results in dramatic movement that can't be countered by in-body image stabilization (IBIS) alone. The camera movement is captured and stored in the video file so even more powerful digital correction can be applied using the extra-cost Sony Catalyst post-production utility software.

The a7C II/a7CR also uses something called *Picture Profiles*, to tailor color, saturation, sharpness, and some video-centric attributes. You can visualize Picture Profiles as Creative Looks for video.

This chapter will show you the fundamentals of shooting video; in the next chapter, you'll learn about some of your camera's more advanced features.

Vloggers and Streamers

Sony hasn't forgotten vloggers and those doing web-conferencing. (Although the days of constant Zoom remote meetings are behind us, live streaming is here to stay.) You can use your a7C II/a7CR for USB streaming, and opt to record your stream for later viewing or editing.

Vloggers have to like the a7C II/a7CR because of its small size, lack of recording time limits, and its fully articulated screen that can be reversed to use as a selfie/monitor screen. The multi-interface shoe on top of the camera allows attaching a microphone like the Sony ECM-B1M shotgun unit that links electronically to the camera through the multi-interface shoe rather than requiring a separate cable. Many of the lenses available for the a7C II/a7CR have virtually silent autofocus, which is excellent for video shooting.

One killer feature is the new Auto Framing mode that lets you set up your video automatically without the need for a second person as a camera operator. With the camera on a tripod, the a7C II/a7CR will identify a subject (say, *you*), and fill the frame with your image. It will even "follow" you around as you move within the frame.

Setting Up Auto Framing

Auto Framing is available only when the Still/Movie/S&Q dial is set to the Movie Position. It cannot be used with S&Q capture or Time-Lapse shooting. To make your settings and activate, navigate to the Shooting > Shooting Option > Auto Framing Settings tab to view the six options shown at left in Figure 10.1. Hold off accessing the first two until after you've specified the last four settings:

- **Auto Framing.** When you're ready to go, choose this entry and select On, and make the settings described below.

- **Crop Level.** This setting tells the camera how tightly to crop the subject being framed *in the final video stream*. The entire original scene with the angle of view provided by the lens' focal length is displayed during shooting. A 16:9 aspect ratio rectangle will be overlaid over the frame

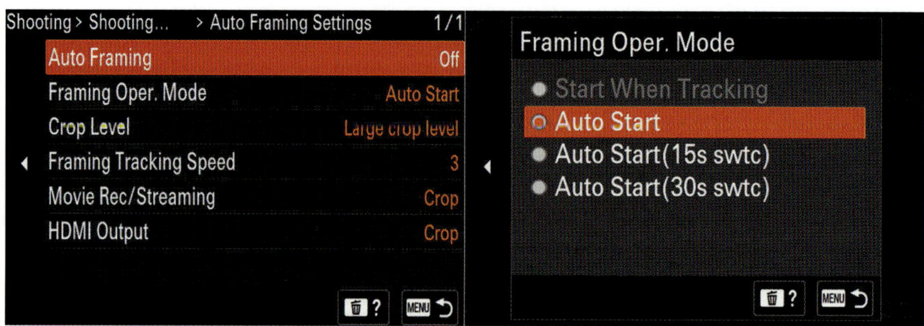

Figure 10.1 Auto Framing options (left). Choose Framing Operation Mode (right).

indicating the cropped area. (See Figure 10.2.) While streaming, the a7C II or a7CR will enlarge the cropped area to fill the video frame from a 4K-resolution capture to maintain image quality.

You can choose from Large, Medium, and Small Crop Levels which, depending on your original framing, may be suitable for head and shoulders, three-quarter-length shots, or full-length views of human subjects, respectively. When Focus > Subject Recognition > Recognition Target is set to Human, frame size will change automatically. With other Target settings, the crop level will be locked at the size you specify here.

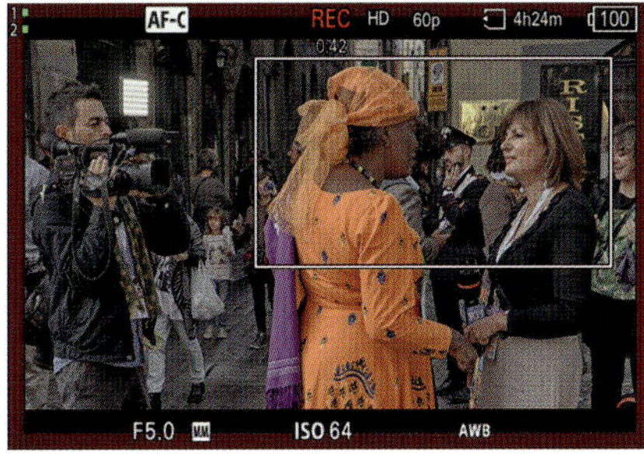

Figure 10.2 The automatic framing will be shown on the camera's display.

- **Framing Tracking Speed.** Here you can select how quickly the camera tracks your subject, from a setting of 1 (Slow) to 5 (Fast). The default is smack in the middle at 3. Slower speeds are your best bet if your subject will be making slight movements and you don't want the auto framing to respond immediately, avoiding distractions. Set to a fast speed if you expect more movement from your subject and you want the camera to follow them as they wander.

- **Movie Recording/Streaming.** This setting is useful if you want the original video to be stored as is on your memory card and not reflect the cropping that auto framing will apply to the video stream. Your audience sees the autoframed stream, but you have the original footage captured on your card for archiving or editing when you select Do Not Crop. If you choose Crop here, both the live stream and the stored version will be cropped.

- **HDMI Output.** This setting functions similarly to the one above, but applies to the video directed to the a7C II and a7CR's HDMI port. If you select Crop, the auto-framed footage is output to your HDMI display, recorder, or other device.

  You can combine the footage captured by an HDMI recorder with that stored on your memory card to create a "two-camera" look—just save cropped video on your memory card and uncropped video on your external HDMI recorder and intercut them in your video-editing software.

When you're ready to activate auto framing, you have several other adjustments to make:

- **Choose shutter speed.** If you expect your subject to be moving a lot or somewhat quickly, you might want to choose a slightly higher shutter speed to avoid blurring. For example, when using a 30 fps rate, a shutter speed of 1/60th or even 1/125th second might be a good idea.

- **Select focus area.** Your best bet most of the time is to set the focus area to Wide. The a7C II/a7CR will locate your target (and choose the highest priority subject) and perform auto framing. You can also use Spot as your focus area to frame the subject located within the Spot, which you can move around using the directional controls as described in Chapter 4. **Note:** You can check framing and perform some other operations using your smartphone and the Creators' App.

- **Framing operation mode.** A final step will be to specify *when* the camera should start using auto framing. Your choices, shown in Figure 10.1, right, are:
  - **Start When Tracking.** The auto framing begins when your subject is identified (automatically or by touching the camera screen).
  - **Auto Start.** Auto-framing starts immediately when your subject is recognized.
  - **Auto Start (15 seconds switch).** After the subject is recognized, the camera switches between the cropped view and full frame view every 15 seconds. This option and the next one produce a single video stream that alternates between the two views (or a single video file, without the need for editing).
  - **Auto Start (30 seconds switch).** After the subject is recognized, the camera switches between the cropped view and full-frame view every 30 seconds.
- **Shooting tips.** Use a wide-angle lens for the most flexibility. That will allow your subject more room to move around and/or approach or recede from the camera. An external mic is a good idea for the best audio, and you should make sure your shooting area is evenly illuminated. Even if the a7C II or a7CR's LCD display is reversed it may be hard to see exactly what is being captured. Consider using an external monitor (or the display of an external recorder) connected to the camera through the HDMI port.
- **Start capture.** You can tap your subject on the screen to begin auto framing, or, if you're shooting selfie-style, let the camera start capture when it recognizes you as the target. If you're operating the camera rather than serving as the subject, you can change to framing a different subject at any time by tapping a different target on the screen.

Some Fundamentals

Recording a video with the a7C II/a7CR is extraordinarily easy to accomplish—just press the black button with the red ring located on the top of the camera to the immediate southeast of the shutter button. Sony has placed it there to minimize the chance that you'll start recording a movie accidentally. That's because video can be captured in *any* exposure mode; there's no need to activate a special Movie mode. After you press the button, the camera will confirm that it's recording with a red REC and numerals showing the elapsed time in the EVF and LCD monitor. Press the button again when you want to stop recording.

The basic movie settings you make most often are found in the Shooting tab. You'll find complete descriptions of your options in Chapter 6, and I won't repeat that information here. I know cross references are a pain, but I have kept all the basic Shooting tab menu entries in one place for easier reference. To recap, you'll need to choose:

- **(Movie) File Format.** Select from 4K and HD movie file formats. Chapter 6 explains about the codecs (coder/decoder), resolution, and compression formats used.
- **Movie Settings.** Here you'll choose frame rates, bit rates, color sampling, and the importance of bit depth. I'll explain frame rates and bit rates later in this chapter.

- **Log Shooting Settings.** Your options are listed in Chapter 6, and I'll return to log shooting in more detail in Chapter 11.

- **Proxy settings.** This entry allows you to create a more compact movie clip at the same time as your full-resolution movie, giving you a second video suitable for emailing, uploading online, or smart device display. I showed you how to do this in Chapter 6.

First Things First

Before you start, though, there are steps to take to prepare the camera to record the scene the way you want it to. I'll show you how to optimize your settings before you start shooting video, but here are some considerations to be aware of as you get started. Many of these points will be covered in more detail later in this chapter:

- **Use the right card.** Because movie capture is, basically, full-time "continuous" shooting, you'll need to use a memory card with sufficient capacity and a fast enough write speed to handle the streams of video you'll be shooting, especially at 4K resolution.

- **Avoid extraneous noise.** Try not to make too much noise when changing camera controls or when using a conventional zoom lens's mechanical zooming ring. Power zooms with a zoom lever on the lens are typically relatively quiet. And don't make comments while capturing that you will not want to hear on the audio track.

- **Minimize zooming.** While it's great to be able to use the zoom for filling the frame with a distant subject (especially the power zoom on lenses equipped with that feature), think twice before zooming. The sound made by a mechanical zoom ring rotating will be picked up and it will be audible when you play a movie. (As I noted, lenses with power zoom are virtually silent.) Also, remember that any more than the occasional minor zoom will be very distracting to friends who watch your videos. And while digital zoom will definitely degrade video quality, the effect is minimized when shooting video because your final video frame (in Full HD mode) will be just 1920 × 1080 pixels and 3840 × 2160 pixels in 4K mode. Digital zoom *is* useful as a way of mimicking a power zoom, as you can "zoom" quietly and digitally by pressing the right button, and then pressing and holding again to zoom continuously.

- **Use a fully charged battery.** A fresh battery will allow at least one hour of filming at normal (non-winter) temperatures, but that can be shorter if there are many focus adjustments.

- **Keep it cool.** Video quality can suffer terribly when the imaging sensor gets hot so keep the camera in a cool place. When shooting on hot days especially, the sensor can get hot more quickly than usual; when there's a risk of overheating, the camera will stop recording and it will shut down about five seconds later. A thermometer icon will appear on the screen as a warning. Give the sensor time to cool down before using the camera again. This limitation generally won't affect serious movie makers, who tend to shoot a series of short scenes that are assembled into a finished movie with an editor. But if you plan to set up your camera and photograph your kid's school pageant non-stop for an hour, you're out of luck.

- **Press the Movie button.** You don't have to hold it down. Press it again when you're done to stop recording.

Preparing to Shoot Video

First, here's what I recommend you do to prepare for a *basic* recording session. More advanced detail settings will be addressed later. Although many movie settings are available when the Still/Movie/S&Q dial is set to the Still photo position, you'll have access to a full range of options if you rotate it to the Movie position as you prepare to capture video:

- **Choose your file format.** Go to the Shooting > Image Quality/Recording > [Movie File] Format entry as discussed in Chapter 6, and select the file format for your movies. (The Still/Movie/S&Q dial must be set to Movie mode to access all the movie-related entries.) You can set it to XAVC S HD or XAVC S 4K to start. File formats determine the transfer rate (roughly equivalent to JPEG compression), which, with resolution, determines the quality of your video. You'll learn more about these and additional options later.

  Which of the options should you choose? It depends in part on your needs. If your plan is to primarily shoot videos that you'll show to friends and family on an HDTV set, choose XAVC S HD. For more professional productions, you'll want to select XAVC S 4K. I'll explain the differences later.

- **Choose Movie settings.** Also, in the Shooting > Image Quality/Recording group you'll find the Movie Settings entry, which allows you to choose the size, frame rate, and image quality for your movies. A Recording Frame Rate of 30p and a Record Setting of 50M 4:2:0 8 bit is a good place to begin.

- **Activate proxy recording (optional).** I described your proxy recording options in Chapter 6. Use the Shooting > Image Quality > Proxy Settings entry. You can choose the higher quality XAVC HS HD to save a proxy video file at Full HD (1920 × 1080) resolution, or select the XAVC S HD standard HD (1280 × 720) version. The same frame rate selected for the main video will be used (that is, 60/50p, 30/25p, or 24p). You cannot create a proxy video file when using the 120/100p frame rate.

  In all cases, your proxy video will be highly compressed. The XAVC HS HD (Full HD) proxy video will be captured with either a 16M or 9M 4:2:0 10-bit transfer rate; the XAVC S HD (Standard HD) proxy will transfer at a 6M 4:2:0 8-bit rate.

  You'll definitely want to use a large memory card when working with this option. When you review your images, the proxy video isn't displayed, viewable, or editable in the camera; the "main" movie will have a Px indicator overlaid on its icon to show you that the clip is paired with a proxy counterpart. Deleting or protecting the main clip deletes/protects the proxy at the same time.

- **Turn on autofocus.** Make sure autofocus is turned on through the Focus > AF/MF > Focus Mode entry. You also have the option of using manual focus, with focus peaking. (Focus peaking also can be used in AF-C autofocus mode, as well, as discussed in Chapter 8.)

- **Try Expand Spot AF Area.** As in still image making, you can use the Expand Spot AF Area while recording a video clip. This feature is most suitable for a static scene you'll record with the camera on a tripod, where an important small subject is off-center and will remain in the same location. By placing the AF Area exactly on that part of the scene, you'll be sure that the focus will remain on the most important part of the scene during the entire recording. (In truth, you could use manual focus for the same purpose.)

If you decide to try this, compose the scene as desired before pressing the record button. Set the Focus Area to Expand Spot. Brackets will appear on the screen, indicating the current location of the active focus detection point. Move the brackets with the directional buttons so they cover the primary subject and press the center button to confirm. Press the center button again any time you want to reposition the focus area. You can now begin recording the video, confident that the focus will always be on your primary subject (assuming it does not move while you're recording).

- **Set useful functions.** Before you start recording, you can set a desired ISO, white balance, Creative Looks, Picture Profiles (explained in the next chapter), any of the three metering modes, and the level of exposure compensation. The DRO feature will not be available, however. You'll recall that these functions are not available in fully automatic modes; if you set them while using another mode and then switch to a fully automatic mode for recording the video, the camera will revert back to the defaults.

- **Decide on a shooting mode.** You can choose an exposure mode (P, S, A, or M) for your movies, either using a menu entry or by rotating the mode dial.

  The P mode works well, allowing the camera to set the aperture/shutter speed and giving you access to the other features discussed above. Program Shift (to other aperture/shutter speed combinations) can be used before you start recording, but it will not be available during actual recording.

  You might prefer to use Aperture Priority (A) mode for full control over the specific aperture; in that case, you can preset a desired aperture and you can also change it anytime while recording. Be careful, however, especially if you have set a specific ISO level. If you switch to a very small aperture while recording in low light, your movie clip may darken; this is particularly likely if you're using a low ISO level. And if you switch to a very wide aperture on a sunny day, especially if using a high ISO, your video will become too bright. Of course, you can see the change in brightness in the live view display before recording a movie and while you're recording.

  Switch to S mode if you want control over the shutter speed; this is a more advanced technique in Movie mode. You can preset a shutter speed and you can change it while recording. Again, be careful as to your settings to avoid a very dark or overly bright video, especially if you have set a specific ISO level. The live view display before and during recording will help to guide you. I don't recommend using the Manual (M) mode initially, but you might want to experiment with it later.

- **Press the record button.** You don't have to hold it down. Press it to start recording and press it again when you're done. Shoot a short test clip and view it to make sure that the settings you made are producing the overall effect you want. If not, change some settings (White Balance or Creative Style or Exposure Compensation, for example) and try again.

Steps During Movie Making

Once you have set up the camera for your video session and pressed the Movie button, you have done most of the technical work that's required of you for basic movie clips. Now your task is to use your skills at composition, lighting, scene selection, and, perhaps, directing actors, to make a compelling video production:

- **Zoom, autofocus, and autoexposure all work.** If you're new to the world of high-quality still cameras that also take video, you may just take it for granted that functions such as autofocus continue to work normally when you switch from stills to video. But until recently, most such cameras performed weakly in their video modes; they would lock their exposure and focus at the beginning of the scene, and you could not zoom while shooting the video. The a7C II/a7CR has no such handicaps, and, in fact, it is especially capable in these areas.

  Indeed, this camera allows you to choose any exposure mode, including Manual exposure, Auto ISO, shutter speed, and aperture.

  Autoexposure works very well, modifying the exposure as the scene brightness changes; the method used depends on the metering mode that you're using. You can zoom to your heart's content (though I recommend that you zoom sparingly). Best of all, AF-C autofocus works like a charm; the camera can track moving subjects and quickly snap them back into sharp focus with speedy continuous AF. Manual focus is also available, with focus peaking to help you zero in on a focus plane. Don't limit yourself based on the weaknesses of past cameras; the a7C II/a7CR opens up new horizons of video freedom.

- **Exposure compensation works while filming.** I found this feature to be quite remarkable. Although the autoexposure system works very well (especially with Multi metering) to vary the aperture when the ambient lighting changes, you can certainly dial in exposure compensation when you need to do so or want to do so for a certain effect. You could even use this function as a limited kind of "fade to black" in the camera, though you probably won't be able to fade quite all the way to black.

- **Use AE lock instead.** Occasionally, you may find that you start having an exposure problem during recording; this might happen when pointing the lens toward a light-tone area that causes the camera to begin underexposing. While plus compensation will allow you to increase brightness, it's preferable to use a defined AE lock button (one you specify using custom keys) to maintain a pleasing exposure during the entire video clip.

- **Don't be a flash in the pan.** With HD and 4K video modes, there is a possibility of introducing artifacts or distortion if you pan too quickly. (This effect is called rolling shutter distortion or the "Jell-O effect.") That is, because of the way the lines of video are displayed in sequence, if the camera moves too quickly in a sideways motion, some of the lines may not show up on the screen quickly enough to catch up to the rest of the picture. As a result, objects in your video can become somewhat distorted or you may experience a jiggling effect and/or loss of detail. So, if at all possible, make your pans are smooth and steady, and slow them down to a comfortable pace.

More About Frame Rates and Bit Rates

Both videos and stills are captured in much the same way, but the technology used for the sensor can cause problems that are most evident when shooting movies. To understand why, it's necessary to understand the difference between a *rolling shutter* and a *global shutter,* and how *interlacing* differs from *progressive scan.*

An image (still or video) captured by the sensor consists of rows and columns of pixels. A "rolling" shutter captures each row one after the other, so that, effectively, the pixels in the top row are captured at a different moment in time than those in the bottom row. This gap is very brief, and typically isn't noticeable in still photographs. But with video this difference can manifest itself as anomalies such as wobble when the camera is moving or vibrating, skew (which is a diagonal bending of an image due to wobble), smear (produced when part of the image, such as an automobile tire, is rotating), and other defects. Even though a video frame is cropped at top and bottom (resulting in a smaller number of rows), the rolling shutter effect is still present.

A "global" shutter, on the other hand, captures the entire image in one instant, eliminating these problems. As I write this, the Sony a9 III is the only camera designed for both stills and videography that has a true global shutter. Fortunately, although your a7C II/a7CR *does* have a rolling shutter, the high speed of its sensor and BIONZ XR digital image processing chip minimizes the rolling shutter effects. However, you should still be cautious when shooting moving subjects; even with improvements the a7C II/a7CR's rolling shutter can produce objectionable effects.

Frame Rates

That leads us to progressive scanning versus interlacing. With a rolling shutter like that found in the a7C II/a7CR, line-by-line scanning during capture and playback can be done in one of two ways. With *interlaced scanning,* odd-numbered lines (lines 1, 3, 5, 7, and so forth) are captured with one pass, and then the even-numbered lines (2, 4, 6, 8, and so forth) are grabbed. With the 1080/60i format, roughly 60 pairs of odd/even line scans, or 60 *fields,* are captured each second. (The actual number is 59.94 fields per second.) Interlaced scanning was developed for and works best with analog display systems such as older television sets. It was originally created as a way to reduce the amount of bandwidth required to transmit television pictures over the air. Modern LCD, LED, and plasma-based HDTV displays must de-interlace a 1080i image to display it.

Newer displays work better with a second method, called *progressive scanning* or *sequential scanning,* and progressive scan modes are the only choices when shooting XAVC S video. Instead of two interlaced fields, the entire image is scanned as consecutive lines (lines 1, 2, 3, 4, and so forth). This happens at a rate of 120, 60, 30, or 24 frames per second (not fields). (All these numbers apply to the NTSC television system used in the United States, Canada, Japan, and some other countries; other places use systems like PAL, where the nominal scanning figures are 100/50/25 rather than 120/60/30.)

The rolling shutter effect I described earlier is even worse when shooting moving subjects with interlaced scanning. Half of the image (one set of interlaced lines) will change to keep up with the movement of the subject while the other interlaced half retains the "old" image as it waits to be refreshed. Flicker or *interline twitter* results. That makes progressive scan (p) options a better choice for action photography. Users of earlier Sony cameras should note that interlaced video frame rates (using the AVCHD recording format) are no longer supported with the a7C II/a7CR. Some of the improvement in the camera's rolling shutter effects come from eliminating the problematic interlaced video options.

Computer-editing software like Final Cut Pro can handle most video formats, and convert between them (although XAVC S/HS 4K and XAVC S HD may not be compatible with the other software you own). The choice between 30/60 fps (NTSC only) or 25/50 fps (PAL only), and 24 fps (available in both NTSC and PAL modes) is determined by what you plan to do with your video. The short explanation is that, for technical reasons I won't go into here, shooting at 24 fps gives your movie more of the so-called "cinematic" look that film would produce, excellent for showing fine detail. However, if your clip has moving subjects, or you pan the camera, 24 fps can produce a jerky effect called "judder." The 30 and 60 fps (or 25 and 50 fps) options produce a home-video look that some feel is less desirable, but which is smoother and less jittery when displayed on an electronic monitor. I suggest you try both and use the frame rate that best suits your tastes and video-editing software.

ABOUT 120/100P

You'll note that when shooting XAVC S HD, you can select 120p (at 100Mbs transfer rates; NTSC only) or 120/100p (at 60Mbs transfer rate; both NTSC and PAL). These high frame rates—amounting to 120 and 100 frames per second—produce video that can be converted to play back at conventional speeds, either 30/25 fps (four times slower than recorded) or 24 fps (five times slower than recorded; NTSC only). The slow-motion video that results can be used for special effects, including clichés like two long-lost lovers running toward each other on a beach.

Bit Rates

Bit rates represent the speed of transfer from your camera to your memory card or external video recorder. The higher the bit rate, the more demands made on your media in storing that data quick enough to keep pace with the video capture. Higher average bit rates range from 16Mbps (megabits per second) to 100Mbps. Note that frame rates of 30/25, 60/50, and 120/100 represent NTSC/PAL systems, respectively. As I noted in Chapter 6, the parameters you need to know are these:

- **Codec.** The 4K HS format uses the HEVC (High-Efficiency Video Coding, also known as H.265) codec. This software produces higher image quality with the same size files as the other settings, which use the less-efficient H.264 codec. The HEIC still photo format is based on HEVC, which is why images captured in that format will better match video captured using the HEVC codec.
- **Resolution.** The 4K and full HD formats provide 3840 × 2160 and 1920 × 1080 pixel resolution, respectively.

- **Movie compression format.** XAVC HS 4K, XAVC S 4K, and XAVC S HD offer long GOP (group of pictures) interframe compression. XAVC S-1 4K and XAVC S-I HD, use All-I compression.

  With long GOP compression, one I-frame (intraframe) is recorded that contains all the information for a frame, minimally compressed. The next frame after this *key frame* is called a B-frame, and it stores *only the changes* from the I-frame, which greatly reduces the amount of information that must be kept. It may be followed by another B-frame, and then a P-frame, which just predicts what the actual frame should look like based on the information from the previous frames, and, eventually, the next I-frame. This type of compression is sometimes called IPB Compression, after the Intra-, Predictive, and Bidirectional frame types.

  The XAVC-I 4K and XAVC S-I HD formats use All-I compression, in which each frame is an I-frame or key frame. While All-I produces larger files and the capability of the camera to support the higher transfer rate they demand, they are more friendly for editing, particularly for those who are doing tight, frame-by-frame editing. For example, if you are capturing a video at a wedding and a still photography flash burst occurs at an inopportune time, you can edit out that particular frame.

Choosing Metering/Exposure Modes

You can use Multi, Center, Spot, Averaging, or Highlight-weighted metering when shooting movies. I recommend sticking with Multi metering, unless you have a special reason for, say, Spot metering. Next, you'll want to select exposure mode, from among Program, Aperture Priority, Shutter Priority, or Manual.

- **Program (P) mode.** The P mode works well for movies, allowing the camera to set the aperture/shutter speed.

- **Aperture Priority (A) mode.** You might prefer to use Aperture Priority (A) mode for full control over the specific aperture; in that case, you can preset a desired aperture and you can also change it anytime while recording. However, remember that your shutter speed may change in Aperture Priority mode, and when shooting movies, it is often desirable to use a specific shutter speed (as I'll explain in an upcoming section).

- **Shutter Priority (S) mode.** Switch to S mode if you want control over the shutter speed; this is a more advanced technique in Movie mode. You can preset a shutter speed and you can change it while recording. Again, be careful as to your settings to avoid a very dark or overly bright video, especially if you have set a specific ISO level. The live view display before and during recording will help to guide you. I recommend Shutter Priority highly, especially for beginners.

- **Manual Exposure (M mode).** Manual exposure may be best when you want to maintain tight control over shutter speed and aperture, say, to maintain exposure as lighting conditions change, or to keep the same depth-of-field in a scene under changing conditions.

As you work, you'll discover that the a7C II and a7CR's Zebra feature can be a marvelous aid in monitoring your exposure. If you are using Shutter Priority, as I recommended, you'll have the shutter speed fixed and, based on what you see in the viewfinder or LCD monitor and Zebra display feedback, adjust the aperture or ISO sensitivity to get the exposure you want. As I explained in Chapter

6, you can adjust the Zebra feature's threshold setting, perhaps specifying 95% so that you're alerted only when the brightest highlights start to clip (making the stripes less distracting) or use 85% so you'll know when human skin starts to be overexposed. Zebra display may not work for you when using S-Log2/S-Log3 gamma settings (described later in this chapter), as those very low-contrast renditions don't lend themselves to that kind of monitoring.

You can also "lock" exposure to keep the same exposure settings as lighting changes or you reframe your scene. As I mentioned, you may find that you start having an exposure problem during recording; this might happen when pointing the lens toward a light-tone area that causes the camera to begin underexposing. While plus compensation will allow you to increase brightness, it's preferable to use the defined AE lock button you specify using Custom Key/Dial Settings (Movie) options in the Setup > Operation Customize tab to maintain a pleasing exposure during the entire video clip.

Why would you need this feature? Let's say you're filming entertainers against grass and foliage, but you're moving the camera and will soon be filming a second group against a white sky. As soon as you do so, the backlighting will cause the video to get darker. Don't let that happen. Before pointing the lens toward the backlit area, press the defined AE lock button and keep it depressed. This will prevent the exposure from changing as you point the lens toward the backlit part of the scene. This is preferable to waiting until an underexposure problem starts and then setting plus exposure compensation that suddenly makes the video brighter.

Stop That!

Both Manual Exposure and Shutter Priority modes allow you to explicitly choose a shutter speed. You might think that setting your camera to a faster shutter speed will help give you sharper video frames. But the choice of a shutter speed for movie making is a bit more complicated than that. As you might guess, in most cases it's best to leave the shutter speed at 1/30th- or 1/60th-second and allow the overall exposure to be adjusted by varying the aperture and/or ISO sensitivity.

Effectively, you're better off working in Shutter Priority mode, so that the aperture or ISO settings are your only way of adjusting the exposure. A "slow" 1/30th- or 1/60th-second shutter speed doesn't mean your movies will have the same amount of blur that a typical still photograph will have using those shutter speeds. We don't normally stare at a video frame for longer than 1/30th or 1/24th second, so while the shakiness of the *camera* can be disruptive (and often corrected by your camera's in-lens and in-body image stabilization), if there is a bit of blur in our *subjects* from movement, we tend not to notice. Each frame flashes by in the blink of an eye, so to speak, so a shutter speed of 1/30th or 1/60th second works a lot better in video than it does when shooting stills. Even shots with lots of movement are often sufficiently sharp at 1/60th second.

Higher shutter speeds actually introduce problems of their own. If you shoot a video frame using a shutter speed of 1/250th second, the actual moment in time that's captured represents only about 12 percent of the 1/30th second of elapsed time in that frame. Yet, when played back, that frame occupies the full 1/30th of a second, with 88 percent of that time filled by stretching the original image to fill it. The result is often a choppy/jumpy image, and one that may appear to be *too* sharp.

The reason for that is more social imprinting than scientific: we've all grown up accustomed to seeing the look of Hollywood productions that, by convention, were shot using a shutter speed that's half the reciprocal of the frame rate (that is, 1/48th second for a 24 fps movie). Movie cameras use a rotary shutter (achieving that 1/48th second exposure by using a 180-degree shutter "angle"), but the effect on our visual expectations is the same. For the most "film-like" appearance, use 24 fps and 1/60th second shutter speed.

Faster shutter speeds do have some specialized uses for motion analysis, especially where individual frames are studied. The rest of the time, 1/30th or 1/60th of a second will suffice. If the reason you needed a higher shutter speed was to obtain the correct exposure, use a slower ISO setting, or a neutral-density filter to cut down on the amount of light passing through the lens. A good rule of thumb is to use 1/60th second or slower when shooting at 24 fps; 1/60th second or slower at 30 fps; and 1/125th second or slower at 60 fps.

In choosing between 30p and 60p, there are several considerations. The 30p frame rate allows you to use a reduced ISO setting for improved grain compared to 60p at a higher ISO value. That's an advantage under low light. However, as I mentioned earlier, at 60p you can safely use a higher shutter speed of 1/125th second, which can produce smoother video of moving subjects. Video editors can *transcode* 60p video to give you 30p video (with files suitable for uploading to websites) as well as the 60i video you might need for DVD/Blu-Ray productions.

Choosing an Autofocus Mode

As I said in Chapter 8, you'll generally want sharp focus in your image—somewhere—but exactly where and how focus is achieved can be an important part of your creative process. On the one hand, while shooting certain types of scenes—particularly action scenes—you'll want the camera to automatically retain focus on your main subjects and keep them tightly in focus. Other times, you'll want to use selective focus to emphasize a subject and de-emphasize the background, or "pull" focus to dramatically change the focus (so to speak) of the scene, say, refocusing to cause a blurry subject to suddenly come into sharp relief.

As with still photography, you have both manual focus and autofocus tools at your disposal, which allow you to specify *when* to focus and what to focus on. An important step before shooting is to ensure autofocus is turned on through the Focus > AF/MF > Focus Mode entry. Only Continuous AF (AF-C) and Manual Focus (MF) can be used when shooting movies. Here are some points to consider:

- **AF-C or MF.** If the Still/Movie/S&Q dial is in the Movie position, only AF-C and MF are available.
- **Presto change-o.** If the Still/Movie/S&Q dial is *not* in the Movie position, and you have selected a focus mode other than AF-C or MF, when you begin shooting movies, the a7C II/a7CR will automatically switch to AF-C.
- **Lock focus.** As video is captured, the a7C II/a7CR's Continuous autofocus will refocus as you move the camera, or subjects in the frame change location. To lock focus, press the shutter release halfway, or use a key you've assigned that function. When you release the button, the camera will refocus. Ordinarily, it does an excellent job of not refocusing constantly, and changes focus only when the a7C II/a7CR detects camera or subject movement.

- **Manual focus.** If you prefer manual focus, you'll need to set it before commencing video capture. I find that manual focus is fine for situations such as a stage play where the actors will usually be at roughly the same distance to your position during the entire performance, and for more professional productions where precise focus is a must, or when changing focus during a shot (*focus pulling*) is used creatively. In other cases, however, you'll probably want to rely on the camera's effective full-time continuous autofocus ability while recording a video clip.

- **Focus area modes.** You can use all focus area modes, as described in Chapter 4, except for Tracking AF. (You can still activate tracking while capturing video, as described below.) If you don't need tracking, try Spot AF. As in still image making, you can use the Spot AF Area (also discussed in Chapter 4) while recording a video clip. This feature is most suitable for a static scene you'll record with the camera on a tripod, where an important small subject is off-center and will remain in the same location.

  By placing the Focus Area exactly on that part of the scene, you'll be sure that the focus will remain on the most important part of the scene during the entire recording. (In truth, you could use manual focus for the same purpose.) If you decide to try this, compose the scene as desired before pressing the record button. Set the Focus Area to Spot. When you press the center button (or designated Focus Standard button), locator brackets will appear on the screen, indicating the current location of the active focus detection point. Move the bracket with the directional buttons so they cover the primary subject and press OK (the center button) to confirm. You can now begin recording the video, confident that the focus will always be on your primary subject (assuming it does not move while you're recording).

Tracking in Video

Conventional tracking available in Still mode is disabled once you switch to Movie mode. When the Still/Movie/S&Q dial is set to the Movie position, the Tracking focus area modes are not available. However, that doesn't mean tracking is totally unavailable in Movie mode:

- **Tracking a subject.** You can still use the *touch screen* to specify a subject and have the a7C II/a7CR continually refocus to track its movement. Navigate to Setup > Touch Operation > Touch Panel Settings > Shooting Screen > Touch Functions in Shooting to select Touch Tracking. Thereafter, you can simply tap a subject on the LCD screen, and the a7C II/a7CR will track it as you capture video. However, if you want to use the alternate touch functions in stills mode (Touch Focus), you'll need to return to the Touch Functions in Shooting entry and revert to your preferred setting when you're finished shooting video.

- **Subject recognition.** If the subject you want to track is a living creature, the full array of subject recognition and face detection features, described in Chapter 8, are available in Movie mode, so you can let the camera find a subject, focus on it, and then track that subject as it moves around the frame as you shoot.

It's tempting to assume that the reason Sony disabled the conventional Tracking AF area modes in video was to discourage shooting movies that involve the kind of motion that produces those awful rolling shutter distortions. Another rationale is that constant focusing and refocusing in video can be extremely distracting, especially at large apertures in which depth-of-field is limited. However, serious filmmakers know ways of putting focus to work in creative ways, as in *pull focus* effects in which the focus plane is manually adjusted in order to change the emphasis from one subject to another. There are even lever accessories that clamp onto lens focus rings with markings that allow precisely moving from one focus point to another.

Tips for Movie Making

I'm going to close out this introductory movie chapter with a general discussion of movie-making concepts that you need to understand as you move toward more polished video production. In the chapter that follows, I'll explain some of the a7C II/a7CR's features that allow you to produce more sophisticated movies. Here are some basic tips:

- **Keep things stable and on the level.** Camera shake's enough of a problem with still photography, but it becomes even more of a nuisance when you're shooting video. While the a7C II/a7CR's in-body five-axis stabilization and stabilizer found in lenses with the OSS designation can help minimize this, neither can work miracles. Placing your camera on a tripod will work much better than trying to hand-hold it while shooting. One bit of really good news is that compared to those hefty pro dSLRs, the a7C II/a7CR, even though it is a full-frame camera, can work very effectively on a lighter tripod, due to its light weight. On windy days however, the extra mass of a heavy tripod is still valuable.

- **Use a shooting script.** A shooting script is nothing more than a coordinated plan that covers both audio and video and provides order and structure for your video. A detailed script will cover what types of shots you're going after, what dialogue you're going to use, audio effects, transitions, and graphics.

- **Plan with storyboards.** A storyboard is a series of panels providing visuals of what each scene should look like. While the ones produced by Hollywood are generally of very high quality, there's nothing that says drawing skills are important for this step. Stick figures work just fine if that's the best you can do. The storyboard just helps you visualize locations, placement of actors/actresses, props, and furniture, and also helps everyone involved get an idea of what you're trying to show. It also helps show how you want to frame or compose a shot. You can even shoot a series of still photos and transform them into a "storyboard" if you want, such as in Figure 10.3.

Today's audience is used to fast-paced, short-scene storytelling. In order to produce interesting video for such viewers, it's important to view video storytelling as a kind of shorthand code for the more leisurely efforts print media offers. Audio and video should always be advancing the story. While it's okay to let the camera linger from time to time, it should only be for a compelling reason and only briefly.

It only takes a second or two for an establishing shot to impart the necessary information. For example, many of the scenes for a video documenting a model being photographed in a rock 'n' roll music setting might be close-ups and talking heads, but an establishing shot showing the studio where the video was captured helps set the scene.

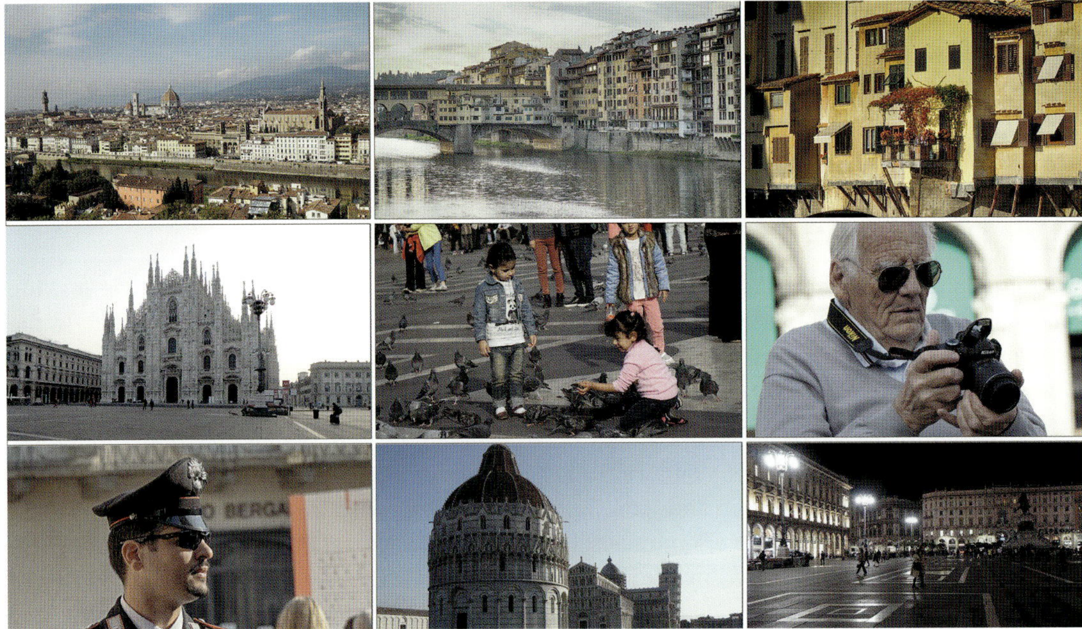

Figure 10.3 A storyboard is a series of simple sketches or photos to help visualize a segment of video.

- **Provide variety.** Provide variety too. Change camera angles and perspectives often and never leave a static scene on the screen for a long period of time. (You can record a static scene for a reasonably long period and then edit in other shots that cut away and back to the longer scene with close-ups that show each person talking.)
- **When editing, keep transitions basic!** I can't stress this one enough. Watch a television program or movie. The action "jumps" from one scene or person to the next. Fancy transitions that involve exotic "wipes," dissolves, or cross fades take too long for the average viewer and make your video ponderous.

Composition

In movie shooting, several factors restrict your composition, and impose requirements you just don't always have in still photography (although other rules of good composition do apply). Here are some of the key differences to keep in mind when composing movie frames:

- **Horizontal compositions only.** Some subjects, such as basketball players and tall buildings, just lend themselves to vertical compositions. But movies are generally shot and shown in horizontal format only. (Unless you're capturing a clip with your smartphone; I see many vertically oriented YouTube videos.) So, if you're shooting a conventional video and interviewing a local basketball star, you can end up with a worst-case situation like the one shown in Figure 10.4. If you want to show how tall your subject is, it's often impractical to move back far enough to show them full-length. You really can't capture a vertical composition. Tricks like getting down on the floor and shooting up at your subject can exaggerate the perspective but aren't a perfect solution.

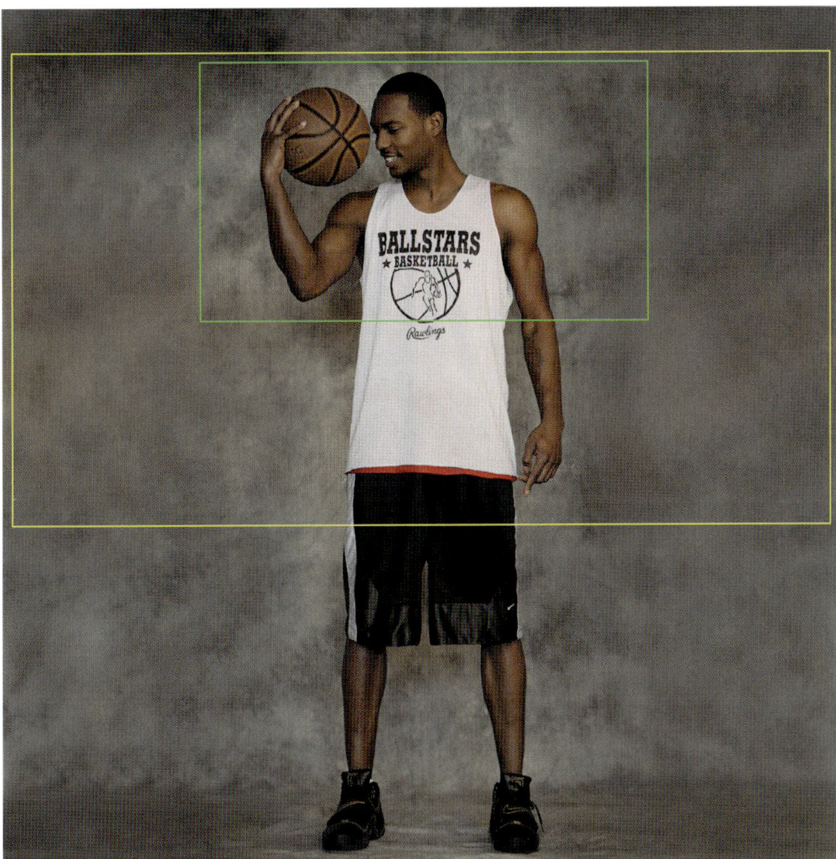

Figure 10.4 Movie shooting requires you to fit all your subjects into a horizontally oriented frame.

- **Wasted space at the sides.** Moving in to frame the basketball player as outlined by the yellow box in Figure 10.4 means that you're still forced to leave a lot of empty space on either side. (Of course, you can fill that space with other people and/or interesting stuff, but that defeats your intent of concentrating on your main subject.) So, when faced with some types of subjects in a horizontal frame, you can be creative, or move in *really* tight. For example, if I were willing to give up the "height" aspect of my composition, I could have framed the shot as shown by the green box in the figure and wasted less of the image area at either side.

- **Seamless (or seamed) transitions.** Unless you're telling a picture story with a photo essay, still pictures often stand alone. But with movies, each of your compositions must relate to the shot that preceded it, and the one that follows. It can be jarring to jump from a long shot to a tight close-up unless the director—you—is very creative. Another common error is the "jump cut" in which successive shots vary only slightly in camera angle, making it appear that the main subject has "jumped" from one place to another. (Although everyone from French New Wave director Jean-Luc Goddard to Guy Ritchie—Madonna's ex—have used jump cuts effectively in their films.) The rule of thumb is to vary the camera angle by at least 30 degrees between shots to make it appear to be seamless. Unless you prefer that your images flaunt convention and appear to be "seamy."

- **The time dimension.** Unlike still photography, with motion pictures there's a lot more emphasis on using a series of images to build on each other to tell a story. Static shots where the camera is mounted on a tripod and everything is shot from the same distance are a recipe for dull videos. Watch a television program sometime and notice how often camera shots change distances and directions. Viewers are used to this variety and have come to expect it. Professional video productions are often done with multiple cameras shooting from different angles and positions. But many professional productions are shot with just one camera, and with careful planning you can do just fine with your a7C II/a7CR camera.

Here's a look at the different types of commonly used compositional tools:

- **Establishing shot.** Much like it sounds, this type of composition, as shown at top left in Figure 10.5, establishes the scene and tells the viewer where the action is taking place. Let's say you're shooting a video of your offspring's move to college; the establishing shot could be a wide shot of the campus with a sign welcoming you to the school in the foreground. Another example would be for a child's birthday party; the establishing shot could be the front of the house decorated with birthday signs and streamers or a shot of the dining room table decked out with party favors and a candle-covered birthday cake. In this case, I wanted to show the studio where the video was shot.

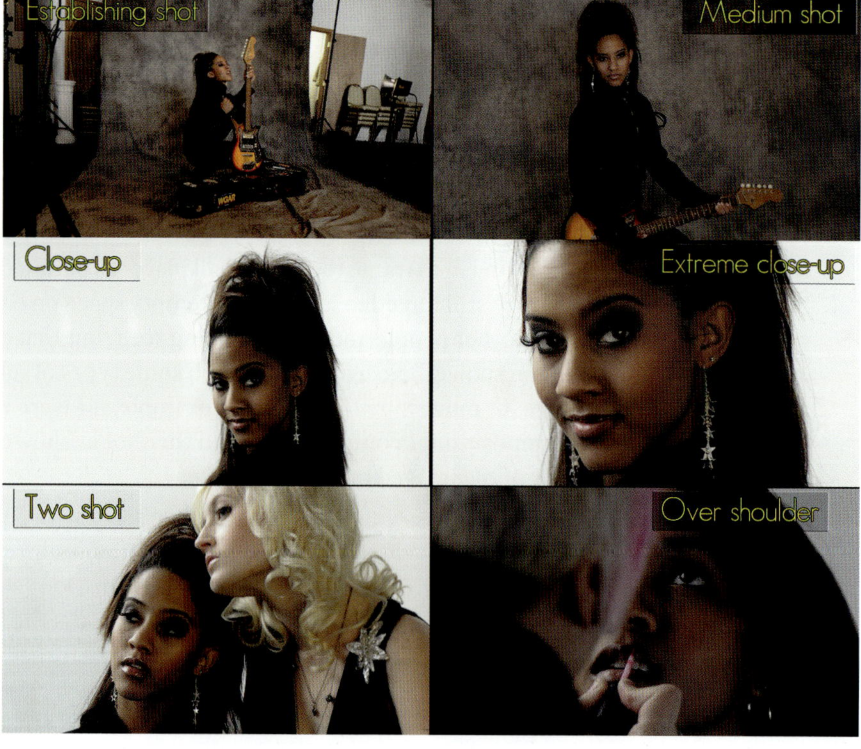

Figure 10.5 Establishing shot (upper left); Medium shot (upper right); Close-up (middle left); Extreme close-up (middle right); Two shot (lower left); Over-the-shoulder shot (lower right).

- **Medium shot.** This shot is composed from about waist to head room (some space above the subject's head). It's useful for providing variety from a series of close-ups and also makes for a useful first look at a speaker. (See Figure 10.5, top right.)

- **Close-up.** The close-up, usually described as "from shirt pocket to head room," provides a good composition for someone talking directly to the camera. Although it's common to have your talking head centered in the shot, that's not a requirement. In the middle left image in Figure 10.5, the subject was offset to the right. This would allow other images, especially graphics or titles, to be superimposed in the frame in a "real" (professional) production. But the compositional technique can be used with a7C II/a7CR videos, too, even if special effects are not going to be added.

- **Extreme close-up.** When I went through broadcast training, this shot was described as the "big talking face" shot and we were actively discouraged from employing it. Styles and tastes change over the years and now the big talking face is much more commonly used (maybe people are better looking these days?) and so this view may be appropriate. Just remember, the a7C II/a7CR is capable of shooting in high-definition video and you may be playing the video on a high-def TV; be careful that you use this composition on a face that can stand up to high definition. (See Figure 10.5, middle right.)

- **"Two" shot.** A two shot shows a pair of subjects in one frame. They can be side by side or one subject in the foreground and one in the background. This does not have to be a head-to-ground composition. Subjects can be standing or seated. A "three shot" is the same principle except that three people are in the frame. (See Figure 10.5, lower left.)

- **Over-the-shoulder shot.** Long a composition of interview programs, the over-the-shoulder shot uses the rear of one person's head and shoulder to serve as a frame for the other person. This puts the viewer's perspective as that of the person facing away from the camera. (See Figure 10.5, lower right.)

Lighting for Video

Much like in still photography, how you handle light pretty much can make or break your videography. Lighting for video can be more complicated than lighting for still photography, since both subject and camera movement are often part of the process.

Lighting for video presents several concerns. First off, you want enough illumination to create a usable video. Beyond that, you want to use light to help tell your story or increase drama. Let's take a better look at both.

Illumination

You can significantly improve the quality of your video by increasing the light falling in the scene. This is true indoors or out, by the way. While it may seem like sunlight is more than enough, it depends on how much contrast you're dealing with. If your subject is in shadow (which can help him from squinting) or wearing a ball cap, a video light can help make him look a lot better.

Lighting choices for amateur videographers are a lot better these days than they were a decade or two ago. An inexpensive incandescent video light, which will easily fit in a camera bag, can be found for $15 or $20. You can even get a good-quality LED video light for less than $100. Work lights sold at many home improvement stores can also serve as video lights since you can set the camera's white balance to correct for any color casts. You'll need to mount these lights on a tripod or other support, or, perhaps, to a bracket that fastens to the tripod socket on the bottom of the camera.

Much of the challenge depends upon whether you're just trying to add some fill light on your subject versus trying to boost the light on an entire scene. A small video light will do just fine for the former it won't handle the latter. Fortunately, the versatility of the a7C II/a7CR comes in quite handy here. Since the camera shoots video in Auto ISO mode, it can compensate for lower lighting levels and still produce a decent image. For the best results though, better lighting is necessary.

I've found a number of lighting accessories that work well with a small camera like the a7C II/a7CR. Several Sony flash units, including the HVL-F43M, HVL-F45RM, and HVL-F60RM have built-in LED movie lights that you can control from the camera. (I cover electronic flash in more detail in Chapter 13.) You'll probably find those too bulky for shooting video during sessions where you have no need for their flash capabilities. Dedicated LED units are smaller and more practical. One I like is the versatile Lume Cube 2.0 (about $90, but frequently found on sale). It's waterproof, it's less than two inches tall (without the optional accessory shoe mount shown), brightness can be adjusted wirelessly, and it has a brilliant 80-degree beam that can light up a room. Battery life is about 1.5 hours at its 100 percent setting. The Lume Panel Mini ($60) is about the length and width of a credit card, has adjustable color temperature, and is provided with a softening diffuser for gentle, flattering light that's useful when capturing video (or stills!) of people. If you need more light, a Lume Panel Go ($99) and Lume Panel Pro ($200) are available. The former has 150 percent of the light output of the Mini, and measures 4.8 × 2.6 × 0.3 inches, while the latter, at 1500 lux (at .5 meters) emits three times as much illumination from its 6 × 3.14 × 0.43–inch form factor.

When I need a lot of light for a long time, I use my trusty Neewer 160 LED panel, available on Amazon and elsewhere for as little as $25. I load mine up with six Panasonic eneloop rechargeable AA batteries and shoot for hours. There are newer ("Neewer") versions that are thinner and use rechargeable batteries from a variety of vendors. All are bulkier than the Lume offerings and have fewer features, but you can't beat their $25–$50 price tags.

Creative Lighting

While ramping up the light intensity will produce better technical quality in your video, it won't necessarily improve the artistic quality of it. Whether we're outdoors or indoors, we're used to seeing light come from above. Videographers need to consider how they position their lights to provide even illumination while up high enough to angle shadows down low and out of sight of the camera.

When considering lighting for video, there are several factors. One is the quality of the light. It can either be hard (direct) light or soft (diffused) light. Hard light is good for showing detail, but it can also be very harsh and unforgiving. "Softening" the light, but diffusing it somehow, can reduce the intensity of the light but make for a kinder, gentler light as well.

While mixing light sources isn't always a good idea, one approach is to combine window light with supplemental lighting. Position your subject with the window to one side and bring in either a supplemental light or a reflector to the other side for reasonably even lighting.

Lighting Styles

Some lighting styles are more heavily used than others. Some forms are used for special effects, while others are designed to be invisible. At its most basic, lighting just illuminates the scene, but when used properly it can also create drama. Let's look at some types of lighting styles:

- **Three-point lighting.** This is a basic lighting setup for one person. A main light illuminates the strong side of a person's face, while a fill light lights up the other side. A third light is then positioned above and behind the subject to light the back of the head and shoulders. (See Figure 10.6, left.)

- **Flat lighting.** Use this type of lighting to provide illumination and nothing more. It calls for a variety of lights and diffusers set to raise the light level in a space enough for good video reproduction, but not to create a particular mood or emphasize a particular scene or individual. With flat lighting, you're trying to create even lighting levels throughout the video space and minimize any shadows. Generally, the lights are placed up high and angled downward (or possibly pointed straight up to bounce off of a white ceiling). (See Figure 10.6, right.)

- **"Ghoul" lighting.** This is the style of lighting used for old horror movies. The idea is to position the light down low, pointed upward. It's such an unnatural style of lighting that it makes its targets seem weird and ghoulish.

- **Outdoor lighting.** While shooting outdoors may seem easier because the sun provides more light, it also presents its own problems. As a general rule of thumb, keep the sun behind you when you're shooting video outdoors, except when shooting faces (anything from a medium shot and closer) since the viewer won't want to see a squinting subject. When shooting another human this way, put the sun behind her and use a video light to balance light levels between the foreground and background. If the sun is simply too bright, position the subject in the shade and use the video light for your main illumination. Using reflectors (white board panels or aluminum foil–covered cardboard panels are cheap options) can also help balance light effectively.

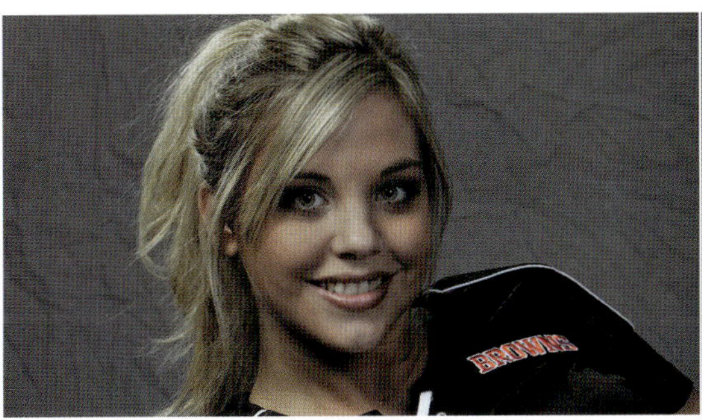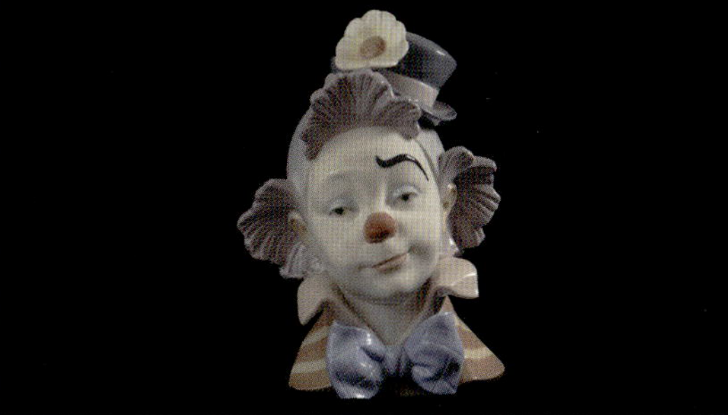

Figure 10.6 With three-point lighting (left) and flat lighting (right).

Audio

When it comes to making a successful video, audio quality is one of those things that separates the professionals from the amateurs. We're used to watching top-quality productions on television and in the movies, yet the average person has no idea how much effort goes in to producing what seems to be "natural" sound. Much of the sound you hear in such productions is actually recorded on carefully controlled sound stages and "sweetened" with a variety of sound effects and other recordings of "natural" sound.

Your a7C II and a7CR have a pair of stereo microphones on its top surface, able to capture Dolby Digital Audio. You can plug an external microphone into the mic jack on the left side of the camera, or work with a microphone designed specifically for Sony cameras, such as the (roughly $130) Sony ECM-XYST1M mic (see Figure 10.7). Hook up Sony's ECM-B1M shotgun mic or XLR-K3M XLR adapter kit with a pro microphone; you'll get professional digital (not analog) audio quality that can match any dedicated camcorder.

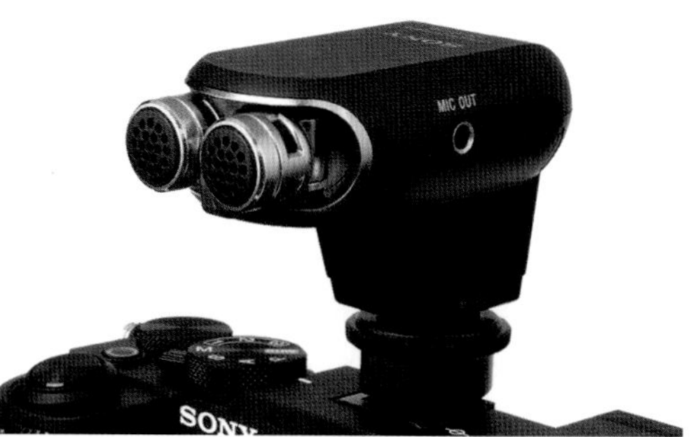

Figure 10.7 An external microphone can significantly improve your audio quality.

If you stick with the built-in microphones, you must be extra careful to optimize the sound captured by those fixed sound-grabbers. In the Shooting > Audio Recording group you'll find entries for Audio Recording, Audio Recording Level, Audio Out Timing (to compensate for a delay when viewing live video through the a7C II/a7CR's HDMI port), and a Wind Noise Reduction on/off entry. The latter is a low-cut filter feature that can further reduce wind noise; however, this processing feature also affects other sounds, making a wind screen on the microphone itself far more useful.

Tips for Better Audio

Since recording high-quality audio is such a challenge, it's a good idea to do everything possible to maximize recording quality:

- **Turn off any sound makers you can.** Little things like fans and air handling units aren't obvious to the human ear but will be picked up by the microphone. Turn off any machinery or devices that you can plus make sure cell phones are set to silent mode. Also, do what you can to minimize sounds such as wind, radio, television, or people talking in the background.

- **Make sure to record some "natural" sound.** If you're shooting video at an event of some kind, make sure you get some background sound that you can add to your audio as desired in postproduction.

- **Consider recording audio separately.** Lip-syncing is probably beyond most of the people you're going to be shooting, but there's nothing that says you can't record narration separately and add it later. It's relatively easy if you learn how to use simple software video-editing programs like iMovie (for the Macintosh) or Windows Movie Maker (for Windows PCs). Any time the speaker is off-camera, you can work with separately recorded narration rather than recording the speaker on-camera. This can produce a much cleaner sound.

I'll explain the half-dozen Audio Recording options available with the a7C II/a7CR in Chapter 11.

Lens Craft

I'll cover the use of lenses with the a7C II/a7CR in more detail in Chapter 12, but a discussion of lens selection when shooting movies may be useful at this point. In the video world, not all lenses are created equal. The two most important considerations are depth-of-field, or the beneficial lack thereof, and zooming. I'll address each of these separately.

Depth-of-Field and Video

Have you wondered why professional videographers have gone nuts over still cameras that can also shoot video? The producers of *Saturday Night Live* could afford to have their director of photography use the niftiest, most-expensive, high-resolution video cameras to shoot the opening sequences of the program. Instead, they opted for a pair of digital SLR cameras. One thing that makes digital still cameras so attractive for video is that they have relatively large sensors. That provides two benefits compared to cameras with a smaller sensor. In addition to improved low-light performance, the large chip allows for unusually shallow depth-of-field (a limited range of acceptable sharpness) for blurring the background; this effect is difficult or impossible to match with most professional video cameras since they use smaller sensors.

As you'll learn in Chapter 12, a larger sensor calls for the use of longer focal lengths to produce the same field of view, so, in effect, a larger sensor allows for making images with reduced depth-of-field. And *that's* what makes cameras like the a7C II/a7CR attractive from a creative standpoint. Shallow depth-of-field makes it easier to blur a cluttered background to keep the viewers' eyes riveted on the primary subject. Your camera, with its larger sensor, has a distinct advantage over consumer cam-corders in this regard, and even does a much better job than professional video cameras.

Zooming and Video

When shooting still photos, a zoom is a zoom is a zoom. The key considerations for a zoom lens used only for still photography are the maximum aperture available at each focal length ("How *fast* is this lens?"), the zoom range ("How far can I zoom in or out?"), and its sharpness at any given f/stop ("Do I lose sharpness when I shoot wide open?").

When recording video, the priorities may change, and there are two additional parameters to consider. The first two I listed, lens speed and zoom range, have roughly the same importance in both still and video photography. Zoom range gains a bit of importance in videography, because you can always/usually move closer to shoot a still photograph, but when you're zooming during a shot most of us don't have that option (or the funds to buy/rent a dolly to smoothly move the camera during capture). But, oddly enough, overall sharpness may have slightly less importance under certain conditions when shooting video. That's because the image changes in some way many times per second (30/60 times per second), so any given frame doesn't hang around long enough for our eyes to pick out every single detail. You want a sharp image, of course, but your standards don't need to be quite as high when shooting video.

Here are the considerations:

- **Zoom lens maximum aperture.** The "speed" of the lens matters in several ways. A zoom with a relatively wide maximum aperture (small f/number) lets you shoot in lower light levels with fewer exposure problems. A wide aperture like f/1.8 also enables you to minimize depth-of-field for selective focus. Keep in mind that with most zooms, the maximum aperture gets smaller as you zoom to longer focal lengths. A variable-aperture f/3.5 to 5.6 lens like the power zoom kit lens, offers a fairly wide f/3.5 maximum aperture at its shortest focal length but only f/5.6 worth of light-capturing ability at the long end. Zooms with a wide and constant (not variable) maximum aperture such as f/2.8 are available, but they are larger, heavier, and more expensive.

- **Power zoom.** An ideal movie zoom should have a power zoom feature, and that's available with Sony lenses with the PZ designation. PZ lenses offer smooth, silent zooming that's ideal for video shooting. Mechanical zooming with other lenses during capture can produce jerky images, even with vibration reduction turned on. If you own a remote with a zoom button, such as the RM-VPR1, I recommend using that with your PZ lenses for smoother zooming. As I mentioned earlier, you can also mimic power zoom using the a7C II/a7CR's digital zoom feature.

- **Zoom range.** Use of zoom during actual capture should not be an everyday thing unless you're shooting a kung-fu movie. However, there are effective uses for a zoom shot, particularly if it's a "long" one from wide angle to telephoto. Most of the time, you'll use the zoom range to adjust the perspective of the camera *between* shots, and a longer zoom range can mean less trotting back and forth to adjust the field of view. Zoom range also comes into play when you're working with selective focus (longer focal lengths produce shallower depth-of-field) or want to expand or compress the apparent distance between foreground and background subjects. A longer range gives you more flexibility.

- **Linearity.** Interchangeable lenses may have some drawbacks, as many photographers who have been using the video features of their digital SLRs have discovered. That's because lenses with mechanical zooming are rarely linear unless they were specifically designed for shooting movies. Rotating the zoom ring manually at a constant speed doesn't always produce a smooth zoom. There may be "jumps" as the elements of the lens shift around during the zoom. Keep that in mind if you plan to zoom during a shot and are using a non-linear lens. In practice, those include virtually all the lenses at your disposal, aside from power zoom lenses (like the Sony FE 16-35mm f/4 PZ G), a special E-mount cine lens, or a cine lens in an entirely different mount that you can use with your a7C II/a7CR with an optional third-party adapter.

Advanced Video Features 11

As I've noted several times in this book, the a7CR and a7C II boast professional-level video features not found in most consumer- or even some pro-oriented digital still cameras. Many of those looking for an advanced Sony camera for video may prefer a dedicated camcorder, like the Sony PXW-Z90V 4K HDR XDCAM. Even so, the a7C II/a7CR is no slacker when it comes to capturing clips that can be assembled into polished video productions.

This chapter will introduce you to some of the most important concepts you'll need to learn as you continue your educational journey toward professional cinematography. Some of this will seem a little technical to those who are just learning about video, so if you're not going to be venturing into serious movie making soon, you might want to skim through this chapter simply to gain some background. I don't normally venture this deeply into tech territory in my books, but the a7C II and a7CR aren't ordinary cameras!

More on Sensors and Crop Factors

In Chapter 10, I described some of the reasons why the large sensor size of a full-frame still camera provides video shooters with some selective focus advantages when compared to the much smaller sensor found on many professional video cameras in the past. I'll be explaining the concept of *crop factor* in detail in Chapter 12. Both aspects are important in the video world, but with a few variations caused by the differences in how video is captured and used.

Sensor Size

Sensor size is important because smaller sensors use lenses with shorter focal lengths to fill their frames, and the shorter the focal length, the larger the depth-of-field. That's why point-and-shoot cameras (or smartphones), with their minuscule sensors, can produce acceptably sharp images for subjects located a few inches from the lens out to infinity. A "normal" lens for a typical smartphone may have a 7mm focal length. Conversely, because a normal lens on a full-frame camera like the a7C II or a7CR is in the 50mm range, it has much less depth-of-field for the same field of view as a point-and-shoot or smartphone camera.

Selective focus is a definite creative plus for videographers. We've all seen shots in which focus initially emphasizes some foreground object that's sharply rendered, and then the camera operator pulls focus out to a more distant subject, which suddenly appears in great detail. Larger sensors make such techniques easier, which is why current video cameras are often segregated into *small sensor* and *large sensor* categories.

Figure 11.1 shows the relative size of the 4K and/or Full HD capture area of some typical sensor sizes, starting with the full-frame sensors (like those found in the Sony a1, a7-series, and a9-series cameras) at upper left, the "small" sensor of typical pro cameras and the $1/^2/_3$-inch sensor of Sony's least expensive pro camera at right, and an APS-C sensor like that found in the Sony a6700 and the RED Raven "large" sensor shown at the bottom right and bottom of the figure. I'll explain more about the crop factor in the next section.

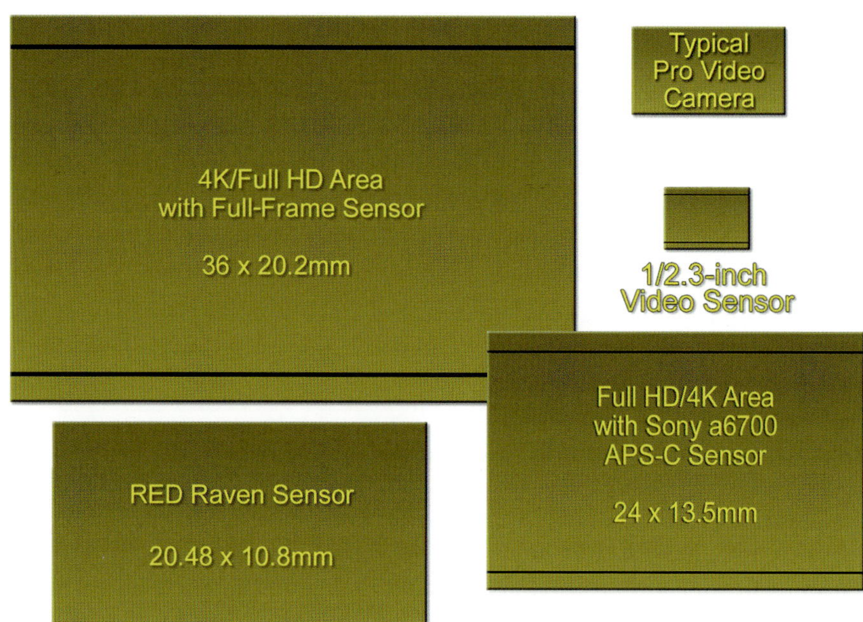

Figure 11.1 Relative video capture areas for example sensor sizes.

Crop Factor

The *crop factor* is important because with any given lens, the field of view will vary depending on how much of that lens's coverage area is used to capture video. (If you're completely unfamiliar with crop factors, skip ahead to Chapter 12 and read about them.) Still photos can be shot in both vertical or horizontal orientations, and most often using the 3:2 aspect ratio used outside the Micro Four Thirds (4:3) world. So, the crop factor for stills is calculated by comparing the diagonal measurement of the frame with the diagonal of the traditional 35mm frame.

For video, clips are normally captured with the camera in a horizontal orientation (at least, outside the realm of the smartphone and TikTok), and the proportions or aspect ratio of the video frame can vary, with 16:9 being the standard for Standard Definition HD, Full HD, and 4K (Ultra HD) video (and beyond).

The 16:9 proportions work out to roughly 1.90:1, which is close enough to the 1.85:1 widescreen cinema aspect ratio that it's easy to show movies captured in either aspect ratio on displays compatible with either. Given the 16:9 standard, it's common to represent the resolution of a video image by its horizontal measurement and scanning method: that is, 720p, 1080p, and 4K (actually 2,160 pixels with your Sony a7C II or a7CR camera) for progressive scan (p) video.

You capture video using the full width of the sensor (effectively a 1X crop) when shooting Full HD (1080p) at up to 120/100 frames per second, or 4K video (2160p) at 30 frames per second. The a7C II/a7CR in these modes use *chroma subsampling,* a type of compression that reduces color information while maintaining luminance (brightness) data to reduce bandwidth requirements without significantly impacting picture quality. (See Figure 11.2, yellow bars.) When the a7C II/a7CR capture video from pixels spanning the full width of the sensor (except when shooting at 120/100p), they do not use *pixel binning,* which takes clumps of red, green, and blue pixels and merges them with others of the same color to create a larger "pixel" at a reduced resolution, resulting in faster capture with reduced noise. The remaining pixels are then *demosaiced,* which interprets the colors of adjacent pixels to produce a full-color image even though each physical pixel actually is sensitive to only one of the three primary colors.

Subsampling is also used to capture 4K 60/50p video, with a slight 1.2X crop applied, indicated by the cyan frame in Figure 11.2. The very best image quality is achieved using *oversampling,* which captures higher-resolution 6.2K footage that is reduced down to a more detailed 4K 60p video file with less noise, but with a 1.5X APS-C Super 35 crop applied. (See Figure 11.2, green frame.) When oversampling, the large number of pixels is demosaiced *first,* and *then* downsized to the required size. Because oversampling happens *after* the RGB pixels have been analyzed and demosaiced, the process allows for better capture of details for a sharper final image. The main drawback of that mode is, of course, that your lenses have the 1.5x "multiplier" applied, reducing wide-angle field of view while adding telephoto "reach."

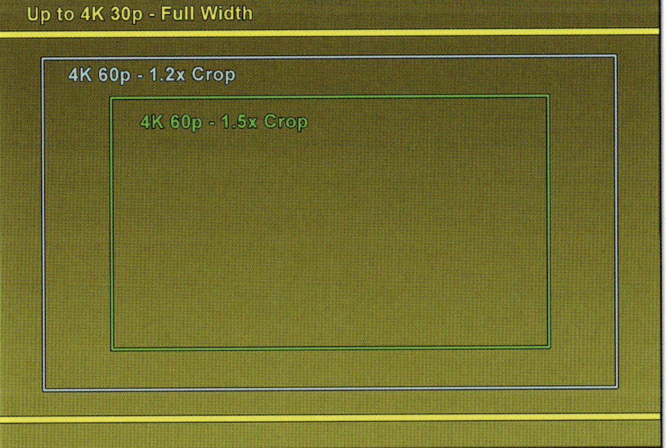

Figure 11.2 Full-width, 1.2X, and 1.5X crops.

Other Important Parameters

But wait, as they say, there's more! The last sections of this chapter will explain some of the other technical details of shooting video, providing enough detail, I hope, to get you reading more complex tomes that cover this information in depth.

Frame Guides

Frame guides are a useful way of visualizing the area that will be captured within a larger visible display. In ancient times, interchangeable-lens rangefinder film cameras that used an optical viewfinder would have bright frame outlines appear, often automatically when a particular lens was mounted on the camera, and sometimes through the use of an attachment that fit over the built-in viewfinder. In the digital age, frame guides have been popular with digital cameras that use an optical viewfinder, providing a masked-off display to preview the actual image area that will be captured in crop or video modes. Cameras with electronic displays, like the a7C II/a7CR, don't necessarily need frame guides, because the capture area can be enlarged and masked off electronically to show only the actual image area.

Even so, frame guides are a popular tool for videographers, because they allow viewing the area outside the actual frame that will be captured (the "look-around area") so you can monitor moving subjects before they enter the frame. In professional productions, it's useful to look at the region outside the captured frame to detect when boom microphones, careless crew members, or other objects threaten to intrude on the frame.

The a7C II/a7CR cameras offer a variety of frame guides that can be turned on or off in the Shooting > Marker Display group. (See Figure 11.3, left.) They include a frame center marker, aspect ratio markers (see Figure 11.3, center), and "safety" areas (see Figure 11.3, right). These markers appear *only* on the EVF or LCD monitor, and not in the captured video itself. The Marker Display group has five entries:

- **Marker Display.** This setting has On and Off options, and simply enables or disables marker display. You can turn any, all, or none of the markers described next on or off independently.
- **Center Marker.** This crosshair can be used to determine whether your subject is placed in the exact center of the screen. (Shown in Figure 11.4, upper left.)

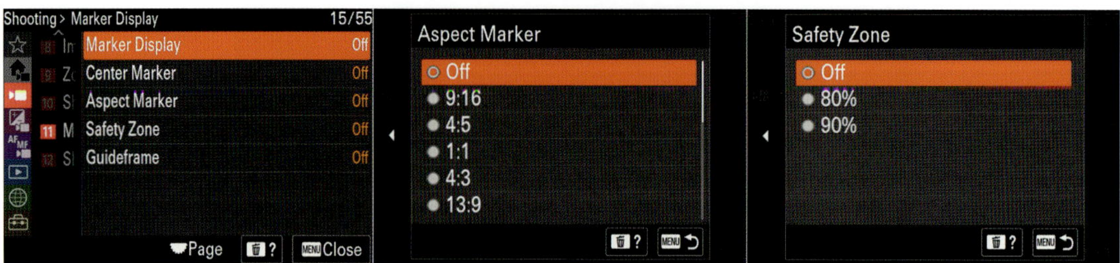

Figure 11.3 The Marker Display group of the (Movie) Shooting tab.

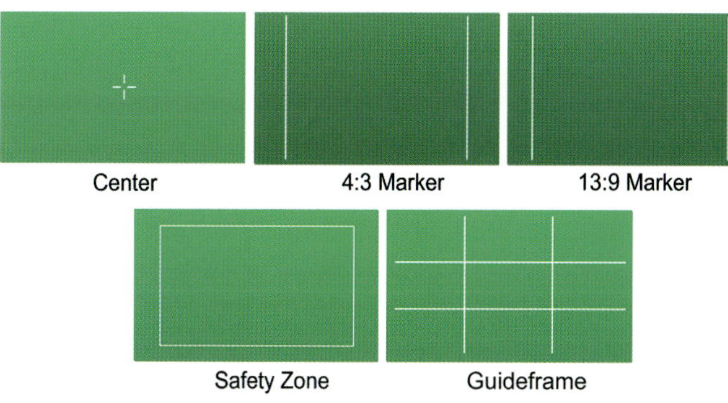

Figure 11.4 Five examples of marker displays.

- **Aspect Marker.** Use these guides to frame your image so the important subject matter is contained within a desired aspect ratio, or to frame the image for later cropping to that aspect ratio. You can select from 9:16, 4:5, 1:1, 4:3, 13:9, 14:9, 15:9, 17:9, 1.66:1, 1.85:1, 1.91:1, 2:1, 2.35:1, or 2:39:1. These conform to various movie formats in common use. (*Star Wars*, for example, was filmed in CinemaScope, with a 2.35:1 aspect ratio.) (See Figure 11.4, upper center and upper right.)

- **Safety Zone.** It's common to shoot movies knowing in advance that they will be cropped down eventually for display in a slightly different format. The director simply makes sure that the important parts of the frame are included in the "safety zone" that will never be cropped out. For example, you wouldn't want to put two characters who are talking to each other at opposite ends of the entire frame but would instead locate them in the safety zone so both would be visible. Your camera's safety zone display can be set for 80 percent or 90 percent of the frame to represent the area that will always be shown when the movie is viewed on a Standard Definition HDTV. (See Figure 11.4, lower left.)

- **Guideframe.** This grid is used to help you determine whether horizontal and vertical lines are skewed and can also be used as a Rule of Thirds guide for composition. (See Figure 11.4, lower right.)

Time Codes and User Bits

The Time Code (TC) and User Bit (UB) settings are information that can be embedded and used to sync clips and sound when editing movies. Advanced video shooters find SMPTE (Society of Motion Picture and Television Engineers)-compatible time codes embedded in the video files to be an invaluable reference during editing. To oversimplify a bit, the time system provides precise *hour:minute:second.frame* markers that allow identifying and synchronizing frames and audio. The time code system includes a provision for "dropping" frames to ensure that the fractional frame rate of captured video (remember that a 24 fps setting actually yields 23.976 frames per second while 30 fps capture gives you 29.97 actual "frames" per second) can be matched up with actual time spans.

Using time codes and user bits is a college-level film school class on its own, but I'm going to provide a quick overview to get you started. If you're at the stage where you're using time codes, you don't need this primer, anyway. However, the a7C II/a7CR's (Movie) Shooting > TC/UB group has six entries (see Figure 11.5):

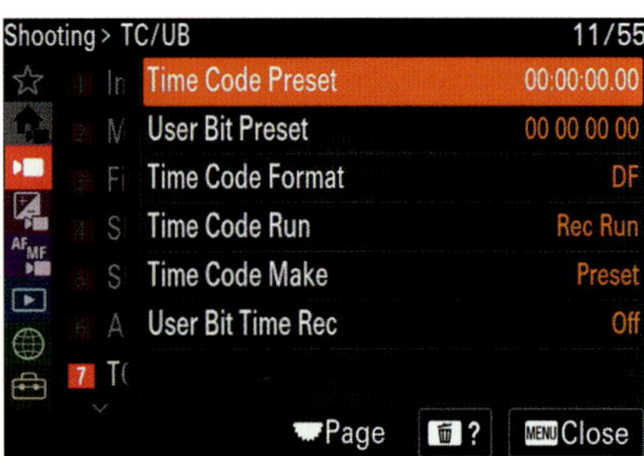

Figure 11.5 TC/UB group.

- **Time Code Preset.** Sets the time code. If you'll be shooting 60i/50i, you can choose time codes from 00:00:00.00 (hours, minutes, seconds, frame) to 23:59:59.29 or 23:59:59.24, respectively. With 24p, you can set multiples of four from 0 to 23 frames. If you own the RMT-VP1K remote commander, the time code can be reset to zero using a button on the controller.

- **User Bit Preset.** Sets the user bit, which is a marker you can insert in your video, say, to designate a scene or take. There are four digits in each user bit (for example, 01:02:03.04), and the digits are each hexadecimal in nature, so you could create a code like C0 FF EE if you were feeling facetious. Everyone will know you're joking because user bits aren't in general use anymore.

- **Time Code Format.** Sets the recording method for the time code. You can choose from DF (drop-frame) or NDF (non-drop-frame) formats. Drop frames are a way of compensating for the discrepancy between the nominal number of frames per second and the actual number (for example, 30 fps yields 29.97 actual frames per second, and 60 fps gives you 59.95 frames per second). In drop-frame format, the camera will skip some time code numbers at intervals to eliminate the discrepancy. The first two frame numbers are removed every minute except for every tenth minute (think of it as a leap year). You may notice a difference of several seconds per hour when using the non-drop-frame option.

- **Time Code Run.** Sets the count up format for the time code. You can choose Rec Run, in which the time code counts up only when you are actually capturing video; or Free Run (also known as Time of Day), which allows the time code to run up even between shooting clips. The latter is useful when you want to synchronize clips between multiple cameras that are shooting the same event. When using Free Run, even if the cameras record at different times, you'll be able to match the video that was captured at the exact same moment during editing.

- **Time Code Make.** Sets the recording format for the time code on the recording medium. Choose Preset to record a new time code, or Regenerate to read the previous time code setting and record the new time code consecutively. When Regenerate is selected, the time code advances no matter what TC Run setting has been selected.

- **User Bit Time Rec.** Sets whether or not to record the time as a user bit.

As explained in Chapter 9, the Setup > Display Option > TC/UB Display Setting entry allows you to determine which of three options are displayed during review. It has nothing to do with what actually is *recorded* onto the Time Code track; it determines how the information is shown:

- **Counter.** When this default value is chosen, the display will include the time counter, which starts at zero and is shown as HH:MM:SS (hours, minutes, seconds).
- **TC.** The SMPTE (Society of Motion Picture and Television Engineers) time code is displayed as HH:MM:SS:00 (hours, minutes, seconds, frames, but the frames are always shown as 00).
- **U-Bit.** A four-character string used to identify the camera that captured the video.

Picture Profiles

If you've been taking photos for a while, you're probably familiar with all the fixes and tweaks you can do with your still images within image editors like Photoshop. It's relatively easy to adjust color tones, contrast, sharpness, and other parameters prior to displaying or printing your photo. Movies are a little trickier, because any given video typically consists of *thousands* of individual photos, captured at 24 frames per second (or faster), with the possibility that each and every frame within a particular sequence might need fixes or creative adjustments.

Shooting video does not preclude doing post-processing during editing. Indeed, many videographers deliberately shoot relatively low-contrast video in order to capture the largest dynamic range possible, and then fine-tune the rendition later using their editing software. Picture Profiles let you do that—and also allow you to adjust your camera so that the video you capture is *pre-fine-tuned* in order to reduce or eliminate the amount of post-processing you do later.

The a7C II/a7CR camera is furnished with eleven "canned" picture profiles, which you can think of as Creative Looks for movies. The parameters included in these profiles can be further adjusted by you to better suit the "look" you are striving for in your videos. You can connect your camera to a TV or monitor using the HDMI Out connector and an HDMI cable, view the image produced by the camera on the larger screen, and then make adjustments to the picture profile.

Needless to say, creating and using Picture Profiles is a highly technical aspect of video making, at least in terms of the amount of knowledge you need to have to correctly judge what changing one of the parameters will do to your video. I hope to get you started with a quick description of what those parameters do, so you'll have a starting point when you start to explore them.

Gamma, Gamma Ding Dong

The eleven Picture Profile presets in the Exposure/Color > Color/Tone > Picture Profile entry already have their own default values, each adjusted for a particular type of shooting, using various gamma and color tone settings. Thanks to our evolutionary heritage, humans don't see differences in tones in a linear manner. An absolutely smooth progression of pixels from absolute black to pure white (with 0 representing black and 256 representing white) would not look like a continuous gradient to our eyes. We'd be unable to detect differences in shadows and highlights that have the same change in tonal values as midtones. So, everything from computer monitors to printers use a correction factor (gamma) to cancel out the differences in the way we see tones.

This correction takes the form of a curve, called a *gamma curve.* If you remember your geometry, the x and y axes on a graph are used to define the shape of a curve, and in the case of gamma curves, the values use logarithmic units (ack!) to define the slope. That's where the terms S-Log2, S-Log3, HLG, and other mind-numbing jargon comes from. The whole shebang is needed to reconcile the ability of sensors to capture, video systems to display, and printers to output a range of tones in a linear way with the actual tones we perceive non-linearly. Gamma correction and gamma compression are used to help make sure that what we get is what we see. While gamma correction between computer platforms (that is, between Macs and PCs) may be different, the actual gamma values defined by video standards like NTSC and PAL are fixed and well-known. Picture Profiles allow you to configure your camera to capture video using a desired amount of gamma and color tone correction.

S-Log2/S-Log3/HLG

S-Log2 is a log gamma curve that is used when the video will be processed after shooting and captures a much larger range of tones (as many as 14 stops!) than standard gamma curves. Indeed, the tones captured using S-Log2 can't be displayed in all their glory on a standard TV or monitor, which are generally adjusted for the broadcast television BT.709 standard. Instead, the unprocessed video will look darker and lower in contrast because all those tonal values have been squeezed into the BT.709 (also called REC.709) range.

Video signals normally encompass brightness levels from 0 percent to 109 percent (you read that right: modern video cameras can record detail in highlights that are actually brighter than was possible when the video age began; the old scale was retained, reminiscent of Nigel Tufnel's 11 setting on his amp). However, even the 109 percent provides too much of a limitation; cameras can capture detail in highlights that are even brighter than *that.* So, a log gamma curve (in this case one called S-Log2) is used to *compress* all that image detail to fit into the space allowed for conventional video signals. Post-processing in a video editor allows working with all that information and produces a

---

VIEWING FIX

Movies captured using gamma profiles appear to be very low in contrast until processed using software on your computer. Because Picture Profiles extend the dynamic range of recorded video, the clips normally appear very low in contrast during review in the camera. The Gamma Display Assist entry in the Setup > Display Option group allows you to adjust playback when viewing images captured using Picture Profiles, so that the appearance on the a7C II/a7CR's EVF and LCD appears more natural, which is useful if you use live view to evaluate your captures. The display is not changed if you're viewing through a device plugged into the HDMI port, and you'll still need to process the video in your video-editing software. You can turn Gamma Display Assist off (Setup > Display Option > Gamma Display Assist), allow the camera to select an appropriate adjustment automatically, or manually set the assist feature to use the gamma you are using. Your choices include Auto, S-Log3->709 (800%), and two HLG (Hybrid Log Gamma) settings, which are used for delivery of video to high-dynamic-range TVs that are currently the rage. (More on HLG later in this chapter.) These are a bit esoteric for the average a7C II/a7CR user who isn't heavily into professional-quality video capture.

finished video that contains the filmmaker's selection of tonal values in a form that can be displayed comfortably. The full dynamic range can be used to produce the finished movie. You might find that useful when exposing for highlights while avoiding blowing out the sky, or for capturing detail in shadows without losing mid tones and highlights.

I know this chapter doesn't tell you everything you need to know to take the next step in movie making with your a7C II/a7CR camera, but my intent was to introduce you to enough of your Sony's capabilities to spur additional exploration of this exciting creative arena.

Select LUT

Options: S-Log3, s709, 709 (800%), User 1–16

My preference: N/A

Look-up Tables (LUTs) are a way of remapping the (typically low-contrast, prior to grading) colors captured during video shooting using a format such as S-Log3, so the footage can be viewed on a standard monitor before color grading has been applied. This entry allows you to choose one of three built-in LUTs, or apply any of 16 different LUTs that you upload to the camera. Of the three built-in LUTs, S-Log3 is the most commonly used; s709 corresponds to the BT.709 specification used with high-definition televisions, and 709 (800%) is an older standard not frequently used. As I noted above, this is an advanced capability beyond the scope of this book, and I won't be showing you how to adjust or create Look-up Tables.

Sony, in its wisdom, has scattered all the entries that manage LUTs among various different menus:

- **Log Shooting.** Navigate to the Shooting > Image Quality/Recording > Log Shooting Setting entry to enable access to this entry. When you do, Picture Profiles, described above, will be disabled.
- **Select LUT.** This entry will allow you to choose one of the three canned LUTs or one you have uploaded.
- **Manage User LUTs.** That's the entry that follows this one, used to import, edit, or delete customized LUTs.
- **Display LUT.** Navigate to Setup > Display Option > Display LUT to enable playback of video footage in the camera using the active LUT.

Manage User LUTs

Options: Import/Edit, Delete All

My preference: N/A

Videographers have access to a wide variety of LUT files that can be found on the internet, both free and with price tags attached. Once downloaded, they can be placed in the /Private/Sony/PRO/LUT folder of your memory card where the a7C II/a7CR can find them when you access this menu entry. They will be loaded into the camera's menu and can be erased from the memory card after they've been imported.

More on 4K Video

It's probably a great time for you to start working with 4K video, especially since 8K video is already on the way. In practice, shooting 4K is not much different than shooting Full HD or Standard Definition HD. The only changes you might make involve your realization that as long as you are capturing higher-quality video, you might as well upgrade your technique (and, perhaps, your auxiliary equipment).

Given the usual pace of technology, it's very likely that your next HDTV will have 4K capabilities (if your current set does not), and cable/satellite/streaming systems as well as Blu-Ray discs have already made the leap sooner than any of us expected.

Shooting in 4K has become more prevalent, even though many households do not own 4K high-definition televisions that allow playing back 4K content at its full resolution. However, the number of 4K-capable TVs is growing all the time, and there are some definite benefits to shooting ultra-high resolution now, even before the ability to take advantage of the format is universal. Simply speaking, if you shoot 4K and then convert it to conventional Full HD, your video will generally be much higher in quality than if you originated in 1920 × 1080 resolution. All you need is editing software like Adobe Premiere Pro, Final Cut Pro, or Corel Video Studio that can work with and edit your 4K clips.

The key thing to know is that your a7C II/a7CR can record 4K video internally, export 4K video to an external recorder, or to *both* simultaneously. If you want to record *only* to the memory card, you don't need to do anything special other than select XAVC S 4K or XAVC HS under the File Format entry and your desired frame/bit rate under Record Setting.

If you prefer to output your 4K video to the HDMI port (say, to a video recorder or other device), or HDMI port *and* the memory card, you need to visit the Setup > External Output > HDMI Output Settings entry described in Chapter 9. Set the Still/Movie/S&Q dial to Movie and attach your camera to the external device using an HDMI-to-micro-HDMI cable. Since the length of your recording time is essentially limited only by the a7C II/a7CR's ability to dissipate heat and avoid shutdown from high sensor temperatures (potentially a problem when shooting 4K video), the extra storage offered by some external monitors can come in handy.

As I mentioned in Chapter 10, you will probably want to use an external microphone, either plugged into the a7C II/a7CR's microphone jack or connected through the multi-interface shoe on top of the camera. As I noted, a move to professional microphones using the XLR interface might also seem prudent. Sony offers the XLR-K3M adapter kit, a dual-channel device that can be mounted in the multi-interface shoe and used to connect XLR mics and other audio sources to the a7C II/a7CR. It's pricey at almost $600, but includes a Sony ECM-XM1 shotgun microphone.

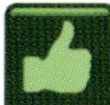

TIP If you read my Chapter 9 advice on redefining the available options in the Function menu, consider using Fn Menu Settings in the Setup > Operation Customize group if you intend to shoot a lot of video. You can define *separate* Function menus for still photography and movie shooting. Among those you might consider substituting are Zebra settings, Audio levels, and Color balance/temperature settings (remember it's more difficult to adjust color in video than in individual still photos). Or, you might want to add Picture Profiles, Wind Noise Reduction, or the Movie setting (which allows you to switch among P, A, S, or M movie exposure modes). Marker Display or TC/UB settings are other entries you might want to add to your Function menu.

Using an External Recorder

If you're truly becoming an advanced videographer, you'll probably be working with the a7C II/a7CR's ability to output "clean" non-compressed HDMI video to an external monitor or video recorder, including the Atomos Shogun lineup, which includes versions that are quite affordable, at least in terms of professional video gear. You can choose models both with and without an external LCD monitor, and capture to solid-state drives (SSD), a laptop's internal or connected hard drive, or to CFast memory cards (the latter chiefly as a nod to those still using the "fast" version of Compact Flash cards). Such equipment allows very high transfer rates and is certainly your best choice if you're shooting 4K video.

Probably the best of the lot for a7C II/a7CR owners is the Atomos Ninja V/V+, and Ultra series, extremely portable units with 5.2-inch screens and priced at $600 to $800. Their size is a definite plus—if you're shooting video with a smaller, lightweight camera, you're going to need an equally compact recorder/monitor, such as the roughly 13-ounce Ninjas. Add a battery, HDMI cable, and a 2.5-inch solid-state drive, and you're ready to go.

The Ninja monitor-recorder has HDMI input and output jacks on its left edge, which you can see in Figure 11.6. The latter allows you to daisy-chain an even larger monitor or other device. A power button, headphone jack, microphone/audio input, and remote jack reside on the other edge. The touch screen enables you to view your video and access the monitor/recorder's menus and controls, which is convenient (except outdoors in cold weather when you're wearing gloves and might wish you had a few buttons to press instead). The only other "defect" of the unit is the noise produced by its fan; even when you're using an external microphone with your a7C II/a7CR, the fan noise may be picked up in a quiet room.

Why use an external monitor/recorder like the Ninja V, when your a7C II/a7CR has its own nifty monitor and can store quite a lot of video on UHS-II-compliant memory cards? From a monitor standpoint, an external unit's screen is larger, easier to see, and offers more flexibility in positioning. The a7C II/a7CR's screen tilts up or down; mounted on a ballhead like the one in the figure, you can adjust an external screen to any angle, including reversing it to point

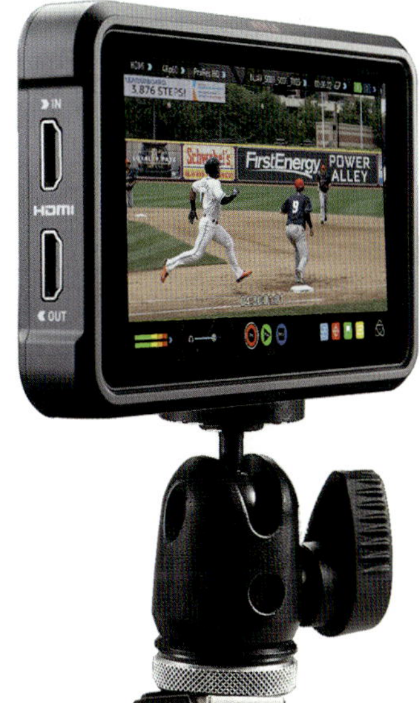
Figure 11.6 The Atomos Ninja V monitor/recorder.

in the same direction as the lens, so vloggers can monitor themselves as they record or stream their video blog.

The HDMI port on the a7C II/a7CR accepts an HDMI cable. I prefer to purchase value-priced third-party cables, which I buy in convenient lengths of 3 feet, 6 feet, 10 feet, or longer. The cable can be connected to the monitor, recorder, or other device of your choice. (Some of the screen shots in this book were output to a video capture device that allowed capturing stills of the a7C II/a7CR's menus, live view, and video.)

When it comes to saving your 4K video files, you have three destination combinations to choose from:

- **Capture to memory card (only).** You can output your 4K video to a memory card in your a7C II/a7CR, but it really should be a fast memory card. Because 4K video files can be so massive, you'll want a 64GB to 128GB (or larger, when they become affordable) card to store your movies. This option is the least expensive, but it comes at a cost.
- **Capture to an external recorder (only).** If you're *really* serious about video, you'll want to consider using an external recorder, linked through the a7C II/a7CR's HDMI port. The video is *not* compressed, and you can take advantage of the fastest transfer rates to optimize quality. You'll want to visit Setup > External Output > HDMI Output Settings > Record Media during HDMI Output and choose Off (HDMI Only).
- **Capture to both.** If you're equipped with a very fast memory card and external recorder, you can opt to save your video to both destinations. Go to Setup > External Output > HDMI Output Settings > Record Media during HDMI Output and choose On.

Audio Settings

I'm going to wind up this chapter with an explanation of the Audio Recording options available in the Shooting menu when the Shooting/Movie/S&Q dial is set to a movie position. There are five entries, shown in Figure 11.7:

- Audio Recording
- Audio Recording Level
- Audio Out Timing
- Wind Noise Reduction
- Multi-interface Shoe Audio Settings

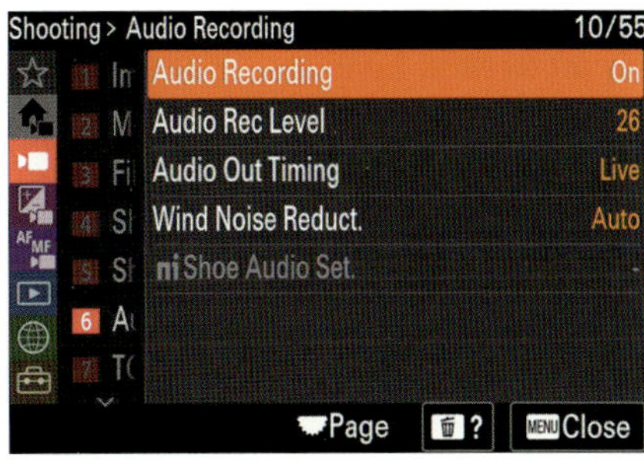

Figure 11.7 The Audio Recording group.

Audio Recording

Options: *On, Off

My preference: On

Use this item to turn off sound recording when you're shooting videos, if desired. In most cases you'll want to leave the setting On, to capture as much information as possible; the audio track can be deleted later, if desired, with software. However, there could be occasions when it's useful to disable sound recording for movies, for example, if you know ahead of time that you will be dubbing in other sound, or if you have no need for sound, such as when panning over a vista of the Grand Canyon. At any rate, this option is there if you want to use it.

Audio Recording Level

Options: Levels from 0 to 31 (default: 26)

My preference: N/A

You can adjust the recording level of the camera's built-in or external microphones using this entry, which also enables/disables the audio level overlay on the screen while movies are captured. To use this feature, just follow these steps:

1. Rotate the Still/Movie/S&Q dial to the Movie position.
2. Navigate to the Audio Recording group, highlight Audio Rec Level, and press the center button.
3. The screen shown in Figure 11.8 appears. Rotate the front or rear dial or control wheel or use the left/right controls to adjust the volume level up or down. There are 32 different levels, from 0 to 31.
4. Press the center button to confirm and exit the screen.
5. Alternatively, you can press the Trash button to Reset to return the recording level to the default value. Then press MENU to exit.

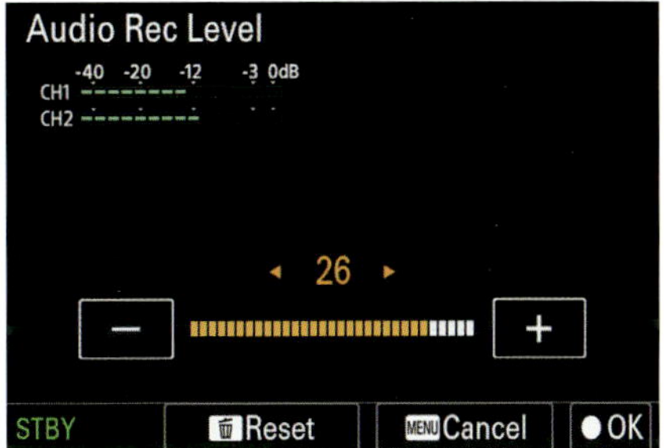

Figure 11.8 Set Audio level.

Audio Out Timing

Options: ***Live**, Lip Sync
My preference: Live

With the a7C II/a7CR, *audio out* refers to the sound signal you hear when monitoring the recording through the camera's headphone jack. In this mode, the sound you hear may be slightly out of sync with the video, because the video must be processed by the camera's digital processing chip before you see it on the LCD or EVF. Using an external microphone may contribute to this delay. Sony offers two different audio modes that can ignore or compensate for this lag.

- **Live mode.** If you are not using headphones and are listening to the audio in real time, this setting allows you to hear the sound being recorded in real time, with no delay. Use this mode if you are watching the action in the scene directly, rather than viewing it through the viewfinder or on the LCD monitor.
- **Lip Sync mode.** In this mode, the audio and video shown while the movie is being captured are delayed by the same amount and will be in sync with each other if you monitor using headphones in conjunction with the EVF or LCD.

Wind Noise Reduction

Options: ***Auto,** On, Off
My preference: Auto

Designed to muffle the howling sound produced by a loud wind passing over the built-in microphones, this item (when On, or set to Auto) is for use when recording video. It's set to Auto by default because Wind Noise Reduction (provided by the camera's processor) does degrade sound quality, especially bass tones, and the recording volume is reduced. You may want to set it to Off when shooting in a location with especially loud wind noises that are not muffled by this feature.

[Multi-interface] Shoe Audio Settings

Options: 48KHz, 24-bit, 4 channel; 48KHz, 24-bit, 2 channel; 48KHz, 16-bit, 2 channel
My preference: N/A

This entry is available only when a multi-interface shoe (MiS)-compatible digital microphone is plugged into the a7C II/a7CR's multi-interface shoe. It allows you to choose audio adjustments that correspond to the parameters of your digital microphone, such as the Sony ECM-B1M camera-mount digital shotgun microphone, or other microphones that have a switch that enables them to toggle between analog and digital operation.

Working with Lenses {.chapter-title}

12

The number of lenses for Sony mirrorless cameras that operate with full autoexposure and auto-focus features has grown dramatically since the E-mount was introduced in 2010. And if you're willing to use an adapter, there are at least several hundred more lenses in Sony/Minolta A-mount, Nikon F-mount, or Canon EF-mount—often available at bargain prices—that can be used on your a7C II and a7CR, with autofocus and autoexposure. And the number of lenses that can be used with *manual* focus and Aperture Priority autoexposure using adapters for Nikon, Yashica, Contex, Contarex, Alpha, and other types of lenses is mind-boggling. Indeed, Pulitzer Prize–winning photographer (and Sony guru) Brian Smith has called the Sony product line the "universal-mount" cameras.

This chapter will help you wend your way through the confusing world of lenses. At the end of the chapter, I'm going to provide an overview of how the camera's impressive stabilization system works with your lenses—and on its own—to provide your steadiest shots, ever. But, before we get into the actual lenses themselves, it may be useful to explore some aspects that affect how you choose and use optics.

Don't Forget the Crop Factor

If your a7C II or a7CR is your introduction to full-frame photography, you may be wondering about the term *crop factor,* or, perhaps, alternate nomenclature such as *lens multiplier* or *focal length multiplication factor.* They're used to describe the same phenomenon: the fact that cameras that do not have a full-frame sensor provide a field of view (or scene coverage) that's *smaller* than what you get with a camera employing the larger sensor. The a7C II/a7CR uses a sensor that's approximately 23.9mm × 35.7mm (roughly 1.0 × 1.5 inches) in size. Many other digital cameras, such as the Sony a6700 (which uses a body configuration similar to the a7C II/a7CR), use a smaller so-called APS-C (Advanced Photo System-C) sensor that measures roughly 16mm × 24mm. In comparison, the APS-C sensor's field of view is *cropped.* Some interchangeable-lens (ILC) cameras from other vendors, including Olympus and Panasonic, may use even smaller sensors (with even greater cropping effect).

Knowledgeable photographers often discuss this effect as the *crop factor* and you'll often find a reference in lens reviews to a *focal length equivalent,* such as 1.5X. In other words, a 200mm lens used on an APS-C camera (or the a7C II/a7CR when in APS-C/Super 35mm mode) captures the same subject area as a 300mm focal length on a full-frame camera. The most accurate expression to describe this concept might be something like *field-of-view equivalency factor.*

Figure 12.1 quite clearly shows the phenomenon at work. The green rectangle, marked 1X, shows the field of view you might expect with a 24mm lens mounted on a full-frame digital model. It provides a very wide-angle perspective, roughly 84 degrees (measured diagonally by convention). The yellow rectangle marked 1.5X shows the field of view you'd get with that 24mm lens installed on a camera like the Sony a6700 that uses a 15.6mm × 23.5mm (APS) sensor. It's easy to see from the illustration that the APS-C rendition is narrower—roughly 61 degrees diagonally—and, compared to the full-frame version, *cropped*.

That 24mm lens on an a6700 or your a7C II/a7CR in APS-C mode has equivalent field of view as a 36mm lens. While you can calculate the relative field of view by dividing the

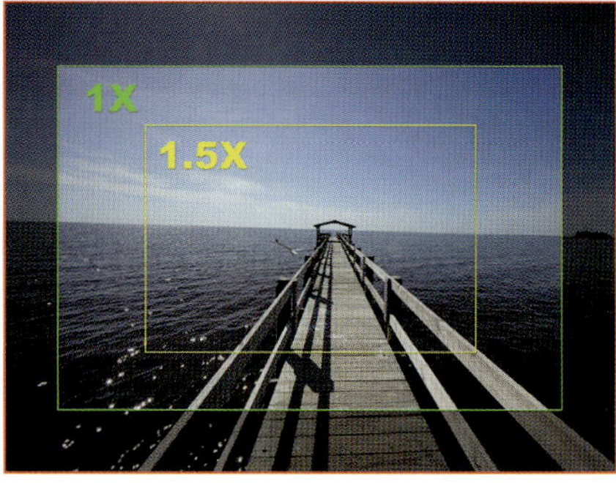

Figure 12.1 This image illustrates the field of view provided by a full-frame camera, as well as the field of view you'd get when using a camera with the smaller sensor (1.5X crop) or the a7C II/a7CR in APS-C/Super 35 mode.

focal length of the lens by .667, we humans tend to perform multiplication operations in our heads more easily than division, so such field of view comparisons are usually calculated using the reciprocal of .667—1.5—so we can multiply instead (24 / .667 = 36; 24 × 1.5 = 36). That's the origin of the misleading term *multiplication factor*. The sensor image is trimmed or cropped—not multiplied.

In any event, I strongly prefer *crop factor* to *focal length multiplier*, because nothing is being multiplied (as I said above). When working with telephoto lenses, a 100mm lens doesn't "become" a 150mm lens; the depth-of-field and lens aperture remain the same. (I'll explain more about these later in this chapter.) Only the field of view is cropped. Of course, the term *crop factor* has a drawback: it implies that a 24mm × 36mm frame is "full" and anything else is "less than full."

I get e-mails all the time from medium-format photographers who own cameras like the Hasselblad H6D-50c, which has a 43.8 × 32.9mm sensor that's 67 percent larger than "full-frame." By their logical reckoning, the 24mm × 36mm sensors found in full-frame cameras are "cropped." Take a look at the outer, darkened area within the red rectangle in Figure 12.1. That represents the whopping 104-degree field of view you'd get with a Hasselblad HCD 24mm f/4.8 ($7,250; body an extra $14,495 if you're compiling a holiday gift list).

Crop Factor Effects

So, what should the crop factor mean to you? Here's a checklist of things you should consider:

- **Reduced resolution.** This is the biggie. In crop mode, your images will have their resolution reduced by more than 50%, producing 14MP shots with the a7C II. That's often sufficient for certain applications, such as real estate photography, or images that will not be extensively cropped or enlarged, posted only on web pages, or emailed.

    However, crop mode (APS-C/Super 35 mode) actually works even better with the a7CR: its 60MP of resolution is reduced to a more-than-respectable 26 megapixels when cropped. Although APS-C/Super 35 mode "transforms" your 70-200mm zoom into a fast 105-300mm lens, the resolution penalty may be acceptable for a7CR owners; for a7C II users, 15MP may not be enough.

- **Shoot now, crop later?** Indeed, many point out that you can always shoot everything in full-frame mode and crop your images, perhaps with greater flexibility, in an image editor. While that's true, it's not *always* the best route. In crop mode, the a7C II and a7CR enlarge the cropped image to fill the EVF and LCD monitor, and it's more intuitive to frame and compose your images already cropped. Sports photographers and photojournalists who fire off 1,000 shots at an event won't be eager to go through their digital files and manually crop images. If the resolution you get in APS-C mode is sufficient, it's easier to crop as you shoot.

- **Lens compatibility.** Lenses designed for APS-C cameras may not cover the entire 24mm × 36mm full-frame camera sensor area, although some zoom lenses may have a large enough image circle at some focal lengths. With most APS-C lenses you will experience vignetting (darkening) in the corners and reduced sharpness along the edges of the image. For full-frame photography, these lenses will usually be less than satisfactory.

- **Enabling mode.** As described in Chapter 6, you'll find the APS-C/Super 35mm crop mode in the Shooting > Image Quality/Recording > APS-C/S35 Shooting entry. It has three settings:

  - **On.** The a7C II/a7CR *always* shoots in cropped mode, regardless of which lens is mounted on the camera. Both full-frame and APS-C lenses will produce images with a cropped field of view. You might use this setting to give your lenses some extra "reach" for sports or wildlife photography.

  - **Auto.** If the camera detects that an APS-C lens is mounted, it will switch to crop mode. Not all lenses will be automatically detected, so you may have to use the On setting instead to manually select crop mode.

  - **Off.** The camera *never* switches to crop mode. Even APS-C lenses will be used in full-frame mode. If you have a lens that *almost* covers the full frame at certain zoom settings, you can use this option and crop out the offending dark corners in your image editor.

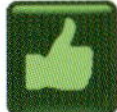

TIP I used the Custom Key/Dial Set entry in the Setup > Operation Customize group to redefine the Custom 1 (C1) button to the function APS-C S35/Full Frame. When shooting sports, I can press the C1 button to toggle between APS-C crop mode (to give my telephoto extra reach) and full-frame mode (when I need a wider perspective) quickly and easily, on the fly. For example, if a wide receiver runs a pattern to the far side of the football field, I can switch to crop mode to get a shot, then return to full-frame mode to get set for the next play with another tap of the C1 key.

Choosing a Lens

Sony's expansion of its lens product line is brisk enough that, while I'm going to provide a quick listing of some of my favorite lenses currently available for the a7C II and a7CR, it will necessarily be somewhat incomplete. I expect additional lenses to be introduced as this book goes into production and, with luck, during the life of the book itself.

I'm going to emphasize only full-frame lenses available from Sony in this chapter. If you read through my explanation of the crop factor, you know that APS-C lenses from Sony and other vendors *can* also be used with the a7C II or a7CR. While there are pros and cons to that approach, and the number of APS-C lenses available is vast, I'm not going to list those options here.

Nor will I provide extensive coverage of the growing number of excellent third-party lenses available in Sony E-mount. I rarely discuss third-party offerings, whether it's lenses, flash units, or accessories in my books, because there are so many of them, and the product churn can quickly make any recommendation obsolete. However, I want to emphasize that, in addition to Sony's own product line, produced internally from the company's own designs or with the cooperation of Zeiss, there are some excellent third-party optics you really should consider from Samyang, Venus Optics Laowa, Mitagon, 7Artisans, TTArtisans, and others. For the very latest information on the full range of lenses available for your camera, I urge you to consult online forums, such as DPReview, as they have constant updates that printed and ebook publications can't match.

As I noted in the introduction to this chapter, you can use a zillion A-mount lenses with the EA-LA3 and EA-LA5 adapters, Canon EF lenses and Nikon F-mount optics with an appropriate auto adapter from Metabones, Commlite, Fotodiox, or other vendors, and adapters for virtually every other possible lens mount if you're willing to forgo autofocus and some other features.

Sony FE Lenses

Enthusiasts of virtually every camera platform settle on a trio of basic, must-have zoom lenses that cover the focal length range from very wide angle to medium telephoto—roughly 16mm to 200mm— and Sony users are no exception. Indeed, as an a7C II/a7CR owner, you actually have multiple options within each range, which enables you to compile a trinity of (reasonably) affordable lenses, or, if you want, spring for upscale deluxe versions that cover the same focal lengths.

I'm going to start off with three excellent, value-priced optics. They all have built-in optical image stabilization that can work in tandem with the a7C II/a7CR's in-body SteadyShot. All have a constant f/4 maximum aperture that doesn't change as you zoom and are reasonably affordable (as far as premium optics go) at $1,200–$1,500 each. Many early adopters of Sony's mirrorless cameras did so for their lighter weight and compactness, compared to traditional dSLRs. As the owner of a super-compact a7C II or a7CR, you're likely still in that camp, so I urge you to consider the optics found in this affordable trio of lenses. Their more expensive G-Master (GM) counterparts have superior optics and builds, but, as a class, are somewhat larger and bulkier. If you don't need a maximum aperture f/2.8 or faster, you'll find these three are very good indeed:

- **Sony FE 16-35mm f/4 ZA OSS lens.** This is the lens you need for your architectural, landscape, and indoor photography in tight quarters. It covers an almost perfect range of focal lengths, from an ultra-wide 16mm to the street/urban photographer's favorite 35mm field of view. Some might prefer Sony's 12-24mm zoom instead (which wouldn't overlap with the 24-70mm lens described later), but I find the extra 11mm useful. I don't have to swap lenses when I need to zoom in a little tighter. One wonderful thing about this optic is that it has *curved* aperture blades, producing smooth circular defocused highlights for great *bokeh*. At around $1,350, you can afford this lens, and if you shoot a lot of wide-angle images, you can't afford *not* to have it. (See Figure 12.2, left.)

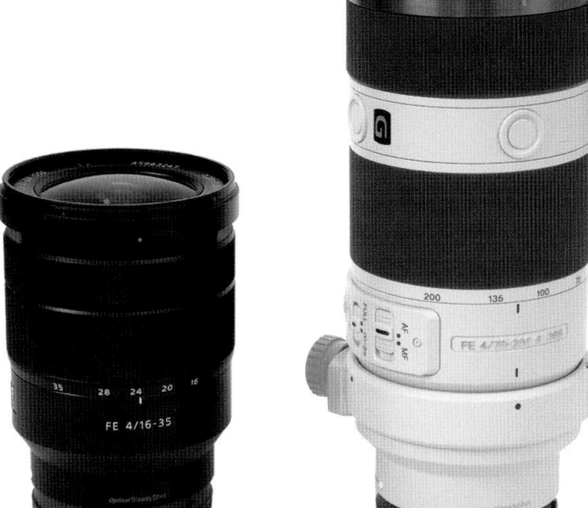
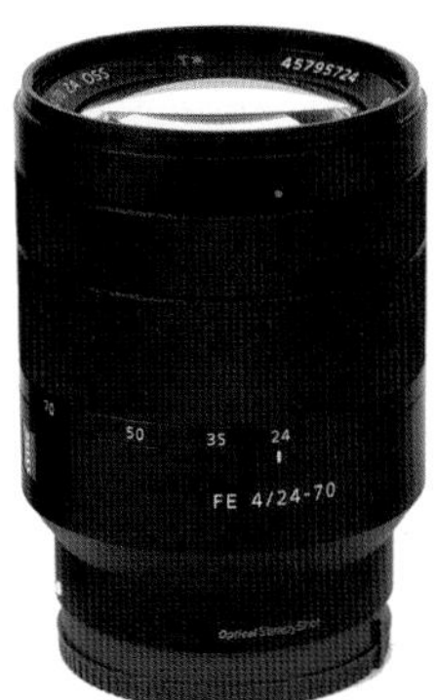

Figure 12.2 Sony's three key FE lenses, left to right: 16-35mm f/4, 70-200mm f/4, and 24-70mm f/4.

- **Sony FE 20-70mm f/4 G lens.** This one has displaced its aging Zeiss-branded 24-70mm f/4 counterpart (discussed later) in Sony's affordable trinity array, thanks to its superior imaging quality, slightly wider 20mm perspective, and some nifty new features. With all that, it's still reasonably priced at about $1,100. It focuses down to 9.8 inches.

  Unlike most lenses these days, this one has an actual aperture ring, with a switch to enable or disable clicks between positions. Videographers can use the feature to perform a smooth ersatz fade-in/fade-out silently. Other movie-friendly features are buttons for focus mode and focus hold (to lock in focus during a shot), and virtual elimination of breathing (an unwanted change in the angle of view depending on focusing distance) when combined with the a7C II/a7CR's breathing compensation feature within the Lens Compensation entry, described in Chapter 6.

- **Sony FE 70-200mm f/4 G OSS lens.** Compared to 70-200mm f/4 lenses designed for other full-frame cameras, this $1,500, 30-ounce lens is almost petite, but it's quite a beast mounted on the tiny a7C II/a7CR. It's well balanced and these cameras do have the new beefed-up mounting bayonet, but you really should consider using the swiveling tripod collar, either when mounting on a tripod/monopod or as a support when hand-holding. It's a Sony premium G lens (the G stands for "Gold") and its optical performance won't disappoint. (See Figure 12.2, center.)

Elite Threesomes

In response to professionals and others who prefer fast, super-sharp lenses with a larger maximum aperture, Sony has heavily invested in what it calls its G-Master (GM) lineup; three of them span the same focal length range as the "affordable trinity." The company has already introduced Mark II versions of its original trio, with each subsequent optic sharper, lighter, and more compact than its predecessor. Many other G-Master lenses are available now, including the Sony FE 85mm f/1.4 GM and Sony FE 100mm f/2.8 SFT GM OSS, offering additional focal lengths and zoom ranges.

Sony's top-of-the-line trio includes:

- **Sony FE 16-35mm f/2.8 GM II lens.** Like all G-Masters, this lens, a replacement for the original Mark I version, is dust and moisture-resistant, has extra-low dispersion elements, and a price to match its high quality: in this case about $2,300. It focuses as close as 11 inches and uses 82mm filters, which is good news for landscape photographers who need to use polarizers or gradient neutral-density filters. The downside? It's a larger lens than its f/4 cousin.

- **Sony FE 24-70mm f/2.8 GM II lens.** Priced at $2,300, Sony touts this lens as "compact," and it is, at 25 ounces compared to its 32 ounce Mark I predecessor. However, it's still 10 ounces more massive than its f/4 sibling. It focuses down to 11.8 inches at 70mm, uses 82mm filters, and is a superb lens for this focal length range.

- **Sony FE 70-200mm f/2.8 GM OSS II lens.** Even though the original Sony 70-200mm f/2.8 GM OSS lens was excellent, the company has outdone itself with this Mark II model, the costliest lens in the elite trinity at $2,800. Get this: at 36 ounces, it's a *full pound lighter* than its predecessor, and is touted as the most compact lens with this zoom range available from any vendor. Featuring a new optical design, it's said to focus 4X faster than the Mark I version, using a pair of linear focus motors to drive two separate focusing elements. It focuses 20 inches closer, too, down to 15.7 inches. The only "bad" news is that it uses 77mm filters, so you'll need a step-down ring to mount the same filters used with the other two members of the top-line holy trinity.

Some Alternate Choices

Whether you're assembling an "affordable: basic trio," or looking to build a premium lineup, Sony has some alternates for the lenses described above that might better fit your needs. Here are some substitutions I recommend:

- **Sony FE 16-25mm f/2.8 G lens.** At about half the price of the FE 16-35mm f/2.8 GM II lens, this optic is a budget alternative for those who need an f/2.8 maximum aperture and are willing to forgo the premium lens's extra 10mm of reach. Unlike most lenses these days, this one has an actual aperture ring, with a switch to enable or disable clicks between positions. (The Sony FE 24-50mm f/2.8 G lens is another.) Videographers can use the feature to perform a smooth ersatz fade-in/fade-out silently. Other movie-friendly features are a focus hold button (to lock in focus during a shot), and virtual elimination of breathing (an unwanted change in the angle of view depending on focusing distance) when combined with the a7C II/a7CR's breathing compensation feature within the Lens Compensation entry, described in Chapter 6.

- **Sony FE 24-50mm f/2.8 G lens.** Another compact, video-friendly zoom (it has the same declickable aperture ring, focus hold/mode buttons, and breathing compensation features as the 16-25mm f/2.8 G lens), this one focuses down to about 7 inches, and is reasonably priced at about $1,100.

- **Sony FE 12-24mm f/4 G lens.** If you need a wider perspective or prefer to have no overlap with the 24-70mm lens in your arsenal, this lens makes an excellent alternative for the 16-35mm f/4 lens I listed earlier. At around $1,800, though, its "affordability" may come into question, and it's a larger lens. But those doing a lot of architectural photography will appreciate its more expansive view. Its chief disadvantage is that it can't accept filters. It might be the most versatile walk-around lens for landscape, architectural, and, maybe, street photographers who love (or need) the wide-angle look. Roughly the same size as the 24-105mm lens, it weighs 20 ounces, but lacks image stabilization (which is less important with wide-angle lenses with most shutter speeds). I'd use this lens if the combination of the Sony 16-35mm zoom and my Voigtlander 10mm f/5.6 manual focus lens didn't give me all the wide-angle flexibility I need.

- **Sony FE 70-300 f/4.5-5.6 G OSS lens.** Cash-strapped enthusiasts who need some extra reach for outdoor sports or wildlife photography may want to substitute this $1,300 lens for the recommended 70-200mm f/4 optic in their "affordable" trio. Its variable maximum apertures are fine when light is plentiful, but not optimum for night photography. It does have Optical SteadyShot, so you may be able to counter the limited f/stop range with slower shutter speeds if your subjects aren't moving rapidly.

- **Sony FE 24-240mm f/3.5-6.3 OSS lens.** On first glance, a 10X zoom lens stretching from a true wide-angle 24mm field of view to the edge of super-telephoto range at 240mm sounds very tempting. With a second look, this optic's $1,050 price adds to the appeal. The reality check comes only when you realize that mating this hefty (1.72 pound), somewhat slow lens (f/6.3 at maximum zoom) to the compact a7C II/a7CR counters the best reason for toting around a tiny full-frame mirrorless camera.

  Given its modest price tag, you can expect this lens will be a jack-of-all-trades and master of none. I've never been a fan of do-everything zoom lenses, as they tend to lose resolution at one end (or both ends) of their focal length range, but those looking to reduce their traveling photo kit to a compact body and a single lens will want to consider this option. It's actually not as bulky as you might think (it's lighter than the 12-24mm f/2.8 G Master described shortly), measures 3.25 × 4.75 inches, and takes affordable 72mm filters.

  If you truly want to walk around with only a single lens and can justify the bulk, this optic does fill the bill. It would also be an efficient choice for photography that might call for extreme wide-angle views and telephoto reach in rapid succession. I tend to prefer Sony's 24-105mm f/4 G lens as my walk-around optic, but this lens's extra reach can come in handy if your travels involve wildlife.

Additional G-Master Lenses

In addition to the superb G-Master zooms already described, Sony offers an extensive roster of GM prime lenses, and two additional GM zooms. You'll want to consider these when expanding your stable of lenses for your a7C II/a7CR.

- **Sony FE 12-24mm f/2.8 GM lens.** The image quality alone puts this $3,000 lens in the "elite" category, but even though Sony touts it as "surprisingly small and lightweight," this fast 12-24mm lens's 30-ounce heft can be a burden. Filters can be problematic with super-wide lenses, but if you rely on certain filters, this lens has a rear-filter holder that accepts inexpensive sheet filters, which may serve certain needs.

- **Sony FE 14mm f/1.8 GM lens.** A wide perspective and large maximum aperture are attractive qualities to architectural, landscape, and astro photographers, and this $1,600 lens checks all the most important boxes. Videographers will appreciate this lens's physical aperture ring, which has a de-click switch that allows smoothly and silently changing the f/stop during capture. It focuses down to 9.8 inches for those amazing close-ups that only an ultra-wide lens can image.

- **Sony FE 24mm f/1.4 GM lens.** This is a prime lens (so to speak) for a wide variety of applications. Architectural photographers will love the $1,400 optic for hand-held interior photography under low-light conditions. Street shooters and photojournalists will find it a relatively affordable option for capturing intimate moments day or night. Landscape photographers will prize its high resolution and useful wide-angle perspective. It's a compact walk-around lens for general-purpose photography, too.

- **Sony FE 35mm f/1.4 GM lens.** Measuring only 3 × 3.9", this fast, compact, wide angle weighs just a smidge over one pound and is a street and candid wedding photographer's dream. Priced at $1,400, it is excellent for photojournalism, landscape photography, and some indoor sports. It has internal focusing (the lens doesn't get longer as you focus) and can shoot macro images as close as 9.8 inches.

- **Sony FE 50mm f/1.2 GM lens.** This $2,000 optic is one of the most versatile in the G-Master lineup. It's got impressive image quality even at the f/1.2 maximum aperture preferred by pros looking to combine selective focus with a creamy background-blur bokeh. The Nano AR Coating II Sony applies to its lenses does an especially good job in reducing flare, reflections, and ghosting even wide open. Autofocus is fast and precise, and, as I mentioned earlier, the de-clickable physical aperture ring will please videographers.

- **Sony FE 85mm f/1.4 GM lens.** This is Sony's other awesome G-Master portrait lens, priced at $1,800. It's good for head-and-shoulders work, too, and a focal length shorter than the 100mm f/2.8 makes it easier to shoot full-length, couples, and group portraits. It has wonderful bokeh, weighs about 29 ounces, and can focus as close as 20 inches. I like this lens's large maximum aperture for concert and performance photography, other subjects under low light, and subjects I want to isolate with selective focus. As mentioned in my descriptions of other GM lenses, videographers will like the ability to de-click the actual physical lens aperture ring (most lenses these days do not have one at all) so exposure can be changed smoothly while a sequence is captured.

- **Sony FE 100mm f/2.8 STF GM OSS lens.** What do you get for $1,500? This G-Master is one of two near-ideal portrait/short telephoto lenses that Sony offers. The f/2.8 maximum aperture makes it easy to defocus the backgrounds, and the STF (Smooth Trans Focus) technology uses something called an apodization filter to produce achingly smooth bokeh with nice, round out-of-focus highlights. (*Apodization* is technical mumbo-jumbo that Sony applies to its use of a radially graduated neutral-density filter that, clear in the center and darker at its edges, in effect, counters the fade-out of those blurry round disks we call "bokeh," for a more pleasing effect.) Reduced flare for greater contrast, fast autofocus, OSS, and focus as close as 1.9 feet (you can switch focus ranges from 2.8 feet to infinity or to a useful macro-only range of 1.9–3.3 feet) make this a formidable lens for portraiture and other subjects.

- **Sony 135mm f/1.8 GM lens.** This fast $2,100 lens is perfect for sports, portraits, and any subjects that can benefit from selective focus and world-class creamy bokeh (for smooth out-of-focus backgrounds).

- **Sony FE 100-400mm f/4.5-5.6 GM OSS lens.** Yet another very welcome G-Master lens, this one covers an ideal focal length range for sports and wildlife photographers, especially since it has OSS and superb weather-sealing. The price, at $2,400, is not even exorbitant considering its likely market and what you get. (Prime and zoom lenses in the 400mm and longer range can easily top $5,000 to $10,000.) It's a little over three pounds in weight, but that's normal in the long tele-zoom territory.

- **Sony FE 400mm f/2.8 GM OSS lens.** This stupendous lens was first used at the Winter Olympics in February 2018. Ordinary humans almost certainly will need at least $12,000 to buy one. It's one of several Sony telephoto lenses with a preset switch that allows specifying a focus plane (say, home plate in a baseball game) and refocusing on that point instantly at the press of a button.

- **Sony FE 600mm f/4 GM OSS lens.** A super telephoto (in many senses of the word), this G-Master has a large maximum aperture that's especially suited for field sports photography. The f/4 aperture can be used wide open at night to allow action shooters to use a motion-freezing high shutter speed, with the added benefit of shallow depth-of-field to throw distracting elements (spectators, or players not involved in the current action) out of focus. This 6.7-pound dream lens has a super price, too: expect to pay $13,000 to add this one to your gear cupboard. Optional 1.4X and 2.0X teleconverters are available. The 2.0X model transforms this optic into a 1200mm f/8 monster (or 1800mm f/8 in crop mode).

Other Favorites

Next up are some of my choices among the other Sony FE lenses. They include walk-around lenses, some fast primes for photojournalism and other available-light applications, and even a stellar macro. Some of the lenses listed next are part of Sony's growing lineup of G-series ("Gold") and a selection of standard lenses that will fit the needs of just about any shooting situation.

They include my own favorite walk-around lens, the Sony FE 24-105mm f/4 G OSS, third in the list that follows:

- **Zoom Lenses:**
  - **Sony Vario-Tessar T* FE 24-70mm f/4 ZA OSS lens.** Another Zeiss-branded product, it has excellent balance with the a7C II/a7CR, making it useful as a walk-around lens for travel photography, full-length and three-quarters portraits, and indoor sports like basketball and volleyball. Unfortunately, it won't be the sharpest optical knife in your toolkit, despite the Zeiss label. I find it perfectly acceptable when stopped down two or three stops from maximum aperture. (See Figure 12.2, earlier, right.)
  - **Sony FE 28-70mm f/3.5-5.6 OSS lens.** This lens is often bundled with Sony full-frame mirrorless cameras as a kit lens, and available separately for less than $400. As I noted above, it's slow (f/3.5) at the 28mm zoom position, and even slower (f/5.6) when zoomed to 70mm. If you favor telephoto lenses or extreme wide angles (as I do), you may find yourself not using the 28-70mm focal length range very often, in which case this lens might make an acceptable fill-in for occasional use.

- **Sony FE 24-105mm f/4 G OSS lens.** This is the do-everything lens for me. I used to rely on the Sony FE Vario-Tessar T* 16-70mm f/4 ZA OSS, and I still use it extensively indoors and for architecture, but for everyday photography I'm willing to give up a little of the wide-angle end of the zoom scale to get the extra reach and selective focus prowess at the long end of this 24-105mm optic's range. It focuses down to 16 inches, uses my full arsenal of 77mm filters, and has Optical SteadyShot. While not petite, I find its 4.5-inch length and 24-ounce weight not burdensome to carry around. As a G lens it has great image quality.

- **Sony FE 28-135mm f/4 G PZ OSS lens.** The specs alone might lead you to believe this is a faster, heavier (5 pounds) walk-around lens with a more restricted zoom range. You'd be wrong. This $2,500 monster is especially designed for pro-level 4K video productions, and if heavy-duty movie making isn't on your agenda, you probably don't want or need this lens. Video shooters, though, will delight in its near-silent, precision, variable 8-speed power zoom, and responsive manual control rings for zoom (with direction reversal for smooth zooms), focus pulling, and aperture.

- **Sony FE 200-600mm f/5.6-6.3 G OSS lens.** Most sports and wildlife photographers will find this hefty zoom lens more affordable, at roughly $2,000. Its maximum aperture varies from f/5.6 to f/6.3 as you zoom to the longest telephoto position, but if you need a 600mm focal length, setting your ISO a stop or two higher can save you $11,000. It is compatible with Sony's 1.4X and 2.0X teleconverters, too.

- **Wide-Angle to Short Telephoto Primes:**
  - **Sony FE 20mm f/1.8 G lens.** Architectural, travel, and street photographers will love this fast ultra-wide-angle lens, especially since it is affordable for most at $900.

  - **Sony FE 24mm f/2.8 G / 40mm f/2.5 G / 50mm f/2.5 G lens.** It's easy to confuse one of these three compact lenses for any of the others in the set that share the same exterior design and $600 price tags. Introduced at the same time, the most significant difference among them is the focal length. They are virtually identical in size and weight (2.7 × 1.8 inches, six ounces) and use the same 49mm filters. They feature fast, accurate, and quiet autofocus, a focus hold button that can be redefined to an alternate function of your choice, and a physical de-clickable aperture ring that has 1/3-stop increments.

  - **Sony FE 28mm f/2.0 lens.** Here's a lens that comes with its own bag of tricks. It's a compact prime lens with a fast f/2.0 aperture, so you can shoot in low light and even gain a modicum of selective focus with its (relatively) shallow depth-of-field wide open. Despite its $450 price, it boasts an advanced optical design with ED (extra-low dispersion) glass elements that improve contrast and reduce troublesome chromatic and spherical aberrations. (You'll find descriptions of lens aberrations later in this chapter.) If that's not enough, you can attach either of two adapter optics to the front. There is a wide-angle version ($250), which converts it to a 21mm f/2.8 wide angle that focuses down to eight inches, and a 16mm fisheye attachment ($300) that I personally find more interesting and fun. But then, I own eight different fisheye lenses, so I'm susceptible.

- **Sony Sonnar T* FE 35mm f/2.8 ZA lens.** This tiny lens is a perfect match for the compact a7C II/ a7CR. At a mere eight ounces and measuring 2.42 × 2.36 inches, it makes a great walk-around lens for stealthy photographers. The image quality is great, but you'd expect that from a Zeiss lens that, at $600, is not bargain-basement cheap.

- **Sony FE 35mm f/1.8 lens.** If you need a little more speed, this compact and lightweight wide-angle prime lens has a fast f/1.8 maximum aperture. The $750 optic is especially suitable for street photography and architecture.

- **Sony Distagon T* FE 35mm f/1.4 ZA lens.** This Zeiss lens is a photojournalist's dream, with a wide-angle focal length that lets you get up close and personal with your subject, and a fast f/1.4 aperture suitable for low light and selective focus. The Zeiss T* (T-star) coating suppresses contrast loss from internal reflections among the lens elements. It's great for video, too, as the aperture ring can be de-clicked with a switch. The only drawback is the price: $1,000, which is a lot to pay for a lens that doesn't give you a range of different focal lengths to work with. However, the shooters this lens is designed for will confirm that it's worth it.

- **Sony Sonnar T* FE 55mm f/1.8 ZA lens.** So, why get excited about a "normal" lens with an f/1.8 maximum aperture and a $1,000 price tag? After all, both Nikon and Canon offer full-frame 50mm f/1.8 prime lenses for quite a bit less. In this case, your ten Benjamins buys you one of the sharpest lenses ever made, with exquisite resolution at every f/stop—including wide open. Given that perspective, this lens is actually a bargain. You'll love using it for head-and-shoulders or 3/4-length portraits using selective focus at f/1.8. You owe it to yourself to get this lens.

- **Sony Planar T* FE 50mm f/1.4 ZA lens.** Faster, sharper, more expensive (at $1,500), and sporting a flare/ghost-reducing T* (T-star) coating, this mid-range ("normal") lens has the Zeiss quality you expect, a solid build, and creamy bokeh from its 11-blade circular aperture.

- **Sony FE 85mm f/1.8 lens.** At $600, this is an affordable, fast, mid-telephoto prime lens that's lightweight and portable.

- **Macro Lenses:**

  - **Sony FE 90mm f/2.8 Macro G OSS lens.** While Sony will continue to make additional macro lenses available, this affordable (in the Sony FE realm, anything in the $1,000 range is considered affordable) $1,100 lens is an excellent choice. Its 90mm focal length gives you a decent amount of distance between the camera and your close-up subject, even at its minimum focusing distance of 11 inches. With internal focusing such that only the internal elements move, the lens doesn't get longer as you focus, avoiding a common problem. You can add a set of auto extension tubes to get even closer. I use Fotodiox Pro 10mm and 16mm tubes. Those tubes are primarily plastic and not especially rugged but are serviceable for light-duty use.

  - **Sony FE 50mm f/2.8 Macro lens.** This is a compact, lightweight standard macro lens with 1:1 (life-size) magnification, focusing as close as 6.3 inches. Priced at $550, it makes a fine, affordable standard macro lens for shooting flowers, bugs, or your coin/stamp collection. If you need to maintain some distance from your subject (say, a skittish creature, or one that requires careful lighting), you would probably prefer the 90mm macro above. But a 50mm is perfect for extreme close-up photography, particularly when mated to a set of extension tubes.

A-Mount Lenses

If you're coming to the Sony mirrorless world belatedly from the SLT/A-mount arena, you may already own some Sony or Minolta lenses that can work very well with your a7C II/a7CR. Sony has discontinued the sale of new A-mount optics, but millions were produced since Minolta originally introduced the mount in 1985. Even if you don't own any of these lenses now, you can buy gently *used* A-mount lenses at bargain prices from reliable sources, such as KEH Camera (www.keh.com). I've purchased more than a dozen lenses from them over the last few years, including the ever-popular "beercan," the Minolta AF Zoom 70-210mm f/4, an ancient optic prized for its tank-like solid build, commendable sharpness, constant maximum aperture, and smooth bokeh.

I'm not sure where KEH gets 30-year-old lenses that are like new, but their selection is huge, and the prices are a fraction of what you'd pay for new A-mount optics. Keep in mind that when Sony took over Konica Minolta's camera/lens technology, it simply rebranded quite a few of the most popular lenses, so you may find a 50mm f/1.4 Minolta lens that's identical to the Sony 50mm f/1.4 lens at a much lower price.

The only drawback to the most affordably priced A-mount lenses is that they probably use Minolta's original screw-drive autofocus technology. To use one of these A-mount lenses that use screw drive on your a7C II/a7CR, you'll need one of the Sony full-frame mount adapters, either the LA-EA3 or LA-EA5 (see Figure 12.3):

- **LA-EA3.** This adapter is suitable *only* with full-frame A-mount lenses that have built-in autofocus motors of the SSM or SAM variety. Autofocus is achieved using the a7C II/a7CR's phase-detect AF system. The designators are included in the lens's official name; check before you acquire. SSM stands for SuperSonic motor, which uses a ring-type ultrasonic driver that is fast and virtually silent and is found on upper-end lenses. SAM stands for Smooth Autofocus Motor, an alternate system built into some lower-end Sony optics introduced since 2009.

- **LA-EA5.** This adapter also works with A-mount lenses built-in autofocus motors of the SSM or SAM variety. In addition, the LA-EA5 has its own motor and can potentially provide autofocus for a much broader range of A-mount lenses. It offers Real-time Eye AF and Real-Time Tracking and its design does not interfere with attaching a vertical grip to your a7C II/a7CR. Check with Sony to see if a particular A-mount lens you are considering is compatible.

Figure 12.3 The Sony LA-EA3 (left) and LA-EA5 (right) mount adapters.

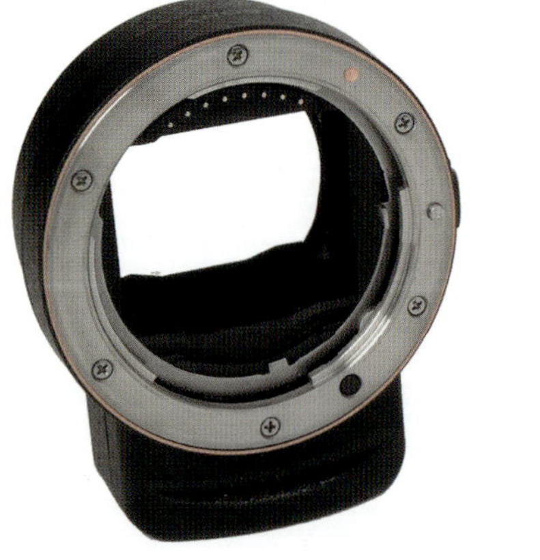
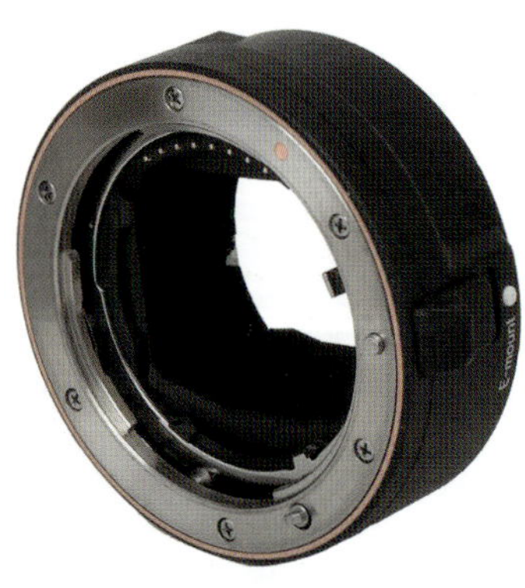

Meanwhile, singling out a few choice A-mount lenses from the vast and varied selection available can be tricky, especially since some of the older lenses are unique, like my 500mm f/8 Reflex super-telephoto lens (available used with either Minolta or Sony badges). It's the world's first (and only) autofocus mirror (catadioptric) lens. (See Figure 12.4.) It has a single, fixed f/8 aperture and that weird "doughnut" bokeh typical of mirror lenses, but it's the most compact long telephoto lens I own, even when attached using an adapter.

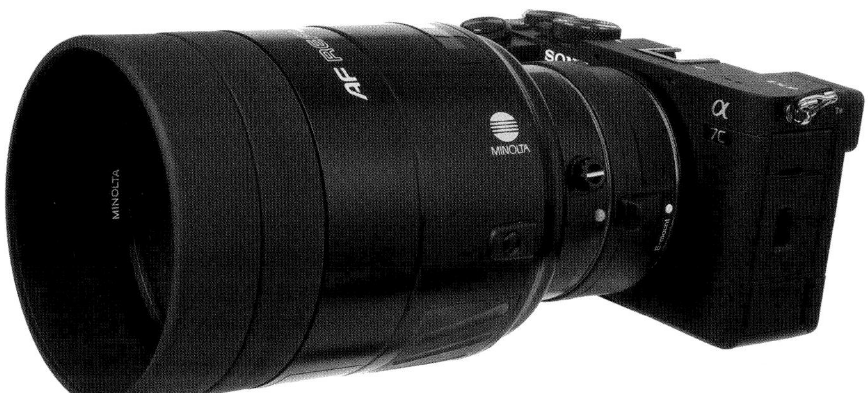

Figure 12.4 The Sony/Minolta 500mm f/8 mirror lens.

Zeiss Batis Lenses

Here we have reasonably priced autofocus lenses from Zeiss. If you're looking for a futuristic touch, they each feature an illuminated OLED (organic LED) display that dynamically shows focus distance and depth-of-field. In the good old days, prime (non-zoom) lenses had etched or painted color-coded depth-of-field markers on the lens barrel, but those largely disappeared when zoom lenses became dominant. Now depth-of-field can be displayed on your lens in a more useful form. The five available Batis lenses are as follows:

- **Zeiss Batis 18mm f/2.8 lens.** Featuring the famed Zeiss Distagon wide-angle design, this optic focuses down to about 10 inches, which is useful if you like wide-angle (apparent) perspective distortion effects. (It's *apparent* rather than *real*, because the distortion is due to the placement of the subject matter within the field of view, not any defect in the lens itself.) At 12 ounces, it's not heavy and makes a good walk-around lens for those who want a prime lens with a wide field of view.

- **Zeiss Batis 25mm f/2.0 lens.** There's a bit of overlap in potential use between this autofocus lens and Sony's own 28mm f/2.0 optic.

- **Zeiss Batis 40mm f/2 CF lens.** Zeiss dubs this a close-focusing (CF) lens; it focuses down to 9.4 inches and is said to work equally well with near and far subjects.

- **Zeiss Batis 85mm f/1.8 lens.** This is a medium-telephoto autofocus lens that's ideal for portraits, and a primo choice for low-light photography and selective focus. It's the first Zeiss lens that has optical image stabilization (the equivalent of Sony's trademarked OSS), giving you hybrid IS when used with the a7C II/a7CR's in-body SteadyShot.

- **Zeiss Batis 135mm f/2.8 lens.** For about $1,600 you get a Zeiss Sonar-design lens with OSS, fast autofocus, and impressive image quality. Some may think this lens verges on being too long for head-and-shoulders portraits, but it's a versatile lens for many types of sports, especially since it has great anti-flare and ghosting properties that are useful when shooting into sunlight.

Zeiss Loxia Lenses

Zeiss also offers the Loxia series, designed specifically for Sony full-frame E-mount cameras. These lenses are among the best we can get; the five available are all manual focus. Not including autofocus helps keep the price down on these otherwise premium-quality super-sharp lenses. Keep in mind that your a7C II/a7CR has a wealth of manual-focus-friendly features, including focus peaking and focus magnification, all described elsewhere in this book.

- **Zeiss Loxia Distagon T* 21mm f/2.8 lens.** This is an extra-compact lens using the famed Distagon design, which overcomes some of the drawbacks of many wide angles to provide consistent sharpness from edge to edge, with little light falloff and excellent correction for chromatic aberrations.

- **Zeiss Loxia Distagon T* 25mm f/2.4 lens.** Another weather-sealed, de-clickable lens, it has two low-dispersion and one aspherical element for excellent image quality.

- **Zeiss Loxia 35mm f/2 Biogon T* lens.** Another name out of the past, Biogon lenses have historically been some of the best wide-angle optics you can buy, and this fast 35mm f/2 lens has been optimized for use with digital cameras (that is, illumination emerges from the back of the lens at a less steep angle, as explained in Chapter 2). This is a well-corrected lens suitable for street photography, architecture, landscapes, and other subjects.

- **Zeiss Loxia 50mm f/2 Planar T* lens.** If you've been involved with photography for any length of time, you'll recognize the Zeiss Planar name, first applied to a symmetrical lens design as far back as 1896. This fast manual focus lens does a good job of correcting for chromatic aberration and distortion.

- **Zeiss Loxia 85mm f/2.4 T* lens.** Its maker describes this lens as portable, inconspicuous, and powerful and urges you to use it for portrait, street, and landscape photography. It is remarkably sharp from edge to edge. Like all the Loxia lenses, the manual aperture ring can be de-clicked, using a supplied tool, for use when constantly varying apertures are desired when shooting video.

Adapters and Third-Party Lenses

Because the a7C II/a7CR has relatively short back-focus distances (the gap between the lens mount bayonet and sensor), it's fairly easy for third parties to adapt their existing full-frame lenses to fit your camera. There are a huge number of adapters that allow mounting just about any lens you can think of on the a7C II/a7CR, if you're willing to accept manual focus and, usually, a ring on the adapter that's used to stop down the "adopted" lens to the aperture used to take the photo. There are also adapters that preserve the automatic features of Canon EF- and Nikon F-mount lenses. You can find these from Novoflex, Metabones, FotodioX, Rainbow Imaging, Cowboy Studio, Vello, Commlite, and others. There are adapters for dozens of different lens mounts, and the same mount adapters are frequently sold by different companies under a variety of names, so your best bet is to use Google to find the exact type you need.

Thankfully, a growing number of lenses are offered in native E-mounts, so you won't need an adapter to use them. Some of the best are described next:

- **Voigtlander.** Probably the oldest name in camera gear, dating back to its founding in Vienna in 1756 (well before the invention of photography itself), this company produces more than a dozen interesting lenses for Sony cameras, including 10mm and 12mm f/5.6 Heliar and a 15mm f/4.5 Heliar. I own the 10mm lens, and it is one of my all-time favorites. On a full-frame camera like the a7C II/a7CR, it's one of the widest rectilinear (non-fisheye) prime lenses available, with a breathtaking 130-degree field of view.

  The company has an impressive array of super-sharp manual-focus full-frame macro lenses for Sony cameras, including an APO-Lanthar 50mm F2 macro that includes electronic contacts that can report EXIF and distance information to the camera for smooth integration with the a7C II/a7CR's in-body image stabilization system and Focus Magnifier. Voigtlander's APO-Lanthar macro lineup also includes 35mm f/2, 50mm f/2, 65mm f/2, and 110mm f/2.5 models. Especially prized are the 35mm f/1.2, 40mm f/1.2, 50mm f/1.2, and 50mm f/1.0 (!) Nokton lenses, which have stellar performance wide open.

- **7Artisans.** This company offers some affordable full-frame manual focus lenses in Sony E-mount, including a 10mm f/2.8 fisheye, an ultra-fast 50mm f/1.05, 35mm f/2, and a 35mm "panfocus" pancake-style lens with a fixed f/5.6 aperture and extremely wide depth-of-field range. I opted for their 50mm f/0.95 APS-C lens, which I use with my Sony a6700. On the a7C II/a7CR, it is transformed into an interesting 75mm (equivalent) portrait optic in crop mode. Other interesting optics from this company include a 9mm f/5.6 rectilinear (non-fisheye) lens with de-clicked aperture ring that's perfect for video.

- **Mitakon/Zhongyi.** This company makes an ultra-fast 85mm f/1.2 manual focus lens, and a hyper-fast 50mm f/0.95 lens in Sony E-mount. The company also offers a 20mm f/2 super macro at a bargain $240 that focuses down to less than one inch! I own this lens and its main drawback is that it focuses *only* at 1.8 inches. There is no focus ring—the lens works best on a focusing rail that allows you to move the entire camera/lens rig back and forth to achieve focus.

- **Sigma.** Sigma is increasingly venturing into FE territory, with a lineup of fast prime lenses having f/1.4 maximum apertures in 20mm, 24mm, 28mm, 35mm, 40mm, and 105mm focal lengths. In addition to a 70mm f/2.8 macro lens, Sigma sells 14mm f/1.8 and 135mm f/1.8 prime lenses. My personal favorite in the Sigma lineup is the company's 100-400mm f/5-6.3 DG DN OS zoom, which has become my mainstay for wildlife photography. It has specs very similar to Sony's FE 100-400mm f/4.5-5.6 GM OSS, at a fraction of the price. It's no G-Master, but I was surprised with its image quality and autofocus speed.

- **Samyang/Rokinon.** This company's manual-focus 12mm f/2.8 fisheye resides in my fisheye collection, and I often alternate its use with my 15mm f/2.8 Sigma fisheye. I use them in manual-focus mode with adapters, but Samyang/Rokinon also sells lenses in E-mount (sometimes under the Bower brand name). They include a 24mm f/1.4, 35mm f/1.4, 50mm f/1.4, 85mm f/1.4, 135mm f/2, and a 100mm f/2.8 macro lens that produce 1:1 (life-size) magnification at a minimum focusing distance of 12 inches. They are starting to issue autofocus lenses in Sony FE mount, including an affordable FE 35mm f/2.8 and a 14mm f/2.8 wide-angle.

- **Tamron.** Tamron, which is partially owned by Sony, has made a move into Sony E-mount autofocus territory, with a total of eight lenses as I write this. Their first FE offering was the Tamron 28-75mm f/2.8 Di III RXD. They also offer telephoto zooms, including a 70-180mm f/2.8, 70-300mm f/4.5-6.3, and 28-200mm f/2.8-5.6. In the wide-angle realm, Tamron has a 17-28mm f/2.8 zoom, plus 20mm and 24mm f/2.8 prime lenses.

- **Venus Optics Laowa.** This company makes a variety of full-frame lenses for Sony E-mount cameras, including the novel Laowa 10-18mm f/4.5-5.6 FE zoom and the weirdest macro lens ever made: the Laowa 24mm f/14 2X Macro Probe, an expensive ($1,800) optic for super-close, bug's-eye views with a waterproof probe that includes a built-in LED ring light. The company also offers a compact 25mm f/2.8 ultra-macro with 2.5X to 5X life-size magnification and focusing down to less than two inches. Other full-frame lenses from Laowa that may be of interest to discerning a7C II/a7CR owners include a 15mm f/2 "Zero D" (zero distortion) lens with a 110-degree angle of view and remarkable image quality. It's not a fisheye—it's a rectilinear lens with two aspherical elements and three extra-low dispersion (ED) elements for impressive optical quality. It focuses down to seven inches, making some interesting, distorted-perspective shots possible.

- **All the rest...** Lensbaby, Thingify, TTartisans, Neewer, and many other vendors are now offering manual-focus lenses in Sony E-mount, at attractive prices. My latest "find" was the 27mm f/2.8 Rockstar, an APS-C lens I ordered simply because it was $59 with free shipping. It's a fixed aperture lens with a very stiff focusing ring (that will take you down to 9 inches) and surprisingly good image quality. I also use my Lensbaby Composer and Thingify Pinhole Pro lenses on my a7C II/a7CR when I want to play around with novelty optics.

What Lenses Can Do for You

A sane approach to expanding your lens collection is to consider what each of your options can do for you and then choose the type of lens that will really boost your creative opportunities. Here's a guide to the sort of capabilities you can gain by adding a lens (using an adapter, if necessary) to your repertoire.

- **Wider perspective.** A 24-70mm or 28-70mm lens can serve you well for moderate wide-angle to medium telephoto shots. Now you find your back is up against a wall and you *can't* take a step backward to take in more subject matter. Perhaps you're standing on the boulevard adjacent to the impressive domed walls of the Mirogoj Cemetery in Zagreb, Croatia, and you want to show the expanse of the walls, as I did for the photo at top in Figure 12.5, made with the Sony/Zeiss 16-35mm f/4 zoom lens. Or, you might find yourself just behind the baseline at a high school basketball game and want an interesting shot with a little perspective distortion tossed in the mix. If you often want to make images with a super-wide field of view, a wider lens is in your future.

- **Bring objects closer.** A long focal length brings distant subjects closer to you, allows you to produce images with very shallow depth-of-field, and avoids the perspective distortion that wide-angle lenses provide. If you find the traffic on the street intrusive, as I did in Zagreb, you can zoom in to eliminate the distraction, as in Figure 12.5, center. A lens like the Sony/Zeiss 24-70mm f/4 can be your best friend. For even more magnification you might want to use a longer telephoto, like the 100-400mm lens I used to zoom in on one of the domes, in Figure 12.5, bottom.

- **Bring your camera closer.** Sony has two excellent macro lenses with f/2.8 maximum apertures, in 50mm and 90mm focal lengths. The Sony 90mm f/2.8 macro lens is preferable to the shorter macro lens in nature photography because you do not need to move extremely close to a skittish subject for high magnification. And you can get a frame-filling photo of a tiny blossom without trampling all the other plants in its vicinity.

- **Look sharp.** Many lenses, particularly the higher-priced Sony and Zeiss optics, are prized for their sharpness and overall image quality. Your run-of-the-mill lens is likely to be plenty sharp for most applications at the optimum aperture (usually f/8 or f/11), but the very best optics, such as the Zeiss 55mm f/1.8, are definitely superior. You can expect to get excellent sharpness in much of the image area at the maximum aperture, high sharpness even in the corners by one stop down, more consistent sharpness at various focal lengths with a zoom, and better correction for various types of distortions (discussed shortly).

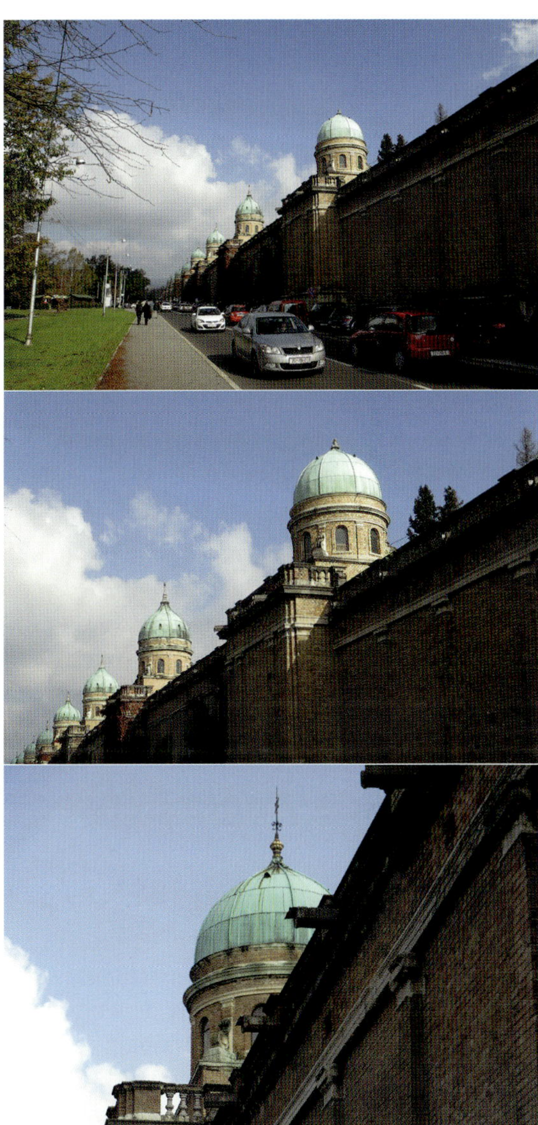

Figure 12.5 A 16mm view shows a broad expanse of wall outside the Mirogoj Cemetery in Zagreb, Croatia (top). A view at roughly the same distance at 100mm (center). A long telephoto lens at 400mm captured this image (bottom).

- **More speed.** Your basic lens might have the perfect focal length and sharpness for sports photography, but the maximum aperture may be small at telephoto focal lengths, such as f/5.6 or f/6.3 at the far end. That won't cut it for night baseball or football games since you'll need to use an extremely high ISO (where image quality suffers) to be able to shoot at a fast shutter speed to freeze the action. Even outdoor sports shooting on overcast days can call for a high ISO if you're using a slow zoom lens (with small maximum apertures).

  That makes the FE-mount lenses with a very wide aperture (small f/number) such as the 85mm f/1.4 optic a prime choice (so to speak) for low-light photography when you can get close to the action; that's often possible at an amateur basketball or volleyball game.

Categories of Lenses

Lenses can be categorized by their intended purpose—general photography, macro photography, and so forth—or by their focal length. The range of available focal lengths is usually divided into three main groups: wide-angle, normal, and telephoto. Prime lenses fall neatly into one of these classifications. Zooms can overlap designations, with a significant number falling into the catchall wide-to-telephoto zoom range. This section provides more information about focal length ranges, and how they are used.

Any lens with a focal length of 10mm to 20mm is said to be an *ultra-wide-angle lens*; from about 20mm to 40mm is said to be a *wide-angle lens. Normal lenses* have a focal length roughly equivalent to the diagonal of the film or sensor, in millimeters, and so fall into the range of about 45mm to 60mm on a full-frame camera like your a7C II/a7CR model. *Telephoto lenses* usually fall into the 75mm and longer focal lengths, while those with a focal length much beyond 300mm are referred to as *super telephotos.*

Using Wide-Angle Lenses

To use wide-angle prime lenses and wide zooms, you need to understand how they affect your photography. Here's a quick summary of the things you need to know:

- **More depth-of-field (apparently).** Practically speaking, wide-angle lenses seem to produce more extensive depth-of-field at a particular subject distance and aperture. However, the range of acceptable sharpness actually depends on magnification: the size of the subject in the frame. With a wide-angle lens, you usually include a full scene in an image; any single subject is not magnified very much, so the depth-of-field will be quite extensive. When using a telephoto lens however, you tend to fill the frame with a single subject (using high magnification), so the background is more likely to be blurred. (I'll discuss this in more detail in the sidebar below.)

  You'll find a wide-angle lens helpful when you want to maximize the range of acceptable sharpness in a landscape, for example. On the other hand, it's very difficult to isolate your subject (against a blurred background) using selective focus unless you move extremely close. Telephoto lenses are better for this purpose, and, as a bonus, they also include fewer extraneous elements of the scene because of their narrower field of view.

- **Stepping back.** Wide-angle lenses have the effect of making it seem that you are standing farther from your subject than you really are. They're helpful when you don't want to back up—or can't because of impediments—to include an entire group of people in your photo, for example.

- **Wider field of view.** While making your subject seem farther away, as implied above, a wide-angle lens also provides a more expansive field of view, including more of the scene in your photos.

- **More foreground.** As background objects appear further back than they do to the naked eye, more of the foreground is brought into view by a wide-angle lens. That gives you extra emphasis on the area that's closest to the camera. Photograph your home with a 50mm focal length, for example, and the front yard probably looks fairly conventional in your photo. Switch to a wider lens, such as the 12mm setting of the 12-24mm f/4 zoom, and you'll discover that your lawn now makes up much more of the photo. So, wide-angle lenses are great when you want to emphasize that lake in the foreground, but problematic when your intended subject is located farther in the distance.

- **Perspective distortion.** This type of distortion occurs when you tilt the camera, so the plane of the sensor is no longer perpendicular to the vertical plane of your subject. As a result, some parts of the subject are now closer to the sensor than they were before, while other parts are farther away. This is what makes buildings, flagpoles, or NBA players appear to be leaning over backward (like the Parthenon shown in Figure 12.6). While this kind of apparent distortion is actually caused by tilting the camera/lens upward (not by a defect in the lens), it can happen with any lens, but it's most apparent when a wide angle is used.

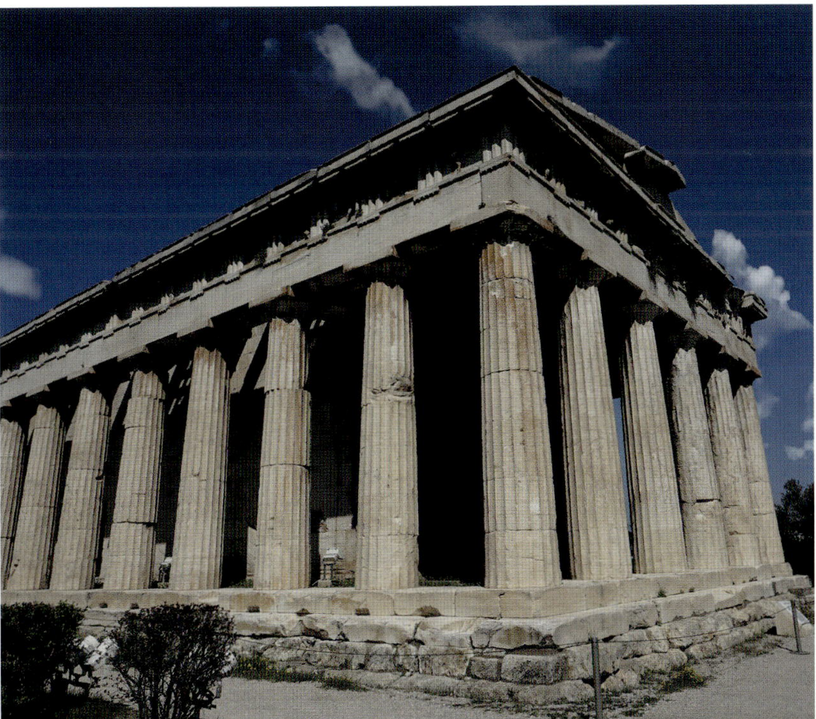

Figure 12.6 Tilting the camera produces this "falling-back" look in architectural photos.

- **Super-sized subjects.** The tendency of a wide-angle lens to emphasize objects in the foreground while de-emphasizing objects in the background can lead to a kind of size distortion that may be more objectionable for some types of subjects than others. Shoot a bed of flowers up close with a 16mm or shorter focal length, and you might like the distorted effect of the nearby blossoms looming in the photo. Take a shot of a family member with the same lens from the same distance, and you're likely to get some complaints about that gigantic nose in the foreground.

- **Steady cam.** You'll find that it is easier to get photos without blur from camera shake when you hand-hold a wide-angle lens at slower shutter speeds than it is with a telephoto lens. And, thanks to SteadyShot stabilization, you can take sharp photos at surprisingly long shutter speeds at a long focal length without using a tripod. That's because the reduced magnification of the wide-angle lens or wide-zoom setting doesn't emphasize camera shake like a telephoto lens does.

- **Interesting angles.** Many of the factors already listed combine to produce more interesting angles when shooting with wide-angle lenses. Raising or lowering a telephoto lens a few feet probably will have little effect on the appearance of a distant subject that fills the frame. The same change in elevation can produce a dramatic effect if you're using a short focal length and are close to your subject.

DOF IN DEPTH

The depth-of-field advantage of wide-angle lenses disappears when you enlarge your picture. Believe it or not, a wide-angle image enlarged and cropped to provide the same subject size as a telephoto shot will have the same depth-of-field. Try it: take a wide-angle photo of a friend from a fair distance. Then, use a longer (telephoto) zoom setting from the same shooting position to take the same picture; naturally, your friend will appear to be larger in the second picture because of the greater telephoto magnification.

Download the two photos to your computer. While viewing the wide-angle shot, magnify it with the zoom or magnify tool so your friend is as large as in the telephoto image. You'll find that the wide-angle photo will have the same depth-of-field as the telephoto image; for example, the background will be equally blurred.

Avoiding Potential Wide-Angle Problems

Wide-angle lenses have a few quirks that you'll want to keep in mind when shooting so you can avoid falling into some common traps. Here's a checklist of tips for avoiding common problems:

- **Symptom: converging lines.** Unless you want to use wildly diverging lines as a creative effect, it's a good idea to keep horizontal and vertical lines in landscapes, architecture, and other subjects carefully aligned with the sides, top, and bottom of the frame. To prevent undesired perspective distortion, you must take care not to tilt the camera. If your subject is very tall, like a building, you may need to shoot from an elevated position (like a high level in a parking garage) so you won't need to tilt the lens upward. And if your subject is short, like a small child, get down to a lower level so you can get the shot without tilting the lens downward.

- **Symptom: color fringes around objects.** Lenses often produce photos that are plagued with fringes of color around backlit objects, produced by *chromatic aberration*. This common lens flaw comes in two forms: *longitudinal/axial*, in which all the colors of light don't focus in the same plane, and *lateral/transverse*, in which the colors are shifted to one side. Axial chromatic aberration can be reduced by stopping down the lens (to f/8 or f/11, for example), but transverse chromatic aberration cannot.

  Better-quality lenses reduce both types of imaging defect; it's common for reviews to point out these failings, so you can choose the best-performing lenses that your budget allows. The Lens Compensation feature in the Shooting > Image Quality group can help reduce this problem. Leave it set for Auto to get the chromatic aberration reduction processing that the camera can provide.

- **Symptom: lines that bow outward.** Some wide-angle lenses cause straight lines to bow outward, an effect called barrel distortion; you'll see the strongest effect at the edges. Most fisheye (or *curvilinear*) lenses produce this effect as a feature of the lens; it's much more obvious than with any other type of lens. (See Figure 12.7.) The mild barrel distortion you get with a conventional lens is rarely obvious except in some types of architectural photography. If you find it objectionable, you'll need to use a well-corrected lens.

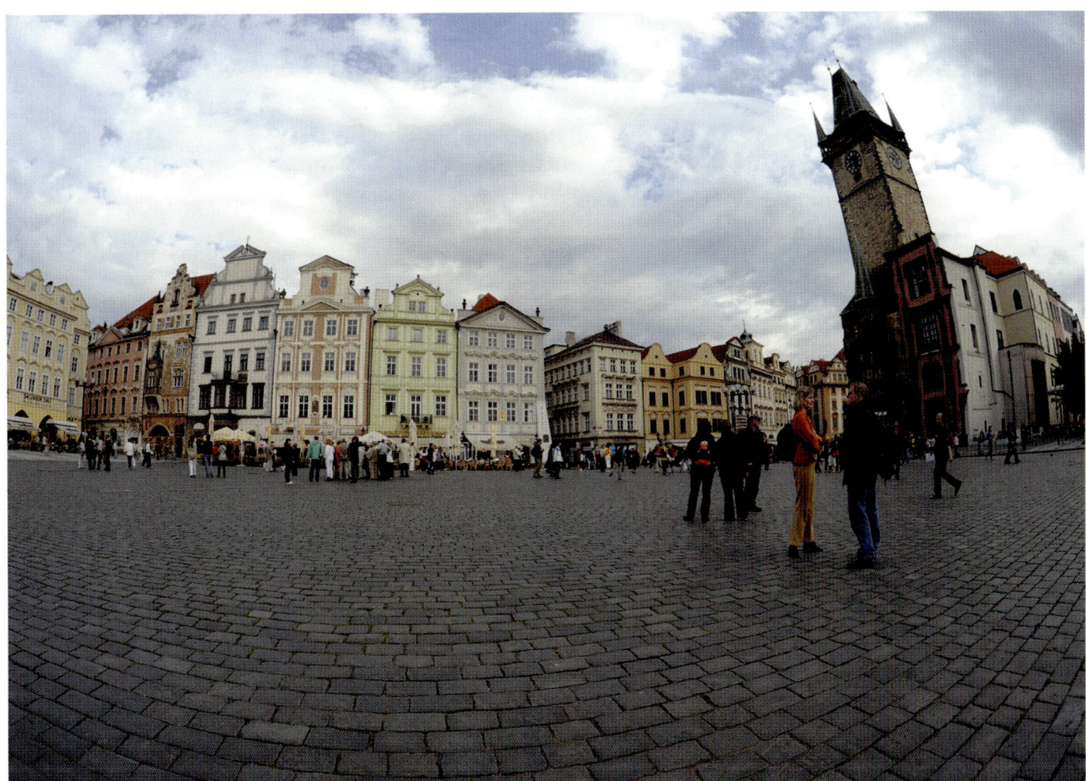

Figure 12.7 Many wide-angle lenses cause lines to bow outward toward the edges of the image. That's often not noticeable unless you use a fisheye lens; the effect is considered to be interesting and desirable.

Manufacturers like Sony do their best to minimize or eliminate it (producing a *rectilinear* lens), often using *aspherical* lens elements (which are not cross-sections of a sphere). You can also minimize barrel distortion simply by framing your photo with some extra space all around, so the edges where the bowing outward is most obvious can be cropped out of the picture. The Lens Correction feature can help reduce this problem, too. Leave it set to Auto to allow the processor to minimize the slight barrel distortion that can occur with the more affordable lenses.

- **Symptom: light and dark areas when using a polarizing filter.** You should be aware that polarizers work best when the camera is pointed 90 degrees away from the sun and have the least effect when the camera is oriented 180 degrees from the sun. This is only half the story, however. With lenses like the 12-24mm or 16-35mm zooms, the range is extensive enough to cause problems.

  Think about it: if you use the widest setting of such a zoom and point it at a part of a scene that's at the proper 90-degree angle from the sun, the areas of the scene that are at the edges of the frame will be oriented at much wider angles from the sun. Only the center of the image area will be at exactly 90 degrees. When the filter is used to darken a blue sky, the sky will be very dark near the center of your photo. Naturally, the polarizing effect will be much milder at the edges so the sky in those areas will be much lighter in tone (less polarized). The solution is to avoid using a polarizing filter in situations where you'll be including the sky with lenses that have an actual focal length of less than about 28mm.

Using Telephoto and Tele-Zoom Lenses

Telephoto lenses also can have a dramatic effect on your photography. Here are the most important things you need to know. In the next section, I'll concentrate on telephoto considerations that can be problematic—and how to avoid those problems.

- **Selective focus.** Long lenses have reduced depth-of-field, a shallow range of acceptably sharp focus, especially at wide apertures (small f/numbers); this is useful for selective focus to isolate your subject. You can set the widest aperture to create shallow depth-of-field or close it down (to a small f/number) to allow more of the scene to appear to be in acceptably sharp focus. The flip side of the coin is that even at f/16, a 300mm and longer lens will not provide much depth-of-field, especially when the subject is large in the frame (magnified). Like fire, the depth-of-field aspects of a telephoto lens can be friend or foe.

- **Getting closer.** Telephoto lenses allow you to fill the frame with wildlife, sports action, and candid subjects. No one wants to get a reputation as a surreptitious or "sneaky" photographer (except for paparazzi), but when applied to candids in an open and honest way, a long lens can help you capture memorable moments while retaining enough distance to stay out of the way of events as they transpire.

- **Reduced foreground/increased compression.** Telephoto lenses have the opposite effect of wide angles: they reduce the importance of things in the foreground by squeezing everything together. This so-called *compressed perspective* makes objects in the scene appear to be closer than they are to the naked eye. You can use this effect as a creative tool. You've seen the effect hundreds of times in movies and on television, where the protagonist is shown running in and out of traffic that appears to be much closer to the hero (or heroine) than it really is.

- **Accentuates camera shakiness.** Telephoto focal lengths hit you with a double whammy in terms of camera/photographer shake. The lenses themselves are bulkier, more difficult to hold steady, and may even produce a barely perceptible seesaw rocking effect when you support them with one hand halfway down the lens barrel. As they magnify the subject, they amplify the effect of any camera shake. It's no wonder that image stabilization like Optical SteadyShot (OSS) is especially popular among those using longer lenses, and why Sony includes this feature in the 18-200mm zooms (and many of the long A-mount lenses).

- **Interesting angles require creativity.** Telephoto lenses require more imagination in selecting interesting angles, because the "angle" you do get on your subjects is so narrow. Moving from side to side or a bit higher or lower can make a dramatic difference in a wide-angle shot but raising or lowering a telephoto lens a few feet probably will have little effect on the appearance of the distant subjects you're shooting.

Avoiding Telephoto Lens Problems

Many of the "problems" that telephoto lenses pose are really just challenges and not that difficult to overcome. Here is a list of the seven most common picture maladies and suggested solutions:

- **Symptom: flat faces in portraits.** Head-and-shoulders portraits of humans tend to be more flattering when a focal length of 50mm to 85mm is used with a full-frame camera. Longer focal lengths compress the distance between features like the nose and ears, making the face look wider and flat. (Conversely, a wide-angle lens will make the nose look huge and ears tiny if you move close enough for a head-and-shoulders portrait.) So, avoid using a focal length much longer than about 60mm with your a7C II/a7CR unless you're forced to shoot from a greater distance. (Use a wide-angle lens only when shooting three-quarters/full-length portraits, or group shots.)

- **Symptom: blur due to camera shake.** Because a long focal length amplifies the effects of camera shake, make sure the SteadyShot stabilization is not turned off (with a menu item). Then, if possible, use a faster shutter speed; that may mean that you'll need to set a higher ISO to be able to do so. Of course, a firm support like a solid tripod is the most effective tool for eliminating camera shake, especially if you trip the shutter with a remote commander accessory or the self-timer to avoid the risk of jarring the camera. Of course, only the fast shutter speed option will be useful to prevent blur caused by *subject* motion; SteadyShot or a tripod won't help you freeze a race car in mid-lap.

- **Symptom: color fringes.** Chromatic aberration is the most pernicious optical problem found in telephoto lenses. There are others, including spherical aberration, astigmatism, coma, curvature of field, and similarly scary-sounding phenomena. The best solution for any of these is to use a better lens that offers the proper degree of correction for aberrations or stop down the lens (to f/8 or f/11) to minimize the problem. But that's not always possible. Your second-best choice may be to correct the fringing using the a7C II/a7CR's Lens Compensation feature, or by using your favorite RAW conversion tool or image editor. Photoshop's Lens Correction filter offers sliders that minimize both red/cyan and blue/yellow fringing. A feature such as this (also available with some other software) can be useful in situations where the a7C II/a7CR's Lens Compensation feature doesn't fully correct for chromatic aberration.

- **Symptom: lines that curve inward.** Pincushion distortion is common in photos taken with many telephoto lenses; lines, especially those near the edges of the frame, bow inward like the pincushion your grandma might have used. You can take photos of a brick wall at various focal lengths with your zoom lens to find out where the pincushion distortion is the most obvious; that will probably be at or near the longest focal length. Like chromatic aberration, it can be partially corrected using tools like Photoshop's Lens Correction filter (or a similar utility in some other software).

- **Symptom: low contrast from haze or fog.** When you're photographing distant objects, a long lens shoots through a lot more atmosphere, which generally is muddied up with extra haze and fog. The dust or moisture droplets in the atmosphere can reduce contrast and mute colors. Some feel that a skylight or UV filter can help, but this practice is mostly a holdover from the film days. Digital sensors are not sensitive enough to UV light for a UV filter to have much effect. A polarizer might help a bit, but only in certain circumstances. I don't consider this to be a huge problem because it's easy to boost contrast and color saturation in Picture Styles (a menu item) or later in image-editing software.

- **Symptom: low contrast from flare.** Lenses are often furnished with lens hoods for a good reason: to minimize the amount of stray light that will strike the front element causing flare or a ghost image of the diaphragm containing the aperture. A hood is effective when the light is at your side, but it has no value when you're shooting toward the sun. On the other hand, you'll often be shooting with the light striking the lens from an angle. In this situation, the lens hood is only partially effective, so minimize flare by using your hand or cap to cast a shadow over the front element of the lens. (Just be careful not to let your hand or cap intrude into the image area.)

- **Symptom: dark flash photos.** Edge-to-edge flash coverage isn't as problematic with telephoto lenses as it is with wide angles. (The built-in flash simply cannot provide light that covers the entire field of view that's recorded by a lens shorter than 16mm.) The shooting distance is the problem with longer lenses. A 210mm focal length might allow you to make a distant subject appear close to the camera, but the flash isn't fooled. You'll need extra power for distant flash shots, making a large accessory flash unit a valuable accessory.

If you do not have a powerful flash unit and cannot get closer to the subject (like Lady Gaga strutting her stuff on a dark stage), try setting the camera's ISO level to 3200. This increases the sensitivity of the sensor so less light is required to make a bright photo; of course, the photo is likely to be grainy because of digital noise. If that does not solve the problem, you will need to set an even higher ISO, but then you'll get even more obvious digital noise in your photo.

Photography is a form of visual art that uses light to shape the finished product. The photographer may have little or no control over the subject (other than posing human subjects) but can often adjust both viewing angle *and* the nature of the light source to create a particular compelling image. The direction and intensity of the light sources create the shapes and textures that we see. The distribution and proportions determine the contrast and tonal values: whether the image is stark or high key or muted and low in contrast. The colors of the light (because even "white" light has a color balance that the sensor can detect), and how much of those colors the subject reflects or absorbs, paint the hues visible in the image.

As a Sony a7C II/a7CR photographer, you must learn to be a painter and sculptor of light if you want to move from *taking* a picture to *making* a photograph. Most of the time, you'll be working with available or ambient light, perhaps with reflectors or other modifiers, or even some additional continuous light sources, such as incandescent or fluorescent lamps. But, at times, you'll want to turn to one of the most versatile sources of illumination you have available, the brief, but brilliant snippets of light we call *electronic flash*. This chapter will show you the differences between working with continuous illumination and working with flash and explain how to use the flash capabilities of the Sony a7C II and a7CR.

Why Flash?

Flash sometimes gets a bad rap, but that's usually prompted by photographers who make poor use of the capabilities electronic flash offers. In some respects, working with continuous lighting instead is easier and more predictable. Continuous lighting is exactly what you might think: uninterrupted illumination that is available all the time during a shooting session. Daylight, moonlight, and the artificial lighting encountered both indoors and outdoors count as continuous light sources (although all of them can be "interrupted" by passing clouds, solar eclipses, a blown fuse, or simply by switching off a lamp). Indoor continuous illumination includes both the lights that are there already (such as incandescent lamps or overhead fluorescent lights indoors) and fixtures you supply yourself, including photoflood lamps or reflectors used to bounce existing light onto your subject.

On the face of things, electronic flash may be uncomfortably *different* from what we are used to, and sometimes considered difficult to use. In practice, you can use flash in all the same ways you use continuous lighting to shape your images, and, in some cases, take advantage of its special properties, such as its action-freezing short duration. Electronic flash is notable because it can be much more intense than continuous lighting, lasts only a brief moment, and can be much more portable than supplementary incandescent sources. It's a light source you can carry with you and use anywhere.

Before moving on to discussing flash in detail, here's a quick comparison of the pros and cons of continuous illumination versus flash:

- **Lighting preview—Pro: continuous lighting.** With continuous lighting, such as incandescent lamps or daylight, you always know exactly what kind of lighting effect you're going to get. If you're using multiple lights, you can visualize how they will interact with each other. With electronic flash, the general effect you're going to see may be a mystery until you've built some experience.

- **Lighting preview—Con: electronic flash.** Compact portable flash units often do not provide a "modeling light" function, although studio flash typically do.

- **Exposure calculation—Pro: continuous lighting.** Your camera has no problem calculating accurate exposure for continuous lighting, because the lighting remains constant and can be measured through built-in light meters that interpret the light reaching the sensor. The amount of light available just before the exposure will, in almost all cases, be the same amount of light present when the shutter mechanism is opened to take the shot. The Spot metering mode can be used to measure brightness in the bright areas of the scene and the dark areas; if you have a bit of expertise in this technique, you'll know whether it would be useful to bounce some light into the shadow areas using a reflector panel accessory.

- **Exposure calculation—Con: electronic flash.** A flash unit provides no illumination until it actually fires so the exact exposure can't be measured by the a7C II/a7CR's exposure sensor before you take a photo. Instead, the light must be measured by metering the intensity of a *pre-flash* triggered an instant before the main flash, as it is reflected back to the camera and through the lens.

- **Evenness of illumination—Pro/con: continuous lighting.** Of continuous light sources, daylight, in particular, provides illumination that tends to fill an image completely, lighting up the foreground, background, and your subject almost equally. A sunlit scene may have shadow areas too, of course, so you might need to use reflectors or fill-in light sources to even out the illumination. Barring objects that block large sections of your image from daylight, the light is spread fairly evenly. Indoors, however, continuous lighting is much less likely to be evenly distributed. The average living room, for example, has hot spots and dark corners. But, on the plus side, you can *see* this uneven illumination and compensate with additional lamps.

- **Evenness of illumination—Con: electronic flash.** Electronic flash units, like the continuous light provided by lamps, don't have the advantage of being located 93 million miles from the subject as the sun is. Because of this factor, they suffer from the effects of their proximity.

  The *inverse square law,* first applied to both gravity and light by Sir Isaac Newton, dictates that as a light source's distance increases from the subject, the amount of light reaching the subject falls off proportionately to the square of the distance. In plain English, that means that a flash or lamp that's 12 feet away from a subject provides only one-quarter as much illumination as a source that's 6 feet away (rather than half as much). (See Figure 13.1.) This translates into relatively shallow "depth-of-light."

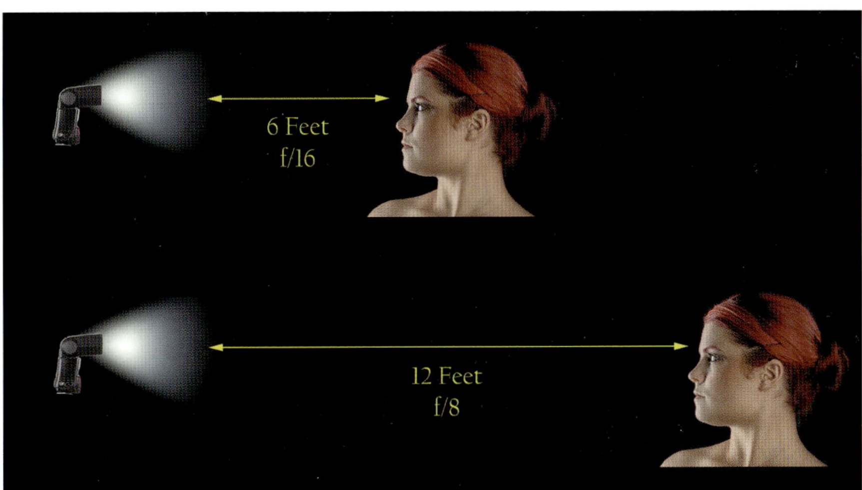

Figure 13.1 A light source that is twice as far away provides only one-quarter as much illumination.

- **Action stopping—Pro: electronic flash.** When it comes to the ability to freeze moving objects in their tracks, the advantage goes to electronic flash. The brief duration of the emitted light serves as a very fast "shutter speed" when the flash is the main or only source of illumination for the photo. In other words, this effect is possible when shooting in a dark area without much, if any, lighting provided by ambient sources but assumes that the subject is not beyond the range of the flash.

  In flash photography, your camera's shutter speed (called *sync speed* in flash photography) is set to 1/160th second, but when flash is the primary light source, the *effective* exposure time will be 1/1000th to 1/50000th second or less; this is the actual duration of the flash illumination. As you can see in Figure 13.2, it's possible to freeze motion with flash of very short duration. The only fly in the ointment is that, if the ambient light is strong enough, it may produce a secondary "ghost" exposure, as I'll explain later in this chapter.

- **Action stopping—Con: continuous lighting.** Action stopping with continuous light sources is completely dependent on the shutter speed you've dialed in on the camera. And the speeds available are dependent on the amount of light available and your camera's ISO sensitivity setting. Outdoors in daylight, there will probably be enough sunlight to let you shoot at 1/2000th second and f/6.3 with a non-grainy ISO of 400. That's a fairly useful combination of settings if you're not using a super-telephoto with a small maximum aperture.

  But indoors, the reduced illumination quickly has you pushing your a7C II/a7CR to its limits. For example, if you're shooting indoor sports in a dark arena, there probably won't be enough available light to allow you to use a 1/2000th second shutter speed unless you use a lens with an extremely wide aperture, such as f/1.8. You can also specify a very high ISO setting, and accept that image quality may suffer. (In truth, the gym where I shoot indoor basketball allows me to do so at 1/500th second at f/4 using ISO 1600.) In many indoor sports situations, you may find yourself limited to a shutter speed of 1/500th second or slower.

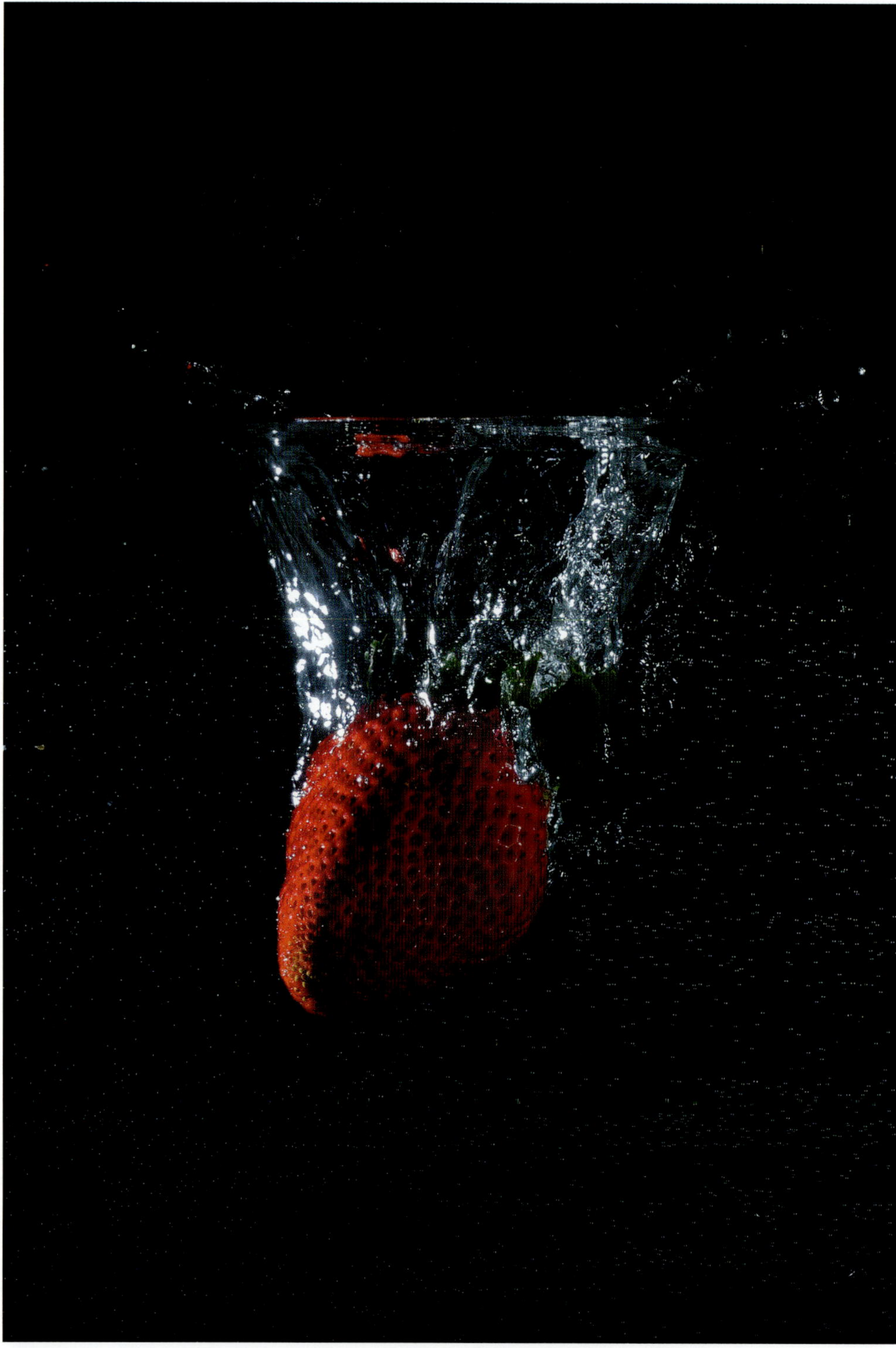

Figure 13.2 Electronic flash can freeze almost any motion because of its extremely short duration.

- **Flexibility—Pro: electronic flash.** The action-freezing power of electronic flash, at least for nearby subjects in a dark location, allows you to work without a tripod; that provides extra flexibility and speed when choosing angles and positions.
- **Flexibility—Con: continuous lighting.** Because incandescent and fluorescent lamps are not as bright as electronic flash, the slower shutter speeds required (see "Action stopping," above) mean that you may have to use a tripod more often, especially when shooting portraits. The incandescent variety of continuous lighting gets hot, especially in the studio, and the side effects range from discomfort (for your human models) to disintegration (if you happen to be shooting perishable foods like ice cream).

Electronic Flash Basics

Until you delve into the situation deeply enough, it might appear that serious photographers have a love/hate relationship with electronic flash. You'll often hear that flash photos are less natural looking, and that on-camera flash in most cameras should never be used as the primary source of illumination because it provides a harsh, garish look. Some photographers strongly praise available ("continuous") lighting while denouncing electronic flash.

As I noted at the beginning of this chapter, that bias is against *bad* flash photography. Indeed, flash—often with light-modifying accessories—has become the studio light source of choice for many pro photographers. That's understandable, because the light is more intense (and its intensity can be dialed up or down by the photographer), freezes action, frees you from using a tripod (unless you want to use one to lock down a composition), and has a snappy, consistent light quality that matches daylight. (While color balance changes as the flash duration shortens, some Sony flash units can communicate to the camera the exact white balance provided for that shot.) And even conservative photographers will concede that electronic flash has some important uses as an adjunct to existing light, particularly to fill in dark shadows.

How Electronic Flash Works

The electronic flash you use will generally be connected to the camera by slipping it onto the hot shoe or linked by a cable connected to an adapter mounted on the shoe. In all cases, the flash is triggered at the instant of exposure, during a period when the sensor is fully exposed by the shutter.

The a7C II/a7CR has electronic shutter options, which I'll describe later, and a conventional vertically traveling physical shutter that consists of two "curtains," one physical and one virtual. The front curtain (which is a physical component in most cameras) is what is called an *electronic front curtain*. Instead of opening and moving to the opposite side of the frame to expose the sensor (which is the case with cameras that have a physical front curtain), the electronic front curtain simply dumps the current live view so the sensor can begin capturing the image.

At this point, the shutter is completely open. Now the flash can be triggered (so-called *front-curtain sync,* which is the default mode), making the flash exposure. Then, after a delay that can vary from 30 seconds to 1/160th second, a second, *rear curtain* (an actual physical component) begins moving across the sensor plane, covering up the sensor again. If the flash is triggered just *before* the rear curtain starts to close, then the optional *rear-curtain sync* is used. In both cases, though, a shutter speed of 1/160th second (or 1/200th second when shooting in APS-C/Super 35 image size) is ordinarily the *maximum* that can be used to take a photo, because that's the speed at which both the virtual and physical curtains are tucked out of the way, leaving the entire full frame exposed to capture the flash burst.

As an exposure is made using the conventional (non-electronic) shutter, the virtual and physical curtains behave as follows:

1. **Both curtains open.** Before the exposure begins, the sensor remains completely exposed, so that the image that's being captured can be viewed on the electronic viewfinder and LCD monitor.

2. **Front curtain dumps image.** The electronic front curtain (dubbed *e-front curtain* for short) dumps the prior image, resetting the pixels so that the exposure can begin.

3. **Both curtains open.** With the sensor fully exposed, the electronic flash's brief burst can fill the frame.

   - If this burst takes place as soon as the curtains are fully open, then *front-curtain sync*, which is the default, has been used. Following the flash, the sensor continues to be exposed for the length of the exposure, which can range from 1/160th (or 1/200th) second to 30 seconds (or longer, with a Bulb exposure).

   - The burst can also take place *at the very end* of the exposure, just before the rear curtain starts to descend. This is called *rear-curtain sync.*

4. **Rear curtain descends.** The rear curtain descends to end the exposure and the captured image is conveyed off the sensor to the camera's internal buffer, and thence to your memory card.

5. **Rear curtain ascends.** The rear curtain moves back to the top of the frame, fully exposing the sensor again and a preview image for the next picture appears in the EVF and LCD monitor.

Why an Electronic Front-Curtain Shutter?

You may wonder why Sony has dispensed with the physical front curtain shutter with the a7C II and a7CR. Recall that the sensor of a mirrorless camera is always exposed and feeding its image to the EVF and LCD monitor; in order to capture an image within a specified period of time, the sensor needs to *stop* collecting the image so the exposure can begin.

In normal operation, as described above, when you press the shutter release down all the way, cameras with physical shutters close the front curtain to remove the image you were previewing, resetting the pixels and leaving the sensor blank and ready to capture an exposure. When the e-Front Curtain Shutter is enabled, the physical front shutter doesn't close: the image is dumped *electronically*, and then the sensor immediately begins capturing an image. The physical rear-curtain shutter then closes at the end of the exposure.

The advantages of the electronic front curtain are that the camera can respond more quickly with less shutter lag, there is no possibility of vibration caused by the physical shutter bouncing at the end of its travel, and an electronic front-curtain shutter is quieter. As a mirrorless camera, it is already quieter than dSLR models, which have a mirror flapping about before and after the exposure.

However, an electronic front-curtain shutter can exhibit problems with certain lenses and very fast shutter speeds. In such cases, when you are using an unusually wide aperture, such as f/1.8, some areas of the photo may exhibit a secondary (ghost) image. The aperture of an affected lens requires the diaphragm's "leaves" to travel a greater distance, and there may simply not be enough time.

Keep in mind that the a7C II/a7CR *always* defaults to e-front-curtain sync unless you explicitly select another sync mode using the Main > Main > Flash Mode or the Exposure/Color > Flash > Flash Mode entries.

And Now for Something Completely Different...

If you've absorbed that, things are about to get *really* interesting. There are two settings *not* found in the Exposure/Color > Flash group that affect how you use flash. They reside in the Shooting > Shutter/Silent group:

- **Silent Mode Settings (No Flash).** As I noted in Chapter 6, your camera has a (mostly) silent mode that eliminates or reduces the most egregious noises emitted by the camera. You can read about options for which noises to suppress in that chapter. Here, all you need to know is that if you've invoked Silent Mode, you cannot use electronic flash.
- **Shutter Type: Electronic (No Flash).** In the Shutter type entry, you can choose Mechanical or Electronic Shutter. You *must* activate the mechanical shutter to use flash. When the electronic shutter is active, you cannot use electronic flash, Bulb exposures, or Long Exposure Noise reduction.

Avoiding Sync-Speed Problems

Using a shutter speed faster than the maximum sync speed can cause problems. Triggering the electronic flash *only* when the shutter is completely open makes a lot of sense if you think about what's going on. To obtain shutter speeds faster than 1/160th second, the camera exposes only part of the sensor at one time, by starting the rear curtain on its journey before the front curtain has completely opened. That effectively provides a briefer exposure as the slit of the shutter (the distance between the front and rear curtains) passes over the surface of the sensor. If the flash were to fire during the time when the front and rear curtains partially obscured the sensor, only the slit that was actually open would be exposed.

You'd end up with only a narrow band, representing the portion of the sensor that was exposed when the picture was taken. For shutter speeds *faster* than the top sync speed, the rear curtain begins moving *before* the image has been completely captured. As a result, a moving slit exposes one portion of the sensor at a time as it moves from the top to the bottom.

If the flash is triggered while this slit is moving, only the exposed portion of the sensor will receive any illumination. You end up with a photo like the one shown in Figure 13.3. Note that a band across the bottom of the image is black. That's a shadow of the rear shutter curtain, which had started to move when the flash was triggered. Sharp-eyed readers will wonder why the black band is at the *bottom* of the frame rather than at the top, where the rear curtain begins its journey. The answer is simple: your lens flips the image upside down and forms it on the sensor in a reversed position. You never notice that, because the camera is smart enough to show you the pixels that make up your photo in their proper orientation during picture review. But this image flip is why, if your sensor gets

Figure 13.3 If a shutter speed faster than 1/160th second is used with flash, you can end up photographing only a portion of the image.

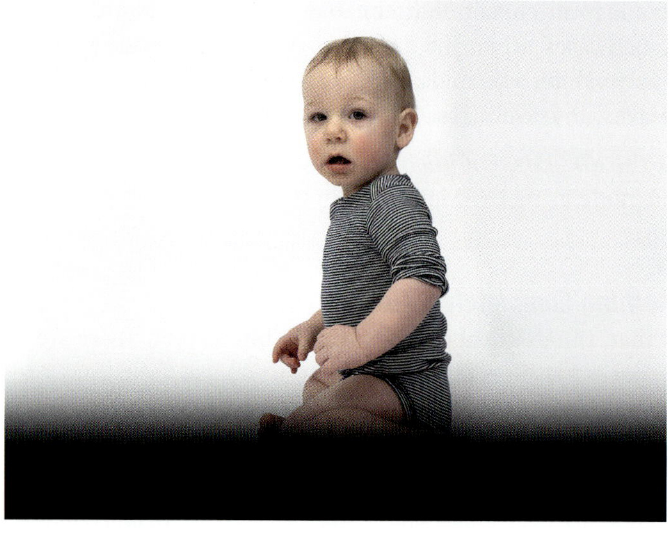

dirty and you detect a spot of dust in the upper half of a test photo, if cleaning manually, you need to look for the speck in the *bottom* half of the sensor.

I generally end up with sync-speed problems only when shooting in the studio, using studio flash units rather than my Sony-dedicated unit. That's because if you're using either type of "smart" flash, the camera knows that a strobe is attached, and remedies any unintentional goof in shutter speed settings. If you happen to set the shutter to a faster speed in Shutter Priority or Manual mode, the camera will automatically adjust the shutter speed down to the maximum sync speed as soon as you attach and turn on an external flash (or prevent you from choosing a faster speed if the flash is powered up). In Aperture Priority or Program mode, where the a7C II/a7CR selects the shutter speed, it will never choose a shutter speed higher than 1/160th second when using flash.

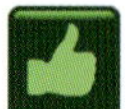

NOTE Both cameras have an APS-C/Super 35 crop mode that is invoked automatically when an APS-C lens is mounted on the camera. It can also be activated manually using Shooting > Image Quality > APS-C S35 Shooting if you want to force the camera to use crop mode with all lenses. In APS-C mode, the flash sync speed is 1/200th second, because the shutter is able to traverse the smaller image area more quickly. For simplicity's sake, I won't be constantly reminding you of this exception to the 1/160th sync speed you'll be working with most of the time.

But when using a non-dedicated flash, such as a studio unit plugged into a PC/X adapter attached to the camera's multi-interface shoe, the camera has no way of knowing that a flash is connected, so shutter speeds faster than 1/160th second can be set inadvertently.

Note that the a7C II/a7CR can use a feature called *high-speed sync* that allows shutter speeds faster than the maximum sync speed with certain external dedicated Sony flash units. When using high-speed sync, the flash fires a continuous series of bursts at reduced power for the entire duration of the exposure, so that the illumination is able to expose the sensor as the slit moves.

High-speed sync is a function of the flash unit and not the camera itself. It is set using the controls that adjust the compatible external flash units, which include the HVL-F60M/RM, HVL-F58AM, HVL-F56AM, HVL-F45RM, HVL-F28RM, HVL-F43AM/HVL-F43M, HVL-F32M, and HVL-F36AM. (Note that all flashes ending in AM use the older Minolta-style foot and cannot be mounted on the a7C II/a7CR without an inexpensive Sony ADP-MAA adapter.) High-speed sync cannot be used when working with multiple flash units. When active, the message H appears on the LCD panel on the back of the flash. You'll find complete instructions accompanying those flash units.

Ghost Images

The difference might not seem like much, but whether you use front-curtain sync (the default setting) or rear-curtain sync (an optional setting) can make a significant difference to your photograph *if the ambient light in your scene also contributes to the image.* At faster shutter speeds, particularly 1/160th second, there isn't much time for the ambient light to register, unless it is very bright. It's likely that the electronic flash will provide almost all the illumination, so front-curtain sync or rear-curtain sync isn't very important.

However, at slower shutter speeds, or with very bright ambient light levels, there is a significant difference, particularly if your subject is moving, or the camera isn't steady. In any of those situations, the ambient light will register as a second image accompanying the flash exposure, and if there is movement (of the camera or subject), that additional image will not be in the same position as the flash exposure. It will show as a ghost image and, if the movement is significant enough, as a blurred ghost image trailing in front of or behind your subject in the direction of the movement.

As I mentioned earlier, when you're using front-curtain sync, the flash goes off the instant the shutter opens, producing an image of the subject on the sensor. Then, the shutter remains open for an additional period (which, as I've noted, can be from 30 seconds to 1/160th second). If your subject is moving, say, toward the right side of the frame, the ghost image produced by the ambient light will produce a blur on the right side of the original subject image, making it look as if your sharp (flash-produced) image is chasing the ghost. For those of us who grew up with lightning-fast superheroes who always left a ghost trail *behind them*, that looks unnatural (see Figure 13.4).

So, Sony provides rear-curtain sync to remedy the situation. In that mode, the shutter opens, as before. The shutter remains open for its designated duration, and the ghost image forms. If your subject moves from the left side of the frame to the right side, the ghost will move from left to right, too. *Then*, about 1.5 milliseconds before the rear shutter curtain closes, the flash is triggered, producing a nice, sharp flash image *ahead* of the ghost image.

EVERY WHICH WAY, INCLUDING UP

Note that although I describe the ghost effect in terms of subject matter that is moving left to right in a horizontally oriented composition, it can occur in any orientation, and with the subject moving in *any* direction. (Try photographing a falling rock, if you can, and you'll see the same effect.) Nor are the ghost images affected by the fact that modern shutters travel vertically rather than horizontally. Secondary images are caused between the time the front curtain fully opens and the rear curtain begins to close. The direction of travel of the shutter curtains, or the direction of your subject, does not matter.

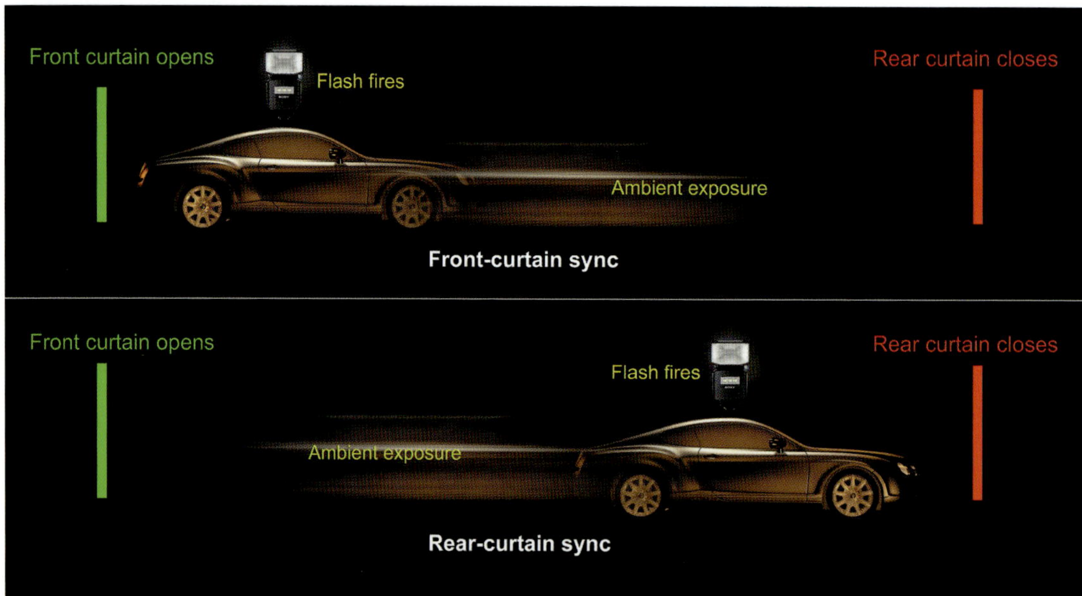

Figure 13.4 Front-curtain sync produces an image that trails in front of the flash exposure (top), whereas rear-curtain sync creates a more "natural-looking" trail behind the flash image (bottom).

Slow Sync

Another flash synchronization option is *slow sync*, which is actually an exposure option that tells the camera to use slower shutter speeds when possible, to allow you to capture a scene by both flash and ambient illumination. To activate Slow Sync, navigate to the Flash Mode entry in the Exposure/Color > Flash group.

Then, the exposure system will try to use longer shutter speeds with the flash, so that an initial exposure is made with the flash unit, and a secondary exposure of subjects in the background will be produced by the slower shutter speed. This will let you shoot a portrait of a person at night and, much of the time, avoid a dark background. Your portrait subject will be illuminated by the flash, and the background by the ambient light. It's a good idea to have the camera mounted on a tripod or some other support or have SteadyShot switched on to avoid having this secondary exposure produce ghost images due to camera movement during the exposure. (See Figure 13.5.)

Because Slow Sync is a type of exposure control, it does not work in Manual mode or Shutter Priority mode (because the camera doesn't choose the shutter speed in those modes). It is not disabled in those modes: you can still select it using the Exposure/Color > Flash > Flash Mode entry or Function menu, but your shutter speed will not be changed.

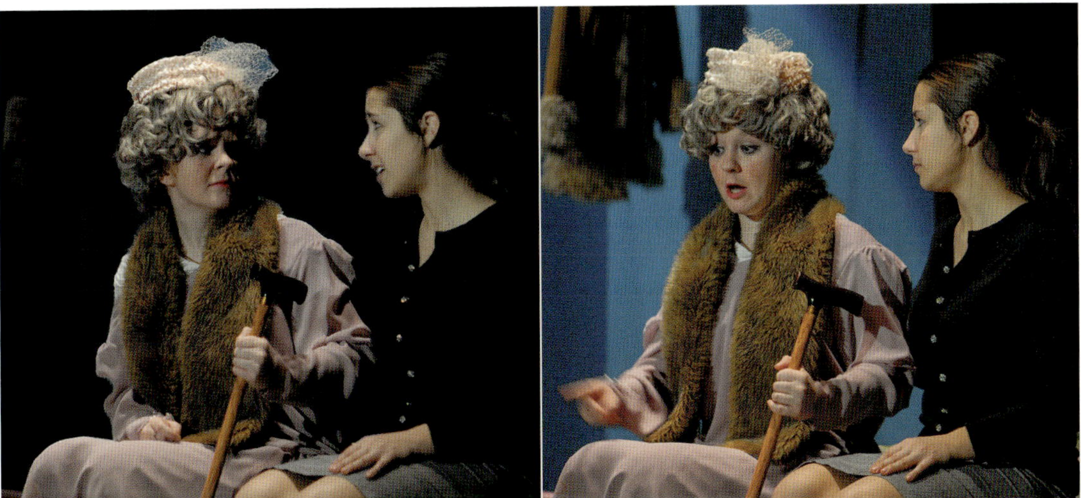

Figure 13.5 Without slow sync, ambient light may not be sufficient to balance with the flash exposure (left). When slow sync is activated, longer shutter speeds are selected, allowing the ambient light to register, too (right).

Determining Exposure

Calculating the proper exposure for an electronic flash photograph is a bit more complicated than determining the settings by continuous light. The right exposure isn't simply a function of how far away your subject is, even though the inverse square law I mentioned does have an effect: the farther away the subject is, the less light is available for the exposure. The a7C II/a7CR can calculate distance if you're using lenses with a *distance encoder chip,* which detects the position of the focusing mechanism as focus is locked in just prior to exposure. The component transmits this information to the camera, which can use it to determine the distance to the subject, and, therefore, how much flash output is required to illuminate the scene. This Advanced Distance Integration (ADI) delivers high-precision flash metering that is unaffected by the reflectance of subjects or backgrounds.

But, of course, flash exposure isn't based on distance alone. Various objects reflect more or less light at the same distance so, obviously, the camera needs to measure the amount of light reflected back and through the lens. Yet, as the flash itself isn't available for measuring until it's triggered, the camera has nothing to measure.

The solution is to fire the flash twice. The initial shot is a pre-flash emitted by the flash mounted on the camera a fraction of a second before the main flash burst. If you are using multiple off-camera flashes, the pre-flash from the on-camera commander tells each of the remote flash units to emit a pre-flash of their own.

The camera analyzes the illumination it receives from the initial pre-flash bursts to calculate the amount of light needed for a correct exposure, taking into account, if necessary, any ambient light also present in the scene. Then, the main flash is emitted, at the calculated intensity needed to provide a correct exposure. The appropriate power needed is also communicated to the off-camera flash. As a result, the primary flash burst(s) may be a longer total duration for distant objects and shorter duration for closer subjects, depending on the required intensity for exposure. This through-the-lens evaluative flash exposure system uses distance information, and it operates whenever you have attached a Sony-dedicated flash unit, and a lens that provides the necessary distance integration information.

Note that you can bypass the TTL autoflash exposure entirely and set some flash for Manual Flash (M) mode, in which you can select a power output level (from 1/1 to 1/128th power). You'll need to calculate exposure manually, but this DIY exposure makes it easy to set up your own flash ratios. One flash can be set to 1:1, and additional flashes triggered wirelessly can be adjusted to provide 1/2, 1/4, 1/8 or another reduced amount of illumination.

You may also have Manual/Multi mode for multiple-shot "strobe" bursts. With Multi, you can select the frequency of flashes, from 1 to 100 Hz (flashes per second). You can also specify the total number of flashes to emit, from 2 to 100, plus "- -" which tells the flash to keep strobing at the frequency you selected, which is useful for exposures longer than one second. The power output level for each flash can be set from 1/8th to 1/128th power in 0.5- or 0.3-stop increments. If High-Speed Sync is deactivated on the flash, an additional 1/256th power level is available. You can calculate an appropriate shutter speed by dividing the number of flashes by the flash frequency. That is, 20 flashes at 5 flashes per second require a shutter speed of four seconds. You can use this multiple-exposure feature creatively, or, more practically, say, to analyze your golf swing. Check your flash's manual to see how Multi is implemented with your unit.

Flash Modes

When using Still photography mode, there are several flash modes available in the Exposure/Color > Flash group:

- **Flash Off.** The flash never fires; this may be useful in museums, concerts, or religious ceremonies where electronic flash would prove disruptive. This option is not available in P, A, S, or M mode; if you do not want the flash to fire, turn it off.
- **Auto Flash.** The flash fires as required, depending on lighting conditions. Not available in P, A, S, or M mode because flash *always* fires in these modes if it's attached and powered up.
- **Fill-Flash.** When this option is set, the flash will always fire when set to P, A, S, or M modes, using one of the two Auto modes or in SCN modes where flash is not disabled. The camera balances the available illumination with flash to provide a balanced lighting effect. (See Figure 13.6.)
- **Slow Sync.** The camera combines flash with slow shutter speeds; the nearby subject can be illuminated by flash, but during the longer shutter speed, there's enough time for the darker surroundings (lit by ambient light) to record on the sensor.
- **Rear Sync.** Fires the flash at the *end* of the exposure time, after the ambient-light exposure has been made, producing more satisfying photos of moving subjects when using a long exposure; light trails will be behind the "ghost" image, as illustrated earlier in Figure 13.4, bottom.
- **Wireless.** This is available from a separate entry in the Exposure/Color > Flash group. (On and Off are your options.) Wireless allows an optional external flash or flash trigger mounted on the camera's multi-interface shoe to activate one or more external flash units that support wireless off-camera flash; there's no need for any cable connection between the camera and the remote flash unit. I'll explain the Sony wireless system later in this chapter.

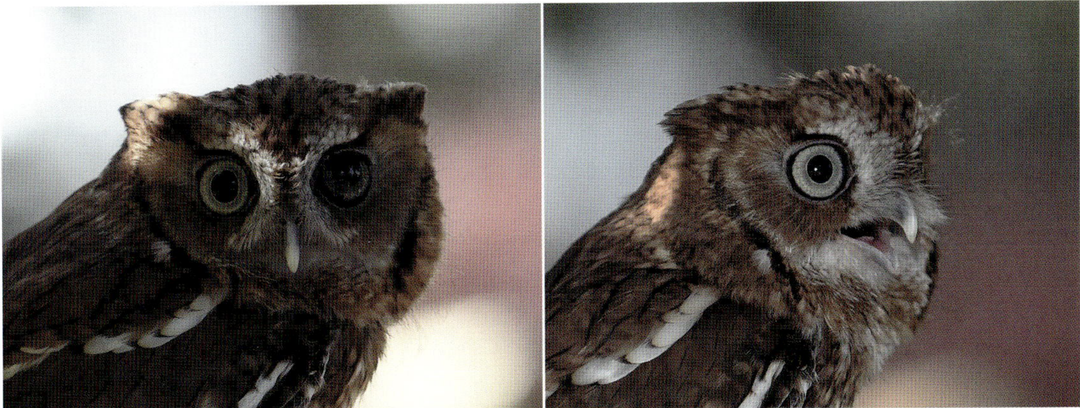

Figure 13.6 The owl's face is in shadow (left). Fill-flash (right) brightened him up, without affecting the background.

Flash Exposure Compensation

This is a feature discussed previously in Chapter 3. It's important to keep in mind how the camera's exposure compensation system works when you're using electronic flash. To activate exposure compensation for flash, visit the Flash Comp. entry in the Exposure/Color > Flash group, and set the amount of plus or minus compensation you want. (See Figure 13.7.) This function is not available when using Intelligent Auto mode. When you find that your flash photos are too dark even after you have set the highest amount of compensation, then the flash simply cannot provide more power; you must move closer to the subject, use a wider

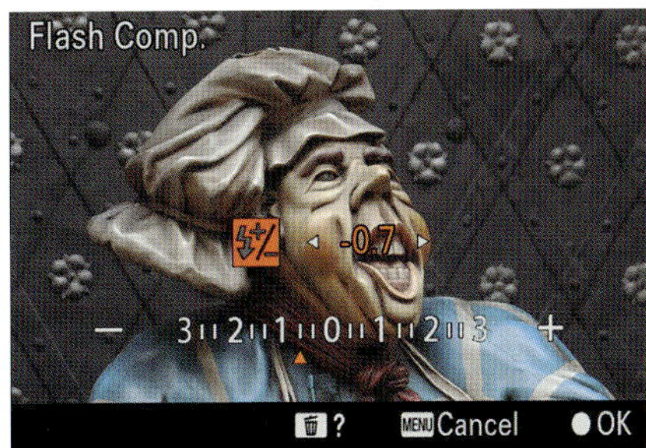

Figure 13.7 Flash exposure compensation can reduce the effect of the flash to provide fill-light.

aperture, set a higher ISO, or take all of these steps. Note too that when a subject is extremely close to the camera, even a –3 setting may not prevent an excessively bright image. You'll probably have to *reduce* your ISO setting in that case.

Flash exposure compensation affects only the amount of light emitted by the flash. If you want to adjust the brightness of the ambient-light exposure, you would also need to use the conventional exposure compensation feature. In fact, you can use both features at the same time, to get a brighter subject and a darker background, or vice versa. Let's say you're taking a photo of a friend posing against a light-toned background such as a white cabana on a beach. A plus exposure compensation setting (perhaps +1 when using multi-segment metering) will ensure that the cabana won't be underexposed while a –1/3 or –2/3 flash exposure compensation will ensure that shadows on your friend's face will be lightened by a very gentle burst of flash. This is an advanced technique that requires some experimentation but can be valuable when used with some expertise.

Red Eye Reduction

When using semi-automatic or manual exposure modes, red-eye reduction is available if Red Eye Reduction is On in the Exposure/Color > Flash group (as described in Chapter 6). The flash will fire four low-power red-eye reduction preflashes to reduce pupil size before the final flash burst that occurs when the photo is actually taken as you depress the shutter-release button. That will theoretically cause your subjects' irises to contract (if they are looking toward the camera), thereby reducing the red-eye effect in your photograph. This feature works only with a flash attached to the camera directly; it is not available when Wireless Flash is enabled.

Using an External Electronic Flash

As I write this, Sony offers nine accessory electronic flash units that are compatible with the a7C II/a7CR's multi-interface shoe. Four of them are triggered optically, that is, by pre-flashes that are emitted before the shot to communicate exposure and setting information between the camera and flash unit. Those are the HVL-F60M, HVL-F43M, HVL-F32M, and HVL-F20M.

In addition, there are five units that can be triggered optically or by more versatile radio-wireless communication. They are the HVL-F60RM/HVL-F60RM2, HVL-F46RM, HVL-45RM, and HVL-F28RM. All these external units can be mounted on the camera, connected to the camera's multi-interface shoe with a cable (I'll detail how later), or (except for the HVL-F20M) used off-camera with wireless connectivity when triggered by another external flash used as a controller. Each can also function as the controller mounted on the a7-series cameras to trigger other flash units wirelessly.

Also, there are earlier Sony flash units designed for the older Minolta/Sony proprietary hot shoe. They can be used with the a7-series cameras if you purchase an inexpensive adapter, such as the Sony ADP-MAA (about $25). Or, you can skip the adapter and use wireless-compatible legacy flash units off-camera in wireless mode, triggered by an on-camera commander/controller. Although they are discontinued, I'll describe some of these earlier flash units because you may already own one or can find one used at a price that's hard to resist. I don't recommend the legacy flash/adapter approach, because older units operate using a more limited communication protocol, which I'll describe later. But because some of you may have an older flash or can pick one up used at a decent price, it doesn't make sense to pretend that these discontinued models don't exist, because they still can work with your a7C II/a7CR, especially as remote/receiver units.

Sony also offers radio trigger/receivers: the FA-WRC1M, which can trigger any of the radio-capable flashes when mounted on the a7C II/a7CR's multi-interface shoe, and the FA-WRR1 receiver, which has its own hot shoe on which you can mount a non-radio Sony flash to give it radio control.

Guide Numbers, Hot Shoes, and More

Before I describe the flash units themselves, there are a few aspects you need to understand in order to compare electronic flash. If you're a veteran Sony (or Minolta) shooter, you can skim over this section, or skip it entirely. Those new to photography or the Sony realm should find this information useful.

Guide Numbers

The first thing you need to learn when comparing flash units is that Sony incorporates the Guide Number (GN) of each flash in the product name. So, what's a Guide Number? The GN designation derives from the good old days prior to automatic flash units and through-the-lens flash metering, when flash exposures had to be calculated mathematically. Those days are very long ago, indeed, as Honeywell introduced Auto/Strobonar flash units way back in the 1960s.

Guide numbers are a standard way of specifying the power of a flash when used in manual, non-autoexposure mode. Divide the guide number by the distance to determine the correct f/stop to use at full power. With a GN of 197 at ISO 100, you would use an aperture of around f/19.7 for a subject that's 10 feet from the camera (197 divided by 10), or around f/9.5 for a subject at a distance of 20 feet. Because most countries in the world use metric measurements, guide numbers are given using values for both meters and feet. Thus, Sony's HVL-F60M/RM unit has a guide number of 60/197 in meters/feet, and the 60 GN is incorporated into the unit's product name.

The Guide Number data is most useful for comparing the relative power of several flash units that you're considering. According to the inverse square law, a flash unit with a GN of 200 (in feet) puts out four times the amount of light as one with a GN of about 100. If your accessory flash has a zoom head, which can change coverage to match the focal length setting of your lens, the GN will vary according to the zoom setting, as wider zoom settings spread the same light over a broader area than a telephoto zoom setting.

Hot Shoes

Starting in 1988, Minolta phased in a proprietary hot shoe, the so-called *iISO* shoe, which was supposedly more rugged and secure than the original ISO 518 shoe, based on a design that dates back to 1913, when it was used to attach viewfinders to a camera (electronic flash hadn't been invented yet). No other vendors, including Canon and Nikon, embraced Minolta's design and continued to use the industry standard shoe. The ISO 518 standard doesn't specify any electronic connections between camera and flash, other than the "dumb" triggering circuit, so when sophisticated electronic flash units with TTL metering and other capabilities were developed, each vendor created their own hot-shoe version with the necessary electrical contacts for their cameras and flash units. The chief consequence for non-Minolta/Sony shooters was that you could mount dedicated flash units from one brand onto the ISO 518 shoe of another vendor's camera, and trigger that flash in manual, non-TTL mode.

When Sony purchased Konica Minolta's camera technology it began redesigning legacy features, and the old iISO hot shoe came under scrutiny. In 2012, Sony introduced a 21+3-pin hot shoe which it dubbed the *multi-interface shoe* (see Figure 13.8), which resembles a standard ISO 518 hot shoe with its "dumb" contacts. However, tucked away at the front of the shoe are additional electrical con-tacts that allow intelligent TTL flash metering communication between the camera and flash, and much more. For example, a whole series of stereo microphones from Sony and others, designed to plug into the multi-interface shoe, are available. As I noted earlier, you can pur-chase adapters that allow you to connect older iISO flash to the a7C II/a7CR, or to attach new-model flash units to a camera that has the origi-nal iISO hot shoe.

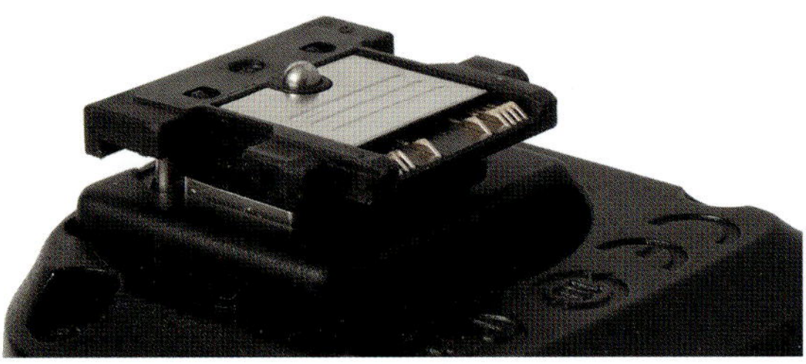

Figure 13.8 The Sony multi-interface shoe.

Cable Connections

In some cases, you can get your external flash off the camera without using a wireless connec-tion by linking an HVL-F60M/RM and a7C II/a7CR with a physical cable. (See Figure 13.9.) The gear needed for the hook-up can be costly, so I don't recommend it, but if you want to go that route, here's the way to go. Purchase the Sony FA-CS1M multi-interface shoe adapter (about $40). It slides into the a7-series camera's multi-interface shoe and has a four-pin TTL socket on the front. Connect that socket to a matching four-pin outlet located on the under-side of the HVL-F60M/RM, beneath a protec-tive terminal cap, using a 4.9-foot FA-MC1AM cable ($60). If you need more length, the FA-EC1AM extension cable ($50) adds another 4.9 feet to your connection. The HVL-F43M does not have the four-pin socket and connecting it

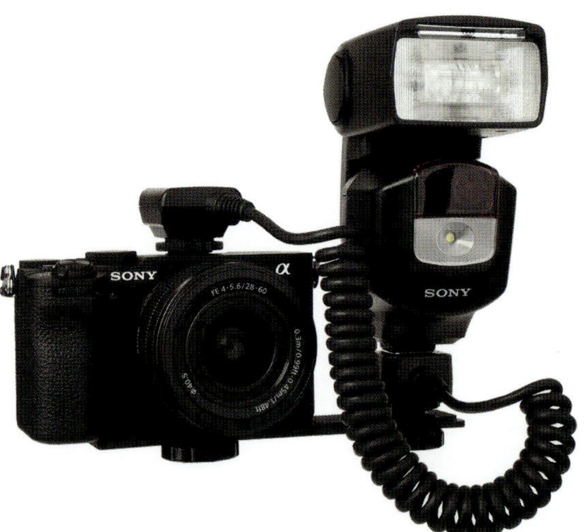

Figure 13.9 Off-camera flash can be linked to the a7C II/a7CR using a cable.

to a cable requires some additional adapters, so you're better off not going that way.

HVL-F60M/RM/RM2 Flash Units

There are *three* Sony top-of-the-line flash units readily available, the HVL-F60M, HVL-F60RM, and HVL-F60RM2. They are similar in output and operation, with some differences:

- **HVL-F60M.** This unit can be used as an optical commander or receiver. It has no radio capabilities. (See Figure 13.10.)

- **HVL-F60RM.** Discontinued, but still widely available, this flash can function as both optical and radio commander and receiver. It has a faster recycling time and at its lowest power level can maintain pace with the a7C II/a7CR's 10-frames-per-second continuous shooting rate. (Note that you'll have to be fairly close to your subject, or use a higher ISO for this low-power mode to be effective.) It also features an LED video light/AF illuminator.

- **HVL-F60RM2.** This latest version functions as a radio command and receiver, but cannot be used as an optical commander. It can be triggered optically, however, by any optical commander. It lacks the LED illuminator. The F60RM2's functions can be set using the a7C II/a7CR's Exposure/Color > Flash > External Flash Settings entry.

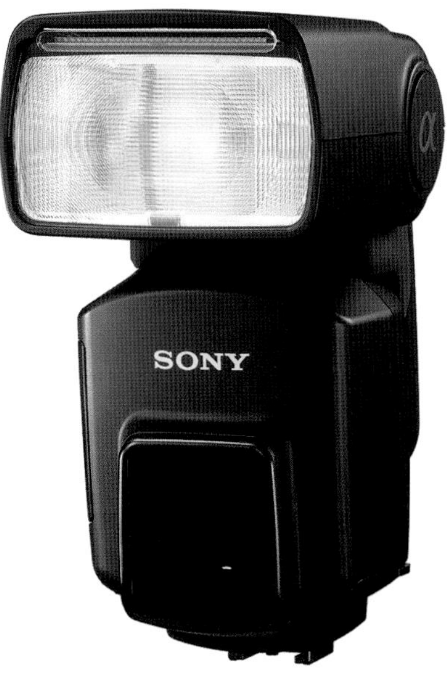

Figure 13.10 The Sony HVL-F60M can serve as an optical commander or receiver.

These are the most powerful units the company offers, with a guide number (GN) of 60 in meters or 197 in feet at ISO 100. As I noted earlier, the GN does not indicate actual flash range but it's useful when comparing several flash units in terms of their general power output. They are all priced in the $550–$600 price range.

Like all Sony multi-interface shoe flash units except the HVL-F20M, the F60M/F60RM/F60RM2 automatically adjust the zoom head to vary the angle of coverage to suit the lens focal length in use. You can zoom the head manually instead, if you prefer. A built-in slide-out diffuser panel boosts wide-angle coverage so it's suitable for photos taken at short focal lengths with the 10-18mm zoom. There's also a slide-out "bounce card" that can reflect some light forward even when bouncing the flash off the ceiling, to fill in shadows or add a catch light in the eyes of your portrait subjects. The dust- and moisture-resistant units use four AA batteries but can also be connected to the FA-EB1 ($250). The new pack is compatible with the 46RM, F60M, and F60RM/RM2 units and is capable of accepting *either* four or eight AA batteries in replaceable magazines, for up to 660 flashes with speedy recycle times of 0.6 seconds. When connected to the flash, it becomes the unit's primary power source. You may find the FA-EB1AM available at reduced prices, which has room for 6 AA batteries for increased capacity and faster recycling. Regardless of power source, the F60M/RM/RM2 automatically communicate white balance information to your camera, allowing the camera to adjust white balance to match the flash output.

You can use these large units as a main flash or allow them to be triggered wirelessly by another compatible flash unit. A pre-flash burst of light from the triggering commander/controller unit causes a remote flash unit to fire. When using flash wirelessly, Sony recommends rotating the unit so that the flashtube is pointed to the location where light should be directed, while the front (light sensor) of the flash is pointed toward the camera. In wireless mode, you can control up to three groups of flashes, and specify the output levels for each group, giving you an easy way to control the lighting ratios of multiple flash units.

HIGH-SPEED SYNC

Those who are frustrated by an inability to use a shutter speed faster than 1/160th or 1/200th second will love the High-Speed Sync (HSS) mode that allows for flash at 1/500th to 1/4000th second! This is ideal when you want to use a very wide aperture for selective focus with a nearby subject with flash; HSS at a fast shutter speed such as 1/1000th second is one way to avoid overexposure. The MODE button on the back of the flash is used to choose either TTL or Manual flash exposure. You can then use the MENU button and plus/minus keys to activate HSS mode; HSS appears in the unit's data panel as confirmation of the mode. (The F60RM2 can be controlled from the camera.)

Keep in mind that flash output is much lower in High-Speed Sync than in conventional flash photography. That's because less than the full duration of the flash is used to expose each portion of the image as it is exposed by the slit passing in front of the sensor. As a result, the effective flash (distance) range is much shorter.

In addition, HSS will not work when using multiple flash units or when the flash unit is set for left/right/up bounce flash or when the wide-angle diffuser is being used. (If you're pointing the flash downward, say, at a close-up subject, HSS can be used.)

HVL-F46RM Flash Unit

This is a smaller, less powerful version of the HVL-F60RM. Like its sibling, it can be used as a radio commander or receiver, but in optical mode only as a receiver triggered wirelessly by an optical controller.

HVL-F45RM Flash Unit

If you want an on-camera flash capable of triggering external flash units optically *and* by radio control and are intimidated by the price of the HVL-F60RM, this flash is an affordable option. It also can be triggered wirelessly by an optical controller, by another HVL-F45RM or an HVL-F60RM mounted on the a7C II/a7CR, or by the Sony FA-WRC1M Wireless Radio Commander mounted on the camera. When using radio control, it uses 14 channels to communicate with up to 15 flash units in five groups. It has a guide number of 45/148 (meters/feet) at ISO 100, and a fast 2.5-second recycle time. Its zoom head adjusts for the field of view from 24mm to 105mm and has an LED video light.

HVL-F43M Flash Unit

This less pricey electronic flash shares many of the advanced features of the HVL-F60M/RM/RM2 but has a lower guide number of 43/138 (meters/feet). Features shared with the high-end unit include HSS, automatic white balance adjustment, and automatic zoom with the same coverage of focal lengths and the slide-out diffuser, as well as a built-in bounce card. Its quick-shift function allows you to direct the flash upward or to the side by rotating the head. This unit also can be used in wireless mode as a commander/controller or remote, and it also offers the quick-shift bounce feature. The HVL-F43M is light (at 12 ounces) and runs on four AAs. This flash replaces the similar HVL-F43AM unit, which uses the older iISO hot shoe.

HVL-F32M Flash Unit

The HVL-F32M is a low-cost wireless-compatible electronic flash unit. It features a high-speed synchronization mode, wireless control, and automatic white balance compensation. In wireless mode, it can be used only on Channel 1 (as I'll describe shortly) but can function as both a controller and remote. The flash is powered by a pair of AA batteries and it is resistant to both dust and moisture. Those who love to use bounce flash will like the built-in bounce sheet and retractable wide-angle panel that spreads the light to cover the equivalent of a 16mm lens.

HVL-F28RM Flash Unit

A most welcome addition to the Sony flash line is this highly affordable external flash that helps bring radio control within the reach of less well-heeled Sony users. It can operate as either a radio commander mounted on your a7C II/a7CR, or as a remote triggered by another RM-series flash or the FA-WRC1M wireless radio commander (which I'll describe later in this chapter). It has a guide number of 28/92 (meters/feet) and sports a compact size that makes it a perfect companion for the a7C II/a7CR whether used alone or with additional Sony flash units. The tilting flash head is adjustable from 0 to 120 degrees for bounce control. You can buy one of these to start out your kit, knowing that it will be fully compatible with additional Sony radio-controlled flash units as you expand your arsenal. Manual power settings from 1/1 to 1/256th power are available. Repeating flash is possible at rates up to 10 per second for 40 flashes, and the HVL-F28RM supports slow-sync, high-speed sync, and front- and rear-curtain sync. (See Figure 13.11, left.)

HVL-F20M Flash Unit

The least-expensive Sony flash (see Figure 13.11, right) is the HVL-F20M, designed to appeal to the budget conscious, especially those who need just a bit of a boost for fill-flash, or want a small unit (just 3.2 ounces) on their camera. It has a guide number of 20 at ISO 100, and features simplified operation. For example, there's a switch on the side of the unit providing Indoor and Outdoor settings (the indoor setting tilts the flash upward to provide bounce light; with the outdoor setting, the flash fires directly at your subject). This flash can serve as a controller on the a7C II/a7CR to trigger off-camera flash units wirelessly but cannot be used as a remote flash. There are special modes for wide-angle shooting (use the built-in diffuser to spread the flash's coverage to that of a lens with a

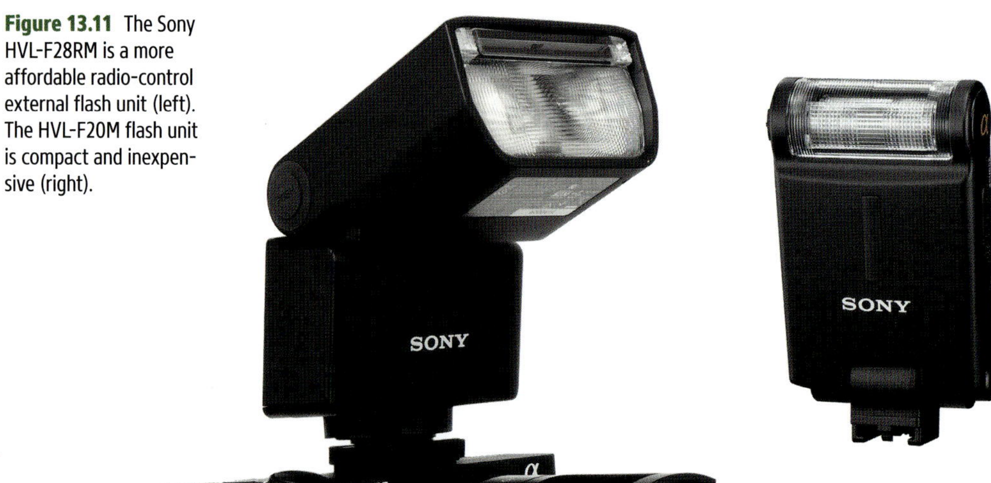

Figure 13.11 The Sony HVL-F28RM is a more affordable radio-control external flash unit (left). The HVL-F20M flash unit is compact and inexpensive (right).

very wide field of view or choose the Tele position to narrow the flash coverage to that of a 50mm or longer lens for illuminating more distant subjects). While it's handy for fill-flash, owners of a Sony a7C II/a7CR camera will probably want a more powerful unit as their main electronic flash.

BATTERY TIP

You may not use your flash very often, but when you do, you want it to operate properly. The problem with infrequent flash use is that conventional nickel-metal hydride batteries lose their charge over time, so if your flash unit is sitting in your bag for a long time between uses, you may not even be aware that your rechargeable batteries are pooped out. Non-rechargeable alkaline cells are not a solution: they generally provide less power for your flash and replacing them can be costly. The Energizer Lithium Ultimate AA batteries last up to three times longer, but they sell for about $10 for four.

I've had excellent luck with a battery developed by Panasonic called *eneloop* cells. They retain their charge for long periods of time—as much as 75 percent of a full charge over a three-year period (let's hope you don't go that long between uses of your flash). They're not much more expensive than ordinary rechargeables and can be revitalized up to 1,500 times. They're available in capacities of 1500 mAh to 2500 mAh. I use the economical models with 1900 mAh capacity.

Wireless Flash (Optical)

Because the Sony a7C II and a7CR lack a built-in flash, in order to sync a flash wirelessly using optical triggering, you'll need to own at least two compatible flash units, such as the HVL-F60M/RM, HVL-F45RM, HVL-F28RM, HVL-F43M, HVL-F32M, or HVL-F20M. One flash will be connected to the camera through the multi-interface shoe and serves as the commander flash or controller. A second (and additional) flash unit can be triggered wirelessly with optical signals, with full exposure control. It is a limited range (about 16 feet) but a useful unit if you want your primary illumination to come from the off-camera flash, and, perhaps, use a less powerful on-camera flash as the commander/controller. In that mode, the HVL-F20M makes a workable controller, especially since it is the least-expensive Sony flash unit. But keep in mind that it cannot be used as a remote flash unit.

To use wireless flash with optical triggering, just follow these steps (I'll address radio control later):

1. **Connect the controller flash unit to the camera.** Slide it all the way into the multi-interface shoe so the connection is solid. Lock it in position.

2. **Position additional flash(es).** Sony flash units come with a mini-stand that lets you set the flash on a table or other surface. You can also purchase third-party adapters so the off-camera flash can be mounted on a light stand or a tripod. In a pinch, you can press a helper into service to hold your supplementary flash units. The remote units must be able to "see" the controller's pre-flash signal, either directly or by bouncing off another surface in the room.

3. **Power up flash and camera.** Note that when you turn off the camera, the flash turns off as well; you don't need to manually turn both on or off simultaneously if you want to save power during a shooting session.

4. **Switch camera and attached commander/controller flash to wireless mode.** Use the Exposure/Color > Flash > Wireless Flash entry. Once the camera is set to wireless mode, press the shutter release halfway, and the attached powered-up flash automatically shifts into wireless mode as well.

5. **Set one or more remote flash unit(s) to wireless mode and choose options.** Turn on the unit and follow the instructions supplied with your flash unit to switch to wireless mode, then select either commander (controller) mode or receiver (remote) mode. Then, choose a group and channel, which I'll explain in the next section.

6. **Test your connection.** Press your defined AEL button, and the controller will emit a burst, which the remotes will respond to with a flash of their own about half a second later.

Key Wireless Concepts

Here are some key concepts you must understand before jumping into wireless flash photography:

- **Controllers/Commanders.** The flash that communicates with and triggers all wireless flash units is called the *controller* or *commander*. Because the camera does not have a built-in flash, wireless communication requires one controller to be connected to the camera's multi-interface shoe.

- **Receivers/Remotes.** The flash units that are controlled wirelessly are called the *remotes* by Sony, or what used to be called *slaves*. There can only be one controller flash, but you can have multiple remote units. All the remotes triggered by a controller must use the same *channel*, but flashes using a particular channel can be divided into one of two *remote groups*, and their power levels specified by group.

- **Channels.** Sony's wireless flash system offers users the ability to determine on which of up to four possible optical channels and up to 14 wireless channels (depending on the flash's capabilities) the units can communicate. (The pilots, ham radio operators, or scanner listeners among you can think of the channels as individual communications frequencies). The channels are numbered 1, 2, 3, and 4 (in optical mode), and each flash must be assigned to one of them. Moreover, in general, each of the flash units you are working with should be assigned to the *same* channel, because the remote flash units will respond *only* to a controller flash that is on the same channel. Note that the HVL-F20M cannot be used as a remote flash, and when used as a controller flash, you *must* use its sole channel, Channel 1.

The channel ability is important when you're working around other photographers who are also using the same system. Photojournalists, including sports photographers, will encounter this situation frequently as Sony cameras make in-roads in these pro arenas. Each Sony photographer sets flash units to a different channel so as to not accidentally trigger other users' strobes. (At big events with more than four photographers using Sony flash, you may need to negotiate.) I use this capability at workshops I conduct where we have two different setups. Photographers working with one setup use a different channel than those using the other setup and can work independently even though we're at opposite ends of the same large room.

- **Groups.** Sony's wireless flash system lets you designate multiple flash units in two separate groups, dubbed RMT (which is selected for all flashes by default) and RMT2 (which must be specified explicitly to change individual flashes from the default RMT group). All the flashes in all the groups use the exact same *channel* and all respond to the same controller, but you can set the output levels of each remote group separately. So, flash in RMT might serve as the main light, while those in RMT2 might be adjusted to produce less illumination and serve as a fill light. It's convenient to be able to adjust the output of all the units within a given group simultaneously. This lets you create different styles of lighting for portraits and other shots.

  Note that these two groups consist *only* of remote flashes. Your on-camera controller/commander flash is effectively a third group. If the controller is a low-powered unit like the HVL-F20M, it may not contribute much to the exposure at all (or, perhaps just add a little fill if pointed directly at your subject); a more powerful unit can become a potential third group. You could, for example, point the on-camera flash at a ceiling or wall to provide additional diffuse illumination.

  If you're using only one group, all the flashes in the RMT group are automatically adjusted based on the settings you specify for the controller, such as flash exposure bracketing and/or flash exposure compensation.

- **Flash ratios.** This ability to control the output of one flash (or set of flashes) compared to another flash or set in groups allows you to produce lighting *ratios*. You can control the power of multiple off-camera flash to adjust each unit's relative contribution to the image, for more dramatic portraits and other effects. Ratios are available with flash units that use the new CTRL+ protocol (described next).

- **Flash protocols.** Older Sony flash units, including the HVL-F20M, used a particular protocol to communicate. More recent units, such as the HVL-F60M/RM, HVL-F45RM, HVL-F28RM, HVL-F43M (with multi-interface shoe), HVL-F58AM, HVL-F32M, and HVL-F32AM/HVL-F43AM (both with the old-style shoe) all have an enhanced protocol for communicating with compatible flash, called CTRL+. They can also revert to the older protocol (CTRL) to be compatible with older flash as well. Because the HVL-F20M uses the original Sony protocol, it cannot be used to adjust flash ratios, as described above.

- **Metering.** In wireless flash mode, advanced distance integration (ADI) is not used (the distance between the flash and subject can't be determined by the off-camera flash), and Sony's P-TTL flash metering is used instead.

Setting Channels and Remote Groups

To specify the channels and remote groups used by each flash in optical mode, you must use the flash unit's controls and menu system. As an introduction to what's involved, I'm going to list the procedures for two of the most commonly used flash, the HVL-F60M/RM and HVL-F43M. For the HVL-F45RM and other Sony wireless-compatible flash units, consult the manual furnished with your strobe.

Setting the HVL-F60M/RM

To choose the group on the HVL-F60M, just follow these steps:

1. Press the MODE button on the flash to display the Mode screen.
2. Rotate the control wheel or use its directional buttons to highlight WL RMT.
3. Press the Fn button and use the control wheel to select the group, either TTL Remote or TTL Remote 2.
4. Press the control wheel center button to confirm your changes.

To choose the channel on the HVL-F60RM, just follow these steps:

1. Press the MENU button on the flash. The Menu screen appears.
2. On Page 1, select the entry to change. Use the control wheel to highlight the entry you want to adjust.
3. Select the wireless channel by highlighting WL CH and pressing the control wheel center button. Then use the control wheel to choose Channel 1, 2, 3, or 4. Press the center button again to confirm your choice.
4. You can also adjust the protocol if needed. Highlight the WL CTRL entry and press the control wheel center button. Use the wheel to select CTRL+ if you are using only compatible flash units (HVL-F60M/RM, HVL-F43M, HVL-F32M, HVL-F58AM, HVL-F32AM, or HVL-F43AM) or CTRL if you are using other flash units in your setup. Press the MENU button again to confirm your choice.

Setting the HVL-F43M

To choose the group on the HVL-F43M, just follow these steps:

1. Press the Fn button on the flash. CTRL or RMT will be blinking.
2. Press the right directional arrow on the flash as needed to highlight RMT or RMT2.
3. Press Fn to confirm your choice.

To choose the channel on the HVL-F43M:

1. Hold down the Fn button on the flash for more than three seconds. The first Camera Setting item (CH01 HSS) is displayed.
2. Press the flash's left/right directional buttons to change to C02: Wireless Channel.
3. Press the up/down buttons to select the channel 1, 2, 3, or 4.

4. Press the Fn button again to confirm your choice.

5. You can also adjust the protocol, if needed. Hold down the Fn button for more than three seconds and use the left/right buttons to select C03: Wireless Controller Mode. You can choose 1 (CTRL, the old protocol) or 2 (CTRL+, the new protocol). Press Fn to confirm your choice.

Setting Ratios

Once you've set up one or more flash for the RMT group, and one or more for the RMT2 group, you can adjust the ratio used between them.

Ratios with the HVL-F43M

Just follow these steps when using the HVL-F43M as the controller or remote. Remember that all flashes in all remote groups must be set to the same channel, as described previously:

1. The easiest way to set ratios is to mount the controller and remote units on the camera in turn. With each flash mounted on the camera set to Wireless Flash as described earlier, press the MODE button on the flash to display WL.

2. Press the Fn button on the flash, then press the left/right directional buttons until CTRL and RATIO are *both* blinking.

3. Press the Fn button again. The line at upper right will display:

   CTRL RMT RMT1

   1 : 1 : 1

4. Use the left/right directional buttons to move the highlighting to CTRL. When CTRL is highlighted, you can press the up/down buttons to choose the relative power of that flash, compared to the others, from 1, 2, 4, 8, 16, or - - (the latter disables the flash). For example, a setting of 16:1:4 would specify that the flash mounted on the camera has 1/16th the power of the RMT group, while the RMT2 group would have 1/4 the power of the RMT group. Selecting - - disables that flash or group. You might want to do that so that the on-camera flash doesn't contribute to the exposure, even though it will still fire a pre-flash to trigger the remote units (see Figure 13.12, left).

5. Press the TTL/M button to display TTL.

6. Repeat for each flash.

Ratios with the HVL-F60M/RM

Just follow these steps when using the HVL-F60M/RM as the controller or remote. Again, all flashes in all remote groups must be set to the same channel, as described previously:

1. You can mount each flash on the camera and set the ratios. Press the MODE button to produce the Mode screen and select WL CTRL.

2. Press the Fn button on the flash to access the Quick Navi screen and use the control wheel to highlight WL CTRL. Press the control wheel center button to access the dedicated settings screen.

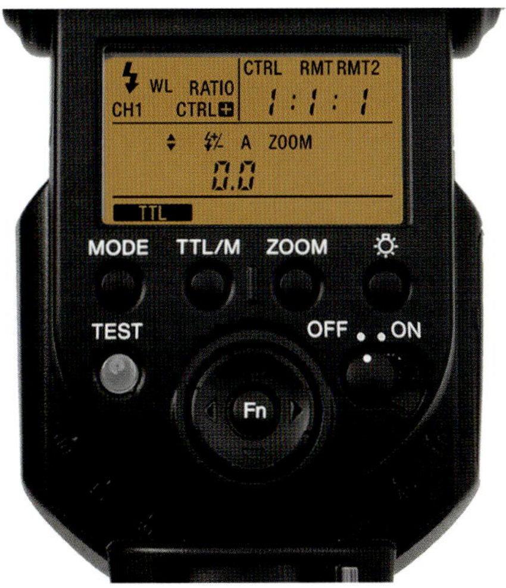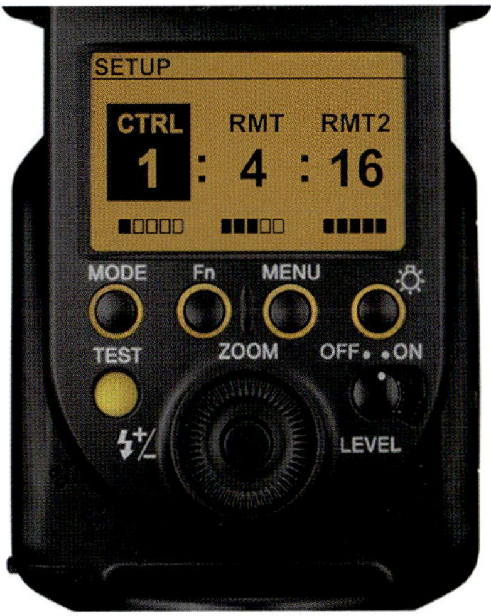

Figure 13.12 Set ratios on the HVL-F43M (left) and HVL-F60M/RM (right).

3. Use the control wheel to highlight RATIO. Press the center button to access your choices, Ratio: Off (the controller flash does not contribute to the exposure), TTL Ratio, and Manual Ratio. You can highlight TTL Ratio and use the control wheel to choose ON.

4. Press the center button to return to the indicator screen.

5. Press the Fn button to display the Quick Navi screen and choose the Wireless Lighting Ratio control indicator located at middle left of the screen. Press the control wheel center button, then use the control wheel to change the lighting ratio of each group. Rotate the control wheel to choose the relative power of each flash, compared to the others, from 1, 2, 4, 8, 16, or - -. The - - setting disables that group. (See Figure 13.12, right.)

6. Press the center button when finished.

Radio Control

Your Sony electronic flash communicate with each other using optical control, via the pre-flashes emitted before the actual exposure takes place. That type of linking requires line-of-sight communication between controller and remote units and works only over limited distances. Early in 2016, Sony introduced its wireless radio commander/receiver duo, which gives you a much greater range, many more channels to work with, and more control. Unfortunately, Sony's radio control solution is expensive, making it impractical for all but the most avid (and well-heeled) shooters. I expect it will be more popular among professionals who can justify the expense, and those, such as photojournalists, who need the flexibility of a larger number of channels to avoid conflicts with other photographers covering the same event. To properly equip yourself, you'll need:

- **Commander.** You'll need one HVL-F60RM flash, HVL-F46RM flash, HVL-F45RM flash, HVL-F28RM flash, or FA-WRC1M wireless radio commander ($350) for every camera you want to equip with radio control. The radio-compatible flash or commander reside in the hot shoe of the a7C II/a7CR and are used to trigger the off-camera electronic flash.

- **Flash units.** You must have at least one Sony flash from those listed above for the wireless commander to trigger. Ideally, you'll have several to allow you to configure multi-light setups, so plan on spending $250 to $600 for each remote flash.

- **Receivers.** As I write this, only the HVL-F60RM, HVL-F46RM, HVL-F45RM, and HVL-F28RM can be triggered by radio controls. So, if you're using any other wireless-compatible (optical only) flash, it must be connected to a FA-WRR1 wireless radio receiver. The flash units are *not* sensitive to radio controls on their own.

- **Light stands or an assistant.** The wireless commander generally resides on the multi-interface shoe of your camera, so you'll need light stands to accept each receiver, which has its own hot shoe your flash is attached to. Alternatively, you can enlist the aid of an assistant to hold the receiver/flash in proper position.

- **VMC-MM1 Multi Terminal cable (optional).** This cable allows you to connect another one of those wireless receivers to a second (or third...) *camera* so the auxiliary cameras fire in unison with the flash and main camera. This very cool feature will appeal to sports and news photographers covering events.

Each commander transmitter can support up to 15 receivers in any combination of flash units and remote cameras, with your choice of 14 different channels (reducing those conflicts at the next Olympics you cover). All the devices on a particular channel can be divided up among as many as five different groups, so you could conceivably have a dozen or more flash units spread among all those groups to provide very sophisticated lighting effects, over a range of more than 98 feet (30 meters). But wait! There's more. The HVL-F60RM, HVL-F46RM, HVL-F45RM, HVL-F28RM, and FA-WRC1M wireless radio commanders give you Manual, TTL, and Group control of flashes, and power adjustment from full power (1/1) to 1/256th power in 1/3-stop increments. The 3.3-ounce commander and 3-ounce receiver each run on two AA batteries. While I don't expect to see many a7C II/a7CR owners springing for this system, it's nice for ambitious photographers to know that these capabilities are there for them to grow into. Eventually, Sony will introduce additional radio-capable flash units and commanders, probably at more affordable prices.

Index